TO: MICHAEL CONNORS,

good friend of the martyred
croatia,

With gratitude

John Prcela
Editor-in-Chief

Cleveland, March 9, 1972

OPERATION SLAUGHTERHOUSE

Eyewitness Accounts of Postwar Massacres In Yugoslavia

Edited By

JOHN PRCELA, M.A.

and STANKO GULDESCU, Ph.D.

DORRANCE & COMPANY

Philadelphia

Standard Book Number: 8059-1406-4
Library of Congress Catalog Card Number: 70-118955
Printed in the United States of America

This book, published on the twenty-fifth anniversary of the Bleiburg Tragedy, is dedicated to the memory of its dead, the victims of a peacetime genocide.

CONTENTS

LIST OF ILLUSTRATIONS

MAPS

PHOTOGRAPHS

FOREWORD

The capture of Adolf Eichmann by an Israeli intelligence unit stimulated a short-lived revival of public interest in the gruesome slaughterhouse procedures which stigmatized World War II. Most of these operations were charged to the Nazis and their allies, and in cases like the Katyn Forest Massacres, where Polish military personnel were butchered *en masse* by the Russians, some awkward facts have conveniently been forgotten. So effectively have even the "democratic" nations maintained their silence, in fact, that another ghastly shambles, which probably represents the greatest single instance of mass murder in modern times, has safely fled the minds of the jaded public. The British and American governments, which were directly involved in this episode, have shown themselves as anxious as the actual perpetrators of the crime to offer only a blank page to the judgment of history. Conceivably, the Eichmann incident constituted a welcome diversion to London and Washington because it drew the attention of the "civilized world" away from the practically unknown Bleiburg-Maribor tragedy, in which 150,000 disarmed Croatian soldiers and an even larger number of civilians were massacred by Tito's Partisans after the end of hostilities in May, 1945, with the mute acceptance of the British and American governments.

This mass murder constitutes a dark stain upon the Anglo-American military and political escutcheon because these nations had the opportunity and the power to prevent it from being carried out. It is the indelible character of this blot upon the war effort of the "democracies" that explains the hood of silence that has been drawn over it. But where nations rather than individuals are concerned, murder eventually will out.

In the spring of 1945 and during the preceding winter months, the Croatians had been trying to find someone to surrender to, but since both Washington and London had committed themselves to Tito and the Russians, this attempt was not crowned with success. At this time, the Croats still had sixteen strong divisions in the field, a force of about 250,000 men, more than enough to wipe out Tito and his much publicized Partisans, whose only real victories during the war were achieved in the pages of the Anglo-American press. Many Croat officers wanted to go after the Partisans lock, stock and barrel—exterminate them, and then fight to the last man against the Russians, who could be expected to arrive at any time. But the civilian leaders of the nation thought that

Bleiburg-Maribor

they could save the Army by surrendering it to the Americans and British. Even if the British refused to recognize the Croatians' political and military independence in their own state, they could conceivably be trusted to observe the international laws of war laid down by the Geneva Convention. No one thought of surrendering to the Russians or to Tito's gangs of professional assassins.

It was May, 1945, and the smell of spring was in the air along the roads that led from Croatia and Slovenia to the Austrian frontier. Long columns of trucks mixed with peasant wagons jammed every highway as uncounted thousands of civilians—peasants, workmen, students, and merchants—joined the retreating soldiers after the evacuation of the Croatian capital, Zagreb, on May 6 and 7. Altogether there must have been a total of close to 500,000 people, military and civilian combined, heading towards the frontier to meet the American and British Armies. They marched on foot and used every kind of conveyance. Now that their leaders had decided not to fight any longer, these loyal Croatians were intent upon only one thing, escaping the murder squads of Tito. The latter had already occupied Zagreb, where they demonstrated their lethal talents by butchering the sick and wounded left in hospitals, along with a good cross-section of the capital's citizenry which had decided to remain behind and trust to the mercies of their new masters, rather than run for the frontier.

For a short time, the fleeing columns forgot the hunger, thirst, cold, and general misery that plagued them. However, towards the middle of May, 1945, word ran down the long lines of trucks, wagons, and pedestrians that the Croatian command and governmental leaders finally had established contact with the British Army. The latter had its headquarters in the Austrian province of Carinthia. The Carinthian nobility was largely of Croatian origin, and the Croats had ties throughout history with these people.

Indeed, the British did let the Croatian leaders believe that they would accept the surrender of the Croat armed forces. On May 15, ten days after the last die-hard Nazis had surrendered and the war was ended, over 100,000 Croatian soldiers and tens of thousands of Croatian civilians encamped on a large field just across the Austrian frontier near the town of Bleiburg. Here the British military authorities requested them to lay down their arms. Most of them did so. Only a few, with some innate suspicion that remained as a heritage from their ancestors' experiences with England, refused, and took shelter in the surrounding forests to see what was going to happen. They did not have to wait long to find out.

Once the British were sure that the Croats were disarmed, they began to herd the unarmed masses back across the border. Was there an agreement between the English commanders and the Partisan leaders, or were the former merely indulging in a form of political ignorance? In any event, Partisan units which had come up during the night and had taken position in the nearby woods opened fire on the refugees as the British forced them back over the frontier line. So well coordinated was this joint Anglo-Partisan action, that thousands of Croatians of all categories, but mostly unarmed soldiers, were shot down on that part of the Bleiburg field which lies within the frontiers of the Tito State. This was the beginning.

Elsewhere, thousands upon thousands of Croat soldiers and civilian refugees also surrendered to the British military authorities on Austrian territory. The procedure was the same. The British totally disarmed them, then jammed them into railway cars and military vehicles like sheep destined for the slaughterhouse. Although the English solemnly assured the refugees that they were being sent to prisoner-of-war camps in Italy, these trains and vehicles rolled back to the Slovenian border. From Villach, Lawamuend, Krumpendorf, Griffen, and other localities along the Austro-Slovene border, these conveyances crowded with human cargo made their way into Tito-held territory. There the prisoners were unloaded—to find themselves in the lethal custody of their Partisan adversaries.

The latter were a little more clever or discreet than those who had carried out the open massacre on the Bleiburg field. Perhaps they thought that the traditionally sporting minded Britons would object to their shooting down unarmed men! Therefore, the Partisans separated the military and civilian fugitives and marched each column well out of sight and earshot of the British. Then specially organized Communist murder squads went to work.

Eyewitnesses who managed to survive the slaughters in one way or another report that the greatest mass butcheries took place near Maribor in Slovenia. There the 17th Partisan Assault Division carried out the wholesale executions under the direction of its Serbian officers, Blaza Yankovich, Rade Corak, commander of the "Proletariat Brigade," and Boza Hinich. The noted Croatian historian, Oton Knezovic, himself a survivor of the death marches, estimates that about 40,000 Croat soldiers were killed near Maribor alone. Knezovic, in his autobiographical account of this episode entitled, *The Massacre of the Croatian Army in 1945*, reports:

> And when after a time, thousands upon thousands of heads, and legs were showing [from the trenches], more horrible scenes took place and stories circulated among our older people [that is, the residents of Slovenia themselves]. A great number of them told me that they would rather have been thrown into those trenches with the Croatians than live any longer in the locality and look at the horrible trench graves for the rest of their lives. . .

But the Maribor charnel house did not end the slaughtering. The death marches from Maribor continued as the British made new deliveries of victims to their proteges. As the trains, trucks and wagons loaded with captives made their daily arrival at Kocevski Rog, Partisans herded the prisoners into the local forests. Soon the abyss-like ravines of the area were filled with the bodies of more than 30,000 Croats and Slovenian White Guards. The massacres in this locality lasted for eight days. A member of the Serbian minority in Dalmatia, Major General Sima Dubajic, commanded selected extermination squads composed of "Old Communists" from the Eleventh Dalmatian Brigade.

To conserve ammunition and time, those executioners devised a truly ingenious plan of mass murder. They arranged coverings of boards over the deep natural ravines that abound in this region, tied the prisoners together in groups of sixes, and then made them "walk the plank." Employing the same technique used in slaughtering cattle, they would hit the end man over the head with a sledge hammer as he stepped onto the board walk. Naturally, his fall would pull others after him into the ravine.

After the massacres at Kocevski Rog, Tito sent a commission of five under the Serbian colonel, Dule Korach, to inspect the places where the bodies had been disposed. To cover up the sea of corpses, Korach resorted to extensive dynamiting of the terrain.

Other huge contingents of the Croat Army were marched all the way across Croatia to Kovin on the Rumanian frontier. They left a trail of scattered bones and mass graves, as first the sick, then the exhausted, and finally the survivors of the march were liquidated.

All of these butcheries were enacted in addition to the planned and unplanned slaughters of civilian elements or military personnel who were unable to reach the Austrian frontier and the "hospitality" offered by the British. At Dolensko, Ptuj, Celje, and Krsko were human slaughter-houses that put the efficiency of any stockyard to shame. At Sestine, near Zagreb, 5,000 soldiers were murdered, near Vrgin-Most about 7,000, close to Dubocac on the Sava River some 3,000, and around Podravski Klostar at least 2,000. In Virovitica, over 1,700 new young recruits, who had been called up and then left without any orders, came to an untimely end at the hands of the Partisans. Many others fell at Bjelovar, Gracani, Sosice, Sisak, Butmir, Kasindol, Podgraci, and innumerable other places.

The henchmen of Tito did not limit their slaughterhouse tactics to the members of the Croatian Army or its civilian followers. As soon as Tito was in power, he set up concentration and slave labor camps throughout the country. Hundreds of thousands of citizens of all ages, sexes, and from every walk of life were imprisoned, tortured, and finally liquidated. Croatia became an immense graveyard—her ditches, ravines, forests, and rivers all crowded with corpses. Few of these people were "war criminals," that is, individuals who themselves had killed Communists. Most such killers were astute enough to know better than to surrender to the British. Indeed, many of these people made their way to safety by devious routes and through hazardous stratagems.

Although Tito and his aides actually carried out this "Operation Slaughterhouse," the British military authorities bear a moral responsibility. The British were obligated by the Geneva Convention and by the laws of war to accept the Croatian surrender and to give the retreating Croat Army and civilian population sanctuary to protect them from Partisan vengeance. Although the American authorities do not bear the same degree of responsibility for the policy of genocide that was put into effect by Tito's Serbian-led and staffed forces, nevertheless American recognition and support of Tito from 1942 to 1945 vied with the assistance offered this usurper by that credulous politician, Winston Churchill. This dual support vitally helped the establishment of Communism in Croatia. And the same support has continued to this day through the truly massive outpourings of the dollars of the American taxpayer!

—Major General Charles A. Willoughby, U.S.A., Ret.

Washington, D. C.
May 6, 1968

PART ONE:

ANALYSIS

Chapter 1

A Survey of Croatian History

Although the Croatians of today are considered to be a predominately Slavic people, it is probable that the original Croats were Iranian tribesmen. Later, they settled in the steppes of what became southern Russia, especially near the shores of the Black Sea. It is likely that this settlement took place in the second century of the Christian era.[1]

About 200 A.D. the Goths conquered the empire established earlier by the Iranian Sarmatians in the steppe country. An Iranian group called the Alans affiliated themselves with the Goths and some ethnic fusion took place between these two peoples.[2] This Iranian-Gothic combine imposed its rule upon masses of Slavic agriculturists in the steppe lands.[3] In the last decades of the fourth century, the invasion of Hunnic nomads disrupted the political life of this area, as well as of those parts of Poland and Bohemia in which Croatian elements appear to have located themselves.[4] During the fifth, sixth, and seventh centuries many Iranians,

[1] On the Iranian theory of Croatian origins see the following: Miljenko Dabo-Peranic, *Teza Istovjetnosti Harvata-Sarmata* (Paris, 1962), and his *Iranska Hrvatska* (Paris, 1962). See also S. Guldescu, *History of Medieval Croatia* (The Hague, 1964), pp. 21, 26, 30, 33-40; M. Rostovtseff, *Iranians and Greeks in South Russia* (Oxford, 1922), pp. 35-146; M. Ebert, *Sudrussland im Altertum* (Bonn and Leipzig, 1921), p. 106; Max Wasmer, *Untersuchungen uber die alteste Wohnsitz der Slaven,* I: "Die Iranier in Sudrussland," (Leipzig, 1923); N. Zupancic, "Prvobitni Hrvati," *Zbornik Kralja Tomislava u spomen Tisucgodisnjice Hrvatskoga Kraljevstva* (Zagreb, 1925), pp. 291-296; Roman St. Kaulfuss, *Die Slaven in den Altesten Zeiten bis Samo (623)* (Berlin, 1842), pp. 6-9; Dr. Luka Jelic, *Hrvatski spomenici Ninskoga podrucja iz dobe hrvatskih narodnih vladara* (Zagreb, 1911), pp. 2-32; Z. Vinski. *Uz problematiku starog Irana i Kavkaza* (Zabreb, 1940), pp. 20-21; S. Sakac, "Iranische Herkunft des Kroatischen Volks-Namens," *Orientalia Christiana Periodica,* XV (1949), 313-340; H. Gregoire, "L'origine et le nom des Croates et leur pretendue patrie caucasienne," *La nouvelle Clio,* IV (1952), 323, V (1953), 3, 466; Ivo Pilar, "O dualizmu u vjeri starih Slovjena i o njegovu podrijetlu i znacenju," *Zbornik za narodni zivot i obicaje juznih Slavena,* XXVIV (1928), 1-86, passim; J. Strzygowski, *Altai-Iran und die Volkerwanderung* (Leipzig, 1917), passim; and his *Starohrvatska umjetnost* (Zagreb, 1927); Archbishop Bohusz-Szestrencewicz, *Precis des recherches historiques sur l'origine des Slaves ou Esclavons et des Sarmates* (St. Petersburg, 1824), I, 193, 223-224, 135; Dr. Dominic Mandic, *Crvena Hrvatska* (Chicago, 1957), pp. 198-199.

[2] E. Beneger, "Der Westgotisch-Alanische Zug nach Mitteleuropa," *Manns Bibliothek, LI* (1931), 118 ff.; Vjekoslav Klaic, "Hrvatska plemena od XI do XVI stoljeca," *Rad* CXXX (1897), 15 ff; L. Hauptmann, "Der Herkunft der Karntner Edlinge," *Vierteljahrschrift* Fur Soz. Gesch., XXI (1928), 263-273.

[3] Guldescu, *History of Medieval Croatia,* pp. 23-26 and footnote references.

[4] *Ibid.,* pp. 26-27.

Goths, and Slavs alike migrated southwards across the Carpathians into central Europe and the Balkans.[5]

It was sometime between the end of the fifth and the early part of the seventh centuries that the descendants of the early Croatians came to present day Croatia, Slavonia, Dalmatia, Istria, and Bosnia-Hercegovina. They founded three principalities in these regions, and in time the name "Croat" (Hrvat) began to be mentioned in various records and chronicles. White Croatia lay along the eastern shore of the Adriatic Sea, taking in parts of the peninsula of Istria and the northern sections of Dalmatia, together with what today is known as western Croatia. South of this entity, Red or southern Croatia stretches well into modern Albania.[6] Between the Sava and Drava Rivers, in the territory of northern or Pannonian Croatia, there arose another section.[7] This territory later became known as Slavonia. Bosnia and the lands that since 1448 have been included in the designation "Hercegovina" (Dukedom) were Croatian settlement areas too, but their political affiliation was of a fluctuating character. The mountainous character of these territories facilitated the perpetuation of a loosely organized tribal system that bore resemblance to the clan arrangement of medieval Scotland.

Between 568 and 791 A.D., an originally nomadic people known as the Avars controlled present day Hungary. Evidently, they subjugated many Croatians, along with other Slavic groups. In a war that lasted from 791 to 796 A.D., the Croatians aided the Frankish king, Charlemagne, to overthrow the Avaric power. The result of this struggle was that both White and Pannonian Croatia became Frankish vassal states while the remnants of the Avars were subjected to the domination of Croatian tribal chiefs.[8] Then, between 812 and 817 A.D., the Franks concluded agreements with the Byzantine or Eastern Roman Empire which brought Red Croatia within the latter's sphere of influence.

Following the death of Charlemagne in 814, the Pannonian Croats revolted against the Franks. But the Dalmatian Croatians under Prince

---

[5] Such evidence as exists concerning these migrations is summed up in S. Guldescu, "Political History to 1526," *Croatia: Land, People, Culture,* ed. F. H. Eterovic and M. Spalatin (Toronto, 1964), pp. 81-84, including footnotes. See also J. B. Bury, *The Early History of the Slavonian Settlements in Dalmatia, Croatia, and Serbia* (London, 1920); Francis Dvornik, *The Making of Central and Eastern Europe* (London, 1949), pp. 268-315 passim, and his *The Slavs: Their Early History and Civilization* (Boston, 1956) pp. 22-24, 47-53. S. H. Cross, "Gothic Loan Words in the Slavic Vocabulary," *Harvard Studies and Notes,* XVI, no. 193; C. Brady, *The Legend of Ermanaric* (Chicago, 1943).

[6] On Red Croatia see Mandic, *Crvena Hrvatska;* St. Stedimlija, *Crvena Hrvatska* (Zagreb, 1937); *Ljetopis Popa Dukljanina* ed. F. Sisic (Belgrade-Zagreb, 1928), pp. 305-307; Dr. N. Z. Bjelovucic, *Crvena Hrvatska i Dubrovnik* (Zagreb, 1929), pp. 5-24; F. Sisic, *Povijest Hrvata u vrijeme narodnih vladara* (Zagreb, 1925), I, 456-457.

[7] For what is known concerning Pannonian Croatia see Guldescu, *History of Medieval Croatia.*

[8] Guldescu, "Political History," p. 87 and footnote references.

Borna aided the Franks to defeat their kinsmen.[9] Just after the close of this struggle the Frankish chronicler, Einhard, noted that the Serbs were known to the Franks only by hearsay. It appears, therefore, that the Serbian people had an origin and development distinct from that of the Croatians with whom they had little or no contact in early times.[10] In any case, the Serbs eventually accepted Christianity from Byzantium, some time after the Croatians identified themselves with the Latin form of this faith.[11]

During the ninth century, White Croatia emancipated itself from the rule of the Italian Carolingians, while Pannonian Croatia threw off the yoke of the Germanic successors of Charlemagne. Red Croatia remained subjected to Byzantine political and cultural influence. Also, the nomadic Magyar nation burst into central Europe in this century. Magyar pressure upon the Croats effected the union of White and Pannonian Croatia under the first Croatian King, Tomislav (d. 928 or 934 A.D.).[12]

Tomislav's Croatia stretched along the eastern Adriatic shore from the Rasa (Arsa) River in Istria to the Cetina stream in Dalmatia. Eastward it reached as far as the Drina, where Serbian principalities were beginning to arise. Most of modern Bosnia and Hercegovina were included within Tomislav's domain. Next to Denmark, Sweden, and Norway, the state established by Tomislav was the oldest continuously existing monarchy in Europe. This fact is of the utmost importance because it explains why the Croatians throughout their history have continued to assert their national independence, even during periods of alien rule.

Medieval Croatia reached the height of its power and grandeur under King Petar Kresimir IV (1058-1074). During his reign and before, Croatia competed successfully with the great maritime Republic of Venice for the mastery of the Adriatic, which was crowded with Croatian shipping. After Petar Kresimir's death, the antagonism between the Latin or Roman Church party and the so-called "National" church group undermined the unity of the kingdom. Although the "National" group wished to maintain ecclesiastical ties with Rome, it was attached to Byzantine liturgical and

---

[9] The Frankish chronicler, Einhard, is the chief authority on this episode. The account of it as given in Guldescu, "Political History," pp. 88-89, is based upon Einhardi Annales, ed. G. H. Pertz, *Scriptorum Rerum Germanicarum,* Vol. I, (1895).

[10] For the ethnic details see Mandic, *Crvena Hrvatska,* pp. 107-123 and 184-186.

[11] Dr. Dominik Mandic, *Bosna i Hercegovina* (Chicago, 1960), Chapter 16.

[12] F. Racki, "Kako i Kada se Preobrazi Hrvatska Knezevina u Kraljevinu," *Rad Jugosl. Akad. Znanosti i Umjetnosti,* CXLVII (1871), pp. 70-89. The oldest Magyar account of Magyar-Croatian relationships in early times, "Anonymi Belae Regis Notarii de Gestis Hungarorum Liber," ed. S. Ednlicher, *rerum Hung. Mon. Arpadiana* (St. Gallen, 1849) p. 118, does not seem too credible. See the discussion of this point in Guldescu, "Political History," pp. 90-91. The account of the "Anonymous Notary" should be compared with more reliable Hungarian sources such as those of J. Thuroczy de Szentmihaly, *Chronica Hungarorum* (Brunn, 1488), and of Simon de Keza.

social practices, and it wished to use the national rather than the Latin language in church services.[13]

With the death of the national dynasty of the Trpimirovici at the end of the eleventh century, the Hungarian dynasty of the Arpads succeeded in imposing their rule upon old Pannonian Croatia which was now called Slavonia.[14] Also the Arpads concluded an amicable agreement with the great Croatian clans living south of the Gvozd Mountains in ancient White Croatia, where the White Dalmatian Croats acknowledged the overlordship of the Arpads, but remained masters of the territory south of the Gvozd. Magyars were not allowed to acquire property in this area, nor were Hungarian laws valid in Croatia unless sanctioned by the Ban and Sabor, the supreme Croatian executive and legislative authorities. Until 1527, the Ban had more power in the Croatian territories proper than had the king himself.[15] Separate Bans for Slavonia and Bosnia appeared in time, and, finally, Bosnia established itself as an independent kingdom under Tvrdko I (1377-1391).[16] Hungarian influences predominated in Slavonia, although Magyar historians of the nineteenth century claimed that this territory was a masterless land when the Hungaro-Croatian union was effected.[17] Eventually, Slavonia developed its own Sabor, or legislature, which met separately from that of Croatia proper.

In medieval times, Venice and Byzantium were the great enemies of both Magyars and Croatians. During the reign of Manuel Comnenos (1143-1180), most of Croatia and Bosnia was conquered by the Byzantines. Although he may have acknowledged the formal overlordship of the Arpads, Ban Kulin (1180-1204) re-established Bosnian autonomy. In the thirteenth century, the rise of the great Croatian noble families of the Subici, later known as the Zrinis, and Kotromanici promised the

---

[13] Guldescu, "Political History," p. 98.

[14] On the Hungarian takeover in Slavonia and the end of Croatian national independence see Dr. Milan Sufflay, "Zu Den Altesten Kroatisch-Ungarischen Beziehungen," *Ungarische Rundschau*, IV (1915); Thomas Archidiaconus, *Historia Salonitana* (Vol. XXVI, *Monumenta Spectantia)*, edited by F. Racki, in *Prirucnik Izvora Hrvatske Historije* (Enchiridion fontium historiae Croatiae), Vol. I to p. 1107 (Zagreb, 1914), pp. 409-423, 462-464, 561-562; Dr. I. Krsnjavi, *Zur Historia Salonitana des Thomas Archidiakon in Spalato* (Zagreb, 1900), pp. 146-169.

[15] An ancient Croatian proverb handed down from the period of the rule of the Arpads and their successors in "Tko sudi, onaj vlada" (He who judges, rules). This adage undoubtedly expresses the Croatian concept of banal authority, although it should not be forgotten that able Hungarian kings such as Charles Robert (1307-1340) of Croatia-Slavonia and Dalmatia were able to impose their authority even upon such powerful Bans as Mladen Subic II. See Miho Barada, "Vrijeme Smrti i Obiteljski Odnosaji Bana Mladena II," *Zbornik Naucnih Radova Ferde Sisica,* ed. G. Novak (Zagreb, 1929), pp. 167-171.

[16] Mandic, *Bosna i Hercegovina,* pp. 100-457, passim.

[17] Stephan Horvath, *Ueber Kroatien Als Eine Durch Unterjochung Erworbene Ungarische Provinz und des Konigreichs Ungarn Wirklichen Teiles* (Leipzig, 1844); F. Pesty, *Die Entstehung Kroatiens* (Budapest, 1882), pp. 71-72. These expositions should be compared with Dr. Miho Barada's, "Dinasticko Pitanje u Hrvatskoj XI Stoljeca," *Vjesnik za Arheologiju i Historiju Dalmatinsku* (Split, 1932), pp. 159-174.

recovery of complete independence of the ancient Triune Kingdom of Croatia, Slavonia, and Dalmatia, which at times had included medieval Bosnia. Old Red or southern Croatia, however, succumbed to the pressure exerted by the Orthodox Byzantine, Serbian, and Bulgarian states and was lost permanently to the Croatian complex.

At the beginning of the thirteenth century, Venice diverted the Fourth Crusade from its original objective, Egypt, to an attack upon the Croatian city of Zadar (Zara) which the Republic long had coveted. After capturing this town, the Crusaders helped the Venetians overthrow Byzantium itself. Enormously strengthened by this accomplishment, the Republic of St. Mark was able to exercise increasing pressure upon Dalmatia. Dynastic strife in Hungary followed the extinction of the Arpad and Angevin Dynasties in 1301 and 1382 respectively. In 1409, the last crowned King of Croatia, Slavonia, and Dalmatia, Ladislas of Naples, sold his hereditary right to Dalmatia to the Venetians for 100,000 ducats.

This transaction inaugurated a disastrous century for the Croatians. Ladislas' chief supporter, Duke Hrvoje Vukcic Hrvatinic, waged war against Sigismund of Luxemburg, who had become King of Hungary, and who asserted his claim to Croatia while reducing Bosnia to the status of a Hungarian vassal state. Hrvoje had to call in the Turks to help him maintain his position vis-a-vis the pretensions of Sigismund.

During the Ottoman intervention, hordes of the Sultan and their Tatar and Mongol auxiliaries repeatedly raided and invaded the Croatian territories.[18] Although the Croatians defeated these adversaries many times in the course of the fifteenth century, the Turks conquered Bosnia in 1463. Nineteen years later Hercegovina, which the Croatian noble family of the Kosaca had formed into a separate dukedom, succumbed to the Ottoman power. In 1493, three generations of the most ancient nobility of the lands south of the Gvozd fell almost to a man on the Krbava Polje, known afterwards as the "Field of Blood."[19]

Under the leadership of Ban and Bishop Petar Berislavic, the "Father of the Peasants," the Croatians again won a series of sanguinary triumphs over the Ottomans during the first two decades of the sixteenth century. But on August 29, 1526, King Louis II, the last Jagellon ruler of Hungary-Croatia, was defeated and killed at Mohacs by the armies of Suleiman II (1520-1566).

The Croatians now accepted as their king a member of the Austrian Habsburg family, Ferdinand, the brother of the Spanish King and Holy Roman or German Emperor, Charles V (1516-1556 of Spain, and 1519-1555 of Germany). Part of the Hungarians recognized the accession of Ferdinand as did the Bohemians. Since Charles V had delegated to his

---

18 Ivan Sakuljevic Sakcinski, *Borba Hrvatah s Mongoli i Tatari* (Zagreb, 1863).

19 On this battle, which had the most profound influence upon Croatian destinies, see Aleksije Olesnicki, "Bezimeni Turski Ljetopisac o Bojevima Turaka sa Hrvatima Godina 1491 i 1493," *Rad* (CCLXV), (1933) pp. 210-219; J. Valvador, *Die Ehre des Horzogthums Krain,* 4 vols. (Laybach, 1689), IV, pp. 390-392.

brother rule over the Habsburg hereditary lands, Upper and Lower Austria, Styria, Carinthia, Carniola, Tyrol, and eastern Istria, the nucleus of a new major power, the Habsburg monarchy, arose.

However, Magyar particularists proclaimed as Hungarian king the voyvoda or governor of Transylvania, eastern Hungary, John Zapolya. The Slavonian Sabor likewise recognized the regal pretensions of Zapolya. This action was taken at the behest of Ban Krsto Frankopan, who originally had agreed to support the claims of Ferdinand. Frankopan fell in battle against the Habsburg forces in 1527, and the Slavonian Croats then followed the example of their kinsmen in Croatia proper and hailed Ferdinand as their sovereign. Unable to maintain himself against the Habsburg power, Zapolya invoked the assistance of the Turks, who carried fire and sword into Hungary and Croatia-Slavonia in his, and their own, behalf. Although Zapolya had to abandon his claim to the Crown of Croatia and Slavonia, he was able to keep Transylvania, which became a Turkish vassal state. Central and southern Hungary were transformed into Turkish pashaliks, while most of Slavonia and the Lika and Krbava districts of western Croatia fell to the Ottomans as well.

The Turkish conquests of the fifteenth and sixteenth centuries exerted a malignant influence upon Croatian national destinies, which continues to be felt to the present day. Material destruction, and the carrying off of hundreds of thousands of Croatians to the slave markets of the Orient, were not the only baneful consequences of the triumph of the Crescent over the Cross.[20] The Turks also brought such alien Orthodox stocks as the Serbs with them into the Croatian territory.[21]

Between 1389 and 1459, the Serbian states were subjected to the yoke of the Ottomans, and the Serbs remained Turkish vassals for nearly four centuries. During the time of occupation they suffered from economic and social exploitation and the effacement of their political identity. Their long period of subjection to the caprices and progressive degeneracy of Turkish rule profoundly affected the mentality and cultural and political life of this Balkanic people, whose national consciousness already had developed within a Byzantine mold.

Since the Serbs were Orthodox Christians, the Turks for a long time dealt more leniently with them than with the Catholic Croatians who continued to live in the territories inundated by the Ottoman tidal wave of conquest. The predominantly Serbian "Martolosi" spearheaded the

[20] On the Turkish-Croatian conflicts in the sixteenth century see especially Dane Gruber, *Borba Hrvata s Turcima od pada Sigeta do Mira Zitva Torokzkoga* (1566-1606) (Zagreb, 1879); R. Horvat, *Borba Hrvata s Turcima za Petrinju* (1592-1596) (Petrinia, 1903). For the effects produced upon the Croatian territories by the raids of the Turkish cavalry see J. Predavec, *Selo i Seljaci* (Zagreb, 1934), p. 69. The more recent study of the Austro-Turkish wars of the sixteenth century prepared by Dr. Gunther Rothenberg neglects almost entirely the part played by the Croatians in these struggles: *The Austrian Military Border in Croatia—1522-1747* (Urbana, 1960).

[21] Dr. A. Ivic, *Migracije Srba u Hrvatsku Tokom 16, 17, i 18 Stoljeca* (Belgrade, 1923).

incessant raids and invasions launched by the Turks against the Croatian national territory. These incursions were an almost daily occurrence from the fifteenth to the end of the seventeenth centuries. During this epoch, the Croatian lands constituted the first line of European defense against the rising tide of Ottoman conquest.

Since the Catholic Habsburg dynasty was the most dangerous opponent that Islam had to face, and since a majority of Croatians remained Habsburg subjects, the Turks regarded the Croats as the least desirable of all ethnic groups native to the conquered Christian lands. Prior to the coming of the Muslims, a religious sect known as the Bogumils had existed in Bosnia and in the region that after 1448 was called Hercegovina.[22] Although the relations of this group with Rome varied from time to time, and although the exact nature of the beliefs and practices of the Bogumils remains a matter of controversy, they were persecuted intermittently by Catholic elements, whether Hungarian or Croatian. Following the Ottoman conquest of Bosnia and Hercegovina, many Bogumils accepted Islam. Others seem to have identified themselves with formal Catholicism prior to the conquest, but many of the Bosnian and Hercegovinian Catholics were converted to Orthodoxy, too, during the sixteenth and seventeenth centuries. It was in this time span of more than two hundred years that the Croatians living under Turkish rule were exposed to systematic persecution and oppression. The Croatians, nevertheless, usually seized every opportunity to identify themselves with their kinsmen in the Habsburg service. Hence, the Catholic Croatian population of Bosnia and Hercegovina was decimated in the Turkish-Austrian wars of these centuries.

Between Habsburg Croatia and "Turkish Croatia," northwestern Bosnia, the "Nicija Zemlja," or "No Man's Land," evolved. Here Habsburg and Ottoman bands of raiders sought one another out as they struck into the territory of one empire or the other. To control the Turkish incursions, the Habsburgs built up the Croatian and Slavonian (Windissch) military frontiers. Later, these defensive bulwarks against the Ottoman flood became known as the Karlovac (Karlstadt) and Varazdin (Warasdin) Military Generalities. Croatian soldier peasants and Habsburg mercenaries collaborated with Serbian refugees from Turkish oppression in holding these military borders against the Muslims.

Relations between the Croatians and Serbian granicari (frontiersmen) were not good, even though they both fought against the Turks and their own kinsmen in the Turkish service with great enthusiasm. Sabor protested repeatedly to Vienna against the policy of settling "Vlachs" on Croatian soil; the Croats used this term "Vlach" to designate any Orthodox people, whether Rumanian, Serbian, Bulgarian, Greek, or Albanian,

---

22 There is a tremendous amount of controversial literature concerning the Bogumils. The definitive work on this subject is that of Dr. Dominic Mandic, *Bogomilska Crkva Bosanskih Krstjana* (Chicago, 1962). The extensive bibliography offered in Mandic's work makes superfluous such notations in this survey.

and sometimes they applied it to the Italians as well. Therefore, the specific meaning of the word as encountered in Austrian, Hungarian, and Croatian documents dating from this era often is imprecise.

Since Vienna had to deal with French, Venetian, Swedish, Prussian, and Bavarian as well as Turkish aggression, she was in no position to dispense with military manpower provided by the Orthodox refugees who came in increasing numbers to settle in the Croatian territories, as the "Nicija Zemlja" gradually was retaken from the Ottomans. Unfortunately, the Viennese authorities separated "Military Croatia" from civil or provincial Croatia and Slavonia, which remained under the jurisdiction of Ban and Sabor. Thus, the Orthodox refugees living in the several " frontiers" were exempted from Croatian political and ecclesiastical control. Like the Croatian borderers in these regions, they held farmland in perpetual and hereditary fief with exemption from all feudal dues. Since their land tenure was conditional upon required military service, Orthodox refugees had to obey only the orders of their officers. Without the defensive wall provided by the military frontiers, Central Europe, and perhaps even Italy, could not have progressed from feudal anarchy and the menace of Turkish invasion to the establishment of relatively peaceful and orderly economies.

The peasants of civil Croatia disliked the Serbian borderers, who were as apt to plunder and ravage the Croatian settlements as they were to fight the Turks. Croatian and Serbian frontiersmen also fought with one another on occasion. But both elements fought fiercely against the "Martolosi," or Turkish irregular troops, many of whom were ethnic Serbs.

In the wars against the French, Venetians, Swedes, and Germans, the Croatians acquired a reputation for loyalty that became proverbial. "Wild as bulls, proud as watchdogs," they contributed significantly to the work of salvage effected by the Catholic, or Counter Reformation, which restored part of Central Europe to the Catholic fold. In the Thirty Years War (1618-1648), the Prussian Wars (1740-1748 and 1756-1763), the French Wars (1672-1679, 1689-1697, 1701-1713, 1740-1748), and Napoleon's War (1792-1814), the Croats fought on every battlefield from the Baltic Sea to the Mediterranean. At the same time they were the vanguard of the Habsburg armies which retook Slavonia, Srijem (Sirmia), Lika, Krbava, and Dalmatia in the wars fought against the Turks between 1683 and 1718. Again in 1848-1849, the Croats battled doggedly to preserve Habsburg control over Hungary and Italy. It is probable that Ban Josip Jelacic expressed the sentiments of a majority of his compatriots when he declared at this time that while others might be able to survive the fall of the House of Austria, which was menaced by Magyar, Italian, Czech, and German republican nationalism, he could not.

Perhaps Jelacic experienced a flash of prophetic insight into the future of his nation. Such was not the fortune of the nascent Croatian intelligentsia which, inspired by French and German romantic nationalism, and by the spirit of the Italian Risorgimento, turned against the Habsburg State.

Between 1849 and 1866, the Magyars succeeded in convincing the Croatian bourgeois and clerical leaders who succeeded Jelacic that the two people should make common cause against Germanic Austria. During the early 1860's, when Vienna had embarked upon an era of constitutional experimentation, the Croatians missed an opportunity to realize their national desires. At this time the Emperor was looking for allies to help in the work of federalizing the monarchy in some degree. Both German and Magyar nationalism were suspect at this moment, and Franz Josef was even willing to see Dalmatia reunited with Croatia and Slavonia if the Hungarians did not achieve control of the coastland as a consequence. As matters turned out, the Croats refused to send representatives to the central parliament in Vienna.[23] The war with Prussia in 1866 obliged the ruler to make his peace with Magyars, and the result of this Ausgleich, or Compromise of 1867, was that the Croatians found themselves included in the Hungarian half of the Habsburg complex, as they had been before 1848. But Dalmatia, whose population was ninety per cent Croatian, remained in the Austrian part of the Dual Monarchy set up by the Ausgleich. Ironically, Dalmatia's fate was determined by the naval victory gained over the Italian fleet at Lissa in the war of 1866. The Austrian squadron which won this battle was manned largely by Croatians, and it was their success which convinced Vienna that Austria-Hungary could become a naval power. But it was essential that control of the navy and the coast should remain in the hands of Vienna rather than Budapest; it did not occur to the Austrians that there was a third alternative, namely, to entrust Zagreb, as the capital of a united Croatia, Slavonia, and Dalmatia, to which Bosnia and Hercegovina could soon have been added, with direction of the navy and the defense of the coast.

In 1868 the Croatians concluded with the Magyars the Nagodba (Compromise of 1868) which established much the same kind of relationship between Hungary and Croatia-Slavonia that the Ausgleich had effected between Hungary and Austria.[24] However, the Nagodba stipulated that the Ban was to be appointed on the recommendation of the Hungarian Minister-President in Budapest, and he was responsible to the Hungarian Government rather than to the Sabor. Furthermore, the Magyars secured an effective control over Croatian finances, and they often thwarted future Austrian plans to develop the economic

---

[23] On the relations of the Croats with Vienna and Budapest during the period 1860-1866, see Dr. Oton Knezovic, *Poviest Hrvata* (Madrid, 1961), pp. 269-279.

[24] Gustave Horn has left a study of both the Ausgleich and the Nagodba which facilitates their comparison: *Le Compromis de 1868 entre La Hongrie et La Croatie-Slavonie Celui de 1867 entre l'Autriche et la Hongrie* (Paris, 1907).

resources of the Croatian lands.[25] This obstruction was particularly exercised in regard to railroad construction, not only with respect to Croatia and Slavonia, but in regard to Dalmatia and Bosnia-Hercegovina as well. The last named region came under Austro-Hungarian control in 1878, when a largely Croatian army was sent into these provinces to suppress a Serbian-inspired insurrection against their transference from Turkish to Austro-Hungarian administration.[26]

Despite the ambiguous role played by chauvinistic elements among the Magyars, the economic prosperity of Croatia-Slavonia increased greatly between 1868 and 1914. Had the Hungarians refrained from trying to impose their language upon the Croats in educational, administrative, judicial, financial, military and transportation facilities, the Croatians might have been satisfied to remain Hungarian citizens. But few Magyars could see why they should grant to the Croats the same political, economic, and linguistic rights that they had obtained for themselves from Austria.[27]

In 1908, Vienna and Budapest decided to do what they should have done thirty years previously—to annex instead of merely administer (in the name of the Sultan) Bosnia and Hercegovina. Although the words "Serb" and "Serbian" rarely were heard in these provinces prior to 1862[28] Belgrade conducted an effective propaganda and nationalistic conversion after that date.[29] Many Hungarian Serbs, descendants of refugees who had fled from the Serbian lands conquered by the Turks. moved into Bosnia and Hercegovina after 1878. They helped to Serbianize such Orthodox elements as the Kutzo-Vlachs (Macedo-Rumans), Greeks, Bulgars, and Albanians, who had followed the Ottomans into these ancient Croatian territories.

---

25 On the rather consistent opposition offered by the Magyars to Austrian aims of economic development see *Hrvatski Dnevnik* (Sarajevo), Nov. 10, 1910. A speech delivered in the fall meeting of the Hungarian Delegation in 1910 by the noted Hungarian politician, Francis Chorins, is quoted in this article. See also Samohrvat (Dr. Djuro Dezelic), *Grudobran Kraljevine Hrvatske* (Zagreb, 1904), p. 408.

26 The best, but almost entirely overlooked account of the resistance offered by the Bosnians to the Austro-Hungarian takeover and the reasons thereof is that of T. Herkalovic, *Die Vorgeschichte der Occupation Bosniens und der Herzegovina* (Vienna, 1878).

27 Enlightening as to the Magyar viewpoint of Hungarian-Croatian relationships is Anonymous, *Die Magyarisierung in Ungarn. Nach den Debatten des ungarischen Reichstages uber den Unterricht der magyarischen Sprache in Volksschulen* (Munich, 1879). See also Jean Provolin (Baron Zivkovic), *Zur Sanierung der verletzungen des kroatisch-ungarischen Ausgleiches* (Vienna, 1886).

28 Herkalovic, *Vorgeschichte,* pp. 16-19. However Grga Martic, who for twenty years represented the Orthodox as well as the Catholic Bosnians on the Sarajevo Council established by the Turks, said that he first heard the designations "Serb" and "Serbian" employed in 1848. K. J. Koharic and F. Sisic, eds., *Zapamcenja fra Grga Martica* (Zagreb, 1906), p. 43.

29 Vladislav Skaric, *Sarajevo i njegova okolina*. p. 223 ff. Skaric was the outstanding local historian of the late nineteenth century. See also Ivan Mestrovic, *Uspomene na politicke ljude i dogodjaje* (Buenos Aires, 1961), p. 91 ff.

Thus, three population groups existed in Bosnia-Hercegovina. In 1878, the Croatian Catholic residents of these provinces welcomed the Austro-Hungarian occupation and the Muslims soon became reconciled to Habsburg rule.[30] By 1908, however, a majority of the Orthodox Bosnians had acquired a feeling of Serbian national consciousness. Therefore, the annexation stirred up an international hornet's nest, since Serbia expected that Russia would back her claim to both Bosnia and Hercegovina. The Montenegrins also had their eye on the last named region.

In 1908-09 Russia could do nothing for Serbia, since she was remedying defects in her military establishment that the recent war with Japan had disclosed; also, she was endeavoring to heal the wounds left by the revolution of 1905. The Russian Foreign Minister himself, Alexander Isvolsky, had proposed to the Austrians that they annex Bosnia-Hercegovina. In return, Vienna promised that she would not oppose the opening to Russian warships of the Straits which connect the Black Sea with the Aegean and the Mediterranean. Isvolsky was such an inept diplomat that he did not realize that it was Great Britain rather than the Dual Monarchy which stood in the way of opening the Straits.

When he found that the Habsburg State had made a meaningless concession, and that what passed for public opinion in Czarist Russia had rallied to the support of Serbia, Isvolsky tried to squirm out of the bargain that he had made with the Austro-Hungarian Foreign Minister, Count Aehrenthal. Isvolsky further accused the Habsburg State of having wilfully disturbed the peace of Europe, of having violated the Berlin agreement of 1878 in regard to Bosnia-Hercegovina, and of having sinister designs in the Balkans. Only when Aehrenthal threatened to publish their correspondence did Isvolsky shut up. The consequence of this imbroglio was that Isvolsky lost his job as Foreign Minister. He was reassigned as Ambassador to France, where he worked to stir up a war of "revenge" against Austria-Hungary and Germany. Other prominently placed Russians developed acute cases of Austrophobia, too, and Isvolsky's successor, Sazonoff, organized a Balkan League consisting of Serbia, Bulgaria, Montenegro and Greece.[31] Originally designed as an anti-Austrian instrument, the League escaped the control of its mentor and attacked and defeated the Turkish Empire.[32]

These developments coincided with the appearance in Croatia-Slavonia and Dalmatia of a new political grouping, the Serbo-Croat Coalition. This peculiar constellation was the result of Magyar nationalistic intran-

---

[30] Filip Juka, "Pavlinovic o Bosni," *Kolo* (Zagreb), XXII. Stjepan Radic, *Zivo hrvatsko pravo na Bosnu i Hercegovinu* (Zagreb, 1908); Ferdo Sisic, *Herceg-Bosna prigodom Aneksije* (Zagreb, 1909).

[31] S. Sazonoff (Isvolsky's successor as Russian Foreign Minister), *Fateful Years* (New York, 1928), pp. 55, 72.

[32] The standard guide works through the maze of diplomatic and military details involved in these struggles still are E. C. Helmreich's masterly *Diplomacy of the Balkan Wars* (Cambridge, Mass., 1928), and W. L. Langer, ed. *Encyclopaedia of World History,* (Boston, Houghton-Mifflin, 1968).

sigence and of Dalmatian poverty. The latter was a consequence of the former, since the Magyars zealously opposed every effort made by Vienna to better the economic situation of the Monarchy's coastal province. In this connection, the prosperity of Istria, in which the Magyars had no particular interest, ought to be compared with the indigence prevailing in Dalmatia, which the Hungarians were determined to prevent from becoming an asset to the Austrian half of the Habsburg State. Of course, the same old element of romantic nationalism that had misled the Croatian intellectuals from the time of Liudevit Gaj to that of Racki and Strosmajer also influenced the formation of the Coalition. Hungarian shortsightedness, and the successes gained by the Serbs in the Balkan Wars of 1909-13, strengthened the Coalition at the expense of more far-seeing political factions in the Croatian lands. Among the latter were included the strongly nationalistic and anti-Serbian elements who adhered in greater or less degree to the program of Croatian national unification advanced by Dr. Ante Starcevic (d. 1894), and the adherents of the newly formed Peasant Party organized by Stjepan and Ante Radic.[33] Although the Coalition succeeded in securing a majority in the Sabor, this achievement was the consequence of the artificially restricted franchise which the Magyars had imposed upon the Croatian Kingdom. Had universal suffrage prevailed, the Coalition would have been swept away overnight by a Peasant-Nationalist combination. As it was, the Coalition drew its chief strength from the numerous Serbian elements resident in the Croatian lands; relatively few Croatians, save for a handful of "intellectuals," backed it. At the same time it ought to be realized that the Coalition had no really clearcut program. Even many of its Croatian Serbian members did not go so far as to desire separation from the rest of the Habsburg State, and union of the Croatian lands with Serbia. Only a minority had this idea in mind, even after the aggrandizement of Serbia in the Balkan Wars.

Meanwhile, Serbian organizations such as the Narodna Obrana and the Crna Ruka or "Black Hand" kept the nationalistic pot boiling in Bosnia-Hercegovina. Russia had promised Belgrade that in a few years time she would be in a position to back up the Serbian claim to these provinces. Chauvinistic Serbian elements counted upon this promise.[34]

[33] Both of the Radic brothers voiced fiery criticism of the policies and objectives of the Coalition. See especially Dr. Antun Radic, *Sabrana djela,* ed. Dr. V. Macek and Rudolf Herceg (Zagreb, 1936), VII, 175-204. See also Vicko Milic, *Postanak Riecke Rezolucije i njezine posljedice (m.p., n.d.);* Josip Horvat, *Stranke kod Hrvata i njihove ideologije* (Belgrade, 1939); V. Skaric, "Die ideologie der kroatische Bauernbewegung,"*Slavische Rundschau,* I (1937), 147-156; Rudolf Horvat *Najnovije doba Hrvatske Povijesti* (Zagreb, 1906), pp. 205-208.

[34] Actually it was "unofficial" rather than "official" Russia, that is the Panslav, ultranationalistic, and Austrophobe elements in the land of the Tsars, that the Balkan Governments, particularly Serbia and Montenegro, depended upon for support. See France, Ministere des Affaires Etrangeres, *Documents diplomatiques francais,* 3rd series, IV, no. 577; Austria-Hungary, Min. des Aussere Angelegenheiten, *Osterreich-Ungarns Aussenpolitik von der bosnischen Krise 1908 bis zum Kriegsausbruch 1914,* 8 vols. (Vienna, 1930), IV, nos. 4020, 4035.

An intellectual proletariat had come into being in these old Croatian lands and there was student unrest of the same kind that has manifested itself in the United States in recent years. From 1910 on, there were a number of Serbian-inspired attempts to assassinate Croatian officials, both in Bosnia-Hercegovina and in Croatia. Finally, on June 28, 1914, the students scored a bullseye – they murdered the Heir to the Throne, Archduke Franz Ferdinand and his wife at Sarajevo.[35]

The Croatians had expected the Archduke to join all of the Croatian territories together when he came to the throne, thus establishing a trialistic instead of a dualistic state. Until, 1906, Franz Ferdinand had intended to do just this.[36] In that year, however, he met with a very chilly reception in Dalmatia when he visited that province.[37] He began to have his doubts about the advisability of resurrecting the ancient Triune Kingdom, and allowing it autonomy and virtual parity with Austria and Hungary. The chief of his military bureau, the highly intelligent and capable Colonel Alexander Brosch, asked him point-blank if the loyalty of the Croats to the Monarchy could be relied upon if they were given virtual independence. Furthermore, the Colonel pointed out that the Austrian province of Carniola, which was inhabited principally by Slovenes, and the predominantly Slovene areas of southern Styria and Carinthia, would have to be given to the "Great Croatian" entity that the Archduke had thought of establishing. Thus, the Croats and Slovenes would have complete control of the Austro-Hungarian coast, and of the navy and merchant marine. If they ever took it into their heads to revolt against Habsburg rule, and the existence of the Coalition suggested that they might, since both Croats and Slovenes seemed to be susceptible to Serbian nationalistic propaganda, they probably would succeed in disintegrating the Monarchy. Further, if the Croats and Slovenes were allowed to have their own state, the Czechs would demand

---

[35] The best presentation of the assassinations per se and the story behind them is that supplied by Dr. Joachim Remak, *Sarajevo: The Story of a Political Murder* (New York, 1959). The well publicized relation by the official Serbian Communist propagandist, Vladimir Dedijer, *The Road to Sarajevo* (New York, 1964), is an artfully constructed attempt to minimize Serbian responsibility for the crime. It is very unfortunate that the factual disclosures of the Serbian Minister, Lyuba Yovanovitch, *The Murder of Sarajevo* (London, 1924), have been so largely overlooked and even discredited by influential publicists and propagandists such as the late R. W. Seton-Watson, who sometimes is referred to, altogether erroneously, as a "historian." Yovanovitch, who at one time or another was Serbian Minister of Education and later President of the Serb-Croat-Slovene postwar Parliament, published the Serbian original of the above cited translation in *Krv Slovenstva* (Belgrade, 1924).

[36] See his letter to Tsar Nicholas II of Russia avowing his support of the Trialist idea, *British Documents on the Origins of the War 1898-1914,* ed. G. P. Gooch and Harold Temperley, 11 vols. (London, 1927-1938), IX, p. 548.

[37] The Fiume Resolutions of 1905, and the formation of the Serbo-Croat Coalition, disillusioned Franz Ferdinand with respect to Croatian political attitudes, even though outside of Dalmatia Croatian elements greeted him warmly as did the Frankist (Rightist) element in that province. See *Hrvatski Dnevnik* (Sarajevo), Sept. 13, 1906.

the same status for themselves and a whole Pandora's box of political evils would be opened. Already there was a deadlock because the Austrian and the Hungarian Parliaments never could see eye to eye with one another or reach any kind of amicable agreement on vital issues such as the status of Bosnia-Hercegovina. It would not help the situation to have three or four parliaments instead of only two.

For all of these reasons Brosch advised the Archduke that the "Great Croatian" or Trialist program could not be realized in the terms demanded by the Croats themselves. Franz Ferdinand decided that the best way to handle the Croatian problem was to maintain the existing Hungarian-Croatian relationship but to have a Habsburg Archduke permanently resident in Zagreb. Thus, the Croatians would have a "direct line" to Vienna which would satisfy one of their chief grievances, the fact that, as a constitutional ruler, the Emperor-King could not deal directly with Croatia-Slavonia nor could the spokesmen of that Kingdom approach him directly; both parties had to go through Budapest to make contact with one another, and the Hungarians placed every possible obstacle in the way of such contact. Therefore, Franz Ferdinand picked out a Croatian-speaking Habsburg and directed him to have his children educated in Croatian schools, in order to fully identify himself and them with the legitimate aspirations of the Croatians and to prepare to reside permanently among that people.[38] Thus, the Croats could present their desires and remonstrances to the Habsburg resident in Zagreb in the future, and that individual had only to pick up his telephone to relay their demands to Vienna. Budapest would be bypassed effectively, and the Croats, in effect, could be masters in their own house without establishing dangerous political precedents.

In 1914 the Croatians did not know all these details concerning their anticipated future, but they did feel sure that Franz Ferdinand had had their welfare in mind.[39] Therefore, they responded to the call to war

---

[38] This was Archduke Leopold Salvator, who had a fair knowledge himself of the Croatian language, and whose sons learned it thoroughly.

[39] The Archduke's attitude towards the Croatians was colored by the fact that he blamed all of the ills of the Monarchy on the Magyars, and considered that the latter managed and made tools of the Croatians. However he never entirely gave up the idea of Trialism, a fact which his letter to Wilhelm II of Germany disavowing this plan does not contradict. Since Wilhelm, and practically all other Reich Germans, were bitter opponents of the concept of Trialism, Franz Ferdinand hardly could flaunt this idea in their faces, even if he did not have doubts about its advisability himself. Although the Archduke, thanks to his tutoring by Onno Klopp and other German nationalists, had the idea that the Germanic stocks were culturally superior to the Slavs in general, he did not particularly like non-Austrian Germans. However, he wished to use the alliance with Germany as a support of European peace, calculating that Russia would not dare attack the Dual Monarchy as long as the latter remained allied with the Reich. Therefore he endeavored to be as diplomatic as possible in his dealings with Berlin, whether in regard to the Croatian question or on other matters. This does not mean, however, that if Franz Ferdinand had ascended the throne and taken it into his head to implement the idea of Trialism, he would have allowed Berlin's opinions to influence his decision. What most commentators on the Trialist

with considerable enthusiasm. It is unfortunate that the Croatian military record during 1914-18 not only has been overlooked by foreign observers but has been misrepresented purposely by Croatian "intellectuals" and politicians, even by many who do not have Yugoslav bias.[40]

The reason for this peculiar circumstance is that a few individuals, who were inspired by romanticist "nationalism" of the Yugoslav variety, formed an Exile Committee which arrogated to itself the authority to speak in the name of the Croatian nation in London, Paris, Washington, Rome, and St. Petersburg. The most sensible member of this exile group was the world-renowned sculptor, Ivan Mestrovic. He lived to acknowledge frankly that the premises upon which the exiles based their policies and actions were monumentally fallacious.[41] They had misinterpreted the nature of the Croatian-Serbian relationship, and this misinterpretation had the most fatal consequences imaginable for the future of the Croatian nation and people.

The thesis of Yugoslav or Serbo-Croatian ethnic identity is a myth that rests upon an artificial linguistic unity established by Croatian "intellectuals" of romantic nationalist persuasion in the mid-nineteenth century. This accomplishment is a story in itself. It will suffice to note here that the authentically Croatian "ca" and "kaj" dialects, both of which had impressive literary monuments to their credit, were discarded in favor of the "sto" parlance which was employed by the Croatians of

issue overlook is that so long as he was only Heir Apparent the Archduke could not publicly avow his support of the Trialist idea because by so doing he automatically would controvert the wish of his uncle, Franz Josef I, who wished to maintain the existing status quo as long as he lived. On the other hand it is sometimes forgotten that Franz Ferdinand never did publicly or definitively repudiate the Trialist scheme. The extraordinarily complicated nature of this question cannot be gone into in detail in this work, and it was this complexity which caused the Archduke to hold it in abeyance prior to his death. It is probable that, had he become Emperor-King, a defeat of the Coalition at the polls would have induced him to put the Trialist concept into operation. The Hungarian opposition to his reign that was anticipated almost certainly would have forced him to take this course. It was his fear that a "Great Croatia" would side with Budapest against Vienna that more than anything else accounts for the Archduke's turning away from the plan of resurrecting the Triune Kingdom. All the Croatians really had to do was to persuade him that their destinies were tied permanently to Austria rather than to Hungary to motivate him to satisfy their aspirations. It is significant that Prince Karl Schwarzenberg and the Belvedere Press continued to press the plan of Trialism and to remain in close touch with right wing Croatian circles.

[40] The best accounts of Croatian participation in the war of 1914-18 are those of Stjepan Pavicic, *Hrvatska vojna i ratna poviest i prvi svjetski rat* (Zagreb, 1943), and General Peter Blaskovic, *S Bosnjacima u svjetskom ratu* (Zagreb, n.d.). Blaskovic was a captain of artillery in 1914. Also there is a great deal of information concerning the Croatian performance in the war scattered through the seven-volume official Austro-Hungarian history of this war, as well as in a multitude of other Austrian and Hungarian writings on this subject.

[41] See his memoirs, *Uspomene na politicke ljude i dogodjaje,* and his article in *The Croatian struggle for freedom and independence,* ed. Mihanovic-Bonifacic (Chicago, 1955).

Hercegovina.[42] The Serbs spoke a subdialect of the "sto", too, and eminent Serbian philologists such as Vuk Karadyitch and George Danitchich had brought the Serbian version of the "sto" to the attention of the outside world in their writings. Thus, a thousand years of linguistic tradition was tossed on the scrap heap, the old "ca" and "kaj" literatures were relegated to the dust bin, and the way was cleared for the emergence of the idea of Yugoslav unity. Some Croatians realized from the beginning that Yugoslavism meant the extinction of Croatian national identity, but their warnings were disregarded.

The settlement of so many Serbians on Croatian soil was another nail in the coffin of Croatian identity. It was the Croatian Serb minority which in the fall of 1918, and with some assistance from the Czechs, stampeded the political representatives of the Croatian nation (Ban and Sabor) into exchanging Hungarian and Austrian political hegemony for Serbian despotism. That is, if we may be permitted to crack a stock joke in this connection, the Croats leaped from the Austro-Hungarian frying pan into the Yugoslav fire.

In essence, this tragically unnecessary and monumentally catastrophic political error was a consequence of the loss of the war and of the starvation conditions produced by the Entente naval blockade. Also, it had become evident by the fall of 1918 that Washington, London, and Paris had made commitments to their Serbian, Italian, and Rumanian allies, as well as to Czech and Polish exile or hyphenated American groups that were prejudicial to the continued existence of the Habsburg State. Furthermore, the Austrian Social Democrats and the Kossuthist, or "1848" faction among the Magyars, were determined to disintegrate the Danubian Monarchy. Since there was no Jelacic or Radetzsky upon the scene to do for the Croats what Mustapha Kemal Pasha did for the Turks and Baron Mannerheim for the Finns, most Croatians allowed themselves to be persuaded by the Croatian Serb minority, and by emissaries sent by the Czech exile leaders, Massaryk and Benes, that they could escape the consequences of having fought on the losing side. The break-up of the Austro-Hungarian Army in the battle of Vittorio-Veneto (October 24 - November 4, 1918) was the decisive factor in motivating the Croatians into accepting the Yugoslav program subscribed to by their "representatives" in exile.

The union of Serbs, Croats, and Slovenes under a common political roof necessarily was effected under Serbian hegemonistic auspices, although the training that the Slovenes had received in the school of practical Austrian politics had taught them how to deal with stronger ethnic elements. This was a lesson the Croats had not learned because of basic differences that existed between Austrian and Hungarian political overlordship.

[42] On the distribution of the several Croatian dialects in the present century see the important series of articles by R. Strohal in *Rad,* nos. CXLVI, CXLVIII, CLII, CLIII, CLXLL, CLXXX, and CXLLX.

Until 1928, most Croatians considered Stjepan Radic to be their political and national spokesman. Unfortunately, Radic's political policies were characterized by instability, although he was always the champion of Croatian national rights. He wavered in his convictions as to whether these could be secured to best advantage under Habsburg, Karageorgevitch (Yugoslav), or republican auspices, and at one time he even flirted with Marxism. In any case, his assassination by a Serbian deputy in a parliamentary session in 1928 was followed by the establishment of a royal dictatorship which was designed to preserve the artificial and unnatural unity created at the end of 1918. A new group of actors, the Ustashas, now appeared on the Croatian political stage. Under the leadership of a fervent nationalist and a trained lawyer, Dr. Ante Pavelic, this element took over the political program elaborated initially by Starcevic and the right-wing Frankist Party of the pre-1919 era. The most important plank in the Ustasha platform was the union of Croatia, Slavonia, Dalmatia, Istria, Bosnia, and Hercegovina in a "Great Croatia" or Croatian national complex. There was nothing new about this concept, but Pavelic added dynamism to it by organizing a campaign of terrorism that was intended to disrupt Yugoslavia, that is, a program to employ against the Serbs the same weapon that they had used to prepare the disintegration of the Habsburg Monarchy. Also, Pavelic endeavored to play off Nazi Germany against Fascist Italy and, therefore, to secure Croatian national independence.[43]

In 1941 the Nazi attack upon the Yugoslav State allowed the Croatians to secure this objective. Croatian units in the Yugoslav Army turned on the Serbs and facilitated the almost instantaneous dissolution of the Karageorgevitch Army. Croatian national independence was proclaimed at Zagreb on April 10 by General, later Marshal, Slavko Kvaternik, a former Austro-Hungarian officer of the (excessively audacious) "Draufganger" variety. Initially the Ustashas enjoyed considerable popularity, and there was little opposition to the setting up of the new state. In practice, however, Croatian independence was limited by the fact that the resurrected kingdom possessed no armament industry whatsoever. It was entirely dependent upon Germany and Italy for military equipment and supplies. Both the Nazis and Fascists took full advantage of this weakness in the Croatian economy which traditionally had concentrated upon producing butter, or at least olive oil, rather than guns.

Although the newly-proclaimed Croatian kingdom had less reason to complain of German harshness and exactions than did other Axis satellite powers, Germans deliberately starved the Croatian armed forces with regard to the supply of guns, planes, tanks, ammunition, and the other appurtenances of modern warfare. Berlin, not desiring Zagreb to become too independent, sabotaged all efforts to create a Croatian war industry.

---

[43] See the article by S. Guldescu, "The background of the Croatian nationalist movement," *South Atlantic Quarterly*, LVI (Summer, 1957), pp. 314-328.

It was with Italy rather than with Germany, however, that the Croatians had their most pronounced difficulties. The Italians claimed Dalmatia and Istria because, in the Middle Ages, Venice had acquired a foothold in these territories which subsequently she expanded and maintained until 1797. The diary of Count Ciano, Mussolini's son-in-law, discloses that the Fascists did not expect to get either Dalmatia or Istria in 1941. They advanced the old Venetian claim to these lands only because they hoped that by so doing the Croatians might be persuaded to yield to them possession of Zadar, Split, and another spot where Ciano's father had distinguished himself in a naval action in World War I. But Pavelic, and whomever he had in the way of advisers, allowed themselves to be cozened into handing over most of Dalmatia and Istria to Italy. This political and diplomatic flabbiness dissipated much of the popularity that the Ustasha movement had enjoyed up to this time. Furthermore, the moral sensibilities of the Croatians were outraged by the brutal treatment that the Slovenes experienced at the hands of both Nazis and Fascists.

Pavelic did not lack intelligence, and years of residence in Italy between 1930 and 1941 had made him aware of the military weakness of Mussolini's Italy. He calculated, correctly, that sooner or later the Italians would have to drop out of the war. Therefore, he expected to be able to take back Dalmatia and Istria at an early date. He did not foresee that when the Italians did throw in the towel in 1943 they would surrender their positions and armament not to his forces but to those of the chief Russian agent in the Balkans, Josip (Tito) Broz.

A sergeant in the old Austro-Hungarian Army, Tito had been wounded and captured by the Russians in 1915. He was converted to Marxism during the Russian Revolution and was sent back to the Balkans later on to organize the Communist Party in the territories ruled by the Karageorgevitch Dynasty. When war came, he brought into the field bands of guerrilla fighters, chiefly Serbs, Slovenes, and Macedonians, who endeavored to aid the Russians by making trouble for the Germans in Croatia, Serbia, and Bosnia. Few Croatians supported Tito. Although his father's side of the family was Croatian, his mother was Slovene. Following the Italian surrender in 1943, large numbers of Italian soldiers joined his bands. Tito camouflaged his Communist affiliation under the misleading titles of "People's Liberation Army" and "People's Liberation Front" in order to impress upon Winston Churchill, Franklin D. Roosevelt, and other Anglo-Americans the conviction that his movement was a democratic one. This tactic paid off, for it secured an immense amount of military aid and political recognition, as well as all kinds of favorable publicity, from the English-speaking world.

Tito's polyglot forces competed with the Serbian Chetniks of General Drazha Mihailovic in slaughtering thousands of Croatian civilians of all ages, religions, and of both sexes. In this process they vied with one another in perpetrating every kind of atrocity, often displaying an ingenuity that aroused the envy of both Germans and Russians. The American and British Governments knew what was going on, but "considerations of higher policy" caused them to turn a blind eye on events in the Balkans and Central Europe. To this day, there has never been any public condemnation of the crimes committed by Tito's Partisans. On the other hand, the Croatians were stigmatized as "war criminals" because they struck back effectively against the Partisans and their sympathizers. Of course, there were "war criminals" among the Croatians, as well as among all other peoples, but their lethal achievements, at least insofar as the killing of non-combatants are concerned, pale into insignificance when compared to the record compiled by the Partisans. After the war, however, Tito's regime brazenly attributed to the Ustashas and other Croatian elements the responsibility for mass butcheries that the Partisans themselves had perpetrated or instigated.

When the Germans surrended in May, 1945, the Croatian armed forces, consisting of seventeen full divisions, plus naval and various irregular units, were still entirely intact, unbeaten, and inspired by high morale, despite their inadequate armament. This military establishment was more than sufficient to deal with Tito's overpublicized forces, although, of course, the Croatian armed forces could not have held out indefinitely against the British, Americans, and Russians. Since history is the record of what happened rather than of what could have happened, there is no point at this juncture in analyzing the strength of the political cards that the Croatians still had in their hands but did not play. What did happen is related by various surviving participants and eyewitnesses in this book.

In the light of historical perspective, it is evident that the slaughter of the Croatian armed forces in 1945 was a delayed action effect of the wholly useless and unnecessary battle of Vittorio Veneto in 1918. The Croatian position was almost the same in 1918 and 1945; they were caught on the losing side in an age of ideological warfare in which a defeated enemy almost automatically is classified as a war criminal. During 1914-18 the record made by the Croatian troops in the field was second to none and, allowing for the sharp limitations in their armament, the same may be said for the years 1941-45. But in the First World War, a handful of exiles were involved with the Entente Powers while in the second global struggle, the nation was divided into anti and pro-Communist factions.

Yet, there was one great difference between the position of the Croatians in 1918 and that which they occupied in 1945. In the former year they still were citizens of a great power, and even when that power dissolved into its component parts, they still enjoyed the status and prestige that Austro-Hungarian citizenship conferred upon them. Both in 1918 and 1945 the governments under which the Croatians were living tried to find someone to surrender to as soon as they realized that the war was lost. Each time, it was loyalty to the German alliance and the disinclination for the victorious powers to deal with Germany or her allies which negated these surrender efforts. In both wars, the major winning powers made commitments to their insignificant allies – Serbia, Rumania, and Italy in the first struggle, the Tito regime in the second – which involved the destruction of the state of which the Croatians were a part.

In the fall of 1918, the Habsburg Army, in which the Croatians fought, was the last intact and unbeaten force that the Central Powers had in the field. If this army had remained intact, it still might have kept at least a part of the Monarchy together, as Radetzsky's forces had done in 1848-49. In such case, Serbs, Montenegrins, Italians, Rumanians, Czechs, and possibly even the Poles, would be unable to realize their national ambitions. Therefore, Great Britain, France, and the United States contributed what forces and material were needed to enable the Italians to win the battle of Vittorio Veneto, a contest that neither the Austro-Hungarian Government nor Army Command wished to fight. The successes gained by the Entente forces were still something less than decisive when, during the night of October 31 – November 2, the Karolyi Government in Hungary recalled all "Hungarian," meaning not only Magyar but Slovak, Carpatho-Russian or Ruthenian, Transylvania Rumanian, Hungarian Serb, and Croatian troops from the front in order that they might defend the southern frontier of Hungary against the Entente forces advancing through the Balkans after the collapse of Bulgaria and Turkey. Still the front line Habsburg troops kept on fighting until, at 3:00 A.M., November 3, the Austro-Hungarian Command ordered its forces to cease hostilities on land, sea, and in the air. An armistice agreement had been signed at Villa Giusti. But then the Italian Command blandly declared that the armistice could not go into effect until 3:00 P.M., November 4, since it would not be possible to communicate the order to advanced Entente units before that time.

Although many Austro-Hungarian troops, including especially the Croatians, fought until the moment their own command instructed them to stop, the tentative break-up of the monarchy into separate compartments already had been accomplished by opportunistic politicians who were able to build upon the good work accomplished in this direction by the Karolyi Government in Hungary and by the Austrian Social Democrats. Romantic nationalism was triumphing everywhere. Loss of the battle of Vittorio Veneto made the dissolution definitive, since there was no Radetzsky or Jelacic on the scene. So the question of the hour was: what country am I going to find myself living in? Austria? Germany? A Czech or a Slovak or a Czecho-Slovak State? Hungary? Rumania? Italy? Poland? Serbia? Croatia? Slovenia? Or some kind of Yugoslav creation? Everyone wanted to get home and find out for himself what was going to happen.

The Austro-Hungarian rear guards were profoundly surprised when they found themselves overtaken by Italian cavalry and armored car units and bombed by British and American planes, and more surprised when their Italian pursuers commanded them to surrender. "The war's over, you damn fools! Just get the hell out of our way and let us go on home. We don't want any part of Italy! You can have it all!"

"The war's not over until 3:00 P.M. tomorrow (after 12:00 midnight on November 3, today)," was the reply of the Italians. The Italian Command's assertion that the armistice could not go into effect immediately was ridiculous, of course. What the Italian Government wanted to do was to strengthen its hand at the approaching peace conference. Therefore, it demanded that all mobile units race forward to occupy as much Austro-Hungarian territory as they could so that Rome might lay claim to it at the conference. All former Habsburg troops found to the rear of the most advanced points reached by Italian cavalry and mobile commands as of 3:00 P.M., November 4, were to be declared prisoners of war.

Some of the Austro-Hungarian troops refused to accept the Entente interpretation of the armistice terms and shot their way through to safety. Most of those who found themselves behind the advanced Italian units could see no point in throwing away their lives now that the country for which they had fought no longer existed. They supposed that if they laid down their arms they would at worst be held prisoners for a few days and then allowed to go on to their homes. Their captors might even feed them, an alluring prospect to the losers of the war, for the Austro-Hungarian troops had been on starvation rations since 1917. Thus by three o'clock on the afternoon of November 4, Italy had 400,000 prisoners on her hands. Three-fourths of these were taken between 3:00 A.M. November 3, and 3:00 P.M. November 4, *after* the Habsburg Army had been ordered by its own command to discontinue hostilities.[44]

The Italians had not expected to win such a decisive victory, even though they had delayed their offensive until they were pretty sure that the Austro-Hungarian Army had lost much of its fighting capacity. Had they realized the actual situation, namely that the Army which had beaten them so often was breaking up into bands of disorganized soldiery more interested in venting their national spites on one another than in opposing the recent enemy, the Italian generals and government undoubtedly would have put the armistice agreement into effect as of 3:00 A.M., November 3, when the Austro-Hungarians did. As it was, the Italians were utterly bewildered to find themselves with 400,000 prisoners on their hands. They had no way of feeding or accommodating in adequate manner this mass of captives. Still, they were afraid to let them go, and the result was that the captured troops were not released

[44] Emperor-King Karl realized that the Supreme Command had neglected to ascertain when the Italians were going to rest on their arms, and therefore he endeavored to countermand the orders issued by his generals. However, his instructions to keep on fighting until the Entente forces stopped doing so reached only a few Austro-Hungarian units.

until the spring of 1919, by which time hundreds, perhaps thousands, had perished from hunger, cold, and disease.

Few of the 400,000 would have surrendered to the Entente had they known the fate in store for them. Still, in 1918, even though Austria-Hungary had ceased to exist, this old and generally respected European landmark extended a protecting shadow over her former fighters. The Serbs, and some Italians, spiritual descendants of Garibaldi's Redshirts and Mazzini's gangs of assassins, might have been willing to massacre the surrendered troops, but they did not dare indulge their lethal desires, except on a small scale. Even in war-happy America, an outraged howl of protest would have gone up had the war to make the world safe for democracy been ended by the wholesale massacre of forces which had fought to make it safe *from* democracy. There were Frenchmen, Englishmen, even some Italians, who rather regretted the disappearance of the international Habsburg state and who certainly felt that its troops could not be treated in the way that the English had dealt with the Sepoy rebels of the Great Indian Mutiny of 1857.

In 1945, most Croatians had in mind the experience of 1918. As losers, they could expect the same treatment they had received in 1918. Since the Serbs had not dared to horrify world opinion then by taking mass reprisals upon their enemies of 1914-18, they hardly would do so twenty-seven years later. What the Croatians forgot was that the war of 1914-18 was a relatively civilized affair. More important, the Communists were among the winners in 1945.

The Croats failed to realize that since 1918 the substitution of the name Yugoslav for Serb, Croat, and Slovene had caused most Europeans and Americans to forget, if they ever knew, that there was an old and time-honored Croatian nation. As subjects of the oldest of European dynasties, the Croatians from 1527 to 1918 had enjoyed a certain status in the eyes of the world which knew of their military achievements, even if it did not always approve of them. In 1945, the Croatians had no such status or reputation. They were branded as willing satellites of what, next to the several Marxist political Frankensteins, was the most monstrous creation of modern times, Nazi Germany. Everyone knew what the Nazis had done to their enemies. Therefore it was open season on both the Germans and their wartime allies, the latter in particular. After all, even though they were defeated "war criminals," there were so many Germans that no one could simply kill them all. German-Americans in the U.S.A. and in Latin America could influence their governments in favor of their kinsmen at home.

But Germany's little allies, particularly the Croats, Slovenes, and Slovaks, had no one to speak in their behalf. And there were enough Marxists among all three of these nationalities to persuade the Western Allies, with their ideological commitment to "popular" government, that this form of regime was being foisted upon all three peoples. Not that Britain and the United States would have fought Russia anyway to save the lives of a few million Croats, Slovenes, and Slovaks, but the "popular" front effected by the Balkan and Central European Communists helped to lull the moral sensibilities of the Anglo-Americans.

The Croatians were in an especially precarious situation in 1945, because they had lost their old international standing. They were not even as well known to the outside world in that year as they had been in 1918. True, no one knew much about Croatian culture even before that year, but at least most literate (and many illiterate) people in the Western World knew that the Croats were good Catholics, invariably the first attacking wave of the Habsburg Armies, and the last to leave a lost field if they left it at all. Furthermore, as citizens of a venerable great power their throats could not be cut, even when they were defeated and captured.

In 1945 this was no longer the case. The replacement of the name "Croat" or "Croatian" by the amorphous designation "Yugoslav" ipso facto made the fighters for Croatian national independence traitors to Yugoslavia. No one had any use for traitors, who since time immemorial have been stood up against a wall and shot, whether with arrows or bullets, or else hung, drawn and quartered, or otherwise butchered. Therefore, the Anglo-American Allies and the world in general accepted without much question the verdict passed upon the Croatians by "popular" justice in the postwar Yugoslav state. Nor has the outside world inquired into the details of this "justice" which was meted out to the losers in the last global conflict.

This work has been compiled to inform the reading public everywhere of the consequences of Communist victory in a war. What happened to the Croatian armed forces and civilian fugitives from "popular" justice will happen in Vietnam, Cambodia, Laos, Thailand, Yemen, or wherever else the hammer and sickle emerges triumphant in a war. And the fate of the Croatians can be that of Americans, too, if native Communists and fellow travelers ever succeed, with foreign assistance, in getting control of this country. Englishmen, too, may live to regret that they did not make use of the Croatian forces in 1945 and afterwards.

But, again, history is the record of what has happened rather than of what could or should have happened. We can only hope that future generations of Americans and Englishmen may not have to rue errors of commission and omission and lost opportunities as we Croatians must to the end of our lives.

— Dr. Stanko Guldescu

Fayetteville, N. C.

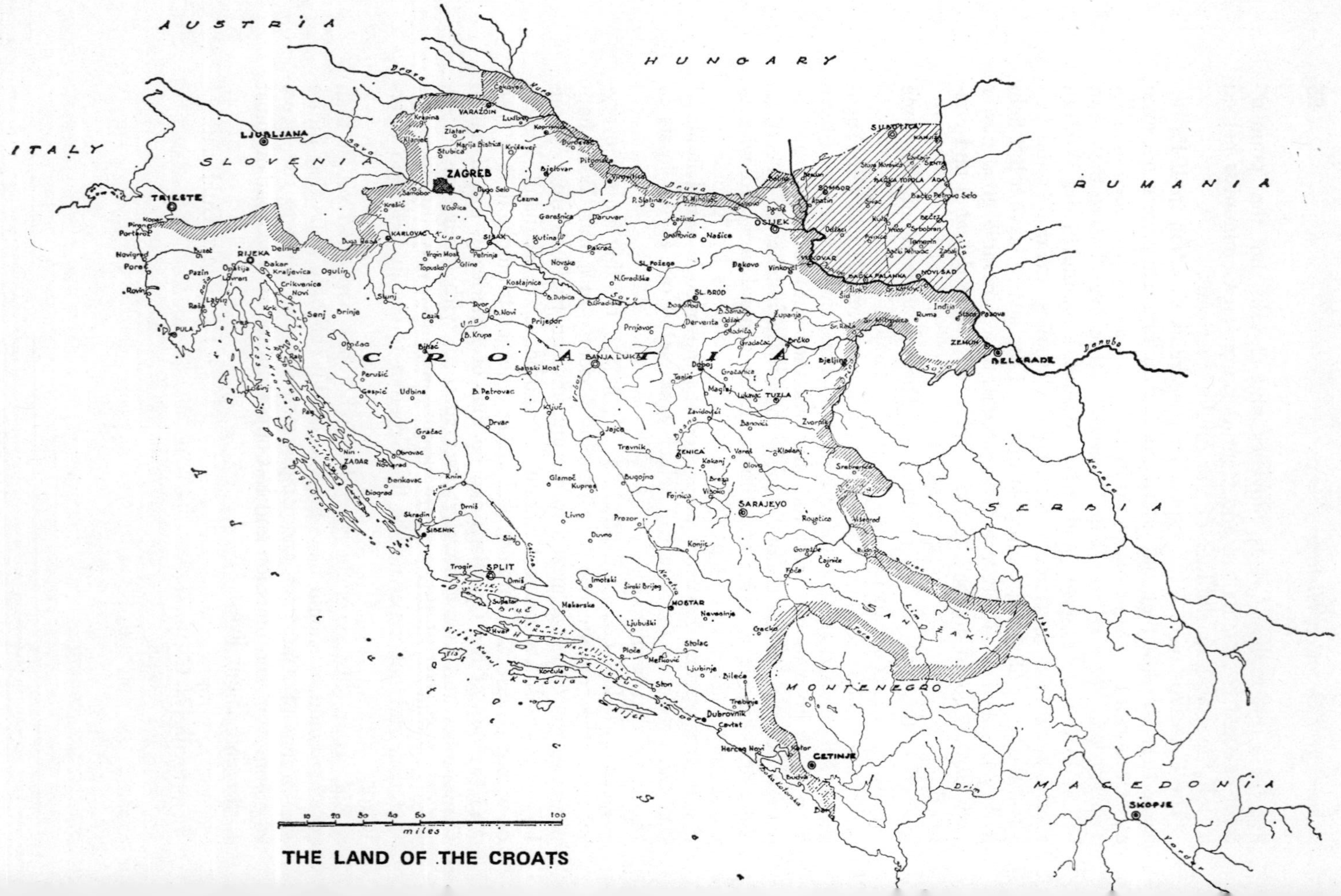

THE LAND OF THE CROATS

Chapter 2

The Serbo-Croatian Antagonism

Although the Croatians and Serbians speak related languages, thirteen hundred years of separate political existence have created a distinct national identity for each of them. During the Middle Ages, these two peoples had little contact with one another. Nor, because of the difference in the religions that they professed, was there much intermarriage. Whether in the medieval or the modern era the Croats intermarried principally with Slovaks, Slovenes, Magyars, and Austrians. They absorbed certain elements of the culture of these peoples who immigrated into the Croatian lands. Naturally the blood infusion of these Croatianized people was accompanied by a cultural interchange which operated within the framework of Latin Christianity. On the other hand, the Croatians neither mixed physically with the Serbs, nor were they influenced greatly by the Byzantine and other borrowed cultures of medieval and modern Serbia.

As stated above, the Serbians were a negligible ethnic factor in Bosnia and Hercegovina before the Turkish conquest of these territories. Those Croatians who remained in the provinces kept aloof from the Orthodox newcomers, except when they were forcibly converted to Orthodoxy themselves. Practically all of the Orthodox stocks in Bosnia and Hercegovina eventually came to think of themselves as ethnic Serbs, whatever their original national orgin may have been. Generally, the Catholic and Muslim Croatians of Bosnia-Hercegovina remained a distinct nationality which had little in common with their Orthodox neighbors.

It was in the military frontiers created by the Habsburg dynasty that Croatians and Serbs came to associate with one another more closely than had been the case heretofore. Often this association was anything but an amicable one. After the reconquest of the Lika and Krbava areas, and of Slavonia and Dalmatia, considerable numbers of Serbian and other Orthodox peoples fled into these territories to escape Turkish oppression. Their descendants have remained to the present day on Croatian soil.

In conclusion, the Croatians and Serbians may conveniently be regarded as "frontier peoples," representing the civilizations of West and East respectively. Essentially the Croatians are Central Europeans in their mores, outlook upon life, and political, economic, and cultural associations and values, while the Serbians are "Balkanese." Even in the twentieth century, and in that great melting pot of peoples (the

United States itself), Croatians and Serbians generally maintain their separate identities, at least until such time as the overwhelming pressure of Americanization makes them indistinguishable from Germans, Frenchmen, Rumanians, Spaniards, and other European stocks.

Despite the profound differences that distinguished the Croatian and Serbian people, during the 1830's and afterwards a group of misguided Croatian idealists devoted themselves to the task of making one people out of these two groups. The spirit of nationalism, diffused throughout Europe by the French revolutionary and Napoleonic armies on the one hand, and by German romanticists such as Herder on the other, provided the inspiration for this endeavor. The idealists were influenced also by the fact that the Croatians were numerically weak because they had shed their blood so freely for the Habsburg dynasty in the wars waged against the Turks, Swedes, Prussians, Bavarians, Saxons, French, and other enemies of the Austrian house. Therefore, the Croatian idealists developed a kind of inferiority complex vis-a-vis the more numerous and economically affluent Germanic Austrians and Magyars who controlled the Habsburg monarchy. Through forging a common identity with the Slovenes and Serbs, it seemed to them that they would be able to overcome the numerical preponderance enjoyed by the two "master peoples." The idealists began to propagate the thesis that Croatians and Serbians were united by ties of ethnic identity. They even discarded the two authentic Croatian dialects, the "ca" and the "kaj," which were spoken and written by a large part of Croatians who did not know Latin, German, or Magyar before the nineteenth century. In the place of these old Croatian idioms they began a new literary language based on the "sto" dialect spoken by the Croatians of Hercegovina. The Serbs used a sub-dialect of the "sto" also. This choice of a common literary idiom for the two peoples provided the concrete base upon which the edifice of Yugoslav unity eventually was erected.

The eventual consequence of the naive idealism of these nineteenth century Croatian intellectuals was that when, in the fall of 1918, their descendants found themselves caught on the losing side in World War I, they allowed the Czechs and the Serbian minority in Croatia-Slavonia and Dalmatia to stampede them into exchanging Hungarian and Austrian political hegemony for Serbian overlordship.

Whoever objectively studies the history of the process of Serbo-Croatian unification in 1918 is bound to arrive at the conclusion that the Serbs, because they had fought on the winning side, found themselves at the end of the "war to make the world safe for democracy" in a position to move into the Croatian lands and to impose their authority upon the Croatians. Croatia-Slavonia, Dalmatia, Istria, Bosnia and Hercegovina all were political derelicts in November and December, 1918, because of the dissolution of the Austro-Hungarian Empire of which they had formed component parts. For the few Croatian expatriate leaders who had identified themselves with the cause of the

Entente Powers during the war, and with whom Serbian spokesmen had concluded various political-juridical agreements, the Serbs had only contempt. Belgrade thought nothing of breaking all of the wartime promises made by her government-in-exile, nor had she any regard for Sabor, Croatia's unique thousand-year-old parliament. On December 1, 1918, Serbo-Croatian-Slovenian "unification" was proclaimed in Belgrade. Four days later Serbian troops sent to the Croatian capital, Zagreb, fired upon the remnants of the Croatian regiments returning from the Austro-Hungarian fronts in Italy, Albania, and Russia.

Most Croatians at the end of 1918 wanted peace at any price. Starved by the blockade imposed by the Entente navies, and decimated again by their service in the Habsburg armies, they were not capable of looking very far into the future. However, as soon as they began to recover from their wartime privations and their war weariness, the Croatians came to view the state of which they now found themselves a part as totally lacking in any legal foundation. Furthermore, its origin and existence brought it into direct conflict with the political-juridical principles and values of the historic national Croatian state which, even under Hungarian and Austrian rule, had maintained a separate identity that the Serbians now denied to it.

As a member of the winning team in the war of 1914-18, the Serbian nation regarded itself as entitled to dispose of the whole Yugoslav complex as it saw fit. As for the Croatians — *vae victis* (woe to the conquered). They ought to be thankful that the Serbians were so gracious as to spare the lives of most of them.[1] Certainly they were not equal partners in the new state brought into being by the events of 1918.

Actually the Croatian territories, together with Slovenia and Macedonia, comprised 78 per cent of the geographical surface of the "Serb-Croat-Slovene" state. Serbia proper and Montenegro constituted only 22 per cent of the total extent of this novel political entity, and a good part of the Serbian-Montenegrin land was seized from either the Bulgarians or the Albanians at that. As to population, the Croatian and other non-Serbian regions contained 75 per cent of the human stock of the Karageorgevitch State, while Serbia and Montenegro could provide only 25 per cent, including those Bulgarians and Albanians who were converted into Serbians by terrorism and indoctrination. Of the total of Yugoslav agricultural production, the Croatian and other non-Serbian lands contributed 83 per cent, the Serbian and Montenegrin territories a scant 17 per cent. The ratio of cattle was 79:21%, of forest wealth 90:10%, mineral wealth 60:40%, trade 77:23%, commerce 82:18%, industry 80:20%, and finance 72:28%.[2] Railway rolling stock and rail facilities

1 Actually, "responsible" political and military authorities of the Serbian nation planned to solve the Croatian question in Bosnia-Hercegovina by massacre. See Ivan Mestrovic, "The Yugoslav Committee in London and the Declaration of Corfu," in *The Croatian Nation* (Chicago, "Croatia" Cultural Publishing Center, 1955), p. 188.

2 Rudolf Bicanic, *Ekonomska podloga Hrvatskog pitanja* (The economic basis of the Croatian question) (Zagreb, 1938), p. 14.

in general possessed by the Croatian and other non-Serbian regions at the end of the war had a value of fourteen billion dinars, whereas the rail wealth of Serbia amounted to an estimated three billion. Croatia-Slavonia, Dalmatia, and Istria had 4,048 public buildings of value as compared to 1,561 in Serbia and Montenegro. Thanks to their improved agricultural practices, the Croatians had more than four times the amount of arable land possessed by the Serbs. On the other hand, however, much of the most productive soil in Croatia-Slavonia was held by the descendants of the eighteenth century Serbian immigrants. Croatia-Slavonia and Dalmatia had 20,087 kilometers of state highways to Serbia's 11,206.

The Montenegrin roads, insofar as there were any apart from those built by the Austrians before or during the war, are hardly worth mentioning. Croatia-Slavonia boasted 871 kilometers of state owned railways and 876 kilometers of privately owned, but state exploited, lines. Serbia had 692 kilometers of railroad course in all; there were no rail facilities in Montenegro. The income of the state forests of Croatia and Slavonia was seven and a half times that of the Serbian owned state forests.[3]

Since the time of her national resurrection in the nineteenth century, Serbia, as a poor agrarian nation, always had owed money to foreign nations. From the above-cited statistics it is easy to see why the Serbians, even though at the start they had been against the Yugoslav idea, were so eager to extend their control over the Croatian lands, and why they mounted the Yugoslav horse to do so. It is less easy to understand why some Croatians were so naive as to accept the Yugoslav thesis at its face value, when it was obvious that a Croatian-Serbian union would be entirely for the benefit of the latter. The noted economist, R. Bicanic, described Serbia's role in international commerce during the postwar years as largely passive, this passivity being compensated for by the international trading ties that Croatia-Slavonia had inherited from her old Austro-Hungarian associations:

> On the active side, on the contrary, the contributions of Serbia to the union are very small. The active role is played by the non-Serbian, especially the Croatian lands . . . furthermore, immigrant remittances have to be taken into consideration. From 1919 to date 1938, the amount of these rose to as high as twelve billion dinars which overcompensated for the three and a half billion deficit or passive balance incurred in foreign trade. According to expert opinion, at least 60% of this twelve billion dinars was remitted by Croatian emigrants. This means that emigrants from the Croatian territories sent back to their homeland over seven billion dinars which sum in itself represents a double coverage of the unfavorable balance of trade or excess of imports over exports accumulated over a nineteen-year period.

Although the economic depression of the nineteen thirties greatly diminished the amounts sent home by emigrants, Bicanic goes on to say that after conditions in America began to improve in the later years of this

[3] *Ibid.*, p. 30.

decade, a million and a half dinars were sent back to the old country by emigrants. No less than four-fifths of this sum represented contributions made by Croatian emigrants. Similarly, of the three hundred and fifty to five hundred million dinars that the Yugoslav state gained annually from tourism, one hundred and eighty-two million were spent in the coastal lands, which are exclusively Croatian. Another hundred million was spent by tourists in the inland Croatian territories. The sum total of the revenues derived from tourism by the whole Karageorgevitch complex was eighty per cent Croatian, and almost all of the remaining twenty per cent came from the other non-Serbian lands.[4] After all, there are few tourist attractions in Serbia or Montenegro, and conditions in those lands were so primitive as compared to those existing in the Croatian and Slovenian regions that tourists who knew what they were doing tended to avoid the Serbian districts, with the single exception of Belgrade.

On the debit side of the state ledger, Serbia brought into the union forged in 1918 debts that were fourteen times greater than those owed by Croatian lands. "Every inhabitant of Serbia was burdened with 4700 dinars of the old foreign debt when he became a citizen of Yugoslavia; every inhabitant of the Croatian and other non-Serbian lands brought with him into the new state only 185 dinars of debt calculated on a per capita basis. This was one quarter the debt burden imposed by the Serbians upon the new political creation."[5]

Later, these debts were paid off from the state treasury. Of the 7,935,000,000 dinars owed in over-all state obligations, 4,114,000,000 were paid out to liquidate the Serbian debts while 3,440,000,000 were expended in behalf of "common" debts. A scant 381,000,000 went to discharge the debts burden borne by the non-Serbian lands. "It can be stated then that out of the revenues of the new state fifteen times as much was expended to pay off the loans incurred by pre-war Serbia than for the debts inherited from the Austro-Hungarian Monarchy."[6]

The Belgrade regime also resorted to chicanery in high finance to promote Serbian financial interests vis-a-vis those of the Croatian and other non-Serbian peoples. When the new Yugoslav dinar was introduced, Belgrade arbitrarily reduced the value of the Croatian kruna by twenty per cent. Then it set up an exchange rate whereby Croatians received one dinar for every four krunas that they had in the old Austro-Hungarian currency.

Bicanic and other economists provide a devastating analysis of the taxation policies introduced by the Serbian authorities. The sum total of taxes paid between 1919 and 1928 for the whole Serb-Croat-Slovene state amounted to 10,112,000,000 dinars (direct taxes only are taken into consideration here). Of this sum, Serbia, Macedonia, and Montenegro paid 1,820,000,000, whereas the Croatian and Slovenian territories

---

[4] *Ibid.*, p. 19.
[5] *Ibid.*, p. 34.
[6] *Ibid.*, p. 36.

paid 8,292,000,000. Their just share, according to the property and income standards applied in the Serbian and Montenegrin regions, would have been only 3,210,000,000 for this period. This means that the Croatian and Slovenian regions paid 5,110,000,000 more in direct taxes than they would have if taxes had been assessed at the same rate as in Serbia and Montenegro, or 260 per cent more than they would have had to pay if they had been part of old Serbia and Montenegro, which had fought on the winning side in the war.[7]

As to the investment policies of the new state, official figures supplied by the Ministry of Construction show that in the period 1925-1934 a total of 2,771,000,000 dinars was invested from state revenues. Of this sum, Croatia-Slavonia and Dalmatia got about 250,000,000, while 1,753,000,000 or 63 per cent of the whole went to Serbia and Montenegro. During this same period, 1,125,000,000 dinars were spent in Belgrade for the erection of military buildings, offices, barracks, etc. "The total that was spent in Belgrade, alone was far more than for all other parts of the state put together." Later the Serbian government expended a billion dinars to build a railroad between Belgrade and Zemun across the Sava River, and for other works that served Serbian interests exclusively. This money could have been used to supply electricity to the entire country. And Belgrade itself did not supply a single dinar to these so-called "state" investments.

The excessive financial discrimination that characterized the Belgrade regime is shown by the fact that to construct the Sava River port at Belgrade, the Government spent 110,000,000 dinars. For sixty-nine major Adriatic ports and three hundred minor ones, all of them Croatian (with the exception of a few in Istria which are Slovenian or Italian), a grand total of 59,000,000 dinars was expended! Under the rule of Belgrade, the Croatian ports retrogressed sharply from the flourishing condition enjoyed by many of them during the period of Austro-Hungarian rule. They became the most backward of all European harbors and ports.[8]

With regard to railroad construction, Belgrade spent 3,377,000,000 dinars in new rail construction between the wars. Of this total amount, 2,852,000,000 was spent on rail lines running through Serbian territory, that is, some 84.5 per cent of the whole. In all of the other lands controlled by Belgrade only 525,000,000 dinars were expended in the building of new lines. This is slightly more than 15 per cent of the total.[9]

Banking, too, constitutes a special chapter in the history of the Serbian domination of the Croatian lands. After the war, a National Bank (Narodna Banka) was organized for the express purpose of serving Serbian state and private interests. Of the 60,000 shares placed on the market,

---

[7] *Ibid.*, p. 52.

[8] *Ibid.*, p. 112.

[9] *Ibid.*, p. 114.

35,000 were picked up by Belgrade interests. Nine Belgrade Serbs owned 25,866 of these shares. During the period 1932-1937, a billion dinars was granted out in credits to Serbian interests, while only a quarter of that amount was conceded to Croatian firms and individuals. In total, Croatian business paid for between 13 and 20 per cent of the dividends issued on the stock of this bank while Serbian business paid for less than six per cent.

A similar state of affairs prevailed with regard to the affairs of the Hipotekarna or Mortgage Bank. According to Bicanic, who bases his judgment upon the participation of Croatian capital in the enterprise and upon the amount of credit granted to Croatian interests, this financial institution gave to the Croatians 412,000,000 dinars less than they should have received. The result was that they had to negotiate loans at high rates of interest from privately owned credit agencies. Sometimes they paid as much as 24 per cent in interest. Of the nine directors of this bank, seven were Serbians. All members of the steering committee were Serbs, as were eleven of the twelve highest clerical officials, and seven out of the nine branch directors. Ninety per cent of the bank employees were of Serbian nationality, too.

This situation was duplicated in most other important banks in the postwar state. Before the war, the Post Office Savings Bank, Postanska Stedionica of Zagreb, was far and away the strongest of all southern Slav financial institutions. As late as 1926, it still was able to give out 77,000,000 dinars in credits. As credit became centralized in Belgrade, however, the position of the Postanska Stedionica declined drastically. Of 1,535,000,000 dinars given out in credits in 1938, firms and individuals in Croatia proper received only 15,000,000, and most of these were obtained at exorbitant rates of interest. The privileged Agrarian Bank, which owned a quarter of all Croatian capital, made loans to 70,000 Serbian peasants, but to less than 10,000 Croatian peasants. The Savska Banovina or Croatia proper contributed 2,777,000,000 dinars to the Yugoslav state treasury during years 1936-1937. Of this sum, some 1,299,000,000 dinars were expended in Croatia. However, 1,279,000,000 dinars went to other parts of the country.

How was all of this financial manipulation possible, in view of the fact that the Croatians had inherited from the Austro-Hungarian monarchy a much stronger economic and fiscal structure than the Serbians could boast? In answer, the Army, the police, gendarmerie, and state of general rank on the active list, and several hundred more who had bureaucracy were all overwhelmingly Serbian. Although the Croatians numbered about a third of the state population and contributed a proportionate amount of soldiers to the postwar military establishment, only about 1000 out of the 10,000 army officers were of Croatian nationality. Serbian Army had only a few generals, in 1938 there were 165 officers Almost all of the high-ranking officers were Serbs. Whereas the pre-1914 retired from service. Only two of the generals on the active list were Croatians, and there was one Slovene. The rest were Serbs.[10]

The defense industry was concentrated in Serbia exclusively. More than four billion dinars were invested in this industry, whereas in Croatia not even a single military building of any value was constructed. Only 120,000,000 to 150,000,000 dinars in all were invested in military installations in Croatia. And even on Croatian soil 90 per cent of the police, gendarmes, and customs and border troops and officials were Serbs.

As to the bureaucracy, only four per cent of the members of the postwar ministries were Croatians, and these usually were handpicked from elements which before the war had belonged to the "Serbo-Croat Coalition" in Croatian political life. In 1938, the state bureaucracy had 350,000 employees, upon whom it expended five billion dinars in salaries. Very few of these officials were Croatians, despite the fact that their past associations with Austria and with Hungary had given them a far better training and foundation for state service than was true of the inhabitants of pre-war Serbia and Montenegro. In this year, 1,058 Serbians and only 152 Croatians were accepted for service in the judicial branch of the government,[11] a field in which Austrian and Hungarian trained logists had long enjoyed supremacy by virtue of the superior education and training that they had received.

Ostensibly, the postwar Yugoslav state was a parliamentary democracy, at least until King Alexander in 1929 established an outright dictatorship to keep the ramshackle complex that had come out of the war from falling apart. Yet, there never was a free election in postwar Yugoslavia. Elections were carefully manipulated to give mandates to a disproportionately large number of Serbians. These Serbians ran the government as they pleased with the help of the army, police, and gendarmerie. No government ever fell because of adverse returns at the polls, nor did parliamentary pressure bring about the fall of one either, even though many of the postwar ministries certainly lacked the confidence of parliament. Exclusively Serbian political and military cliques operating behind the scenes were the only force in Yugoslav political life that could bring down a government.[12]

In order to assure a Serbian majority in parliament, the Serbians resorted to electoral geometry. The principal Croatian political party after the war was the Peasant Party, founded by Stjepan and Ante Radic. A representative of this group had to get 11,300 votes to be elected to the legislature, whereas a spokesman of one of the several Serbian polit-

---

[10] *Ibid.*, pp. 120-121. On the fate of the Croatian officer corps after 1918 see also S. Guldescu, "The Habsburg hysteria," *Social Education*, Vol. XII (November, 1948), pp. 293-297.

[11] Bicanic, *op. cit.*, p. 77.

[12] *Ibid.*, p. 59.

ical groups had to obtain only 8,000 votes. Thus, the Serbs, who numbered 23 per cent of the total population of the state, at all times had at least 37 per cent of the parliamentary mandates. To illustrate the political mathematics employed at election time, the Croatian Peasant Party, whose electoral list was headed by Dr. Vladko Macek, received 1,076,345 votes in the 1935 elections to parliament, but elected only 67 representatives, whereas the government's list returned 303 deputies by virtue of 1,746,952 votes secured.

The mentality of the Serbian rulers of the state is evidenced by the action taken by the Yeftitch-Stoyadinovitch Government when Croatian parliamentary representatives withdrew from the sittings of the Skupshtina, or parliament, to protest the assassination of several leading Croatians by Serbian thugs, and other injuries done to Croatian interests. These Croatian delegates did not resign; they simply refused to attend parliamentary sessions because this seemed to them to be the most effective means of protesting against the illegal procedures that had become a customary feature of postwar Yugoslav political life. The Yeftitch-Stoyadinovitch parliamentarians simply appropriated the salaries of the Croatian deputies and distributed them right and left to individuals of their choosing.

Forty-six per cent of the state income collected in the Savska Banovina or Croatia proper, as distinguished from the Primorska Banovina, which included the Croatian coastal territories such as Dalmatia, was spent outside of Croatia. Croatian economists estimated that over a twenty-year period the inhabitants of the ancient Triune Kingdom of Croatia, Slavonia, and Dalmatia had to contribute more than thirty billion dinars in taxes to the central government in Belgrade. In other words, the Croatians were obliged to pay out approximately two and a half times as much to their new Serbian overlords as they had to pay when they were under the rule of Austria-Hungary. Yet, the agencies of the Croatian administration as such had at their disposal in the years that followed 1918 only one half of the sums that they had been able to devote to domestic needs before 1914.[13]

A French member of parliament has supplied some startling statistics relative to the Croatian-Serbian relationship after the "war to make the world safe for democracy." According to his detailed findings, of 1500 students enrolled in the Military Academy, which prepared officers for the Army, 1300 or 85 per cent were Serbians. There were only 140 Croatians and 50 Slovenians enrolled. Of the clerks of the Royal Palace, 30 out of 31 were of Serbian nationality. The Bureau of Decorations, quite naturally, was staffed entirely by Serbs. All 13 members of the Ministerial Council were of Serbian stock. In the Ministry of the Interior 113 out of 127 officials were Serbs, as were 120 of the 180 employees of the Ministry of Foreign Affairs, 150 out of 156 in the Min-

[13] *Ibid.*, p. 223.

istry of Public Instruction, 115 of 137 Ministry of Justice officials, and 115 out of the 116 generals on the active list of the Army.

The picture is identically reflected in regard to religion. In the post-war Serb-Croat-Slovene state 38 per cent of the population was Catholic, 42 per cent Orthodox. A representative confessional budget was that for the year 1922. It provided 17,000,000 dinars for the Orthodox cult, 6,000,000 for the Catholic. Orthodox bishops were subsidized to the extent of 40,000, while Catholic bishops had to be content with 15-20,000. The Protestant parish in Belgrade, which boasted 900 communicants, received 115,000 dinars from the government, while the Catholic parish in this city, which administered to the religious needs of 10,000 people, got 66,000.[14]

In some respects, discrimination in favor of the Orthodox Church was almost comical. Thus, Article 21 of the laws relating to the Serbian Orthodox Church provided that this institution should be indemnified "for the damages suffered under the Turkish yoke and for the service of the Church to the Serbian national cause." The indemnity requested by the Church for "damages" and "service" was no less than four billion dinars. These said "damages" and "service" were construed as extending for more than a century into the past of the Serbian nation.

The constitution of the Orthodox Church provided that the Patriarch should receive 35,000 dinars over the amount provided for in the budget, thus giving him a total income of 420,000 dinars annually. Furthermore, he received an automobile for his personal use, this being provided by the state budget. A magnificent building for his use also was erected in Belgrade at state expense, even though he already had a truly royal patriarchal residence in Karlowitz (Karlovci) in Srijem (Sirmia). On top of all this, during the year 1921 alone the state allotted 20,354,590 krunas for Serbian religious schools. Catholic educational institutions received just 3,951,275 krunas.[15]

The Croatians did not take all of this rank discrimination lying down. They resorted to legal means of protest, such as sending petitions with many thousands of signatures to the League of Nations and supplying the governments of the victorious Great Powers with memoranda. Croatian deputies for a time abstained from participating in the sessions of the Skupshtina or parliament. Some attention was paid abroad to the Croatian claims, which received a certain amount of publicity in the foreign press, but the only result of such legal expedients was that the Serbian authorities used brute force to strangle Croatian opposition.

The murder in open session of parliament of Stjepan Radic and two other Croatian M.P.'s in 1928 was followed by the establishment of an

---

[14] Ernest Pezet, *Stepinac-Tito. Contextes et Eclairages de "l'Affaire"* (Paris, 1959), p. 15.

[15] Dr. R. Rogosic, *Stanje Katolicke Crkve u Jugoslaviji do Sporazuma* (Sibernik, 1940), pp. 25-26. (The state of the Catholic Church in Yugoslavia up to the conclusion of the compromise.)

outright dictatorship on January 6, 1929. All Croatian political parties and associations were prohibited from continuing their activities, and even the use of the Croatian flag and of the name "Croatian" was forbidden. Police and military terrorism were rampant. Serbian gendarmes and soldiers slaughtered Croatian youths in Senj and peasants in Sibinj. Parliamentary delegates Brkljacic and Predavec were murdered, also. Police killed the noted Croatian savant, Milan Sufflay, and they tried to kill the distinguished writer, Mile Budak.

Even the loyalist foreign friends of the Serbs were aghast at the terrorist methods that were employed to stifle the Croatian opposition. Henry Wickham-Steed, foreign correspondent of the London *Times* and one of the spiritual godfathers of the Yugoslav state whose creation he had championed so ardently during the war of 1914-18, compared Serbian political procedures to those of the Turks at their worst.[16] The French publicist, Ernest Pezet, acknowledged that Archbishop Stepinac of Zagreb had showed him first a photostatic copy and then the original document of a receipt written by a Serbian fiscal agent. This receipt acknowledged payment by a Croatian family for the cost of the ammunition used by the Serbian police in executing, for political reasons, the father of the household. The ostensible excuse for this deed was that the man had broken the official regulations governing the crossing of the border. It so happened that he owned property on both sides of the frontier and was supposed to have legal access to the land that he owned across the state line. But the Serbian police considered that he was a Croatian patriot, should be liquidated, and that the expenses, something over thirteen dinars, should be charged to his family.[17]

Such world celebrities as Albert Einstein and the author, Thomas Mann, spoke up on behalf of the Croatians. Neither their sponsorship nor the memorandum sent by Croatian emigrants abroad to the League of Nations improved the lot of the Croatians at home. The memorandum stated that between January 6, 1929, and June, 1930, 76 Croatians were murdered in the prisons to which the Serbian police conducted them. During the same period, 69 trials were held for persons accused of endangering the security of the Yugoslav state. Only two individuals were condemned to death and one to life imprisonment, but 319 other persons received terms of imprisonment which totaled up to 1201 years and nine months. The chief offense committed by various culprits was that they happened to have been born Croatians.

The Serbians were able to justify, at least to their own satisfaction, the treatment of the Croatians described above. After all, they had "liberated" the Croatians. The Serbs argued that they had set up the Yugoslav state in which they had allotted the Croatians a place, and, having done so, they of course had to protect and defend this state. Even one of the greatest enemies of the Croatian cause, the Croatian Serb,

---

[16] *Review of Reviews,* August 15, 1930.

[17] Pezet, *op. cit.,* pp. 20-21.

Svetozar Pribitchevitch, leader of the pre-1918 Serbian minority in Croatia-Slavonia, was disgusted by the naivete of the Serbian justification of their policies. Although he was one of the creators of Yugoslavia in that, in the fall of 1918, he helped to stampede the Croatian political leaders into giving their assent to the acceptance of Serbian hegemony, and although he had aided in the postwar campaign of terrorism launched against Croatians who opposed the merger of their land with Serbia, he spoke up in favor of the Croats after the murder of Radic:

> This "liberation" thesis is impossible. There's no use in advancing it in a serious conversation. First of all, in Austria-Hungary the Croatians had their own parliament (Sabor) and their own Government which was headed by the Ban (viceroy) who was responsible to the Croatian Parliament[18]. . . besides Croatia possessed complete autonomy with regard to the administration of its domestic affairs, including education, justice, and national commerce.

Pribitchevitch then went on to point out that it was the Western Powers, France, England, the United States, and Italy, which had played the decisive role during the war of 1914-1918 and therefore in the so-called "liberation." He added: "When these facts are examined what sense is there in asserting that Serbia liberated us (the Croatians and Croatian Serbs or Serbs living in Croatia) and to justify on this basis the exercise of absolute power by the Serbian minority which numbers a little over a fifth of the population of our entire nation? This isn't reality, it's megalomania, and small nations have to be on their guard against megalomania."[19]

There were elements among the Croatian people who quite agreed with Pribitchevitch insofar as the necessity of guarding against Serbian megalomania was concerned. The answer to the establishment of Serbian dictatorship was the formation of the *Ustasha*, a strongly nationalistic organization.[20]

On October 9, 1934, the Ustasha revolutionaries, along with Macedonian nationalists, assassinated King Alexander Karageorgevich in Marseilles, France. Since no other Western countries would support the cause of Croatian independence, this group turned for support to Italy and Germany. When the Italians and Germans invaded Yugoslavia in April 1941, the Ustashas found that their hour had come.

It should be understood that at this historic juncture the entire Croatian people rose unanimously against the Serbian tyranny that had op-

---

[18] He was responsible also to the Hungarian Minister President in Budapest. This was one of the chief grievances that the Croatians had against Magyar rule, since the Minister President thus was able to intervene in Croatian political life.

[19] S. Pribitchevitch, *Diktatura Kralja Aleksandra* (Belgrade, 1952), pp. 46-47.

[20] On the appearance of this group, see S. Guldescu, "The background of the Croatian independence movement," *South Atlantic Quarterly*, LVI (Summer, 1957), pp. 314-328.

pressed them for the past two decades.[21] Croatian soldiers serving in the Yugoslav Army turned on the Serbs and completely disorganized the resistance that was being offered against invaders. A few years before, Einstein and Mann had asked the world to protect the "cultured and freedom-loving Croatian people." Now the Croatians took their protection into their own hands and proclaimed the resurrection of the ancient Triune Kingdom of Croatia, Slavonia, and Dalmatia.

The Serbians and Tito's Partisans furiously indicted the Croatians as "traitors." Remnants of the Yugoslav Army, that is, Serbian units which escaped from invading Italians and Germans and from their erstwhile Croatian "comrades," attacked defenseless Croatian villages in Bosnia and Hercegovina. One of the Serbians who took a leading part in these attacks lives in Canada today. He has admitted that the Serbian military perpetrated many outrages against the Croatians of Bosnia and Hercegovina in the spring of 1941. But still today he continues to justify the crimes that were committed by his compatriots on the ground that they were necessary for the "defense of the state." Why soldiers who could not defend the Yugoslav state against the Italian, German, and Croatian military elements considered that they could do so by slaughtering defenseless Bosnians is hard to understand.

Merciless guerrilla warfare followed the complete break-up of the Yugoslav Army. Serbian Chetniks under the command of General Drazha Mihailovic carried fire and sword to Croatian villages and towns. After the war, when he was tried by the Communists whom he also had opposed, Mihailovic declared that his primary objective in the war was to destroy the Croatian State set up on the ruins of Yugoslavia or "Greater Serbia," in which he believed.

The Croatians struck back viciously at the Serbs, intent upon settling old scores. The Communist bands organized by Tito Broz then appeared, and a three-cornered war developed. Most of Tito's followers at that time were Serbs, although some Slovenian and Croatian Socialists and Communists along with a sprinkling of "intellectuals" of indeterminate political affiliation were found in his ranks, too.

Although the Chetniks and the Communists or "Partisans" fought one another as well as the Germans, they often joined hands in attacking the Croatian State. The Government set up by Dr. Ante Pavelic in Zagreb was able to organize a highly effective Croatian Armed Forces, however, and soon both the Chetniks and Communists were on the defensive. What the Croatian Government wanted was for the Germans and Italians to keep out of Croatian territory but to supply the Croatian Armed Forces with the weapons they needed to crush the Serbian and Communist forces. Both the Nazis and Fascists, however, persisted in intruding themselves into this Croatian-Serbian-Communist war. Since neither

---

[21] See the statements of Archbishop Stepinac and of other eminent Croatians in Richard Pattee, *The Case of Cardinal Aloysius Stepinac* (Milwaukee, The Bruce Publishing Company, 1953), pp. 415-418, 442-446, 476.

Berlin nor Rome had any idea of how to fight the type of war that was being waged, the effect of the Nazi-Fascist intervention was to interfere with the Croatian prosecution of the struggle and to give the Communists, in particular, a new lease on life. Even though the Germans and Italians refused to supply the weapons and munitions that the Croatian Forces needed, the latter could have made short work of both the Chetniks and Partisans if only the cohorts of Hitler and Mussolini had stayed out of their way. As it was, the incomparable facility of the Germans and Italians for bungling military operations seriously endangered the Croatian State at times. The situation is rather well described in an American legal document which gives the highlights of the Croatian situation:

> The Croatians never forgot their ideal of an independent state, and, when the Germans and Italians invaded Yugoslavia during World War II, they had their first opportunity to set up their own government.
> On April 10, 1941, the Croatian leaders declared their independence and started to establish their government. This was opposed by the Serbians and others, and civil strife was rampant. The leaders of the Independent State of Croatia called upon the Croats to support the new government and took steps they considered necessary to further its struggle for political power . . . Factions of the Chetniks and Partisans were doing everything they could to defeat the aims of the new government.[22]

According to statistics published by the Tito regime after the war, about 1,700,000 people lost their lives during the three-faced Croatian-Chetnik-Partisan conflict. A great many polemics have been written to indict the Croatians as mass murderers of Serbs and Partisans. Although the Croatian military forces in the field were more efficient than the predominantly Serbian elements[23] that they had to face, the number of victims was highest on the Croatian side.[24] This was because the operations of the Serbo-Croatian war with its accompanying cruelties against the civilian population were carried out exclusively within the borders of the State of Croatia. The climax of this Serbo-Croatian conflict was reached only after the war was over and after most of the Chetniks and other Serbian nationalistic formations had converted themselves into Communists to escape vengeance at the hands of Tito and his Anglo-American-Russian supported Partisans.

---

[22] Theodore Hocke, judge of the U. S. District Court of Los Angeles, Docket 9, Case 283 of Jan. 15, 1959.

[23] After the withdrawal of Italy from the war in 1943, a great many of the Italian soldiers stationed in Dalmatia and other Croatian and Slovenian localities joined Tito's forces. From this time on they contributed considerably to the success of Yugoslav Communists.

[24] Typical of the diatribes written to accuse Croatians of pursuing a policy of genocide towards the Serbians is the semi-official publication of the Government of post-1945 Yugoslavia, edited by Joza Horvat and Zdenko Stambuk, *Dokumenti o protunarodnom radu i zlocinima jednog dijela Katolickog klera* (Zagreb, 1946).

The collapse of Germany in the early spring of 1945 caused the Croatian political authorities to order the withdrawal of their intact and unbeaten Army to Austria. They had the extraordinarily naive idea that the British forces which had entered Austria would accept the surrender of the Croatian Armed Forces and accord them prisoner-of-war status. Instead, the British supported the Communist demand that the Croatian Army, and about 200,000 civilians who had followed it into exile, surrender to the Tito regime which had established itself in Belgrade.

As long as the prisoners remained within sight of British forces, the largely Serbian Communists detailed to escort them across the Austrian frontier back into the newly resurrected Yugoslav State behaved fairly well. However, as soon as they were out of sight and hearing of the British, Tito's people began to murder the prisoners wholesale. The details of these gruesome death marches are told elsewhere in this volume. Here it is necessary only to stress that these postwar massacres of unarmed men, women, and children mark the climax of the tragic relationship between the Croatians and the Serbians.

This relationship, initiated by short-sighted Croatian "intellectuals" before World War I and brought to fruition by Entente propaganda and military success during that war, established the Serbo-Croatian union of 1918. This union was born in blood on December 5, 1918, was continued in blood during the years 1918-1941, was dissolved in blood in 1941, and finally in 1945 was reestablished in blood. After the murder of Stjepan Radic, the Montenegrin national representative and martyr, Dr. Sekula Drljevitch, said that the entire thread of Serbo-Croatian relationships is blood-spattered. Whoever wishes to accept the rule of Belgrade, Dr. Drljevitch asserts, will find himself spattered with martyrs' blood.

In 1941, the Croatian people rebelled against Serbian injustice and tyranny; they demanded their right of national self-determination, the principle which President Woodrow Wilson of the United States declared World War I was fought to realize. After their bitter experience with Serbian overlordship, the Croatians knew that the human and national rights they cherished would always be trampled underfoot by the Serbs so long as the latter had the power to so deal with them. If ever they are given any freedom of choice, the Croatians never will accept any kind of union with the Serbians.

The statesmen and military leaders of the free world handed over the Croatian people to the Serbian and other Communists to do with as they pleased. Thus, after the war was supposed to be over, several hundred thousand disarmed Croatian soldiers and civilians, including many women, children, and elderly people, were slaughtered under circumstances of the most atrocious brutality. Dr. Giuseppe Massucci, secretary of the Vatican emissary to the Croatian Episcopate, on November 23, 1945, put a significant note in his diary that even after the mass murders in the first seven months of the Communist regime were over, still, day in and day out, Croatian patriots were condemned to death and shot or hung. "This is obviously a policy carried out by the new regime itself and it is not a series of acts committed by irresponsible elements. There is no one who does not mourn someone."[25]

But to the outside world the Communist regime in Belgrade played the role of angelic innocent. Over the concentration camps established by Alexander Rankovic, the most efficient murderer that Yugoslavia had produced in the past quarter century, there fluttered flags of "liberty." And under the slogan "Love for man," a much misused catchword of international Communism, the Belgrade Government set up a collection of farcical "People's Courts" which carried out a work of wholesale genocide. Tito's bloody assizes were effected under the excuse and pretense that the Croatian people had betrayed their "own" state, Yugoslavia.

Justitia fundamentum regnorum (Justice is the foundation of kingdoms) was the motto of the old Habsburg state, in which no Croatian was condemned to death for political reasons between 1867 and 1914. This old adage was not peculiar to Austria-Hungary, however, and it represents a lasting truth. In the light of the facts that have been set forth in these pages, who can expect the Croatian people to be loyal to Yugoslavia, which for them has been a charnel house? For almost fifty years the Croatians have had to fight the inherent Serbian propensity for lawlessness and violence. This propensity reached its climax at Bleiburg, Maribor, Kocevski Rog, and at the other places of wholesale postwar massacre in the year 1945.

Just as the United States prosecutor declared at the Nuremberg trials of the German war criminals that the chief accuser of these men was CIVILIZATION, so we may say that the chief accuser of the Serbian elements who carried out the super-crime known as the Bleiburg Tragedy is CIVILIZATION, rather than the Croatian people themselves.

— Dr. David M. Baxter

Rogers, Arkansas

---

[25] Dr. Giuseppe Massucci, *Misija u Hrvatskoj* (Valencia, 1967), pp. 234-235.

Chapter 3

The End of The Croatian Army

Chronology

March, 1945	Croatian South Army defeats elite Partisan troops in series of battles in Bosnia.
Mid-April, 1945	Croatian Intelligence discovers that the German Wehrmacht is planning to evacuate Croatia.
April 30	Croatian Government adopts final decision to abandon the homeland and forego offering large scale resistance in order to spare the civilian population Anglo-American air raids, and punishment at the hands of the Partisans and former Serbian Chetniks who have rallied to Tito.
May 1	Decision of the Government communicated to General (Military) Headquarters. Generals elaborate details of plan to retreat into Austria by way of Slovenia and to surrender to the British, claiming prisoner-of-war status under terms of the Geneva and Hague Conventions.
May 5	Minister of State Vrancic and Captain Vrkljan leave for British General Headquarters to ask the British Command to accept the surrender of the Croatian Armed Forces.
May 6	Evacuation of Zagreb by the Croatian Armed Forces begins.
May 7	South Army retreats northward and bypasses Zagreb.
May 7	In the evening, General Luburic returns to Zagreb to evacuate die-hard troops that wanted to fight to the last man.
May 8	At dawn, General Luburic himself leaves for Slovenia. First Partisan units enter Zagreb.
May 7-12	Vanguard of Armed Forces and accompanying civilians arrive in Slovenia and Austria without special molestation by the Communist forces which are beaten back everywhere by Croatian elite units. Dis-

	integration of the Balkan Wehrmacht blocks the roads all the way from Zagreb to Celje in Slovenia.
May 12	Croatian peace mission is detained at Forli in Italy by a Captain Crawford. Thus, no direct contact with British Field Marshal Alexander's Headquarters at Caserta is established.
May 14-15	Croatian Armed Forces and accompanying civilians reach British lines in Austria.
May 15	General Patric Scott, British spokesman in the talks at Bleiburg, refuses to accept surrender of Croatian troops. Informs Croatian generals that Croatian military personnel and civilians will be extradited into the hands of the Yugoslav Communists. Commissar Milan Basta, Serbian representative of Tito, promises that military personnel will be treated in accordance with laws of war, and only convicted war criminals will be punished. All civilians will be allowed to return to their homes immediately.
May 15	Croatian representatives (Herencic, Crljen, etc.) accept the British-Communist demand for unconditional surrender.
May 16	Massacres of soldiers and civilians begin.
May-August, 1945	"Death Marches" of the Croatian prisoner columns throughout Yugoslavia.
August, 1945 to fall, 1947	Massacres continue as Austrian and Italian Socialists repatriate Croatian refugees to Yugoslavia.

During March, 1945, our Croatian Armed Forces[1] waged a series of hard-fought battles against the Partisan troops of Josip Broz Tito along the ridges of the Ivan Planina in southeast Bosnia. In grim, bloody encounters the Croatians smashed the elite Partisan troops that the English and Americans had trained and equipped in Egypt and Italy and then transported to the Balkans. Although the Partisans' armament was superior, what artillery we had was able to outgun theirs and to beat off the attacks launched by the Red motorized and technical assault units. Croatian patriots had unearthed hidden stores of arms, some of which dated from the war of 1914-18. Outmoded though these weapons and

[1] Regardless of what General Luburic's enemies, adversaries, or critics say, write, or think about his World War II record, the editors of this volume feel that it is essential to include the following account of the events and reasons which led to the surrender of the Croatian Army in 1945. Luburic's account provides an insight into the tragedy of this year which otherwise would be lacking from this presentation of the chain of causes and results that constitutes the story of the great Croatian national disaster. It cannot well be omitted from this book. It is more than a footnote to history; it is history and, to date, virtually the only unvarnished report of what really happened during the last days of the war in the northern Balkans.—Editor's note.

munitions were, they were used to re-equip the militia formations which earlier in the present war had won signal victories over the Partisans and Chetniks.

Our left flank spread out over the Ivan Planina. Here we prepared defense positions and organized mobile units which maintained a liaison between the numerous Croatian militia bands in western Hercegovina and our detachments in southwestern Bosnia. Aid supplied to them by General Headquarters enabled the "Rakicanska Vojska," the Rakicanska Army commanded by Colonel Dragicevic and the "Suicka Vojska," to combat various offensives that the Partisans threw against our flank.

The constant inspection tours that I made of our positions on the Ivan Planina gave me full assurance that we could hold our ground here against ten full Partisan divisions. A concentration of 100,000 men in this sector would secure our flank against the attacks of all of the Yugoslav Communists and Serbian chauvinists in the Balkans.

That portion of our front located around Banja Luka was also rock-solid. I had established garrisons in central Slavonia, and in the areas between Gradiska, Dubica, and Sanski Most. These commands secured the unimpeded transit of troops and materials from Brod to Zagreb. Thus, communications between the Southern and Northern Armies were kept open, as well as those linking the Srijem (Sirmian) front in eastern Slavonia with our national capital, Zagreb. In the north, General Moskov had under his command the elite units of Dr. Pavelic's Bodyguard Brigades (Tjelesni Sbor). Together with the divisions led by General Boban, veterans of the bitter fighting along the Drina, these troops held the front against the Russian and Bulgarian masses who were concentrating in this theater of war.

I kept in direct touch at all times with the Croatian Chiefs of Staff, and with the Poglavnik, or Head of State, Dr. Ante Pavelic. Over the telephone, as well as in formally written reports, I advised these authorities that I had successfully executed the task with which they had charged me—the organization of the defense of the Croatian State on the Ivan Planina. Our victories over the Communists in this zone of operations had convinced everyone who had participated in these actions that we could and should defend Croatia on the ridge of the Planina.

There was much talk at this time about the building of a "Zvonimir Line"[2] which would run from Varazdin and Koprivnica in Slavonia

[2] King Dimitar Zvonimir, who reigned from 1076 to 1088 or 1089, was the last great Croatian King of national blood. The Zvonimir line was to consist of three principal sectors of which General Luburic was to have command of the central front, based in Sisak and Petrinja. General Moskov's First Army, with Pavelic's Bodyguard Brigades, was to hold the left wing at Varazdin, while General Sertic had the task of arranging the defense of the right wing. For this purpose he was to use those Croatian forces which were retiring from the south and from the Lika territory in western Croatia. His headquarters were to be at Karlovac. The decision taken by the civil authorities to evacuate the country cancelled these operational plans.

through Sisak and Petrinja, and south of Karlovac to the sea. This projected line of fortifications was to serve as a last bastion of defense against the anticipated Russian drive into our country from the north. Many optimists thought that Great Britain and the United States would recognize the danger posed by the advance of Soviet Russia and international Marxism into Central Europe and the Balkans. These people even believed that the Anglo-Americans would give us the military equipment that we needed to stop the Russians from overrunning us. Today, this line of reasoning may seem naive, especially in the light of subsequent developments, but in that spring of 1945 not a few Croatians had convinced themselves that the Western Allies surely would realize the value of the Croatian Army for the coming world struggle against Marxism.

The high morale displayed by our troops and by the civilian population impressed me greatly. On one occasion I made a personal inspection of some units that had retreated from Hercegovina owing to the unexpected flight of the Germans from that region. I found these Hercegovinian Croats to be imbued with the conviction that soon they would return as victors to their native land.

When the Germans abandoned Hercegovina, they did so without making prior arrangements with the Croatian military authorities there. Consequently the Croatian troops stationed in that part of the country were in a difficult position. To try to save the imperiled units from being cut off by the advancing Partisans, all Croatian military and civil authorities in Hercegovina and adjacent regions were subordinated to my authority. All those Croatian forces which had to retire from Hercegovina in the wake of the German retreat, as well as the various units withdrawing from southern and central Dalmatia, and from eastern and central Bosnia, were incorporated into our Southern Army.

I should like to take this opportunity to render a personal tribute to the Croatian population of Hercegovina, whether Catholic, Muslim, or Orthodox. From April, 1941, until those last grim days in May, 1945, all Hercegovina was a military reservoir for the Croatian Army. Every one of our regiments drew volunteers from this old Croatian land, the only part of the Croatian State which did not have to enact formal mobilization measures or to provide for regular drafting into the Armed Forces. Every Hercegovinian Croat, whether Catholic or Muslim, and some Orthodox Hercegovinians as well, *volunteered* for service. Even those who were under or over age asked to be allowed to serve. When I was in Konjic to inspect the columns withdrawing from Hercegovina, I saw with my own eyes how three generations marched side by side under the Croatian banners. To this day I remain convinced that we should have defended the Domovina homeland to the last man on the Ivan Planina. The hundred thousand soldiers whom I had under my command shared my convictions, as did the civil population in the south.

No one seemed to realize that the war was lost. It was 1918 all over again, when the Croatians were the last of the Habsburg nationalities to read the handwriting on the wall and thus were not prepared to take advantage of the political situation of the moment. Civilian delegations came before me to express their readiness to defend the Croatian frontiers on the Ivan Planina. Many prominent citizens brought their sons, some of them still in their teens, to serve as volunteers in the defense of the national soil. Our women's organization, the *Zenska Loza,* asked that all Croatian women be armed. The arrival of fresh troops from the northern part of the country raised to an even higher pitch the spirit of martial enthusiasm that prevailed everywhere. So stimulating was the atmosphere, that I brought back from Brod to Sarajevo military equipment and artillery stores that were on the point of being shipped northwards. Officers and soldiers had only one idea in mind—to get at the enemy and to destroy him. Some Austrian and German officers requested permission to fight in our ranks if Germany surrendered. Albanians, Macedonians, and Bulgarians arrived in Bosnia in increasing numbers, as did men from the old Sandjak of Novi Pazar. The Montenegrin followers of Sekula Drljevitch sent emissaries to ask that they be permitted to join us.

At Sarajevo, I conferred with the local military and civilian authorities. I had lengthy discussions with Minister of State Frkovic, with Dr. Spuzevic, the veliki Zupan (local governor), and with the Ustasha representative, Scepa Barbaric. I also had consultations with Minister Vjekoslav Vrancic and with Dr. Meho Mehicic. Both of these able officials labored to secure for our troops all available military equipment. They also were trying to help the "muhadzirs" (Muslim refugees). The six generals in the Bosnian theater of operations, headed by General Markulj, Commander of the Sarajevo Military District, placed themselves at my disposal. So did Colonel Hadjic, Chief Imam or Chaplain of Dr. Pavelic's Muslim Bodyguards, and Imam ef. Aganovic, an outstanding theologian and national leader of the Bosnian Croat Muslims. A Captain of the General Staff and a number of officers and officials whose services I had requested arrived by plane to assist me with the proposed defensive organization, and a special Assault Battalion arrived by truck. I noted that the Croatian military columns arriving from Lika and Krbava in western Croatia exceeded all other formations in their iron determination to fight to the death against Communists of whatever variety.

But while morale soared at the front, in the capital the Government was drawing up plans for the evacuation of Croatia. Major —,* a Military Police Commandant, and Major —,* of Military Intelligence, had

*The names of these officers have to be withheld in order to avoid prejudicing their subsequent careers.

discovered that the German forces in the Balkans intended to retreat through Croatia into Slovenia. The Balkan Wehrmacht preferred to surrender to the Slovenian Partisans rather than to Tito's southern forces. These two officers supplied reliable data concerning the German intentions to the Government and to Croatian Military Headquarters.

As soon as I had wind of what the Germans were planning behind our backs, I contacted certain Austrian officers who had served in the old Imperial-Royal Army and who esteemed the Croatians greatly. These people informed me that some German and Austrian commanders did not favor the idea of surrendering to the Partisans, whether in Slovenia or elsewhere.

Nonetheless, there was a real witches' brew in the making. As at all other times in this war, Drazha Mihailovic's Chetniks were playing a double role. Our security units caught two of them who pretended to collaborate with the Germans by day, but discharged errands after nightfall for the Partisans. This precious pair were busying themselves preparing the slaughter of wounded Croatian and German soldiers who would be left behind in the Sarajevo hospitals if we had to abandon this city. Our security men broke up a number of other Chetnik-Partisan conspiratorial nets, and apprehended some Croatian traitors as well.

Despite these sinister forces in the background, the morale of the Armed Forces and the patriotism of the civilian population had reached its highest pitch of the entire war. I reported this to the Chief of State and to the Defense Minister, Admiral Steinfl, who came to inspect our positions on the Ivan Planina. Steinfl agreed with my analysis of the situation and quite obviously wished to remain with us rather than to return to Zagreb. Even in these trying days he contrived to maintain the merry sense of humor that never left him under the most difficult circumstances. During World War I, he had been wounded in the right leg and was now unable to walk without the use of a cane. When he visited the positions on the Ivan Planina he would call attention to this disability. He joked about it, telling the soldiers that he wanted to remain with them because he was bound to be the bravest of the brave. Why not, since he couldn't run away anyhow?

Steinfl and I had been good friends for many years. When we were alone I told him frankly that I felt that he wasn't telling me everything he knew. I surmised that the Government had sent him down here for a specific purpose and most likely this purpose was related to the intention to retire from Sarajevo and the southern part of the Croatian state. It was with great zest that I informed him that here in Bosnia we would establish a real Croatian Kingdom. General Boban, Colonel Sudar, Colonel Bogdanic, Colonel Pjanic, Colonel Dragicevic, and Colonel Hadjic would help us do it. So would the Muslim Hodzas, the Franciscan and Dominican friars, and the descendants of the old Pashas, viziers, and agas of Turkish days. We joked together about how we were going to set up a new Croatian King[3] in Sarajevo. As for the Croats on the other side of the Sava, they could do as they pleased about forming a state. The outcome of our many conversations was that Steinfl returned to Zagreb with the conviction that I would not retreat from the Ivan Planina unless the Government and Military Headquarters ordered me specifically to do so.

Sarajevo was alive with national fervor at this time. Preparations were being made to celebrate the day of National Independence, April 10, on a scale that Bosnia had not yet seen. The most prominent citizens, together with many normally reserved and withdrawn "begs" (noblemen), congratulated me upon the successful defense of the Ivan Planina and upon the military successes that we had scored against the Communists. They also expressed their satisfaction in the apprehension and punishment of the traitors and enemy agents who had been uncovered by my men.

As is ever the case when the summits of joy and enthusiasm seem to have been attained, there appeared upon the horizon of our momentary happiness an ominous cloud which warned us that all the joys of the world have their inevitable end.

Though they were doing their best to assure us that they would not leave us, we knew that the Germans were preparing to do precisely this. When I had all the facts at my disposal, I invited the German commanders to a gala dinner which was attended by Croatian generals and civilian high officials. During the meal I informed my guests quite bluntly that I knew their plans. I told them that if their efforts to effect a general retreat threatened the effectiveness of the Croatian troops, I would disarm all German formations. And I would hang any German officers who were immediately responsible for actions that proved harmful to our national interests.

Evidently the Germans did not doubt that I meant what I said. They asked the German Consul in Zagreb to mediate between them and the Croatian High Command. Consul R. was the right-hand man of Siegfried Kasche, Berlin's Ambassador to the Pavelic regime. R. was a sincere friend of the Croatian people and enjoyed good personal relations with me. On several occasions he turned over to me the originals of complaints submitted to the Ambassador by German officers from whom we Croatians had taken arms and ammunition. Hence these complaints never reached the higher German authorities and did not bring about the break between us and the Germans that might otherwise have been expected. I must note, too, that soon after Consul R's arrival in Zagreb a number of German officers, whose presence in Croatia was objectionable to us, either were recalled by Berlin or assigned to other fronts.

---

[3] When Croatian national independence was proclaimed in 1941, a member of the Italian House of Savoy was accepted as King by the Pavelic Government. The Duke, however, was aware that the Croatians were anti-Italian by tradition, and he had never set foot upon Croatian soil.

Because of the uncompromising stand that I took with respect to Croatian state sovereignty, I was not well-regarded by many Germans. I accepted them as wartime allies and as anti-Communists, but never at any time did I subscribe to the practice of giving the Nazi raised arm salute, with which they habitually greeted me, nor did I ever attend Nazi Party meetings to which Croatian officers and officials sometimes were invited. Likewise, I refused civic distinctions offered me by the German Government. In general I avoided all contact with the Nazi Party as such, including the S.S., S.D., Nazi militia formations, etc.

The Croatian Government had decided, however, that if Germany collapsed it would be unwise to continue our own military operations upon Croatian soil. Therefore the warning that I had issued to the German generals was not well received in Zagreb. In mid-April of 1945, Dr. Pavelic telephoned me to come to the capital to participate in a discussion that was to be held concerning the military and political situation that confronted us.

Colonel Rogulj placed a plane at my disposal and I went to the airport without even opening the day's mail. My Chief of Staff, Colonel Muhammed Ridjanovic, remained in charge at Sarajevo. I instructed him to take vigorous action to avert the rise of any suspicion that I was deserting my command. If a rumor of this kind had begun to circulate, its effect upon military and civilian morale could have been calamitous.

Due to unfavorable weather conditions, I had to wait for some time at the airport before we could take off. During this period of enforced inactivity my security service surprised and captured a fully-armed Communist Assault Group, which was charged with the agreeable duty of effecting my assassination.

Finally, my plane was able to get off the ground. Two pilots and two personal bodyguards were aboard besides myself. Over the Kozara area we ran into a bad storm. Hardly had we left this behind us than two British planes dived down upon us. We had to fly at a low altitude and change our course several times to escape their attacks. It was already quite dark when we found ourselves approaching Zagreb. An air alarm was in progress in the city, which placed us in a difficult situation, as we were low on fuel. We could neither turn back, go on to another destination, nor land. If we flew around above the city, our own anti-aircraft fire might bring us down. The pilots decided that the only thing they could do was to try to set the plane down at the airport, even though it was known to be damaged, and there would be no lights to guide us.

They got our craft to the ground safely, but after we were down we ran over a hole made by a bomb. The plane lurched violently and seemed to tip over sideways. I am not sure what happened except that I remember throwing myself backwards and lying on the floor with my legs thrust out ahead of me. One of the pilots was injured, while the other pilot and one of my guards sustained slight concussions. Fortunately, the other guard was uninjured and he quickly summoned medical assistance.

I awoke on the third day after the accident in the hospital at Rebro. I had a brain concussion which promised to be a "grave" matter, as Shakespeare might have put it. The director of the hospital at Rebro, however, was Colonel Cvitanovic who, earlier in the war, had been one of my closest associates in the fighting that had taken place along the coast. He saw to it that someone remained at my bedside at all times, and that I received every attention.

In his book published several years ago, Dr. Jerome Jareb[4] states that as soon as I had recovered consciousness I asked to see Dr. Pavelic. He came to my bedside and I informed him that the Germans intended to abandon Sarajevo and probably all of Croatia as well.

After Dr. Pavelic had left the hospital, I was transferred to Command Headquarters at Pantovcak. Here I was treated by Colonel Cvitanovic and by our family friend and physician, Dr. K. I was still so weak that I could not stand on my feet without assistance. There was constant activity around me because military operations were in full swing. So, despite my debilitated condition, I was entrusted with the organization of the Army Command at Sisak. The entire personnel of the Croatian Navy joined the forces placed under my orders at this point. Riparian units, the cadets of the naval academies, all of the naval forces which had withdrawn from the coast into the interior, and the complete staff of the Naval Ministry passed under my command. Also the Honor Work Service units were assigned to me. Some of the naval and Work Service formations were incorporated without delay into the regular military units.

It seems that the duties connected with the Army Command at Sisak may have been thrust upon me in order to prevent my return to Sarajevo. Orders were given to the authorities who were in charge there during my absence to institute preparations for a retreat to the north. Thus perished the plan of defending Croatian soil on the line of the Ivan Planina, and of organizing national resistance behind the Partisan lines. General Markulj was now the ranking general in the Bosnian sector. Zagreb ordered him to arrange the withdrawal of all our forces in Bosnia, including the para-military militia and home defense units, to the northern bank of the Sava River. From here they would be able to take up positions along the "Zvonimir Line."

But this line existed only on paper.[5] The Government had no serious intention of continuing the war on the national territory. Significant

---

[4] *Pola stoljeca Hrvatske politike* (Half a century of Croatian politics) (Buenos Aires, 1960), p. 116.

[5] According to the plan prepared by the Croatian General Staff, General Luburic was to have charge of the central sector of this line which was to be defended by his Second Army and the Obrana formations. Sisak was designated as headquarters for this operation.

resistance to the Partisan advance would be offered only after the bulk of the Army had entered Slovenia. This calculation was based upon the supposition that the Germans would have to concentrate large bodies of troops in Slovenia as their various units withdrew from Italy and Trieste.

Most of our military leaders wanted to organize a bitter last-ditch resistance in the homeland. The civilian administrators felt, however, that if we chose to fight to the end on our own soil, the Chetniks and Partisans would receive so much assistance from Russians, English, and Americans that the struggle could only result in the extermination of the bulk of the civilian population of Croatia, women, children, and old people alike.[6]

Thus the plans for the withdrawal to Slovenia were elaborated. As soon as I was physically able to do so I was to take command of the Southern Army. This operational group included my own Second Corps and the Third and Fourth Corps. General Moskov with his First Corps was to take over the Northern Army which would form the vanguard of the retreat. Already Moskov was busy organizing receiving stations for the members of the State Council, Sabor (Parliament), and the Government officials who expected to leave Croatia. These reception centers were located in Austria and Germany.

The plane accident had left me virtually paralyzed, but thanks to the efficient care that I received I recuperated rapidly, and soon was able to devote my attention to concentrating my Obrana forces in the vicinity of Sisak. Colonel Lisak and my personal representative, Lieutenant-Colonel Ivica Matkovic, went to Sarajevo to assist General Markulj in preparing for the withdrawal northward.

Since early in the war I had commanded the Obrana or Defense Formations, which had the responsibility of organizing resistance in those Croatian territories which, because of the visissitudes of war, fell under Communist control. As a rule, Tito's forces were able to control authentically Croatian regions only when they succeeded in negotiating local agreements with our "allies," the Italians especially. The Obrana units employed against the Partisans the same guerrilla tactics used by the Reds themselves in the areas that we controlled. As soon as I knew that our Government was planning a retreat, I took quick measures to organize the Croatian National Resistance behind the enemy lines. I hoped to be able to protect the withdrawal of the Regular Army by delivering surprise attacks, ambushing advancing Partisan columns, and instituting general sabotage. Such tactics were designed to throw the Serbian and Communist forces into confusion and to paralyze their pursuit of our retiring troops.

---

[6] It is desirable to call attention to this motivation for the evacuation of the national territory because the Serbian Jew, Mosha Pijade, has written a very tendentious and erroneous account of the final military events in 1945. Pijade's narrative is designed to lend a halo of military glory to the Partisan armies which actually were in a state of near paralysis whenever they could not count upon massive Russian, American, and English support.

To facilitate this objective, I collected and regrouped the remnants of several foreign anti-Communist forces which were retreating westward through the territory of the Croatian State. Up to the time of the German collapse, these elements had formed the rearguards, vanguards, and flanking and covering forces of the German Armies operating in the Balkans. In World War I, the Germans had used Croatian and other Austro-Hungarian troops to do as much as possible of the dirty work and hard fighting, while they spared their own men and took all credit for the successes gained. Now, in the second global conflict, the Wehrmacht was repeating its unscrupulous employment of its allies.

Large groups of Albanian nationalists came to Sarajevo to join our columns. These people were fleeing from the Kossovo Polje, the famous "Field of the Blackbirds" of Serbian legend, as well as from Macedonia and the Sandjak, in order to escape the total extermination that the Partisans were carrying out in some Albanian areas. Serbian Communists and Chetniks alike understood that the only way to secure a Serbian numerical preponderance in the Kossovo region, Macedonia, and Novi Pazar was to kill off as many Albanians as possible. From these fugitives I formed a special unit, the "Skanderbeg Legion."[7]

This Albanian formation should be distinguished from the Sandjak Brigade which was led by Colonel Suleiman Pacariz, and from still another Albanian guerrilla unit commanded by Omar Pasha which was operating on the Serbian side of the Drina; the so-called "Prekodrinska Grupa" (Trans-Drina Group). Colonel Pacariz was a Croatian of Albanian descent who had organized the national resistance in the Sandjak. His command was included in my Second Army.

The Montenegrin followers of Sekula Drljevitch also succeeded in reaching us. Calling themselves the Montenegrin Army, they formed two brigades which were commanded by Colonel Agram.[8] There was also a Hungarian Legion led by Major Kovacs. It was composed of refugees from Hungary proper, a Magyar group from Osijek, and various individual Hungarians who had deserted from the German Army into which they had earlier been drafted. During the latter part of the war, these Magyars fought side by side with the Croatian troops, as they had in the war of 1914. Until the Germans began to evacuate the Balkans, the Hungarian Legion had its headquarers at Lepoglava, an ancient seat of Croatian learning and culture.

During this final phase of the war, I also had to negotiate with General Dyukitch, the military representative of Drazha Mihailovic's so-

[7] Skanderbeg (George Castriotes), who died in 1468, is the great national hero of non-Communist Albanians. He won many victories over the Turks in the fifteenth century.

[8] Until the nineteenth century, Montenegro was the only independent Slavic state in the Balkans. Conquered by the Austrians in 1916, it was incorporated in the postwar Serb-Croat-Slovene state in 1918. Some Montenegrins remained loyal to old King Nikita, however, and wished to reestablish the independence of their country.

called "Royal Chetniks." The Croatian High Command wanted to know if these Serbian royalists would collaborate with us in carrying out operations against the Communists on Croatian and Slovenian territory. Together with General Moskov, I conferred also with the Slovenian military delegation sent by General Rupnik, Commander of the Slovenian White Guards or Domobrans. Bishop Rozman and a Mr. Horvat, a Slovene resident of Zagreb, were members of this delegation.

In addition to the task of integrating these several foreign elements with the native troops under my command, the Government directed me to gather together and incorporate into our ranks all Croatians who, for technical reasons, had been serving in German units. Throughout the spring I remained in close touch with General Metzger[9] who was the commanding general on the Srijem (Sirmian) Front. In answer to his requests, I sent to him a number of experienced and brave young men whom he needed for his tank units. They had to meet the push of the powerful Russian tank columns which were converging upon the Srijem front to help the Serbians attempting to establish themselves there.

Metzger advised me that Mihailovic's Chetniks were up to their usual tricks. So expeditiously had they transformed themselves into Partisan Brigades that they had not even taken the trouble to remove the royal Serbian insignia from their caps and uniforms. Metzger told me that he would not retreat even if every Serb, Russian, and Bulgarian in the Balkans attacked him. He was no youth susceptible to bursts of unreasoning enthusiasm or fits of futile defiance, but a seasoned warrior who meant seriously every word that he uttered. I was greatly encouraged by the messages I received from him. Especially was I elated to learn of the brilliant successes gained by our Colonel Stir in the Valpovo district. Here, Stir had beaten and dispersed a Russian regiment which had reached the right bank of the Drava. In notifying me of this action, General Metzger added that he had carried out total mobilization in Srijem, the easternmost part of the Croatian national territory.

Following the great battles which were fought at Sisak and Petrinja to stop the Partisan advance, I launched an attack from Sunja upon the rear of Tito's masses. Before I could carry this operation through to a completely successful conclusion, I received an urgent call to report immediately to General Headquarters at Zagreb. A special transport plane was sent to bring me to the metropolis which, this time, I reached without mishap.

Grim news awaited me in our capital. On April 30, Dr. Pavelic and Minister-President Dr. Nikola Mandic had presided over a meeting of the Croatian Government. A decision was made at this meeting to abandon Croatian soil and to retreat into Austria by way of Slovenia. In Austria, the Croatian Armed Forces would surrender to the British Army. Everyone seemed to think that the English military authorities would honor the stipulations of the Hague and Geneva Conventions relative to

[9] See footnote no. 1 in Part Two, Document V.—Editor's note.

military prisoners of war. Yet even the civilians, some of whom had a touching confidence in the much-publicized British spirit of fair play, agreed that under no circumstances should Croatian military personnel capitulate to the Partisans, Serbian Chetniks, or Russians. With such enemies it was war to the death, and everyone knew it.

A meeting at General Military Headquarters was scheduled to follow the Governmental session. I had been called to Zagreb expressly to attend this conference. General Headquarters was the supreme military forum for determining the conduct of the war and for co-ordinating the operations of the several Croatian Armies. Dr. Pavelic himself held the post of Commander-in-Chief, General Grujic had charge of actual field operations, and General Dragojlov was Chief of the General Staff. General Percevic, head of Dr. Pavelic's Military Bureau, General Herencic, Commander of the Ustasha troops, General Skoliber, Commander of the Security Forces, and General Sertic, Chief of Staff of the Armed Forces in the field, were other members of General Headquarters. Air Force Commander General Rupcic, Gendarmerie Commandant General Pecnikar, and General Moskov also belonged, and as Commander of the Obrana formations I was a member, too.

The Headquarters conference convened on May 1. It was in session for only thirty minutes following my arrival. Dr. Pavelic personally informed us of the decision reached by the Government. The assembled generals were asked to submit suggestions and objections relative to the plan of retreating into Austria and surrendering there to the British.

All of the soldiers present received with grave and quiet dignity the depressing intelligence that meant the end of their professional careers and of the lives of most of them as well. As one of the few survivors of of this historic meeting, I am glad to be able to testify that in this moment of imminent disaster not one Croatian General appeared to be concerned about his own fate. Their sole consideration was how to save the lives of the 200,000 young Croats who formed the seventeen regular divisions and the auxiliary troops of the Croatian Army.

Since our competence was limited to military affairs, we had nothing to say about political decisions taken by the Government. Hurriedly we calculated the strength of the total forces at our disposal. I reported briefly on the results of the negotiations that I had carried on with the Slovenians, the royal Chetniks, and the several Balkan anti-Communist groups. Everyone agreed that the morale of our forces had remained unaffected by the withdrawal of Germany; our chief worry was the shortage of guns and ammunition, not to mention planes, tanks, and technical equipment. This was the same weakness that had plagued our Armed Forces throughout the war. Although Croatia was the most industrialized part of the southern Slav territory, there was not a single large armament plant located in our country. Therefore we had to depend upon the Germans for military supplies. Sometimes we secured guns and munitions from them, not by purchase or agreement, but through outright theft or through the expedient of redirecting into our own hands arms shipments sent from the Reich to the Balkan Wehrmacht. Such tactics were justified, because it was the deliberate German policy to starve our Army; Berlin wanted to make us entirely dependent upon her. Of course we occasionally succeeded in capturing American, British, or Russian weapons supplied to the Partisans by those countries, but never at any time in the war did the Croatian Armed Forces have the equipment that they needed to realize their full potentiality.

Since the Communists were killing all Croatian patriots who fell into their hands, the urgency of establishing early contact with the British, who presumably were more civilized, was apparent to everyone. It was a firm reliance upon the military honor and integrity of the English that induced most of our military authorities to accept without argument the plan of retreating by the shortest route into the Austrian province of Carinthia. Here, we could lay down our arms before the British rather than the Partisans.

Our surrender decided, almost everyone seemed to hope for the best. No one was so naive as to think that the Western Democracies would do what we really wanted them to—equip us with the artillery and tanks and planes, that we needed to stop the westward advance of the Russians. But certainly it was felt that the British and Americans would accept our surrender and accord us prisoner-of-war status.

Perhaps I was the only military man at the conference who put little faith in British military honor. Our generals seemed to forget that in 1918, the Austro-Hungarian military authorities had tried to surrender to the British and Americans for almost two months prior to the totally unnecessary battle of Vittorio Veneto (October 24-November 4), and that British planes in particular had had great sport in bombing the retiring Austro-Hungarian columns after the fighting was over. I knew that the English possess a sense of "sacro egoismo" that is as acute as that of the Italians, and that in wartime, their only concern is to reach a victorious conclusion as quickly as possible. In doing so they have no regard for anyone's interests but Britain's. Just as we had taken allies wherever we could find them, calling on Germany and Italy, so the British Lion had laid down in the same bed with the Communist Serpent. It appeared to me to be very unlikely that London would risk incurring the displeasure of her Soviet ally merely to save the lives of a few hundred thousand Croatians.

I expressed to the other generals and members of the Government my conviction that if the Englishmen did accept the surrender of our troops it would be "Auf Gnade and Ungnade." They would disarm our men and then turn them over to the Partisans to be slaughtered in the same way that the British themselves had massacred the Hindu and Muslim rebels after the suppression of the great mutiny of 1857.

Since I was sure that this would happen, I suggested that rather than surrender we divide our forces into three segments. The first of these would not surrender to the English or to anyone else, but would force its way through the Allied lines in Austria. Croatian troops had faced the British before when, after Caporetto in World War I, a number of Tommy divisions were sent to Italy to prevent the further collapse of the Italian Army. I did not underrate the Tommies, but I believed that our men could break through their lines. Once our vanguard had done so it would be able to disperse in all directions towards France, Germany, Belgium, Switzerland. By taking shelter in forests, hills, and fields, the individual survivors of this first segment of our Armed Forces would have a good chance to make good their escape. Undoubtedly, some men would be rounded up or would have to surrender at their discretion, owing to hunger, cold, and exhaustion, but such individuals almost certainly would receive trials for whatever they might be accused of, and most likely they would be accorded prisoner-of-war status. General Moskov was the logical commander for this first wave of the Croatian Army, which would have the task of throwing aside the British troops who sought to bar our way to safety.

I recommended that the second wave of the Armed Forces be constituted from those forces which were withdrawing from Dalmatia, the Lika and Krbava areas of western Croatia, and the zone around Karlovac. Since many Italian-speaking Croatians would be included in this body, such as priests, intellectuals, and bilingual Dalmatians from the coastal zones that had been occupied by the Italians, they might in some contingencies be able to masquerade as Italians. I proposed that General Herencic assume command of this second military segment. He could count upon the aid of the Slovenian nationalists who were concentrating around Kranj. The Slovenes would aid the withdrawal of his forces into Istria by way of Rijeka and Ljubljana. Once Herencic's Army was in Istria, he would be able to establish contact with the Americans. If the latter proved impossible to deal with and I, for one, expected them to hold to the tradition of "Unconditional Surrender" established by Ulysses S. Grant in the American Civil War of 1861-65, then the Croatian inhabitants of Istria, and probably the Slovenes as well, would assist his men to disperse and to escape as individuals into Italy and Austria. The fact that most Croatians spoke either Italian or German was bound to facilitate the success of such endeavors.

It was my idea that I should take command of the third wave or segment of the Armed Forces myself. We would don our black uniforms and hit the Partisans before they ever reached Zagreb. Certainly we would be able to damage their columns enough to insure the escape of the first two segments of our Army. I counted upon receiving help in this task from Vanca Mihailov's Macedonian Revolutionary Organization, and from such German troops as might be trailing behind the main Teutonic body.

The other Croatian Generals did not approve my plan; they displayed blind faith in the sense of fair-play and the benevolence of the British and Americans. They did expect that they themselves would be extradited into the hands of the Communists, but they could not believe that this would be the fate of the lower grades in the Army as well. They were sure that, at the very worst, the bulk of the soldiers and civilians would be confined to prison camps for some time until their cases could be examined individually.

I asked my colleagues point-blank what they supposed would happen if the British took our weapons and then turned us over to the Partisans. I added that I had no doubt that the latter would kill all of the young men whom the other generals were so concerned about saving. To my query and foreboding Dr. Pavelic himself replied succinctly, "They (the British) will be responsible then."

Thus, the meeting of May 1 ended with an irrevocable decision to go ahead with the retreat and surrender plans. I wish to stress the fact that this commitment was prompted by an ingenuous trust in the honor of the Western Allies. The war had been lost long ago, when the responsible civilian authorities had made up their minds to forego massive resistance in the homeland if worst came to worst. They thought we might be able to hold out indefinitely against the Partisans, if the Bulgarians did not back them up in force, but the Russians, once they had finished with the Germans, could overwhelm us from the north. Protracted resistance in Croatia, with the inadequate armament that the Germans had allowed us, could only serve to worsen the lot of the civilian population. Nor would a savage, last-ditch resistance be of any advantage to our Army in the long run, except to give our Army a chance to die fighting. And yet, after all, that is what an army is supposed to do when it possesses no other honorable or hopeful alternative. If the other Generals had shared my apprehensions, I knew that they too would have chosen to fight to the end, however hopeless the prospect of ultimate success.

Instead, we obeyed the orders of the civilian authorities and instructed the troops under our command to retreat along the shortest routes available to them towards the British lines in Austria. I received express orders to abandon my intention of conducting guerrilla operations in the rear of the Partisans. My instructions were to group my Obrana units around Zagreb in order to cover the withdrawal of the main body of the Army to the north and west.

As Commanding General of the Southern Army, I had under my orders all forces located south of the capital, as well as those concentrated in the city itself. General Grujic had general direction of the withdrawal. He conferred with Colonel Helbich, Chief of the Operational Division of the General Staff, as soon as the Headquarters meeting was over, to arrange the general details of the retreat.

Meanwhile, our relations with our German allies were taking an unpleasant turn. Colonel-General Loehr, Supreme Commander of the German forces in the Balkans, came to Zagreb expressly to consult with me. Dr. Pavelic had advised him that I was going to concentrate the forces at my disposal to secure the flanks and rear of the retiring German units, as well as those of the main Croatian Army.

Loehr and I met at the house of Dr. Mile Budak, who, along with Minister of State Ivica Frkovic, was present during our conversations. It was difficult to negotiate with Loehr because he did not understand Croatian nor was my command of German adequate for the discussion of the technical details that the general retreat involved. Dr. Budak and Minister Frkovic were able to interpret for us, however.

Loehr came to see me because he knew that once the Chief of State, the Government, and General Headquarters had crossed the Slovenian frontier, I would be ranking commander of all national forces left on our home soil. As such I would be free to make decisions *ad hoc* according to the necessities of the moment. Of course what he wanted me to do was to sacrifice my Croatian troops to protect the withdrawal of his German units, just as in 1940 the British expected the Belgians to die to the last man to make possible the Dunkirk operation.

He got an unpleasant surprise when, at the commencement of our conversation, I had Budak and Frkovic remind him that the Wehrmacht, by surrendering a bridge near Petrinja, had exposed one of my regiments to the danger of encirclement by the Partisans. The German authorities had not advised the local Croatian commander in time for him to make the dispositions necessary to insure the safety of his own troops. We were not going to stand for any more of this sort of thing. I told him bluntly that the German Command would have to notify me personally of all of their evacuation plans and the time schedules for them.

Despite the best efforts put forth by Budak and Frkovic to mediate between us, Loehr and I parted in an unusually cold manner. I never had cared much for Loehr personally, because he seemed to me to be a typical Nazi opportunist, and no more trustworthy than the usual run of such people. Nevertheless, I did cover the retreat of his columns by fighting a holding action on the outskirts of Zagreb some days after we had our talk, and his troops were able to leave Croatian soil without experiencing serious molestation at the hands of the Partisans. We also saved some isolated German formations by delivering an attack upon a Communist concentration near Podsused. I was unable to prevent other German contingents from being cut off by Tito's troops, or by local "Fifth Column" and Communist Party militia.

Following the termination of the Headquarters meeting, I returned to Sisak. Despite the desperate efforts of the Partisans to impede the retreat or turn it into a rout, the retirement of our forces from Bosnia had been effected successfully and with little loss. Unfortunately, however, the special commandos, whom I had previously sent to General Metzger, could not rejoin my Southern Army. They fell to the last man in the bitter and protracted fighting on the Srijem front, where they held out to the end against massive Russian tank columns and their Bulgarian artillery support.

In accordance with my orders, I concentrated my forces to cover the withdrawal of the main Army and the Government from Zagreb. As the units under my command converged on the capital, I received a message from the Metropolitan of Croatia (later Cardinal) Stepinac. He asked me to call upon him at the Archepiscopal Palace. The Metropolitan's request was delivered to me by his secretaries and by Colonel Cvitanovic. I suggested that I wear mufti when I went to see him. Through donning such garb, I trusted that I might be able to avoid creating for him an unpleasant situation *vis-a-vis* the Communists, who would take over Zagreb as soon as we left it. His secretaries said, however, that he wanted me to visit him in my official capacity as ranking commanding general on Croatian national soil. He was willing to accept the consequences of according a formal reception to the Commander of the Croatian Armed Forces, of which he was supreme chaplain.

Since this was the way he wanted it, I attired myself in dress uniform, complete with all the Croatian and foreign decorations that I had received. When I presented myself at the Archepiscopal Palace, the secretaries received me on the staircase. They conducted me into the presence of Archbishop Stepinac, who received me most cordially. A long and friendly talk followed.

The Archbishop began the conversation by thanking me warmly for the aid that I had given to refugees during the course of the war, as well as for that rendered to a number of monasteries and convents. He expressed particular gratification for the help that I had supplied to the Church authorities in caring for the many homeless children whom we had brought in from the several fighting fronts, or from war devastated regions. The identities of many of these little waifs were unknown, but some of them must have been of Orthodox parentage. Many such children were encountered in the forests, or found huddled along the streets of ruined and burned-out towns and villages. All through the war, the Archbishop-Metropolitan had tried to arrange for the care of such children, and the Croatian Army had donated food from the Military warehouses for their support. On several occasions I had been instrumental in providing material assistance for these forlorn orphans. So now, "before the night falls," as the Archbishop himself put it, he wanted to thank me for the efforts I had put forth in behalf of the little foundlings.

Our conversation then touched upon politics and was carried on in a direct, simple, and sincere vein. Questions asked were brief and to the point, and answers were given in all honesty. Archbishop Stepinac asked me to give up the idea of defending Zagreb. He informed me that the Germans had occupied churches and historical and cultural points of interest which should never have been utilized for military purposes. I promised him that I would see to it that the Germans evacuated these places immediately.[10] Also, I agreed that I would not make Zagreb a battlefield, as the Wehrmacht had made of Vienna and Budapest. The Archbishop was greatly worried about the fate of the Croatian capital, which was the historic center of Croatian culture and national consciousness. He knew that Keserevitch's Serbian Chetniks, who suddenly had transformed themselves into Partisans, wanted to raze the hated Croatian metropolis to the ground and to kill the entire population in doing so. He feared that Tito would find it necessary to "give satisfaction" to his new Serbian recruits. The Archbishop considered it likely that the Communists would revert to the old practice of the mercenary armies of the Thirty Years War of 1618-48, when the soldiers who captured a town were allowed three full days in which to murder, rape, burn, and pillage at their pleasure. Both Msgr. Stepinac and myself were familiar with the directive issued by the Partisan Commander, General Yovanovitch. It was a model of clarity. "If Zagreb resists, our liberating army on its way to the final liberation of our country, and our combat-ready air force, will turn it into ashes and cinders."

The Archbishop-Metropolitan seemed greatly relieved when he found out that I intended to evacuate the city without a fight. We discussed the plan of a general retreat into Austria. I explained to him that the Chief of State, the Government, and the Military Command all had agreed upon this scheme, and in doing so had forbidden me to conduct large-scale resistance on the territory of the Croatian State. They had opposed my desire to employ large-scale guerrilla tactics against the Partisans because they believed that such resistance, however successful it might be, would serve only to give Tito the excuse he needed to have the British and American air forces smash our cities flat. Certainly the greater part of the urban Croatian population would meet the same fate that befell the Japanese residents of Hiroshima. We knew that the war was lost and that the Anglo-American victors saw in us nothing but fascists, thugs, and murderers. Therefore, it could be anticipated that the English and American commands would give the Partisans all the military help they needed to effect the massacre of the Croatian people. None of the Governmental or military authorities was willing to accept the responsibility for ordering "war to the knife" resistance under such auspices.

When the general war picture had commenced to darken, Dr. Pavelic had declared that, if for any reason the regularly constituted State authorities could not carry out their official functions, then the Archbishop of Zagreb would take charge of the Government of the Croatian Nation. Such a procedure was rooted in historical precedents. Part of the Croatian Archives, including the State Archives of 1941-1945, were housed in the archdiocesan buildings. Therefore, at precisely this mo-

---

[10] My orders to this effect were executed immediately after I left the Archepiscopal Palace. My men discovered that the Germans had brought explosives into these places, evidently intending to blow them up during the evacuation.

ment, when the political authorities were withdrawing from the country, most Croatians considered Archbishop Stepinac to be both *de facto* and *de jure* head of the Government.

This eminent cleric assured me that he shared the views of the Government and the High Command in regard to the defense of Zagreb, and the avoidance of large-scale resistance on our national soil. When he said this I looked him straight in the eye and inquired:

"What do you think will be the fate of those who surrender to the British?"

"General, do you intend to surrender?"

"No, neither to the English nor to anyone else. But as a soldier, I shall carry out the orders that have been given to me to cover the retreat of our Armed Forces, and to send all troops to the points designated for surrender. When the fighting is over, I will assemble the survivors of our rear guards and will go with them into the forests to organize resistance and to save the lives of everyone we can. In the woods I shall await what may come and, guided by my conscience and reason, I shall decide what to undertake, that is, of course, if I remain alive."

"My dear General, there is nothing that divides us; God and Croatia unite us. I give you my blessing. Go in the Name of God, and do what you can. Do not surrender! As for those who do surrender, have no illusions concerning their fate!"

He kissed and blessed me and personally accompanied me to the door of the Palace. We parted knowing that we would not see one another again in this world.

Certainly, my talk with Archbishop-Metropolitan Stepinac was one of the most interesting experiences that I have had in my life. Still, it was only one of a number of momentous encounters that I had with eminent personalities in Zagreb "before night fell." There stands out in my mind today a particularly vivid recollection of a long and friendly conversation that I had with Dr. Dzaferbeg Kulenovic, Vice-President of the Croatian Government. Throughout the war our relations were most cordial. In Government circles he always defended my policies and actions. Dr. Kulenovic's concern was the care and placement of war refugees, and my men often were able to assist his efforts in this direction.

On the morning of May 6, Dr. Pavelic himself had a lengthy and intimate talk with me. I told him about my conversations with Archbishop Stepinac and with Dr. Kulenovic. I assured him that no matter what the future might hold, I would remain loyal to him, to my military oath, and to the Croatian State to the day of my death. Also, I would execute the orders that I had received to lead the Armed Forces placed under my command out of our national territory, though I should do this most unwillingly and against my own better judgment. If I had to, I would sacrifice the entire Obrana to cover the rear and flanks of the main Army in order that he, as Chief of State, might present himself to the Western Allies at the head of 200,000 armed soldiers. Thus, it could not be said by our enemies that a puppet Government had sought to secure its own safety by sacrificing the Army and the nation that it purported to represent.

Then I told Dr. Pavelic that the only command that he could not give me was to surrender my own person. He asked what I meant by this statement. I gave the same answer to him that I had to Archbishop Stepinac: when the fighting had ended I would go alone into the forests. Even my personal guards would not have to accompany me if they did not wish to do so. In the woods I would endeavor to collect all stragglers or individuals who refused to surrender. I reminded him that I was a Jankapuszta man and Jankapuszta "alumni" were not in the habit of surrendering.[11] On this occasion I reaffirmed my loyalty to the school which I had entered as a recruit, and which later I had come to command.

We agreed that I should consider myself commander of the armed forces left on Croatian soil until the general surrender had been effected in Austria. Then I should act as I deemed best under the existing circumstances. I reiterated to Dr. Pavelic my conviction that the British would hand our Army over to the Communists if we were so foolish as to surrender "Auf Gnade und Ungnade" to the representatives of "perfidious Albion."

Dr. Pavelic seemed to understand my attitude in this matter. He asked me if I thought that General Boban would follow my example and go into the woods to rally all die-hard elements. I thought that Boban probably would do so, even though he was one of those who believed that the British would accord prisoner-of-war status to all Croatian military personnel except our higher-ranking officers. As a matter of fact, Boban even cherished the hope that the English might see the advantage of employing our tough Croatian units to check the Communist steamroller that was crushing all of Central Europe under its wheels.

During this talk, Dr. Pavelic gave me his final orders relative to the evacuation of Zagreb and the retreat to Austria. He approved my plan of sending General Junus Ajanovic, my assistant in command of the Second Army, to take command of the vanguard in the withdrawal of the Southern Army to the north. Ajanovic's staff had available a radio transmitting apparatus which they hoped would enable them to contact the British quickly in order to arrange terms of surrender. At the same time, this apparatus would facilitate the maintenance of a liaison between the Second Army and the other Croatian Field Armies.

---

11 Jankapuszta was a camp for Croatian refugees established in Southern Hungary during the 1930's. Some of its inmates were trained in terroristic tactics for the purpose of being able to reply in kind to the Serbian terrorism that was inflicted upon the Croatian people during these years.

Dr. Pavelic agreed that Minister Vrancic should accompany the Second Army. Vrancic realized that the British and their American allies might refuse to accept the formal surrender of our Army on political grounds. Unfortunately, neither the Englishmen nor the Yankees had the wit to perceive how valuable an independent Croatian State could be for the West *vis-a-vis* the Marxist complex that was taking form in East-Central Europe and the Balkans. But Vrancic did cling to the hope that the Anglo-Americans would at least allow our men individual prisoner-of-war status which would preclude their being extradited into the hands of the Communists. I had no illusions on this score myself, but there were few others in positions of authority who shared my apprehensions. For me, the bitterest element in the situation was not that we were going to die and that the war was lost; it was rather the fact that our soldiers would have to lay down their arms, not because they were unwilling to fight to the end, but because their own Government commanded them to do so. I was convinced that the Government had made a terribly wrong decision, but as a soldier, I could only obey the orders received from my superior officers.

Minister Vrancic returned to Zagreb from Sisak to execute the role assigned to him by Dr. Pavelic as peace emissary to the Western Allies. He presented himself before me in military uniform and with a knapsack and a machine-gun slung over his shoulder. Vinko Nikolic was with him, and I assumed that they would go together to contact the British High Command. Captain Vrkljan of the General Headquarters Staff was also detailed to accompany Vrancic and the Second Army, since he had lived in England before the war and spoke fluent English.

Dr. Pavelic's last orders directed me to cover the flanks and rear of the forward columns. Once the latter had surrendered to the British or other Western troops, I was to gather together all dispersed groups and individuals and would initiate, according to prearranged plans, such resistance as might appear feasible. We had in mind the probability that the Russians might sweep down in force from the north. As far as the Partisans and their recent Chetnik converts were concerned, we apprehended little danger. Both of these enemies knew better than to press us too closely. Dr. Pavelic gave me a free hand to deal with whatever circumstances might arise. We parted after arranging to remain in touch through trusted emissaries who would contact one another at designated addresses in the fatherland.

And so the great retreat began. Since both Archbishop Stepinac and Dr. Pavelic had asked me to see to it that as many of our units as possible went around the capital rather than through it, the withdrawal took longer than would otherwise have been the case. It was not to prevent desertions that I had our troops avoid taking the direct route through the metropolis, even though it is only to be expected that individuals and even whole groups may fall out and disappear when a retreating army passes through a city of any size. In our case, volunteers were so eager to join the colors that some of our battalions which did have to go directly through the city entered it only five hundred strong, and left with more than seven hundred in their ranks.

General Servatzi, Military Commander of Zagreb, shared with me the responsibility for clearing the city of those elements who were determined to fight to the last gasp. Of course, Archbishop Stepinac was right in thinking that if we turned the metropolis into a battlefield it would be destroyed in the course of the fighting, regardless of where the victory fell. Both the Partisans and their new Serbian allies would welcome such a denouement. On the other hand, most Croatians felt that as long as Zagreb remained intact, the idea of a free Croatia would persist. We have the same regard for our capital that the French do for Paris or the Austrians do for Vienna. All the same I thought that the Austrians had made a mistake in not fighting in 1938, and by the same token we were making an even worse mistake by not doing so now.

Yet I had to obey my orders, and so, to discourage local resistance activities, I detailed special units to remove from the capital those contingents and groups which wanted to die where they stood. It was especially painful to have to deal with the wounded and with the invalids. Many of these Croat patriots had hobbled, dragged themselves, or had themselves carried to advantageous points, where they proposed to fight on as long as there was breath in their bodies. Some of these men flatly refused to be evacuated. When they realized that we were not going to allow them to carry out a house-to-house resistance, they shot themselves or detonated bombs which blew them to pieces. What a horrible waste we made of our manpower in these critical days!

Dr. Kumicic, a member of a renowned family who remained in Zagreb, organized a popular militia force which helped my men and Servatzi's to clear the town of the die-hards. Kumicic's militia wore the Croatian coat of arms on their caps and coats and carried rifles issued to them from the arsenals. Their chief task was to prevent looting and the perpetration of other crimes that might occur between the time of our evacuation and the Partisan entry into the city.

Those Croatian forces which were withdrawing from the eastern and southern parts of our nation had orders to retire through Zidani Most. To reach this point, they either had to pass through Zagreb or pass around it to the north or south. Our retreating columns thus presented a funnel-like formation, the wider ends of the funnel being based upon Varazdin and Karlovac. From these points, the funnel narrowed down via Podsused and Sljeme in the direction of Zidani Most. Beyond this city, our Army formed a huge column which reached out towards the Slovenian and Austrian frontiers.

Because the roads were blocked by every kind of vehicle imaginable, it was not humanly possible to maintain any kind of effective order. So thickly packed together were wagons, tanks, ox-carts, carriages, automobiles, trucks, and vans of all descriptions that at many points no ground could be discerned between them. This state of affairs was largely the fault of the Germans. They had concentrated in the vicinity of Zidani Most not only the convoys accompanying their twelve or fourteen divisions, but also the vehicles belonging to a hundred or more detached units. Hence the retreat to Zidani Most presented the spectacle of a mass migration such as the Ostrogoths under Theodoric the Younger had achieved fifteen hundred years before when they passed through this region enroute to Italy. Women, children, old people, and all kinds of animals were mingled with Croatian, German, White Russian, and Albanian troops. Peasant carts stood alongside the most modern "tiger" tanks. It was the most magnificent chaos imaginable, but in my opinion it was no way to finish a war.

Nonetheless, the Partisans and their Chetnik converts were unable to take effective advantage of this unparalleled confusion. My so-called "fleet winged" Obrana battalions protected the flanks and rear of the forward columns converging on Zidani Most. These troops were commanded by such men as Kreso Majic, the Primorac brothers, Major Miro Matijevic, Captain Kresic, Captain Nikica Kardum, Captain Joja Sudar, Captain Tiho Kordic, and Major Hadzija Mataja. Their men were all veterans, seasoned, elite fighters. Whenever either the Partisans or the Chetniks collided with these units, they did so to their sorrow.

However, two important factors became evident to me in the first hours of the retreat from Zagreb. First, the much vaunted German discipline was breaking down altogether. Individual German soldiers were slipping off by themselves, deserting their units. Relations between the Austrians and the Germans were deteriorating. Small Austrian contingents were looking for any opportunity that might present itself to surrender to the Partisans, or to anyone else. On the other hand, some of the Germans attached themselves to our units and announced their intention of escaping over the Alps whether their officers ordered them to surrender or not.

The second aspect of the situation that impressed itself upon me was the necessity of taking the most ruthless measures to relieve the congestion that was clogging the highways between Zidani Most and the second main objective of our planned withdrawal, Celje, in Slovenia. Despite the traffic tie-up, we suffered few casualties en route to Zidani Most. To clear the road from here to Celje, I carried out several "excursions" along both sides of the thoroughfare to kill or disperse the Partisan groups that were trying to harass our retiring columns.

The Germans were abandoning their vehicles everywhere. They left heavy trucks and tanks standing in the middle of the road while they tried either to make their way forward on foot or to escape into the woods. I sent our pioneer units along the main highway to collect the ammunition abandoned by the Wehrmacht. The pioneers had to explode much of it to get rid of the stalled trucks and tanks that were blocking the thoroughfare. Parenthetically, I feel impelled to remark that, if earlier in the war the Germans had equipped us with the kind of weapons that they now were so wantonly abandoning, we could have pacified the entire northern Balkans in record time, whatever the English and Americans did to help the Communists there. It is my conviction, too, that had the Wehrmacht turned over to us their weapons and military supplies when they fled from the Balkans, we could not only have secured their unmolested withdrawal, but we could also have held out in our country until the English and Americans became tired of financing Tito. Of course I have to admit that we could not have resisted indefinitely against the Russian and Bulgarian pressure that unquestionably would have been applied against us had we fought to the end in the Domovina. Still, the possession of good German weapons would have made us a far more effective force than we were in our actual condition, a military stepchild of the Axis.

As far as Zidani Most, the retreat was primarily a military withdrawal, even though there were civilian refugees from Zagreb and other points included in our columns. Beyond Zidani Most, however, crowds of fugitive civilians, Magyars, Slovenes, and other non-Croatian nationalities pressed into our ranks. This heterogeneous mass had only one thought in mind, to reach the British lines in Austria and surrender there. Although the unseasonably hot weather produced a horrible thirst, and the refugees were half-dead from lack of sleep, these human masses kept hurrying on towards their goal – the British lines.

Another meeting of General Headquarters was supposed to take place on May 7. I was on my way to attend it, driving with my chauffeur in an Army car. I had placed my own car at the disposal of General Begic, when alarming news concerning the disintegration of the German units caused a change in plans. Dr. Pavelic and some other Government and Headquarters personnel hastened ahead towards Austria. Instead of the meeting taking place at Tuskanec, as intended, it was held at Rogaska Slatina. I did not go to the latter place, since I considered that it was more important to continue clearing out the Partisan nests along the Zidani Most–Celje road, and on the route to Maribor.

As soon as I had satisfied myself that our pioneers and flying columns were performing their tasks effectively, I returned to Zidani Most. Here I issued my last orders, not to the troops as a whole, but to individual commanders. Whenever I saw a high-ranking officer in the retreating columns, I would summon him to me and tell him:

"Do not travel to Celje over the main road. Already it is overcrowded all the way from Zidani Most to the Karawanken Alps. Abandon your vehicles and get rid of whatever luggage you have right here. Have your men follow the little country roads and paths and tell them to keep heading north! Do not be in a hurry to surrender to anyone and be sure that you do not allow everyone under your command to lay down their arms at the same time! After you see what happens to those who surrender ahead of you, make your own decision. I now am Supreme Commander of all Croatian Armed Forces remaining on our national soil. As such I have been directed to order our soldiers to yield their arms to the enemy. But if you see that those who surrender before you are being killed or turned over to the Partisans, then you will know that you have no choice but to fight to the end and die like men! Go in groups and keep in touch with all other groups in your vicinity. The time for maintaining regular military formation is past now. From here on, the initiative will be in the hands of those who know how to deal with the situations that may arise and *who want* to deal with them."

It was only now that our unbeaten Army began to break up. Many officers committed suicide as soon as they crossed the border into Slovenia. They knew that suicide was no solution to the Croatian problem, but as patriots, they could see no other way out of the dilemma in which they found themselves. Their Government forbade them to continue fighting, and they would not surrender.

For the last time I embraced my cousins and other relatives, all of whom wanted to go with me into the forests. Every man of the Defense Brigades and the regiments and divisions of my old Second Army would have done the same. Colonels Pjanic, Hasic, and Pacariz wanted to take to the woods, as did our Albanian, Montenegrin, and Hungarian allies. Those Croatian generations who will come after us should not forget that all of these peoples shed their blood with ours and perished with us. The Croatian generations of future days should no more forget them and the bravery that they displayed to the very end than they should forget the fate of our own troops.

It is some consolation to those of us who had the fortune or misfortune to survive the debacle of 1945 to know that not all Croatians or other anti-Communists were so deluded as to place their trust in British military honor. The "fleet-winged' battalions, the veterans of 1941, and the Defense Brigades did not surrender. One battalion, which was commanded by a much-decorated officer, deliberately marched towards Ljubljana to distract the attention of the Partisan forces which were preparing to attack our rear guards. A huge Partisan mass came out of Trieste to overwhelm this already weakened battalion which died fighting to the last man.[12] In this encounter, the Communists killed even those Croatians who were too badly wounded to continue fighting. This was an augury of what was to happen to those Croatians who did surrender.

---

[12] The Partisan forces from Trieste were composed partly of Italian troops of the old regular Italian Army. When Italy surrendered to the Allies in 1943, many Italian officers and men in Dalmatia and Istria joined the Partisans. From this time until the end of the war they helped considerably the overpublicized Partisan formations commanded by Tito.

Thanks to the protection afforded by the "fleet-winged" battalions, the great mass of the military and civilian refugees reached Celje in safety, and from there made their way into Austria. As for the men of the "fleet-winged" battalions themselves, the bones of these veterans of the first days of Croatian national independence in 1941 are scattered throughout the area between Zidani Most and Maribor, especially along either side of the Zidani Most-Celje road. And there are plenty of Partisan bones to keep them company.

I should mention, also, that a battalion of naval infantry took an especially brilliant part in clearing the way for our main columns by routing the Partisans repeatedly in a series of hot actions. This unit was heavily engaged east of Zidani Most on May 11-12. In an attack upon numerically superior Partisan concentrations, they lost more than three hundred men, including many officers and non-commissioned officers. The Communists fled in confusion, and the survivors of the naval battalion joined Major Matijevic's command. He told me later that he believed that never before had men anywhere in the world displayed such valor in battle as had these naval soldiers. I am mentioning this fact in order to render a deserved tribute to the heroism displayed so consistently by our naval personnel. Likewise, our Honor Work Service displayed the most heroic qualities.

In accordance with my orders, I parted with the last detachment of my personal guards at Celje. They left me with tears in their eyes. They were accompanied into Austria by two Croatian ladies, members of the Sarajevo Ustasha Youth organization, who shared the soldiers' fate.

I remained in the vicinity of Celje until our last units had marched out of the town en route to the Karawanken Alps. There remained with me two men whom I met in the woods. Also, I had with me my faithful "Askerica," a machine gun that we had fabricated ourselves, and twelve hand grenades. Such was the force disposed of by the last Commander of the Croatian Armed Forces. For the first time in days I washed my face in a brook and got some sleep. When I awoke, I felt somewhat refreshed and began my journey back towards the Croatian border.

As soon as I re-entered the fatherland, I established contact with a commando post. Since I had sustained wounds in the fighting that had taken place during the retreat, I decided that I had better go to Zagreb for treatment. Later on the Partisans learned where I stayed during my last visit to our capital. I believe that the wife of one of our officers may have betrayed the people who sheltered me.

By the time this happened, I was back in the forests in the company of other Croatian nationalists who wanted to continue the war against the Communists as best they could. Our first concern was to save all other patriots who had taken refuge in the woods. Once we had brought together all of these people we could find, we commenced our resistance activities. These were based upon the erroneous calculation that sooner or later events on the international scene would develop in a manner favorable to Croatian national interests. At the time, even a skeptic like myself could not help but feel that before long the professedly free Western World would have to take a decided stand against Russian and international Communism if it did not wish to suffer the same fate that had befallen the Croatian State and people. Needless to say, our hopes were illusory. The "free world" afforded material and moral assistance to the Communists everywhere in order to insure the establishment of the Marxist dispensation not only in Croatia, Slavonia, Dalmatia, Bosnia, Hercegovina, and Istria, but also over the other lands and peoples of Central and Eastern Europe. When the Americans finally began to oppose the spread of Communism, they did so in the Far East, precisely the area in which they had the least chance of success in their belated effort to contain the Communist menace.

Since I am a Croatian myself, it is perhaps natural that I should feel that the lot of the Croatians has been a harsher one than that of any other people who have been subjected to Marxist domination. Because of the role that I was called upon to play in the frightful denouement that awaited our Armed Forces and the civilians who accompanied them into exile, I have especially bitter memories of the events of 1945. As a soldier, I was trained to obey orders. And I received express orders to (1) direct all of our military personnel to retire into Austria and (2) to refrain from organizing a massive resistance movement in the rear of the retreating Army. The result of the mistaken decision made by our Government was that most of the soldiers and civilians who surrendered to the British in the belief that they would be treated as prisoners-of-war were handed over to the Partisans by the English military authorities. As soon as the "Yugo-Communists" had their victims out of sight and hearing of the Western allies, they tortured and slaughtered them in ways that would have commanded the admiration of the Red Indians of America two hundred years ago.

And despite the fact that the massacres of both Croatian military personnel and civilians continued to occur for weeks, months, and years after the end of World War II, the press of the "free world" maintained a conspiracy of silence concerning Tito's abattoirs. The "free world" was too intent upon enjoying the fruits of victory to care about the fate of losers in the recently played game.

The Committee for the Investigation of the Bleiburg Tragedy is to be commended for its endeavor to make known to the professedly civilized world the facts concerning the Bleiburg, Maribor, and other post-World War II massacres.

I hereby give my word of honor as a soldier that I have recorded in this account of the end of the Croatian Army only that which I myself experienced, saw, and felt at the time. I personally composed the original Croatian text of this report in the belief that it might be helpful in preserving for posterity the truth about the events in which I, by virtue of my nationality and rank, played a part of some importance.

Signed General Vjekoslav Luburic

Carcagente (Valencia), Spain
August 15, 1967

General Luburic did not live to see his own analysis and this volume in print. On April 20, 1969, he was murdered in Carcagente, near Valencia, the victim of recent "hunts" in which many prominent Croatian exiles in West European countries were murdered by agents of the Yugoslav Secret Police, the UDBA. Lengthy articles on Luburic's life and death can be found in all major Spanish newspapers and magazines. We recommend especially *La Actualidad Espanola* of May 1, 1969, because of its thorough article on Luburic. To our knowledge, Luburic's assassination was not even reported in the American news media. – Editor's Note.

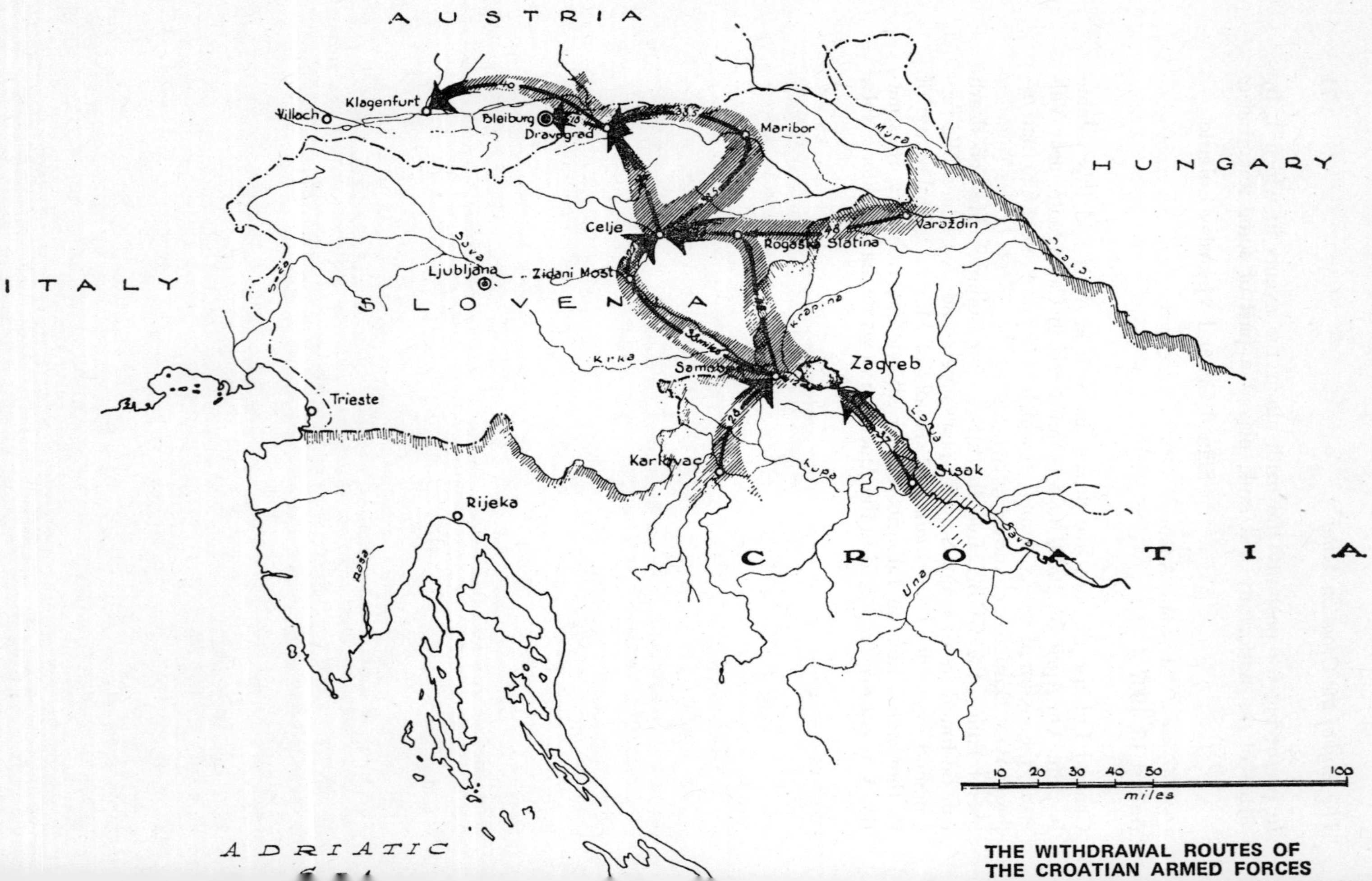

THE WITHDRAWAL ROUTES OF
THE CROATIAN ARMED FORCES

Chapter 4

Extraditions of Croatian Victims

On May 5, 1945, the Government of the Independent State of Croatia[1] sent a memorandum to Field Marshal Alexander, Commander-in-Chief of the British forces in Italy, asking that troops of the British Eighth Army enter the territory of the Croatian State and occupy the capital, Zagreb, along with other key points. The Croatians also asked that this British force accept the surrender of the Croatian Armed Forces, which were still unbeaten and intact and quite able to deal with Tito's Partisans and all of the other Communist forces in the Balkans.[2] The Government in Zagreb wanted the English to save Croatia and Slovenia from Communism, as they actually did save Greece from this blight. As stated, the Croatian forces were able to overpower Tito's bands, but obviously they could not hold out for long against the Russian armies that would come to the help of the latter. Therefore, Zagreb wished the British to beat the Soviets into Croatia and Slovenia.

According to Dr. Vjekoslav Vrancic, a copy of this memorandum was taken to Field Marshal Alexander's headquarters in Caserta, Italy, by two American airmen who had been captured by the Croatian troops. Dr. Vrancic himself, in his capacity as head of the mission for negotiating

[1] The Croatian people took advantage of the German invasion of the synthetic Yugoslav state to revolt against the Serbian hegemony that had prevailed since 1918. Croatian troops of the Yugoslav Army thoroughly disorganized that force through sabotage, desertion, and armed rebellion. On April 10, 1941, the resurrection of the ancient Triune Kingdom of Croatia, Slavonia, and Dalmatia was proclaimed in Zagreb. Dr. Ante Pavelic, leader of the nationalist Ustasha organization, founded in 1929, became Poglavnik or Head of State, pending the selection of a King. Unfortunately, the choice of the Italian Duke of Spoleto as ruler became coupled in the minds of the Croatian public with the cession of a large part of Dalmatia to Mussolini's Italy. This wholly unnecessary sacrifice of Croatian territory also did much to discredit the Pavelic regime in the eyes of Croatian patriots generally.

[2] The Croatians had seventeen full divisions still in the field, in addition to various auxiliary and technical units. Croatian military morale remained unaffected by the military collapse of Germany, and in fact most Croatians were glad to get rid of their late "Allies." Undoubtedly one of the great mistakes made by the Croatian Supreme Command at this time was that it did not compel the German forces retreating from the Balkans to turn over their weapons to the Croats. Although the latter were dependent throughout the war upon Germany for supplies of weapons and munitions, the Nazis were very niggardly in meeting the requirements of the Croatian Armed Forces, who received arms and equipment that were often defective. This was the German way to keep Zagreb from becoming too independent vis-a-vis Berlin.

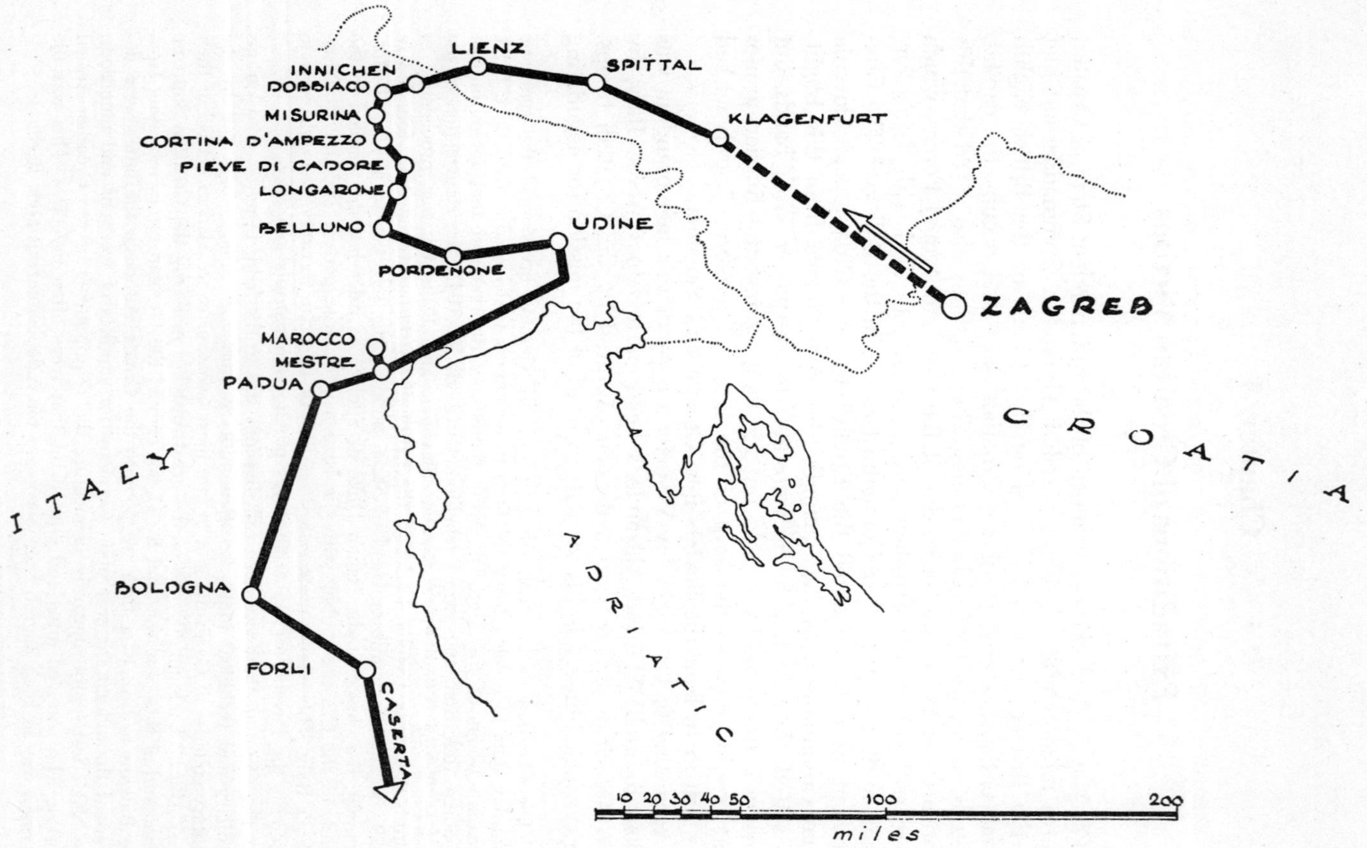

ACROSS THE ALPS UNDER A WHITE FLAG

the surrender of the Croatian Armed Forces, set off for Alexander's headquarters with the original copy of the memorandum. He was accompanied by Captain Andre Vrkljan, who had lived in England before the war and spoke English fluently. He was to act as interpreter for Dr. Vrancic. Also, the Reverend Giuseppe Massucci, personal secretary of the envoy sent by the Vatican to the Croatian Episcopate, was to accompany the Croatian mission.

When Dr. Vrancic's plane was ready to take off from the Zagreb airport, Dr. Ramiro Marcone, the Vatican envoy, forbade Rev. Massucci to board it. Therefore Dr. Vrancic and Captain Vrkljan left with the rest of the mission at 2 P.M. on May 5. They arrived safely in Klagenfurt, Austria, from which point they were taken by automobile to Linz. The Austrian authorities in this city placed an almost new Mercedes at the disposal of the Croatians here, because the car they had been using was in a bad state of repair. A veteran Austrian driver was assigned to chauffeur the Croatian mission across the Alps.

In the mountains separating Austria from Italy, the mission was allowed to pass through the outposts of the United States Fifth Army and then through those of the British Army with relatively few difficulties. As late as May 9, Dr. Vrancic had every reason to expect that he would be flown to Alexander's headquarters in Caserta. High-ranking British officers indicated as much in conversation with Captain Vrkljan.

But suddenly on this day the situation changed catastrophically. The Croatian peace mission was imprisoned in a war prisoners' camp located in Mestre near Venice. On the following day, however, they were released and permitted to continue their trip southwards towards Caserta, only to be confined again for the night in another prisoner camp at Cesena. Although these brief incarcerations may have been only a convenient way of providing overnight lodgings for the peace mission, both Dr. Vrancic and Captain Vrkljan were affected unpleasantly by them.

On May 11, they were allowed to travel further south to Forli, where they came under the surveillance of British Field Security Outpost #313. A Captain Douglas had command of this unit of the British Army. He seemed to be quite interested in the Mercedes that the Croatians were using and to have no concern whatsoever for the surrender mission they had come to discharge. He held the peace emissaries virtually incommunicado until May 18. On that day, they were allowed to see the Bishop of Forli. They asked this ecclesiastical dignitary to inform the Croatian Government, through the medium of the Vatican, of the failure of their mission.

Two days later (May 20), Captain Douglas broke the pole of the white flag the Croatians had displayed on their car all the way from Austria. He threw this internationally recognized symbol of a peace mission in the dust of the streets of Forli. Then, with the help of an Italian accomplice, he confiscated the Mercedes and left Forli in it for northern Italy. Before he departed, however, he had Dr. Vrancic and

Captain Vrkljan incarcerated in the war prisoners' camp at Forli. Such was the denouement of the Croatian peace mission.[3]

In the meantime the Croatian Armed Forces and civilian refugees had entered Austria with the belief that their government had made an arrangement with the British, whereby the latter would grant them prisoner-of-war status in accordance with the stipulations of the Geneva Convention and other internationally accepted agreements regulating the laws of warfare. Dr. Pavelic and his Government seem to have assumed that Vrancic and Vrkljan would execute their mission successfully, providing for the safety of more than 400,000 Croatian patriots who had left their native land rather than submit to Marxist tyranny.

But while the Croatian peace mission was vainly endeavoring to reach Field Marshal Alexander's Italian headquarters, the English earnestly began to extradite Croatian refugees, who had sought sanctuary in Austria, into the hands of the executioners of Josip Broz Tito. As early as May 10, 1945, the Britons in a limited, but highly prophetic sense, had begun this process.

On that day a Croatian group, consisting of approximately 500 troops and several priests, stopped on a small plain in front of a local church in Velden. Since May 10 was Ascension Thursday, the priests and most soldiers attended a solemn Mass. A little later, British military police drove a group of the fugitives into cars in which the fugitives previously had arrived from Croatia. The British military police then drove the captured fugitives to the city of Villach. The first batch was halted and disarmed in front of the local British headquarters. The second contingent was disarmed at the outskirts of the city on a road leading to Spital; then it was returned to Villach to join the rest of the original column. The prisoners were taken from Villach to Arnoldstein, to the Austro-Yugoslav frontier, and extradited. After this extradition, a Croatian priest in Villach demanded to be informed about the fate of this first party to reach Austrian soil. The British commander there replied that he knew nothing about them whatsoever.

A few days later British military police went to Turacher Heights to "take care" of another Croatian group, including about 130 members of the Croatian Government. These prominent men were lodged in two hotels of this scenic Alpine resort. Some of them were convinced, others compelled, to move from Turacher Heights to another place. Among the 130 officials were Minister-President, Dr. Nikola Mandic, Ministers of State, Dr. Osman Kulenovic and Dr. Mile Budak (a famous literary figure), Ademaga Mesic, Drs. Makanec, Puk, Canki, and others. All of them were told by the British military police that they would be transported to Italy by way of the shortest possible route. Escorted by the

[3] The full details concerning the journey of the peace mission to Italy are described vividly by Dr. Vrancic in *S Bijelom Zastavom preko Alpa* (Under the white flag across the Alps) (Buenos Aires, 1953). See also Dr. G. Massucci, *Misija u Hrvatskoj* (Mission in Croatia) (Valencia, 1967), pp. 195-196.

British military police, these men were first driven to Turach; they were then taken through Tamsweg south to Rossegg, Sankt Jacob, Maria Elend and Rosenbach. At the Rosenbach railroad station, the victims were loaded into a train which took them through a Karawanken Alps tunnel onto the Yugoslav territory.

Some men now began having doubts about the British promises. One of them, General Vilko Pecnikar, foresaw the whole treachery. Therefore, he jumped from the moving train and fled into a nearby forest. Other victims still believed in the British promise. They thought that their trek was to take them to Italy via Yugoslavia, because railroad tracks further west were destroyed in the war and were not yet repaired.

The fact was that the prisoners, on reaching Jesenice, were completely in the hands of Tito's Partisans. From Jesenice the victims were driven to Zagreb and were "marched" through its streets. Days later, the members of the government and other prominent personalities of the extradited group were mock-tried and shot or hanged.[4]

The principal objective of Tito's Partisans was to induce their English allies to turn the entire Croatian Government and Army over to them. Wherever and whenever the British proved willing to do this, the Communists removed the Croatians from Austrian soil as quickly as possible and then either executed the victims outright or exposed them to intense misery and suffering in the infamous "Death Marches," which are described elsewhere in this book. One of the survivors, Captain Josip Hecimovic, has already compiled a detailed account of these marches.[5]

Since the war was irretrievably lost, the Croatian Military Command, in accordance with the orders it had received from Dr. Ante Pavelic and his government, did not feel that it could order its troops to throw away their lives in a last, useless fight. The English had at their disposal hundreds of planes and tanks, against which the Croatian Army, hopelessly encumbered by thousands of civilian refugees and never too well armed to begin with, had little chance.

When the military spokesmen finally realized that the English were going to turn the whole army and the great mass of civilian refugees over to the Partisans, it was too late to organize anything but a militarily useless last-ditch fight in behalf of an already lost cause. Thus, the beginning of the greatest tragedy in the entire history of the thirteen-century-old Croatian State was initiated.

The series of mass slaughters carried out by Tito Broz's executioners is commonly referred to by Croatians and Slovenians as the "Bleiburg Tragedy," or, more succinctly, the Bleiburg Massacres. It was to Bleiburg, which is located near the Austro-Slovenian frontier, that the bulk

---

[4] Dr. Charles Kamber, "Moja Sjecanja na Exodus (My Remembrances of the Exodus)," *Danica*, Chicago, June 14 and 28, 1961, p. 3.

[5] Joseph Hecimovic, *In Tito's Death Marches and Extermination Camps* (New York, 1962).

of the Croatian refugees, both military and civilian, fought their way through Communist resistance. It was at Bleiburg that the British Military Command in Austria demanded the unconditional surrender of the Croatian troops and civilians. It was at Bleiburg that the Croatian generals allowed themselves to be bluffed into accepting such a surrender and relegating themselves to the role of sheep in a slaughterhouse. It was at Bleiburg that most of the long columns of Croatian refugees originated which later developed into "Death Marches."

On May 15, 1945, at about 4:00 P.M., some 120,000 members of the Croatian Armed Forces and countless thousands of civilian refugees were assembled on a great field or meadow close to Bleiburg. They knew that their military and civilian leaders had been negotiating with the local British authorities for days past. Thus, when they suddenly received orders to run up the white flags of surrender and stack their arms for delivery to the British, they did so in the expectation that they would be English prisoners-of-war.

The surrender procedure lasted from 4:00 P.M. until 10:00 P.M., when the Englishmen ordered that an end be put to it until the following morning. From the place of surrender, the columns of captives were marched into Bleiburg itself. Here, the civilians were separated from the military, the former being lined up on the left and the soldiers on the right in columns of fours. Before dark on the night of the 15th, many thousands of prisoners were led off to Lawamuend. British soldiers accompanied them as far as this town. The columns grew steadily in number as more captives joined them.

The surrender at Bleiburg involved approximately 30,000 other Croatians who had reached the valley of the Meuse River nearby. Most of these fugitives were concentrated around the villages of Prevalje and Gustanj. Those taken prisoner near Prevalje formed a column which set off towards Bleiburg. The first section of this column passed through Bleiburg during the night and early morning of May 15-16. All other sections of the Prevalje column were taken across the Drava in the morning hours and directed towards Dravograd. There were some small prisoner groups which lagged behind the others.

The bulk of the Croatians who surrendered in the vicinity of Gustanj were sent to Dravograd also. Here, they were distributed among the several "Death Columns" organized by their Communist captors. Some of these flocks of human candidates for Tito's abattoirs were marched towards Maribor; others were directed to Celje.

Several thousand Croatians refused to surrender when they received the command to do so on the field near Bleiburg. They hid themselves in the woods. Those refusing surrender either found an opportunity to penetrate into the interior of Austria, where there were no Communists to whom the British or the Austrian Socialists* could hand them over,

*The term "Austrian Socialists" refers to the Marxist-orientated Social Democratic Party, not to the old Christian Socialist Party which, after the war, transformed itself into the conservative and strongly Catholic Peoples' Party.

or made their way back to Croatia. General Rafael Boban, aided by over 2000 determined fighters, went back to the Domovina. About 1000 of General Boban's men, who wanted to join him on the night of May 15-16, fell into the hands of the Partisans who included them in the "Death Columns" which were being sent towards Maribor and Celje. Among the other officers who also took their men with them into the forests, Major Noso, Commander of the Officers' School of the Second Ustasha Assault Group (Zagreb), and First Lieutenant Buhin should be mentioned especially. A large part of the Fifth Brigade of the "Black Legion" from Koprivnica and the Military Academy at Kerestinec decided to make their way deeper into Austria. They by-passed the British tank columns, but while they were marching towards Klagenfurt, they ran into strong British forces. Like so many other Croatians, the "Black Legion" and the military cadets did not realize that surrender to the English meant surrender to the Partisans. Had this been known, the Englishmen would have had a fight on their hands. As it was, the Croats supposed that they were going to be British prisoners-of-war and allowed themselves to be disarmed. Their captors then sent them back to Bleiburg, where the Communists took charge of them and herded them towards Dravograd and the Red slaughterhouses, along with other victims of the supposed English reputation for decency.

Many Croatian officers grasped the situation more realistically than their less sophisticated countrymen. People who had been brought up on an English literary diet went around among the fugitives on the night of May 15-16, warning them of what was going to happen. They urged all who were able to accompany them into the woods, to escape extradition into the hands of the Communists. There were at least fifty officers who devoted themselves to trying to prevent those who had not yet surrendered from placing their lives at the mercy of the Britons, who cared not at all what happened to Croatians individually or collectively. They succeeded in persuading many soldiers and civilians to return with them to Croatia, where they either continued guerrilla warfare against the Reds or endeavored to lose themselves individually among the postwar population. Most of the fugitives who were still in the hills and forests near Bleiburg at the time of the surrender were led back to the Domovina by their officers. Those who gave themselves up on the morning of the 16th lived long enough to bitterly regret their folly.

Sunrise on the 16th revealed a strange sight, as thousands of men who had spent the night in the thickly-wooded hills began to descend to the highway below. Some came down of their own free will from the recesses where they had taken refuge, while the Partisans rounded up others who had not listened to the warnings of their officers. Many Croatians still thought they were going to be British prisoners-of-war. The Englishmen contributed to this persistent delusion, because the British Headquarters were located at Bleiburg and the prisoners taken on the morning of the 16th were lined up and disarmed at a crossroads a little north of that town. These people still could not believe that the Partisans were going to be allowed to have a free hand with them.

The Eighth Croatian Standing Brigade had not surrendered on the previous day. It had concealed itself in the woods along the right side of the road in order to see what happened to the people who did surrender. But when the British proposed on the 16th that the brigade give themselves up to the English Command, they made the same mistake so many other Croatians had made; they supposed that they were safe from Partisan vengeance. Of course, the Britons promptly extradited them into the hands of the executioners. Other Croatian units, which were detached from the main body of the Army and did not know what had occurred so far, met an equally disastrous fate.

After they had turned over the main body of the Croatian fugitives to the Communists on May 15-16, the British began to extradite the multitudes who surrendered to them in the Klagenfurt Valley. There were tens of thousands of Croatians who had made their way from Zagreb into this part of Carinthia. Thousands of Croatians who had escaped from the Bleiburg field also came here. These people were crowded into prisoner-of-war camps at Klagenfurt, Krumpendorf, Toschling, Rosseg, Ferlach, Viktring, Maria Saal, Tamsweg, Grafenstein, Volkermarkt, Griffen, and Wolfsberg. In all, there were at least 90,000 Croatians distributed throughout the Klagenfurt Valley. In order to make the extradition proceed as smoothly as possible, the Englishmen assured the Croatians that they were going to be sent to prison camps in Italy. Some of the Britons even persuaded the naive Croats that they would be trained to continue the fight against Communism in these Italian prison camps!

On May 15, the English took 3000 Croatians from the town of Klagenfurt itself to the railroad station at Rosenbach. Their number grew to 5000 while they were waiting for the trains that the British said would carry them to Italy. Actually the trains were going to Jesenice. When the Slovenian border was reached, the English guards were replaced by Partisans. At last, the Croats realized how they had been tricked and a great many jumped from the already moving train; they had no illusions now as to what was in store for them.

Dr. Pavelic's bodyguards were among the first Croatian troops to arrive in Carinthia. There were approximately 1000 men in this unit. They surrendered as a body to the English who took their weapons and conducted them to Krumpendorf, where they were lodged in temporary barracks close to the railroad station. On the 16th, the entire group, including a few civilians who had joined them, were transported to Villach. There they were added to another Croatian group which was under the command of First Lieutenant Babic. The combined detachment was loaded into locked boxcars by the English. In this manner, these particular victims were delivered into the hands of the Partisans.

On May 17, the British extradited 3000 more Croatians who had been brought to Krumpendorf. Among them were a high-ranking officer, Colonel Markovic, and a number of other commissioned and non-commissioned officers. These prisoners were taken through Unterferlach to Sankt Jacob, where they were loaded into British military trucks which brought them to the rail station at Maria Elend. Here the Englishmen put them on a train which, they said, was going to Italy. Since the train pulled out of Maria Elend after dark, the prisoners could see nothing and did not realize that they were being sent, not to Italy, but to Slovenia. Only when they arrived at Jesenice did they realize the horrible truth. Had they divined it sooner, they would certainly have overpowered the British guards at Maria Elend and taken their chances in the surrounding countryside.

Colonel Petrovic guessed what the fate of the fugitives was going to be and tried to lead the column that he commanded deep into the interior of Austria. Some 2000 of his troops did not follow him, but remained scattered along the Ferlach road. The British rounded them up, disarmed them, and locked them into boxcars at the Maria Elend rail station. From this point, they were extradited into the hands of Britain's wartime allies, the Yugoslav Communists. Taken by train to Jesenice, they were marched from there to the places of execution.

On May 18, another Croatian group, this time of some 800 soldiers and civilians, was ordered by the British Command to leave Krumpendorf. Leaving, they were joined by approximately 500 Croatian soldiers who came from the temporary camp established at Maria Saal. Another 300 fugitives who had assembled at Tamsweg also attached themselves to this column. Major Stipe Milinkovic, Captain Djuro Markovic, First Lieutenant Sindik, and other officers were included in this combined group. At the Rosenbach railroad station, 250 Croatian gendarmes were brought from a camp north of Krumpendorf to join the column. All of these people desired to fight, rather than to place themselves in the hands of the Partisans. But they were deceived by the British, who told them that they would be taken to Udine in northern Italy. Only when they found themselves in the hands of Tito's troops did they realize they had been tricked. In this particular group of victims of English duplicity and Yugoslav barbarism, there were more than sixty seasoned and combat-ready Croatian officers, among them General Tomislav Sertic.[6]

Between May 19 and 23, the British extradited a large number of Croatians from Grafenstein. As usual, these victims were told they were being taken to Italy. Therefore, they allowed themselves to be conducted to the Maria Elend station without offering any resistance. Their British captors searched them thoroughly at the station to make sure they had not concealed any weapons on their persons, and then loaded them into

[6] Dr. Fra Oton Knezovic, *Pokolj Hrvatske Vojske 1945* (Chicago, 1960), pp. 91-92.

boxcars. The Croats were transported in two separate trains to Rosenbach, where the Partisans were waiting for them.

On May 20, English tanks brought another 2000 Croatians to the same station. General Ajanovic and Lieutenant-Colonel Oreskovic-Gandi were in this group. When their British captors confiscated the revolvers carried by these officers, these Croats also began to have some doubts about the reliability of British "military honor" and the much-advertised Anglo-Saxon sense of fair-play. But, when the English solemnly assured them that they were being transported to Italy, they believed them. After an all-night train ride, the captives awoke in the morning to find themselves in the hands of the Partisans, who drove them on foot to St. Vid.

Two more prisoner groups were transported from Grafenstein on the 21st. The first of these consisted chiefly of family groups, although there were some individual civilians with them. They were loaded into English military trucks about 8:00 A.M. and driven to Bleiburg. At 11:00 A.M. a mixed military-civilian batch of refugees, among whom were a number of priests, were put into additional trucks and sent after the first group of victims. There were about 1500 people in the two groups. The convoys were escorted by British military police mounted on motorcycles; there were tanks at the front and rear of each column. The Croatians were conducted to the rail station at Bleiburg, where they were searched.

By this time, the captives had become convinced that they were not going to be sent to Italy as the British had told them previously, and they began to break away and take shelter in the nearby wheat fields. Rev. Dr. Kranjcec, who spoke English, asked the English Commandant to let the prisoner column take care of itself and find refuge where it could. The Englishman replied that the Croats would have to be extradited to Yugoslavia, but, if they were maltreated in any way, they could file complaints with the British Consul in Zagreb!

Was this British officer only a naive and stupid military man, ignorant of everything outside his own profession, or was he being deliberately hypocritical and sarcastic? Whatever his intellectual status, his remark brings to mind a saying of the late George Bernard Shaw who liked to fancy himself a Marxist at times:

> There is nothing so good and nothing so bad that you will not find an Englishman doing it somewhere. But you will never find an Englishman doing the wrong thing.

The English soldiers who were escorting the fugitives warned them that they had orders from their superior officers to shoot any prisoners who tried to escape. At dusk, all Croatians who had not succeeded in getting away were handed over to the Partisans. The captives were herded into boxcars and taken off to the shambles at Maribor accompanied by much shooting of rifles and machine guns. Besides Rev.

Kranjcec, the Superior of the Franciscan monastery in Karlovac, Dr. Ribic was extradited with these unfortunates.

On the following day, May 22, another 1000 people were taken from Grafenstein. Again, the British promised that they would be transported safely to Italy. And again the victims believed what they were told until they arrived at Bleiburg and heard rumors concerning the fate of those who had preceded them.

Finally, on May 23, the prisoner-of-war camp at Grafenstein was deactivated; the last 800 Croatians lodged there were assured of transport to Italy, but sent instead to Bleiburg. At the Grafenstein railroad station, they were lined up in columns of fours and then kept waiting out in the hot sun for more than two and a half hours. The pistols carried by the Croatian officers were confiscated in direct violation of the provisions of the Geneva Convention concerning the conduct of international warfare. Some soldiers and civilians who had initially taken shelter in the forests were forced by hunger and exhaustion to attach themselves to this last group of Grafenstein detainees. Finally, the whole mass of captives was driven into boxcars and taken by rail to the next station on the line, where the Partisans boarded the train and conducted it to Maribor.[7]

Another Croatian party, consisting chiefly of members of Dr. Pavelic's bodyguards and headquarters personnel, came by truck all the way from Zagreb to Lawamuend, Volkermarkt, and Griffen. They had about twenty Croatian Army trucks at their disposal. Individuals and groups kept joining the original unit. To avoid a collision on Austrian soil with the Partisans who were at Klagenfurt in some force, the 2000-odd Croatians in this party went to Toschling. Colonel Petrovic, Chief of Staff of the Bodyguards, was the ranking officer in this band of fugitives, although Colonels Aladar, Bidler and Jagnjic, Lieutenant Colonel Sladovic, and other high-commissioned officers were also with the group. Petrovic was accompanied by his wife. He surrendered the party to the British, who put two armed guards in each truck and sent the convoy to Rosenbach, where the usual extradition process took place on May 20. Petrovic himself, however, was not extradited on this day.

One small contingent succeeded in overcoming many difficulties after leaving Zagreb and won its way to the British zone of operations in Austria, arriving finally at Volkermarkt. Included in this party was Slavko Truhli, a well known anti-tank artillerist, who had won wide acclaim among the Croatians because of the heroism he had displayed in the battles around Dravograd. Because of the arrival at Volkermarkt of individual refugees and small isolated groups, the number of this band rose to over 1000. Following their surrender to the British, these people were extradited without exception.

---

[7] See Doc. XIX of R.G.G. See also the article, "Na Marsu Smrti od Klagenfurta do Ivanjcice," *Drina* (April, 1954), nos. 3-5. (On the Death Marches from Klagenfurt to Ivanjcica.)

Some contingents of the 369th Legionary Division and other German units also arrived in the British zone. The Germans numbered 4000 men in all; there were some Croatian volunteers serving with them. An English armored regiment accepted the surrender of these men. On May 16, the entire group was taken to Lawamuend under the escort of British guards and some Partisan detachments. The Englishmen abandoned the party at Lawamuend and left the prisoners to the mercies of the Communists.[8]

A number of individuals who had left Colonel Petrovic's command in time to avoid capture, and some remnants of the First Defense Brigade, were rounded up by the British in a large prisoner-of-war camp at Viktring, five kilometers south of Klagenfurt. There were approximately 4300 Croatians at Viktring. On May 21, the British transported these prisoners to Maria Elend. Before they started on their journey, an English Colonel addressed them. He told them that they were being sent to Italy where they would be trained to take part in the coming fight against Communism. The Englishman's speech was translated into Croatian and all of the Croats, including Colonel Petrovic, who had joined the group, were greatly encouraged by this talk. After the Briton had spoken, these heroic veterans of anti-Communistic action boarded two trains which began rolling southward. Only when the trains passed through a tunnel on the Austro-Slovenian frontier did the Croats realize that they had been delivered into the bloody hands of the Partisans. They were forced off the trains at Jesenice and driven like sheep to the slaughterhouse towards Radovljica, where many of them were murdered.[9]

A considerable number of the Croatians who fled from the vicinity of Bleiburg to avoid surrendering there, made their way towards Klagenfurt. About 700 of these people were captured by the British close to the city itself. The Britons escorted them to Krumpendorf. On the 22nd they were conducted to Maria Elend under the pretense of being sent to Italy. At Maria Elend, once again, they were turned over to the Partisans. P. Bjondic, Ivan Carevic, Josip Krizic, Ivan Ivanovic, and other well known Croatian personalities were among these captives. The four men mentioned above, more fortunate than many of their fellow prisoners, were enslaved for three months in Tito's Yugoslavia, but finally succeeded in escaping to Italy and then overseas.

After the extradition of the above-mentioned group, large numbers of soldiers and civilians, lacking food and shelter, were forced to give themselves up. By May 25, there were around 2000 of these people at Krumpendorf. They were visited on this day by a British Commission of Inspection, which was headed by a high-ranking officer. He gave them the usual "fight talk" which was translated into Croatian by General Rupcic. Of course, the customary promise of safe conduct to Italy was forthcoming. Once they arrived at Maria Elend rail station, this new batch

[8] E. Schmidt-Richberg, *Der Endkampf auf dem Balkan.* (Heidelberg, 1955), p. 146.
[9] See the account of Hasan Selimovic, Doc. XXVII.

of prisoners suffered the same fate as those who had gone before. They were placed on trains which took them to Jesenice. Before arrival at this station, however, the officers were pulled off the train, many of them to be murdered immediately afterwards. Others were attached to the "Death Columns" which were moving towards Kranj.[10]

At Viktring there was a prisoner-of-war camp which was designed to accommodate anti-Communist Slovenians. However, there were at least 2500 Croatians in this place too. On May 27, the Croats, together with 600 Slovenians and some Serbian royalists, were conducted to the rail station at Rosenbach. Here, they were handed over to the Partisans who led them off to the Communist butcher shops. In 1960, a well-documented book, *Vetrinjska Tragedija*, appeared, commemorating the fate of these Slovenes, along with thousands of other victims of this nationality. Anti-Communist Serbians have also published a book, *Kocevje*, which describes the liquidation of the Serbs, Slovenians, and Croatians who were turned over to the Partisans by the British, as related above. Both of these works stress the fact that the English authorities promised prisoners of all three nationalities safe conduct to Italy, and single out the infamous Major William Johnson, who seems to have been the principal author of this deceit. By constantly assuring the captives that they would be taken to Italy, Major Johnson contributed materially to the liquidation of thousands of men who would never have submitted to extradition had they known what it meant in advance. Recently, government circles in London launched a discreet inquiry into the accuracy of the facts reported in *Kocevje*. The findings of this inquiry were published in Canada, and official authorities in Ottawa informed their British interlocutors that the story told in *Kocevje* "is essentially correct."[11]

In Rosseg approximately 2000 Croatian fugitives were herded together by the British. Although some of these people came directly to Rosseg from Croatia, others made their way here from Villach, Spital, and other smaller Austrian towns located in the western part of the Klagenfurt basin. On May 31, all of these unfortunates were delivered to the Partisans at the Arnoldstein railway station.[12]

Most interesting and enlightening is the fate of some 3000 Croatians who had about 150 motor vehicles with them when they left the Domovina. They got to Reichenfels, were declared captives by the British, and then were sent to Sankt Stefan, two and a half kilometers from Wolfsberg. Only a few of these people were extradited. The lives of the great majority were saved thanks to the clear-sightedness and honesty

---

10 Hecimovic, *op. cit.*, p. 24.

11 See *Vetrinjska Tragedija* (Cleveland, 1960) p. 59. See also Bor Karapandzic's book, *Kocevje* (Cleveland, 1959), pp. 36-40, and Lubor J. Zink's article, "For Titoist Crimes: A Latter-Day Nuremberg," which appeared in the *Toronto Daily Telegram* of July 22, 1966.

12 Knezovic, *Pokolj Hrv. Vojske god. 1945*, p. 80.

of the British commander here. He told the Croatians quite frankly that he had orders from higher English authorities to turn all fugitives over to the Partisans. Then he proceeded to drag out the extradition process, repeatedly telling the Croatians that only those individuals who considered themselves soldiers had to be sent back to Yugoslavia. Major Braco Tomljenovic took advantage of the delay to gather 200 soldiers together. This entire party took to the woods, eventually making their way back to Croatia where they continued the fight against the Communists as best they could. The hesitation of the English in carrying out the extradition at this point enabled most of the other Croatian soldiers in this group to transform themselves into civilians, whom the British officer refused to let the Partisans capture.

Meanwhile General Tomislav Rolf, his wife, and General Dragojlov decided to commit suicide. The responsibility the generals had incurred by trusting to the good faith of the British and ordering their soldiers to surrender instead of fighting to the death weighed heavily upon their minds. Again, the British Commander in the St. Stefan-Wolfsberg area displayed his quick-wittedness and humanitarianism by rushing all three to a hospital. The lives of General Dragojlov and of Madame Rolf were saved. General Rolf died of his self-inflicted wound.

On May 18, about 150 soldiers and 450 civilians of this group were extradited. Among the military men, there were two high-ranking officers, one of whom was Lieutenant Colonel Steinfl, who did not attempt to take advantage of the deliberate delay in the extradition procedure, but decided to return to the Domovina to face whatever charges might be directed against them. Steinfl, for example, was so outraged by the earlier extradition of his brother, Admiral Steinfl, that he was unwilling to accept any courtesies whatsoever from the British.[13]

At the last moment, a hundred people who had decided to return to Yugoslavia changed their minds and their British guards allowed them to escape. Later this group was joined by other Croatians who came out of the woods and hills, where they had taken refuge.

The action taken by this one courageous, intelligent, and humane British commanding officer saved the lives of at least 2500 Croatians. Even more could have escaped the return to Yugoslavia, if they had wished to take advantage of his kindness. Certainly this officer risked court-martial by controverting or disregarding the orders concerning extradition received from his superiors; the example that he set shows what could be done by military personalities on the winning side if they possess a modicum of decency and political sensitivity. It was the misfortune of the Croatians that there were apparently few such individuals serving in the British Army in Austria or Italy at this time.

---

[13] The Admiral surrendered to the English on the night of May 12-13, and was handed over to the Partisans the following day. As noted in the account of General Luburic, he was a high official of the Croatian Government.

Because of the presence of a garrison of four companies of Partisans at Lawamuend, several small extraditions of prisoners took place here with greater facility than proved to be the case in the St. Stefan-Wolfsberg region. Both the English and the Partisans kept picking up individual fugitives and isolated little groups who were moving from place to place in the eastern part of the Klagenfurt basin, especially around Jaunthal and Lawanthal. Most of the people taken in these areas were moved to Bleiburg or Lawamuend and extradited from these places. Sometimes, without troubling to go through a formal process of extradition, the Britons handed them over to the first Partisan detachment they encountered. On occasion, Tito's executioners killed fugitives as soon as the original British captors were out of sight and hearing. They took others to the "Death Columns" at Dravograd.

One of the first attempts made to effect such on-the-spot killings involved a group of sixty Croatian Air Force officers who had escaped the surrender on the Bleiburg field and were attempting to make their way towards Klagenfurt. They fell into the hands of the Partisans near Ebendorf and were stripped of all their clothing. Then, they had to watch while a mass grave was dug for them. Before the execution could take place, however, a prisoner column passed by and the Communist commander of the escort had the sixty intended victims included among his other prisoners. This Communist official reportedly was himself a Croatian or a Slovene.

On the other hand, a small contingent of General Ajanovic's forces had a series of successful encounters. They fought their way through mountainous territory, dispersing Partisan bands which tried to stop them, and on May 13 were joined by another band of Pavelic's Bodyguards. Among the latter were First Lieutenants Rolf and Pejic, and Color Bearer Ivan Svatos. The combined group was attacked by a larger force of Partisans, but the latter were routed by artillery fire directed at them by a unit of the Croatian Obrana, which happened to be in the same vicinity. When Partisans found their retreat cut off, the Obrana made them promise they would take care of the Croatian wounded, along with some women and children who had come this far with the soldiers. When the Obrana men left this area, the Partisans murdered all of these non-combatants.

Partisan military formations remained in Carinthia from May 8 to May 24. During this period, they murdered many Croatians on Austrian soil. These butcheries were performed under cover of darkness. Machine-gun firing could be heard every night in the Carinthian valleys. One of the intended victims of these murders survived to write an account of his experiences during these Carinthian killings.[14] The late Sir Winston Churchill evidently heard something about the massacres, which occurred while British troops had effective control of Carinthia and therefore could have stopped the slaughters, if he had wished to do

[14] See the account of Pero Martic, Document VIII.

so. Churchill remarked that both the English and American troops witnessed with their own eyes the perpetration of various cruelties by the Partisans. Undoubtedly, he was thinking about these incidents when he compared Hitler's tactics with those employed by Tito.[15]

The hills and valleys of Austria are dotted with the graves of unknown Croatian victims of the slaughters of May, 1945. Carinthia was the principal scene of these deaths, but a few isolated butcheries occurred (by grace of the Russians) elsewhere in Socialist Austria, too. Four known graves are located at Unter-Loibach, three kilometers distant from Bleiburg. Twenty-four Croatian unknown soldiers are interred in one of these graves, and more than thirty bodies have been found in the other three burial grounds. Austrian witnesses have revealed that one Ustasha lieutenant was murdered in the house of a local inhabitant and that the Partisans cut his throat after he was dead to make sure they had not bungled the job. Not far from the locality in which this incident occurred, there are seven Croatian graves. At Homberg, above the railroad tracks, there is a mass grave which contains the bodies of 200 murdered Croatians.[16] Because of the conspiracy of silence which has been maintained by all authorities, British, American, and Austrian Socialist alike, concerning the great tragedy which occurred principally on the field of Bleiburg and in the surrounding areas of Austria, many other instances of torture and slaughter remain undescribed. However, the records kept by the Catholic Rectory at Galizien mention that the bodies of six Croatian soldiers who had been shot in the back of the head are buried here. This same account also states that at least one Croatian soldier was starved to death by his captors.[17]

Some of the witnesses who have contributed accounts of their experiences in this volume have told how the Partisans sometimes hid behind the British troops so that the Croatians would not realize that they were really giving themselves up to Tito's people. This sort of thing happened many times. As soon as the British had accepted the surrender of the Croatians and had collected their weapons, they would appoint one of the captive officers as commander of the group. Then they would march off, and the Partisans would appear to take charge of the disarmed men and force them to join the "Death Columns," which contained so many thousands of other unfortunates.[18]

While the Partisans perpetrated many isolated butcheries at different places and on a smaller scale, the camp they maintained at Ebendorf,

---

15 W. Churchill, *Triumph and Tragedy* (Boston, Houghton Mifflin, 1953), pp. 557 and 561.

16 On the details see the article "Bleiburg," *Hrvatska Drzava* (Munich, 1955), No. 1, p. 5.

17 *Hrvatska* (Buenos Aires), May 20, 1951. The late Fra Oton Knezovic, who survived the Death Marches, mentions the mass starvation of Ustasha prisoners, in particular.

18 See particularly Document XXIII.

eight kilometers south of Volkermarkt, was their main slaughterhouse. Approximately 350 Croatians were confined here at one time. Among the other prisoners were four Croatian military officers and a journalist, Ivo Mrakovcic. The Partisans captured these people before they could make contact with the British and forced them into the Ebendorf camp without telling the local English authorities. Mrakovcic and the four officers got away and succeeded in reaching Klagenfurt. Later they went to Krumpendorf and reported the incident to a unit of the Croatian Red Cross, which had found asylum there. The Red Cross notified the English authorities of what had happened, and the British did intervene to take the rest of the prisoners at Ebendorf away from their Partisan captors, only to extradite them at Maria Saal a little later on!

There was a Partisan encampment at Eisenkappel, too, through which 5000 Croatian captives passed en route to the "Death Columns." They were sent from here to Kranj and St. Vid for assignment to these grim Calvaries. Hundreds, perhaps thousands, of Croatians are also known to have been murdered in the Leibl defile on the Austro-Slovenian border during the bloody sojourn of the Partisans in Carinthia. Later, the bodies of many of these victims were exhumed from their temporary resting places and interred in Austrian cemeteries. Today there are thousands of Croatian graves in the Lawamuend-Rosenbach area, in particular. Since the Social Democrats enjoyed Russian protection, and English, French, and American patronage after the war, this party dominated Austrian civil life for a time. Therefore, the Austrian newspapers had nothing to say about the mass reburials or the events of May, 1945. However on August 28, 1953, the Swiss paper, *La Liberte*, attracted attention to the exhumation of the corpses so hastily disposed of by the Partisans before they left Carinthia. The correspondents of this sheet conducted an investigation which resulted in the publication of a lengthy article entitled "Un 'Katyn' Yougoslave."[19]

Austria was not the only non-Yugoslav territory in which the British allowed the Partisans to conduct a reign of terror. As early as May 1, 1945, the 30th Partisan Division, commanded by General Dushan Kveder, reached Trieste.[20] It was accompanied by the 43rd, or Istrian Division, of Tito's over-publicized forces. Of course, the English already held the city. The British Commander there, Lieutenant-General Freiburg, allowed the Partisans to remain in the town for a full forty days. Kveder's troops, which were joined by many isolated Partisan units, utilized this interval to perpetrate a number of massacres in the city and its environs.

[19] The Katyn Forest was the scene of the massacre of over 10,000 Polish army officers and civilian authorities. For some years this slaughter was supposed to have been perpetrated by the Germans after their conquest of Poland in 1939. Eventually, it was discovered that it was the Russians rather than the Germans who killed these Poles.

[20] The Tito Government claimed that Trieste was Yugoslav territory, basing this contention upon the fact that many of its inhabitants were Slovenes or Croatians.

They killed at least 7000 inhabitants of Trieste, several hundred wounded men belonging to various anti-Communist nationalities, and 1100 German prisoners-of-war.

For a long time the general public in Trieste and the surrounding territory did not know what the Partisans had done with these victims.[21] The truth did not come out until 1954, when it was discovered that thousands of bodies had been thrown into a great abyss, which for years had served the city as a dumping ground for garbage and refuse disposal. Of course, only those scenes of slaughter which lay on the Italian side of the Italo-Yugoslav frontier could be investigated. Naturally, Tito's officials have prevented the opening-up of the mass graves of postwar victims which lie on the Yugoslav side of the frontier line. Nor have the Italian authorities displayed any desire to uncover all of the burial places of Tito's victims on Italian soil. It is known, however, that the remains of about 3600 Italians, both soldiers and civilians, have been unearthed both near Bazovica and in a great pit or hollow called Rudnik or Bunar. It is estimated that some 800 German prisoners-of-war were contained in these mass graves, too.

Near Opcina a mass sepulcher holding close to 1300 corpses has been unearthed. This abattoir is designated as the one hundred forty-ninth such burial ground in this area. The victims here included 400 sailors of the Croatian Navy, 100 Croatian soldiers, 350 German prisoners of war, and some hundreds of civilian refugees from the Croatian Primorje (coastland), Lika, and Istria. Among the latter were a number of nurses and other hospital employees.

Certainly the Americans, as well as the British, knew what was going on. On May 12, 1945, President Harry Truman sent an angry telegram to Sir Winston Churchill denouncing the Hitler-type tactics that were being employed by the Partisans under the protection of the British Army. In a letter that he wrote at this time, Truman spoke of the need of preventing Communist domination of Europe. Two days after he sent the message to Churchill, however, Truman's ideas seem to have changed

[21] John (Ivan) Prcela, one of the editors of this book, and Chairman of the Committee for the Investigation of the Bleiburg Tragedy, was attending the Franciscan Seminary in Makarska in 1944-45. Tito's forces gained control of the Makarska territory at the beginning of the fall of 1944 because of the impending German collapse, the beginning of the withdrawal of the Wehrmacht in the Balkans, and the consequent shortening of the lines held by Croatian Armed Forces. Prcela was forcibly drafted into Tito's Army on April 3. He was stationed first on the islands of Ciovo and Rab, then at Bazovica and later in Trieste. He heard rumors concerning the large scale slaughter of war prisoners and distinguished anti-Communist citizens. While posted in Trieste, he heard a great deal of shooting every day from the direction of Bazovica, and in the environs of this city. He got some information about what was going on from members of the execution squads and learned other facts from less trustworthy elements among the Partisans. On June 10, Prcela deserted from the Communist forces and hid in a monastery in Trieste. On the massacres in the vicinity of Trieste see also "Hrvatski Krizni Put," *Slobodna Hrvatska* (Free Croatia) (Munich), May-August 1961, p. 3.

CARINTHIA: EXTRADITION POINTS OF THE CROATIAN VICTIMS

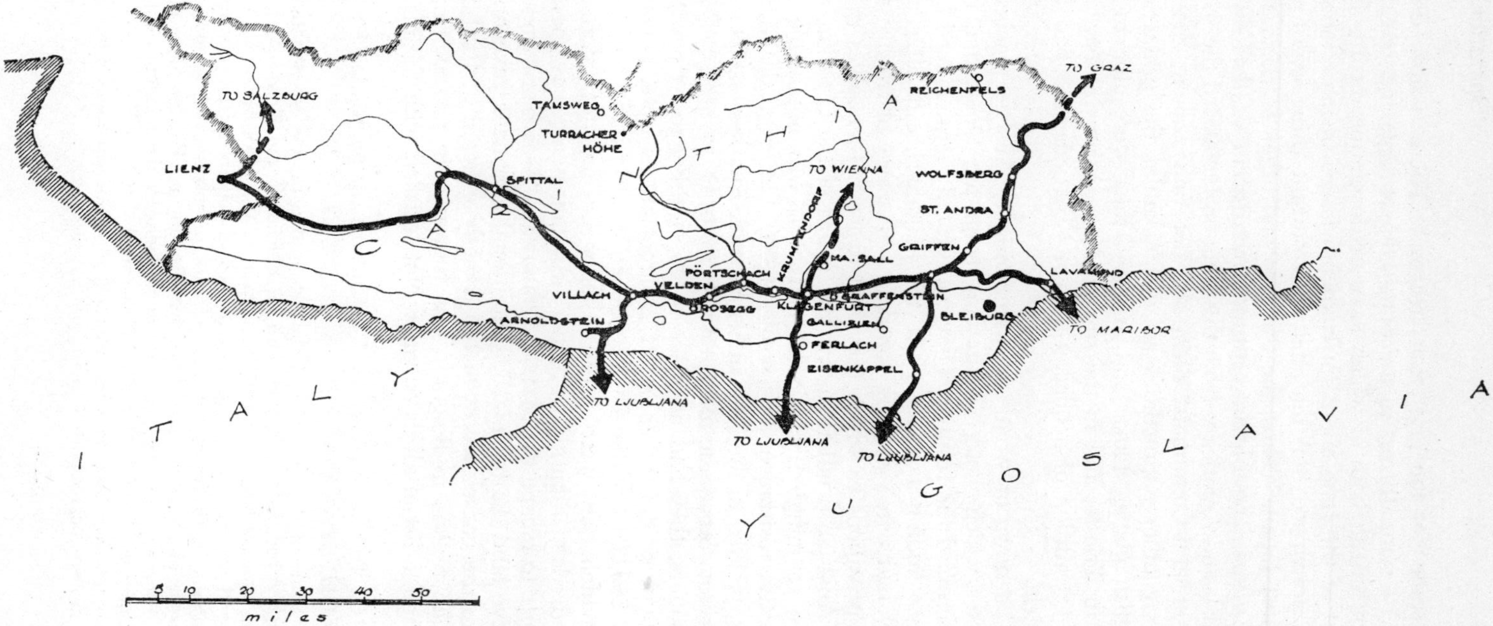

for some not too mysterious reason.[22] There is little doubt that Communist sympathizers in the State Department, and possibly in the War Department, both of which have made unique records by being wrong most of the time about international issues of importance, "got to him" and convinced him that the all-important thing was to finish the war against Japan.[23] Thus, the Russians and other Marxists had a clear field in Europe. The tolerant attitude towards Tito's killers displayed by both British and Americans from this time on facilitated the wholesale slaughter of anti-Communist elements, not only among the Croatians, but among other nationalities as well.[24] Under the protection afforded by English planes, tanks, and artillery, they were able to do a thorough job in Trieste, and in the surrounding districts of Istria. They effected the extradition of a quarter-million Croatians who had taken refuge in Austria.

The news of what was happening in Austria reached the Croatian masses which were withdrawing from the Domovina, but had not as yet crossed the frontier. They were totally demoralized by their despair at not finding a sanctuary in the neighboring country, especially since they had eaten nothing for days and were physically exhausted from the privations to which they had exposed themselves in order to reach the Austrian frontier. In this rear guard of the Croatian exodus, civilians were so mingled with soldiers that it was impossible to organize an effective resistance. As a result, 20,000 soldiers, and about as many civilians, yielded to the Reds at Dravograd. Another 60,000 surrendered near Maribor. Since the British were refusing to accept Croatians as war prisoners, they had no place to go, nothing to fight with, and nothing to fight or die for either. It is important to note, however, that if the first 250,000 Croatians who reached Austria had been given the asylum to which they were entitled under the laws of international warfare, hundreds of thousands of other Croatians would have persevered in their efforts to escape the Marxist tyranny that was being imposed upon their native land. Perhaps 60,000 additional Croatians gave up at Celje. Such were the consequences of the tragedy enacted at Bleiburg.

The regime in Belgrade was thorough in endeavoring to compile a complete list of all its enemies. Not satisfied with the masses of captives

---

22 On Truman's message, see Churchill, *op. cit.*, pp. 554 to 557.

23 *Ibid.*

24 Some of the members of the Committee for the Investigation of the Bleiburg Tragedy became acquainted with an official of the Truman administration a few years ago. He told them that there were in the office of the United States Attorney General a great number of documents and reports relating to the massacre of the Croatians in 1945. On the basis of this information, the Committee asked Senator Lausche of Ohio and Representatives Bolton and Feighan, also of Ohio, to request the Attorney General's office to turn the relevant documents over to them. The Congressmen were told by the Attorney General that his office did not possess any documents which related to large-scale slaughters of Croatians after the war. Nor were any such papers reported in the military archives.

placed in its hands by the policies and actions of the British, it prepared a list of "war criminals" for the edification of its Western Allies. The names of 20,000 people who had eluded extradition were on this list. Both the British and Americans, who thought they had done a good job of obliging Tito's henchmen, were stunned by the extent of this list. If these were the "war criminals," whom had they turned over to the Partisans? Naive as both Englishmen and Yankees were in their conceptions of non-Western peoples, there were few among them who seriously believed that the entire Croatian nation consisted of "war criminals." The authorities of both nations refused to accept the Yugoslav list as valid. Not at all put out, Belgrade cut the list to 2000 names. By this time, however, even the Britons and the Americans were beginning to have qualms about the rectitude of the attitude they had adopted in the matter of the Croatian refugees. They turned down this list too.

Nothing daunted, Belgrade reduced the number of "war criminals" whose extradition it demanded, to 150 well-known Croatian personalities. Perhaps because they were tired out by the persistent Communist importunities and perhaps because they didn't care about the Croatians anyway, the Western Allies accepted this smaller list at face value. Later the Tito regime added another 660 names to it. On the basis of the data supplied, the Allies, Great Britain and the United States, began hunting down the people indicted.

Those Croatians whom the British had not turned over to the Partisans at Bleiburg and other places in Austria were kept in camps maintained by the English and Americans at Klagenfurt and Salzburg, respectively. The British also had a camp for Croatians at Wolfsberg. There they sent the "war criminals" whom they picked up in the Klagenfurt area and in Spital, Villach, and Graz. From Wolfsberg, this new batch of victims was extradited piecemeal to Yugoslavia. The English kept on sending their driblets of "war criminals" until well into 1948.

Five-hundred Croat refugees of the exodus of 1945 remained at Camp Lehen in Salzburg. There were also a number of Croatians here who had worked in Germany during the war and who did not wish to return to Tito's Socialist Paradise after the end of hostilities. The headquarters of the Croatian Red Cross, directed by the Reverend Vilim Cecelja, was located at this place, also. Vladimir Bosiljevic, secretary of this organization, was an indefatigable worker, too. The endeavors of the Red Cross to ease the life of the imprisoned exiles greatly irritated the Yugoslav Committee, which had its offices across the street from the Lehen barracks. This committee labeled all anti-Communist Croatians as Nazis and Fascists. Under this pretext, the Communists tried to hinder the activities of the Red Cross.

The Croatians confined in the American zone of occupation in Austria had to suffer persecution also from the American Counter Intelligence Corps. This force was directed by an American Serb, Major Milovanovich. On the night of August 29-30, 1945, Major Milovanovich brought fifty of his men in bullet-proof armored cars to the Lehen Camp. He had fifty of the prisoners taken by truck to the Provincial Court building on this night. Also he carried off some fifty eyewitness accounts of the massacres that had taken place at Maribor, Celje, Kocevje, and other places in Slovenia.

The arrestees were confined in the Provincial Court building for two weeks. The majority were then sent to Camp Marcus W. Orr at Glasenbach. This center was the place of detention for "war criminals." Two such individuals were extradited from here into Communist hands on February 11, 1946. Some other arrestees suffered the same fate on September 9.

Worse yet was the fate of Major Ciril Kralj. Since Kralj could not be convicted of having committed any crime other than killing a number of Partisans during the war in open battle, he was released from the camp and told to take a short-cut that would bring him to Salzburg. He was hardly 150 meters away from the camp when Tito's agents seized him, forced him into their car, and transported him across the frontier. Once they had him in Yugoslavia he was promptly hanged. *This incident could not have occurred had there not been collusion between Americans such as Milovanovich and Tito's police.*

Field Marshal Slavko Kvaternik was among the Croatians who were extradited on September 9, 1946. Before his execution on June 13, 1947, in Zagreb, he managed to smuggle out a "last message" which constitutes Appendix A of this volume. It throws additional light upon the common practices of the Tito regime.

Italy, too, witnessed a great hunting down of Croatian refugees, even those who had taken no prominent part in the life of the independent Croatian State of 1941-1945.

Major Stephen Clissold of the British Intelligence Service was a principal activator of this witch hunt. Before the war, Clissold had represented the British in Zagreb. He married a woman of apparently "Yugoslav" orientation, who must have helped to color his view of the Yugoslav situation. On the evening of March 27, 1947, he personally effected the arrest of 120 Croatians who had escaped extermination in 1945.[25] He functioned in this affair as Secretary of the Commission for the Investigation of War Criminals. This body was headed by General Fitzroy McLean, the author of an incredibly naive book on the wartime activities of Tito and his Partisans. McLean is a worthy compatriot of the late R. W. Seton-Watson, who perhaps has done more than any other one individual to muddy the Central European and north Balkan historical waters.

In April, 1947, the English carried out a real military offensive against the displaced persons camp at Fermo in Italy. There were at least 2500

---

[25] John Prcela, one of the editors of this volume, was in Rome at the time and suffered from this persecution, along with his brother Paul.

Croatians in Fermo; many were well-known athletes or men of letters and the camp as a whole fostered Croatian cultural life and encouraged sports. Fifteen Croatians were taken from this camp by the British and thrown into the "Queen Elena" prison in Rome, which housed a number of other supposed Croatian "war criminals" also. Some Croatians were extradited from this place to Belgrade.[26] Others were sent to Germany for trial and were returned to Yugoslavia from there. The "war criminal" witch hunt in Italy was carried on not only in Rome and in Fermo, but also in Bagnoli, Modena, Berlatti, and other places. General Vladimir Kren, Colonel Janko Vernic, Dr. Vladimir Zidovec, and the Croatian newspaper men, Milivoj Magdic, Vilim Peros, and Dane Uvanovic were among prominent Croatian personalities who were turned over to the Yugoslav Communists at this late date (1947).

Major Clissold and Uvanovic, both journalists, had established friendly relations in Zagreb long before the Croatian catastrophe of 1945. Their friendship was renewed during Uvanovic's exile in Rome. Uvanovic, however, learned what the Englishman's "friendship" was worth when he found himself en route to the land from which he had fled two years before.

Clissold also distinguished himself by securing the extradition of General Ante Moskov on May 8, 1947. Moskov was one of the most dangerous of Tito's foes. He had opposed the evacuation of Croatia in 1945, and counseled fighting to the end against all odds. This Englishman directed the capture in the harbor of Genoa[27] of some Croatians who had secured passage to Argentina. These people were sent to Trieste and then returned to Yugoslavia. According to the noted Croatian ecclesiastical historian, Dr. Krunoslav Draganovic, the authority on both post-war extraditions and the resulting butchery of hundreds of thousands of Croatians, thirty-five very distinguished Croatian political leaders and intellectuals were either extradited from Trieste or kidnapped by Communist police in the vicinity of Trieste and spirited off to Yugoslavia. Some Croatian "war criminals" were sent from Italy to Germany. Later, they were extradited to their Yugoslav executioners. Governor Josip Markovic, Consul Professor Seliha Baljic, and Minister of State Zivan Kuvedzic were among those who, long after the war was over, were taken from the German prisoner camp at Esterwegen and delivered over to Yugoslav justice.[28] As late as 1948, Croatians were still being sent back to the Yugoslav hell from Esterwegen. Finally, in 1967, while engaged in the task of collecting further evidence concerning the mass

[26] Spiridion (Dr. Dusan Zanko), "Nevini u 'Regina Elena'" (The Innocents in 'Queen Elena'), *Novi Zivot* (Rome), Nov. 2, 1967.

[27] This witch hunting maneuver, resulting in the extraditions of leading Croatian figures to Yugoslavia, prompted Dr. Branimir Jelic, President of the Croatian Refugee Committee in London, to send a lengthy and documented report to the British Government not only on the Croatian victims of May, 1947, but also on those of May, 1945. Dr. Jelic charged Tito's regime with Nazi-like brutalities and genocide.

[28] Dr. K. Draganovic, "Popratna Rijec," *Novi Zivot,* No. 2 (1967), p. 123.

murders of 1945-47, Dr. Draganovic himself was abducted by Tito's police near Trieste.[29]

Only in 1948 did some Catholic representatives raise in open Parliament the question of British responsibility for the extradition of war refugees into the hands of the Communist regime in Belgrade. In answer to their inquiries, His Majesty's Government declared that at the end of May 1945, 600 "Yugoslav Collaborationists" had been sent back to their homeland! Subsequently the British Foreign Office solemnly confirmed the "accuracy" of this official government statement.

This declaration of the English Government needs to be preserved in letters of gold as a permanent reminder of the mendacity of which official Britain is capable when it desires to avoid political embarrassments. This official statement of 1948 is on a par with the Government thesis of 1914 concerning the entry of Great Britain into the war in that year, and with the superb dishonesty of British wartime propaganda in both World Wars. The English always know how to smear their opponents effectively and how to whitewash their own conduct. History

---

[29] On September 10, 1967, Fr. Krunoslav Draganovic disappeared in the vicinity of Trieste, which presently is held by Italy. He was engaged in adding to his collection of documents and personal testimonies received from survivors of the postwar massacres carried out by Yugoslav Communists in 1945 and subsequent years.

Newspapers and periodicals in Austria, Italy, Switzerland, Germany, and the English-speaking countries commented on this incident, as did the Yugoslav Press. The majority of the European press organs have displayed a more intelligent comprehension of the case than has the press of the United States and Canada, or Great Britain. Informed Europeans everywhere share the convictions of Dr. Draganovic's thousands of Croatian friends, who are scattered throughout the world, that this most eminent of Croatian exiles was kidnapped by the Yugoslav secret police. Almost all Croatian news organs abroad have expressed their certainty on this point.

On the other hand, the Yugoslav Press printed a seven-page letter, supposedly written by Dr. Draganovic, together with alleged interviews that he gave to their correspondents following his reported "return" to Yugoslavia, two months after his initial disappearance. According to the officially inspired Belgrade Press, Dr. Draganovic came back "voluntarily" to face trial for his "war crimes" and for the hostile propaganda that he has directed for years past against the Tito regime.

During mid-November, 1967, American newspapers such as the *New York Times*, the *Cleveland Plain Dealer*, as well as other prominent news organs in the United States and Canada, printed the official report of the Draganovic case that was disseminated by the Yugoslav regime. Neither the American nor the Yugoslav press mentioned the real issue involved in the disappearance of the Croatian savant.

This issue revolves around the fact that for the past quarter-century Fr. Draganovic has devoted himself to uncovering the facts concerning the war and postwar crimes committed by Yugoslav Communists. During this long span of years, Fr. Draganovic has interviewed hundreds of Croatian, Slovenian, Montenegrin, German, Austrian, Magyar, and Serbian survivors and eyewitnesses of the massacres decreed by Tito and his Government.

Naturally the Communist "Marshal" and his regime are anxious to keep their achievements of the war and postwar years unknown to the Western Powers which made these slaughters possible, through the help they gave to "Tito and his gallant warriors," as the late Sir Winston Churchill put it before he found out what these allies of Anglo-Saxon righteousness were doing. In their attempt to cover up their is replete with manifestations of this Anglo-Saxon talent. It is the peculiar success achieved by the Britons in this department of political warfare that has caused Europeans, who understand the British official mind, to designate the island kingdom as the "vampire of the continent." The Croatians are neither the first nor the last people to rue the admiration for things British that the diplomatic and literary representatives of "perfidious Albion" are so successful in inculcating in the minds of the naive among all nationalities. Because of their four centuries of membership in the Habsburg community of nations, the Croatians acquired a "favorable image" of the British which was a consequence of the long-standing friendship and alliance that existed between Great Britain and Austria-Hungary. In the course of time, most Austro-Hungarians acquired the extraordinarily fatuous idea that the British Union of Nations had all the virtues and advantages possessed by the Austro-Hungarian Union, but none of the faults and weaknesses of the latter. Thus Austria-Hungary herself, and then the individual peoples included in that complex, joined a host of former friends, allies, and admirers of the English on the historical scrapheap.

---

own record, the Yugoslav Communists have labeled Fr. Draganovic a "war criminal." In their eyes of course, his crime is that he, more than any other living man, has dug up evidence which damns the whole wartime Partisan organization. This same evidence must also damn the regime in power in Belgrade, Zagreb, Ljubljana and other capitals of the Yugoslav republics today.

Prior to his disappearance on September 10, 1967, several attempts were made by Tito's secret police to kidnap and liquidate this intrepid Croatian patriot. Earlier in the year, he wrote friends that he knew that he was a marked man and that no credence should be given to any reports that might be disseminated by the Tito regime concerning his "return" to Yugoslavia. If Belgrade reported that he was back in that country, or if he should be murdered, "accidentally" killed, or listed as an apparent suicide, all patriotic Croatians would know what had happened and who was responsible for it.

Croatian exile organizations have quietly investigated Fr. Draganovic's disappearance. Two Yugoslavs, Petar Galic and Asim Sahimpasic, obviously agents of the infamous Secret Police, the UDBA, gained the confidence of the aging scholar by convincing him that they were against Serbian domination of the present day Marxist regime in Yugoslavia. The evidence in the case indicates that Galic and Sahimpasic lured the Professor to a spot near Trieste on the pretense of showing him where some of the mass killings had taken place in 1945.

It was believed that UDBA agents, and particularly Commissar Nikola Cimesa, who for years had been determined to bring Fr. Draganovic "alive or dead" into Yugoslavia, killed the priest as soon as they had him in their hands. The fact, however, is that he is still being held incommunicado, although this is not the way that Communists of any nationality ordinarily do things. Reliable reports from Zagreb declare that the man who gave the above-mentioned interviews to the Yugoslav Press, and who is supposedly residing in Yugoslavia today while the authorities decide whether or not they ought to try him for "war crimes," is someone other than Fr. Draganovic. Handwriting experts at the Police Department in Cleveland, Ohio, and elsewhere have pronounced the facsimile of Dr. Draganovic's alleged letter, the contents of which were publicized in the Yugoslav press, to be a clever forgery of the Croatian's actual handwriting. Dr. Draganovic is, therefore, one of the most distinguished victims of the Yugoslav masters of deceit.

Of course, there are many Englishmen who deplore both the hypocrisy and deceit of which the British official mind is capable and also its inordinate capacity for self-justification. British Welfare Officer John Cornellis, shocked by the declaration made by his Government concerning the extraditions of 1945-48, challenged the accuracy of the statements made by British officialdom. He was in a position to do so, because he had seen with his own eyes how thousands of Croatians, Slovenians and Serbians were sent back to Yugoslavia from the Viktring camp alone. He protested publicly against the official lie that was being disseminated by British ministers to clear the good English name of any suspicion of complicity in the wanton and indiscriminate slaughter of hundreds of thousands of losers in the recently concluded war. The Foreign Office invited him to visit its sacred precincts to see the original list of the 600 Yugoslavs who were repatriated by courtesy of the English military authorities.[30] But the Foreign Office found that Cornellis knew too much to be taken in and, therefore, simply ordered him to keep his mouth shut. To insure his silence, it brought upon him irresistible pressure in the inimitable manner that English authorities have used since the days of the Tudors.

One of the members of the Committee for the Investigation of the Bleiburg Tragedy is acquainted personally with an official of the British Foreign Office. This Englishman has informed him that there are in the Foreign Office archives a great many documents and statistics which refer expressly to the massive extraditions and ensuing mass murders of Yugoslavs who sought refuge in the British zones of control in Austria, Italy, and Germany. John Prcela, Chairman of the Committee for the Investigation of the Bleiburg Tragedy and the co-editor of this book, requested Representative Frances P. Bolton (R-Ohio) to approach the British Foreign Office with the request that the materials in its archives concerning the postwar extraditions and massacres be placed at the disposal of the editors of this work. On October 19, 1966, the Foreign Office replied to Mrs. Bolton as follows:

> Thank you for your letter of 13 October about the documents relating to the massacres of Croatians in which your constituent, Mr. John Prcela, is interested.
>
> I personally have conducted a search of the Foreign Archives for the reports which Mr. Prcela believes us to have, but I am sorry to say that I have found nothing. I can well imagine that such reports were prepared by our military people in Austria at the time, but like so many of our administrative records, they were not sent back to London, but were kept locally and subsequently destroyed. (It is only during my own last four years in the Foreign Office Library that we have been able to bring home the records of the British Element in the Control Commission for Austria, which had hitherto mouldered away in the basement of our Embassy in Vienna!)

---

30 *Vetrinjska Tragedija,* p. 133.

I am sorry not to be able to help Mr. Prcela, but if any of the reports come to light in the future I will bear his interest in mind.

C. J. Child

Under date of November 25, 1966, Mr. Child wrote another letter to Mrs. Bolton, who had continued to pursue this matter. The text of this communication is the following:

Thank you for your further letter of 16 November about the information concerning the Bleiburg Tragedy which your constituent, Mr. John Prcela, is interested in obtaining.
As I have said, we do not have anything in the Foreign Office archives, but I am now asking the military authorities if they will make a search to see if any of the material has been preserved in their files. I will let you know the result in due course.

A third letter from Mr. Child to Mrs. Bolton was written on January 3, 1967. In his capacity as Librarian and Keeper of Papers of the Foreign Office Library, Mr. Child averred:

Further to my letter of 25 November I have now heard from our military authorities the result of the search for material relating to the Bleiburg tragedy which I asked them to make on behalf of your constituent, Mr. John Prcela.
Mr. E. H. G. Richardson of the Ministry of Defense now writes: 'with reference to your letter of 25th November 1966—your reference LS 8/68, regarding a request from Congresswoman Frances P. Bolton whether certain reports dealing with the massacres of Croat war prisoners could be traced, I write to let you know we have been unable to trace these references to or evidence of them in Army Department records.'
This, I am afraid, seems to leave me no possibility of pursuing the search further. *As I said in my letter of October 19, many records were retained locally in Austria after the war and were eventually destroyed instead of being sent home. This may well have happened to papers dealing with the Bleiburg Tragedy.**

Clifton J. Child

It can be seen from the above-cited letters that official London gave a less satisfactory reply to Representative Bolton's repeated requests than it did to Lubor J. Zink, correspondent of the *Toronto Daily Telegram.* Mr. Zink, who knew something about the vicissitudes suffered by Welfare Officer Cornellis in his endeavor to uncover the truth concerning the extraditions, concentrated his inquiries on the forced repatriations that had taken place from the Viktring prisoner-of-war camp. The Serbian account, *Kocevje,* also deals largely with extraditions from this camp. Through the Canadian Government in Ottawa, Mr. Zink received the answer from official London that the facts reported in *Kocevje* are "essentially correct." Of course, Canadians rate considerably above

*The above lines are emphasized by the editors of this volume.

Americans in the estimation of most Britons, whether they are members of the legislature of their respective countries or not. Mrs. Bolton got nothing but politely negative answers or, as the Americans put it, a "run around." Of course, the personal good faith of Mr. Child is not to be questioned, but it is clear that either Communist sympathizers in the British Foreign Office, or officials who are above all else concerned with keeping the British name unsullied, have quite evidently removed all incriminating evidence, or destroyed it.

It has taken almost five hundred years for the truth concerning the murder of the sons of Edward IV of England and the systematic elimination of all the legitimate claimants to the throne of England by Henry IV, Henry VII, and Henry VIII to come to light. It may not take this long to prove the responsibility of official Britain for the mass slaughters of 1945-47 and the isolated killings perpetrated by the regime in Belgrade thereafter. But if typically egoistic and self-righteous Britons in Government and military circles can cover up the facts for more than half a millennium they certainly will do so! There's always an England, and who cares about the Croats anyway?

Yet as early as May 23, 1945, the *Times* of London contained a lengthy editorial written by a British soldier who lately had been in Yugoslavia. These comments in the *Times* made pointed reference to the fact that British political and military circles were thoroughly acquainted with the details of what was taking place in Austria, Slovenia, the environs of Trieste, and in Yugoslavia itself:

> . . . We have, in our thanksgiving for victory, reaffirmed the fact that we are a Christian nation and have solemnly and severely dedicated the peace to Christian principles. Within a few days of these ceremonies we are invited to acquiesce in a gross extension of a spectacle which touched the conscience of our grandfathers—the subjection of the Christian peoples of the Balkans to non-Christian tyrannous rule. The peoples now overrun by the forces of Marshal Tito are predominantly Roman Catholic. The attitude of his regime to their Church is not a matter of conjecture: it has long been evident in Croatia; but the knowledge is confined to those who, owing to official sources, may not speak. Has the time not come to proclaim the truth? During the German war it was thought convenient to attribute heroic virtues to any who shared our quarrel and to suppress all mention of their crimes. There can now be no honorable reason for further concealment.
>
> If, when the truth is published, it is revealed that the regime of Marshal Tito has all the characteristics of Nazism—a secret political police, an unscrupulous propaganda bureau, judicial murders of political opponents, the regimentation of children into fanatical, hero-worshipping gangs, the arrest and disappearance of civilians for no other reason than that they spoke English and had exchanged civilities with British troops, the kidnapping of political opponents on allied territory, the arrest and disappearance of a national leader who came under safe conduct to discuss cooperation, that, above all, the Church is subject to persecution aimed at its extinction, that great numbers of priests whose

> only offense was popular esteem, have been done to death, religious houses closed and religious associations abolished, that the elaborate and violent machine propaganda is employed to vilify the religions, that no expression of opinion is possible outside the party machine—if these things are true, the nation will see where its duty lies toward people threatened with an extension of this regime.
>
> We have been obliged to make many painful compromises with justice during the past 10 years, some of which seem irreparable; here is a question where we have the power to do right. . . . [31]

In its feature article dealing with the fanaticism of Tito, *Time* also corroborates the mass persecutions perpetrated after the war in Yugoslavia and attributes the liquidations and imprisonments of an estimated total of 300,000 victims to the Partisans and Alexander Rankovic's state security police.[32]

A concise statement made by Sir Winston Churchill on the subject of postwar crimes perpetrated by the Yugoslav Communists is enlightening concerning the question of British involvement in the massacres of 1945-47. It reveals that leading British circles were well informed about the butchery that was going on. Churchill declared in very succinct terms:

> Their (the Partisans) behaviour both in Austria and Venezia Giulia (that part of the old Austrian province of Carniola and the Kustenland which Italy got after the war of 1914-18) made a bad impression on the Allied troops, both United States and British. Our men were obliged to look on, without power to intervene, at actions which offended their sense of justice, and felt they were condoning wrong doing.[33]

It is evident from the foregoing material that the Western Allies, though they were not themselves the perpetrators of the Bleiburg-Maribor complex of slaughters, materially facilitated the execution under the most atrocious circumstances of hundreds of thousands of people, Croatians and others, who had committed no crime save that of being anti-Communists. As for those Croatians who might with some excuse have been indicted as "war criminals," the worst they had done was only what many soldiers on the winning side, that is in the armies of the Western Allies, had done – they had killed. In Victor Hugo's great historical novel, *Ninety-three,* there is a scene in which a band of Vendean royalists, who have been surrounded by republican troops, kneel before a priest to request absolution for their sins before waging their last fight against overwhelming odds. When the priest asks each one to confess his sins, they reply individually with the simple statement, "I have killed." The troops who fought or are fighting in Vietnam and

---

[31] "Letters to the Editor," *The Times of London,* May 23, 1945, p. 5.

[32] *Time,* "The Nations: Proletarian Proconsul," September 16, 1946, Vol. 48, pp. 26-30.

[33] Churchill, *op. cit.,* p. 557.

Korea, the Vendean royalists or French republicans of 1793-1800 and the Croatian freedom fighters of 1941-1945, are all "war criminals" or, except for extraordinary brutes, none of them are war criminals. In the twentieth-century the real crime is to be caught on the losing side!

On the twentieth anniversary of the Bleiburg tragedy, Senator Frank J. Lausche, D-Ohio, declared in a session of the United States Senate that the large scale extraditions and delivery of uncounted thousands of victims into the hands of Tito's executioners was one of the "many tragic blunders" made by the Western Allies toward the end of World War II. His solemn declaration reads as follows:

> Among the many tragic blunders committed by the Western Allies toward the end of World War II is one that is too often forgotten or overlooked today. That blunder is the unstinting aid given by Western forces to the Communist guerrilla bands of Tito. At the time, there was every indication that Tito was not only fighting against the Nazis but also conducting a ruthless campaign against all the anti-Communists within the borders of prewar Yugoslavia. It was already evident that political and civil liberties and minority rights would be trampled upon in a Communist-dominated Yugoslavia. Nevertheless, those brave freedom fighters who seeking to hold back the Communist tide in Yugoslavia and to protect the right of distinct nationalities to self-determination received scant sympathy from Allied authorities. In May, 1945, British military authorities in Austria extradited to Tito's bands thousands of anti-Communist Slovenes and Croats who had surrendered to the British in the hope of receiving protection and support. These patriots were ruthlessly slaughtered by Tito's forces.
>
> The mass extermination of Croats who were surrendered to Tito by British authorities in May, 1945, has come to be known as the Bleiburg tragedy. Croats who have scattered throughout the world in order to escape terrorism in Communist Yugoslavia set aside a day in mid-May to mourn their countrymen who were the victims of Allied blindness. I am convinced that continuing investigation of the Bleiburg tragedy is necessary in order to help lift the veil of illusions surrounding the Communist dictatorship in Yugoslavia. I wish to salute those who are engaged on this task, and to extend to them my heartfelt sympathy on a sad occasion.[34]

Undoubtedly, the victims of that great slaughterhouse operation would agree with the distinguished Senator from Ohio. They would, however, raise the Senator's "thousands" to hundreds of thousands of victims. Almost an entire generation of Croatian men had to die horribly, and their families were similarly affected during the savagery of 1945-47 and the succeeding twenty years of Red tyranny. Tito and his henchmen wanted to kill not only their contemporary political opponents, but also the Croatian State idea, which had survived all the centuries of Hungarian and Habsburg rule.

---

[34] The *Congressional Record,* May 13, 1965, pp. 10068-10069.

Whether the massacres of 1945-47 were carried out on a massive enough scale to annihilate Croatia remains to be seen. Whatever destiny may await the Croatian people, the non-Communist world can learn some valuable lessons from their experience.

The first lesson is one that should be ingrained into the consciousness of every soldier and civilian in all of the non-Communist nations of the world. It is:

Never surrender to the Communists on the battlefield or anywhere else whether you are in a winning war or a losing one. Many of the men who fought or are fighting in Korea and Vietnam have come to this realization themselves without knowing anything about the events of 1945-47. But the anti-war nonsense in the United States is indicative of the fact that there are a great many people who are living in a pacifist fool's paradise. Unfortunately, few human beings seem to be capable of learning from the experiences of others; they learn only through their own misfortunes. What the world needs today is to become intimately acquainted with the details of what happened to the Croatians as well as to the other victims of world Marxism after 1945. Then, perhaps, citizens everywhere will be able to apply the teachings of the British poet and spokesman for the Empire, Rudyard Kipling, when in the coming Armageddon the Communists attempt to dispose of unbelievers once and for all.

When yer officer's dead and the sergeants look white,
Remember it's ruin to run from a fight.
So take open order, lie down, and sit tight,
And wait for supports like a soldier,

Wait, wait, wait, like a soldier,
Wait, wait, wait, like a soldier,
Soldier hof the Queen!

When yer wounded and left on Afghanistan's plains,
And the women come out to cut up what remains,
Just roll to yer rifle and blow out yer brains,
And go to yer Gawd like a soldier.

Go, go, go, like a soldier,
Go, go, go, like a soldier,
Go, go, go, like a soldier,
Soldier hof the Queen!

The Croatian experience of 1945-47 shows that there is only one way to deal with Communism — fight it, wherever and whenever the opportunity offers — and *Vae Victis!*

Such is the lesson taught by the Bleiburg Tragedy.

— John Prcela and Stanko Guldescu

April 10, 1969

Chapter 5

The Bleiburg-Maribor Massacres in the Press, and Eyewitness Accounts

Josip Tito Broz's Partisans initiated the policy of mass murder of the Croatian people in August 1941. It was at this time that the so-called "Liberation" movement or "Popular Revolution" began in the territories formerly included in the Yugoslav state of 1918-41. The Partisan campaign was launched in obedience to instructions received from the Government of Soviet Russia, which had sent Tito to the Balkans years before the war to organize the Communist Party in Croatia and other parts of the royal Karageorgevitch State. The Yugoslav Marxists viewed with indifference or positive rejoicing the breakup of the Yugoslavia of 1918-41, but as soon as its conquerors, the Germans, turned on Russia, they began to do all in their power to divert Nazi troops from the Russian front. Thus the war came to the Croatian Kingdom, whose nationalist leaders had hoped to make their country another Sweden.

Even before the Partisans offically launched their campaign against the fundamentally anti-Nazi and anti-Communist Croatian people, royal Serbo-Chetnik bands under the command of Drazha Mihailovic and other intensely chauvinistic leaders had already been attacking Croatian non-combatants indiscriminately, particularly along the coast where they had a free hand under the Italian occupation forces. From August on, however, the Partisans and Chetniks collaborated against what they considered to be their most dangerous enemy, the Independent Kingdom of Croatia. Both Partisans and Chetniks wanted to restore Yugoslavia, the artificial and unnatural creation of World War I propaganda and military fortune. Although they had different ideas concerning the auspices under which such restoration should be accomplished, they both knew that it was the Croatian desire for national independence which stood immovably in the way of such a recreation, far more than the German Nazis or the Italian Fascists. Since Berlin and Rome would have preferred to deal with a united Yugoslavia under a government acceptable to them, they were not happy with the proclamation of Croatian independence on April 10, 1941. With the Croatians taking matters into their own hands, the Germans and Italians were faced with a *fait accompli* which they could not alter without creating enormous complications in the south, at the very moment that they were engaged in all-out struggle in Russia, North Africa, and Greece. Therefore, they made the best of a bad bargain and contented themselves with denying the newly-established Croatian Army and Navy the war materials and supplies needed to make Zagreb independent from Berlin and Rome. Being aware of this, the Partisans and Chetniks understood that at worst they could settle with the Nazis and Fascists on the basis of a restored Yugoslavia, if they could weaken the Croatian element enough to make its support of no account to Hitler and Mussolini.

The Partisan-Chetnik cooperation against the Croats continued until the spring of 1942. At that time, the political differences between the Russian-inspired Marxists and the Serbian nationalists came into the open and they began to fight one another. By warring against the Partisans the Chetniks were also able to secure arms from the Nazis through General Nedich, head of the war-time Serbian state. Both Chetniks and Partisans, however, continued to attack undefended Croatian villages and butcher the women, children, and old men left behind in these settlements, since the young men had gone to enlist in the Croatian Armed Forces. With the Croatian State being a special target, the war was consequently carried out mainly on the Croatian State territory with the victims mostly Croatians.

Some of the Serbian minority in Croatia (descendants of Orthodox elements which centuries before had found shelter on Croatian soil fleeing the night of Turkish despotism and fanaticism which had descended upon the Balkans) joined the Partisans and Chetniks in attacking Croatian non-combatants. On occasion they also dared to strike at Croatian military detachments. As a consequence, the enraged Croatians struck back, and a merciless three-cornered war began: Partisans against the Serbs and both against the Croats. Even in 1941 and 1942 as in the closing days of the war when Chetniks joined the Partisans en masse, Tito's Partisan forces were composed mostly of Serbs; so the Partisan-Chetnik struggle was in reality a conflict of Serbian Marxists against Serbian nationalists, and both hated the Croatians with equal intensity. Unfortunately, there were some elements among the Croatians, chiefly "intellectuals" or urban workingmen, who were susceptible to the Marxist line of argument. In addition, Socialist and Communist party members and fellow travelers were even stronger among the Slovenes, the third national element making up the pre-war Yugoslav state. With the inclusion of these peoples and those Croatians along the coast reacting against Chetnik horrors and the occupational exploitation of General Roatta's Italian Army, the Partisans were thus able to maintain the fiction of a united front.

In September, 1943 the comic opera Fascist state set up by Benito Mussolini in Italy collapsed ignominiously, having lasted just long enough to harm the Croatians. In a moment of weakness, Dr. Ante Pavelic, head of the Croatian State (its King was supposed to be a member of the Italian House of Savoy), had ceded Dalmatia, the cradle of the Croatian national tradition and civilization, to Italy. In the Middle Ages, the great maritime Republic of Venice had acquired this Croatian territory, and from the end of the seventeenth century until 1797, the greater part of it had remained in Venetian hands. For this reason, among others, Mussolini laid claim to its control in 1941. Pavelic was willing to cede Dalmatia, because he expected Italy to collapse under the strain of the war, and supposed that the Croatians would then move into Dalmatia as the Italians left it.

Matters turned out differently than had been anticipated. When Italy surrendered, most of the officers and men stationed in Dalmatia surrendered themselves and their ultramodern weapons to the Partisans and, in some instances, to the Chetniks. Thus, these two groups, rather than the Croatians, benefited from the collapse of Croatia's so-called "ally."

It was not until the last quarter of 1944, however, that the Partisan movement became a serious menace to the Croatian nation. Contrary to the glowing propaganda printed in the Anglo-American press through Russian connivance, the Partisans were no match for the Croatian Armed Forces, despite the abysmally ineffective tactics of the German Balkan Wehrmacht, which severely limited the Croatian war effort. The Germans did not know how to fight a guerrilla war in the mountains and their bungling often hampered the Croatians from destroying Partisan formations.

In the fall of 1944, the Balkan Wehrmacht began to retreat northwards. As in the war of 1914, the Germans did not cooperate loyally with their allies. Often a German unit would withdraw from a locality without notifying the Croatian force in the near vicinity. Thus, the Croatians found their flanks uncovered and would have to fall back to avoid being cut off by the advancing Partisans, now joined in large numbers by the Chetniks who, detecting the shift in political winds, exchanged the "royal" insignia for the red star. As villages, towns, and cities in the southern part of the Croatian State were left unprotected, the Partisans' tactic of murdering non-combatants, pursued throughout the war, assumed the character of genocide.

All Croatian localities that came under Partisan control between October 1944 and April 1945 had their "Katyns."[1] The population began to comprehend what was in store for them if they waited for the Partisan murder bands (armed and financed by the United States, Great Britain, and Soviet Russia) to take over their communities, so multitudes of people abandoned their homes and possessions and fled northwards. During the first months of 1945, the population of Zagreb doubled as hordes of these destitute refugees poured in. Meanwhile, Dubrovnik

[1] See footnote 19 in Chapter Four.

(Ragusa), Split, Sinj,[2] Imotski, Mostar, Siroki Brijeg,[3] Travnik, Sarajevo, Nasice, Mitrovica, Gospic,[4] and other Croatian localities fell into the hands of the American and British-backed Reds. In all of them, scenes of massacre and atrocity were enacted such as the Croatian territories had not witnessed since the days of the Mongol and Turkish invasions. Tito's followers were intent upon liquidating all Croatian patriots, male or female, old or young, rich or poor, well or poorly educated.

These pre-Bleiburg massacres could well enter into this book, but they form a story in themselves. Therefore we, the editors, have limited our documentation to the incidents that occurred *after* the formal end of hostilities in 1945 and *after* Tito's own official proclamation of "final victory." The documents used in this book deal, therefore, with the *postwar* massacres of the Croatian people at the hands of the Partisans. It should be noted, however, that in a few cases the testimonies describing postwar massacres also refer to those which occurred before the end of the war.

Factual eyewitness testimony and other details concerning the wholesale slaughter of the inhabitants of the Croatian territories of Croatia, Slavonia, Dalmatia, Istria, Bosnia, and Hercegovina can be found in many Croatian newspapers and periodicals of the period 1941-1945. The pre and post-Bleiburg massacres are best described by the Reverend Krunoslav Draganovic in his many writings on this subject.[5] Such Croatian emigrant papers and magazines as *Danica, Hrvatska Drzava, Hrvatska Revija, Studia Croatica* and *Novi Zivot* have printed Dr. Draganovic's observations.

---

[2] Since the author of this section of the present book comes from the vicinity of Sinj, he is acquainted with the intimate details of the fate of this area in 1944 and 1945. The files maintained by this Committee contain long lists of people who were murdered by the Partisans in Sinj proper, in its surroundings, and in the writer's own village of Kosute. Among the victims, were many teachers of the author and numerous other Franciscan priests from the surrounding countryside. We have not told the story of the fall of Sinj in the autumn of 1944 in these pages, because we wished to concentrate upon the postwar massacres.

[3] Siroki Brijeg, seat of a famous Franciscan gymnasium which has turned out many generations of eminent Croatians, was the scene of the most notorious of the pre-Bleiburg massacres. Twenty-eight Franciscans were murdered by the Partisans, who burned alive thirteen of these fathers. Dr. Oton Knezovic, who was a member of the Franciscan community there, escaped from Siroki Brijeg shortly before the massacres took place and lived to write his gripping *Pokolj Hrvatske Vojske 1945.*

[4] This Committee has in its files detailed survivor and eyewitness accounts of the massacres that were perpetrated at all of the places named, as well as in many other localities. Worthy of particular note is the slaughter at Virovitica of 1718 Croatian youths whose only crime was that of being called up for military service by the Croatian Government at the end of the war. None of them had fired a shot in this conflict. See Document LXXX.

[5] See Draganovic's study published in C. Mihanovich and A. Bonifacic, editors, *The Croatian Nation in its Struggle for Freedom and Independence* (Chicago, 1955), pp. 293-308.

Works dealing with the Partisan slaughters at the beginning and towards the end of the war include:

Martyrium Croatiae (Rome, 1946).

Reverend Thedore Benkovic's *Tragedy of a Nation* (Chicago, 1946).

Dr. Oton Knezovic's *Pokolj Hrvatske Vojske 1945* (Chicago, 1960).

Dr. Ivo Omrcanin's *Martires de la Fe* (Bs. Aires, 1962).

Dr. Ivo Bogdan's *La Tragedia de Bleiburg* (Bs. Aires, 1963).

La Croatie Martyre (Paris, 1968).

Bernard George's *L'Occident Joue et Perd: La Yougoslavie dans la Guerre* (Paris, La Table Ronde, 1968).

Worthy of special mention is the contribution of the late Safet Jaskic, *Srbokomunisticki Zlocini nad Bosnom* (Serbo-Communist Crimes in Bosnia) (Valencia, 1968). After thirteen years of imprisonment, Jaskic finally escaped to West Germany, where he died before he could see his book in print. But he left behind him an invaluable first-hand account of the martyrdom of Bosnia, particularly concerning the Muslim inhabitants of that much disputed land.

Apart from these several eyewitness accounts published by Croatian survivors, innumerable other written testimonies have been assembled by Croatian committees and organizations in Austria, Italy, West Germany, the Argentine, and in the United States, particularly in Cleveland. These various depositions could fill many volumes. It is a tragedy that most of them will remain unread, because their stories might well parallel the fate of the above-mentioned countries, should the Communists ever succeed there as they did in Croatia. This material is available in the files of the several committees or organizations referred to, and it is to be hoped that future historical or social investigators will have recourse to it.

With regard to the butcheries of 1945 and afterwards a score of volumes the size of this one could be prepared, granted there were free access to the various massacre sites existing in the present Yugoslav state. Of course, only the United Nations could arrange such an investigation, and it could do so only after the overthrow of the Tito regime. Time and again we have petitioned this body, as well as the Congress of the United States, to take action to bring out the truth concerning the slaughterhouse tactics employed by the Yugoslav regime before and after 1945. At first we directed our pleas to Dag Hammerskjold. Then we approached U Thant, Secretary General of the UN. We also contacted individual delegates of various "Free World" states who had seats in the United Nations. But this international body had no more interest in the fate of the Croatian victims of Communist aggression than it has in the sufferings of the Yemeni people under Egyptian and Soviet invasion. Despite our many letters, we did not receive one acknowledgment from the authorities of this most futile and ill-conceived of all international bodies. Obviously it no more wants an investigation of the pre and post-Bleiburg butcheries than it does of the Yemeni tragedy, or that of the Kazahks of Russian Central Asia who, along with the sheep they tended, were wantonly slaughtered by the Soviets.

We have had a little more luck with the American Congress. During the past nine years, the Committee for the Investigation of the Bleiburg Tragedy has on two occasions appealed to every single member of the United States Congress to initiate a formal and official investigation of the Bleiburg-Maribor-Zagreb postwar massacres. We have asked them to do this not so much for the sake of the hundreds of thousands of victims whom the Communist allies of the United States and Britain murdered in 1945 and afterwards, as for the education of American taxpayers, who since 1941 have been brain-washed continuously by their own government. Officials of the American government and the news media, almost without exception, vied with one another in impressing upon the gullible American public the "moderate" character of the Tito experiment, which is no "real Marxism."

Times without number, this Committee has urged the most prominent members of Congress, including the senators from Ohio and the greater Cleveland congressmen, to open Congressional hearings on crimes committed by the Yugoslav Communists whose methods made Nazi concentration camps seem humane in comparison. Our efforts in this direction have been attended with less success than those of the anti-vivisectionists or the several other advocates of prevention of cruelty to animals.

On June 2, 1960, however, Congresswoman Frances P. Bolton, acting in accordance with the request of Mr. Glenn, introduced into the *Congressional Record* a brochure compiled by Stephen W. Skertic, *The Bleiburg-Maribor Massacres–Croatian Golgotha,* together with a resolution adopted by the United American Croatians in regard to the massacres.[6] This agreement was the outcome of the 15th Anniversary Commemoration of the Bleiburg Tragedy held in Cleveland. This Committee itself was formed during the original commemoration of the slaughter of the Croatian Army.

On the Twentieth Anniversary of the Massacre (that is, of the date on which the British accepted the surrender of the Croatian Armed Forces and began to turn the disarmed men over to the Communists), Senator Frank J. Lausche of Ohio made a significant statement on the floor of the Senate. Senator Lausche's speech, delivered on May 13, 1965, is reproduced in Chapter Four. Also recorded there are the steps taken by Rep. Frances P. Bolton to help bring to light the complete truth concerning the Bleiburg-Maribor murders and subsequent horrors.

Again and again Representative Michael A. Feighan has given to us his wholehearted support through speeches he delivered at the memorial programs we have organized to honor the victims of the Bleiburg massacres. In 1961, following the Memorial Day Commemoration of the

[6] See the *Congressional Record* of June 2, 1960, pp. 10922-10923.

slaughters of 1945, Representative Feighan went so far as to request several high-ranking officials in the United States Government to deport the Yugoslav Consul in Pittsburgh, Ivan Mirosevic, because this Communist representative attempted to stigmatize the writer of this chapter as a "war criminal." Mirosevic similarly endeavored to smear most of the members of the United American Croatians, and also tried to talk Mr. Feighan out of addressing our Memorial Day assembly. Naturally, Feighan ignored Mirosevic, and in addressing the assembly the congressman cited Mirosevic's letters in order to discredit both the Consul and his Moscow-trained boss, Tito Broz.

The consequence of this imbroglio was Mirosevic's removal from his post. Belgrade then launched vicious verbal attacks upon Mr. Feighan, the undersigned, and the other organizers of the Memorial Day assembly. Tito himself honored all of these individuals with expressions of his venom during the twentieth anniversary of the beginning of the Communist revolution in Yugoslavia.

On the twentieth anniversary of the Bleiburg Tragedy, Congressman Feighan declared:

> Tito and his Communists should have been brought before the Nuremberg Court and convicted for the sad, disgraceful incident of the Bleiburg massacres and many other inhumanities committed by man against man—inhumanities that were committed by him and his Communists against good, God-fearing people whose only fault, if any—and I can see no fault in this—was that they had the love of God and Country in their hearts and the desire to have a homeland, freedom, and national independence. We must keep alive, sad though it may be for us to do so, the memory of this terrible tragedy, this attempt at genocide by the Communists, because, by keeping that memory alive, eventually this memory will help win freedom and independence for the great homeland of the Croatians and it will help to destroy the tyranny of Communism and enable all of Yugoslavia to be free and to be able to determine its own destiny so that it will no longer be shackled by the Russian-dominated Tito regime, which is the worst sort of Government imaginable.

A special word should be said concerning the lack of press coverage given to the "Death Marches" and to the torture and massacre of hundreds of thousands of Croatians and other victims of defeat in 1945. All that appeared in the British Press at the time of the catastrophe was a letter to the editor of the London *Times,* a newspaper which before 1918 did much to bring into existence the Yugoslav political Frankenstein. The text of this communication is reproduced in Chapter Four of this book. One day after the publication of this revealing testimony, however, the publishers of the *Times* issued a retraction in the following words:

> In the *Times* of May 23 (1945), a British soldier lately in Yugoslavia submits a terrifying list of unspecified charges against Marshal Tito's regime for mass shootings, arrests, deportations and kidnappings of civil-

ians, murders of priests, and vilification and persecution of religion. I returned from Yugoslavia recently, having spent many months in various parts of that country, including Roman Catholic Croatia, and I am afraid that as an eyewitness on the spot I must firmly contradict these unsupported wholesale accusations. Futhermore, during my long stay in Yugoslavia I kept in constant personal touch with the office of the British Military Missions, and I never once heard such accusations from their lips. Some of these officers are now in London, free to testify before their authorities.

Sincerely yours,
An American War Correspondent[7]
Lately in Yugoslavia.

This letter is worthy of some careful attention. Who was the "American War Correspondent Lately in Yugoslavia?" It could have been Ray Brock, Robert St. John, Leigh White, or any of the numerous other American journalists who sent back inaccurate, uninformed, and sophomoric encomiums of the Tito regime, although White later realized the truth about this "deviationist" Marxist dispensation. The British war correspondent, Lovatt Edwards, a Serbophile of long standing, was capable of writing such a letter in order to whitewash his beloved Serbians, whether Marxist or royalist. The fact is that we do not know who this unnamed correspondent was, and presumably neither does anyone else except the individual himself and the publishers of the *Times*, if they have kept the original letter or a record of the name of its composer.

As to the content, it is something that someone brought up in the Anglo-Saxon tradition could be naive enough to dictate. Did this "eyewitness on the spot" expect to be invited by the Partisans, whom he so obviously admires, to take part in or to witness the operation of the abattoirs they were conducting? Or to pitch in as a member of the burial details?

If the "American War Correspondent" really spent any time in any part of Croatia, he was obviously being wined and dined and shown more edifying sights than that of numbers of dying people. The Communists, of course, weren't as crude or forth-rightly honest as the late King Carol II of Rumania who shot Iron Guards out in the open street and left their bodies lying there—not that the majority of the victims didn't deserve what they got. So the "American War Correspondent" was an "eyewitness on the spot." Of what? Dinners, drinking parties and officially conducted tours? These do not usually include visits to execution sites or to concentration camps.

As for the officers of the British Military Missions, it could be only said that the English have an unmatched ability to disassociate themselves from brutalities committed by their allies. They closed their eyes to Russian, Serbian, and Italian atrocities in World War I, because an ally of Britain automatically becomes sacrosanct and can do no wrong.

---

[7] For this correspondence see the London *Times*, issues of May 23 and 24, 1945.

British military men are about the most slavishly minded in the world in this respect. History has shown that they know how to maintain the most discreet silence concerning barbarities practiced by allies of England, and expect the same service from their allies in instances where the British themselves are guilty of atrocities. Examples are the Great Sepoy Mutiny of 1856, the Boer concentration camps of 1900-1902 in South Africa, and the British naval blockade of 1914-18. To therefore suppose that any British officer—rather, almost any British officer—would testify "before their authorities" to any misdemeanors on the part of Britain's allies against her enemies is almost comic. To also fancy that the authorities would do anything but carefully hide, if not destroy, the report of any officer who did have the temerity to deny that all's fair in war as long as Britain or her allies do it, would be even more grotesque. Thus the value of this "eyewitness on the spot" testimony, is obvious to anyone familiar with the nature of British military political theory and practice.

With few exceptions, the news media in the Anglo-American countries either responded as gullibly, as the "American War Correspondent," or else vied with one another in glamorizing the "gallant warriors" of Tito. For the benefit of their reading publics, they described in the most eulogistic terms the rich fruits produced by the planting of Marxism on Croatian soil.

It was this astonishing spectacle of how a free press could systematically delude its readers by glorifying Tito and his Partisans that led to the foundation of our Committee. Moreover, we were appalled by the way in which billions of dollars, contributed by U.S. taxpayers, including ourselves, was being channeled to Belgrade to consolidate Tito's so-called "national Communism." (Remember Hitler's National Socialism—Nazism?) We felt that it was our inescapable duty to inform our fellow Americans and other citizens of the world of the real nature of Tito's rise to power and the actual character of the rule that has prevailed in Yugoslavia since 1945.

The preliminary spade work for the Committee's establishment was a consequence of the speech delivered by Dr. Charles Kamber at the fifteenth anniversary of the Bleiburg Tragedy, commemorated in Cleveland on May 30, 1960. By this time a few American publications, in addition to the British periodical *Tablet,* began to print accounts of what really happened before, during, and after 1945. On May 31, 1960, the *Cleveland Plain Dealer* published a relevant article pursuant to our commemoration ceremony. This article touched, necessarily, upon the Partisans' (allies of America) liquidation of 150,000 Croatian prisoners-of-war.

Then on June 18, 1960, the periodical *America* recommended to its readers the previously cited brochure, which was read into the *Congressional Record* by Congresswoman Bolton. *America* made the following comment on the Croatian tragedy:

> Historians now recognize that after World War II many murders were glossed over by the facile charge that the victims were collaborators or Fascists. Better documented than most cases of this kind is the fate of the Croatian soldiers, victims of Tito.[8]

Still almost all other American newspapers and magazines refused to let their readers have the facts, even though we were exerting ourselves to supply the American press with the most authentically documented information. A real conspiracy of silence existed in the journalistic world concerning the Bleiburg-Maribor slaughters and subsequent happenings, as is now the case with the Egyptians and their Communist sponsors in Yemen since 1962. Virtually without exception, the slavishly uniform American press continued to favorably present Tito and his executioners, among whom, it is true, both Croats and Serbs were numbered. The Serbs have told their own story of the mass liquidations inflicted upon those Serbians who were anti-Communists. At Kocevje, for instance, in addition to 20,000 Croatians, 10,000 Serbs and Slovenes were slaughtered by Tito's Marxists. But this "unity in the brotherhood of death," and the fact that the remains of both Croats and Serbs moulder together in many common graves is no more reason for the establishment of "solid basis of unity" between surviving Croats and Serbs than there is for the unity between the Croats and the Magyars on the basis of their both being butchered in the old Banat and Backa provinces by Tito's killers in 1945.

Still, we will admit that mass murder is an effective way of establishing unity of a sort, if it is comprehensive enough. The old Assyrian Kings, Genghis Khan, Tamerlane, and the late Adolf Hitler all used this tactic with much success—for a while. To be sure these great historical criminals did not have at their command the voice of the Anglo-American press. Right to the present day, this presumably free and incorruptible press, and the radio and television media as well, have kept on trying to sell their readers and listeners the Tito Myth. The news media project the image of Tito's Yugoslavia as a model for the peaceful evolution of peaceful coexistence between the Marxist and non-Marxist worlds. As Frederick Wilhelmsen said in 1962:

> This Myth is altogether mindless of the fact that otherwise decent human beings are led to condone the continuous suppression of a Western people—who were separated from the tribes to their immediate south and east by chivalry of manner and a high courtesy in letters and life that are one with Europe. I refer, of course, to the Croats. But the Eastern Myth sees nothing specifically western as being worthy of salvation.[9]

---

[8] "On All Horizons," *America* (June 18, 1960), p. 369.

[9] Frederick D. Wilhelmsen, "Babylonian Meditation," *National Review* (April 10, 1962), p. 246.

In 1962, Joseph Hecimovic published a book which described the Bleiburg-Maribor massacres and the subsequent "Death Marches" in explicit detail. Hecimovic was himself a survivor of the horrors overlooked by that other "eyewitness on the spot," the "American War Correspondent Lately in Yugoslavia." As expected, neither the British nor the American press in their various book review sections gave any notice to Hecimovic's work, which so powerfully contradicted the established journalistic myth accepted in the Anglo-American nations. Nonetheless the appearance of Hecimovic's volume, *In Tito's Death Marches and Extermination Camps,* helped to lift a corner of the ominous veil of silence drawn over these mass peace-time crimes. *America, The Catholic Universe Bulletin,* and several other religious periodicals did comment sympathetically on Hecimovic's work. Dr. David M. Baxter, who has contributed Chapter II to the present volume, reviewed Hecimovic's contribution favorably in a number of Catholic and Protestant periodicals. Dr. Revilo Oliver also gave Hecimovic's book a sympathetic review in *American Opinion.* To our knowledge, that vast segment comprising the popular liberal press did not bring this book to the attention of the public. Yet, genocide is an international crime against humanity, regardless of who commits it, and should be the concern of all.

In the fall of 1963, Tito was permitted to make a state visit to the United States. Our Committee welcomed him by sending both him and his host, the late John F. Kennedy, a carefully documented booklet that we had prepared. We also sent copies of this expose of "Yugo-Communist" crimes to members of the United States Congress, delegates of the United Nations, many American newspapers and periodicals, and all three major TV networks. Our booklet bore the title *Postwar Massacres in Yugoslavia.* Rudolph Erich, the secretary of the Committee, with several other members, and many individuals who have supported our efforts to destroy the myth of Titoist rectitude, joined the Croatian pickets who demonstrated against Tito's official reception in the White House. These picketeers and demonstrators bore posters which told of the mass butcheries of 1945. *The New York Times* finally took some notice of the Croatian story by photographing the pickets and the placards they carried. Thus, we were able to make the front pages of the *Times* and other leading American newspapers, but this was to no great avail as the press printed no details relating to Tito's prison camps or Tito's executions.

The next step in attempting to bring the truth to light was taken by Berislav Dezelic, Director of the Croatian Social Service organization in Dusseldorf, West Germany. Acting in agreement with his refugee organization, as well as with the Committee for the Investigation of the Bleiburg Tragedy, Dezelic asked the International Red Cross in Geneva, Switzerland, to demand the exhumation of the massacre sites where Croatian victims of the postwar murders were known to be buried.

Unlike the English and American press, the Swiss, Austrian, and German newspapers supported this demand.[10] Of course, Tito and the regime in Belgrade refused to comply with the request for exhumation eventually made by the International Red Cross; but the interest of the Red Cross in investigating the occurrences of 1945, nevertheless alarmed them. They were able to envision the consignments of American taxpayers' dollars vanishing into thin air especially if the reading public in the United States was to learn that the money was used to finance a notorious collection of murderers. Agents of the UDBA, the Yugoslav secret police, shot and seriously wounded Mr. Dezelic and his wife and daughter. If Mrs. Dezelic had not fought off the assailants with her fists, the killers would probably have murdered her husband. As it was, he remained hospitalized for many weeks.[11]

The end of eventful 1963 saw another Croatian attempt to bring the facts relating to the Bleiburg-Maribor slaughters to world attention. *Studia Croatica,* published in Spanish in Argentina, produced a special edition entitled *La Tragedia de Bleiburg.* Many documents from the files assembled by our Committee were placed at the disposal of the editors of this volume. Periodicals and newspapers in Spain, Latin America, and elsewhere reviewed this work sympathetically. However, the United Nations and other supposedly competent international investigating bodies remained silent.

On the occasion of the twentieth anniversary of the Bleiburg Tragedy in May 1965, we made another attempt to bring the record of Communist crimes in Tito's state to public attention. Apart from the statements made by Senator Lausche and Congressman Feighan quoted above, the *Cleveland Plain Dealer* published two articles sympathetic to our cause.

Meanwhile, we continued our work of compiling and translating the testimony of survivors of the massacres and "Death Marches." Occasionally, we supplied statements or data on these matters to various American newspapers and magazines and also to TV and radio networks. Early in April 1967, the *Plain Dealer* again gave us some space. It printed formal charges that we made concerning the murders of several hundred thousand Croatians, Slovenes, Serbs, Magyars, and "Volksdeutche" of German minorities in the Croatian or other Yugoslav territories.[12] Un-

[10] See especially the long and comprehensive article by Othmar Wettinger, "Ein 'Solferino' fur das Rote Kreuz im Jahre 1963," *Der Republikaner* (Zurich), May 18, 1963. The International Red Cross was founded in consequence of the sufferings experienced by the wounded at the battle of Solferino in the Franco-Italian-Austrian war of 1859.

[11] For detailed accounts of this incident see the Croatian emigrant newspaper *Obrana* (Madrid), issue of October, 1965. On June 28, 1969, the day before the contract for the publication of this book was signed, Nahid Kulenovic, Dezelic's son-in-law, was brutally murdered in his Munich apartment by Yugoslav Secret Police agents.

[12] See the article "Group Here Accuses Tito of Genocide," *The Cleveland Plain Dealer,* April 3, 1967.

doubtedly the reason that the *Plain Dealer* proved so accommodating on this occasion was that Tito had just been imprudent enough to accuse President Johnson and the United States forces fighting in Vietnam of pursuing a policy of "genocide" in that country!

Tito's righteous blast at Johnson caused us to send a copy of our booklet, *Postwar Massacres in Yugoslavia,* to the American President. We also sent him a letter in which we pointed out that Tito certainly was an authority on the subject of genocide. As could be expected, the White House sent us a conventionally trite reply of the most general character. This acknowledgment did not even mention the topic dwelt upon in our own letter.

However the Akron *Beacon-Journal* reacted to Tito's defamatory charges by publishing an editorial that cited some of the documentary evidence that our Committee had assembled concerning Tito's own genocidal policies in Croatia.[13] On April 8, the *Plain Dealer* printed Dr. Zvoninir Maras' pointed Letter to the Editor concerning the genocidal tactics pursued by the Belgrade establishment.

The publication of Maras' letter elicited a response similar to that made twenty years earlier in the London *Times* by an "American War Correspondent Lately in Yugoslavia." The 1967 effort to whitewash Tito came from a Mr. Harold Ticktin who, as a lawyer, could not refrain from tacking the label "alleged" to our charges and those made by Mr. Maras. Mr. Ticktin pointed out that the charge of committing war crimes had never been directed against the government in Belgrade, either at the famous Nuremberg Trials or in any other official connection. Therefore he concluded that this and other international tribunals had given Tito and his regime a clean bill of health.

Regarding the Nuremberg Trials, we believe it appropriate to call the reader's attention to a significant volume written by F. J. P. Veale. Although this writer does not deal specifically with the Bleiburg slaughters, the following passage states the Nuremberg-Bleiburg relationship very explicitly:

> It is indeed hard to realize, when studying the proceedings at Nuremberg and the terms of the judgement ultimately delivered with such enormous solemnity, that, all around at that very time, deeds of unparalleled horror and brutality were taking place. The following experience (the persecution of Germans by Red Poles) which was repeated tens of thousands of times and sometimes under even harsher conditions, and involved around fifteen million persons altogether, was in some ways even more horrible and cruel than the bombing of Dresden, Hiroshima, and Nagasaki, or Hitler's extermination of Jews. . . . The Tribunal listened with tireless patience to descriptions of the conditions which had existed at Belsen, but expressed no concern over the fact, which was common knowledge to everyone, that there existed between the Iron Curtain* and the Arctic Circles scores of similar concentration

[13] Editorial "Look Who Is Talking," *Akron Beacon Journal,* March 29, 1967.

> camps in which conditions were as bad or worse. Unpalatable facts, such as these, were rigidly excluded from the dream world in which the Nuremberg Tribunal had elected to live.[14]

Veale also discussed at considerable length the well known Katyn massacres of Polish military and civilian personnel in 1939. He cited the attempts made by the Russians to cast the guilt for these butcheries onto the Nazis and concluded:

> The International Military Tribunal, however, rose grandly to the occasion: at the close of the trial, the judgement of the Tribunal contained no reference to the Katyn massacre.[15]

Of course the august Tribunal dismissed the Bleiburg-Maribor massacres in an even more facile manner than the way in which it wrote off the Katyn slaughter. It appears, however, according to rumors that circulated in Rome and elsewhere in Europe at this time, that United States Justice Robert Jackson questioned the Yugoslav accusers at Nuremberg about the Bleiburg-Maribor "deal."

Nothing was done and little said at Nuremberg about the crimes committed by the Communists, because they were on the side that won the war. As British Field Marshal Montgomery said at Paris on June 9, 1948, "The Nuremberg Trials have made the waging of unsuccessful war a crime: the generals on the defeated side are tried and then hanged."[16]

This is precisely what happened to thirty-three Croatian generals who received a mock trial conducted by individuals whose own war crimes defy the imagination. According to the definition enunciated at the Nuremberg trials, these Croatian commanders were not "war criminals." Nonetheless, they were hanged or shot as such.[17] And this in spite of the incontrovertible fact that they had led the Croatian Army in a strictly defensive war that had as its objective the achievement of the delusive promise of national self-determination propounded by President Woodrow Wilson in World War I. Yet the greater part of the Croatian Armed Forces received far worse treatment than was meted out to most notorious Nazi war criminals, or to the twenty-seven Japanese leaders who were tried in Tokyo. Nor were Mussolini's Fascist henchmen even tried for their guilt in leading Italy into a war of pure aggression which was inspired by expansionist ambitions. But the Croatian soldiers and their

---

*Winston Churchill's definition of the 'Iron Curtain' definitely placed the Tito state behind it.—Editor's note.

[14] F. J. P. Veale, *Advance to Barbarism* (Appleton, Wisconsin, C. C. Nelson Publishing Co., 1953), pp. 246-248.

[15] *Ibid.*, p. 189.

[16] *Ibid.*, p. 195 (direct quotation of Montgomery's words).

[17] See Colonel Korana's article, "Kako su osudjena 33 hrvatska generala, How 33 Croatian Generals were Sentenced to Death," *Drina* (Madrid, 1962), No. 2-3, pp. 17-20.

supporters from every Croatian village, town, and city had to die, usually with every refinement of suffering.

Why?

So that a new Marxist version of the political monster brought to life at the end of 1918 by the midwifery of the Creel Committee, Crewe House, the Maison Blanche and other wartime propaganda agencies, by the Northcliffe Press and, for that matter, by the rest of the Anglo-American newspaper world, might live. This modern vampire could only live on blood, the blood of those who hated and opposed it because they knew what awaited the Croatians and other non-Communists in the Yugoslav People's Republics.

The Reverend Inge in his foreword to Mr. Veale's book, *Advance to Barbarism,* declared that one of the nations which functioned as a judge in the Nuremberg Trials—Russia—should have been in the dock herself and not on the bench. The Yugoslav judges, too, should themselves have been judged for their crimes, even if these were only judicial in nature. But these Yugoslav legists were guilty of more than condemning men to death without valid reason. They also helped supply the Nuremberg Tribunal with photos taken by the Partisans showing the execution or massacre of their victims in 1945. The Tito regime forwarded these photographs of crimes which Belgrade itself had ordered. With supreme audacity, Tito's officials and agents identified as "Ustasha crimes" the revolting scenes recorded by the cameras of the Partisans themselves as they butchered the postwar victims.[18]

As noted in Chapter Four, in the early fall of 1967, Reverend Krunoslav Draganovic disappeared mysteriously while visiting 1945 massacre sites located in the vicinity of Trieste. Italian, Austrian, Swiss, and German newspapers in their comments on this occurrence expressed the view that the reason for his sudden disappearance, which was presumed to be a simple kidnapping by agents of the Yugoslav Secret Police, was his unrivalled knowledge of the massacres and massacre sites of 1945. He had accumulated an astonishing quantity of evidence in the form of oral and written testimonies taken from survivors and eyewitnesses of the events of 1945 and subsequent years.

---

[18] The writer during his travels has been able to meet and converse or correspond with a number of former Partisans who are Croats by nationality. These individuals gave him specific details of how the Belgrade authorities had pictures taken of their own victims and then labeled these photographs as "Ustasha crimes" and sent them to Nuremberg, or even showed them in theatre newsreels in Yugoslavia itself. One of these eyewitnesses of the butcheries of 1945 disclosed that pictures taken by the Partisans of massacres they committed at Sisak were so utilized. Some other former Partisans have consented to have their accounts published in this volume, while a few have been quoted in other news media. All of these people— whose names cannot be revealed for fear of reprisals—stressed the fact that Belgrade again and again has endeavored to present to the outside world its own victims as "martyrs to Ustasha brutality."

But in November 1967, American newspapers fed their readers the Yugoslav Communist version of the Draganovic case. The *Cleveland Press*, for instance, in its issue of November 13, asserted the official Belgrade line, that Father Draganovic had returned "voluntarily" to Yugoslavia in order to face trial for his "war crimes." This article prompted me to write a letter to the Editor in my capacity as Chairman of the Committee for the Investigation of the Bleiburg Tragedy. The *Cleveland Press* nationalities columnist, Theodore Andrica, in an article intitled "Nationality Groups Seek Word on Priest Who Has Disappeared," which was published in the issue of December 1, gave a shortened and misquoted version of my letter. I demanded from the Editor-in-Chief that Andrica's distortions be retracted and passages from my letter be quoted as I had written them. Otherwise, I would bring the matter to the attention of the reading public. Since the *Press* has ignored my protest, it will be to the benefit of our readers to reproduce the original letter in its entirety. It reads as follows:

> The article, "Anti-Yugoslav Priest Returns To Face Trial," published by the Cleveland Press on November 13, distorts many facts of Rev. Fr. Draganovic's personal—and his native country's—history. It would take too much space to accurately answer every distortion, but the true reasons for Fr. Draganovic's kidnapping by the agents of the Yugoslav Secret Police, the UDBA, must be made known to the American public. On August 25, 1967, Fr. Draganovic signed a contract in Munich, Germany, for the publication in his native Croatian language of his book, *Bleiburg. Bleiburg* deals with the extradition from Bleiburg and other places in Austria of several hundred thousand Croatian refugees and their subsequent liquidation in the forests of Slovenia, Croatia, and Serbia. Before publication of this important work the noted Croatian historian was kidnapped from Trieste, Italy. The manuscripts of his scholarly book, which Rev. Fr. Draganovic had worked on since 1945 by interviewing hundreds of Croatian, Slovenian, Montenegrin, German and Serbian eyewitnesses of the *postwar* massacres in Tito's "new" Yugoslavia, were stolen, perhaps destroyed. He exposed his own life on many occasions but he never stopped doing his research. Some of his studies were published in Croatian (emigrant) periodicals, newspapers, symposiums, and books. Fr. Draganovic was also to be one of the main contributors to our book, *Operation Slaughterhouse,* which is in preparation. His chapter, "The Factual And Critical Analysis Of The Bleiburg-Maribor Massacres," would, as he wrote me a few days before his kidnapping, contain the highlights of his own book and would be mailed to us by the end of September, 1967.
>
> The real issue behind this entire tragedy is not Fr. Draganovic's "war crimes." The crime lies with the postwar genocide operations of the Yugoslav Communists. The Yugoslav Communists plan to cover up their crimes by labeling this exemplary priest, an ardent Croatian patriot, a "war criminal." If he had been a criminal, the Croatian Bishops would not have sent him to work in the Croatian Mission to the Vatican in the critical World War II years, nor would Pope Pius XII have accept-

ed his appointment. Further, when World War II was over, the Allied authorities would not have allowed him access to all POW camps and prisons. Thousands of Croatian and non-Croatian refugees from the Communist European onslaught now living in the United States, Canada, Australia and many Latin American countries owe their lives to the dedication and determination of this zealous Catholic priest. Father Draganovic is a citizen of Austria. Never was he a subject of Communist Yugoslavia. His kidnapping and the stealing of his historical research, as well as the mock trial which he is now facing in Yugoslovia, constitute grave international crimes perpetrated by the Yugoslav Government. Very likely this treacherous incident will produce serious and necessary repercussions throughout the Western World. Therefore, every God-fearing American should raise his voice in defense of this historian and priest whose reputation has been calumniously smeared—man now in serious danger of his life and unable to defend himself.[19]

In closing this note on the general bibliography of our volume we should like to call attention to a few other journalistic comments on Croatian and Yugoslav events.

In July 1966, the *Chicago Tribune* commented upon the deposition of Alexander Rankovic, UDBA Chief, and a principal director of the charnel house operation described in this book, and reported in regard to the liquidation of anti-Communists in the postwar Yugoslav state:

He (Tito) gave Rankovic his due for service during the war and *early postwar years* and noted the meritorious service of the secret police in the liquidation of class and all other enemies who tried to play any role in our country during the war and after.[20]

In Ljubo Sirc's article, printed in the *New Individualist Review*, more revealing comments concerning the postwar liquidations of Yugoslav anti-Communists are expressed:

During 1945 and 1946 hardly any reforms were introduced; the time was spent on tracking down the "collaborators" and bringing them to justice, but the definition of collaboration was so wide that practically anybody, patriot or no patriot, whom the Communists did not like, could be fitted in. If somebody could not, there was always the possibility of trumping up charges.

In addition many people were killed without any trial at all. Although the Nazi rule in Yugoslavia was extremely ruthless, the Germans are quite right in pointing out that a large part of over 1.5 million Yugoslav war victims were due to internal strife, and a substantial number of these were liquidated by the Communists, sometimes for good reason,

---

[19] A faithful reproduction of the spirit expressed in the above letter, and exact quotations taken from it, can be read in the article, "Says Arrested Priest Was To Write Book," *The Catholic Universe Bulletin*, Dec. 1, 1967.

[20] "Bugging Big Issue Purge in Yugoslavia," *Chicago Daily Tribune*, July 17, 1966, Section 1B, page 2. Similar Titoesque statements can be found in many other newspapers and periodicals that covered the ousting of Rankovic.

> sometimes only in preparation for the final take-over. The massacres continued when some 300,000 people were done away with; the prisons overflowed, and many people, mainly members of the German minority in Yugoslavia were driven over the border to Austria. There was sufficient terror around to terrorize the population into silent submission.[21]

In further corroboration of these figures, Tito's former Press Chief, Bogdan Raditsa, stated that since the "liberation," the Communists themselves had admitted that they had gotten rid of 500,000 Yugoslavs, whether by detention, disappearance, or death.[22]

Both the late Dr. Oton Knezovic, author of *Pokolj Hrvatske Vojske 1945* (Massacre of the Croatian Army in 1945), and the present writer calculate that the Tito regime murdered 600,000 Croats after the end of hostilities in 1945. German Attorney Wilhelm Schottler, who for years has tried to bring to justice the Serbian Communist General, Kocha Popovitch, former Yugoslav Foreign Minister and ranking member of the Belgrade regime, is of the opinion that twenty per cent of the population of Croatia was liquidated after the war.[23] Parenthetically, it should be remembered that at least 12,000 anti-Communist Slovenes were also murdered in 1945, and many more Montenegrins, Albanians, White Russians, Magyars, Macedonians, and Germans or Austrians.

It seems appropriate to quote at this point a statement made by the late Cardinal Stepinac. On July 21, 1945, the then Archbishop of Zagreb wrote a lengthy letter on the persecution of the Catholic Church in Yugoslavia. In this letter he dealt with the fate of the Croatian Army:

> The question is asked where does there exist a moral justification for the persecution of thousands of Croatian officers and hundreds of thousands of Croatian soldiers who, in the greatest good faith and with many sacrifices in order to serve the Croatian people, fulfilled their duty as soldiers? In conformity with the moral principles of war *not one of them should be punished except those who violated the international rules of war or unjustly attacked the peaceful population who took no part in military operations.*[24]

Dr. Giuseppi Massucci, Secretary of the Vatican's envoy to the Croatian Episcopate, noted in his published diary that the policies pursued by the new Yugoslavia were diabolical. He compared the "liberated" city of Zagreb to a huge cemetery and referred to the prisons "overflowing with

[21] Ljubo Sirc, "Two Decades of Economic Planning in Yugoslavia," *The New Individualist Review* (University of Chicago), Winter, 1968, Vol. V, No. 1, pp. 23-24.

[22] Bogdan Raditsa, "The Tragic Lessons of Yugoslavia," *Reader's Digest,* Oct., 1946. See also Raditsa's article, "How Terror Rules Yugoslavia," *The Catholic Digest,* February, 1947.

[23] "Die Kroaten Rutteln an dem Gewissen Europas" (The Croats are shaking the conscience of Europe), *Deutche Wochen-Zeitung,* April 14, 1967, p. 11.

[24] Richard Pattee, *The Case of Cardinal Stepinac* (Milwaukee: Bruce Publishing Co., 1952), Document LXVI, pp. 441-442 (Italics are ours.—editors)

victims" as a sheep's den. Included among prisoners were many priests. Massucci observed, too, that around Zagreb masses of people were being executed. He pointed out that because of the commission of wholesale murders, the foundations of justice in Tito's state were completely obliterated. Also he recorded under the date November 22, 1945:

> Bitter tears are flowing without pause. New punishments continuously send men to death by hanging. The entire land is inundated by streams of tears. *After the massacres of several hundred thousand Croatian soldiers and civilians in the first months of the Communist regime,** shootings and hangings still are being carried out day in and day out. Evidently this policy of mass execution is that of the new regime rather than a series of acts committed by irresponsible elements. There is no one who does not mourn someone.[25]

Whatever the total number of Croatians murdered by orders of the Belgrade regime may have been, all extant Croatian sources agree that between 150,000 and 180,000 Croatian soldiers, most of them extradited by the British into the hands of their Partisan executioner allies, were murdered in cold blood by the "victorious" legions of Josip Broz Tito. The slaughter of these soldiers was drawn out over a period of four months.

Since an enormous number of victims were massacred by express orders of the Belgrade regime, it would be logical to expect such authors as the late Sir Winston Churchill, Fitzroy McLean, Field Marshal Alexander, Stephen Clissold, and other commentators on the Yugoslav scene to say something about these slaughters in the works that they have written on World War II and its aftermath. *All of these individuals were directly involved in the British-Yugoslav deal at Bleiburg in one way or another. All of them,* except for Sir Winston, who wrote the brief statement cited in Chapter Four, maintained complete silence in regard to the massacres, both during the war and afterwards. Clissold exerted himself for years after the war to hunt down survivors and escapees and deliver them into the hands of Tito's executioners. Whatever his motives, he certainly did his best to cover up the truth of the "Whirlwind" he described so eulogistically. Not only Clissold, but McLean and other Anglo-Americans could become quite verbose when it came to describing the faults and shortcomings of the Croatian State and the Ustasha regime.

Of course, it has to be granted that such commentators are still laboring under the impressions created by Anglo-American propaganda. In this connection it must be remembered, too, that Britain and the United States are the two greatest "advertising" countries in the world. Their economies are founded upon the ability of the British or American advertising man to sell people things whether they need them or not.

*Italics are ours.

[25] Dr. Giuseppe Massucci, O.S.B., *Misija u Hrvatskoj* (Mission in Croatia) (Valencia, 1967), pp. 234-235.

British and American wartime propaganda are superior to the propaganda disseminated by other nations precisely because of the plethora of advertising talent that can be mobilized to sell the moral righteousness of the British-American cause to friend and foe alike. And every ally of Britain or the United States is a sacrosanct paragon of virtue as long as the war lasts, and afterwards too, in many cases.

But the Marxist world has a propaganda technique of its own which is very effective with the more naive categories of "intellectuals," as well as with the herd-minded of all social and national groups. Between them, the British-American and Communist-Socialist propaganda swayed all countries; capitalizing upon the military events of 1945, they succeeded in imposing upon the Croats a regime which did not and probably still does not enjoy the support of anything but a minute fraction of the Croatian people. No British-American officials, journalists, or publicists want to admit that they were taken in by Marxist pretences, nor do they wish to acknowledge that they "backed the wrong horse" in the Balkans in 1941-45 and afterwards. Therefore, they do not want to uncover the circumstances which produced such tragic consequences for the Croatians and other Balkan and Central European peoples. They prefer to swallow the untruths disseminated by Pan-Serbian Chetnik and diplomatic spokesmen, Yugoslav Partisan apologists, and the official propaganda line relayed from Belgrade and Moscow throughout the rest of the world, where it is picked up and faithfully echoed by the increasingly "liberal" and Socialist-oriented press. Although the Serbian royalists and the Communists have no love for one another, they do agree that nothing should be left undone that may contribute to villifying the Croatian nation, its historical past, its national aspirations, and its record in the two world wars.[26]

The silence of Anglo-American news media, particularly of that "free press" which the British and Americans like to boast about, and even of the governmental and educational authorities, is a tribute to the efficacy of Marxist propaganda in covering up the events of 1941-45 and their background and consequences. Even in a rather good book like Charles Zalar's *Yugoslav Communism. A Critical Study of Its Socio-Economic, Legal, and Political Aspects,* the Bleiburg-Maribor and other Croatian tragedies are referred to only in the passage cited below:

The British extradited also *several thousand** Croatian soldiers.[27]

Not even a complete sentence is given to the topic of the Croatian massacres, although there are sections entitled "Liquidation of Chetniks and Other Anti-Communists," "Annihilation of Anti-Communist Fighters," "The Role of the Red and British Armies," etc. But Dr. Zalar, however,

---

26 Dr. Branko Jelic, *A Report on the Croatian Refugees and Displaced Persons* (London, 1947).

* Italics ours (editors).

27 Dr. Charles Zalar, *Yugoslav Communism. A Critical Study on Its Economic, Legal, and Political Aspects* (Washington, U. S. Govt. Printing Office, 1961), p. 115.

is not as parsimonious with words when he endeavors to discredit the Ustashas and their short-lived regime.

Despite the fact that the press, other news media, and individual writers, as well as official comment, tend to carefully avoid writing or talking about the Partisan massacres—*these massacres did take place.* These wholesale murders were perpetrated not only at Bleiburg and Maribor, but also at countless other places as the surviving eyewitnesses and their testimonies recorded in this book will prove. It will always be the shame of the Croatian nation that more Croatians died after the official end of the war, than during the bloody years between 1941 and 1945. In these years, nine different armies fought inside the borders of the Croatian State and the Croatians gave as good or better account of themselves as did any other army in the field, including Germans and Russians. But, thanks in part to the incompetence and lack of vision of their own leadership, the Croats found themselves trapped in a vast chain of abattoirs.

Instead of finding safety in Austria which, it must be acknowledged, did provide a refuge to Croatian fugitives from Balkan and Italian aggression and calculated barbarism for four centuries, close to half a million Croatians, who made their way back to the old hereditary lands, encountered only death and suffering. Prisoners of war, wounded men, women, children, and old people of both sexes met the same fate, unless they managed to elude the vigilance of the Partisan executioners to whom they were turned over by the British.

For over two decades, various Croatian groups and individuals, including our own Committee, have devoted themselves to collecting the evidence that still exists concerning the mass slaughters perpetrated by Josip Broz Tito, most successful of modern-day Attilas, Genghis Khans, and Tamerlanes. Depositions have been obtained from eyewitness survivors of the massacres that were carried out by Tito's express orders. Individuals who were serving in the ranks of the Partisans during the war and later have also contributed their accounts of the happenings of these eventful years. Therefore, there is no secret—other than that enforced by the world press and communication agencies—about what went on.

Through reading these documents, any interested individual can piece together the whole gruesome picture of those hellish days. Thus one is able to learn first-hand that from the middle of May, 1945, to the end of August of that year, large and small groups of anti-Communist Croatians who were not butchered immediately after the end of the war were marched throughout the length and breadth of the political Frankenstein known as Yugoslavia. As they "marched," they were decimated systematically and brutally. Those who had escaped being shot, knifed, or bludgeoned to death in the first days after the end of formal hostilities were allowed to die of thirst, hunger, and exhaustion. Many died of illnesses that could have been easily alleviated. Others were fortunate enough to have guards shoot them or beat in their skulls. Many other victims were unable to keep up with the rest of the human cattle who were being driven to concentration camps. These unfortunates were picked up by special "ambulances" and taken to more efficient abattoirs. Those men who were strong enough to be able to survive all hardships had boiling hot water poured over them, because nothing else could give their captors the satisfaction of hearing them scream or evince signs of pain. Thousands of victims were burned alive in ovens, a gruesome practice that the press of the democratic and Marxist worlds has tried to limit to the Nazis. Other thousands were thrown down mine shafts while still alive, or were pitched into abysses in the mountains. Many were drowned like rats in public baths. Some were poisoned deliberately or had lethal doses injected into them by Tito's medical men.[28] And the irony is that the American taxpayer helped finance these mass slaughters because of the deceitful propaganda and military and economic aid that the U.S. Government contributed toward maintaining the Tito regime in power.

We do not contend that all who were members of the Partisan forces participated in or approved of the wholesale murders ordered by their commanding officers. Certainly, the great majority of Croatian Partisans were sick at seeing the life blood of their nation destroyed and were powerless to stop the wanton killings. Yet, enough of their units were involved, along with the extremist units provided by Serbian, Slovenian, Albanian, Macedonian and other varieties of Balkan and European Communists, to make this a shameful as well as a tragic period in Croatian history. Since most of the top-level positions in the army, government and secret police were held by men of Serbian background, the planning and the relaying of the execution orders as well as provoking and inciting the masses into action was mainly their doing, even to the propaganda cover-up afterward. Thus, at Maribor, "Proletariat Brigade" Commander, Rade Corak, in collaboration with his fellow Serb, Kocha Popovitch, and other high-ranking Reds directed the murder of tens of thousands of captives. Among these predominantly Croatian victims, there were smaller numbers of other Yugoslav nationalities and also Germans, Austrians and Magyars.

The cadavers were thrown into a two-mile long anti-tank trench built by the Germans during the war. Another major butchery took place at Kocevski Rog in Slovenia. The principal executioners here were Dalmatian Croat Communists, but a Serbian Marxist, Sima Dubajic, was in charge of the whole operation. As many as 20,000 Croatians may have

[28] See especially in these connections the work of the late Safet Jaskic, *Srbokomunisticki zlocini nad Bosnom* (Serbo-Communist crimes in Bosnia) (Valencia, 1968), *passim*. This book is particularly valuable because it relates precise details concerning the task assigned by the Communists to Dr. Jovo Drzitch, General Mihailovic's personal physician. He had to administer lethal "shots" to sick and wounded Croatian prisoners.

been slaughtered here, along with several thousand Slovenes as well as Serbs. The killers were rewarded for their lethal efficiency with an expense-paid vacation at a luxury hotel on scenic Lake Bled.

While the long columns of prisoners were being driven over the Slovenian, Croatian, and Serbian countrysides, the Communist authorities in the villages through which they passed organized mobs for the purpose of humiliating and maltreating the captives. The population of Serbian rural and urban settlements especially distinguished themselves by reviling and abusing the exhausted and starving losers of the war. Apparently, these unfortunates were deprived deliberately of food and drink for days and even weeks at a time. They finally would drop in their tracks and thus provide their guards or the officially incited mobs with an excuse to finish them off.[29] That this procedure was systematically planned is apparent from the fact that the Croatian soldiers often were taken back to localities in which they had inflicted heavy defeats upon the Partisans or Chetniks during the war. At places of former triumph, the Croatian soldiers were now brutally tortured and subjected to every kind of degrading mistreatment.

Many of the prisoners of war were marched time and again through the streets of Zagreb and other Croatian cities. Their guards took pains to deliberately aggravate the sufferings which were already horrifying. The idea behind this was to impress upon the Croatians the completeness of the Communist victory and to deter them from further resistance to the march of Marxism.

Survivors of the "Death Marches" who live today in the United States, Canada, Latin America, Australia, Italy, Austria, Germany, Sweden, and other countries tell their stories in this book.

A number of the accounts reproduced here were smuggled out of post-1945 Yugoslavia at great risk to the narrators and other persons concerned. Over ninety such testimonies are included in the "Documents" section. Our files contain hundreds of other first-hand relations which, for one reason or another, we have not been able to include in this book. Some of these reports can be found, however, in such works as *La Tragedia de Bleiburg, Pokolj Hrvatske Vojske 1945, Srbo-Komunisticki zlocini nad Bosnom, In Tito's Death Marches and Extermination Camps, Four Years in Tito's Hell,* and also in Mato Tovilo's *Croatia's Way of the Cross* (Toronto, 1966). Hecimovic and Pintar both have devoted many pages of their books to the ghastly slaughter which took

[29] The most conclusive evidence against the Serbian civilian population is provided by the Muslim Croats, Safet Jaskic and Safet Bayin, which are reproduced below. The last named individual had a personal interest in investigating the most horrifying and repugnant of all the massacres, the one which was committed at Gornji Podgraci. He had a particular motivation for wanting it to be described in detail in these pages because his own brother was among the victims of this mass slaughter carried out by Bosnian Serbs in the Kozara mountains. See "Documents" section of this volume, Docs. XCI and XCII.

place as late as July, 1948, within the walls of the Lepoglava prison.[30] The late Cardinal Stepinac, the most publicized victim of the postwar Croatian catastrophe, was confined at Lepoglava at the time of this butchery.

Despite a discreet silence of the Anglo-American press, such emigrant newspapers as *Obrana, Danica, Nasa Nada, Hrvatski Glas, Nezavisna Drzava Hrvatska, Nova Hrvatska, Slobodna Hrvatska, Hrvatski Narod, Hrvatska Drzava,* and many others have provided a wealth of articles, editorials, and eye-witness accounts of many of the postwar enormities engineered by Tito and the regime in Belgrade. These emigrant sheets have never stopped publishing the names of Croatian soldiers who were last seen or heard of at one or the other of the massacre sites. Thousands of surviving relatives are still anxious to ascertain the location of the mass graves which may contain the mortal remains of their own loved ones, even though it would be impossible now to identify such remains. Tito's Government has long since invoked the well known criminal subterfuge of removing evidence of *corpus delicti.* Quicklime and dynamite are the agents employed to efface, as far as possible, the factual evidence in the case. Even the Croatian military cemeteries of World Wars I and II were plowed up in the endeavor to wipe out all memory of past Croatian valor which Tito himself has compared favorably to that of the Germans.

A number of Croatian periodicals such as *Hrvatska Revija,*[31] *Hrvatska Misao, Osoba i Duh, Drina, Hrvatska Gruda, Glasnik Srca Isusova i Marijina, Mlada Hrvatska, Vjesnik Uj. Am. Hrvata, Novi Zivot, Jadran,* and many almanacs published by Croatian emigrant societies, have also dealt in great detail with the postwar massacres. There are even entire volumes of poetry dedicated to this most terrible of Croatian catastrophes. Among others we should like to bring to the attention of the readers of this volume *Izgubljena Domovina* (Lost Homeland), and *Oskrvnuto Proljece* (Dishonored Spring). Both of these works are from the pen of Vinko Nikolic. Also worthy of translation into better known languages are Lucijan Kordic's *Pod Tudjim Nebom* (Under Alien Skies) and *Exodus.* There is a novel, too, written by Marijan Mikac, the noted Croatian writer and literary critic, entitled *U Povorkama Smrti* (In the Death Parades). This story reproduces in fictional form much of what we have given here. Mikac also is the editor of the revealing diary of Dr. Giuseppe Massucci, whose account of the wartime regime in Croatia

---

30 See Chapter V of Captain Joseph Hecimovic's book, *In Tito's Death Marches and Extermination Camps,* pp. 182-185. See also Chapter V of John Pintar's work, *Four Years in Tito's Hell* (Buenos Aires, 1954), pp. 169-171.

31 On the tenth anniversary of the beginning of the Bleiburg-Maribor-Zagreb massacres, the editor of the *Hrvatska Revija* of Buenos Aires prepared a bulky volume which dealt with the individual tragedies sustained by some fifty renowned Croatian poets, writers, historians, journalists, and professors who were murdered after the "liberation" of Zagreb.

shows that it was not as black as the Tito regime and the Anglo-American and Marxist presses have painted it.

We have had to neglect almost all of the vast amount of material printed in the emigrant Croatian press, not only in the "Analysis" and "Documents" sections of our volume, but also in this bibliographical chapter. We have had to limit the size of the present work in order to avoid repetition, even though such repetition actually is the best corroborating evidence of the truth of the accounts that we have reproduced in these pages. Even so, there is inevitably a good deal of repetition in the "Documents" section of this book. Especially the accounts given of the "Death Marches" may sound much alike since, after all, the survivors had pretty much the same experiences. We can only point out that we are not writing fiction which would allow us to come up with a different plot and diverse experiences for every character. We can also stress that it is constant repetition which corroborates the truth of what Croatian, Slovenian, Montenegrin, Austrian, German, and Serbian eye-witnesses say about the things which they saw with their own eyes.

In arranging the documents and testimonies at our disposal, we have given precedence to those which deal with the events that took place at Bleiburg or which were an immediate consequence of the British-Partisan "deal" effected there. We could have included the account of General Luburic in Part II of the present volume, but instead we have put it in the "Analysis" because it sheds light upon the background of the tragedy of 1945. It will be noted that we have allowed Tito's bombastic pronouncement of "final victory" to head the list of "Documents." In fact, this typical Tito harangue, together with the account of the Bleiburg negotiations given by Lieutenant Colonel Basta, a Serbian Partisan commander, has been permitted to set the tone for this entire volume, or at least that has been our intention. Following the Basta account is one provided by Professor Daniel Crljen, the civilian representative of the Pavelic regime in the Bleiburg talks. It ought to be noted that, except for the anti-Communist and Croatian national viewpoint expressed by Crljen, his relation agrees substantially with that of Basta.[32]

Basta's story was taken from his book *Rat Posle Rata* (War After the War). He concludes this work with the statement, "The Partisans then left the valley of the Drava and went hurriedly homeward in order to discharge new tasks."[33]

---

[32] Professor Crljen gave his testimony concerning the Bleiburg "negotiations" to Professor Draganovic in Austria in 1945. Dr. Oton Knezovic reproduced this testimony in his *Pokolj Hrvatske Vojske*. *Obrana* (Madrid) also published Crljen's account in 1962. It was given again in the "Studia Croatica's" *La Tragedia de Bleiburg* and likewise in an issue of the *Hrvatska Revija*. All of these Croatian, Spanish, and English language edition of Crljen's account are essentially the same, but he has added to the Croatian version in *Hrvatska Revija* of Spring-Summer, 1967, details taken from the various articles and books that have been written on the Croatian national catastrophe of 1945.

[33] Milan Basta, *Rat Posle Rata* (Zagreb, 1963), p. 153.

Basta does not say what these "new tasks" were. Their nature is revealed by the people who speak in these pages, some of them his own Partisan wartime "comrades."

Because of the fact that tens of thousands of Croatians and members of other nationalities were murdered at Maribor, this city is considered by most survivors to be the most important abattoir operated by the Tito Government. A large percentage of the eyewitnesses whose testimonies are given here went through Maribor en route to other points and saw one part or another of the shambles enacted there. Therefore, we believe that the section of the present volume which deals with the Maribor massacres is the most thoroughly documented of all. We feel also that the "Death Marches" described herein, particularly the principal ones, which are delineated on Map No. 5, rival the Maribor massacres in thoroughness of eyewitness description. It may appear that the estimates of the number of victims of the several incidents described by survivors are exaggerated. However, we have not taken it upon ourselves to reduce the figures given since, after all, the survivors were in a position to know better than anyone else how many lives were lost in one place or another.

There is a noticeable weakness in some of the reports that we have reproduced in regard to dates and the identification of the perpetrators of the crimes described. It should be realized that in the terrible situation in which eyewitnesses found themselves in 1945 and afterwards, they did not expect to survive. Despite such a conviction, they were concerned almost exclusively with trying to preserve their own lives by any means that came to hand. They did not have the time nor the facilities with which to carefully record precise data — the "who, when, where, why and how" of newspaper reporting. Certainly, none of these people who lived through the holocaust that followed World War II had any idea that some day they would be a principal source of information on the happenings of this period.

Despite these shortcomings and the inevitable blurring of recollections over the years, we believe that any objective analysis of the eyewitness testimonies that we have selected, though they may refer to different dates and places, will concede that these testimonies complement and corroborate rather than contradict one another. Therefore, we feel at long last we have been able to present a well-filled-in picture of what happened during the Yugoslav Reign of Terror.

Anyone who is inclined to doubt the basic truths set forth in the personal accounts which we have brought together in this work should read Dr. Massucci's diary which is referred to both above and below. His description of the "nesretni grad" (unfortunate city) of Zagreb in the months after the war is simple reporting such as the "American War Correspondent" and his colleagues at Tito's banquet tables apparently did not have time to concern themselves with. Massucci says that Zagreb became a huge cemetery for its murdered victims. For largely sentimental reasons, because Zagreb in the nineteenth and twentieth centuries has been the focal point of Croatian culture and national aspirations, we have reserved a special section in this book for "The 'Liberation' of Zagreb." Even though the available testimonies on this part of the Croatian tragedy are not as plentiful as the reports dealing with the Maribor slaughters, we feel that all Croats, and many foreigners who were acquainted with the peculiar charm of the Croatian metropolis in pre-war days, will want to know about its fate.

As to the sites of the various massacres, we have asked our informants to describe them in as minute detail as possible. Yet, there is no doubt that many of these sites, especially those within the borders of the Croatian lands, are not referred to in this work. It has not been possible to uncover the facts in regard to all of the Croatian "Katyns," whether large or small. In order that the long succession of massacres ordered by Tito might be investigated in the detail that they deserve, most of the billions sent to Belgrade by Washington would have to be paid back and devoted to this specific purpose. In addition, such an investigation would have to be carried out by an international body capable of imposing strong sanctions against any interference attempted by the Tito regime.

The writer of these lines wishes to emphasize that through his travels in Europe, the United States, and Canada during the past nine years, and through appeals printed in the Croatian emigrant press and personal correspondence, he has endeavored to collect as much documentary evidence as possible. In the process he discovered that most of the survivors and other knowledgeable persons feared what would happen to their surviving relatives and friends in Yugoslavia, if they told what they knew. Many such people flatly refused to allow themselves to be quoted or to provide the writer and his collaborators with signed depositions. Quite a few of the testimonies that are contained in this volume were secured only after pleas and requests that had to be repeated many times. Even some of those who did allow themselves to be persuaded to record their experiences in writing asked that their identities remain secret until such time as a competent international forum might decide to look into the gruesome series of postwar killings.

Often enough, too, this writer has been warned not to expose to the outside world the story of Tito's crimes. Threats of physical violence were interspersed with malicious attempts to blacken his reputation, and UDBA questioning of his parents in the homeland.

The latter are deserving of special mention. Under continuous pressure exerted by the UDBA, the parents of the writer repeatedly tried to talk him out of going through with the publication of this record of the *postwar* crimes committed by the Tito Government and its backers. Likewise, the Yugoslav authorities endeavored to convince both federal and local authorities that the writer and his collaborators in the investigation were Ustashas. As far as the writer personally is concerned, he spent the years between 1935 and 1949, that is the days of his boyhood and youth, in minor or major Franciscan seminaries in Sinj, Visovac, Makarska, Venice, Bologna, and Rome. He served in Tito's army for sixty-nine days of this period, also. Since it was not possible to construct a very convincing indictment of him as a "war criminal" on the basis of this record, Belgrade demanded that Washington prohibit our Committee from continuing its activities. Meanwhile, however, the UDBA came up with another idea. Its agents disseminated "information" concerning his past which made him out to be an officer in Tito's forces, who had indeed murdered a great many people in 1945! Although they have not been able to silence him, they have succeeded in making it more difficult for him to travel in the United States than it is for known Yugoslav Communist agents to do so.

In the face of these and innumerable other difficulties that have been placed in the way of the publication of this book, one can recall the immortal words spoken by Cardinal Stepinac in Croatia's darkest hour, "Even if fall we must, we'll fall by performing our duty."

These words have been and still are the guiding motto for this Committee. Someone has to speak up and to speak up effectively to show to the Anglo-Saxon world in particular the true face of Communism and the meaning of Communist victory whether in Croatia, Thailand, Yemen, Spain, the Far East, Russia, China, or – some day – America and England. What happened to Croatia and the other victims of Marxist fanaticism can happen here, and it already has started to happen thanks to the progressive degeneration of the educational process in America and the coming into existence of the "New Left," whose leaders have become either conscious or unconscious tools of international Marxism.

Frankly, there would be a certain poetic justice if Communism triumphed in the United States and the rest of the English-speaking world, because Washington and London as well as uninformed and misguided public opinion throughout Anglo-Saxondom, made possible the Communist takeover in Croatia and in other parts of the world. For us who formed this Committee on the occasion of the fifteenth anniversary of the Bleiburg Tragedy, it is enough that the mountain ravines, the woods, the rivers, and even the blue waters of the Adriatic be allowed to tell the story which an international investigating commission and tribunal of justice can get from them easily enough, even at this late date.

There is another, personal purpose that we have, too, in presenting this volume to the reading public. We want to introduce to this foreign public, as well as to the younger Croatian generations both at home and abroad, those Croatian anti-Communist fighters who during four years of war shed their blood profusely, not because they had any affection for the German Nazis or Italian Fascists, but because they knew that the delusive premises on which the Marxist creed is based constituted a greater and subtler threat to everything that is worth while in modern civilization than did the cruder ideology of the other totalitarianisms. This is a lesson that most of the rest of the world still has to learn.

— John Prcela, Chairman of the Committee for the Investigation of the Bleiburg Tragedy

Cleveland, May 15, 1969

PART TWO:

DOCUMENTS

CHAPTER 6

The Bleiburg Talks and Extraditions

Document I

The Commander-in-Chief praises the Third Army and its leading officers.

With a fast, energetic drive toward the upper course of the Drava River, the troops of our Third Army cut off the retreat of the remaining German and Ustasha-Chetnik bandits, and after surrounding them in the area around Gradec-Gustanj-Dravograd in Slovenia, destroyed them and forced them to surrender after a bitter three-day battle. In this massacre the last enemy forces to offer organized resistance to our troops have been liquidated. Over twenty thousand Ustashas, whose ranks include a great number of notorious criminals, have been taken prisoners. Along with the Ustashas, a great number of Chetniks have been captured, and the last remnants of German groupings of Field Marshal Loehr have been forced to capitulate, over ten thousand Germans having been taken prisoners. In the course of the battles, over five thousand enemy soldiers and officers have perished, while eight thousand civilians, whom the Ustasha bandits had taken by force, were liberated. A large quantity of arms and war material has been seized. The Third Army's troops during the last fifteen days have captured about one hundred thousand enemy soldiers and officers.

For winning this victory and also for a fast, successful and complete performance of the set task, my thanks go to the brave troops of our Third Army under the command of Lt. General Kosta Nadj, Colonel Branko Petricevic, and Colonel Vukasin Subotic. I express my gratitude to all the fighters and commanders of the units which have won this victory and successfully executed the mission. We will remember our heroes, fallen for the liberation of our fatherland!

Death to Fascism – Freedom to the People![1]

–Commander-in-Chief
Marshal of Yugoslavia
J. B. Tito, M. P.
(Belgrade, May 15, 1945)

---

[1] The official organ of the People's Ministry of Defense, F.N.R. of Yugoslavia (Sluzbeni List Ministarstva Narodne Obrane), Year I, April-July, nn. 4-7.

Document II

The Bleiburg talks are described by a high-ranking Serbian Commissar.

Our conversations with the Commander of the British Expeditionary Corps took place in an old feudal castle located in a pine forest not far from Bleiburg.

Many vehicles were parked around the castle. Gathered near them were large numbers of Allied officers and soldiers. Since they regarded us with evident interest and admitted us into the castle without delay, we decided that they were expecting us.

An officer received us in an antechamber of the castle and told us that we would have to wait a little while before the Allied Commander would be able to see us. I was stunned to see four Ustasha generals[1] standing in a corner of the same room that we were in. We were unprepared for their presence here. Up to this time we had no inkling that the representatives of Pavelic's Army had already made contact with our allies and had offered to surrender to them. Apparently, they did not notice us when we were shown into the castle antechamber. I was surprised that the liaison officer made no reference to their presence. Of course, we could comprehend the anxiety of the Ustasha chiefs who desired to contact the English as soon as possible; the ground was burning under their feet!

I was so worried by this unexpected development that I could not stand still but strode up and down, and back and forth through the antechamber. I could feel the blood mounting to my head as I asked myself: Why had our allies kept silent about the presence of enemy negotiators at their headquarters? I began to feel that I had made a mistake in accepting the invitation of the British to come here. I had come in the expectation that I would have to deal only with Englishmen and, perhaps, their other allies. Now I was faced with the prospect of having to deal directly with the enemy. What's more our allies were likely to put pressure upon us in behalf of these same enemies! There couldn't have been a worse beginning to the proposed negotiations! At this critical moment I had no authorization from my headquarters to enter into such complicated maneuvers.

I felt I had been tricked. It occurred to me that it would be helpful to inform the British Commander as soon as I got to see him that I knew the enemy plenipotentiaries personally. My first task would be to let him know that the Yugoslav public would be informed in the event that these men were allowed to go abroad under Allied protection.

I had only a few moments to consider this subject. I did not even have time to discuss this contretemps with the comrade from Slovenia

---

[1] Actually only three of the Croatian officers who had preceded the Communist emissaries into the castle were generals (Herencic, Servatzi, and Metikos). As indicated in the next section, Daniel Crljen, although holding the wartime rank of colonel, actually was a civil rather than a military official – Editor's note.

before we were conducted into an old reception hall of the castle where the British commander awaited us.

He was a tall, slender, completely British type. Quite gray and clean cut, he had a stern military look about him. He shook hands with us with some cordiality, saying that he was very pleased to finally have made contact with Tito's troops and high Partisan commanders. He remarked that he had heard much about us during the operations in Italy in which he had participated, and that he admired us for our heroism and the privations we had endured.

I replied that we, too, had followed closely the operations of the Allied Army in Italy and on other fronts and that our men greatly appreciated the aid we had received in the way of war material sent to us by the British and the Americans. I stressed the fact that our fighters had frequent contacts with Allied airmen who had been forced to land in our country on their way back from bombing raids. We sheltered them and took care of those who were wounded, because for years past we had waged war with them against a common enemy. This circumstance contributed to the creation of a feeling of war comradeship that we greatly cherished. While my words were being translated to him the general kept nodding his head in agreement.

Pointing to a long table that stood nearby, he indicated that we seat ourselves. I did so, and the Slovenian comrade sat down on my right. The British General himself took the chair to my left. Five or six British Headquarters officers stood near the window. Immediately behind the British commander stood the liaison officer who had conducted us to the castle; he acted as interpreter for us.

I took advantage of the slight pause that followed to say that I was surprised to find that Pavelic's generals had been received without my having been notified of such a procedure. I added that I was personally acquainted with all four of the enemy emissaries. The general at once replied that the Croatians had come in order to surrender, and that this was the reason he had sent for me to come here.

Then he went on to say that before us there were 300,000 enemy troops. "For reasons that are quite understandable, these troops do not want to surrender to you. Moreover they are prepared to continue fighting if their negotiations with us turn out unsuccessfully. However, the war is over and there is no sense in shedding more blood. They want to surrender to us, and, since you are our allies, we can resolve this matter easily."

Since I was unaccustomed to this kind of talk, I was quite nervous. I told him that the Croatian Ustasha-Domobran units did not number more than 30,000 men. Indeed, at this time, I had no idea that there were about 100,000 of Pavelic's soldiers around Bleiburg. I advised the General that he was misinformed in regard to the strength of the enemy forces which were decimated, demoralized, and pressed on all sides by our troops. Then I made a brief statement concerning our viewpoint in regard to the prospective surrender. It was a purely Yugoslav affair; the Allies had to regard it as such. We had the strength to solve the situation facing us without any help. If our British and other Western Allies did not wish to help us deal with the enemy, then we desired that they would not hinder us in doing so.

The Briton smiled and then insisted once again that it was difficult to convince men of the necessity of dying when they know they have won a war.

"On the contrary," I replied, "for we are dealing now with an enemy who has inflicted great damage upon our country. Because of this, our men are ready to keep on fighting until final and complete victory is achieved regardless of how long the struggle may last. Besides, by the same logic, it might be asked who will convince the majority of the weary and demoralized enemy troops, who have spent many days and nights in retreating from their country, that they ought to continue fighting when there is no prospect of their being ultimately successful? Why should they fight any longer to protect Pavelic and his commanders who have sought safety abroad in order to avoid being called to account for the crimes they have committed?"

Instinct told me that the General was undecided about what he ought to do. Therefore, I continued talking, bringing in the element of military pride. I stressed that the enemy must understand that he was completely beaten by those forces whose continuous attacks had brought him to his knees. In the interests of military solidarity, our allies should refrain from taking victory from the hands of those who were most deserving of it. I added that the majority of the Croatian forces were still on Yugoslav territory and had no great prospect of being able to cross the border.

Finally, I said very bluntly:

"I have express orders to compel the enemy troops to capitulate if they do not wish to do so willingly. As I am a soldier, I must respect these orders and do everything that I can to carry them out whatever the circumstances that prevail. I came here to discuss the best manner of doing this."

After a brief silence the general asked me when, in my opinion, the surrender should start. I replied that at the latest it should be within an hour after the return of the enemy delegates to their camp. It was now about 2 P.M. The British General expressed doubt that the surrender of such a large number of enemy troops and war material could be effected before nightfall, and suggested that the capitulation proceedings be postponed until the following morning. During the night the necessary preparations could be made for the surrender to proceed in an organized manner, that is for the registration of personnel, weapons, and so on.

I quickly made it clear to him that it was not a question of carrying out the surrender by a roll call in an hour's time. But within an hour after the conclusion of the negotiations, that is after the negotiators had returned to their respective camps, the capitulation must begin. While it was important for the surrender to begin in the shortest possible time, the process could extend over several days, if necessary.

With what struck me as being a "controlled" smile, the General replied that it would be necessary to prolong the time limit set for the capitulation. In an hour's time the commander of the Yugoslav forces himself would not be able to advise all of his units of the result of the negotiations or to issue the necessary instructions to his subordinates. I replied that we had at our disposal American jeeps, and the British themselves had supplied telephones to our headquarters. Therefore, it would require ten or fifteen minutes at most to inform all of our units about the time for the capitulation. Our units already knew what their duties were with regard to taking charge of the enemy captives and their arms and other materials, and where they were to escort the prisoners. "After all," I concluded, "it is not difficult to herd together and control a defeated and disarmed enemy. It is more difficult to wage war against him while he still has arms in his hands."

This last remark seemed to convince the general. "I heard about the alertness and readiness of the Partisans," the gray haired Englishman said, "but anyway I would like to talk again with the representatives of the enemy troops about all of these conditions."

He asked that we wait for a moment in the adjoining room before the final negotiations got under way. These repeated delays affected us unpleasantly enough. My feelings were mixed. On the one hand I saw that things were going much better than I had imagined they would. While we had stated our viewpoint clearly and firmly, we had not closed the door on the possibility of receiving the collaboration of our allies in conducting the surrender negotiations. On the other hand why should our allies want to talk again with the enemy plenipotentiaries? I thought at the time that Allied commander was misinformed about the numerical strength and material and moral state of the enemy units, as well as of our own. It appeared to me that he might have given the Ustashas some kind of promise or guarantee. Otherwise, why would he constantly adopt an attitude that differed from ours? Even now, when he had received from us accurate information concerning our own state and that of the enemy, and was able to see for himself how resolute we were in our view of the situation, it was evident that he was not certain about the decision he should make in regard to the surrender. Obviously, to accommodate his position to ours, he had to change his previous position. It occurred to me that he might have contacted his superiors in the Allied Command, and on the basis of his talks with us and with the Croatians was requesting a new decision from above concerning the surrender of the enemy. Perhaps he was interviewing the Ustasha generals again so that he might talk alone with them and thus gain time until he could receive definitive orders from Field Marshal Alexander's Headquarters. In any case, his intentions were anything but clear to me.

A high-ranking British officer conducted us into the adjoining room, the antechamber of the castle. We seated ourselves, and nervously awaited the resumption of the talks. Our escort was unacquainted with our language, so the Slovenian comrade and I were able to converse frankly, though in very low voices. Although we did not have time to discuss the situation in any detail, the Slovenian comrade seemed pleased with what I had said to the British general.

Nonetheless, both of us felt concern over the fact that the Allied commander seemed to feel or believe that he had to play the role of arbitrator between the Croatians and ourselves. For the second time he was conferring with the delegates of these, our enemies, without informing us, his allies, about what was being said between them. Nor had he asked for our view of these discussions with our foes.

The dubious outcome of the negotiations, and concern over the state and position of our own forces vis-a-vis the enemy, combined to make me extremely nervous. Even though hardly ten minutes had actually passed since we left the presence of the British general, it seemd to me that an eternity had gone by. I walked up and down, looked out the windows, and expressed my apprehensions to the Slovenian comrade.

Finally we employed a mixture of French and German words to advise our escort that we had waited too long. We asked him to inform the general that the talks must be speeded up. He left the room only to return in a few minutes with an incomprehensible message. We then told him to advise his superior officer that if he did not summon us for the final talks concerning the surrender in five minutes, we would break off the negotiations and return to our camp.

While we were waiting for the answer to this ultimatum, my Slovenian colleague suddenly called me to the window. I looked out and saw, about a hundred meters in front of the castle, a moving column of infantry and artillery. At once, I identified them as the 12th Proletarian Brigade bringing the divisional artillery sent on from Dravograd by the divisional commander, Kolja (Colonel Sreta Savic).

"These are our men, these are our men!" I exclaimed joyfully. I embraced the Slovene who also was elated, though a little confused. He asked me what these units were. It was only then that I realized that he was not acquainted with our military dispositions. He had been brought to our headquarters at Hrust by the Allied liaison officer and had joined us a little less than two hours before. I told him that I had accepted the offer of the British to participate in negotiations with the Croatians to give the troops from Dravograd time to arrive.

"Then these surely are ours (our troops)?" he asked me.

"Yes, of course they are ours, who else could they be?" I replied.

He smiled and rubbed his hands. Like me he felt now that the fight against time had been won. Victory was ours and it was within reach of our own hands.

When we were brought into the presence of the Allied commander for the second time, Pavelic's generals were not in evidence. The Englishman said nothing to us concerning his talk with the Croatians, but he did tell us that the definitive negotiations for the surrender would start at once. He indicated the seats that we were to take at the conference table. I felt that we were making progress, because it seemed that the British commander had decided to cast himself in the role of an objective, neutral observer, whereas a while ago he had expressed his intention of receiving the surrender of Pavelic's forces himself. But, we had not come here to talk with the enemy through the assistance of an arbiter! Circumstances of the moment had brought us to the point of negotiating; it was necessary to get the conversations over with as soon as possible. After all, the reinforcements that we had hoped for were now here. Time was working in our favor, and we already had stated our conditions. Whatever the outcome of the negotiations, they must be brought to a conclusion in half an hour's time at the most. After that we were going to return to our camp whether an agreement had been reached or not.

The Final Talks

The enemy generals, only two in number now, were brought into the room. They bowed to the British general, without taking notice of us, and remained standing at attention. The Englishman gestured to one of them to take a seat at the table opposite us. I took this individual to be Chief of the General Staff of the Armed Forces of the NDH (Independent State of Croatia). Later, I learned that he was Tomislav Sertic.[2]

The British Commander gave no introductions, but made it known through an interpreter that he was giving the floor to the Yugoslav commander to state his conditions for the proposed capitulation. I was a little confused, because I was not prepared for this kind of negotiation. However, I remembered the conditions for the surrender elaborated previously at our headquarters. After a brief silence, I began dictating these conditions in what I knew was a dry and rough manner. After the arrival of the 12th Brigade and the artillery I felt that we were now masters of the situation, at least to a considerable degree. Therefore, I did not mince any words in exposing the facts of the situation:

"The remnants of your Ustasha-Domobran troops are in a dead-end street situation. You are surrounded on all sides by the strong forces of the Yugoslav Army. I believe that you know that the four armies of the Yugoslav Liberation Forces have tightened their encirclement of you on

---

[2] From Document III and several other documents, it is obvious that Commissar Basta was mistaken in identifying General Sertic as one of the two final Croatian negotiators at Bleiburg. These Croatians actually were General Herencic and Professor Crljen.

all sides. We know that you do not have at your disposal combat ready forces that would be capable of breaking through our lines. Time is working in our favor too. We have the power to compel you to surrender unconditionally or to destroy you, as we choose. Some of our new troops have arrived in this sector and others are continuing to arrive. It is both in your own interests and in those of the civilians whom you caused to emigrate with you that you surrender without attempting further resistance. On behalf of the Command of the 51st Division of the Third Yugoslav Army, I demand your unconditional surrender. The time limit allowed for this surrender is one hour from the time of your return to your units, that is by 4 P.M. at the latest. The signal for surrender is to be given by raising white flags. The surrender will continue until we have taken charge of all personnel and weapons. As to certain other details, we will talk them over on the spot during the surrender process itself."

I paused a moment for breath and then went on:

"I can, however, inform you definitively concerning the following matters: we will return to their homes the civilians who have fled with you; all of your military personnel, in the event that you surrender unconditionally and without resistance, will be escorted to prisoner-of-war camps; the members of your Armed Forces will be treated in accordance with the stipulations of International Law provided for prisoners of war; the most necessary belongings will be left to all officers and soldiers; the generals may retain their valets and their personal weapons until further notice. If you do not accept these conditions, you will be considered—taking into account the fact that you are continuing war operations after the war itself has ended officially—as unprotected by the rules of international law governing prisoners of war. In such case we will treat you as rebels in whose liquidation our allies will assist us."

I was careful to stress the point about the help that our British and other allies would give us, because I wanted to impress upon the Ustashas the fact that their fate was decided regardless of the course they chose to take concerning the surrender.

The Ustasha Chief of General Staff repeated the capitulation conditions after me in a loud and energetic voice. Then he lowered his voice and said: "Sir Commissar (of course he knew the ranks in our Armed Forces, although the British General kept referring to me as 'Commander'), your propositions are well expressed from your standpoint, but we cannot accept the time limit set for the capitulation. First of all, it would be impossible for us to acquaint all of our troops with the capitulation conditions in an hour's time. Besides that, a great number of our men have been fighting against you for four years, and it will not be easy to convince them of the necessity for capitulation on such short notice. In spite of our orders, individual units are likely to continue to resist. Such incidents could very well cause you to think that the Croatian Army as a whole was refusing to capitulate."

I interrupted him to say that if the enemy forces, as a whole, accepted the terms of surrender, instances of isolated resistance that might occur would be treated as such.

While the Ustasha general was talking, a high-ranking Allied officer came into the room. He spoke to the British general in a low voice. Since the Englishman was sitting next to me, I could hear the words but couldn't understand them. I realized that something was being said about us Partisans and about Yugoslavia. I noticed that the General listened with great interest and that he asked several questions in a low voice. It seemed probable to me that he was being informed of the arrival of our reinforcements.

The second Ustasha general present at the interview had been standing all this time. Now, he suddenly addressed the British commander directly. Speaking in an highly emotional tone of voice, he said that history would never forgive him if he allowed three hundred thousand Croatians to be delivered into the hands of the Communists.

To end his interruption, I stood up and asked the interpreter to tell the British General that we were leaving, as we had stayed too long already. Everyone stood up, although the Ustasha general kept on shouting and arguing. Obviously in a disturbed frame of mind, the Briton turned to me and said: "Sir Commander, my tanks are at your disposal."

This utterance shook me. I was quite surprised that the Englishman should so unexpectedly have taken a stern, clear stand on our side. It is probable that his sudden sternness was a reaction to the Ustasha's appeals to the judgment of history. I must say that this appeal to history in behalf of the Croatian people sounded grotesque in that it was voiced by an Ustasha general. I am sure that the British General knew something about the crimes committed by the Ustashas against innocent people. Unquestionably, it was because of such knowledge that he had reacted in the way that he did. But at the same time, he must have known about the arrival of our forces on the scene. Thus, had he taken a different stand, or intervened in behalf of the Ustashas vis-a-vis our brave troops, he would have incurred a responsibility for the consequences that might have ensued. He evidently wished to escape this responsibility. I assume that these are the reasons which induced the British general to abandon his previously expressed intention of receiving himself the surrender of Pavelic's troops.[3]

---

[3] It is interesting, however, to note that other motivational interests may have been involved. For instance, Alexander Keller has written an article in *Die Furche* (Vienna, Austria) of June 7, 1958, entitled "210,000 Menschen fur Ein Auto—Vergessene Kroatische Tragodie." The title itself is self-explanatory. Ivan Mestrovic, the late renowned Croatian sculptor, in his memoirs also mentions conversations with leading Communists in Yugoslavia. Here, it was boasted that the Croatian Army had been delivered from Austria for the price of an American Packard. See Ivan Mestrovic, *Uspomene na Politicke Ljude i Dogadjaje* (Buenos Aires, 1961), pp. 392-393.

The second Ustasha general finally gave up his attempt to alter or modify the verdict that had been passed. After bowing to the British commander, both of the enemy commanders quietly withdrew from the room. In the doorway, Sertic turned and asked that we synchronize our watches, since theirs were set according to German time, an hour ahead of ours.

Encounter With the Slavonian Proletarians

I thanked the Allied Commander for his collaboration, and asked him to give me his name so that I might inform my superiors of the help that he had given us. He did so, and made a memorandum of my name also. Unfortunately, I lost the note that he gave me and I cannot now recall his name. We parted on cordial terms, after an exchange of compliments concerning the wartime alliance between our respective countries.

When we left the castle, we hastened to make contact with the 12th Slavonian Proletarian Brigade and the divisional artillery units accompanying it. I found Dushan Ostojitch, nicknamed "Osman" and Rade Knezevitch ("Tihi"), Assistant Commander of the 12th Slavonian Division, to whom I rendered a brief account of the results of the negotiations. I informed them of the situation of the enemy, and also advised them about the positions that my own command was holding at the time when I left for the conference with the British and the Ustashas. Then I explained how they were to receive and escort the prisoners. I stressed particularly the necessity of enforcing strict military conduct and discipline upon their soldiers. They must issue express orders and explain to their men that no mistakes in regard to the prisoners would be tolerated. Since incorrigible and notorious Ustasha criminals would be included among the prisoners, our people might easily get out of hand. Among our fighters, there were many whose entire families had been wiped out by the Ustashas. Therefore, I told Dushan Ostojitch and Rade Knezevitch to explain to their troops that our higher authorities would examine the degree of guilt borne by all of the prisoners. Those who had bloodied their hands by killing the innocent would be brought before the People's Court and punished as they deserved.

Also, I warned them to take all precautions to see that none of the enemy escaped from the prisoner columns. If any of the local Allied Commanders tried to interfere with our handling of the prisoners, they would have to be informed of the decisions reached at the headquarters of the Commanding British General in this sector.

All in all, it was a difficult task that we had before us. To escort back to Yugoslavia a multitude of prisoners-of-war, and a still greater mass of civilians, was no light responsibility. I knew that formal agreements could be broken; we had had recent experiences of this kind. Until the enemy soldiery was disarmed and back on our territory, we could not really be sure how the affair would turn out. However, I felt that the arrival of units such as the 12th Brigade, and especially of its artillery, would be of decisive influence in insuring a favorable outcome for this whole complex situation.

Stancer's Attempt to Conduct New Negotiations

When we arrived at our own headquarters, we found that our long absence had given rise to much nervousness. The time limit that we had set for the enemy surrender already had been passed. I had hardly seated myself and begun to tell our staff of the result of the negotiations when word came that four other Ustasha generals were requesting a word with the "Chief Commander."

The Commander of the Guard showed these new arrivals into the garden house where we were conferring. They approached the table where our officers were seated, stood at attention, and saluted. The oldest of them, Colonel General Slavko Stancer, was Commanding General of the Regular Army of NDH (Independent State of Croatia). He was a tall, slender old man who had lost an arm in the war. He told us that he and his companions were looking for a British or other high Allied commander with whom they could negotiate surrender terms for the Croatian Army and civilian refugees. He added that four other generals had preceded them in seeking to negotiate with the British, but that they had not returned from these talks.

I informed the new enemy plenipotentiaries that we officers assembled here represented the high command of the Yugoslav Army. Surrender could be made only to us. I then advised them that I had already negotiated with their other generals and the spokesmen of the Western Allies, and that it had been decided that all Ustasha-Domobran units would have to surrender to our command and to the troops that we had at our disposal. Once I had made these points, I related the conditions of capitulation to them.

On this occasion, I laid particular stress on the fact that we were allowing the enemy generals to retain their personal weapons, luggage, automobiles, and attendants. It occurred to me also that I should say something to them about their own probable fate, which was undoubtedly their primary interest at the moment.

"All that I can tell you in regard to your own fate is that you will be treated according to the stipulations of international law. A mixed commission of Allied representatives will be formed to examine such charges as may be made against you and to determine your degree of guilt. I cannot give you any assurances. I repeat that we, too, are a regular army and we will observe all the laws of war."

What seemed to perturb the enemy generals most of all was the stipulation relative to the display of white flags in sign of surrender. One of them – I think it was General Tomasevic – said that they had no white flags. One of our officers replied, "Well, display your shirts and underwear then — you certainly have those articles!"

The Croatians consulted briefly among themselves. Finally, Stancer, who showed obvious signs of doubt as to the accuracy of what we had told them, declared: "If all this is the way you say it is, and if an agreement really has been reached with our other representatives, I will order the surrender. But I am a soldier and I am accustomed to receive my orders from our Chief of Staff. Since there appears to be no other alternative, if I do not receive such orders from him soon, I will proceed on my own initiative in the spirit of the conditions enumerated."

We warned him that any delay in accepting the terms offered would cost the Croatians dearly. I said to him in terms that admitted no ambiguity: "It is likely that your higher commands already have issued, or will issue the orders for surrender in the spirit of the conclusions reached at the aforesaid negotiations as soon as possible. But regardless of whatever orders and instructions you receive, or whether or not you receive them at all, I command you in the name of the Yugoslav Army to halt all attempts at resistance within one hour's time, to lay down your arms, and to carry out our orders in a disciplined manner. If you do not obey these orders, we will destroy you, and you will bear the responsibility for the fate of your troops and civilian population. I think you should realize that if you do not surrender now, you will expose yourselves and those of your men who fall into our hands to very harsh treatment. It has been announced that the continuation of resistance after the end of the war will be considered rebellion. We are offering you a last chance to save the lives of yourselves and your men. If you capitulate in an organized manner and see that our orders are carried out, you will contribute materially to the betterment of your present and future situations."

After a further moment of thought Stancer came to attention, saluted, and asked that he be dismissed to convey the surrender orders to the Croatian troops and civilian population. We allowed the four generals to go back to their encampment.

Since there were many proven war criminals among the enemy, we really did not expect that the surrender would proceed very smoothly. But, about fifteen minutes after Stancer had left our headquarters, it was announced that white flags were being displayed all over the nearby fields and surrounding hills in which the Croatians had taken position. Our troop units were ordered to begin receiving the surrender of weapons and prisoners. Then everything went forward at a dizzying pace. A column of prisoners was quickly lined up on the road in front of our headquarters. From the generals who were brought to our quarters, we learned with great surprise that there were over 100,000 men of the Croatian Army in the immediate vicinity. There were many civilian refugees, also. Because of the battles that had taken place recently, and

Old castle of Bleiburg, Austria.

Bleiburg Field—the scene of the Croatian Troops' surrender to the British and Yugoslavian Partisans.

Left: Barracks of the Austrian Frontier Guard.

Background: The Austrian-Yugoslavian Frontier and the mountain Petzen, part of the Karawanken Alps.

Bleiburg Field–The Partisans knifed Croatian victims under the pinetrees (right, foreground).

Left: Unter-Loibach Cemetery, burial place of the first Croatian victims—Right: Tavern Hrust where one phase of Bleiburg talks between the British and Tito's Partisans was conducted—Center: Pinetrees under which Croatian victims were knifed by Tito's Troops.

Hamlet of Unter-Loibach with cemetery where first Bleiburg victims are buried.

Bleiburg Custom House at Austrian frontier–Background: church, forests, and mountains of Slovenia.

the losses sustained in the retreat from Zagreb, the enemy commanders themselves could only guess at the approximate strength of their army.

And so it was that on May 15, 1945, between 4:00 and 4:30 P.M., the organized resistance of the enemy came to an end, and World War II was over in the territory of Yugoslav state.

Signed: Milan Basta, Lt. Colonel,
Political Commissar of the
51st Voyvodina Division

Document III

The Bleiburg talks and the beginning of the Bleiburg Tragedy are described by a Croatian negotiator who is now living in Buenos Aires.

On May 6, 1945, long columns of the Croatian Armed Forces began to evacuate the capital city, Zagreb, and other strategic points in the northern part of the Croatian State territory. Already the Croatian troops had withdrawn from Bosnia, Hercegovina, and most of Dalmatia. Now they had orders to retreat through Slovenia to the Austrian border.

Military catastrophe necessitated this gigantic withdrawal of 200,000 officers and soldiers after months of bitter fighting in Bosnia, Hercegovina, and other sectors. But it was not a Croatian military catastrophe which caused the withdrawal. The Croatian military operations against the much over-rated Communist Partisans, commanded by the half-Slovene half-Croatian Tito Broz, had been almost uniformly successful, although it would be difficult to infer from the absurdities concerning the Partisans that continued to appear in the Anglo-American Press. Farther north, in Sirmia and Slavonia, the Croatians also helped stiffen the defense that the Germans were putting up against the advance of the Russians and Bulgarians. But the outcome of the war of 1939-45 was not being decided in these combat theatres. In the view of the political authorities in the Croatian State, the inability of the German Wehrmacht to cope with the Russians, Americans, and English made further defense of the Domovina (homeland) useless in that final victory could never be achieved.

Yet, "hope springs eternal in the human breast." A great multitude of civilians, men, women, old people, and children hastened to leave Croatian soil together with the undefeated Army. They hoped to escape the long night of Marxist domination that soon threatened to blacken the Croatian homeland, by obtaining asylum in Western European countries, Austria and Italy to begin with, and then farther afield. The troops themselves were led to believe that if they surrendered to the English, Americans, and French, they could claim the protection of international law, and prisoner-of-war status as defined by the Geneva Convention.[1] While neither the Russian nor the Serbian or Slovenian Communists cared anything about such abstractions as international law and the Geneva Convention, the Western Allies did profess to recognize and practice the principles they stood for.

Huge civilian masses impeded the progress of the military columns. Every highway, secondary road, rail line, and footpath was packed and jammed beyond belief. Under such circumstances, it was impossible for the military authorities to keep in direct touch with all of their units. Information and instructions had to be transmitted orally along the columns which stretched out for miles and miles. En route through these columns, orders were likely to be altered in context or to be lost altogether. Communications between the various commands were uncertain, sporadic, and casual. It soon became evident that the generals could not control the situation created by the retreat, and that catastrophe was likely and imminent.

Two days after the evacuation of Zagreb, the officers commanding the advanced units decided that it would be necessary to take the direction of the retreat into their own hands. They were primarily concerned with the maintenance of military order and discipline, and with regularizing communications and arriving quickly at decisions that would have to be made according to the immediate circumstances.

As a Colonel of the Regular Army charged with the direction of the Education Section in the Defense Ministry of the Croatian State, I was included in this officer group. General Ivan Herencic, Commander of the Fifth Army Corps which had its General Headquarters at Karlovac, assumed the leadership of this improvised military group. Several other generals and General Staff colonels constituted its core, while a group of military motorcyclists was charged with the task of carrying crucial orders up and down the long lines of the columns. Especially pressing was the necessity of maintaining the precarious contacts with those units which were protecting the flanks and rear of the retiring masses.

There weren't enough Communists in either Croatia or Slovenia to make it advisable for them to bother us during the first five days of the retreat. However, those who took part in the great exodus from the Domovina were not spared want and suffering. We had only as much food as we had brought with us. We suffered acutely from thirst because of the unseasonably hot weather during the daytime. On the other hand, as soon as night fell, there would be a twenty or thirty degree drop in temperature to which we were not accustomed. We slept uncovered on the ground exposed to all the whims of nature. Because of

[1] The Geneva Convention is an international agreement which was made in 1929 for the protection of sick and wounded soldiers and also for the just treatment of prisoners of war. The Independent State of Croatia joined the Convention on January 20, 1943. All the signatory states, including the United Kingdom, were informed of this by the Political Department, Foreign Affairs Division, in Bern, Switzerland. See *La Tragedia de Bleiburg* (Buenos Aires, 1963), pp. 214-215.

the lack of doctors and medicines, the plight of the previously wounded and the people who fell sick en route became desperate. The growing disorganization brought on by the interference of the civilian masses with the military columns accentuated the gravity of the situation. Our new officer group was able to place a number of trucks at the disposal of the wounded and sick and to help with the problem created by the presence of so many children and old people. They would pick up these various categories of refugees, transport them for a few miles, and then go back to pick up other truckloads and help them along their way. Although this procedure did something to alleviate the distress of the weaker members of the retreat, it frequently resulted in the separation of families. In many cases this separation was permanent.

At the end of five painful days we arrived in Slovenjgradec. This Slovenian town is located on the road to Dravograd, which is only a few miles from the Austrian border. Here the front of the column stopped to enable the rearward sections to join it. We ascertained that a detachment of the Yugoslav Communist Army was holding the bridge that led across the Drava River. Bulgarian troops were also in the vicinity; they had accompanied the Russians during their advance into Austria in pursuit of the beaten German formations. Our improvised group of officers held a hurried council-of-war. The council decided that General Metikos and I should undertake negotiations with the Bulgarians to see if they would permit us to cross the Drava into Austria without a fight. We knew that the Bulgarians had no love for the Serbs or Yugoslavs, and that they even chased away many of Tito's people from this locality.

General Metikos, General Servatzi, and I succeeded in establishing contact with the Bulgarian military authorities whom we met at their General Headquarters in a village near Dravograd. Bulgarians and Croatians usually get along well enough with one another, but I found myself engaged in a harsh exchange of opinions concerning the war and our present situation with a political commissar who was accompanying the Bulgarian forces. Of course, he was a Communist, and the Bulgarian military officers present could hardly conceal their disgust at some of his utterances. We military men carried on our negotiations with mutual politeness. The Bulgarians informed us that a conference was to be held the next day to deal with our situation. Some British and Russian generals were coming to Bulgarian General Headquarters for this purpose. The Bulgars invited us to be present at the meeting. As it turned out the British delegates did not show up and, therefore, the prospective conference never took place.

In the meantime some Yugoslav Partisan units had occupied the terrain immediately ahead of us. We could have brushed them aside easily enough, but we feared that such an encounter might involve us in a large scale combat with the Russians, Bulgars, and British. Since the war was irretrievably lost, there seemed to be no sense to such an involvement if it could be avoided. Therefore, after some desultory skirmishing, the commanding officers decided to give up the idea of forcing the Drava crossings. Instead we would direct our columns to the Miess, a tributary of the Drava. Once across the Miess we could proceed towards our destination, Bleiburg, and enter Austria by another route.

We managed to ready various units for action in a few hours time. They delivered an attack upon the Yugoslav troops who tried to bar our advance to the Miess. In less than two hours our men cleared the way for our columns. The Communists left several hundred dead on the field, while we had over two hundred wounded to further encumber our movements.

Eight days following our departure from Zagreb, we encountered the first British troops in the vicinity of Bleiburg. The Britishers had moved into Austria during the general breakup of the Wehrmacht. Now they were arranged along the Austro-Slovenian frontier line. We sent an officer to their headquarters to negotiate the surrender of our Army under the stipulations of the Geneva Convention and the general provisions of International Law.

This negotiation occurred on May 14. The first messages that we received from British Headquarters were encouraging. The British seemed willing to accept the surrender of the Croatian Army, and to provide asylum for the refugees.

But from the early morning of the following day, May 15, contradictory information began to reach us. As the hours passed, our mood became more and more pessimistic. British military planes hovered over our encampment, evidently for the purpose of intimidating us. We had no air cover, as the few planes that our Air Force had available after the surrender of Germany were short of fuel or had been commandeered for special purposes.

The liaison officer whom we had sent to British headquarters notified us that we were to send delegates to confer with the commanding general[2] of the English Expeditionary Corps. He had just arrived from Klagenfurt, the capital of Austrian Carinthia. Generals Herencic and Servatzi were detailed to carry on the negotiations with the Englishmen. I accompanied them in the capacity of political negotiator.

We went to the meeting with somber forebodings weighing heavily upon our minds. The British headquarters was located in an ancient castle, and to reach it we had to pass through lines of British combat ready tanks.

Surrounded by a large group of officers, the English general awaited us in the castle. An American sergeant of Croatian descent served as interpreter. He informed the British commander that General Herencic was the chief of our delegation. Hearing this, the Englishman offered

---

[2] According to numerous Croatian emigrant sources, that English general was Horatius Murray. In August, 1967, however, information leaked out from the Foreign Office in London that the English negotiator at Bleiburg was General Patric Scott.

Herencic a seat immediately in front of him. The rest of us remained standing, the British officers at one side of the table and we at the other.

There were no introductions. Without formalities of any kind, the British general pointed with his hand to General Herencic, thus indicating that he was to speak. Herencic told the interpreter in Croatian that we came in the name of the Chief of the Independent State of Croatia to offer the Western Allies the surrender of our Army, and to ask that the right of political asylum be granted to the mass of civilian refugees.

Moments of disturbing silence followed the interpreter's rendition of this statement to the British commander. It seemed to me that the so-called "conference" was at the point of breaking up without any further discussion. I asked the interpreter to tell the Englishman that I wanted to add something to Herencic's remarks.

The General nodded to me and indicated with a wave of his hand that I might take a seat beside General Herencic. I spoke bluntly and pointedly. The problem concerning us could not be judged from only the military standpoint. "From the moment we left our own country, without undertaking the offensive actions of which we were still capable, we exchanged our role of warriors for one of political exiles. It is the custom of all civilized nations to receive and protect political exiles. We expect from the United Kingdom, the United States of America, and France this kind of protection."

Through the interpreter, the British general replied that as a soldier he could not deal with political problems. His duty was limited to executing the orders received from Field Marshal Alexander, Commander-in-Chief of the Allied Armies operating in the Mediterranean area.

General Herencic interrupted the interpreter's transmission of this information to ask that we be given the opportunity to send a delegation to the General Headquarters of Field Marshal Alexander. This request was refused with the observation that Alexander had already issued orders to cover the situation and that he had certainly received instructions from Prime Minister Winston Churchill.

I answered the British Commander by pointing out that he was faced with a situation that Allied General Headquarters had been unable to foresee. Hence, a consultation with this Headquarters was justified. In addition to the Croatian military personnel whose surrender had perhaps been foreseen by the British and other Allied Governments, there were hundreds of thousands of civilians, who had not fought in the war, now trying to escape wholesale massacre at the hands of the Communists.

It was with apparent nervousness that the Englishman replied that the civilians had fled from Croatia without reason. He declared that the Yugoslav allies of the British respected human rights and international conventions with regard to waging war. Therefore, the civilians were safe from illegal persecution.

Disturbed by his obvious ignorance of Marxist tactics I said:

> I am extremely sorry to have to express a contrary opinion. The flight of hundreds of thousands of civilians from Croatian territory is the consequence of crimes perpetrated by the Communists against the Croatian people upon this territory. Since the great migrations of peoples of fifteen hundred years ago that attended the break-up of the Roman Empire, there has been, right to the present day, no mass movement of similar proportions to the Croatian exodus that now is taking place before your eyes. There has been no such instance of a people abandoning their own country as the Croatians are doing today in the face of the Serbian and Soviet Communist advance. Not only had we [the military element] no desire to have the civilians flee the land and so hamper our own withdrawal [I was referring here to an allegation that he had made a few moments previously to "propaganda" that we military men were supposed to have employed to scare the civilians], but also we had no way of preventing such a mass exodus. In the course of the apocalyptic journey that they undertook, many people committed suicide owing to despair or to nervous and physical exhaustion. But *there was not one individual who decided to return to take his chances with the Communists.* This is an evident proof of the fact that our people prefer death to the prospect of returning to their Communist-subjugated country. Today these suffering political refugees of Croatian nationality are addressing their pleas to England, which is in a position to be able to decide their fate. On her, therefore, falls the moral responsibility of whether our defenseless people are to be turned over to the Communists to be slaughtered.

While I was speaking, the British commander tried to interrupt me several times, saying that he had no interest in the political problem that I was posing. The poor interpreter became so bewildered during this crossfire that I was able to add prophetically: "There is no doubt that sooner or later the free world will have to take a stand against Communism. It is our misfortune that we have opposed it too soon to be able to ask for protection against it in order to prevent the most terrible catastrophe that has ever happened to the Croatian people."

The general replied, almost nonchalantly, that a delegation of the Yugoslav Army was expected to arrive and that we would have to meet with it in his presence to arrange the conditions for surrender.

The "conference" ended at this point, and we retired to the antechamber of the castle. Here we found General Metikos, who had been worried about our long absence and had come to get news. All of us were very agitated and depressed. We discussed the advisability of staying for further conversations with the victors, or of simply abandoning all attempts to reach an understanding and organizing a last ditch resistance. We decided that it was now too late to choose the latter alternative, although I am sure that all of us deeply regretted that our

Government had not determined to fight to the end to defend the soil of Croatia. Anyway, it appeared to us that we ought to stay where we were for the purpose of gaining time. Since conditions could not be much worse, perhaps events might take a favorable turn for us in time. Besides, the English troops might not let us rejoin our own forces at our pleasure.

While we were talking, two Communist Yugoslav officers passed through the antechamber to enter the room used as an office by the Commander of the British Expeditionary Corps. A few minutes later, a British officer told us through the interpreter that two of us were to come into the office to confer with the Commander and the two Communist officers. Generals Servatzi and Metikos urged that General Herencic and I continue the conversations with the enemy representatives, while they awaited the outcome in the antechamber.

Accordingly, Herencic and I found ourselves facing the two Communists across the same table at which we had confronted the British general so recently. They were both colonels in the Yugoslav Communist Army and political commissars. One was a Serbian, although he bore the Italian surname of Basta, once a famous name in the Habsburg service. The other Communist representative did not tell us his name, but judging by his accent and vocabulary he must have been a Slovene.

Without formally introducing himself, and speaking in a very insolent manner, Basta asked for our credentials. We answered his request by introducing ourselves and then suggested that he reply in turn. He did so with evident displeasure. The British general had the interpreter translate our conversation to him. It is worth noting that no record was being kept of the talks in which we were engaged.

Commissar Basta began to dwell upon the military situation. He said that a number of Communist divisions had encircled us and that our generals had surrendered. He claimed that General Frane Sudar, commander of a division that had become legendary because of its consistent heroism, was already his prisoner. His manifest intention was to stifle any ideas concerning further resistance that we might be nourishing. Finally, after much verbiage, he declared pompously:

> We demand that you surrender unconditionally within an hour's time. If you do this, the women and children who have accompanied you will be allowed to return home. Officers and soldiers will remain prisoners of war. The officers will be sent to Maribor where those who may be charged with crimes will be tried. If you do not accept these conditions within a quarter of an hour, our general attack will begin and you no longer will have the right to invoke the agreements effected through the instrumentality of the International Red Cross.

General Herencic pointed out that it would be impossible to notify all of our units about the conditions of surrender in an hour's time. The length of our columns in itself precluded such a possibility. He proposed that twenty-four hours be allowed for the dissemination of the surrender order.

Basta refused to make this concession. He said: "You are in command of an organized army and to get the news around it is necessary only to make the decision known to your unit commanders. It will not even be necessary for you to return to your encampment. You can send a liaison officer to transmit your instructions."

I interrupted his discourse to say that whether we decided to accept his terms or not, under the ordinary conventions of military law and practice, we were entitled to return to our own camp.

The British Commander now suggested that we be given two hours to effect the transmission of the surrender orders. Both commissars flatly rejected this concession, trivial though it was, and the Englishman did not insist upon the point. Instead, he evidenced a quite obvious displeasure with our opposition to the short time limit. He told us we were surrounded by British tanks that were at the disposal of his and Britain's ally, Communist Yugoslavia. Then he turned to the Yugoslav delegates and asked them if they needed help in dealing with us. They declared that they did not, but quickly added that in case of urgent need they would request such help on their own initiative.

The action of the British general seemed to us to be a calculated atrocity and cheap attempt at intimidation. It shattered effectively any illusions that we had cherished up to this time about the proverbial British spirit of fair play. This spokesman of official Britain had offered the aid of British arms to delegates of the Yugoslav Communist Army to coerce us into a premature and unconditional surrender. He also proposed that a British commission assist the Communists in carrying out the details of the surrender process. General Herencic at once said that we would be pleased to have the British supervise the surrender process. To this, the British general replied flatly that we were in no position to solicit anything; he had offered the help of an English commission just in case his allies needed such aid.

This was the end of the negotiations. All doors were closed to us. There was no hope for our Army or for the refugees. The only alternative that we had left was to decide whether to surrender, fight, or flee. And we had just sixty minutes to make up our minds which to do.

As we were preparing to leave, I asked that the one hour period of grace begin *after* our return to the Croatian encampment, that is about twenty minutes after our departure from the castle. With some reluctance the Yugoslavs agreed to make this concession. All of us set our watches in unison. Then Herencic and I arose, bowed coldly to the Englishman, and took our leave without further words.

We returned to our encampment with all possible haste. General Herencic took upon himself the task of informing the high-ranking officers and unit commanders of what had transpired during the interview. Immediately a division of opinion manifested itself in our ranks. Some officers advocated an immediate withdrawal into the neighboring forests and a fight until the last throat was cut on one side or the other. Others proposed that a new delegation be formed under the leadership of General Stancer. As a gravely wounded general, he might receive more consideration from the British officers than we unwounded men had. Although their counsel prevailed, Stancer's delegation was not even received by the British Commanding General. Instead, it was sent under armed escort to the general headquarters which the Yugoslav troops purported to have established in the vicinity.

General Herencic charged me with the responsibility of conveying the depressing intelligence concerning the surrender to the political functionaries and other civilians who had assembled together in groups apart from the military. I fulfilled his orders to the best of my ability in the short time allotted.

But soon after the time limit had expired, I felt that I was entitled to look after my own safety. I joined a group of soldiers who were determined not to surrender to the Communists, and went with them towards the nearby mountains.

Signed: Daniel Crljen

Document IV

The surrender at Bleiburg (Austria), extraditions to the Yugoslav Communists, and subsequent "Death Marches" as seen by a Croatian civilian.

I joined the Croatian exodus as a civilian, departing by train from Zagreb on May 7, 1945. We passed through Zidani Most, and arrived at Celje on May 10. At Celje Slovenian and Yugoslav flags, all bearing the red star, had been hoisted to signal the end of the war. From Celje, we went on to Slovenjgradec and then crossed the Austrian frontier en route to Bleiburg. In spite of losing the war, we were in good spirits. So we spent the long, tedious hours on the train singing all of the old Croatian songs.

On the morning of May 15, we left the train and assembled in the fields near Bleiburg. Everyone was ready for a march into the interior of Austria, where we expected to be interned. We lined up in columns and moved across the fields. But soon we received orders to halt. Since we had no idea what was happening, we awaited further developments with some anxiety.

About 9 A.M., English tanks and military vehicles approached our left flank and began to form a circle around the packed Croatian masses that had assembled on the Bleiburg field. While the motorized English units were completing this maneuver, twelve British planes flew very low over the field. No one knew the purpose of this flight, but many people shouted and waved friendly greetings to the planes. Everyone seemed to be in a happy mood. Croatian flags were hoisted here and there and a generally festive atmosphere prevailed.

Around 2 P.M., we heard that the Commander of the British troops had requested our generals to meet him for a discussion of the conditions of surrender. From the moment that this news arrived, the cheerful attitude displayed by almost everyone suddenly disappeared. Our glum faces clearly reflected the silence and apprehension that prevailed in our ranks.

It was perhaps 3:45 P.M., when the first tidings of the coming disaster reached us. We were told that our leaders had signed a treaty of surrender with the British. The terms were onerous indeed. The entire Croatian Army had to give up all of its arms and ammunition to the Englishmen. Then the latter would turn our soldiers over to Tito's Army. The Communists had promised the British that no reprisals would be taken. All Croatians would be allowed to return to their homes without any hindrance or molestation.

Promptly at 4:00 P.M. the order came to lower the Croatian flags and raise white ones in their place as a signal of surrender. This was a bad augury of things to come. Everyone began to feel that the situation was taking the worst possible turn. Soon after receiving this order, we saw several British officers, accompanied by a number of Yugoslav Communist officials, passing along the vehicle line that had been drawn up around us. They eyed us with visible satisfaction as the surrender began.

Not far from my position, there was a Croatian Army officer who was acquainted with a friend of mine. I sent my friend to ask this military man about the details of the surrender. My friend soon returned from his talk with the officer. Even from a distance, it was evident that he had depressing news. The officer had told him that everything was lost. The British would turn us over to Tito's people who would do with us as they pleased. Since the officer had his wife and son with him, he was especially upset. However, many of our officers had decided not to surrender. My friend told me that they were going to hide in the woods and fight to the end.

I would have liked to go with them, but my wife and son were with me. While I was racking my brain trying to find a way out of this desperate situation, I saw General Boban coming towards us. He held an automatic rifle in one hand and a small suitcase in the other. His face was pale and serious, and he was vigorously talking with several other officers who accompanied him. About twenty yards from my position, Boban and his group stopped and exchanged a few words with a colonel in our Army. After a short conversation, they saluted one another and went off in different directions.

A number of other officers joined General Boban, and I saw Danijel Crljen and Professor Irena Javor approach his group. After an obvious exchange of information, they followed Boban and his officer contingent towards the nearby woods.

During the previous eight days of our exodus, not a drop of rain had fallen. Now, however, it began to drizzle. Although it was not a heavy downpour, it served to further dampen everyone's spirits and add to the general funereal atmosphere that prevailed among us.

Since the British had not completed the circle they had tried to draw around us, and the rain showed no sign of stopping, I decided to go into the forest to pick up some wood for tent poles. In the woods, I encountered several Montenegrin National military units watching the drama being enacted on the Bleiburg field. These Montenegrins had come under General Boban's command during the retreat from Croatia. They observed attentively the surrender procedure that was going on, and so did I.

The multitude of Croatians assembled on the field were composed of a heterogeneous mass of officers, soldiers, women, and older people of both sexes. They were ordered to draw up in a column of fours and to be ready to leave at once.

Until this moment, I had not made up my mind what to do. The truth of the matter is that I was on the verge of a nervous breakdown. My friend said to me that surrendering would be the worst thing we could do. If we went into the forests, we could at least fight until we were killed. But I knew that my legs were not up to a flight into the woods, and I felt that I might as well give myself up and get killed as soon as possible without any argument.

My friend flatly refused to surrender to the British since they were turning us over to the Partisans. Encouraged by his example, I decided to follow him into the woods. We took a few of the belongings that we had brought with us from our bags and turned the pack horses loose. Before making our final break, we crept up a little hill which afforded us a view of what was going on in the field below us. It was a terrible and dramatic scene of the final separation of families, husbands, wives, sons, and fathers. Many soldiers were determined not to surrender and were only waiting for night to fall before they tried to get away into the mountains. Partisan soldiers and officers were pushing in among the crowds, trying to separate the officers and soldiers from the civilians. Whenever they could isolate military personnel from their families, they marched them off to an unknown destination. A huge mountain of arms and ammunition was arising on the field as our men laid down their arms.

At 6 P.M., the British halted the surrender procedure, saying that it would begin again at 8 A.M. on the following day. By this time about a third of the refugees assembled on the field had passed through the "gate of surrender."

As darkness fell, large numbers of people started to move into the woods and towards the nearby mountains. Rain was still falling, and we were fortunate indeed to find an empty building where we could take shelter. We were extremely weary, both mentally and physically, and almost entirely without food. Weary though I was, I could not sleep because of the excitement of the day and the uncertainty of our situation. Finally, towards dawn, I dozed off from sheer exhaustion.

When I awoke, the sun was already high on the horizon. To the surprise of everyone in our little party, we found that the whole vicinity around us was deserted. Even on the field below us there were few people. As we were descending from the hill, we ran into some men who told us that during the night many of our officers had gone around advising everyone not to surrender. We regretted that we had not encountered these officers. Had we done so, we would have taken their advice to lose ourselves in the mountains.

After a long discussion of the predicament in which we found ourselves, we decided that the best thing we could do now would be to surrender to the British. I accompanied a friend to the lower part of the slope, where we found a few small groups who were angry with themselves because they had not joined those who had fled to the mountains during the night. Many Yugoslav Communists wearing red armbands were standing or walking around, but the big piles of guns and munitions were gone.

We remained on the lower slope for about twenty minutes. Some seventy other individuals joined us there. They, too, had seen that it was too late to get away to the mountains and had decided to give themselves up. After a time, we moved off in the direction indicated to us by the British the night before. We had gone hardly a mile when a Yugoslav Communist patrol came up and took us prisoners. Some of them remained with us while the others in the patrol went on to pick up more prisoners at the designated place of surrender.

About ten o'clock on the morning of May 17, all civilian refugees and soldiers were told to line up in columns of four. We moved off escorted by heavily armed Communist soldiers who lined up on either side of us. As we marched, we saw British soldiers here and there. We were marching along the right bank of the river Drava, the historic northern boundary of our country.

After an hour's march we came to a wooden bridge that spanned the river. An English military detachment was guarding the crossing. Since the bridge was in very poor condition, we had to cross it in small groups rather than in column. On the far bank of the Drava, armed Communists mounted on horseback met us and took over escort duties.

From this moment on we saw no more English soldiers. Now we began to realize how desperate our situation really was. We understood clearly, although unfortunately much too late, what lay before us. The emergency measures we might have tried a few days earlier were useless.

As long as the Communist units were in sight of the British troops, they refrained from maltreating us. But the moment that Englishmen were no longer in evidence, the Communist units began to behave as though we were wild beasts and they were the same, but bigger and stronger. The first thing they did was to start us off at a run. Whenever some converted trackman could not keep up, the Communist guards fell upon him and beat him unmercifully.

With this fast-paced march, we arrived in the vicinity of Dravograd about 5 P.M. This was a short stop since Tito's Partisans quickly took over from our former escorts. These Communists were wild beasts, too. They took all valuables that we had on our persons, and, in robbing us, the animals did it with clear assurance that we would have no further use for material possessions. On the outside of my line there was a young soldier of the regular Croatian Army. This boy wore a ring with his father's picture set into it. The father had given it to his son when the boy was sixteen, and now, a few years later, the ring was very tight. Several of the Communist soldiers tried to remove the ring, twisting his hand so that he had to scream with pain. When they saw that the ring would not come off, they gave up and left him alone. This little act was repeated several times. Finally, a Serbian Partisan came up. He took one look at the ring and told the boy that he wanted it right away. The lad replied that he would be glad to give it to him, but that it fitted too tightly to be removed from his finger.

"Well, you bandit," said the Serb, "come here. I'll show you how to take it off."

The boy went off with him into the surrounding woods. He never came back; we knew that his life had ended and the Serb had cut off his finger somewhere in that leafy expanse.

A few hundred yards from the scene of this tragedy stood a storehouse. As we approached it, two husky Partisan soldiers grabbed me. They held a pistol to my head and took everything that my previous escorts had not discovered on my person. They threw me out of the storehouse just as our column began to move off again.

Our Communist captors escorted us to Slovenjgradec, where we joined a large column of refugees who had been brought there the day before. All of us spent the night in the streets of the village under the guard of armed soldiers. There were strong Communist forces in Slovenjgradec. Among the refugees, we saw some of the people who had wanted to join General Boban in the mountains. They had lost their bearings and been picked up somewhere by the Communists.

Soon we reached another bridge that crossed the Drava. Our guards separated us into two columns, one of which followed the left bank while the other proceeded along the opposite shore of the river. Beyond the bridge we could see two roads. One of these led to the rail station; the other went straight on to Celje. When we came to the crossroads, two soldiers began to direct the sick, the elderly, and the very young to the railroad station. The others were sent on up the main road.

I suggested to my friend that we pretend to be sick. It was our only hope of escaping the massacre in store for all prisoners sufficiently healthy to be possible opponents of Tito's proposed state, supported by Soviet Russia, Britain, and America.

At first, my friend refused to agree to my suggestion. At last, however, he agreed that we might as well try this subterfuge in lieu of any better course of action. But as soon as the Communists saw us mingle with the old and sick people, they yelled at us: "Where are you going, bandits?" My friend replied that I was dying and that he did not know what to do with me. The Partisans swore and shouted at us but, at last, they did let us go on to the rail station.

There, several hundred refugees were milling around. Among them were other young people who probably had the same idea and employed the same kind of trick that we had to get to the station. The rest of our column was driven by the Partisan guards along the main highway towards Celje.

Signed: J. U.

Rome
April 7, 1955

Document V

A Croatian officer gives his account of how Croatian Armed Forces surrendered to Yugoslav Communists in the British zone of Austria.

Shortly before noon on May 6, 1945, I received an oral command to evacuate the school during the night from Captain George Markovic, who had arrived at Kerestinec from Zagreb. He directed me to take all of the students and as much of the equipment as possible to Celje. Here our group would join the staffs and student bodies of the several officers' schools. We would receive further orders and instructions once we had reached this Slovenian locality.

I set to work immediately to organize the retreat. Besides our own students, I brought with us part of the Fourth and Seventh Lieutenants' Corps as well as the members of the Female Work Service employed on the state properties at Kerestinec.

We left Kerestinec on foot on the morning of May 7. Our route lay through Hrvatsko Zagorje. We encountered no obstacles in our two-day march to Celje. We arrived at this town on May 9, and found Communist Partisan bands in possession of Celje. They wanted to disarm us, but we drove them off and joined other Croatian columns which were proceeding towards Dravograd.

My own group consisted of 300 civilians and 220 well equipped military cadets and officers. We reached Dravograd on May 13 without much difficulty. There must have been 80,000 people, soldiers and civilians mixed together, in and around this town. After we arrived, more military and civilian columns kept coming. The whole vicinity was unbelievably crowded.

At Dravograd, I saw Generals Herencic, Servatzi, Boban, Tomasevic, Metzger, Gustovic, Metikos, and, as I recall, General Stancer, also. There were many other high officers of the Croatian Army there, too. I reported to General Herencic, who ordered me to try to supply food to units which lacked it and then to place myself under the orders of General Gustovic, our operational chief.

I asked General Herencic how serious he considered our situation to be. He replied that he had initiated negotiations with representatives of the Bulgarian Army, as well as with the commanding generals of the Partisan Army in the vicinity. These negotiations were conducted to ascertain whether the Bulgarians and Yugoslav Partisans would allow the Croatian Army to withdraw into Austria where it could surrender to the English and the Americans, or whether we would have to fight our way through to Austrian territory. He told me that on the following day our representatives would confer with a mixed commission of English, Russian, Bulgarian, and Partisan generals to decide this question.

I told General Herencic I didn't think it was wise to give the Partisans another day to bring up new forces. I suggested that we give all Communists who stood in our way a two-hour ultimatum. If they did not withdraw within that period of time, I further suggested that we break through their lines. General Herencic refused to accept my advice and said that he would wait until the following day, as pre-arranged with the enemy representatives.

When I reported to General Gustovic, he attached me to the Fourth Division. General Begic was supposed to be the commander of this operational unit. However, for reasons unknown to me, he had declined the command, and it was taken by a supply officer. Since he was not a field or "fighting" officer, his subordinates assumed the active direction of the various units of the Division more or less at their own discretion.

On the evening of May 13, we received orders to set out for Bleiburg, because Partisan units had opened fire on us despite the truce arrangement that was to last until the following day. At once, Generals Boban and Herencic and Colonel Sudar led forward units which swept the Partisans aside and opened the way to Bleiburg for our columns. Sporadic battles continued throughout the night, during which Colonel Sudar's men brought in more than a hundred captives. On the following morning, the Partisans attacked again. They were now supported by the Bulgarian artillery, whose fire was very effective against our closely packed columns. Although we lost several hundred men in this cannon fire, we broke through the Partisans again, and established a rear defense line to protect the withdrawal of our masses from Dravograd to Bleiburg.

My division took a side road which ran westward out of Dravograd, and reached the outskirts of Bleiburg without much trouble that same evening, May 14. We found a great number of civilians and members of the Croatian Armed Forces assembled there. We found that English, as well as Partisan troops, were blocking our entrance into Bleiburg through which we intended to pass in order to reach Klagenfurt in Carinthia. These troops were awaiting orders concerning us from their respective commands.

A number of our higher generals arrived in our midst. On May 15, Generals Herencic, Servatzi, and Metikos, and Colonel Crljen went to negotiate with the British Commander. I do not know how the negotiations were conducted, but I remember that on this same afternoon these officers ordered us to hoist white flags as signs of surrender.

Great emotional confusion prevailed among our officers and soldiers following the reception of this order. Many officers, myself included, wanted to take their units into the adjoining woods and wage a last-ditch resistance. However, General Metzger[1] and Lieutenant-Colonel Bobinac thought we should obey the surrender order that our superior officers had given us. Metzger said the British and Partisans were capable of firing deliberately upon the women and children that we had with us, if our military effectives offered resistance. I talked with a number of other officers who foresaw the worst from the British. Some of them disregarded the surrender order and led their men into the nearby forests. I also heard that General Boban and Colonel Sudar were already returning to Croatia to arrange fighting groups. Their intention was to take shelter with their bands in the great beech and oak forests of the Domovina which they would now defend to the bitter end. This is what all of us should have done when our lines were still intact and our soldiers still confident. At that time, despite German collapse, the Croats were still confident that they could hold out almost indefinitely against Tito's Communists and their Anglo-American, Russian, and Bulgarian allies.

After considerable hesitation, I got rid of my weapons and joined the column which was going to surrender at Bleiburg, from which point I understood that we were to be returned, ultimately, to Croatia.

To our great astonishment we had to surrender to the Communists rather than to the British. At first it seemed they were going to treat us decently and conduct us safely back to Croatia. As soon as the columns of prisoners had left the British lines behind, however, the Reds started to loot our belongings. Then they commenced to disband groups of officers and shoot or otherwise dispose of them. As soon as I saw what was going on, I made up my mind to escape before my turn came to experience the lethal attentions of our captors.

---

1 As a member of the Austro-Hungarian General Staff in 1914-15, Metzger bore a heavy share of responsibility for the disastrous mistakes made in the conduct of the Russian and Serbian campaigns during the first months of that war. Later on, he distinguished himself as a divisional commander in the front line fighting.—Editor's note.

"Kaj Bog dade i sreca junacka!" (What God may give and a soldier's luck!) The parole given to our Army by Ban Jelacic in 1848 when it crossed the Drava into Hungary held good for me now, almost a century later. I got away into the woods and after eight days of wandering and privations arrived at Villach in Carinthia. Here I enjoyed Austrian hospitality for three months before I sought final safety in Italy.

Signed: B. J.

Fermo, October 22, 1945

Document VI

A Croatian mariner, who was a celebrity in the United States in September, 1926, describes his first contact with the British troops in Austria. He gives a revealing eyewitness account of how hundreds of Croatian troops were saved from extradition to Yugoslavia.

My first conversation with the British took place in the Alps, which their advanced units had reached in the course of their march from Italy into Austria. The initial contact that I had with them made a most unfavorable impression upon me. While I was trying to explain our reasons for abandoning our homeland and was expressing our doubts about the equity of the "justice" likely to be meted out by Tito's Communist courts, they informed me that, in spite of everything I was saying, we Croatians would have to make our peace with Tito as best we could because sooner or later we would be placed under his jurisdiction.

After this interview, I went on into Austria and arrived at Wolfsberg on May 12. This place was occupied by various formations of the British Army. Their number of effectives kept increasing steadily. Here we also encountered some compatriots who told us that a large group of Croatian fugitives would arrive from Judenburg near nightfall. In fact, it was just about dusk when the first of a column of some one hundred and fifty vehicles pulled into the town square. Between 2500 and 3000 refugees were loaded into the various automobiles and trucks which made up this column.

We attached ourselves to this caravan as it left Wolfsberg. The caravan proceeded in a southerly direction towards Sankt Stefan, about two and a half miles distant. Here our column halted, and we camped out in the open on meadows that met the road on both sides.

On the morning of the following day, General Tomislav Rolf called me to him. He informed me that during the previous night the British had captured our Minister of Defense and Naval Affairs, Admiral Steinfl. Rolf asked me to go back to Wolfsberg in order to ascertain Steinfl's fate and to do something in his behalf if possible.

In accordance with his request, I made the round of the British units, asking everywhere about the Admiral. Finally, I met a junior officer of Irish descent who cautiously conducted me to the building in which Steinfl was confined. I introduced myself to the guards stationed at this structure and asked them to take me to the officer-in-charge. After hesitating briefly, they offered to do so. The officer-in-charge of the guard then brought me before a British major.

In moving words I explained to this officer who the Croatians were and how we had struggled to obtain our freedom from the Serbian dictatorship. I also told him about the persecutions and sufferings that our people had endured at the hands of other Communists, as well as the Serbians. In particular, I endeavored to impress upon him the situation of the Croatian people vis-a-vis the Communists and their leader Tito. I bluntly said that if Admiral Steinfl were extradited to Yugoslavia, he would be murdered with every cruel refinement of which Marxists are capable. I also asked this officer to do everything he could to prevent the general extradition of our people.

Apparently the information I gave him made some impression upon him, because he went off to consult with superior officers, by telephone, I think. When he rejoined me he said, "Your Admiral is in this unit. He is not a prisoner but, unfortunately, he cannot leave here right now. His situation is considerably different than that of your group. Keep your group where it is now but have them dispose themselves so as not to block traffic on the road."

He spoke to me in a resolute, though friendly tone, and my further pleas in behalf of Admiral Steinfl had no effect upon him. It was evident to me what the Admiral's fate would be. Our own probably grave destiny preoccupied me too. I told the Englishman that we had no food at all, and he at once said that we should send two trucks to pick up supplies of food every second morning. The English would give us food enough for two days on every such trip.

When I returned to our roadside camp, I informed General Rolf of Admiral Steinfl's plight and expressed my apprehension about the fate that awaited all of us.

On the evening of May 16, a British first lieutenant came to where our cars were parked and told us, "Tomorrow, at 8 A.M., your group must be ready to move. Before you set out, all soldiers will be disarmed. Do you have a sufficient number of vehicles to carry your whole group?"

When I asked for information about our destination, he flatly replied that he did not know where we were being sent. The harsh manner in which he delivered his orders increased my fears concerning what was in store for us at the hands of the English and their allies. From this moment on the size of our group began to decrease steadily. A number of people shared my feeling of foreboding and slipped off by themselves to seek their safety as best they could.

General Rolf, however, continued to believe quite firmly in the military honor of the British. Therefore he simply refused to entertain the idea that they might hand us over to the Communists. Nonetheless, he did accept the advice that I gave him concerning hiding some of our small arms. Also, he further put Major Hodko's unit, a tough fighting force, at the head of our column. It was agreed that Hodko and his men would halt at the junction of the highways leading to Wolfsberg, Klagenfurt, and Lawamuend. If we were directed to proceed towards the last mentioned place, that is in the direction of Yugoslavia, they would then be ready for trouble.

At the appointed hour on May 17, a detachment of the British Army, commanded by a captain of Irish descent, arrived at our campsite. The captain commanded us to surrender our arms, which we did in accordance with the plan that we had worked out among ourselves the previous night. No individual registration or general inventory of the weapons was taken by the British. Their soldiers made a rapid inspection of all the yielded arms, and then either loaded them into lorries or destroyed them.

I questioned the captain about our destination. He replied that he had no idea where we were being sent. When I remarked that I could believe the statement made to this effect by the officer who had visited us the night before, but could hardly believe he had orders to take us somewhere without knowing where, he remained silent.

According to our pre-arranged plan, Major Hodko's fighters started off at the head of our column. After we had gone about two miles, a halt was made near Sankt Andrea at the Klagenfurt-Lawamuend road crossing. We understood at once that we were going to be sent to Yugoslavia. Hodko and his men were ready to fight, but it appeared useless for them to try to do so because the Klagenfurt road was blocked by a powerful British tank formation. With pistols or other light weapons they had concealed, what could our men accomplish against these iron monsters which were well equipped with machine guns and cannon?

We then asked the English point-blank to simply shoot us down where we stood rather than send us back alive to that Communist hell, Yugoslavia. I myself approached one British officer and explained to him as briefly as I could the history of our nation, the struggle for freedom from Serbian tyranny that we had waged since 1918, and our anti-Marxist sentiments. Since he and most of the British soldiers who had charge of us seemed to be Irishmen, I stressed our firm Catholicism, the common religion of our forbears as well as his. I believe that he himself was convinced that I was telling him the truth. He seemed to be torn between his sense of military duty, which required the execution of orders he had received from his superiors, and his Christian feelings and the dictates of his conscience. Finally he asked us to be considerate of the position in which he found himself and to continue our march without forcing him to resort to armed violence to compel us to do so. He assured us that at least as far as this day, May 17, was concerned, we would not be extradited into the hands of our enemies. He pointed out also that the road to Lawamuend passed through forest country, that there were several villages along the way, and that neither he nor his soldiers could have their eyes everywhere. In this way, he invited us to leave the column if we wished to and seek safety in the woods or among the Austrian villagers who were, of course, anti-Communists, Catholics like ourselves, and before 1918, our fellow citizens, at least in a sense.

So we decided to continue our journey without putting up a fight at this point. As we went along, I could see for myself how the seats in our vehicles gradually emptied. As the Irishman had promised, his soldiers saw nothing of what was going on. About 4 P.M., we came to a forest a half mile away from Lawamuend. The remainder of our column halted here, the British soldiers remaining with us while their commanding officer went on into the town. Soon he returned, accompanied by a British first lieutenant who was attached to their Intelligence Service. They had me accompany them back into Lawamuend, where they brought me before an English colonel who, I found, was charged with the job of extraditing us into the hands of our enemies. I repeated to him what I had said to other English military men concerning our status as Croatian patriots, and I appealed to his conscience in asking him to do what he could to prevent extradition proceedings from going forward. I urged that the British Army take us under its official protection. Finally he promised to do what he could for us. After this talk, I returned to the remains of our group with the officer in command of our guards.

The British colonel visited us several times that evening to acquaint himself with the details of our situation. It was about 9 P.M. when he called our leaders together and said, "Tomorrow, at 10 A.M., all of you military men will be extradited. Let the civilians who do not want to return to Yugoslavia remain under my protection."

I told him bluntly that I doubted the veracity of the statement that he had just made. Obviously much displeased he said sharply, "Who are you that you do not believe the words of a colonel of the British Army?"

I replied that I had no intention of offending him, and that I knew he was a soldier and therefore obliged to carry out the orders that his superiors gave him.

"That is true," he replied, "but I assure you that your civilians will not be forcibly extradited tomorrow. They will remain under my protection. What will happen to them later on depends upon the resolutions taken by His Majesty's Government."

His words convinced me that at least the civilian members of our group would not be delivered against their will into the hands of the Communist butchers who I knew were preparing a holocaust for every Croatian who came under their control. While I was reflecting upon the significance of his speech, Mr. Bogdan[1] asked me to introduce him to the Colonel. When I had done so, Bogdan handed the Englishman the text of a telegram which he wanted to send to the Holy Father. The proposed telegram contained information concerning the extradition proceedings to which we were exposed, and requested the intervention of His Holiness in our behalf. I explained all this to the colonel, who accepted the text of the wire and promised to forward it.[2]

An hour or so after this scene had been enacted, the Irish officer who had charge of our escort came up to me and said goodbye. He seemed to be deeply affected, but he assured me that the Colonel had told us the truth. He added that he and his men were being sent back to Wolfsberg and that another officer had taken over our custody. He also said that he had spoken to the colonel in our behalf, as far as his military rank allowed him, and that the officer who was replacing him was a man of good feelings and would look out for us in the same way that he himself had tried to do. He wished us good luck and took his leave, obviously quite moved by the circumstances in which we were involved. I feel that he certainly fulfilled his promise to do what he could to prevent our extradition.

As soon as he left us, tanks belonging to another English unit surrounded us. Their commander called me to him and said quite frankly:

> You can believe the words of the colonel in their entirety. That is, only your army personnel will be extradited tomorrow. As far as I am concerned I am letting you know right now that you should not consider the tanks that I have placed around you as enemies. This means that those of you who consider their lives endangered by the extradition proceedings have a whole night at your disposal. There [pointing with his hand] is the forest and [covering his eyes with his hands] my soldiers don't see anything they don't have to see.

He invited me to have tea and biscuits with him. This refreshment did a good deal to cheer me up, for I had eaten nothing all day long. Of course we were not slow to follow the oblique advice that he had

---

[1] Ivo Bogdan is now residing in Buenos Aires; he is editor of the *Studia Croatica*, a quarterly review in Spanish. *Studia Croatica* published a 400-page volume, *La Tragedia de Bleiburg*, on the postwar massacres of the Croatian anti-Communist troops and civilians.—Editor's note.

[2] On August 31, 1966, we wrote directly to Pope Paul VI, because in 1945 he was the Vatican State's charge d'affaires. We asked him whether the said telegram had reached Pope Pius XII. We also requested copies of the documents on the postwar massacres in Yugoslavia, a large number of which, according to the diary of Dr. Giuseppe Massucci, O.S.B., can be found in the Vatican Archives. On October 21, 1966, our request was parsimoniously answered by Bishop Egidio Vagnozzi, the Apostolic Delegate in Washington, D. C., in the following terms: "It has been the policy of the Holy See not to give out any documents from the Archives that are dated after the year 1870."—Editor's note.

given us, and by morning our group counted barely six hundred people, hardly a fifth of our initial figure.

I slept for a while that night, but was awakened early in the morning by the announcement that Tito's Communist Army had taken up positions around us, but that the British troops were still between us and them, our mortal enemies. I was also informed that both General Rolf and his wife had taken poison while General Dragojlov had tried to commit suicide by slashing the veins in his wrists. I advised the British captain in command of our escort of what had happened to Rolf and Dragojlov, and he immediately asked the intelligence officer to arrange the transfer of Dragojlov to the hospital at Wolfsberg. He said quite forcefully that people who were dying should not be extradited before they received medical assistance, whether they were military men or not. Because of his intervention, all three of the attempted suicides were taken to the hospital. The Partisans protested this action, but the British paid no heed to their arguments.

General Rolf died en route to the hospital, but his wife and General Dragojlov were hospitalized and so saved from being extradited.[3] After they had left in an ambulance, Dr. Gomez told me that Rolf had poisoned himself and his wife in a fit of despair because he felt that he was responsible for leading all of us into a death trap from which there was no escape. I was so angered by this comment that I seized Gomez by the shoulders, shook him roughly, and asked if he had taken leave of his senses. I told him that I had received permission from the intelligence lieutenant himself for General Rolf and others to go to fetch water from a nearby spring. Therefore, the general who still had his revolver, could have put himself out of reach of the Partisans easily enough.

While all this was happening, the Partisans surrounding us were glaring at us with undisguised ferocity. But whenever any of them tried to approach us, the British soldiers turned them back. Shortly before ten o'clock that morning, May 18, the British colonel came to us in the company of a Montenegrin Communist lieutenant by the name of Tomitch. The colonel called me over and declared, "As I informed you last night the military personnel will be extradited now, while the civilians who do not want to return to Yugoslavia will stay here under my protection."

I asked him who was a soldier after a war is over. "Whoever considers himself as such," he answered, adding, "let those who do not wish to go back to Yugoslavia separate themselves from those who are being extradited."

As soon as the Communists saw that most of our soldiers were joining the group that did not want to go back to Yugoslavia, they began to pro-

---

3 Many months later General Dragojlov told me, following his recovery, that the British and Austrians had given him back the money he had with him as well as his automobile and all other personal belongings.

test that these soldiers were officers who had to be extradited because of agreements concluded previously between the British and Yugoslav Governments. The English colonel called me to him again and asked if what the Communists were saying was true. This was no time to stick to the letter of the truth, so I told him that the men wearing military uniforms were returnees from German work camps, and that they had exchanged their ragged civilian clothes for discarded uniforms of the Croatian Army. This improvised explanation could hardly have sounded convincing to anyone, let alone to an astute observer like the English colonel. But he appeared to accept it at its face value, and interrupted the yelling and screaming of the Partisans to tell them that all of the people who were not going back to Yugoslavia were civilians and were under his personal protection and that of the British Army. At the same time he gave orders that about four hundred people, most of them women and children, who had sufficient faith in Communist justice to accept extradition, should begin their journey back to the old Domovina.

The British now encircled the group that was remaining on Austrian soil, not for the purpose of extraditing us, but in order to protect us against the Partisans. There was a noticeable change of countenance among the British soldiers. Up to this time they had worn very glum expressions, knowing that military discipline required them to perform an unpleasant duty. Now they openly rejoiced at being converted from our gaolers into our defenders. Undoubtedly, the savage looking Serbian and Montenegrin Partisans had impressed them unfavorably.

Sometime later, the British fed those of us who had remained in their custody. About 3 P.M., our group, numbering some one hundred fifty people, was taken to a barracks located within the British camp at Lawamuend. Our captors told us that what they had done was contrary to British military regulations. But they had to do it to save us from the Partisans who had four companies encamped around Lawamuend.

Thus, thanks to the traditional sense of fair play for which the British have a reputation they do not always deserve, but which was mainfested by the officers and men with whom we had to deal, more than two thousand Croatians were spared slaughter at the hands of Tito's soldiery.

Signed: Ilija Perusina[4]

Ramos Mejia, Buenos Aires
June 10, 1961

---

[4] On September 5, 1926, Ilija Perusina and several other sailors on the Yugoslav steamship *Izabran* had rescued the crew of the American schooner *Albert W. Robinson*. President Coolidge himself decorated Perusina with a gold medal in recognition of his heroic services. American newspapers on several ensuing days gave the hero considerable publicity.—Editor's note.

Document VII

The following account corrobrates what Ilija Perusina has stated in the previous document.

My group left Zagreb on May 6, 1945, just about midnight. We traveled in trucks, which had great difficulty in making their way through endless masses of pedestrians who also were seeking safety in flight abroad. We arrived at the Slovenian town of Brezice at noon on May 7, and remained there until evening, since we sent trucks back to pick up as many people as possible and help them on their way.

That evening, we continued on towards Celje. Again the going was very difficult because the roads were crowded with both troops and civilians. We arrived at Celje on the morning of May 8. Here we received orders to go on at once towards Austria. There was danger that Communist troops might cut off our retreat. However, we reached Ruden and the vicinity of Volkermarkt about 4:00 P.M., without encountering any special difficulties. Here we stopped again and once more sent our trucks back to help those who were traveling on foot.

We felt safe now because we were in Austria and within the British occupation zone. After an overnight's rest, many of us proceeded on foot towards Klagenfurt the following morning. We wanted to contact the British troops as soon as we could. Some of our group remained at Ruden and Volkermarkt, however, awaiting the return of our trucks. I don't know whether these vehicles succeeded in making it back to Austria with loads of pedestrian refugees or not.

I had joined General Rolf's column which came to the Volkermarkt-Griffen crossroad, and continued on towards Griffen. News reached our leaders that the Yugoslav Communist units had penetrated into Austria and were now in Volkermarkt, Klagenfurt, and all through Carinthia. Therefore, we decided to head for Salzburg. To do this we had to go through Wolfsberg and Judenburg.

On the afternoon of that day, May 9, we arrived in Wolfsberg and there, for the first time, we saw British troops. General Rolf sent an English speaking naval officer to inform the British Commander at Wolfsberg of our arrival and to ask for instructions about how we should proceed. After we had waited alongside the road for some time, an English officer appeared and asked us in a sarcastic tone who we were and whose army we belonged to. We told him that we were Croatians and members of the Armed Forces of the Independent State of Croatia. He then said that we were neither troops nor citizens of any political state, but only members of an association that the British did not recognize. He added that we should have surrendered to Tito. General Rolf told this British fool that we were Croatian nationalists who had fought against the Communists because we could not accept the Marxist way of life. Rolf also told the Englishman that we could not surrender to the

Communists because we knew that they would deal with us in an unprincipled and barbarous manner.

On the morning of May 10, we were allowed to go on towards Judenburg. At about three in the afteroon we came to Reichenfels. We stayed here until May 12. Then, the British sent us back to Wolfsberg where we stayed until May 19. On the morning of that day we surrendered our arms to the British. We were loaded in trucks and conveyed southward. Although we did not know where the British were taking us, our immediate future did not seem promising.

When we came to the crossroads near Sankt Andrea, we were dismayed to find that our captors were directing the vehicles transporting us towards Maribor in Slovenia, rather than towards Klagenfurt, as we had hoped they would. As soon as we realized the direction in which we were traveling, we stopped our vehicles and refused to go any further.

The British troops escorting us had blue and violet feathers on their caps and were commanded by a captain who was of Irish descent, probably a Catholic like ourselves. After an argument that lasted for more than an hour, he told us to continue on to Lawamuend where there was an English general to whom we could talk. Our column halted in a meadow a short way to Lawamuend, and General Rolf sent some officers ahead to negotiate with the English commander.

After we had remained there for a while, the Irish captain came back from Lawamuend to tell General Rolf that he had received orders to extradite us to the Yugoslav Communists. Rolf tried to explain to him that two-thirds of the people in our column were civilians, and that many of them were women and children. To extradite these non-combatants would be to violate the laws of both God and man. When he saw that his words were having no effect upon the Irishman, Rolf ceased his arguments. Instead, he asked the officer to have his men shoot us immediately. That way we would be spared the tortures we knew awaited us at the hands of the Communists now that we were disarmed. The British captain refused to order his men to carry out the mass execution for which we asked. General Rolf then requested that our revolver and a little ammunition be returned to us so that we could all commit suicide in preference to extradition.

Apparently this plea made a deep impression on this Irish officer since it came from Catholics like himself whose religion does not permit self-destruction, whatever the circumstances that induce it. He turned away from us, perhaps to conceal his tears.

However, when my friend I.R. and I found that we were indeed going to be extradited into the hands of the Yugoslavs, we made up our minds to escape. So did most of the other 200-250 soldiers contained in Rolf's column, which numbered 800-900 in all. My friend and I quietly absented ourselves from the column at 5:00 P.M. Eventually, we reached safety.

My knowledge of what happened to the rest of our group after our departure is confined to what other survivors, that is, those people who in one way or another managed to avoid extradition, told me long afterwards.

Signed: Eye-Witness #188

(This participant in the tragedy of 1945 does not wish that his identity be revealed because he still has relatives in Croatia who might be made to pay for the disclosures that he has made in the above lines.)—Editor's note.

Document VIII

A Clevelander, himself a survivor of a horrifying massacre on Austrian soil, relives his experiences.

From the fall of 1944 until the great retreat in May 1945, I served as an enlisted man in the Ustasha Railroad Battalions. About the middle of April, my unit was ordered to withdraw from Dubocac because our High Command in Zagreb had decided to evacuate Bosnia and to retire northward. We withdrew to Zagreb by way of Bosanska Kostajnica, Sunja, Sisak, and Petrinja. From the capital, we retreated northwards towards Celje early in May. We had a couple of hot battles with the Communists at Bosanska Kostajnica and near Petrinja. I was wounded in an action between Sisak and Petrinja, and still boast a scar on my leg to remind me of the encounter.

When we were close to Celje, about three thousand Ustashas, Domobrans, and civilians left the main highway and went across a hill in order to avoid having the same trick played upon them that the Partisans had used to capture the German troops who had preceded us into this sector. When they saw that we were not going to allow ourselves to be disarmed as the Germans had, the Communists concluded a truce with us. This agreement provided for a mutual ceasefire, and allowed us to go on past the disarmed Germans without meeting resistance.

A day later, the Communists broke the truce and began to fire upon us. They quickly found out that they could not stop our march, and disappeared when we pursued them. But a little further on, we came to a railroad bridge near the village of Kamnik, and discovered that British troops were holding the far end of this span. The leader of our column, a Domobran colonel, negotiated with the commander of the British troops. The Englishman demanded that we lay down our arms. Then, he said, we could cross the bridge to the far side. The Domobran colonel flatly refused to surrender to the British or anyone else. He knew that Yugoslav Communist forces were concealed in the woods in back of the Englishmen and that Croatian troops which had come through there previously had been turned over to these Reds.

While the talks were going on, we rested in the vicinity of the bridge. While doing so, we heard that there was another bridge near Felkemark. But the civilians who brought this information also told us that this second bridge had been mined, and that the British were on the other side of it, too. While we were talking, we heard explosions in the distance and concluded that the bridge had been blown up.

Since the war was supposed to be over, we decided that it would be unwise to force the passage of the bridge. It was decided that rather than die here, our column should break up into small bands which would make their way back to Croatia to die with arms in their hands. On the evening that this decision was reached, either May 13 or 14, another Croatian and I hid out in a peasant's stable, where we spent the night.

When morning came, we awoke to hear someone asking the peasant if there were any soldiers around. Since we were stupid enough to assume that it was our own people who had come here, we left our belongings and weapons in the stable in order to climb a little hill from which we could see what was going on at the peasant's house. Suddenly we heard someone cry out: "Hello, comrades!"

We realized too late that the intruders were Communists, because they intercepted us when we tried to return to the stables to get our weapons. They told us to load all of our belongings on the peasant's horses. Then they took us to their brigade headquarters. Here, four Partisan officers interrogated us in an effort to find out what we knew about the movements of the Croatian military columns. My friend, who was very young and inexperienced, was quite ingenuous in his answers. I gave my interlocutors plenty of information, but garbled it so much that they were bound to be misled.

Finally, one of the Communist officers asked my friend where he came from. He replied, "From Gracanica near Ozren."

"Oh, you're my close compatriot then. I'm also from Ozren," the officer replied.

Another short heavy-set officer offered me a cigarette saying, "Take and smoke our Partisan cigarettes."

"Thank you! I have cigarettes in my knapsack," I told him.

"I know you Ustashas don't like us Partisans," he remarked with something like a sneer.

"I like everyone whether he's a Ustasha or a Partisan, if he's a good man," I answered him.

After this exchange, the Communists told us to go up on a hill that overlooked the house they were using for headquarters. Another Communist began to question us here. He wore no insignia of rank and looked like a private, but I suspected that he was a commissar. He asked us all kinds of questions about our column. When we left, a group of twenty-five or thirty Ustashas and Domobrans were brought to where we were sitting. There were three women and an Ustasha first lieutenant among them. These people were guarded by Partisans who kept their guns leveled at them at all times.

The Ustasha lieutenant was taken off to be questioned while the rest of us remained together. Suddenly, a Partisan began yelling out, "I am a Serb!" Then a high-ranking Communist officer who wore a red shirt asked if there were any Serbs among us. As there was no answer, he commented bitterly, "It is only you Croats who are fleeing. Woe to the food that you ate and the shoes that you wore. You don't know what is in store for you." Other Communists now began to threaten us openly with death, but some of them tried to reassure us. Perhaps they feared that we would attack them and take their guns away from them. Indeed we should all have tried to do just this. Perhaps all of us would have been shot down, but at least we would have had the satisfaction of fighting for our lives instead of allowing ourselves to be killed like sheep in a slaughterhouse.

After a time, the Ustasha lieutenant returned. He told the men in his group that they had an obligation to aid in the reconstruction of their war-devastated country. He lined up his people and invited my friend and me to join them. The Communist commander asked seven men from the group to volunteer to remain with him. All of them were willing and anxious to do so, but he arbitrarily picked out my friend, myself and five others from the lieutenant's group. The rest were taken towards a nearby lake where, as civilians told us afterwards, the Communists tortured them, cut the letter "U" on their foreheads and chests, and finally killed them.

While this was going on, two higher ranking German officers were brought to brigade headquarters. These men had been promised a safe conduct back to the Reich. But, after they were questioned, guards led them off towards the lake which happened to lie in a different direction than the road they would have had to take to go to Germany. The Germans stopped and refused to go any farther along the path pointed out to them. Their guards cried out loudly, "Comrade Commander, they don't want to go where they're ordered to. They want to go toward Germany."

The commander bellowed blasphemous oaths and told the guards to bring the officers back to headquarters so that he could show them where Germany was located on a map. But the Germans threw their knapsacks down and bolted into the woods. The guards fired a hail of bullets after them, and both of them fell fatally wounded. The Communist officer then remarked, "There! They've arrived in Germany!"

Half an hour later, the Communists brought in four German privates. The Communists questioned them, made a lot of false promises, and took them off towards the lake where I presume they killed them.

After a time, two Croatian Domobrans and an Ustasha were brought to headquarters, also. The Ustasha man had been discovered hiding in the house of a peasant. He was forced to don a Communist uniform. As dusk came on, I was sitting with the other Croatian captives in front of a stable. We were guarded by armed Partisans. There was also a large group of other Communists in the vicinity. They sang derisive songs about Croatia and Germany. However, one guard who was a Croatian, slipped some cigarettes to me in the dark.

Since the Communists were afraid that we would take advantage of the night to escape, they made us go into the stable. There were horses and cows on one side of this building, and pigs on the other. Between them ran a small corridor. About half an hour after we had been incarcerated there, two Communists armed with light machine guns came into the building. They told us to give them our watches, fountain pens, and rings; we had already been relieved of any money we had. I hid my watch and fountain pen in the straw. The Reds yelled at one man because he did not have a watch to give to every Communist who wanted one.

The Communists left with our valuables but soon returned and ordered us to undress right down to our underwear. The Ustasha said to me that he was not afraid to die, but that he didn't like to die a slave's death and one that without doubt would also be accompanied by atrocious torture. I tried to persuade him that nothing so tragic was going to befall him, but I had hardly spoken when two more armed Partisans came in and shone their flashlights on us. "Bosnian, go out for the examination!", they said to the Ustasha man. He gave them an argument, but they succeeded in tying his hands with wire, and took him off. For the next twenty minutes, I could hear nothing but the Communists in the courtyard singing and amusing themselves. Then the guards came back and told us, "Now let's have a Dalmatian go to be examined!" They took another of our group for "examination." At the end of twenty more minutes they led out another Dalmatian. I heard this man ask them something, but they told him to keep quiet.

At similar intervals, the Reds conducted a fourth and fifth victim from the stable. It occurred to me that if I should be killed trying to escape, at least I would avoid being tortured. I examined the stable windows. All save one had bars on the outside. This one unbarred window was nailed shut, too, but while the Partisans were disposing of the sixth man, I pulled out the nails, opened the window and jumped out. The remaining Croatian soldiers followed me, just as the Communists returned to get their seventh victim.

"Pobegli! Pobegli!" (They've fled!)

A hail of bullets came after us, and two of our number fell. I came to a little stream, ducked into it, and pulled branches down over my body. The Reds thrashed all around through the woods and fired haphazardly into the dark, but they never found me. When everything quieted down, I crawled further into the forest, but was still close enough to the stable to hear the Communist officers cursing their men because they had allowed us to escape. I think they may have shot some of the guards to punish them. Later, I heard sounds indicating that they were digging graves for the victims of this macabre night.

I did not feel at all safe in the forest, because the firing of machine guns in the general vicinity was almost incessant. I presume that other Croatian prisoners were being killed in the same general area. Moving very cautiously, I made my way out of the forest and climbed a hill. There were wolves prowling about here, but I had less fear and loathing toward them than I did toward the Reds who were hunting me. I spent a whole day on this hill, and another day and night hidden in another forest. Since I was clad only in my underwear, I suffered greatly from cold as well as hunger.

On the third night after my escape, I saw what I thought was a house. When I reached it, I found that it was a church. In the yard, I tripped over a statue of the Virgin, one of several that the Communists had thrown out of the church.

From the churchyard, I could see a light nearby. I went towards it and found that here there really was a house with people in it. Since I was cold, hungry, and exhausted, I was in no mood to be cautious, so I went right up to it. Fortunately, the people who lived here had almost as low an opinion of the Communists as I did. They told me what they knew concerning the murders and robberies that the Reds had committed. The lady of the household referred to them as "prokleti hudici" (cursed devils). I learned that the Yugoslav troops had withdrawn to the old Yugoslav-Austrian border. Also, I found out that there was another Croatian hiding out in the vicinity.

I had hoped that these anti-Marxist people would give me some clothes. They did not, but at least they fed me and allowed me to sleep in their stable. They provided me with a grease-soiled blanket, too. The Croatian turned up the next morning, and thanked me for saving his life by breaking out of the stable when I did. The peasants had told him where the murdered Croatian soldiers were buried. I wanted to see the place, and went to it. A peasant was standing near it. When he saw me come up he said, "Eto tam su v detelini" (There they are in that clover!). The clover and the grass around it were red, as though scarlet paint had been poured over them. I was told by the peasant that the British had given orders that no one should disturb this resting place of our dead, for they were going to bury the remains themselves. Although I felt like unearthing the corpses to let all the world see what had taken place there, instead of allowing the Englishmen to cover up the evidence, I was afraid that the nearby peasants would denounce me to the British if I did so. Therefore, I contented myself with saying a prayer over the grave. Near it, I picked up some decent underwear, since my own had gone through a rough time of it in the woods and hills the past three days and nights. I also found a pair of old shoes which I put on.

Peasants living nearby found a job for me on the property of Joseph Pusnik. This man took care of me for several days while I hid from the

British, who were looking for me in order to turn me over to the Communists, as they had done to so many other Croatians. At the end of this time, Pusnik passed me along to another peasant. This individual followed regulations, and duly reported my presence to the local authorities. Perhaps the latter let the English know where I was. Pretty soon a British patrol came along and questioned me.

Whatever reasons may have induced them to turn Croatian refugees over to the Communists to begin with, the British knew now that their allies were massacring all Croatian soldiers and civilians that they could lay their hands on. Therefore, the Englishmen showed no disposition to extradite me back to the homeland, but let me keep on working here in Austria.

I confirm the truth of the atrocities described above under oath. I am ready to take this same oath before any competent forum which devotes itself to the investigation of the butcheries of 1945, which I was fortunate enough to survive. Furthermore, I am prepared to point out the places of massacre with which I am familiar any time an interested commission wishes to see them, and acquaint itself with the facts concerning the murders perpetrated there. I should like to stress the fact that I can provide such a commission with many more details concerning Communist atrocities in 1945 than I have set down in this account.

The foregoing statement was read to me twice after I had dictated it. I did not want to sign it after the first reading because there were some inaccuracies in the reporting. When it was read to me for the second time, I did sign it because everything was in accord with my oral recitation.

Signed: Pero Martic

Cleveland, Ohio, December 4, 1960

Chapter 7

Death Marches*

Document IX

I.H. opens his account with a brief analysis of the Croatian troops' surrender at Bleiburg and then describes the brutalities committed by the Partisans against women, children and war prisoners. The witness was much more impressed by individual tragedies than by the sufferings of the entire group; therefore, throughout the testimony he has very touching passages about individual victims. Before reaching Maribor, our eyewitness' "Death March" was forced to run in spite of the physical incapability of hundreds of victims to do so. These "death marchers" were shot for this on the spot. In Maribor itself, I.H. saw masses of prisoners taken to be slaughtered. When he had left Maribor, in the woods along the Maribor-Ptuj road, he saw several freshly covered mass graves. During his further trek towards the Croatian territory he marched past some sixty corpses of the murdered captives and witnessed many atrocities of the Tito troops. When he arrived in Zagreb, our witness was confined in the Maksimir extermination camp where he saw two hundred and fifty of his co-sufferers tied with wire and taken to be liquidated. In Maksimir he heard continuous screams coming from torture chambers. After a seven-day stay in this abattoir, the witness was transferred to the Kanal concentration camp. Here he saw a young prisoner shot for displaying joy at seeing his mother. Towards the end of the account I.H. dedicates a few pages to his and two friends' unsuccessful attempt at escaping. During this attempt he witnessed horrifying liquidations of large groups of prisoners in and around the Kanal camp. Later, our witness was taken to a Zagreb people's court. This time, however, he was neither interrogated nor tried. His trial, during which he refused to sign a false declaration about himself, took place in Zrinjevac. After the trial I.H. was first sent to forced labor in Popovaca and then in Osijek. In both places he saw unbelievable atrocities committed by Tito's people against prominent Croatian personalities and war prisoners. The account closes with a dramatic presentation of the tortures and mass murders at Osijek.

During the first years of the war of 1941-45, I served in the Croatian Armed Forces as a sergeant in the Second Preparatory Brigade which was stationed in Zagreb. By 1945, I had attained the rank of Color Bearer, in which capacity I participated in the final battles fought by the Croatian

* The "Death Marches" chapter includes a wealth of material that belongs not only to this part of our volume, but also to the following chapters of the documentation.—Editor's note.

Army and in its retreat into Austria. On May 15, I was among the Croatian soldiers who laid down their arms at Bleiburg under the impression that we were surrendering to the English.

Soon after giving up our weapons, however, we found to our complete consternation that the British had an agreement with the Partisans, that the latter were to take charge of us. As the column of which I was a member returned from Bleiburg to Dravograd, we came to a wooden bridge which spanned the Drava River. Fifty Partisans armed with automatic weapons were waiting for us on this bridge. They separated the commissioned and non-commissioned officers from the private soldiers and advised the former that they were being sent to Zagreb by train.

As Color Bearer, I was included in the commissioned and non-commissioned group. We were taken to the rail station indeed, but then were led on past it, ostensibly to a more convenient place to answer to roll call. Our Partisan guards conducted us into the courtyard of a building which stood on the left hand side of the street and ordered us to sit down. We were not allowed to converse with one another and became suspicious that we would be liquidated.

Suddenly several people who were passing down the street which ran by our halting place cried out simultaneously, "Run away! They are going to shoot you!"

Five or six guards ran out onto the street to apprehend the individuals who had given us this warning. Many of the prisoners took advantage of this confusion to make a dash for liberty. They got outside the courtyard and tried to lose themselves among the crowds in the street. However, the guards opened fire with their machine guns and mowed down about a hundred people, soldiers, civilians, men, women, and children alike. As an experienced soldier, I did not join this exodus because, when you serve in a war long enough, you acquire a kind of sixth sense that tells you when to take a chance and when not to. My instinct and snap judgement of the situation told me that I would never get past the gate of the fence which surrounded the yard. From this spot I was able to see what happened outside the enclosure. I remember that I watched a woman who was running in the direction of the Drava, dragging along with her an eight or ten-year-old girl. They had gone fifty paces when a burst of machine gun fire cut them down.

After this grim episode was over, we were formed into a column and marched off in the direction of Maribor. On the afternoon of this day we came to a small hamlet somewhere between Dravograd and Maribor. I saw a girl leave the column a short distance ahead of me and go toward a well to get a drink of water. A mounted Partisan shot her without warning the moment she stepped off the road. He must have pumped at least ten shots into her body, which was left lying where it fell.

It took us two days to get from Dravograd to Maribor. When we were about eight miles away from Maribor, the mounted Partisans who guarded us began to yell at the top of their voices, "Bandits! Run forward!"

They also started to shoot at us quite indiscriminately. Although we were dead tired, and our tongues were stuck to our palates as a result of going three days without a drop of liquid (or food either), we tried to run. Many people could take no more than fifty or sixty strides before they became exhausted and fell out of the column. The guards shot them down with their automatic weapons. It is difficult to say how many of us were killed in this manner. I know that between forty and fifty men in my section of the column were slain. Since the entire column stretched out for a length of at least six miles, it is anybody's guess as to how many lives were lost in all.

There was a sixty-five year old Catholic priest in my own group in this column of misery. I do not know his name. He could not continue running very long, so some of the younger men seized him by the arms and carried him along with them to keep him from dropping out of line and thus exposing himself to immediate execution. We tried to persuade him to take off his clerical garb so that he would not be identified as a priest. He adamantly refused to do this. We all prayed aloud to the Lord to give us strength to endure this hardship. But that evening the Partisans sought him out and led him off somewhere. I have no certain information concerning his fate, but it is my opinion that he was killed.

When we entered Maribor we found the streets filled with Croatian prisoners of war. I saw perhaps twenty Germans also, three of them officers. These officers had already suffered terrible beatings. Since my part of the column halted for a few minutes because of the congestion ahead of us, I saw these Germans of commissioned rank being led into a garden close to the street down which we were proceeding. I could see how the Partisans robbed them in the garden. One officer had a ring and a watch which he had concealed in his cap, the second had a can of food in his pocket, while the third appeared to have nothing of value on his person. The Partisans made all three of them lie down with their faces to the ground. Then they killed the hapless trio, turned the corpses over on their backs and smashed in the faces of the dead men with their gun butts. Presumably they did this in order to keep the victims from being recognized.

We were not placed in a concentration camp at Maribor. Instead we spent the night out on the streets. At about 10:00 P.M. the Partisans began to seek out specific categories of individuals among the multitude of prisoners. Every one who bore an insignia of rank, or who wore a uniform that looked as if it might be that of an officer with such insignia removed, was separated from the rest of us and led off to a place of no return. This process of "selection" lasted throughout the night. Finally, about 4:00 A.M., the rest of us were ordered to get up and continue our journey.

We proceeded in the direction of Ptuj without knowing from one minute to the next what would happen to us. There is a pine tree forest on the right hand side of the road that leads from Maribor to Ptuj. At this stage of our "march," the guards did not prevent us from going behind trees along our line of march when we had to relieve ourselves. When I had gone forty or fifty paces into the forest to do this, I came upon a horrifying sight. Before me there were three large craters that had evidently been made by the explosion of bombs. They were about ten feet or so away from each other. All three were completely filled with the bodies of murdered Croatian soldiers. A thin covering of earth was thrown over the top of each hole, but arms and legs were sticking out from this inadequate shroud. Shaken by this discovery, I threw myself to the ground at the edge of one of the holes and dug up a little of the earth with my fingernails. I uncovered a very young man whose head had been smashed in with some kind of sharp object. Since the corpses did not smell, it was evident that the slaughter had taken place recently, probably the previous night or the day before.

I made the sign of the Cross over this mass abattoir and rejoined the column, determined to keep my eyes open for a favorable opportunity to escape. Again my warrior's instinct told me that this was not the time to try to do so.

A little farther on we came to the junction of two roads, one leading to Varazdin, the other to Krapina. On a field that extended between these highways, some forty meters from their intersection, there lay the corpses of perhaps sixty men who may have been killed during the preceding night. Some of the bodies were completely nude.

During the two days that we followed the Krapina road, we found opportunities to pull up very young potatoes from the fields, thus relieving our hunger to some extent. Many prisoners ate grass and snails too. As for myself, I kept my eye out for young ears of corn which grew here and there. I want to stress that in contrast to the experiences that we had in other parts of Slovenia, the Slovenes of this region displayed great sympathy for us. Sometimes they would toss pieces of bread to us. Their conduct was altogether different from that of the Slovenians who lived along the Dravograd-Maribor highway. That population not only refused to give us food or drink, but also stole from us whatever our Partisan escorts had not already helped themselves to.

When we arrived at Krapina, a large Partisan unit took charge of us. On the night of our arrival, this crew drove us like a herd of cattle in the direction of Mirkovci through the small village of Trgoviste. I remember that there were barracks that the Germans had constructed during the war at the last named place. From Trgoviste we went on to Luka where we spent the night camped around the village schoolhouse. And here, for the first time in six days, our captors fed us. We all received a small head of green onion and a piece of bread. To compensate themselves for their munificence towards us, the Partisans took everything of value that our previous captors had missed.

From Luka we were herded down the railroad tracks which led to Zagreb. We had to get off the tracks to allow a slow-moving train to pass us just after we had left Luka behind us. Someone on this train tossed a piece of bread in the general direction of our column and three railroad conductors who were marching with us ran to pick it up. The Partisans killed all three of them near a fruit tree which stood by the railroad tracks.

On this same day we arrived at the concentration camp of Jankomir, which was located close to Vrapce. Since there had been a model horticultural establishment in Jankomir during Habsburg times, there had been many transplanted fruit trees here. We stayed at the Jankomir camp for two days. While we were there one young man became so ill that he was unable to stand up unassisted. Blood trickled from his mouth almost continuously. Another youth who remained constantly beside him asked the guards to get a doctor to examine the sick man. Instead of doing so the guards, who were Serbian judging by their language, took the sick youth aside and smashed in his head with their rifle butts. Then they threw his body into a brook.

We received no food at all while we were at Jankomir. One enterprising non-commissioned officer occupied himself by boiling tree leaves in a can to relieve his hunger. A guard saw what he was doing and ordered him to extinguish the fire; he then dealt the Croat a blow with his gun butt. The NCO was knocked senseless and fell to the ground. As soon as he recovered consciousness, the Partisan ordered him to get up and led him to a stone building where other Partisans joined in beating the unfortunate man with metallic rods. Eventually they beat him to death and threw his body onto a dungheap.

After the two day stop at Jankomir, we were sent towards Precko, a suburb of Zagreb. As far as I can recall we reached the concentration camp here on May 24, but found that it was too crowded to accommodate us. So we remained in it for only two or three hours. During this time the hands of about two hundred and fifty prisoners were bound with wire, one man's wrist tied to that of another.

From the Precko camp, we were marched to the camp at Maksimir, another Zagreb suburb. Six trucks were waiting for us here. Two hundred and fifty of the wire-bound men were thrown (quite literally) into these vehicles. Those of us whose hands remained untied were herded into the camp. We were aware of the fate that awaited our bound comrades. Some twenty minutes after they were taken away we heard machinegun fire from the direction of the Stara Ciglana (the old brick factory). When we heard the shots, we recited an "Our Father" in unison for the repose of the souls of the victims.

We remained at Maksimir for six or seven days. A very young Communist came among us every day and looked us over while we stood lined up in military formation. He would select certain individuals who would be pulled out of line and tied with wire. Then they were taken to a building which had formerly served as a stable. It was perhaps a hundred and fifty feet away from the camp. In this broken down edifice,

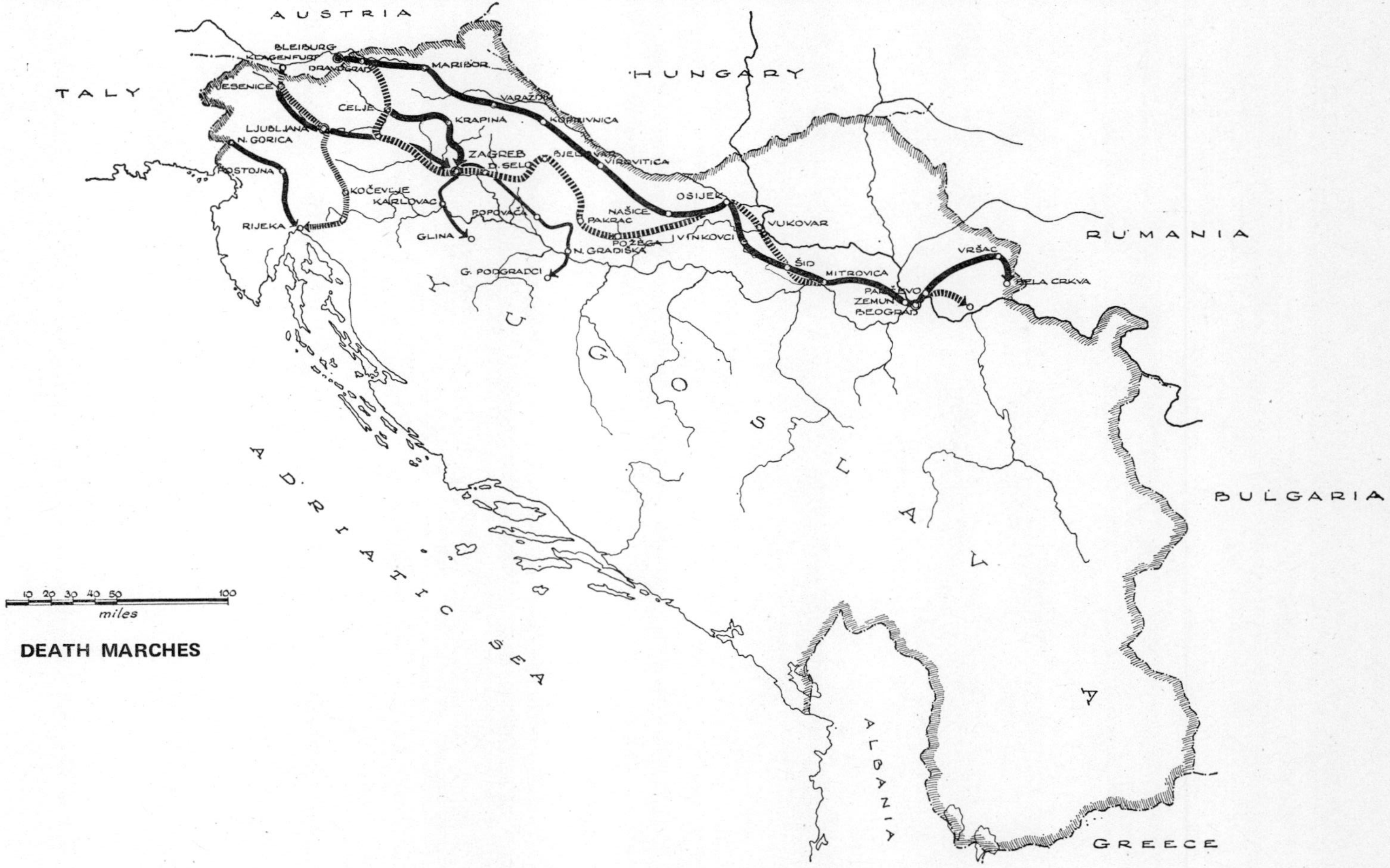

DEATH MARCHES

the bound prisoners were subjected to the most brutal tortures. Every day we could hear cries of pain and anguish coming from this building. Some men probably died from the beatings and planned torture to which they were exposed. Most of them, however, were only half dead when they were loaded onto trucks which conveyed them to their final execution.

On the sixth or seventh day of our stay at Maksimir, two hundred of us were bound with wire as the preceding victims had been. I was in this batch of candidates for slaughter, but for some reason we were not killed as the others had been. Instead we were taken to the Kanal concentration camp which was also in the suburbs of Zagreb.

I remained at Kanal until June 29. The regimen here was extremely severe. Every building in the place was surrounded by thickly interlaced barbed wire. Guards were stationed fifty paces apart along a stretch of road that ran between the camp and the nearest residential sites. During the nights that I spent there, patrols made constant inspections.

One morning sometime in June, I happened to see two women walking along the road that led by the camp. One of them was young while the other was considerably older. A young Color Bearer shouted to them from a barracks window, "Mother!" The older woman stopped and waved to her son. Immediately a Communist guard opened fire with his machine gun upon the young Color Bearer who was so delighted to see his mother that he had lost all sense of precaution. The boy fell from the window and died in full view of his mother and the other woman, who perhaps was his sister or fiancee. Individual tragedies are always more poignant than group ones and make a deeper impression upon those who have the misfortune to witness them. So it is really impossible for me to convey in appropriate words the horror of this grim little episode.

Soon after this incident, a general alarm was sounded in the camp. Probably someone had escaped in one manner or another. The guards were reinforced and everyone was confined to the barracks for the remainder of the day, nor was anyone allowed to receive any packages of food or clothing that might be brought to him by relatives and friends.

On the following day, the Partisans brought a skilled worker from Zagreb to repair the lavatory. Three prisoners, myself included, were assigned to help him. He had with him a very powerful scissors which he used to cut sheet iron; it was a sharp instrument with which I was not familiar, but we all saw at first glance that it could be used to escape this hellhole. So, when no guards were watching us, we took this cutting tool. Probably the workman saw what we did, but he said nothing. He was a good Croatian who understood our situation, though constrained to serve the Tito regime in order to save his own life. On leaving he said to us, "Good luck!"

Three of us prepared to make our escape by following an old uncovered canal which ran toward the railroad shops; fortunately, I was well acquainted with this part of the city. It was bad luck for one of us,

Ivan Herceg, an interior decorator from Zagreb, that we were obliged to wait for suitable weather before we risked an escape. The night before we committed ourselves to this undertaking, Herceg was taken off by the Partisans and shot near Stara Ciglana. Later I learned that he was murdered in the company of the Orthodox Metropolitan of Zagreb, Germogen. I have vivid recollections of the Stara Ciglana, even though I had the luck not to visit it during the month of June, 1945. During the period of my incarceration in the "Ustasha" barracks of the Kanal camp, however, our Partisan guards would say to us again and again, "It is a waste to use bullets on you bandits! We shall knife all of you at the Forestry College (Sumarski Fakultet)!" Stara Ciglana, that is, the old brick factory, is located right behind the Forestry College.

On the night after Herceg's disappearance, one other prisoner and I crept stealthily out of the barracks about 1:00 A.M. It was dark, rainy, and windy, the kind of night that we had been waiting for. I led the way, and cut an opening through the first and second barbed wire fences that we came to, using the tool we had stolen with the tacit consent of the Zagreb plumber. Once we got through the second fence we were at the edge of the canal, which was filled with dirty water and various kinds of refuse. We plunged into it just in time to escape the notice of a patrol which was passing by. A five minute trudge through the canal brought us to the last barracks building in the camp. I saw a number of men out of this barracks and heard someone say, "When that's done, let one guard remain!" Then I saw Partisan guards drag twenty bound men into a concrete installation which looked like a bunker. Two Partisans armed with machine guns stood at the entrance to this place and discharged several bursts of fire into it. Screams, terrible swearing, and prayers could be heard coming from within. Someone shouted, "Fire again!" After they had done so, the two machine gunners entered the bunker and fired two or three more times. Absolute silence followed.

Overcome with horror, I felt my skin sweating although it remained cold as ice. My hands and feet were numb and I must have lost consciousness for a moment. I came to my senses when my companion, Luke, who had crept along behind me, pulled me by the leg. We crept cautiously along to the last fence, which stood on the brink of a larger canal. Our spirits lifted, for we knew that in two minutes we would be outside this abattoir—then suddenly we stopped abruptly, stunned by the discovery that this last barrier between us and freedom was composed of thick metallic rods which our scissors could not cut. There was nothing we could do but return to our own barracks unobserved before the lights were put on.

On June 29, I was sent with nineteen other Croatians, both men and women, into the so-called OZNA II prison which was located at 2 Gjordjic Street in Zagreb. Here I was held for two days in a kind of windowless cave. Two other men were imprisoned with me. We received no food during our confinement here.

On the morning of July 2, I was taken to the present day district court at 2 Amruseva Street where trials for so-called "offenses against national honor" were conducted. I awaited trial at this place in the company of the industrialist, Masina, who, as far as I can recall, owned a sock and stocking factory. Later on I heard that he was eventually shot, but I have no certain information regarding his fate.

As it turned out, I was not tried at the court on 2 Amruseva Street. Instead I was transferred on July 8 to the district court at Zrinjevac where the military court of the Second Yugoslav Army conducted the trials of prisoners accused of "offenses against national honor." Because of the long period of privations and maltreatment to which I had been exposed, and especially because of the inadequate nourishment I had received for the past two months, I was already gravely ill at this time. A young man from Srijemski Karlovci and a Domobran Major carried me from the ground level of the Zrinjevac court building to the third floor. I cannot remember the major's name but I do recall that it had sounded Italian, Martini, Zorini, Dorini, or something like that.

At the Kanal camp, a written statement of my "guilt" had been prepared by one Ivan Suster, who was charged with investigating my past. Since I refused to sign this carefully concocted document Suster nearly beat me to death on three occasions. These beatings were a major reason for the poor state of my health when I arrived at Zrinjevac. I had refused to sign the written statement that Suster drew up because he did not record my declarations, but on the contrary used his own imagination so effectively that if ever I had affixed my signature to such a confession, I would have been condemned to death by far more impartial courts than those of the Second Yugoslav Army. As it was, when I was brought to trial I had not acknowledged the truth of the accusations brought against me. This fact caused some confusion to the prosecution because most of the prisoners who stood trial were coerced beforehand into signing a written confession of their guilt.

On July 17, I was tried together with Dr. Kumicic, Lovro Matacic, who was director of the Zagreb Opera, General Lukic, Colonel Canic, and a young priest from Srijem (Sirmia). The court was composed of four Partisan officers, a Captain Vlado Ranogajec acting as presiding judge.

The procedure was as follows: first I was brought into an empty courtroom. Next the judges filed in one by one. The prosecuting or state's attorney, a Major Molnar, read out the accusation made against me and concluded by saying, "Let the prisoner be judged according to articles one or three or one through three." A hurried consulation among the judges followed and one of them yelled at me, "Bandit! Have you understood? Bow your head! Now revenge will be taken upon you!" Another judge shouted, "You don't have a defender and you don't have any right to defend yourself!" Finally, Presiding Judge Ranogajec declared: "Since it has been ascertained that you are an enemy of the People and an Ustasha by conviction, there is no place for you among honest men—Guard, take him out!"

The whole proceeding took less than an hour. By 4:00 P.M. I was back in my cell. Two hours later I was brought into another room where a Partisan first lieutenant confronted me. The only question that he asked me was if I knew how many entrances there were to the Ustasha concentration camp at Jasenovac during the war. I answered that I did not know. Then I was led back to my cell.

At 8:00 A.M. on the following day, Captain Ranogajec entered my cell accompanied by a strong detail of prison guards. He read out to me the decision reached by the court. I was sentenced to eight years' imprisonment. Of course, I was fortunate to escape the death penalty but at the moment I didn't appreciate the leniency shown to me. I was so sick that I really would have welcomed death because it promised a relief from further sufferings.

Not everyone brought to Zrinjevac was as lucky as I was. Every night those sentenced to die were hung in the courtyard of the district court. Such victims invariably were thrown headfirst down the stairs by the guards. Some of them suffered broken backs or heads and the rest of us had to wash the bloodstains from the stairs on the following mornings.

The day after my trial I was taken with Dr. Kumicic, Director Matacic, General Lukic, Colonel Canic, and the priest from Srijem to another military court which was located at Sesvete near Zagreb. The data that our captors had compiled was checked here, and Dr. Kumicic and General Lukic were again interrogated. Director Matacic was cursed roundly for refusing to go to Moscow to conduct a concert there.

On July 19, we were put to work in an old mill which was located at Popovaca. Since there was no room for us to sleep inside this building, we had to get what rest we could at nights on the lawn outside. The work to which we were assigned involved cleaning the nearby railroad station which had suffered severe damage during the war.

One day a husky man whose arms were bound with wire was brought in among us. The guards hung him from the limb of an oak tree which stood near the camp buildings. That evening they took him down but again tied his hands and feet so that he was unable to move or to defend himself from the ants which crawled into his ears, nostrils, mouth and eyes. He cursed and yelled for some time but finally was silent. When morning came the guards unbound his feet but he was unable to stand up. There was a woman in the camp who could not endure seeing this treatment of a helpless man. She ran at the Partisans and hit one of them in the face. The guards then tied her up and dragged her off somewhere. We never saw her again. Her heroic gesture was all in vain, because the man whose plight had aroused her pity and anger seemed to be little daunted by the sufferings to which the Partisans exposed him. He was still able to laugh at them and ask them when they were going to get serious and really try to hurt him. We were told that he was the *veliki zupan* (High Count or Governor) of the county of Bjelovar-Krizevci. His captors could not break his spirit. Finally he was sent to Zagreb to stand another "trial."

From Popovaca, I was sent with a group of two hundred other prisoners to work in the village of Struzec. Because of the maltreatment and hunger which I continued to suffer, I became sick here once again. I managed to drag myself around until August 15, on which date I was allowed to go to my home to convalesce. This unexpected boon was granted to me because there was no space for me in the Communist-run hospitals, and the authorities probably preferred to have me die at home rather than on their hands. Back at my home in Zagreb I fooled everyone by making a rapid recovery. I got about the city during my period of convalescence, but was expelled from the capital when Tito issued an amnesty towards the end of the summer. Together with my family I went to Osijek, where I found employment as a chimney sweep.

A real reign of terror still prevailed in Osijek. Every night people were executed and buried in the so-called Stara Tvrdjava (old fortress) which dates from Habsburg times. It is located on the left bank of the Drava, that is on the side of the old Hungarian Baranya province. Many touching scenes were enacted here as the parents, brothers, sisters, or children of the victims came to visit the freshly dug graves. However the Partisan guards would not allow these sorrowing relatives to approach the places where their loved ones lay. The mourners could only throw flowers toward the bodies of their sons, fathers, or brothers, or else kneel on the road leading to Kistarda and pray for them.

In the capacity of chimney sweep, I had access to the prison buildings in Osijek. Thus I was able to see a number of happenings which the authorities had no idea that I might witness. There was a Partisan officer nicknamed "Bubalo" (The Drummer). He liked to use a knife on the Croatian prisoners who were given to him to dispose of. Several times from an unseen vantage point in the prison building I saw him place a person in a prone position. Then he would lift up his victim's head with one hand, while slitting the man's throat with a knife that he held in the other. I do not know how many Croats this fiend butchered, but I am certain the number was considerable. Probably "Bubalo" was insane all along, as were many of the Partisans who had served under Tito. In any case he went stark raving mad one day during the winter of 1945-46, and his colleagues took him away.

Forty-eight Croatian intellectuals were tired and condemned to death at the Osijek prison while I was employed there. Among them was one man named Seper whom I knew before the war; he was an outstandingly patriotic Croatian. These victims were packed all together into a single cell which was designed to accommodate only a few prisoners at most. Once they were jammed inside, the guards tossed hand grenades through the bars into the cell. This novel method of murder was used because the families of the victims were waiting outside on the streets, expecting the Communists to lead prisoners to the Stara Tvrdjava to be executed.

I guarantee on my life and honor that everything that I have described above is true.

Signed: I. H.

Sweden
November 8, 1965

Document X

M. Gavran first describes the massacre of two hundred wounded Croatian soldiers near Maribor. He then describes the German surrender to the Partisans at Celje and the Croatians' refusal to surrender there, at Dravograd, and two miles before Bleiburg. He depicts in detail the Croat surrender at Bleiburg. On the very first night after the surrender, Tito's troops murdered Croatian officers, looted the prisoners' column and identified and killed various people. Past Dravograd, hundreds of victims, including women and children, were liquidated. During the subsequent trek, large groups of "Death Marchers" were murdered each night. Gavran noticed mass graves at Celje, observed the corpses of fifteen Croatian Marines slain at Zidani Most, and witnessed the extremely brutal end of a considerable number of Croatian captives at Samobor. At this point in the account he emphasizes the Croatian population's hospitality toward the prisoners. Not far from Zagreb, Gavran hid for a day, but the Partisans found him and forced him to march to Sisak. On this stretch, too, he saw a great many prisoners murdered. At Sisak itself he witnessed a liquidation of a hundred and twenty members of the legendary Croatian Black Legion. Gavran, among seven hundred prisoners, was then transferred from Sisak to Karlovac. On the Sisak-Karlovac march he saw over sixty of his co-sufferers killed by the Serbian Partisan guards. During his transfer to Ogulin, he escaped to Italy.

In 1945, I was serving as a Color Bearer of the Second Battalion of the Second Marine Division of the Croatian Army. My immediate superior was First Lieutenant Franjo Luksic. Two days before Germany capitulated, I suffered a neck wound in a battle fought against the Partisans at Kostajnica. On Wednesday, May 9, I was evacuated by truck from the hospital in Zagreb along with a number of other wounded men. At this time the Partisans already were entering the city and engaging in local fights with rearguards of the Croatian Army, or die-hard elements who refused to leave the capital.

Since many thousands of civilians were fleeing northwards to escape the Partisans, we did not reach Krapina until very late on the evening of the 9th. I was among two hundred and fifty wounded Croatian soldiers who were placed aboard a German hospital train. We arrived at Celje on the morning of the 10th and received food at the railroad station there. Following this meal we moved on towards Maribor.

Four stations away from Maribor, our train came to a halt. The German guards began to shoot and soon a regular battle seemed to be developing. We thought that the Russians had attacked the train, but it turned out to be Partisan formations that had ambushed it. Soon the Partisans broke into the first car and began to loot and murder the wounded. From our position farther back in the train, we could hear cries of anger, pain, and desperation coming from this car. Later on, Marko Klujevic, one of the wounded soldiers in this wagon, told me that when the Serbian and Slovenian Partisans first got into the car they plundered the wounded men and beat them with their gun butts. Then they shot them, using both machine guns and revolvers to finish this grisly work. Some of the Serbs used knives on the wounded too. Mainly severely wounded men were killed in this car, because the less badly injured jumped out of the windows and doors and got away into the woods. Among the invalids who were massacred by the Serbian and Slovenian Partisans were Joseph Krajinovic from Foca, Anton Grlic, and Ljubo Nikolic. I believe that in all, two hundred wounded Croatian soldiers and about a hundred German guards were slaughtered in this tragedy that befell our train.

I escaped from the car in which I was riding, together with fifteen other wounded men. We ran into the woods and headed back towards Celje and the general direction of the Croatian Army. Among the men accompanying me were Mijo Kurtusic and Ivan Galic.

On the evening of this day we reached Celje. Here I witnessed the disarmament of the German troops. Some of the Germans would not give up their arms to the Partisans and fought them. Our Croatian troops likewise refused to surrender to Tito's people and shot their way through wherever they had to. Finally the Slovene Partisans agreed to let the Croatians pass on through Celje without laying down their arms. However they refused to grant this permission to the Germans.

When I passed through the center of the town, I found that Croatian troops had complete control of the downtown section. The Partisans had withdrawn to the outskirts and suburbs. I spent the night close to the highway which runs towards Dravograd. The next day I started marching and got to Dravograd two days later. Since I was wounded, I made slow progress when I had to depend on my feet to take me places, but fortunately I got a number of rides along the way, sometimes in trucks, and usually in private motor cars belonging to Croatian military officers or civilians.

As we neared Dravograd, we ran into strong Partisan forces again. They summoned us to surrender, which we refused to do. The column with which I was traveling penetrated the Partisan lines and went on towards Bleiburg.

When we approached this town, we heard that the negotiations with the British initiated by General Herencic had been repudiated by General Boban. The latter ordered his men to attack the Partisans who were trying to bar their way into Austria. I was an eyewitness of the battle that ensued and saw some twenty of our men and as many or more of the Partisans fall before my eyes.

Another bitterly fought conflict took place just three or four kilometers out of Bleiburg. Cannons were employed in this battle. Our men won and we moved on over the bodies of the Partisans to the field that lies outside Bleiburg. We passed fifteen or twenty burned-out trucks, most of which were still smoking. I saw the corpses of German soldiers in these trucks. It was a horrifying scene; the stench of burnt flesh lay heavy on the air.

We remained all night long on the Bleiburg field. At 4:00 P.M. on the following day, orders were received to report the number of effectives in each unit. At the moment that this order arrived I was sitting with the battalion commandant of my own outfit. I ran to our company and counted seventy-six men. Fifteen days before we had numbered two hundred and twenty. We had lost heavily in the fighting around Zidani Most where we had protected the withdrawal of the main columns of our army. It is probable that my brother Frank, a boy of only nineteen, was killed in the combat that took place there.

Our battalion commandant reported our numerical strength to the commander of the brigade and was told that we were to surrender to the British. We also learned that we were going to receive newer and better weapons from the English because they wanted us to help them fight the Russians.

In accordance with the instructions that came, allegedly from the High Command of the Croatian Army, some units hoisted white flags denoting surrender. Other detachments and individuals hid their weapons and threw away their medals and decorations. I saw First Sergeant Ante Krizic, a much decorated veteran from Tohovac, throw away his machine gun along with his decorations and burst into tears because of the incomprehensible order that we had received. Our column, again in obedience to instructions from some unidentified source, began to move forward past a pile of discarded weapons. Suddenly we heard a mine explode. An officer had blown up his own car and killed himself, his wife, and his children by so doing. Undoubtedly he had heard that we were going to be extradited into the hands of the Partisans.

Not all of our officers behaved in this utterly inexcusable manner, but it did seem that a great many of them were overcome by despair when they realized that the British were not going to accept the surrender of our Army. What they should have done at this juncture was lead us in an attack upon the British lines and upon any Communist troops that dared to get in our way. Although the English had planes, tanks, and artillery, I think that we could have penetrated their lines in a night attack and fought our way through into the interior of Austria where we certainly would have had a better chance for survival than we had here on the frontier of Slovenia.

On the evening of the surrender we were brought to a large fenced enclosure. Before this place stood a huge British tank with an English soldier sitting atop it calmly puffing away at a pipe. Around him were a number of Partisans.

As long as there were British troops in our immediate vicinity, the Partisans behaved relatively well towards us. After the nightfall they sent an invitation to our officers to dine with theirs. Immediately our superiors divined what was in store for them. My own lieutenant, Jelic, told me with a gloomy look on his face: "My dear Gavran, if you survive, go to my house and tell my wife that I am not alive anymore."

We never saw the officers who responded to the supper invitation again.

After this incident, our column turned back towards Maribor. When we came to Dravograd, the Partisans evidently thought that they were far enough away from the British to begin looting us. They took our pens, watches, rings, boots, shoes, other valuables, and all good clothing that we had on our backs. While so engaged they held revolvers trained on us and threatened to kill us if we resisted. They stripped me of my uniform, giving me a lice-ridden one in exchange. However they assured us that we would soon receive the clean white uniforms that are worn by prisoners of war.

Once the looting process was completed, a new group of Partisans appeared. They identified various people, took them to the edge of the woods, and shot them there. Some of the victims were killed close to the highways and settlements, but others were conducted deeper into the woods to be disposed of. We could hear cries of pain and shots coming from the forest, and often we could see men being killed. In my own section of the column alone, I saw six or seven men shot before we entered Dravograd. As we crossed the bridge leading into this town, a group of accordion-playing gypsies greeted us with mocking and ribald songs.

At Dravograd, the column in which I was marching was split into two sections. One part continued on towards Maribor, while the other turned in the direction of Celje. I was in the Celje group and, like many other prisoners, feared that we were being sent to Russia. At the Dravograd rail station I encountered a group of Air Force men who asked me to join them. I was lucky I did not because I discovered later that half of them were murdered only a few kilometers beyond Dravograd. Pilot Penjak from Brcko, who survived this massacre, told me that the Partisans ordered the airmen to lie down along the bank of the Drava. When they did so, the Communists opened fire on them with machine guns. Other survivors confirmed his story.

Our guards told us that any members of our column who were too tired to proceed any further on foot could be taken by train. A number of exhausted and starving men reported for such transport, even though they knew that they might be boarding their last train. Of course, they were not even put on a train. The Partisans led them to the bank of the Drava, machine gunned them, and threw their bodies into the river. Among the victims were many women and children who were too fatigued to walk any further and who therefore had taken the chance that the Partisans might actually send them on by train. A soldier who escaped from this butchery hid nearby and witnessed all of the details. I noticed myself that a good many people in our column reported voluntarily for the special rail transport promised them, even though they realized that they were asking for a passage to death.

We were now only a herd of starved, naked, and confused remnants of what had once been human beings. Overconfident and bold Partisans, mounted on horses and armed with machine guns, escorted us. Often they beat us or took some individuals aside and shot them. Anyone who fell behind the main column was murdered without warning or delay. Many times I had to witness the slaughter of my companions in misfortune. Women and children experienced the same fate as men when they could not keep up.

On one night, our Partisan guards took off groups of twenty prisoners at a time and shot them a hundred meters away from the place where the rest of us had laid down. I do not know how many groups were massacred in this manner before I was awakened by the shots, but I do know that three such detachments were "liquidated" during the time that I was awake. In order to avoid being included in one of the clusters of prisoners destined to be executed, I crept into the center of our column. The same thing happened on many other nights.

Near Celje I saw a number of pits which had been dug three or four meters off the road. Dirt was thrown on top of some of them. I was told that dead horses were thrown into these places along with the bodies of murdered Croatians and Germans.

At Zidani Most, fifteen men of the Marine Division were murdered, and, still clad in their own blood-soaked uniforms, left along the road. A few branches had been thrown over them but their bodies were still plainly visible to passersby. I observed these and other gruesome details with great attention because I was looking for the body of my brother. However, I did not find it.

The most horrible scene of my "Death March" took place at Samobor where the Partisans had identified a number of Ustashas. Those whom they recognized were bound and led into a house where they were murdered under extremely brutal circumstances.

We did not receive a bite of food until we reached Zagreb a week or more after the surrender. Some of us managed to survive this long only because the Germans had abandoned many cans of food along the road and occasionally we were able to pick up one of these and share it between us under cover of darkness. Sometimes, too, we found oats and were able to mix these with sugar beets. The Partisans did not allow us to get a drink of water, but we were able to gulp a few hurried mouthfuls from puddles along the side of the road once in a while. The guards made us run through the villages, killing everyone whose wind gave out. After we entered Croatian territory, the people would bring food and drink to us whereas the Slovenians removed the buckets from their wells so that we could not use them. It is some consolation to me to remember that in these days of national disaster the civilian population of Croatia did everything it could to alleviate our plight.

When we were about seven kilometers from Zagreb, I got away from the column in broad daylight and hid in the woods for a day. A woman who sympathized with the Communists reported my presence in the vicinity of her home and a Partisan patrol picked me up in a village near Velika Gorica. They took me to the concentration camp that was located there. I declared that I was a civilian laborer who had worked in Germany during the war. Of course, I gave my captors an assumed name. Nevertheless, I was forced to march to Sisak where I found the miserable remains of the column with which I had set out from Dravograd. On the way to Sisak I saw the bodies of a great many murdered people, and heard Partisan girls sing mocking songs filled with hatred for everything Croatian.

I was confined in a concentration camp at Sisak for three days. On the first day, a hundred and twenty members of the Croatian Black Legion were shot. Among them were my relatives, Adam Tolic, Stipo Peric, Ivan Peric, Anton Mandic, and others. These victims were taken off during the night, and we heard gunfire coming from the direction in which they had gone. Some of these prisoners had identified themselves as Ustashas even though they were not members of that organization and did not belong to the Black Legion. They wanted to put a quick end to the sufferings to which they were exposed.

There were 4500 prisoners in the Sisak camp when I arrived there but soon 700 of us were transferred to Karlovac. A Serbian captain, who carried a machine gun, was in charge of our guard detail. He went around asking the names of the units in which the individual prisoners had served. He grinned widely as he shot those who acknowledged attachment to commands against which he had a grudge. He shot so many people that he ran out of ammunition and left to get more, telling us that our turn would come as soon as he came back. In my estimation, he and a few other guards shot sixty or seventy captives in all. One young boy of sixteen or seventeen fell dead at my feet. I must admit that the Serb saw to it that his victims did not suffer because he put two or three bullets into each one of them. My friend, Ivan Galic, witnessed these killings along with me.

From Karlovac we were forwarded to Ogulin. Together with three other prisoners I got away at Ogulin and made good my escape to Italy. Two of my companions, Mirko Bodrusic and Ivan Fucik, are in the camp at Fermo at the present time, while Mate Gadza is in Naples.

I am ready to declare under oath that everything that I have said in the foregoing account is true to the best of my knowledge, belief, and observation.

Signed: M. Gavran

Rome
September 5, 1947

Document XI

This eyewitness describes the hopes of Croatian troops that the British would accept their surrender. He accuses General Herencic and other leading Croatian officers of not telling their troops that they were to be extradited to Yugoslavia. Lootings by the Partisans, a running "death march," and circumstantial evidence of massacres in Maribor are also described. The eyewitness *saw* mass murders of Croatian victims in Precko and Cazmanska Suma. Finally, he and a group of captives were saved by a ranking Partisan officer.

I retreated from Zagreb to Celje on a motor scooter early in May, 1945. At Celje I was captured along with General Brozovic and a small group of P.T.S. men by the local Slovenian Communists who were under the command of a Partisan officer. A few hours after this mishap, oncoming Croatian troops under General Servatzi set us free. The Croatian soldiers did not commit any acts of violence in Celje, but they tore down the red flags that the Communists had run up and later burned them.

From Celje I proceeded with the other freed prisoners to Dravograd. We traveled with General Boban's column and had an easier time getting through the Red lines than we had at Celje. Nevertheless, we engaged in bitter fighting in a mountain pass through which flows a small river. I believe this pass, or the valley behind it, was called the Huda Lukna. We battled Partisans there for one entire afternoon. When we broke through, we still had skirmishes with the enemy all the way to Dravograd.

Just before our arrival at this town, we found Bulgarian troops blocking our passage across the Drava River. The Bulgars sent three mounted officers to negotiate with our commanders. I personally guided them to General Boban's headquarters where he and General Herencic talked with them at some length. Afterwards, I escorted these officers back to the river.

As a result of our negotiations with the Bulgarians, we went around Dravograd and on the night of May 14-15, arrived on a plain which was close to the Austrian town of Bleiburg. Besides the great masses of our troops which had reached this point, there were countless thousands of civilians assembled there. Peasant carts loaded with women and children could be seen on every road. I noted the presence of an extraordinary number of railroad conductors. Although most of the refugees were Croatians, I saw quite a few Montenegrin royalists and Chetniks, or nationalists. The refugees also had their families with them.

British planes hovered overhead. The people on the field waved to them, not suspecting that the English still regarded us as enemies at this time even though the war was over. British tanks were also in evidence, and American as well as British flags were flying here and there. All of this display lulled us into believing that we had nothing to worry about now except incarceration as prisoners-of-war. We were anxious to accept this fate, since the only alternatives to it were to continue to wage a hopeless fight against the victors in the war, and thus expose ourselves to summary vengeance at their hands as soon as we ran out of ammunition, or else to bow our heads beneath the Communist yoke that we knew was being imposed upon our own country.

I attached myself to the student body of the Officers' School of the Croatian Armed Forces. This formation was under the command of General Petanjek. I joined it with the hope that I might receive the food ration that they did. All of these boys were between sixteen and eighteen years old, and one hundred of them were ready for graduation and promotion to officer rank in our Army. Of course, the end of the war and the evacuation of Zagreb had ended their hope of taking part in the defense of the Domovina against the forces of world Communism. As could be expected of boys of that age, however, they had no comprehension of the predicament in which they were involved. Therefore, their morale still remained at a very high level. For that matter, most of us at this time, whether military or civilians, were looking forward to only a temporary exile which we regarded as a preparatory training period for our triumphant return to the Fatherland.

Grim reality soon stared us in the face, but only by degrees. General Herencic was one of the spokesmen who had contacted the British command in Austria. He returned from British Headquarters to the Bleiburg field to inform us of the outcome of his talks with the English Commander, calling together both Ustasha and Domobran officers for this purpose. About two hundred officers quickly assembled around him. Since I myself was standing no more than ten to fifteen feet away from Herencic, I could hear every word that he said quite clearly. He told us that the only condition set for our surrender by the British Command was that we must lay down our arms. *He did not utter one word intimating that we were in effect surrendering not to the British but to Tito's miserable Partisan bands.* Therefore, we viewed the proposed surrender as the normal procedure we could expect in our circumstances. I do not know of anyone around me who had the slightest apprehension that the British had refused to accept our surrender themselves, but told Herencic and the other negotiators that we would have to be sent back to Yugoslavia.

I believe that my testimony on the events of this most tragic day in the entire thirteen-hundred-year history of the Croatian nation is important. I hereby accuse General Herencic and our other ranking military commanders of being responsible for the disintegration and subsequent massacre of our Army, which on May 15, 1945, was still ready to fight anyone that it was ordered to fight, whatever the odds against it. As a matter of fact, neither the British nor the Partisans could have barred our further progress into Austria at this point, had our commanders possessed the wit to launch a night attack in which we could have knocked out the English tanks and artillery and, with a bit of luck, perhaps destroyed their planes on the ground.

On this day I did not see a single Partisan on the Bleiburg field except for a few whom we had taken prisoner during our retreat. General Herencic ordered an Ustasha officer to return the Partisan insignia which we had stripped off their uniforms to these prisoners. Also he excused himself to them with great courtesy for having taken them prisoner! The Partisans were allowed to depart to join their troops without molestation on our part. I remember that one of them was a former Ustasha officer who had deserted to Tito toward the end of the war.

After we had heard what Herencic had to say, all officers returned to their units. At 4:00 P.M., we began to stack our arms on the plain. When we had done so, my group, together with other formations, marched off by column in an unknown direction. At sunset of this same evening, we passed an encampment of British troops and spent the ensuing night in an Austrian village, where the inhabitants greeted us kindly. We conversed for some time with one old man in this place who was a veteran of the war of 1914-18, during which he had served alongside Croatian units. So far as I know we were escorted by neither British or Partisan troops. I do remember that we encountered a number of Partisan soldiers enroute to the village where we passed the night, but they had no weapons, and I assume that they were prisoners whom our troops had released following our own surrender. In any case, they did not bother us, nor we them.

On the next day we continued our march towards an unknown destination. We went through another village which was adorned with Austrian flags, both the red-white-red of the post-1918 Austrian state, and the old black and yellow Habsburg banner. The sight of these standards gave me assurance that we were not heading back towards Yugoslavia.

Our column was a very long one. I could not see where it ended behind me although I tried to do so several times. Hardly had we got past this flag-decorated village when we began to meet armed Yugoslav Partisan troops in increasing numbers! Since they behaved courteously towards us, however, we were not unduly alarmed, even though we began to realize that we were their prisoners instead of being captives of the English.

For the next three days we traveled by night and by day. The women and children were separated from us while the troops and older male civilians learned that we were being taken to Maribor. We followed the course of the Drava River, and finally crossed into Slovenian territory near the site of an electrical power plant. On the second day of this journey, the Partisans began to take our valuables, but I must say that at first they observed a modicum of courtesy toward us in doing so. I took a ring that my parents had given me when I got my Maturity Diploma and put it on the second toe of my left foot. It took off the skin right down to the bone, but I saved the ring!

Soon the Partisans who now were guarding us began to kill everyone who collapsed from fatigue. At this stage of the march I was accompanied by a seventeen-year-old nephew, and I had to slap him in the face continually in order to keep him from falling asleep right on his feet and so exposing himself to the fate that met the others who stopped marching.

When we were about a mile out of Maribor, the Partisans took all of the railroad conductors out of the column. They started the rest of us at a running pace towards Maribor and murdered everyone who could not keep up. We had to throw away whatever knapsacks, blankets, or other articles we had left to maintain the pace they set for us. Often we tripped over objects that people ahead of us had discarded, or stumbled over the bodies of those shot by the guards because they could not move faster. I saw Second Lieutenant Knez, Director of the Clothing Institute of the Croatian Armed Forces, gunned down right before my eyes. I must have seen ten other dead men before we entered Maribor, although I was pretty well towards the head of our column.

On the afternoon of our arrival in Maribor, we were taken to a park which stood in front of a two or three-story building that strongly resembled the edifice housing the University of Zagreb. Here we were separated into three distinct categories: officers, students, and private soldiers. Then the officer group was split up into Ustashas and Domobrans. Partisans armed with rifles, to which bayonets were attached, were assigned to guard the Ustashas, while the Domobrans were dealt with less stringently. I accompanied the Domobran group to a modern three-story building which had been a German school. The seating arrangements in this place resembled those of a theater.

Here we remained for four or five days. Although we received no food during this period, we were not too badly treated otherwise. I do not know whether or not any of us were killed while we stayed in this place. Finally, we were taken to a large government warehouse which stood in between two or three industrial railroad tracks. In this building we were required to supply general data concerning our identities. Also, we had to state the identity of the units which had made us prisoners. We informed the Partisans that we had not surrendered to them to begin with, but were the prisoners of the English. Of course, they paid no attention to this assertion, and ultimately we had to sign all sorts of nonsensical statements which gave their army credit for having captured us.

As I have said above, I do not know whether any of the Domobran group in which I was included were killed up to this time or not. From the moment of our arrival in Maribor, however, there was plenty of shooting to be heard all over town. From several sources, we learned that the Partisans were massacring their prisoners, but as far as I am personally concerned this was only hearsay since I did not see anyone being killed.

While we were undergoing interrogation in the warehouse, we received the first food since our surrender almost two weeks before. It consisted of a kind of tea with a small piece of bread floating in it. I can't say much about the attitude of the citizens of Maribor toward us, but I should like to stress, however, that on the outskirts of the city, after we were allowed to stop running, many women brought water to us. The Partisans drove them off, and threatened to shoot them. Among these women was the wife of Second Lieutenant Knez; she herself was a native of Maribor. She asked me if I had seen her husband, but I couldn't bring myself to tell her that I had seen him killed only a few minutes before.

Since I was a P.T.S. man, I spent an uneasy time of it in the Maribor camps, because I was afraid that someone might tell the Partisans that I wasn't a Domobran. Therefore I was really glad to leave the place aboard a train composed of cattle cars. Fifty or sixty of us were packed into each of these wagons used to transport animals to slaughterhouses. Naturally, the conditions under which we traveled were terrible. There was no room to sit down, even though many of us were sick, and everyone was exhausted. We had to relieve ourselves right in the car, and since some men were suffering from diarrhea, it was a frightful mess. One captain was suffering internal hemorrhages. It was unbearable to have to breathe the air in this car, and I suppose the air in all of the other cars on the train was just as bad.

After a wait of several hours under these conditions, we pulled out of the Maribor station. On the following day we arrived at Zidani Most, from which we went on to Zapresic and Zagreb. In the afternoon, we drew into the main railroad station in the Croatian capital city. Here, we had to wait for a long time while the Partisans stripped us of practically all of our clothes, since they couldn't find anything else to steal. They were furious because other comrades had beaten them to our valuables, and treated us more brutally than they might otherwise have done.

We had to spend the entire night on the train which shuttled to and fro between Kanal and the main railroad station. When morning dawned, we were unloaded and taken to the Precko concentration camp. If anything, living conditions were worse here than any that we had experienced to date. Fortunately, the weather was warm so we could get some sleep on the bare ground. Also, I had the luck to receive a package of food from my relatives who came there looking for me. I almost had a nervous breakdown because I was afraid that they would betray my real identity to the guards. They didn't, but a Domobran captain by the name of Racic did give me away. I was, fortunately, forewarned of this development. Therefore, when the Partisans came looking for me, I was not to be found in the group with which I had identified myself since the surrender. Ustasha officer Dusper and others advised me to go to the Ustasha or some other non-Domobran part of the camp, because the Reds certainly would expect me to stay with the Domobrans who were more likely than the Ustashas to get off easily. That evening I sneaked around asking for the location of the Ustasha section in the camp. Those prisoners whom I approached with this question shuddered openly and told me to stay away from that area under any circumstances. Nevertheless, since I knew that I now was a marked man among the Domobrans, I persisted in my efforts to find the Ustashas. When I did make my way to their barracks, the first thing that met my eyes were Partisan details carrying corpses out of the building and loading them onto trucks. In the darkness I could not see very well, but I noticed no signs of life among the Ustashas who were being removed from the building. I decided that this was no place for me either. I could think of nothing better to do than to go back to the Domobran barracks. Fortunately, by the time I got there the Partisans had given up looking for me, and I was able to remain undetected by not staying very long in any one place.

After several days, a column of ten thousand prisoners was formed for evacuation from Precko. The comrades started to tie us up with wire, but we suspected the worst and offered resistance. They then changed their minds and herded us out of camp at curfew time. The Partisans marched us through Zagreb during the night hours and on to Dubrava and Cazma. At Cazma, the column halted while the Partisans instituted a furious search for Ustashas who might be among us. Also, they murdered everyone who tried to get a drink or collapsed from exhaustion. These killings were performed in broad daylight.

That evening we were marched into a forest. It began to rain, and a terrible hailstorm followed, which must have lasted for two or three hours. In the forest, the water came up to our knees in many places, and when we stepped into holes it sometimes reached our waists. Since the earth was very slippery underfoot, we frequently stumbled and fell. Some of our Partisan escorts were mounted, but others had to accompany us on foot. Since they were as drenched as we were, they were in a furious mood and kept firing away quite indiscriminately with heavy machine guns. The continual flashes of fire produced a horrifying effect in the dripping darkness of this gloomy wood. How many men fell dead and wounded during the course of this ghastly night, or how many got away into the blackness that surrounded us, I do not know. I do know that I saw hundreds of bodies, and it was rumored among the survivors that the Partisans were butchering masses of us deeper in the forest.

Certainly, our number was considerably decreased when we approached Bjelovar the following day. We were also completely exhausted and half insane because of the night of horror through which we had passed. The guards now mockingly called us the "Zuta kolona" (yellow column) because we were plastered all over with the yellow mud of the Cazma woods. Nor was there an end to the killing of the previous night. A short distance in front of me, a soldier knocked a Partisan commissar off his horse and seized the machine gun the Red was carrying, but was killed himself as were a few other prisoners in his vicinity. As we were going through the streets of Bjelovar, a young man saw his mother and ran to embrace her. The Partisans shot him down at her very feet, then beat all of us savagely, ordering us to keep our eyes on the ground and not to look for relatives or friends in the crowds that watched us pass. They also made the population of the town get off the streets and draw down the window shades in their homes.

If it is true, as Tito's historians maintain, that the inhabitants of Bjelovar welcomed the Partisans when they entered the city at the end of the war, they certainly were disillusioned now. Almost every civilian face expressed open hatred of the Reds.

Something unexpected happened next. A well-known Partisan official by the name of Cop arrived in Bjelovar, bearing an order for the removal of a number of captives from the column. On the pretense that I was sick (this was actually no pretense, although my condition was no worse than that of the rest of our group) I got myself included in this group. Cop seemed to be in a big hurry. He gave orders right and left to the local Partisans and then left the city. We were brought before the OZNA, interrogated, and, after two or three days, began to receive better treatment than we had heretofore. We were even able to obtain permission to roam about the city. Meanwhile, the column from which we had been extracted was driven on towards Osijek, where they met with more suffering, and, for most of the prisoners, eventual execution.

In Bjelovar I visited a number of acquaintances who supplied me with false identification papers and a suit belonging to a railroad conductor. Thus equipped, I took a train to Zagreb, arriving on June 6.

In the capital I hid in a cellar for a hundred and six days. I decided to try to reach Papuk, where the Krizari (Crusaders) were organizing to fight the Communists. A friend found new identification papers and, with God's help, I succeeded in escaping from the metropolis. However, I found the way to Papuk barred, and I was forced to flee via Rijeka to Trieste.

Signed: I. S.

January 1, 1956

Document XII

This woman's account describes the brutalities committed by the Partisans at Klagenfurt, Horoska Bistrica, Jesenice, Skofja Loka, and also the St. Vid extermination camp. At Maksimir in Zagreb, women and children are drenched with boiling water. Stories of mass slaughters in many Croatian and Serbian cities are also included.

On May 6, 1945, I joined a column of the Croatian Army which was retreating towards Austria under the command of Col. Joso Mrnic, Lieutenant Colonel Dragutin Kamber,[1] and a major whose name I do not remember. This small column was surprised and disarmed by Serbian Royal Chetniks commanded by Colonel Yovanovitch on May 7, after we had entered Austria and presumed that we were safe from any pursuit. On the following day, both we and our Chetnik captors were taken prisoners by Yugoslav Partisans six miles out of Klagenfurt.

Several hundred of us were crowded together into a narrow lane adjacent to the road. Many of the men brought here had head wounds inflicted by the gun butts of the Partisans. Among these casualties was a Russian priest. The Partisans cursed us and threatened us with every kind of horrible death. They beat several of our number in the sight of all the rest. Our situation was miserable, but all we could do was keep quiet, tear up our identification papers, throw away our money and valuables, and wait for what might come.

At 5:00 P.M. on this day, May 8, each of us received "supper". It consisted of a spoonful of dough. While the Partisans were distributing this savory refreshment, they relieved us of all the valuables that they had not already taken.

About 8:00 P.M., trucks arrived to convey us to an unannounced destination. We passed through several villages and forests and halted finally in Horoska-Bistrica, where we got some fairly decent food. However, the two nights that we spent at this place were made horrible by the sound of shots, screams, yells of rage, oaths, and the thud of gun butt blows. Just before dawn on the first night of our stay there we heard someone cry, "I was thrown through a window. The whole night I kept begging them to kill me with a bullet. I have a wife and am the father of two children. I was a mechanic at 25 Palmoticeva Street in Zagreb." The truck motors were turned on to drown out the noise of this and other last laments. However, some prisoners were close enough to the man who made the statement cited above to see the Partisans kill him with axes. When day broke, we saw that a number of prisoners had cut the veins in their wrists in the hope that they might bleed to death. There were many wounded and sick men among us, too.

---

[1] Dr. Kamber, recently deceased, was in the past decade pastor of Our Lady the Queen of Croatia Church in Toronto, Canada, but at the time of his escape from Yugoslavia, he belonged to the Catholic Archdiocese in Sarajevo, Bosnia. Fourteen priests and one seminarian of this Archdiocese were murdered by the Partisans.

On May 12, we were taken towards Villach in Austrian Carinthia. Late that night, while we still were ten miles outside the city, we stopped and waited for two whole days. We had received no food since leaving Horoska-Bistrica and were crowded together in one room where we had to stand up because there was no room to lie down.

After two days we were taken to a place about a mile away where we had more room, but still received nothing to eat. Since the number of prisoners increased from day to day, our living conditions worsened accordingly. Interrogations were held daily; beatings were administered occasionally.

One morning — I can't remember the precise date — we were sent in the direction of Rosenbach. It took us half a day to get there. At this town we were loaded onto a train which passed through several tunnels and eventually brought us back to Croatia.

When we were taken off the train, we proceeded on foot to Jesenice. Here we spent several days under conditions similar to those I have described above. The number of Croatian prisoners kept increasing.

From Jesenice, we were taken to Kranj, where we were given good food, which helped us recuperate somewhat. As our numbers continued to increase we were formed into a long column which was driven to Skofja-Loka, where an old cemetery is located on a hill. We remained in this place, sleeping in filth, while our fellow prisoners were being subjected to continuous interrogations. Many people did not return from these examinations; they disappeared. Most of the prisoners were soldiers, although they had donned civilian clothes in an attempt to disguise their true identities.

On the first floor of the building which housed my group, and directly below our own place of detention, about four hundred Croatian war prisoners were quartered. We were told that there was not enough room for us in the building. As we left the building, the men on the first floor whispered that the Partisan guards were maltreating them horribly.

My group left for Sent Vid near Ljubljana. We arrived there late one evening. Since there was no room for us to sleep elsewhere, we women were packed inside a chapel. The military prisoners in our column were left out in the open, and exposed to rain, and wind. When day broke I saw how these poor fellows were soaked to the skin by the heavy rains that had fallen during the night. They were chilled to the bone and shivering as though they had the ague or St. Vitus' dance.

I was told that there were 30,000 prisoners packed together in the St. Vid camp. Among them I met many acquaintances; I gathered together about twenty-five of these men and asked a Partisan officer to let them come into the quarters we were occupying. He permitted them to do so, and I succeeded in placing them in a corner where they could warm up a little. In this group were Col. Josip Mesic, First Lieutenant Rukavina and his brother, First Lieutenant Slavujevic, Color Bearer

Zrinjko Superina and others whose names I do not recall now. Only a few hundred of our men got into the building; all of the rest had to stay out in the open, day and night, rain or shine.

We heard that food was being prepared for us, but because of the rain and strong gusty winds we could not get it. Some men died of cold or fever brought on by the terrible conditions to which we were subjected. One day a group of P.T.S. men were introduced into the courtyard. They had their camp kitchen with them, and in accordance with directions given to them by some of the prisoners who were medical doctors, they cooked linden tea for us. This daily "food" saved the lives of many people.

Every day the Partisans made up a list of prisoners whom they removed. Seven men were taken from a room adjacent to mine, and were not seen or heard of again. We were locked in our rooms to prevent us from seeing what was going on in this hellish place, but almost all the time we could hear screams, groans, howls of pain and anger, and every other kind of nerve-shattering noise.

This camp at St. Vid was a sort of central concentration point to which prisoners were brought from every quarter. They were interrogated here and then sent off to various destinations. I managed to mingle with a group of women and children who were being treated with more consideration than the rest of the captives. I learned that they were soon to leave for Zagreb. We were lined up at 4:00 P.M. one day – I don't remember the date – and stood waiting until 3:00 A.M. Finally, sixty-two women and a number of children were loaded into a railroad boxcar. The doors were locked from the outside and we were off for a twelve-hour ride which was memorable because of the excessive heat, thirst, and hunger from which we suffered. Although we cried and pounded on the doors, asking our guards to let us have air and water, our pleadings were of no avail. Many women and children fainted during this terrible journey.

At 3:00 P.M., we pulled into the Zagreb station. Four hours later we were taken to the concentration camp at Maksimir. Here we were told that we had to be disinfected and so had to report to the Disinfecting Institute. We certainly were in need of some kind of cleansing treatment because no one had been able to bathe or even wash for a month past. At the Disinfection Institute, a hundred and fifty of us were crowded into ten wash stalls. We had to undress, then our clothes were taken outside and boiling hot water was showered down upon us. In less than a minute the stalls were hellish because of the steam given off by the water. It was a real steam bath, but at a much higher temperature than any we had ever experienced. This ordeal lasted for two hours. Three children died during the course of it. Almost all of the women fainted at one point or another in this grueling bath. Never shall I forget their screams, or how the eyes of the children were wide with agony. All of us, and especially those who were the mothers of small children, cried out for release from this torture, but only after a full two hours of such treatment did three youths turn off the water. After they had done so they returned our clothes to us.

Three days after our arrival in Maksimir all of the children who were left alive, and some of the women, were released from the camp. Those of us who remained were grouped according to our districts of residence. I was in the Zagreb district. We were able to feed all the other groups because the good people of Zagreb, even those who had no relatives or friends in the camp, brought food to us continually, and we shared it with all of the other district groups. Several days after the first batch of prisoners were set free, I was allowed to go to my home, too.

I remained at liberty for only three weeks. Then I was rearrested and brought to the concentration camp on Savska Street. There were a number of people from my former group in this place. I remained here for twenty-three days. Some women had to stay there longer than I did, while others were set free before me. I do not know why the OZNA kept after me unless it was because I was a known Croatian patriot. Of course, this was enough to merit their persecution, for they hounded every true Croatian, often to the death.

When I was allowed to go home again, I was told that the OZNA was going to pick me up once more unless I gave up my apartment. Therefore, I let some of Tito's "democrats" have it. After all, every Croatian anti-Communist was subject to eviction at a moment's notice and likely to be killed. This is what the triumph of "democracy" has meant in Tito's Yugoslavia.

I heard stories about the wholesale massacre of Croatian prisoners at Dravograd and many other places in Slovenia. Also, I was told of the "Death Marches" and the mass slaughters that had occurred around Zagreb and at Bjelovar, Nova Gradiska, Osijek, Petrovaradin, Zemun (Semlin), Belgrade, Bela Crkva, and elsewhere. Tito and his henchmen did a thorough job of decimating the Croatian nation. A young Croat who had escaped from the concentration camp in Martinovac near Koprivnica told me that the Serbs and other Partisans knifed and slaughtered the Croatian war prisoners as if they were chickens rather than human beings. I was unable to ascertain the details of the fate of eight hundred captives who were taken from the Virovitica concentration camps into the Borovo Forest. They were never heard from again after they disappeared into this gloomy woods. Masses of other prisoners vanished from human sight in the same way.

Many priests were arrested and imprisoned during these days. One evening I saw a column of two hundred clerics being taken in the direction of Nova Ves, a Zagreb suburb.

What I have related above is only a small part of what I know about the systematic genocide that is being practiced by the Tito regime in the Croatian lands. If I supplied all the details that I knew, I could fill an entire volume. It would be truly melancholy reading for anyone who knew old Croatia, to learn what it is like now.

Signed: Franciska Blazevic

Rome
October 4, 1945

Document XIII

This witness, a California Croat, tells how he and his group were disarmed by the British and extradited to Yugoslav troops. He reveals valuable details on the Partisan atrocities in Sent Vid during his eleven-day stay there. When he arrived in Zagreb, this eyewitness of so many Partisan brutalities and mass murders escaped from "death marches" but was recaptured. A ranking Partisan officer, probably a Croat, saved him and a group of other captives from imminent death. Later, the author of this account joined Croatian guerrilla fighters, the Krizari. He explains why their guerrilla warfare was not successful. He also relates how his immediate family and many other relatives were liquidated by Yugoslav Communists.

At the beginning of May, 1945, I was hospitalized in Zagreb. When the city was evacuated, I was able to leave the hospital and succeeded in reaching Krumpendorf in Austria. When I arrived in this town, there was a rumor circulating that the British were going to accept volunteer anti-Communist fighters into their service. Since most Croatian soldiers were eager for such duty, we allowed the Englishmen to load us into trucks which took us to Sankt Jakob. In the plum orchard near this town, the British relieved us of our weapons. Somehow we had the idea that they were going to supply us with newer and better ones; otherwise, we would have baulked at giving them up. But we understood the British spokesmen to say that we were going to Udine, Italy, and that as soon as we arrived there we would be re-equipped.

Still laboring under the impression that we were going to Italy to become auxiliaries of the British Armed Forces which, now that the Germans were beaten, had to worry about the Russians, we let ourselves be loaded onto trains. The train on which I was riding did not get very far down the line before it came to a halt. We found that it had stopped at Kranj in Slovenia, and to our consternation we saw Partisan troops all around us. They made us disembark and drove us like a herd of sheep into a barbed wire enclosure. Since we had given the British our weapons, we were in no position to put up any kind of resistance.

During the three days that I remained in the Kranj enclosure, I received food only once. Its quality was as unmentionable as its quantity was inadequate. On the fourth day I was sent with other soldiers to Sent Vid near Ljubljana. My first day there I was astonished and enraged to see Partisan soldiers, some of them dressed in uniforms they had taken from our own men, walking among the prisoners with machine guns, rifles, and revolvers in their hands and shooting in cold blood anyone who complained of wounds or illness. I saw about thirty men killed in a period of only a few minutes.

The Partisans continued this summary procedure of execution, and, as the number of victims increased, trucks were brought to the camp to carry away the dead. Now the Partisans began to throw two live victims into the trucks along with every dead one. At the end of a couple of hours, the trucks would come back empty to pick up more bodies and living candidates for the slaughterhouse. This routine went on during the entire eleven days that I stayed in this inferno.[1]

After the first few days here we all knew that we were doomed to die. Since our captors did not feed us, we had to break branches from the trees and eat the bark. Also, we found some potato peelings on dung heaps in the camp. During the whole eleven days that I was there, the Partisans fed us only twice. I became so weak that I was unable to stand up unaided.

On the eleventh day, those of us who were still alive were packed into railroad boxcars. Our train started off for some unknown destination but, as far as we were concerned, we knew that our tickets read "Station Death." Because of both the crowded conditions that prevailed in the boxcars and the debilitated state of our health, four men died in the boxcar in which I was riding.

It was May 25th or 26th when we pulled into the west rail station in Zagreb. As soon as the train stopped, the guards threw the doors of our car open. I had anticipated this action on the part of our captors and had made up my mind that I might as well die trying to get away as to wait passively for the axe to fall. Therefore, I summoned up what strength I had and, as soon as the doors opened, I threw myself to the ground outside and rolled under the car and then scrambled to the other side of the train. I expected to be riddled by a hail of bullets, but either my precipitate action surprised the guards, or perhaps some of them were Croatians and deliberately let me get away unscathed. I managed to make my way to a house in Kustosija. However, my hiding place was discovered by the Partisans, and they took me with twenty-five other escaped prisoners, whom they had recaptured, to a barbed wire enclosure where they beat us and bound us tightly.

During the entire night that we spent in this enclosure the Partisans kept telling us one minute that we would soon have enough to eat and drink, and the next that we were soon to die. We resigned ourselves to

[1] Details on the massacres of many thousands of Croatian soldiers and civilians at Sent Vid can be found in Hecimovic's book, *In Tito's Death Marches and Extermination Camps* (New York, 1962), pp. 32-37.

our fate and regretted only that we had not chosen to die while we had weapons in our hands and strength enough to fight.

Towards dawn, the Partisans took us out of the enclosure and marched us across a meadow. Soon we were ordered to halt and we guessed that our captors were preparing to butcher us. Then we saw some kind of light in the distance, which seemed to be approaching us. We thought it was an execution squad, but when the light came near enough we could see that it was only a Partisan officer who had two soldiers with him. He asked the first sergeant in command of the detail escorting us where he was taking us. The Partisan sergeant replied, "Comrade Lieutenant, I am taking them to the Central Command!" When he heard this remark, the lieutenant said curtly, "No! Take them to the school building at Kustosija. I will question them tomorrow morning and find out the charges against them. Then we shall punish them!"

Believe it or not, the first sergeant actually gnashed his teeth in anger. I had read about people doing this but it was the first time that I actually saw or heard it happen. Of course, he was furious because now he did not dare to kill us as he had intended.

That morning we were taken to Precko and after interrogation and a period of imprisonment were assigned to work brigades. The task entrusted to us was to clean up the areas adjacent to the banks of the Sava River.

Two cousins of mine who lived in Zagreb, Marko and Scepo Mucic, brought food to me a few times while I was in the capital. They had a restaurant, the "Zalogajnica Jelacic," on Jelacic Square. One night, a month or so after the end of the war, they were arrested by the Communists and never heard from again.

At the beginning of July, I was allowed to return to my home in Hercegovina. The war was still going on there because many Krizari or Crusaders were fighting tenaciously against the Communists. A great number of these anti-Marxist fighters were personal friends of mine. About the first of September my sister, Sima, and I were accused of supplying food to these last defenders of Croatian independence. One morning I awakened just in time to see that Yugoslav troops had surrounded my house. Fortunately, Sima was in Sarajevo, so she escaped arrest. I also succeeded in eluding the soldiers. That same evening I joined the Krizari in the forests.

The rest of my family were less fortunate than Sima and I. One of my female cousins was arrested and sentenced to ten years of imprisonment. My mother was also imprisoned, and my father was beaten so terribly that he died from the effects. Some of our other relatives or friends got word of what had happened to Sima in Sarajevo. Therefore, she did not try to return to Hercegovina for a full year, and when she did go back she stayed well away from our old home. The Partisans forced my younger sister, Jela, a girl of only seventeen years, to guide them into the mountains in order that they might find me. They made her spend several nights without shelter standing out in a heavy rain because she would not reveal my hiding place. Finally, the Partisans became so furious because they could not catch up with me that they beat her with clubs until she lost her senses. She died in delirium and misery. Her fate was worse than that of any other member of the family, although my older brother, Martin, was killed by the Partisans at Bela Crkva after he had survived a "Death March" made by a prisoner column. My two brothers-in-law died fighting during the retreat to Austria.

Thus, all of my ties with home and family were severed. As a "Crusader," I operated from Siroki Brijeg and Brotanj all the way to Popovo Polje. For some time, too, I fought the Communists in Dalmatia around Ston. Many and bitterly fought were the battles in which I engaged long after the war had officially ended. We used the same tactics against the Partisans that they had employed towards us during the war, except that we endeavored to spare the civilian population all the suffering we could. In 1941-45, the Partisans did everything they could to terrorize civilians into joining or supporting them, stopping no crime to achieve this end. They also murdered German and Italian soldiers and officials in a way that deliberately threw suspicion upon anti-Communist peasants, villagers, or townsmen living in the vicinity. The Nazis and Fascists were so stupid that they retaliated indiscriminately against the population of the locality without making any serious attempt to find out whether or not their victims had anything to do with the murders committed. As a result, Tito's forces picked up many recruits who joined the Partisans only to escape death at the hands of the Germans or Italians. We never made use of tactics of this kind.

Also, whereas the Russians, Americans, and British competed with one another in supplying Tito's murderous hordes with the most modern weapons, we had no source from which we could secure new arms and ammunition, let alone any kind of supplies, when what we had wore out or was exhausted. Of course, we sometimes captured arms and ammunition from Tito's troops, or took them from dead bodies after a battle, but a guerrilla force cannot hold out indefinitely against the resources that a modern government can command, unless the guerrilla force is getting help from somewhere. Since we were not getting any help, our situation became more and more hopeless.

Early in 1947, two of the best of the Krizari, Grgo Vasilj (Kekusic) and Nikola Jerkovic (Zovkusic) were badly wounded. Grgo died, while I nursed Jerkovic back to health. In February of 1947, however, we both were in very poor condition, he because of his many wounds, I because of a cold that I had contracted while caring for him up in the mountains.

The Yugoslav authorities issued an order at this time requiring that all the people in Bijakovici, my native village, move outside the community unless Jerkovic and I surrendered. Since some of our neighbors knew our various hideouts, we were afraid that we might be betrayed. No one did so, but when Tito issued another of his numerous "amnesties," some of our fellow villagers advised us to give ourselves up because sooner or later we were bound to be caught or die of hunger and exposure. By this time we had no other alternative than to follow their advice, because we were both in such terrible condition that we could not move about without assistance, and I could no longer take care of either Jerkovic or myself.

Therefore, we let men from our village carry us down to the nearest command post of the regular Yugoslav troops. Fortunately for us, there were some Croatian officers among them who insisted upon literal observance of the terms of the amnesty; their Serbian and Montenegrin colleagues would have killed us out of hand, amnesty or no amnesty.

While we were convalescing, the anti-Communists who had taken advantage of the "Marshal's" declaration of an amnesty were arrested one by one. This is a typical Communist trick. The fact is that you cannot do business with the Communists any time, any place, or for any reason. Peace with them is impossible because they will not keep their promises any longer than they find it convenient. The moral standards which some people try to live by mean absolutely nothing to these Marxist fanatics. It is to be hoped that what is left of the non-Communist world will learn something from the experiences of the Croatians, but to date I see no sign of its doing so. There are still too many people who think that Communists are just ordinary human beings, and that they will honor peace or other agreements made with anti-Communists when they find it expedient to do so. This is a fundamental misunderstanding of the true nature of Communists everywhere, for which the rest of the world may pay as dearly as Croatia did.

A friend of mine advised me to get out of the country before it was my turn to be arrested and disappear forever as had so many other Croatians before me. Since I was well enough to travel by this time, I left without delay for Rijeka, where I concealed myself while making preparations to flee abroad. On April 30, 1948, I made good my escape to Italy. Towards the end of 1950, I came to the United States where I now live.

My fellow crusader, Jerkovic, also got away safely and now lives in Canada. I understand that my fellow prisoners on the train from which I escaped were taken to the Kozara Mountain where they were tortured and murdered by Serbian elements. This information I secured from train conductors whom I was able to contact before I left the Domovina, perhaps forever.

Signed: Ivan Ivankovic

Los Angeles, California
August 10, 1961

Document XIV

This Croatian soldier and his group surrendered to the Partisans at the village of Prevalje, but his "death march" column was lined up at Bleiburg. He eyewitnessed murders of large groups of disarmed Croatian soldiers at Dravograd, Slovenjgradec, Celje, Zidani Most, Samobor and Sisak. On this long trek a total of about 2000 men were slain. At Daruvar he saw how Tito's troops tortured a fifty-four-year-old priest to death and also how they abducted twenty-five additional victims.

I was drafted into the Croatian Armed Forces on February 9, 1942, and was assigned to the First Automobile Battalion which had its headquarters at 207 Ilica Street in Zagreb. My service with this unit lasted until 1944 when I was transferred to the technical section of the automobile department attached to the War Ministry. I was still in this unit when, on May 8, 1945, we received orders to leave Zagreb and go through Slovenia to Austria.

It is not my intention to give an account of our retreat through Slovenia because others have said all that I could say in this connection. What I do want to do is to give my own personal testimony concerning our forced return to Croatia. I do feel, however, that it is necessary to point out that our leaders, that is, General Headquarters, bore the responsibility for the various individual surrenders made by our troops. It was our officers who proved unworthy of discharging the responsibilities entailed by their rank. I can certify that the morale of both non-coms and private soldiers, as well as that of lower ranking officers in general, was so high that they would never have surrendered to anyone if General Headquarters and our generals in the field had ordered them to fight to the end.

On May 15, I was at the front end of a column of troops and civilians which had reached the village of Prevalje in Slovenia. At 4:00 P.M. on this day, we were ordered to empty our arms and surrender them to the Partisans. Apparently our commanders knew that we would not do this, orders or no orders, so they added to this message the information that after the Partisans had taken our arms the British would take charge of us as their prisoners-of-war. After a little while most of us concluded that this was the best treatment we could expect in view of the fact that we had lost the war. Even though we hated to lay down our weapons before a mangy crew like Tito's Partisans, we finally did so. When we were disarmed, we went on to Bleiburg.

I shall skip over some details in order to pick up the story when we were ordered back from Bleiburg to Prevalje. Nothing particularly unpleasant had happened to us so far, but when we repassed Prevalje I noted that more and more Partisans were appearing around us. Now, for the first time, they supplied an escort for us. Hitherto, we had marched unguarded.

We next came to a bridge that crossed the Drava River. Once we started to cross it, the Partisans closed the gates at both ends. They began to search us and to confiscate everything we had that was of the slightest value or utility.

Following this confiscation, the column, now only 4000 to 4500 strong (since many soldiers had slipped off into the woods at various points), headed for Dravograd. That night we stopped on the road and were allowed three or four hours of rest. Every time we had such a respite, the Partisans would shoot fifteen or twenty men whom they suspected of being Ustashas.

At Dravograd, the civilians were separated from the soldiers. Then we soldiers were subjected to a process of registration during which we supplied our captors with data concerning ourselves. When this business was completed, two columns were formed. One set off toward Maribor, the other in the direction of Slovenjgradec and Celje.

I was in the second column, which contained about 4000 people. With me were Alfonz Knez, Marijan Jerbic, Zvonko Koncevic, Josip Rogina, Srecko Cerecki, Drago Sautner, and a fellow by the name of Majstorovic. We arrived at Slovenjgradec about 8:00 P.M. and spent the night in a sawmill there.

My friends and I found room to lie down behind a pile of boards. Hardly had we done so when a Partisan came up to me to say that he knew that I had worked for the Domobran Automobile Battalion because he, too, had formerly served in that unit. He advised me to find another location because the Partisans were likely to shoot everyone whom they could lay hands on easily during the night. He told us that the Partisans would probably begin shooting right where we had stationed ourselves. All of us heeded his warning and moved to another part of the mill.

What he had told us proved to be true; a number of men were awakened and led away during the night. After they had left the mill we could hear shouts of "Halt!" in the distance, and then staccato bursts of gunfire. This could only mean that the Partisans were butchering our luckless comrades.

At 8:00 A.M. the next day, our column moved on towards Celje. We estimated that we were two hundred fewer than when we had arrived the night before. En route to Celje, the Partisans killed fifteen or twenty more who lagged behind or tried to go aside to relieve themselves.

It was 2:00 P.M. when we arrived in Celje, or rather at a meadow just outside the city. Fifty men were picked out, ostensibly for the purpose of bringing food to us from the city. Since this was the third consecutive day that we had received nothing to eat, we accepted this explanation at face value at first. However, we were not fed and the chosen fifty never rejoined us. We later realized that they must have been killed.

Around 7:00 P.M., we were told to move on. We left Celje and after a three-hour march came to a small forest where we were allowed to stop and sleep for a while. This wood was approximately one kilometer from Zidani Most.

At 4:00 A.M., we were roused by the curt order, "Get up and do not say a word!" Many men were so exhausted that they remained sleeping on the ground. Those of us who had heard the order were lined up and marched towards Zidani Most. We had gone hardly a hundred and fifty meters from our resting place when we heard shots ringing out behind us along with screams of pain.

Later, I talked to one of the sleepers we had left behind us. He had awakened in time to escape deeper into the woods, but the Partisans had shot about a hundred and fifty of his companions in cold blood.

At Zidani Most, I met an old acquaintance, an officer by the name of Zdravko Spehar. I believe he was from Vinkovci. We stayed together all the way from Zidani Most to Sevnica on the Sava, where the Partisans regrouped us into battalions of a sort. I was beaten and tortured at this place, but was able to rejoin my group and go on to Samobor.

Following our arrival in this city, we had to go through another registration process which was conducted by local Communists and Partisan troop details. Whoever could not provide convincing proof that he was neither an Ustasha or a commissioned officer was beaten mercilessly and then tortured. It was about 6:00 P.M. when the registration ended. We were turned out in a meadow to spend the night; it was filled with prisoners who had preceded us to Samobor. Others were sent to a prison inside the city itself; no one ever found out anything about their fate.

We remained in Samobor for two days. Then we were taken to Velika Gorica, and confined on the fair grounds of this town. We were told that we would get supper here and, in fact, some food was distributed to us. I got nothing myself because there was not enough to go around. Besides the scanty rations, we got a sound beating from club-wielding civilian Communist sympathizers. They spat not only on us soldiers but also on the women in our column, calling us traitors, Fascists, and the like.

From Velika Gorica we went on to Sisak, arriving at 9:00 P.M. Here too, the Communist hangers-on used clubs on us. Some men were pulled right out of the column, and we saw no more of them. It was in Sisak, too, that I saw the Partisans throw prisoners into the river and then shoot at them to make sure they did not swim to safety.

All survivors were placed in the "Viktorovac" prison camp. Here, each of us received a kilogram of corn flour, but no water in which to cook it. Everyone was searched very carefully, and anyone who incurred the displeasure of the Partisans for any reason was locked up in the barracks. Later, such individuals would be loaded into trucks guarded by machine gun armed Partisans and driven, allegedly, to Petrinja. I am positive myself that they were killed in the forests that lie between Sisak and Petrinja. Thousands of other Croatians, also lost their lives in Sisak. My column was so decimated here that when we left the town we numbered no more than 2000 to 2500, all told.

On the afternoon of the second day that we spent at Sisak, we started off for Banova Jaruga. When we were about three kilometers from Sisak, I saw the Partisans kill three men because they had stopped to relieve themselves. Also, I was an eyewitness of the death of a fifty-year-old priest. He was killed near Daruvar because he could not walk any further. Along with some other men, I carried him on my back for quite a distance, although by this time, I was weak from lack of food. Finally, we were allowed to stop, and the priest got off my back and sat down in a ditch while we were resting. A Partisan came up and kicked him in the stomach for no reason at all. When the priest doubled up, the Partisan blew the back of his head off with a revolver, shooting at point-blank range. All the men whom I have mentioned above, and another friend of mine, Engineer Vedrina from Zagreb, witnessed this wanton murder.

On the eleventh day of our march, we came to Daruvar. The Croatian women of this place brought food to us, but the Partisans would not let us accept it. However, they did give us a two-kilogram loaf of bread to feed every twenty-six men.

At Daruvar, we were lodged on the fair grounds where we remained for five days. On each one of these days five men were taken away from the rest of us, allegedly to sweep the streets of the city. None of them came back to us. I presume that they were murdered.

After five days on the fair grounds, we camped in a meadow for another forty-eight hours. On each of these days we received approximately one deciliter of corn mush. Then we were shifted to a saw mill in Pakrac, where we passed another eight days. From here we were herded onto the state grounds in Lipik, where we received food twice a day. Although these "meals" were deficient in quantity and quality, at least they were warm.

On the evening of the second day that we spent at Lipik, the Partisans called roll and then sent us to Daruvar and on to Bjelovar via Grubisno Polje. Before we left Daruvar, the Partisans tried to force Drago Sautner's wedding ring off his finger. A female Partisan in this town asked for two men to help her with something. These men were taken to the local People's Committee. Needless to say, they never came back from their meeting with this self-appointed body.

When we got to Bjelovar, we were lodged in the Vojnovic barracks which was being used as a prisoner-of-war camp, and were questioned there by the OZNA. After this ordeal, most of us were assigned to work battalions.

I was detailed to the Fourth Work Battalion which labored in Varazdin, Sarajevo, Banja Luka, Prijedor, Planciste, Jajce, and then was sent back to Banja Luka where we were discharged on October 1, 1945.

The identities of our escorts during the movements that I have described above were as follows: from Prevalje to Sisak – Montenegrin Partisans; Sisak to Daruvar – 12th Krajina Brigade (mostly Serbs); Daruvar-Bjelovar — Montenegrins again. The commander of the Fourth Work Battalion was Rado Uzelac, and its commissar was a Serb, Sava Savanovitch. Both of these men came from Raic.

Signed: M. Stankovic

La Fraschette, Italy
April 26, 1952

Document XV

Over 30,000 Croatians surrendered to the British and their Yugoslav proteges in the Klagenfurt Valley. The huge "death march" was driven by the First Serbian Proletarian Brigade. Not far from Maribor, an estimated 4500 Croatian officers were murdered by the Serbian Proletarians. In Maribor itself, this eyewitness saw thousands of Croats tortured and led to be slaughtered. A new "death column" was lined up and sent from Maribor to Croatia under the guard of the Sixth Bosnian Brigade. During this trek, several thousand Croats were murdered. The eyewitness ends his "death march" at Ludbreg in Northern Croatia. Later, he learns of the horrifying experiences of other captives who were led through Croatia into Serbia.

During the retreat of the Croatian Armed Forces to Austria in May, 1945, I reached Klagenfurt. This Carinthian city extends across the length and breadth of a valley, for three square miles. When I arrived here, I found the entire valley thronged with anti-Communist troops of all nationalities. The majority of the eighty or ninety thousand refugees, whom my colleagues and I estimated were in this place, were Croatians and included civilian non-combatant as well as military personnel. However, stretched out along the main highway, one could discern Slovenian, Albanian, Montenegrin, White Russian, and German formations too.

On May 16 and 17, I noted that many tanks had entered the Klagenfurt valley. The tank park was two miles away from my own location, so I could not make out to whom these tanks belonged. I was told that they were British, but rumors were also going around that some of them were Yugoslav, i.e., Partisan. At about 9:00 A.M., May 17, six British airplanes flew over us at the low altitude of approximately six hundred feet. They circled above us three times, but did not bomb or machine-gun us, or make any kind of signal to us whatsoever.

After this incident, conjecture was ripe about our fate. It was evident from the bearing and attitude of our high ranking officers that they were dejected and greatly worried. In the course of the next two hours, the news of the successful breakthrough of the main body of our Armed Forces into Austria spread among us. It was said also that our Supreme Command and the Government had negotiated our surrender to the British.

Even though we did not like losing the war, and grumbled quite a bit about the military incompetence and political blundering of the Germans, we resigned ourselves to the idea of giving up our arms to the English and becoming their prisoners for a while. We thought we would soon be free men, even if exiles, for we could not see what the Britons would gain by holding us for any length of time. Of course, we might have followed up this reasoning and deduced from it that the simplest thing for the Englishmen to do from their own point of view would be to collect our weapons and then turn us over to their Communist allies. However, I do not know of anyone who thought far enough ahead to realize that we were in a *cul-de-sac* from which we could escape only by fighting our way on through into the interior of Austria, perhaps all the way to Switzerland. To us at the moment, however, the mere fact that we were on Austrian soil seemed to provide us with a guarantee of safety. In other words, we were convinced that we enjoyed the same status in Austria that we would in Switzerland.

Of course, we were overlooking the obvious fact that the English and their Communist allies had troops in Austria, whereas they had none in Switzerland. Therefore, the postwar Austrian authorities could not offer us the asylum that we might have been able to obtain from their Swiss contemporaries even if they had wanted to do so. The Social Democrats among them didn't want to, but were willing and even eager to turn us over to their fellow Marxists.

The first real intimation of the national catastrophe that awaited us came when we saw, to our stunned surprise, that our higher officers were beginning to strip off their insignia of rank. This process began when we received orders to unload our weapons and display white flags. On every hand, the soldiers began to shout, "Why are we to run up flags of surrender? To whom are we showing this signal of capitulation after we have shed so much blood in so many battles?" I had the same thought as my comrades, but at this critical juncture we had absolutely no leadership. No one came forward to take charge and to bring order out of the sudden confusion that reigned among us, as our higher officers simply resigned their authority. As a result, some soldiers and officers kept their arms and went off into the forests, although I could not see what they hoped to accomplish by doing so, while others stood around and argued about whether or not to surrender.

Meanwhile, explosives and hand grenades were being collected by some of the men who were determined not to give themselves up. Others, including myself, hurried about to give a helping hand where we could and to try to find out what was really going on. Most of our troops moved slowly forward along the long plain in accordance with confused instructions we were receiving from unidentified sources. All of a sudden, we came upon two Partisans, a woman and a man, standing on opposite sides of the highway. Both were armed with light machine guns of British make. They did not menace us with these weapons, but simply stood motionless in the attitude of sentinels. Behind this pair, we saw six huge piles of assorted weapons. British troops were also lined up on both sides of the highway with their weapons ready. Other English units were ranging up and down the road, apparently keeping an eye on us. Our troops began to destroy or render useless their weapons, but neither the English nor the occasional Partisans whom we met interfered, although they kept telling us to just lay down our arms.

As we moved on further, British tanks accompanied us, but the English soldiers kept telling us through interpreters: "The war is over. Everyone is going home. Don't be afraid of anything. You are free men now!"

However, the British troops and tanks stayed with us for only a few miles. Around 5:00 P.M., the First Serbian Proletarian Brigade took over our custody. I do not know who the commanding officer of this Brigade was, but I remember that a Captain Nikola Krnjoc was in command of the First Company of the Second Battalion of this outfit. All of the Serbs were mounted on horseback and heavily armed. They told us, "You thought the British would stay with you all the time, eh? Now you're where you're supposed to be, and now you'll see what Communist Partisans are like."

The Serbs lined us up in a column of fours. There must have been close to 35,000 captives in all under the charge of the First Proletarian. They made us travel without pause at a fast run a great part of the time. The mounted Partisans used clubs and whips upon us to keep us going.

We got our first rest at dawn on May 19. By this time, we were not far away from Maribor. Some 4500 officers were now separated from the rest of the column. Captain Krnjoc came to look them over and told them: "You are those I had to pursue, and on account of whom we have suffered so much. You have caused us much woe during the past four years, and now I will repay you for it!"

Then, he called a number of subordinate officers together and told them that since the war was over, these Croatian officers had to be separated from their men and had therefore been pulled out of the column. After this, Krnjoc took one hundred heavily armed Partisans and led the officers into a ravine that extended along the highway for a distance of three miles. For the next two hours we could hear yells, oaths, shots, and screams of pain coming from the direction of this ravine. Then Krnjoc's men came back with their hands and clothes dripping blood. Breathing hard, they told us "There's nothing better in store for you than there was for them. They went 'home' before you common soldiers because they were officers and so deserved the honor of being first!"

The memory of this tragedy is engraved indelibly upon my memory; I shall never be able to erase from my mind the recollections of its details if I live to be a hundred. The flower of our brave youth was butchered here at Maribor without having a chance to put up a fight for their lives. None of the officers who died in this slaughter had reached his fortieth year. I myself heard some of them shout as they died, "Farewell, my beloved Croatian land, I am leaving you!"

We arrived in Maribor at 10:00 A.M., May 20, and were confined in a barracks painted red. As we were driven through the gates of the barracks yard, we were searched with great care so that no one was able to conceal a watch, fountain pen, ring, weapon, or any other article of value. There were almost 10,000 other war prisoners in this place. Despite the huge size of the barracks and the grounds around it, there was not room for all the prisoners. During the war, Maribor had been bombed and the craters made by the explosives dropped by Allied planes were filled with corpses. Some dirt had been thrown over them, so that it was hard to tell whether men or animals were piled into these holes. However, the earth covering them was so scanty that it was apparent that many bodies had been stripped of all their clothing.

The Partisans took everything but the underwear of the living, too, and most of us were barefooted. We suffered greatly from hunger and thirst, since they did not feed us and seldom allowed us to get water. It is utterly impossible to describe in words all the hardships that we had to endure there between May 20 and June 5, when I left the camp. The daily routine included roll call, separate groupings according to years of service in the Croatian Armed Forces, additional or sub-groupings by home districts, and so on. Meanwhile, starvation, sickness, and maltreatment took their toll, while the guards killed many prisoners more for sport than any other reason. The dead were buried in the bomb holes within the camp itself, and new pits had to be dug to accommodate the many victims of the triumph of "democracy" and "the people."

At 4:00 P.M. on May 27, a roll call was held and all Ustashas were commanded to report. An estimated 5000 men, my brother among them, obeyed this summons and were separated from the rest of us. On the evening of this same day, all of these unfortunates were taken to a forest that was two miles distant from the camp. That night we heard continuous firing from the direction of this woods.

Since we now had no illusions about our fate, some two hundred prisoners devised a plan to escape. The chief organizers of this attempt were Stanko K., Marko B., Pero K., Venco Z., Stanko B., and some other men whose names I do not remember. There were three rows of wire around the camp, and guards armed with machine guns stood at three foot intervals all along the wire. Therefore, we planned to overpower and kill these guards as we broke through the wire. This undertaking may seem foolhardy in print, but since we knew that the Partisans were going to kill us anyway, we had nothing to lose by attacking the wire with our bare hands.

As casually as possible, we assembled close to the wire on the night of June 3, and at a prearranged signal made a dash for the wire and the guards. Some of the captives boosted their mates right over the top of the first fence row; others scaled it unaided. Someone hit a guard over the head with a club or stick. The guards nearby yelled out warnings before they went down under the weight of the infuriated and desperate prisoners. Shots rang out everywhere. Over a hundred men got away in the confusion. I wasn't among them since I was in the rear of the escape group and, by the time I reached the fence, the Partisan machine gunners were firing so heavily and continuously that there was no chance of getting out alive. Therefore, I threw myself flat on the ground, and together with other inmates who had been unable to get over the wire, crawled stealthily back in among the multitude of other prisoners. During the night about forty of those who had escaped were hunted down and killed.

On June 6, I was one of some 32,000 starved, thirsty, exhausted, and sick prisoners who left Maribor under the escort of the Sixth Bosnian Brigade, commanded by Rade Corak. This outfit distinguished itself by its efficiency in maltreating and killing the captives entrusted to its charge. The dead were left lying in ditches along the road or were thrown into the fields that adjoined this highway of death.

We were only moving skeletons when we passed through Varazdin on June 10. The Croatian inhabitants of this city wept when they saw our condition. They were ordered to place pails filled with water in front of every house along our route. When the parched prisoners made a rush for these pails, the Partisans beat them with the butts of their guns. Some captives suffered broken ribs or arms while others had their skulls smashed in or their spines fractured. At other places, our captors would not allow the population to give us water.

By the time we reached Ludbreg, we were 6000 fewer than when we started out from Maribor. Most of the 6000 were murdered between Maribor and Ludbreg, but quite a few men succeeded in escaping despite the vigilance and ruthless brutality of our Partisan guards.

We spent a night encamped at a field near Ludbreg. During this evening of misery, the Partisans maltreated and mocked us. Some prisoners who came from the locality around Ludbreg tried to get away by hiding in nearby oat plantations, but guards found and killed most of them. On the following morning, we were divided up into groups. I had attached myself to the youngest Domobrans, who were formed into a separate group and sent back to Varazdin. Here we were clad in Yugoslav uniforms and forced to pursue our brothers, the anti-Communist Krizari or Crusaders, all around the Varazdin area and through the forests in the vicinity of Lepoglava. Because of my youth, I was soon released from this service. I was told later that the prisoner column from which I had been separated at Ludbreg was taken over by the Slavonian Partisan Brigade led by Josip Mihajlek, nicknamed "Kos" (Blackbird). He served with the Communists from 1942 on, and today is chief of the UDBA or secret political police of the 36th Proletarian District. I served my regular military term under him at Varazdin in 1949.

It was at this time I learned that following my departure, the prisoner column continued its "Death March" to the notorious concentration camp at Bela Crkva in Serbia. When a cousin of mine returned from a year's stay in this hellhole, he had four broken ribs and weighed barely eighty pounds. He told me that following my departure for Varazdin with the young Domobrans, he had marched in a column of 12,000 Ustashas. Only 5000 of them survived to arrive in Pancevo, and they numbered only 2400 when they reached Bela Crkva. Another 8000 Ustashas had preceded them to this place. Every day men died of starvation, thirst, or sickness in this imitation of the German Dachau camp. The dead were buried on the grounds of the camp itself. My cousin's best friend was thrown into a hole beneath the barracks in which they were quartered. Only about a hundred and fifty men survived to return to their homes.

As indicated above, I was inducted into the regular Yugoslav Army in 1949. I happened to be assigned to serve in the unit commanded by the same Captain Nikola Krnjoc who had perpetrated the massacre of our officers near Maribor after the end of hostilities. I was still serving my term of military service when a military court of the Fifth District in Zagreb sentenced me to eight years' imprisonment and three additional years of deprivation of civil rights (not that civil rights mean anything in Tito's Yugoslavia, since no one who is not a member of the Communist Party has rights, and even Party members who fall out of favor with the powers do not enjoy them). This sentence was imposed on me because of "hostile activities against the people and State."

I served six years of this sentence and then was sent to my home, following which I was drafted into the army for the second time! Since my term of service had been interrupted in 1949 by my imprisonment, I had to complete my military service following my release! On my second tour of duty I was sent to Boljevac where I again served under Krnjoc, who was born in this vicinity.

Finally, I was discharged from the Yugoslav service and found a way of escaping into the so-called Free World. Certainly it is a great deal freer than Tito's Socialist Inferno.

Although I have given my name and address to the Committee for Investigation of the Bleiburg Tragedy, which has its center here in Cleveland, I have asked this body not to reveal these facts at the present time. This precaution is necessitated by the fear that disclosure of my identity would mean the death of relatives who are still living under Tito's domination. As to this report itself, I have written it with the same frankness with which I make my confessions to a priest. It is in this spirit that I hereby confirm this record of atrocities committed by the Yugoslav Communists with my oath and signature.

Survivor of the P.T.S.
Signed: I. K.

Cleveland, Ohio
December 1, 1961

Document XVI

This eyewitness and his group surrendered in the vicinity of Krumpendorf. A few days later, the British conveyed them to the city of Villach and extradited them to Yugoslavia. The victims were unloaded in Kranj and placed in a concentration camp where they saw women and children suffer and die. From Kranj, the captives were taken to Sent Vid and after a few days, sent to Zagreb. From the Croatian capital, they marched to Samobor, then to Precko and again to Samobor.

On May 3, 1945, I was called into the Headquarters of the P. T. S. (Pavelic Bodyguard Brigades), which was located on the Kulin-ban Square. I was here informed that preparations were being made for the evacuation of the capital and for the withdrawal of the Armed Forces northwards through Slovenia into Austria.

My detachment left Zagreb, fully armed and equipped, on May 5. We traveled by bus to Podsused, but there the vehicle developed engine trouble and had to be abandoned, since we did not have parts to fix it. I then joined a German transport which was heading in the direction of Slovenia, and thus reached Celje. Here we received food, changed uniforms, and joined a military column. Again, I traveled by truck for about twenty miles, and then *this* truck broke down! Together with a friend, I attached myself to another German transportation unit. We made it to Dravograd aboard one of their trucks, arriving there on May 7.

A skirmish with the Partisans took place at Dravograd; after the fighting ended, I joined a Croatian column which was moving quite slowly towards the Austrian frontier. When we arrived in the old land of the Habsburgs, who for four centuries had ruled us, too, we took shelter in an abandoned German airport. It was while we were resting here that we heard of Germany's capitulation.

On the following day, we went on towards Krumpendorf. Enroute, we suddenly found ourselves surrounded by Partisans and British troops. The latter had two tanks to halt our further progress. They opened negotiations with us and the "Yugoslavs" demanded that we surrender our arms. This we would not do unless both the British and Partisans agreed to let us go on to Krumpendorf and Klagenfurt. Finally a compromise was reached. We threw our weapons into nearby ditches and the ill-assorted Allies let us continue our march. Some of us kept our weapons too.

When we arrived in Krumpendorf, we were lodged in a temporary barracks which was constructed out of boards, cardboard, paper, and other improvised materials. A considerable number of Croatian soldiers, government officials, and officers assembled at this place, which was close to the railroad station. On May 13, the Partisans tried to attack the camp, but the British troops prevented them from doing so.

I do not remember whether it was May 15 or 16 when we were told to get ready to move. Trucks conveyed us to Villach in the Austrian province of Carinthia. Here we found Second Lieutenant Babic, who was on General Moskov's staff. Most of the rest of the P. T. S. units were there too. The British took us to a meadow where they gave us dry food and some money. Then we had to get aboard the trucks again and go to the railroad station where we found a great many boxcars waiting for us. We were loaded into the cars and the doors were locked behind us.

In my car was an old friend, Djuro Zvonko. Both of us were attached to P. T. S. Headquarters during the war. His companionship made the sixteen-hour ride more bearable than it would have been otherwise.

We were in Slovenia, near the town of Kranj, when the car doors were opened. Outside Partisan troops were waiting for us. I do not know how this happened. When we got on the train, we thought we were going to Italy. If we had suspected that the British intended to send us back to Slovenia and the hands of our deadly enemies, the Englishmen would have had a fight on their hands. As it was, most of us were unarmed and the few pistols that some men had concealed were of little use against the heavy machine guns and rifles which we found trained upon us. So we had to submit and allow the Partisans to lead us across a bridge into the town of Kranj, where we were placed in a prisoner of war camp, encircled by barbed wire and heavily guarded.

The first thing that the Partisans did when they got us into the camp was to rob us of everything we possessed. During this procedure, I encountered Lieutenant Babic and my own commander once again. Babic was seriously ill and I was not feeling well myself. There were women and children in this camp. Many of them became sick and some of the children died. I presume it was lack of food and the hardships entailed by the retreat that caused this epidemic of sickness. We received no food until the third day that we were in this camp. An individual who managed to hide something of value on his person was lucky, since he could sometimes bribe one of the guards to give him a piece of bread in exchange for it.

On the fifth day of our stay in Kranj, we were lined up in a column of fours. There were thousands of us, all starving and completely exhausted, who started out from Kranj on foot. Partisan guards surrounded us on every side. As we "marched" along, curses, sighs, and shots could be heard on every hand, for those who could not keep up were slaughtered mercilessly by the Partisan escort.

When we came to Sent Vid, near Ljubljana, the women who had accompanied us that far were taken away somewhere. All men were crowded into the courtyard of a hospital, where we dropped to the ground from sheer exhaustion. A cousin and a relative of my brother-in-law, both officers, were already in this place, so I kept close to them. On the third day of our incarceration, a Partisan officer addressed us, saying that nothing would be taken from us from this time on. I don't know whether this was just his idea of a joke or whether he really didn't know that his fellow Marxists had robbed us of everything we had long before. Also, he said that the younger prisoners were going to be sent to Russia "to study."

Two days after this talk, the civilians were separated from the military, and the latter were divided into officer and private soldier groups. Furthermore, men born in 1927 or later were segregated from the older males. We realized what these several divisions meant, because the Partisan officers often killed prisoners right out in the hospital courtyard. Women Partisans seemed to take a specal delight in killing the already half-dead prisoners whenever they were allowed to do so.

One morning, those of us who were eighteen or under were jammed into boxcars and sent to Croatia. When we pulled into the west railroad station in Zagreb, we were so weak that we could hardly stand up. Despite this fact, the Partisans made us march to the Samobor rail station. Mothers, sisters and wives brought food to us, but the Partisans would not allow us to have it.

At Samobor, we again were loaded into railroad boxcars and rode across the Sava bridge to the Precko concentration camp. In this camp, Ivica Loncarevic and other friends of mine were murdered by the Partisans for accepting food that a peasant offered to them. The Precko camp was terribly overcrowded; in fact there was simply no room in it for new arrivals like ourselves. So we were sent back to Samobor on foot.

On the second day of our stay in Samobor, we were interrogated. Those of us who came out of this questioning in good shape received identification cards which served as passes to our homes. However, my friends Ivica Novak and Josip Farkas were imprisoned instead of being allowed to return home. Never have I seen or heard of them since I left Samobor.

When I got to my own home I was confined to my bed because, in addition to my generally weakened condition caused by the hardships of the period following our retreat, I had contracted a severe dysentery infection.

Signed: Eyewitness #284

Document XVII

The author of this account, survivor of one of the most horrifying "Death Marches," analyzes the precarious situation that had caused the Croatian Exodus and subsequent surrender in Austria. A detailed description of lootings and killings by Slovenian and Croatian Communists who guarded the victims from Austria to Bjelovar in Croatia, is also given. From Bjelovar to Osijek, Montenegrin Partisans guarded the marchers and treated them fairly well. From Osijek on, however, maltreatment and murders of the captives at the hands of Serbian Partisans and civilians increased. The eyewitness glowingly praises the Croatian population in Bjelovar, Osijek, Pozega and elsewhere for welcoming the prisoners generously with food and water. He further states that his "Death March" ended in Tuzla, Bosnia. Over 30,000 Croats were murdered during this long trek.

In the last major encounters of the war of 1941-45, the Croatian Armed Forces cleared a way for themselves into Austria by throwing back Tito's Communist forces in bitter battles that were waged around Slovenjgradec (Windischgratz) and the Dravograd bridge. The objective of the Croatian Command was to bring the Army onto Austrian soil and to surrender it there to the Western Allies. There was no intention of yielding to the Tito faction under any circumstances.

What our Command had overlooked was the possibility that the Western Allies, particularly the British, might not wish to accept our surrender because of commitments they had made to their ally, Josip Tito Broz, and his Communist backers. Hardly had we crossed the Austrian border, than rumors began to circulate that the English had massed their planes, tanks, and cannons to bar our further progress. However, we thought at first that they were doing this only to make us wait until such time as the negotiations that our spokesmen were carrying on with their commanders could be completed.

We arrived on the great field that adjoins the town of Bleiburg at 4:00 P.M., sometime around the middle of May, 1945. Here we camped for the night. Early in the afternoon of the following day, our Command announced that we were to lay down our arms. Unfortunately, most of us still did not understand that our spokesmen had yielded to the British demand that we surrender, not to them, but to the Partisan forces commanded by Tito.

At twilight of this eventful day, rain began to fall. As word concerning the true nature of our surrender spread, general disorder set in among our troops. Some officers and soldiers warned everyone not to give up their arms to the Partisans, or to the British either, now that it was evident that the latter were only acting as an agency of the former. They suggested that we all go into the woods and fight a guerrilla-type war. Others pointed out that the war was lost in any case, because the evacuation had given the Communists possession of our homeland so that we had no prepared base from which to operate, and no one from whom to get ammunition, other necessary military supplies and food. On the other hand, Russia, England, and the United States would supply Tito's people with everything they needed, and to judge from their actions here at Bleiburg, would undoubtedly come to the assistance of the Yugoslav Communists, if by some miracle we succeeded in recapturing our lost country. Croatia could not hold out against the entire democratic and Marxist world. This is the reason why our Government and Military Command had decided to abandon the Domovina when our Armed Forces were still intact and had artillery and some planes and tanks at their disposal. What could we do now if we decided to fight? When our ammunition ran out, where could we get more? We would then be in a worse position than we were now and much more likely to incur severe punishment at the hands of the several victors in the war.

So the argument continued, with each element trying to rationalize their particular view of the situation. Since we were very hungry, we slaughtered some of the cattle that we had brought with us.

As darkness approched, the first Partisan units that we had seen on Austrian soil came into view. They were barefoot, clad in rags and tatters, and hungry, but well armed. That night, Partisan Captain Pecikozic came to visit us. Until 1943, he had served in the Croatian Army as a first lieutenant of anti-aircraft artillery. Today he is a clerk attached to the Ministry of Transportation of the People's Republic of Croatia in Zagreb. I remember him vividly as he appeared on this May evening in 1945. He wore a large five-beam red star with a sickle and hammer insignia on his military cap, but he told us not to worry about the red star because he was our friend.

That same evening I listened to a debate that was going on between an Ustasha sergeant and a Partisan Commissar. The Commissar asked the Ustasha, 'Why and to whom did you surrender? Surely not to us, as many of you and as well clad and well armed as you are? If there were iron gates reaching all the way from earth to heaven, you could break them down and pass through them. Why did you quit fighting? Certainly you could overcome us!"

Those of us who had decided to obey the surrender order had ample opportunity to appreciate the cogency of the remarks made by this Communist official.

On the following morning, we began to stack our weapons and remove the Croatian insignia from our military caps. Most of the officers took off their marks of rank, but many of them were foolish enough to insist on retaining their decorations. Perhaps this stubbornness more than anything else provides a clue to some basic faults in the Croatian national character. As individuals and as a nation, we often seem to have no grasp upon reality. We had lost a war and were in the hands of our sworn enemies, yet some of us were determined to flaunt in their faces decorations that no longer meant anything and were bound to enrage Partisans who had often taken a beating at our hands during the war.

That morning, I sat down in one of our military trucks to await my turn to deliver up my arms. Meanwhile I ate meat procured from the slaughter of the cattle, using a can for this purpose. I ate about half a can and threw the rest away. A Partisan picked up the remnant of the meat and used his fingers to extract it from the can. Then he came up to me and asked: "Comrade, have you any bread? I have not eaten anything for three days."

Since I had no ordinary bread, I gave him some biscuit bread. I asked him where he came from and he replied that he was a Serb. He was dressed in the fashion affected by the people of Shumadiya,[1] so I presume that he was a Serb as he claimed to be.

---

[1] A part of the pre-1914 Serbian state.

My turn to surrender my weapons came around 12:00 noon. On the road that leads to Maribor, I descended from my truck and in view of many Partisan officers laid down my light machine gun along with my revolver and a couple of German hand grenades that I was carrying. All of our troops who had not gone into the surrounding forests did likewise.

This was the stupidest thing I have ever done in my entire life. When I think back upon this incident and what followed it, I sometimes feel that all of us who gave up our arms in this way got just what we deserved for such cowardice. The only excuse for our action I can offer is that, as soldiers, the habit of obedience to the orders of our superior officers was ingrained into us. Had our officers commanded us to fight we would have fought, whatever the odds against us. Since they directed us to surrender, we did so. It was as simple as that.

After we had given up our weapons we were told to start moving back towards Maribor. When we were within a few miles of the Drava River we had to leave our trucks and form a column. This was the beginning of what was later referred to as the "Death March." Now the Partisans began to take everything that we had on our persons. Shoes, uniforms, watches, money, and all valuables had to be yielded to them, just as we had surrendered our weapons. To keep this fine crew from getting what I had, I threw everything that I possessed, except the clothes on my back, into the Drava during a rest period. Also I used a Gillette razor blade that I was carrying to slash holes in my trousers so the Partisans would not take these away from me as they had taken the pants of other captives. One Partisan noticed what I was doing and clouted me on the back with his rifle butt. He hit me so hard that I fell into the ditch which ran beside the road. Then he told me that I was guilty of sabotage because so many of the "heroes of the liberation" had only rags to wear.

After we had been looted of our possessions, the column proceeded further in the direction of Maribor. I saw the Partisan guards take Captain Sindek out of our column in order to kill him. Thousands of other Croatian war prisoners suffered a similar fate. The guards kept us moving at a rapid pace and often made us run at full speed in the blazing sunlight. Since they would not give us water, our thirst soon became unbearable. When we asked the Slovenes who lived along the route that we were following to bring water to us, some of them refused outright to do so while others demanded thousands of cigarettes in exchange for a glass of water. The Slovenes are the Scotchmen of Yugoslavia! Anyway, those who had plenty of cigarettes sometimes could get a few swallows of water while the rest of us went thirsty.

It was evening when we arrived in Maribor. We were herded into a military barracks which contained more than forty thousand prisoners in its immediate vicinity. Barrels of spoiled beans were given us to eat. Many prisoners refused to eat this mess; those who were hungry enough to put up with it became ill in consequence.

On the following day we started out for Zagreb. During that day's march, many thirsty, starved prisoners were killed by the Partisan escort or the Commissars. During the afternoon, we came to Novo Mesto, where we were loaded onto trains and transported through Zagreb to Dugo Selo. We camped on the fair grounds at the last-named place. Here we received our first food since the spoiled bean issue two days before. The Dugo Selo rations consisted of bread and a little weak broth.

After we had eaten, we went on towards Bjelovar, escorted all the way by Croatian and Slovenian Communists. We spent the night in a meadow where our Partisan guards began to shoot whole groups of prisoners at a time. At dawn, however, two Partisan officers came up in an automobile and issued orders to stop the killing.

Around 3:00 P.M. on this same day, we entered the Vojnovic gendarme barracks in Bjelovar. Here we waited three days for new guards to take charge of us. During this period of rest, the Croatian population of Bjelovar supplied us with food and drink. Since the guards prevented them from coming into the camp itself to bring us these welcome gifts, they had to toss the food and containers of liquid over the fence that surrounded the barracks. This activity caused the guards to yell to the prisoners to keep away from the fence, and their gun butts enforced this command.

More prisoner columns arrived daily from every direction. On the evening of the third day, the procession to which I belonged left Bjelovar and proceeded towards Osijek. Partisans belonging to a Montenegrin brigade now guarded us. Before we started this stage of our "Death March," a Montenegrin Commissar delivered an address in which he asked us to obey orders and accept our captivity without fear. Both Croatians and Montenegrins were soldiers, and the latter would not harm us.

I should like to acknowledge that this Commissar and his men kept the promise that he gave us. Whenever a mob of Serbs or other Communist sympathizers tried to beat or kill us along the line of march that we followed, the Montenegrins kept them away from us. They would shout incessantly, "Keep away from this column! We are responsible for these men until we hand them over to others!"

A day's march with an overnight halt brought us to Zeleno Polje, in the ancient Croatian town of Osijek. Here we stayed for two whole days. While our Montenegrin escorts were granted time off from watching us, we had a bad time of it. Mainly Serbs from Croatian Slavonia relieved the men of the Black Mountain. They searched everyone to see if they could find money, watches, rings, or photos that our previous captors might have missed. Besides these camp guards, young Serbs, only fifteen to seventeen years old, beat us with heavy clubs. These fellows belonged to the Slavonian Partisan Brigade, recruited from among the descendants of Serbs whom our ancestors had been so foolish as to allow to settle in Slavonia centuries before. While we were on the

Zeleno Polje, a train filled with Partisan troops passed by the camp about 4:00 P.M. The Partisans fired upon us from the moving train, killing or wounding some two hundred prisoners.

However long I may live, I shall not forget what the Croatians of Osijek and the vicinity did for us while we were involuntary "guests" in their city. Many of them traveled great distances to bring us huge quantities of food, fruit, and water. The continued starvation to which we had been exposed since the surrender had shrunken our stomachs so much that we could not eat or drink all that they brought us. This was a shame because I know that most of these people made severe sacrifices on their own part to relieve our misery. In our column there were several men who were natives of Osijek. Their relatives tried to locate them, but the Serbian guards would not permit them to talk with their loved ones.

After two days on the Zeleno Polje, we proceeded towards Slavonska Pozega by way of Krndija and Papuk. As we left Osijek we could hear children crying behind us, "Daddy! Come back!" The guards obliged the women and children related to the prisoners to remain, and the parting was a sad one since the captives knew that they probably would never see their families again.

On the way to Slavonska Pozega, we passed through the village of Cerin, which is chiefly a Serbian settlement. The Serbian inhabitants of this place gave us poisoned milk to drink and beat us with pitch or hay-forks. If the Montenegrin escorts had not protected us, many of us would have been killed. The Black Mountain men kept shooting into the air to frighten the mob away. Despite this action, some of us left our bones to blight the Slavonian landscape.

We arrived in Slavonska Pozega during the evening hours, and were placed immediately in the Glotez camp, which occupied the site of a former military shop and warehouse. I believe there must have been forty thousand prisoners here. Now the Montenegrins, of whom we had good memories, handed us over to other escorts.

In the Glotez Camp, the prisoners suffered beyond description from starvation and typhoid fever. They died quietly side by side or in the arms of the stronger members of the column. Although there was a stream of water scarcely sixty feet outside the barbed wire fence of this camp, the Partisans never gave us any water themselves or allowed us to get any from the stream. They stood outside the wire, and as the captives pressed forward to beg for water, the Reds shot at and killed some of these parched wretches. When the Croatians of this vicinity brought food to us, the Partisan guards took it for themselves. Fortunately, there was more food than they coud eat, and sometimes when it spoiled because of the summer heat, they would toss what remained to us. One of my fellow sufferers got hold of the head of a red onion in this way and gave part of it to me, saying that it would help to prevent my contracting typhoid fever. Oh how hard it was to eat that onion, suffering from thirst in all the heat to which we were directly exposed!

We remained at S. Pozega for three days, then left for Pitomaca. Members of the Zagorska Brigade were our new escorts. They rode horses while we "marched," half clad, barefoot, starved and dying of thirst. They forced us to run by beating us with long poles. Whenever a prisoner could not keep up with the rest of the column, he was killed by Partisans who were following the rear on motorscooters. Peasants in the neighborhood had to bury the dead. The Croatian population living between S. Pozega and Pitomaca attempted to give us water, but the guards killed everyone who tried to take a drink. Then they would empty the water containers, telling the people who were trying to help us, "These Ustasha bandits do not need water!"

We stayed in Pitomaca for only two hours, but while we were there, individual prisoners who were identified as belonging to Ustasha units were taken out of the column and shot in front of the church. I shall never forget how the Croatian population of the place were moved to tears by this sight and how they shouted angrily at the Partisans, "Why are you killing them now? It's easy to kill them when they're disarmed like this, isn't it? Where were you when they had their weapons?" One group of women braved the threats of the guards to provide us with bread and milk. As they fed us, they cried bitterly, "Soldiers, our soldiers, to whom did you surrender—to these lousy criminals from out of the forests?"

Late on the same evening that we left Pitomaca, we arrived in Koprivnica, where we stayed on the fair grounds. The Partisans began to look among us for men of General Boban's command. They had bitter memories of these fighters who had given them solid trouncings here at Koprivnica itself as well as elsewhere in the Posavina. Throughout the night, the Croats of Koprivnica brought food to us, tossing it right over the heads of the guards. On the following morning we were driven further, through the villages of the Podravina. Everywhere the Croatian population displayed sympathy for us and helped us as much as they could.

When we came to Djurdjevac, however, about a hundred Communist sympathizers, men and women alike, had assembled for the purpose of stoning and beating us. They killed some captives by striking them with heavy clubs. Those who lived went on through Lipik, Pakrac, and Daruvar to Slavonski Brod. Some men collapsed, but others picked them up and carried them to keep the guards from killing them on the spot. For instance, my friend Dragec was unable to walk any further, so together with other prisoners, I carried him for twenty miles. That he is still alive and residing in Zagreb resulted particularly from the good services rendered him by a headquarters' sergeant who happened to be a friend of mine from Sibenik in Dalmatia.

Our stay at Slavonski Brod lasted for two days. Although we were given bean soup and bread, we could not eat it because we all had either diphtheria or typhoid. Nevertheless we had to go on from Sl. Brod through Prijedor, Doboj, and the valley of the Bosna River, the cradle of the medieval Croatian Kingdom of Bosnia. Many were carried by the current of the Bosna to their last resting place. After a week of journeying through the towns and villages of Bosnia, we arrived in Tuzla and were lodged in the former military barracks.

This was the last concentration camp that I had to put up with on my own personal "Death March." I remained here with other survivors of the column until December. During this time we all had to work at the hardest physical tasks imaginable, despite our emaciated and diseased condition. Among other labors that we performed were stone breaking, working on the roads, and lumbering jobs in the forests. While so engaged, we received one meal a day. Every night we were exposed to the attacks of former Serbian Chetniks who had joined Tito's forces at the end of the war. They posed as loyal Communists during the daytime, so they could more easily revert to the role of Mihailovic men after darkness fell, and they had leisure to liquidate Croatian soldiers and civilians.

On one occasion, I was sent with a prisoner group back to Sl. Brod to disassemble some German artillery there. When we had completed this job, we returned to Tuzla. In this Bosnian city we slept out in an open meadow during the fall months, and when winter came, were allowed to take shelter in former horse stables. Since this lodging was wholly inadequate for the bitterly cold Bosnian winter, all of us contracted one kind of illness or another. After a long day of arduous work, we were subjected to military drills on the "Sloboda" soccer field. While we were drilling, a Communist Colonel who had lost an arm in the war tried to make us sing Partisan songs but we were not only unable (because of the colds from which we were suffering) but also unwilling to comply with his commands. Because of our obstinacy on this point, he called us traitors (to what?), cursed our Croatian mothers, and vilified us in the most obscene terms imaginable.

One day we were told that we were to be issued military uniforms. We were lined up and marched to the Tuzla hospital. When we arrived there, we were given torn and bloody uniforms that had belonged to Partisan soldiers who had fallen fighting against us Croatians during the war. Many of these uniforms were pierced with bullet holes. Actually the "uniforms" consisted only of trousers made of woolen cloth known as "coha." Also, our Communist captors gave us typical Serbian peasant moccasins whose original owners probably had no further use for these articles of footwear. Although many of us were still barefoot and almost naked, we did not want to don either these moccasins or the uniforms that went with them.

At long last, we were assigned to regular units of the Yugoslav Army. Out of forty thousand some three thousand of us had survived to deserve this boon. We survivors were loaded into boxcars and sent off by train in various directions. I was one of a group of three hundred prisoners who were assigned to the notorious 7th Banija Division. This outfit's chief claim to fame, or rather to infamy, was that it had slaughtered 15,000 German war prisoners near Nova Gorica, after the war was over. The officers and soldiers of this division boasted not only of this exploit but also of knifing Ustasha prisoners following the end of formal hostilities. Colonel Gruber, who despite his German name, was a Captain of Serbian Chetniks until 1943 when he went over to the Partisans, was the Divisional Commander. It is easy to imagine how the officers and men of this command treated us during our six months stay at Idria, where the entire division was quartered as a form of punishment for some transgression.

I endured this suffering, too, and eventually was able to return to my home. Those of my relatives who were still alive did not recognize me because I weighed just 107 pounds! It is perhaps fortunate that at the time of my homecoming my father and mother both were still in prison. I believe that if they had seen me when I first got back they would have died of shock, because before and during the war I was a fairly robust young man.

The account that I have given above is only a part of the recollections that I retain of the end of the war and the following years. I am sorry that I cannot recall the exact dates when the events I remember occurred.

I request that neither my first nor my last name be appended to this account so that reprisals cannot be taken by the present regime in Belgrade against my relatives who are still living in Croatia. Since they are Croatians and Catholics, the Yugoslav Communists consider them to be outlaws, precisely because they are loyal to the Croatian homeland. Should my experiences appear in print, and my identity become known, they would have to undergo more persecution, and possibly "liquidation." However, some of the members of the Committee for the Investigation of the Bleiburg Tragedy know who I am and can vouch for the reliability of my story.

Signed: V. F.

Chicago, Illinois
September 3, 1962

Document XVIII

After the British had refused to accept the surrender of several thousand Croatian troops and civilians, the whole contigent had to return to Dravograd where General Kocha Popovitch's troops took charge of them. Past Dravograd, the eyewitness and many other women were separated from the "death column" of their husbands and were driven to Maribor in a "death train." Later, they were placed in a concentration camp for women and children. Our witness saw the horrifying sufferings of her inmates and another "death transport" of female prisoners. She also describes the well-known anti-tank trenches at Maribor, and the Red Cross trucks which carried the Croatian prisoners to that infamous place. Brutalities of Tito's troops against pregnant and even laboring women are especially stressed in this account. The testimony closes with a vivid description of extermination camps and massacre sites in Pozega.

On May 6, 1945, I left Zagreb on foot in the company of my husband who was retreating with a military column that proceeded to Dravograd via Savski Marof, Celje, and Slovenjgradec (Windischgratz). There were many battles along the way, but we fought successfully against the Partisan forces which tried to stop us, and eventually arrived safely on Austrian soil at Wolfsberg.

Here the British Army refused to accept our surrender! On May 17, they ordered us to go back towards Dravograd. On the following day we were back at the bridge that crosses the Drava River to Dravograd, where we had been a few days before. But then we were headed towards what we thought was political asylum on foreign soil; now we were returning to our native land. But did we have a future to look forward to?

The British did not escort us back to Dravograd. However, twelve English planes hovered threateningly over our heads, and English guards at the Drava bridge ordered us, very harshly, to lay down our weapons at a place which was 300-400 meters away from the bridge. Near this spot some fifty poorly-dressed Partisans were hovering.

We had four thousand well-equipped troops who were ready to fight anyone whom they were ordered to fight. But there was no one to give orders! All of the officers with us seemed to have lost their heads, or to have convinced themselves that since the war was lost in any case they might as well make the best of it and make their peace with the victors as well as they could. Many of the soldiers were very upset by the predicament in which they found themselves and hesitated to obey the orders of the British until their own officers told them to do so. Then they cursed or wept according to their individual temperaments as they kissed their weapons and piled them alongside others which earlier formations had evidently left there. My husband wanted to commit suicide at this point, but Captain Merkic, who had fought as a volunteer in Russia, dissuaded him, saying, "S., don't be crazy! You weren't born with weapons in your hands! Now lay them down!" Then he took my husband's pistol away from him. Captain Merkic certainly was a brave man, proved by his war record on the Russian front. But two days earlier he had negotiated with the Bulgarians, who were aiding Tito's armies, and the talks he had engaged in with the Bulgars evidently had influenced him to take an optimistic view of the consequences of surrender.

I would like to stress the fact that if we had possessed any kind of determined leadership, we could have instantly overpowered both the British and the Partisans, and perhaps held the survivors as hostages. Had we taken such action, however, we would have been a target for the bombs of the British planes, against which there was no cover in the vicinity of the bridge.

While we were stacking our weapons, another Partisan unit came up. We were told that they were Kocha Popovitch's men. They were well armed and dressed in German and Domobran uniforms. Although they displayed a very stern attitude towards us, they did not plunder our belongings at first. They shouted, "Officers, go ahead!"

Together with the wives of several other officers, I asked permission to accompany the officer group. The Partisans granted our request. They placed the officers and their wives at the head of the column, the non-coms and private soldiers behind. Ustasha, Domobran, and Gendarmerie officers all were grouped alongside one another, their wives with them. Then the plundering started. The Partisans took everything that had gold or silver in it, all watches, boots, overcoats and the like. They did not beat us at this time, however.

After sunset on this same day, May 18, Kocha Popovitch's men started the prisoner column moving towards Maribor. Because of road blocks and the attempts that some of the captives made to escape, we made slow progress. Sometimes we stood for hours at a time without moving at all, while the escapees were being rounded up or killed. On May 20, we still were only six miles out of Dravograd. At about 11:00 A.M. on this day we arrived at a brick factory where the wives of the officers were separated from their husbands. Most of us wanted to continue with our men, but the Partisans used force to stop us from doing so. When I refused to leave my husband, a Partisan struck at me with the butt of his gun. I carried his blow with my arm which consequently remained numb for two days afterwards. At the time I was only eighteen years old and already three months pregnant.

Those of us who were the wives of officers were loaded onto a four-car train filled with members of the Ustasha Female Youth. These young girls were from fourteen to sixteen years of age, but many of them looked even younger than this. They were dressed uniformly and came from Virovitica, Osijek, Bozjakovina, Krizevci, and Zagreb. There were a few older girls also, their age ranging from twenty to twenty-two years. Among them I recognized an old acquaintance, Vilma Kuzmek, from Bozjakovina. We were so crowded together in the cars that there was no room to sit down, so we had to stand, packed like sardines in a can. We had received nothing to eat for the past three days and were suffering from thirst and exhaustion as well. Many of the younger girls fainted and we had to hold them up in our arms since we had no place to lay them.

On the evening of this day, May 20, we arrived at the main railroad station in Maribor. Standing at the front of my car was the wife of Ustasha Second Lieutenant I. C. of Bihac. As we pulled into the station she yelled to us: "Get off the train! Hide underneath the cars! Your life is in danger!" All of us heard her words, but we were too exhausted and discouraged to care whether we lived or not. I think that her words were meant particularly for me, because when I did not move at first, she reminded me specifically of my mother for whom I had cared since the death of all four of my brothers in the war. Then I did exert myself to get out of the car. I jumped down and hid in the semi-darkness underneath it along with Maja Budjak from Senj and her fiance, First Lieutenant Jerko Sliskovic, a Croat from Hercegovina, who somehow had gotten in among this carload of women, or rather girls. I took off the trousers and jacket that I was wearing and put on a dress which the wife of the Ustasha lieutenant brought to me. She had called out the warning to us because she had overheard the Partisans conversing among themselves during the train ride and thus learned that they intended to kill all of the Female Ustasha Youth. The rest of us also had heard the Partisans yell at us both during the trip and from the Maribor station platform, "Tonight you'll ride on the tide of the Drava!"

The train stopped for only fifteen minutes at Maribor and then got under way again. I heard later on that all these young girls were slaughtered by the Partisans and indeed thrown into the Drava! The Partisans and their fellow travelers spoke quite openly of this incident for years afterwards.

Meanwhile, those of us who had escaped from the train could find no shelter in Maribor because we knew no one was there. After a while, a Partisan patrol picked us up and took us to the concentration camp which was close to the railroad station. Of course, they did not guess that we had been on the death train, since we were older than the young Ustasha girls.

The concentration camp in which we found ourselves possessed ten barracks which were used by German troops during the war. However, the Partisans bolted up the doors and windows so that we could not use these buildings, even when it rained. There were about five thousand of us in the camp, all civilians, most of whom were women and children. Left out in the open as we were, we suffered exceedingly from heat, rain, thirst, and hunger. We received absolutely nothing to eat while we were in this place. The wife of the Ustasha lieutenant and I succeeded in getting out of the barbed wire enclosure once in order to look for food and water—the latter commodity also denied to us by the Partisans. They had blocked up all the water pumps and faucets in the camp, though hundreds of young children were crying and begging for a drink of water. I remember vividly the sufferings endured by one old lady, Mrs. Marija Mikel, who came from Vrlika near Sinj. She had with her a girl by the name of Krista, who was her daughter-in-law, and her five little grandchildren. They were all between five and twelve years of age. They cried bitterly and constantly because their throats were parched. The Serbian Partisans were particularly brutal towards this family because Mrs. Mikel's father had fallen fighting against the Chetniks of Mihailovic at Bosansko Grahovo in 1941; some of these Partisans probably were ex-Chetniks. Although I often have inquired about them during the past ten years, I never have been able to find out the ultimate fate of this pathetic group.

During the two days that I remained in the Maribor camp, another transport of female prisoners was butchered by the Partisans. Some of the victims were members of the Ustasha Youth, while others belonged to officer families. There were several carloads of these women and girls, all of whom were taken from the train at Maribor and subsequently liquidated. Among them were the following: Miss Ljubica Srsen of Zagreb; Nevenka Cigic, sister-in-law of General Marko Pavlovic, a Croat from Mostar; Miss Danica Tomas, sister of the wife of Ustasha Major Tomas; Mira Matkovic, wife of the well-known Ivica Matkovic; Ankica Kardum from Prijedor, and a Serbian girl, Bozica, who during the war had escaped from the Chetniks and joined the Croatians. Mrs. Matkovic was hung in Gradiska, according to what I heard from another lady, D.M., and her mother. These two were not killed, for some reason, but were sent back to Zagreb to be "tried." They eventually were liberated, because of the intercession of a Jewish physician, Dr. Spitzer, on their behalf. He was either a Communist himself or else had succeeded in getting himself into the good graces of the Tito Regime in one way or another.

On the evening of May 23, the guards emptied the entire concentration camp at the rail station. They lined up the entire prisoner population, women, children, old men, and invalids in column and started them out on foot for Zagreb. Since almost all of us were completely worn out, we could only proceed slowly. As twilight came on, we were approaching Ptuj. On the right hand side of the road that we were following, anti-tank trenches had been dug out during the war. They were about eight feet deep and equally wide, with white sand strewn along their floors. They stretched out in zig-zag fashion for about a kilometer, running to the east of four two-story military barracks and a couple of smaller buildings attached to them. We were led along the side of these trenches towards the barracks.

As we approached them, two Red Cross ambulance trucks passed by our column. They were so filled with passengers that the doors could not quite be closed. At the door of each truck stood a Partisan armed with a light machine gun. Six feet in front of me in the column was a fairly young woman who had little twin girls. They were about two years old I should judge. The woman recognized her husband, whose hands were tied behind him with wire, and who was standing at the door of one of these Red Cross ambulances. She left her children in the ditch near the road and tried to board the slowly moving ambulance. A guard shoved her away from the machine and she fell onto the road where she lay weeping and tearing her hair. We picked up the children and brought them to their mother who seemed to be completely drained of life. All of us had seen that her husband was a young Croatian soldier and we realized that he was going to be shot along with the other captives in the Red Cross ambulances. This incident caused everyone nearby to break into tears, because we not only sympathized with this woman and her husband and children, but also realized that our own men would fare no better than he. We guessed that their bodies would be thrown into the anti-tank trenches. This was our only consolation, for at least we knew where we could come to mourn them.

Another lady, the wife of officer Franjo Vrbicevic, also saw her husband in one of the Red Cross trucks. She asked the Partisans what was going to happen to him, and they drew their hands across their throats, meaning that his was going to be cut.

Just before sunset the guards pushed us through the big iron gate which led into the yard of the barracks. We were taken to the first building, which probably was a relic of Habsburg times, since it was painted yellow.[1] All of the buildings were crowded with prisoners. From time to time a large truck loaded with men whose hands were bound with wire would pass by the barracks yard. It was evident to us that most of the passengers in these vehicles were Croatian officers. The Partisans did not hide from us the fact that they were going to be shot. The anti-tank trenches extending to the east of the barracks continued on over a hill which was covered with vineyards and trees. We could see the trucks go on past the barracks and continue uphill. A little while after they disappeared from view, we heard the continued firing of machine guns. Before darkness fell on this first day at the barracks, I saw ten trucks loaded with prisoners pass by and go up the hill. After dark I still could hear the noise of the motors as other death transports passed by. The shooting lasted until dawn. All one thousand of the people in our column were aware that our husbands, fathers, sons, or brothers were being massacred; we wept throughout the night. There were those among us in the barracks who were slated for execution too. The Partisans made no secret of this fact, or of the slaughter that already was being enacted, so most of us were convinced that we too would be shot during the night. Therefore we prayed and commended our souls into the hands of our Maker.

At sunrise on the next morning, May 24, the Partisan guards burst in among us yelling "Get up, bandits!" They took us to the point at which we had left the road the day before. Again we were started off towards Zagreb. There was a column of young men, most of them between the ages of sixteen and eighteen, standing alongside the road. As they were members of the Croatian Honor Work Service, they carried shovels and other tools. Many of them were bleeding from wounds inflicted by blunt or pointed instruments. I saw an acquaintaince, Marko Kardum, in the very first row of this column. He had a wound over his eye and blood

[1] Yellow was the usual color of the old barracks of the Austro-Hungarian Army, as well as of the Imperial and Royal Government buildings throughout the Dual Monarchy. The colors of the House of Habsburg are yellow and black.

was running down his face. I went up to him and tried to stop the bleeding but couldn't because the Partisans had taken even my handkerchiefs. He told me he had been injured when Maribor women stoned the prisoners. These feminine Partisan sympathizers had closed up all the wells so the prisoners could not drink from them, and they kept calling out mockingly to the youths, "Ustashas! Ustashas!"

This attitude displayed by the women of Maribor was fairly common among the Slovenes. When some of the women in my prisoner column asked for bread at Slovenian houses along our line of march, they received only the scoffing answer, "Let your Pavelic give you bread!"

It took us the whole day to get to Ptuj, where we spent the nights of the 24th and 25th. On the 26th, we arrived in Krapina; a day later we were in Oroslavlje, and finally, on the fourth day of our enforced hike, we reached Zagreb. It was the 27th of May.

When I look back upon those terrible nine days that followed the surrender at Dravograd, the whole period seems like a nightmare to me. During all this time our Partisan captors gave us nothing to eat or drink. I remember that at the concentration camp by the Maribor railroad station, Dr. Petar Glavas[2] managed to smuggle in a loaf of bread to us. There were fifteen of us who shared this treasure, each getting a couple of mouthfuls. Also we did encounter one sympathetic Slovene along our route who gave us some cooked potatoes. Thirst bothered us more than lack of food. The only water that we got came from little pools that had collected in holes in the road. We would kneel beside these to get a few hurried gulps before guards noticed what we were doing.

When it came to the plundering of our persons, the Shkipetars (Albanians) were our worst tormentors. They also led out men from the barracks to be shot. We could not understand what they said to us, for none of them spoke Croatian, and we did not know Albanian. I remember how one of these fellows stripped the boots off the swollen feet of a Croatian woman from Travnik. He did this so brutally that she screamed with pain. She was pregnant at this time and later had a miscarriage, probably as a result of this man's brutality. Actually, I thought he meant to break both of her legs because of the way he forced off her boots.

There were many other women who had miscarriages, as I did myself. All of us who were pregnant had to drag ourselves along, half dead. We did not dare fall behind the column because we knew that we would be killed without mercy if we did so. All along our route we passed the bodies of previous stragglers. Most of them were soldiers, but there were some civilian corpses among them. I myself saw an old Croat from Lika sit down right in the road and declare that he was too tired to

[2] Dr. Glavas, member of the Croatian Franciscan province in Bosnia, was later killed. He is one of forty-six Franciscans of this community who were murdered by the Tito troops.

go any further. A mounted Partisan officer ordered another soldier of Tito, who was on foot, to kill this man. The infantryman did so without hesitation.

At this point in my narrative, I want to mention two other episodes that occurred during the march to Zagreb. Along the stretch of road that lies between the barracks where we spent the night of the 23rd and Ptuj, an officer's wife had labor pains. She had to lie down in a ditch alongside the road. Here she gave birth to twins, a girl and boy respectively. The Partisans did not molest her, but they did not allow anyone in the column to give her any help, either. Finally, the guards made her get up and follow along with the tail end of the column, while other prisoners carried her babies for her. Later on when I tried to do what I could for her, she told me that she had asked the Partisans to let her go to a nearby peasant house but they had refused her request. I do not know what happened to her.

The second incident that stands out in my mind occurred as we were crossing the Drava bridge at Ptuj. We could see that the waters of this stream were running red with blood. Many corpses were floating on the surface of the water. Some thirty meters in front of me a woman by the name of Jelena from Novska, who was married to a second lieutenant from Split, was carrying two little children who were only two or three years old. Suddenly she climbed over the bridge railing, still holding the infants in her arms, and jumped into the river with them. The guards did not even try to stop her.

When we reached Krapina, we were interrogated concerning our flight from Croatia. Then when we got to Oroslavlje, the Croatian inhabitants brought warm food to us!

Those of us who survived the grueling ordeals to which we had been subjected met various fates after our arrival in Zagreb. Maja Budjov was hung along with her fiance, Lieutenant Mirko Sliskovic. As for myself, I managed to escape from the column with one of my girl friends. Since we didn't know where else to go, we entered the capital, going by way of Tuskanec. I found that the Partisans had already taken over my apartment.

I stayed in the city for six months, but then was expelled from it. I had contacts with the Krizari (anti-Communist resistance fighters) commanded by Nikola Vulic and other former officers of the Croatian Army. I was arrested at Garesnica and taken to Bjelovar where the UDBA chief, a Serb by the name of Gugitch who came from Pisnik, exercised every ingenuity in torturing me in order to extract information concerning the whereabouts of the Krizari. His assistant and fellow townsman, Lazhitch, gave him all the assistance he needed to execute this undoubtedly congenial task.

Following my "interrogation," I was tried before the Divisional Military Court at Nova Ves (in Zagreb). I was sentenced to two years imprisonment in the K.P.Z.[3] prison in Pozega. There were perhaps five thousand female inmates of this prison. Besides the male guards, there were some illiterate Serbian women from Banija and Kordun who also served in this capacity; their conduct was worse than that of their male colleagues. The prison director was Jovan Radic from Kistanje.

While I was confined at Pozega, I often was sent outside the jail to work. Sometimes I had the opportunity to pass quite close to the concentration camp, which was located two miles outside the city, between "Cesma" and "Trenkovo."[4] We prisoners who were doing outside work could see a barbed wire fence about a quarter of a mile away from the Orljava River. Several hundred of us managed to get close enough at one time or another to see arms, legs, skulls, and bits of uniforms protruding from the ground in back of the fence.

Informants told me that for several days Croatian patriots were brought by truck to be executed at this place. The majority of the mass graves around Pozega are located at the "Pozeski Jarak," near the vineyards which used to belong to the nuns. Everyone living in Pozega knows about the mass shooting of prisoners carried out by Tito's Partisans. Sometimes hungry dogs would dig up the bodies and drag parts of them through the fields. Probably it was for this reason that the Communists slaughtered even dogs after the war.

This report was read to me in the original Croatian text and I have signed it. I am ready to testify to the truth of all the facts that I have described above, and to do so under oath.

Signed: S. M.

Munich, West Germany

July 20, 1955

Document XIX

The Exodus of elite Croatian troops and civilians of all categories, who in mid-May 1945, surrendered to the British in the Klagenfurt Valley, is described. Under the pretense of being transported to northern Italy, the victims were extradited to Tito's troops, and the "Death Transport" began at Bleiburg, On May 22, it arrived in Maribor. On May 24, in honor of Tito's birthday, the eyewitness and his group were saved from execution. Two days later they were shipped to Zagreb where they were imprisoned in the Savska Street. Here, as they did in Maribor, the victims either saw or heard of slaughterhouse procedures which were meted out even to pregnant women, and children. The author of this account joins the Yugoslav Army and later sees how the people of the village of Ruda were expelled from their home. The account concludes with a description of massacre sites near Zagreb.

---

[3] Kazneno Popravni Zavod (Poenal Reformatory Institute).

[4] See also Doc. XXX.

We started out by train from Zagreb towards Maribor on May 7, 1945. Since some cars were filled with wounded soldiers who had been removed from the military hospitals in the capital and places nearby, four cars did carry Red Cross markings. Other passengers on the train included girls who belonged to the female section of the Ustasha Youth Organization in Zagreb, Krizevci, and other localities, women, children, and old people who belonged to official families, and other assorted civilians. There were also some fifty priests and seminarians. Among these refugees were people who had not a single relative in the Croatian Armed Forces or in the Pavelic Government. They were fleeing the homeland, because they knew what Tito Broz's Partisans were capable of doing to anyone who could not fight back effectively. Just as we were approaching Celje, one old man committed suicide by opening a vein in his wrist and bleeding to death. Before we crossed the Slovenian border, many other older people got off the train whenever it stopped in order that they might secure and carry with them into exile a small lump of Croatian soil.

All along the route, we heard explosions as the Croatian Pioneers blew up trucks or other vehicles that the German Wehrmacht had abandoned along the highways. Although the four cars mentioned above were clearly marked by the Red Cross, frequent air raids were made upon our train. I believe that both Partisan and British and perhaps Russian planes participated in these attacks. Because of the delays caused by these raids and other reasons, it took us two full days to get to Celje, where we arrived on Wednesday, May 9, at 4:00 P.M. Here German troops forced us to leave the train. They told us that peace had been concluded and that only Germans would be permitted to stay on this train which was going to continue on to Germany.

Thus, we had to walk from Celje to Sant Petar near Maribor. Here we joined other refugees and soldiers and formed a regularly organized column. We understood that we were to proceed to Austria, part of which was already occupied by English troops to whom we would surrender. General Ajanovic assumed command of our column. He was assisted by Lieutenant-Colonel Minic.

Some people had gloomy presentiments about what lay ahead of us. While we still were at Sant Petar, the son of Professor Stahuljak of the University of Zagreb shot himself and his fiancee, a young woman by the name of Maria Devide. He was not a soldier but an employee of "Merkur."[1]

Along with the refugees from the train, P.T.S. (Pavelic Bodyguard Brigades) units, members of the Honor Work Service, members of the Ustasha Women's Organization, and great numbers of civilians of all categories were included in the column. There were mothers with small

---

[1] An association of privately employed clerks which, like countless other Croatian organiations, was abolished at the arrival of Tito's Partisans.

children in their arms and their other children walking beside them. There must have been five thousand people in all.

We set out along the valley of the Savinja River. As we followed its course, we climbed high into the Slovenian Alps until we came to the Austrian border. Here we saw many demolished homes. To the left of us, far off in the distance, we could see the peak of Grintovac Mountain disappearing into the clouds. On May 14 or 15, we arrived safely at the Austrian town of Eisenkappel, worn out and hungry. All we had to eat since leaving Zagreb was a bit of horse meat and leaves stripped from beech trees.

On the day after our arrival at Eisenkappel, we started out for Klagenfurt. En route to that point, we met British troops who demanded that we surrender to them unconditionally. Since we were on Austrian soil where the Communists had no jurisdiction, or where, even if they occupied some places, they could be expected to behave more decently than they were likely to in their homelands, we saw no reason to refuse the English demand. We had lost the war but, after all, Englishmen didn't murder prisoners, at least they hadn't been known to do so since the Indian Sepoy Rebellion of 1857. We would have done well, however, to remember the fate of the Boers of South Africa, whom the British crowded into concentration camps where thousands died miserably during the war of 1899-1902. However, we were too concerned with our present circumstances to recollect what we had learned from our history books in school.

After we had surrendered our arms, the English put the older people, women, and the children into trucks. The rest of us continued our march on foot. On May 16 or 17, we arrived at Grafenstein where we had to camp in an open field. Since it was raining, the weather made it bad for us civilians who had no tents. The military men had tents with them and they allowed us to share these as much as possible. However, there were just too many people to be accommodated in the few tents that they had at their disposal.

Through interpreters or sign language, the British soldiers told us that we were going to be transported by way of Villach into refugee camps in Italy. Some of our own people spoke English, among them Dr. Matej Kranjcec,[2] formerly pastor at the old Frankopan stronghold of Ozalj, and K. J., a Franciscan priest. Thus there was no doubt about what the Englishmen told us. Perhaps, they were just trying to cheer us up and had no idea themselves what was in store for us.

Early on the morning of Saturday, May 19, British military trucks arrived to take the disarmed Croatian troops in our column to Villach for, as we understood, further transport to Italy. It took all of Saturday and Sunday to remove the military personnel. In the forenoon hours of Mon-

[2] Dr. Kranjcec, member of the Zagreb Archdiocese, was later killed. He is one of fifty-six of this Archdiocese's priests who were liquidated by the Yugoslav Reds.

day, May 21, Croatian State officals were transported. Family groups and single civilians were taken about 8:00 A.M. We climbed aboard the trucks willingly, glad that we were going to Italy. The farther we could remove ourselves from Tito the better.

A heavy British tank rolled along in front of our column while another brought up the rear. British military police on motorcycles escorted us also. We assumed that they had come along to protect us from Partisan troops, likely to become extraordinarily valiant as soon as they found out that our own soldiers were disarmed.

Our first doubts came when we passed a Croatian soldier who was coming from the direction in which we were going. He stared at us with horror on his face and put both hands to his head, yelling out "Oh, God, where are you going?"

Soon after this incident, we were unloaded onto a field which was close to the Bleiburg railway station. Then the British guards lined us up in double file. They made us raise our hands over our heads, and despite our loud protests, they searched us and took away our cameras, watches, and other valuables. They answered our complaints by saying, "Better that you give these things to us than to the Partisans."

Only now did we really begin to comprehend the fix we were in. But it was too late to remedy matters. Some of us tried to get away in order to hide in the nearby wheat fields, but the English soldiers threatened to kill us, saying they had orders to shoot all escapees. Dr. Kranjcec went to the British Commander to ask him to let the column go and allow the fugitives to save themselves if they could manage to do so. The Briton replied that he had been ordered by higher authority to turn over all captured Croatians to the Yugoslav Army. In case the Croatians had any grievances concerning the treatment given them by this Army, they could bring their complaints to the attention of the English Consul in Zagreb.

At dusk, the British took us to the Bleiburg rail station where Partisan units were waiting to take charge of us. They threw us into freight cars and locked the doors. The prisoner trains pulled out to the accompaniment of volleys of rifle shots and bursts of machine gun fire. I think that the Partisans were firing away not so much with the intention of hitting anyone, although of course they didn't care if they did, but rather to discourage any escape attempts.

A number of men were delivered into the hands of Tito's executioners at the same time I was. I have already mentioned the name of the English-speaking priest, Dr. Matej Kranjcec. There were also Dr. Richard Ribic,[3] Superior of the Franciscan Monastery in Karlovac, the seminarian Ante Dunatov and Martin Macukat of the Sibenik diocese, and a young man by the name of Kulisak who belonged to the diocese of Senj.[4]

[3] Dr. Ribic, a member of the St. Cyril and Methodius Croatian Franciscan Province, was later killed. He is one of ten priests of this community who were liquidated by the Partisans.

[4] Twenty priests of the Senj diocese were killed by the Yugoslav Communists. Kulisak's name, however, is not on the list.

Our train arrived at Maribor at 4:00 A.M. on May 22. As soon as we unloaded, we were taken to a large camp which was located close to a partially destroyed military barracks. A great number of Croatian soldiers and civilians were already assembled in this camp where we remained until May 26. We stayed out in the open without any covering to protect us from the rain, which sometimes fell in torrents. Some of us gathered up pieces of brick from the ruined barracks, so we could lie on them instead of directly in the mud. Men, women, and children were herded together in this camp, all suffering equally. Such food as we received was of miserable quality and altogether insufficient in quantity. We had to submit to being looted of all of our remaining possessions, but we were not much misused in other ways. The commissars at this camp assured us that "those whose hands are not bloody" would be set free. A minor annoyance was the Partisan habit of firing machine gun bursts over our heads at night. In consequence, we were afraid to get up at any time. This tactic unquestionably inhibited plans of escape.

Fellow sufferers who already had spent time in this camp told us that every night trucks loaded with prisoners went into the woods nearby. In due time they returned empty. The older prisoners said that mass executions took place in the forest every single night. We ourselves heard the firing of automatic weapons from the woods. Our military personnel now paid with their lives for allowing the British to disarm them. Civilians, too, and many women, particularly those belonging to the Zenska Loza or Women's Branch of the Ustasha movement, were liquidated also. The old prisoners alerted us to the fact that certain death awaited anyone who was taken to the barracks and confined there.

Thus, we had the gloomiest presentiments when, on the evening of May 25, our group was transferred to the ruins of this building. However, we were glad that the women and children who had accompanied us so far were separated from us and sent by train to Zagreb. In the big dining hall of the barracks we found many military overcoats, officers' coats, knapsacks, and other articles that had belonged to the officers and soldiers who had preceded us into this place. We knew what awaited us. The priests who were with us heard confessions and gave final absolution to all prisoners who wished this last consolation.

We could hear the town clock striking one A.M., when a number of trucks pulled up before the building. "This is it!" we muttered to one another, and shook hands silently in the darkness. Some of us prepared to fight for our lives, while others accepted their fate passively.

Time passed and nothing happened. One hour succeeded another, and still none of us were obliged to get into the waiting vehicles. We saw the commander of the camp exchanging whispered comments that seemed like arguments with other Partisan officers. Dawn broke, and we were still alive and in the barracks.

Later, I found out why our lives were spared from an old acquaintance, L.P., who had joined the Partisans at the end of the war. L.P. told me that the British and Americans had exerted pressure upon the government in Belgrade to put a halt to the orgy of killing that had followed the English extradition of prisoners. This intervention on the part of the western Allies happened to coincide with the date of Tito's birthday, which I understand is May 24. Belgrade did not want to acknowledge that it was susceptible to pressure from the West; thus, the Yugoslav Army was advised that no prisoners were to be killed on the "Marshal's" birthday.

My acquaintance also informed me that there were mass executions between May 10 and 24. Usually groups of a hundred people were killed at a time. The victims were stripped of their clothes and sometimes had to dig their own graves. They were mowed down by machine gun fire. The first group to be shot would be buried by the next and so on. According to L.P., it was chiefly Albanian Partisans who served as executioners.[5]

On the morning of May 26, I had an opportunity to converse with an Albanian guard. He did not know Croatian very well, so we had some difficulty in understanding one another. I did find out, however, that he had been on duty in this camp for three days and nights. He said that during this period captured soldiers and civilians were executed continually. I succeeded in winning the sympathy of this guard and gave him a letter for my relatives. This letter actually reached the addressee, although only after considerable delay.

About 10:00 A.M. on this same morning, Partisans armed with submachine guns loaded us into Red Cross trucks. The guards threatened to gun down anyone who dared to lift up the tarpaulins which covered the trucks. We later learned that the reason for this injunction was that we drove right by the places where thousands of captives had been massacred.

At 8:00 that evening we arrived in Zagreb, and about 10:00 we were taken to the prison on Savska Cesta. In the truck in which I rode from Maribor to Zagreb, there was a young Partisan guard who was a Croat from Lika. He sat quite close to me in the truck and, being a Croatian himself, talked freely with us. There was genuine sadness in his voice when he told us that we were going to be taken to Belgrade or to Ada Ciganija where all of us would be executed. I remember that he said among other things: "Just think how terrible I feel, for I shall have to be killing my own Croatian people who have harmed no one. I myself was an Ustasha but, after being taken prisoner, I saved my neck by joining the Partisans who killed my father, mother, and relatives."

I was taken with a group of eighty other prisoners to a basement room in the Savska Cesta prison. It measured sixteen by eighteen feet. We

---

[5] In Knezovic's *Pokolj Hrvatske Vojske,* pp. 90-91, Ivan Zivkovic charges the thirteenth Montenegrin Brigade with massacres at Maribor. Other eyewitnesses attribute these massacres to various Serbian units of the Third Army, as well as to the high-ranking Serbian Communists, particularly Kocha Popovitch, Blaza Jankovich, Uros Kukolj, Nikola Vracar, Milan Sekulic and others. After all, not one but many of Tito's brigades were needed for murdering 40,000 captives.

were left crammed together in this place without food, water, or sanitary facilities until Monday, May 28. On this day interrogations began. We were asked why we had fled to Austria, who had organized this flight, and other questions. Obviously, our captors wanted to secure the names of all who had taken a leading part in the evacuation of Croatia.

One man was set free on this same day, but the rest of us were not so lucky. Later I discovered that eight men who were taken from our room were executed. Four of these were disposed of in the Savska Cesta building itself, the others were taken to the Square "N." Others were transported from Zagreb to the provinces; and I have never learned their fate.

As for me, I remained for some forty days in this indescribably filthy cellar. Every night trucks drew up in front of our building at about 9:00 P.M., and various prisoners were taken off in these vehicles. We were later able to confirm our suspicions that they were murdered. The guards would call out the names of the prisoners who were to be taken on a particular night and they would give these poor wretches a good beating before they threw them into the trucks. One night, a pregnant woman was included among the victims. She pleaded with the guards not to manhandle her because of her condition, but they only swore and continued to abuse her. Usually the windows of our cell were blocked with boards and wooden boxes to prevent us from seeing who was taken off from the other cells. Prisoners were taken mainly from our level. After about ten days, I was transferred to another room where I was not able to find out what was going as well as I had when I was in the basement. In the more than forty days I spent in the Savska Cesta prison, it constantly was overcrowded. New batches of captives were brought in daily to take the places of those who were exterminated the night before.

One day a couple of Dalmatian Partisans entered our cell. They were both in their early forties and wore decorations which showed that they belonged to the oldest group of Partisan fighters, those who had been continually in the field since 1941 or 1942. They began to interrogate us and in the course of this task found themselves face to face with one of their close relatives, a Domobran or Croatian Regular Army man. "Martin! What are you doing here!" they exclaimed.

"I wanted to get out of the Domovina," he answered.

They scolded him, saying, "While we were fighting you were collaborating with an enemy regime. Don't think that we shall rescue you. The people will sentence you."

And, indeed, the "people" did. Martin the Domobran was taken off one night and eliminated for being caught on the losing side. He was one of the eight men taken from the basement cell that I mentioned above.

Often, the interrogations conducted by the Partisans were very superficial. I myself know of instances in which friends of mine were sentenced to death even though they had never served in the Croatian Army. The fact that they happened to be wearing army shoes when captured was enough to doom them, since the Partisans catalogued the owners of all such footgear as enemy soldiers.

Following some forty days of imprisonment, I was set free. The catch was that I either had to serve in the Yugoslav Army for six months or put in this time at hard labor. I chose the army and was sent to Samobor. Since my data file showed "negative characteristics," I was assigned to the company office. My superiors did not allow me to participate in field maneuvers or other duties which were entrusted only to old Partisan fighters or to dependable Marxists of other categories.

"Field maneuvers" or "actions" involved so-called "clean-up jobs." On one occasion, trustworthy Communists and Socialists who belonged to my company were ordered to effect the evacuation of the village of Ruda. This was a settlement of Germanic origin, so it was considered a German village, although, as is usual in Croatia, many of the original foreign stock had been Croatianized for some time. The inhabitants were given only a half hour's notice to get ready to move. Men, women, and children were then herded into trucks and taken to a "Volksdeutsche" camp. Apart from such unpleasant incidents, my term of military service passed without notable happenings. I was one of the lucky ones, for during 1945-47 a real "Reign of Terror" prevailed in all of the Croatian lands as Tito and his henchmen deliberately endeavored to eradicate the Croatian nation, that is, the people who wished to designate themselves as Croatians rather than Yugoslavs. Perhaps the following anecdote will illuminate the conditions that prevailed in my native land during the days when I was holding down a relatively safe and easy job in the office detachment of a military company.

In 1948, I visited a peasant from the village of Granesina who had done me some favors during the war. We were strolling in the vicinity of the Maksimir woods, the great Zagreb public park. I noticed that he seemed gripped by some inner agitation. His face became gloomy and he even began talking to himself. When I asked him what was troubling him he replied:

> During the months of May and June, 1945, the Partisans were executing people every night. They brought these people by trucks from the camps and prisons. The executions took place right here, in these woods of Maksimir, and also in the close vicinity of Granesina, about two thousand feet away from the woods. Automatic weapons were used to shoot the prisoners down. Every night the Partisans would pick up groups of peasants from the villages around here and make them dig graves and bury the people who were executed in them. I myself had to bury these unfortunates in mass graves on several occasions. Right here is one of those graves!

He took me to a spot which lies in the direction of Zagrebacka Gora and showed me where this particular massacre had taken place. As I looked over the grass covered hillside, it seemed impossible that beneath the lush greenery lay the remains of hundreds of victims of the defeat of 1945. Yet, everyone who lives in this vicinity knows what happened here and where the corpses were interred.

Also, I wish to testify from my own experience and observations, as well as from eyewitness reports, that after the Partisans took Zagreb, they established the worst sort of prison and concentration camps in Precko, in Kanal, at Maksimir, where women, children, and older people were confined, in Kalinovac near Samobor, and in Samobor itself. The camp at Samobor was located next to what is now known as the Dom Kulture (House of Culture).

Unnumbered thousands of victims were taken from these camps to be executed at Rakov Potok near Samobor, Anindol, Sestine, Gracani, and Dubranac. Many of the residents of Zagreb today know what went on, as do peasants forced to bury masses of corpses by the Communists.

This written report was read to me and found to be in accordance with what I had orally recounted. Declaring myself willing to repeat the same under oath before an international tribunal, I confirm the truth of this report with my own signature.

Signed: R. G. G.

Buffalo, New York

Document XX

Eyewitness No. 36 and sixty other Croatians fled from the surrender at Bleiburg and went towards Klagenfurt. On the way, they were ambushed by the Partisans and captured. The captors were digging a hole for their burial when a Croatian Partisan officer came, saved them, and sent them on to Dravograd and Maribor. Just before arriving in this city, they reached a long "death march" which was guarded by the the troops of the Twelfth Proletarian Division. In addition to indecent manhandling and murdering of four Croatian girls, the Proletarians took about 3,000 officers from the column and shot them. Later, our eyewitness and a few friends tried to hide in Krapina, but were recaptured and taken to the extermination camp in Sveti Kriz, near Mirkovci. Here, thousands of Croatian prisoners died of thirst or starvation, and a considerable number of captives were shot by the Partisans. The witness also saw the atrocities in the extermination camp in Precko, from which he was taken to Sesvete, and then to Bjelovar. The witness "marched" from Bjelovar through Virovitica and Daruvar to Pozega. Only 3,000 captives, out of 4,000 who had left from Bjelovar, arrived in Pozega. The "death march" then went through Vinkovci and Osijek to Petrovaradin, and on to Vrsac where eighteen to twenty prisoners were daily led out to death. On August 8, 1945, the witness was set free in Kovin.

On May 6, 1945, the day of the retreat of the Croatian Armed Forces from the Domovina, I had orders to fly to the Austrian provincial capital of Klagenfurt. Since my plane developed engine trouble and there were no facilities for repairing it speedily, I joined a motor column which was enroute to Austria. I traveled with this cavalcade to Bleiburg.

We remained near this city for one night. On the following morning, a Major Tecic, who earlier had served as a captain in the Croatian Air Force, appeared dressed in a Partisan uniform. He told us that we were going back to Zagreb; he had arranged everything, and we had nothing to worry about. The commanding officer of our column, Colonel Djal, argued with Tecic, telling him that he had orders to surrender only to the British. While they were heatedly disputing one another, I collected my gear and set off with a group of sixty other men, most of them officers, to reach Klagenfurt on foot. In our group, were the brothers Vlado and Branko Maric and their father. I do not recall the latter's given name but he was an Ustasha senior captain. A Colonel Gaveza was also with us.

We had gone about nine miles into the woods when we blundered upon a Partisan ambush. We were captured, robbed of our clothing and valuables, and forced to lie flat on the ground. Some of the Partisans began to dig a big hole in the ground.

A while later, a Partisan major approached us. I recognized him as a doctor whom I had seen in Zagreb before the war. Apparently the units that had captured us had not heard of the surrender and extradition proceeding that was going on at Bleiburg, since he proceeded to acquaint our captors with this information. He told them that we had surrendered our arms to the British and that they had no right to shoot us. Then he assumed command of the Partisan group, and we set out towards Dravograd under their escort.

From Dravograd we went to Maribor. Near this town we joined a larger prisoner column which must have contained 20,000 men. It stretched out for a length of at least seven miles. It left corpses behind it every mile of its journey. Just before we got to Maribor, the Partisans took four young girls, who were students at the University of Zagreb, out of the section of the column in which I was marching. They took them into a house nearby, raped them, then stripped off their skirts and other clothing and brought them out stark naked in front of the house which my part of the column was passing at this moment. There they shot them right in front of us.

The Twelfth Proletarian Division came along to take whatever possessions our previous captors had left us. I noticed that some of the Partisans were carrying bags full of money, watches, rings, and whatever other valuables they had been able to find. Mounted members of this Division rode alongside the column, firing into it with machine guns. They forced us to proceed at a run, first towards Maribor, then back again. The weaker ones among us could not keep up this pace for long. As they stopped or fell down, the Partisans shot them.

After they had tired of this diversion, the guards commanded all officers and "intellectuals" to step forward. Perhaps three thousand people so identified themselves. Later we heard that they were shot en masse. Along the way to Maribor, too, I saw the bodies of many members of the Montenegrin National Army which had been allowed to join our retreat and which had surrendered with us.

From Maribor, we were allowed to go on towards Zagreb without any armed escort. Many prisoners took advantage of this circumstance to leave the column and go off individually or in groups. I was among those who hastened off to their homes. With a few friends, I tried to reach Krapina.

As long as we were in Slovenia, the populace treated us in a beastly manner. Although we were perishing from hunger and thirst, they would give us neither food nor water. They told us that they had no water to give to Croatians. This statement, which we heard so frequently from their lips, ought to be remembered by those Croatians who persist in regarding the Slovenes as "a brother Slavic people."

Finally we reached Krapina, where the Croatian inhabitants showed every kindness to us. However, the Communist authorities in this place confined us in a schoolhouse, where we remained for seven days. An epidemic of typhus broke out and many people died. Perhaps because of this plague, we were transferred to Mirkovci, or rather to Sv. Kriz, near Mirkovci, where the Croatian Honor Work Service had quarters during the war. Here the Communists separated the Domobrans from the Ustashas. For ten days we received no food or water whatsoever. Since all prisoners had been on short rations for an extended period of time, many could not survive this experience. I know that thousands died of thirst or starvation.

The camp commander was a shoemaker from Krapina with whom I had had a slight acquaintance before the war. By the grace of Tito, he was now a Partisan first lieutenant. When I heard that the Ustashas were going to be shot, while the Domobrans were to be sent to Zagreb, I managed to persuade him to shift me into the Domobran group. A day later I left by train with the Domobran officers for Camp Precko near Zagreb. The Ustasha officers remained in Mirkovci or Sv. Kriz and were heard from no more.

We stayed at Precko for five days and received food here for the first time since we had left Krapina. Every day the Partisans made up lists and took away small groups. We never found out what was done with these people, but I assume that they were murdered.

On the sixth day of our stay at Precko the guards loaded six hundred of us onto a train and sent us off towards Zagreb. At dusk we arrived in Sesvete. About eighty of us were crowded into each car, so that we had no room either to stand or to sit down in comfort. We were covered with one another's excrement and urine. When we asked them to open the car doors at Sesvete so we could get out to relieve ourselves, the Partisans fired into the cars, killing or wounding many of us. Finally, they did let us out of the cars, however, and we marched off towards Bjelovar. Along the way the guards shot at us again for no reason at all. Seven of our number went mad and committed suicide by throwing themselves into wells that were close to the highway.

We arrived at Bjelovar about noon on June 7. As we were going through this town, a woman, carrying a child in her arms, saw her husband among the prisoners and ran to greet him. A guard took the man out of the column and shot him just a little distance away from me. Standing over the corpse, the Partisan then yelled out mockingly to the horrified woman, "Here's your man!"

There were now about four thousand people in our column. We went from Bjelovar to Virovitica, then on to Daruvar and from Pakrac to Pozega. Whenever we passed through a Serbian village, the inhabitants maltreated us in every way possible. Unfortunately, there are many such villages in Croatia and Slavonia, because the ancestors of these Serbians were allowed to find refuge here when they fled from Serbia proper before the Turks. Before we arrived in a village or town, whether the population of the place was predominantly Croatian or Serbian, the guards would announce our arrival; individual residents who wished to establish themselves in the good graces of new Communist authorities could identify any officers or outstanding Croatian patriots whom they happened to know. Such "identified" persons were taken off; we do not know what happened to them. But every night there was a lot of shooting on either side of our column; perhaps this was just random firing to discourage us from attempting escape.

Only three thousand of us reached Pozega. After three days here, the officers were isolated and marched to Vinkovci. As was the case elsewhere, the Croatian inhabitants of this town did all they could for us. In fact, they were so friendly that the guards would not allow us to remain here overnight but started us off on the evening of our arrival towards Osijek. Here we remained out in the open fields, without any shelter, for five days. Rain fell during a good part of our stay in this place. We were drenched to the skin, cold, and thoroughly miserable. Typhus again broke out among us, and since the Communist authorities were afraid that this dread malady might spread to them, we received inoculations.

From Osijek we went on to Mitrovica and then to Petrovaradin. Since we were joined by a group that had come here a month before, there were seventeen hundred officers in our group now. During the fifteen days that we spent at Petrovaradin we saw a number of women from Dubrovnik (Ragusa). They were looking for their husbands or sons so that they could supply them with food and clothing.

At the end of fifteen days, the entire prisoner camp was transferred to Vrsac. On the way to this place, we passed through burned-out villages in which not a single living soul remained. Formerly, these villages were inhabited by German colonists (Volksdeutscher). The ancestors of some of these Germans had come here long ago.

We were in Vrsac for another fifteen days. Here we were told that if anyone had Communist acquaintances, he could mention this fact in a petition for release directed to the Commander-in-Chief of the Yugoslav Army, "Marshal" Tito Broz. Such a petition would insure an earlier release. Every day, fifteen or twenty officers who thought they might be able to take advantage of their pre-war acquaintances with Marxists were taken off. They did not rejoin us, and we assumed that they were liquidated.

The Communists had selected one of our number, a Colonel Mirik, to act as commanding officer of the prisoners. Mirik indeed held the rank of colonel in the Croatian Army during the war, and I believe that, until the end of hostilities, he had a good service record. He was a Croatian Serb himself, however, and after the surrender he was able to ingratiate himself with the new authorities by identifying some of our officers who tried to pass themselves off as civilians, or Ustasha officers who pretended to belong to the Domobrans or other formations. While he was set free as a reward for services rendered to the victors, men whom he betrayed were liquidated. A Captain Barbir succeeded him as our commander.

From Vrsac we were taken to Kovin, where we remained until August 8. The Political Commissar who had charge of the prison camp here was a young peasant, only about twenty years old. His name was Sertic. He saw to it that we received good food; we were even allowed to read newspapers and listen to the radio. Later we found out that the reason for all this kindness was that an international committee had arrived at our camp to inspect its conditions.

On August 8, 1945, "Marshal" Tito granted an amnesty of a sort to his recent opponents. I was one of those who had the luck to be set free. I went from Kovin to Belgrade and from there to Zagreb, where I was reunited with my family. But I found that a number of my friends who had been set free ahead of me were being rearrested. Since I had no prospect of making a living in Zagreb, and since I thought that I, too, might again be arrested and denounced as an "Enemy of the People" because of my wartime service in the Croatian Air Force, I left our ancient capital and my home on September 11. I succeeded in making my way to Trieste, where I was interned for three days by the British authorities. Then I was sent as a war refugee to Camp Fermo in Italy.

Signed: Eyewitness #36

Fermo, Italy
October 20, 1945

Document XXI

Ivan Skoro who, when he was 17 years old, was drafted into the Croatian Army, describes the withdrawal from Zagreb, the surrender and also his "Death March" from Maribor to Varazdin, Podravska Slatina, Vinkovci, Sriemske Laze, Sid, Kukujevci, where he met his mother in a most painful manner, Kuzmin, Mitrovica, Ruma, St. Pazova, all the way to Pancevo and Bela Crkva. At almost all these places more prisoners were murdered by the Serbian population than by the Partisans themselves. Of the 5,000 captives who had left Osijek, only 1,000 arrived in Pancevo. The youth, who at the end his "Death March" was 18 years and 3 months old, was saved because of an amnesty issued by Tito.

During the retreat of the Croatian Army in May 1945, I was serving in the Second Company of the Pavelic Bodyguard Brigades. We retired towards Slovenia and experienced no difficulties in reaching Zidani Most. Wherever the Partisans attempted to dispute our progress, we sent them running with a few volleys and a following charge.

On May 8, we were approaching Celje. Since the Reich was quitting the war, the Yugoslav (Slovenian) Partisans were disarming the German soldiers here. Partisan units tried to block our way at Celje, too. They demanded that we turn our weapons over to them, but when we refused to do so they got out of our way in a hurry. Soon however, the Slovenian Partisans were reinforced by Serbians and Communists of various other categories and nationalities. They began attacking us from every side.

The battalion in which I was serving suffered heavy casualties, among them, our commanding officer, Captain Mate Vodopija. The column of civilians which retreated with us had it much worse than we did. Partisan artillery shelled them while they were crossing an open field. It was frightful to see the bodies of men, women, and children, as well as horses and wagons, being thrown into the air by the force of the explosions. All of us were so infuriated by this terrifying spectacle that in a few hours of bitter fighting we smashed through the ring the Communists were trying to draw around us and paid them back for the sport they had had with our civilians.

Carrying all of our wounded with us, we continued on into the Slovenian mountains. The broken Partisan units kept us under continuous fire in order to hamper our progress, but we reached the Austrian border without serious trouble. At about 9:00 A.M., May 16, we bivouacked on a field close to the frontier line. There was an Austrian town nearby, but I do not remember its name.

At 4:00 P.M. a courier whom we had sent out returned bearing a command from our generals that all soldiers must take the ammunition out of their guns. A little later we received another command to run up white flags and furl our Croatian standards. We supposed that the British were going to take our weapons, accept our surrender and intern us as prisoners of war.

As soon as the white flags were displayed, the infantrymen were ordered to march forward, while the transportation vehicles had to remain where they were. As we laid down our weapons, the Partisans immediately appeared. All officers, non-coms and private soldiers were formed into a column which was directed to turn back towards Maribor. The Partisans forced us to take off our uniforms and shoes. They also confiscated our money, watches, rings and everything else of value. Anyone who protested against this robbery was shot down immediately. Immediately they also initiated a process of identification. This Marxist innovation in the time-tried tactic of delay allowed anyone who disliked a neighbor, or held a grudge against someone for any reason, to accuse the object of his resentment of committing war crimes. Such an accusation, regardless of its source, was enough to insure the slaughter of the accused party.

As we approached Maribor, the guard details accompanying us were strengthened by mounted patrols. They forced us to run continuously. Of course, not everyone could keep up such a pace, and those who halted to get their breath lost it forever. When we came in sight of Maribor, the guards made us about-face and run away from the town, then race back towards it again. They were intent upon seeing how many of us they could tire out, force to stop, and then kill.

We were taken to a concentration camp which had printed signs at the entrance. These posters directed Ustashas to go to the left and Domobrans to the right. I was an Ustasha but I chose the right hand side.

In this camp there was a water fountain with about ten spigots. There were so many prisoners, however, that everyone could not get a turn at the fountain, even once a day. On the second day of our arrival, the camp administration started to prepare us for the slaughterhouse. They grouped us in companies of 120 men apiece, saying that they were doing this so we could draw food rations regularly. Actually, those who were so registered did receive two pounds of corn bread for every ten men. When the bread was distributed, guards took these men off to another camp, or so they said. No one knew what camp they went to.

I suspected that the registered men were being taken off to be massacred. Therefore, I took care not to register in any company. For several days I kept shifting my location from one part of the camp to another. Finally, hunger got the best of me, and I had to register in a company in order to get something to eat. New arrivals were coming into the place all the time, and new companies were being formed constantly, so it was easy enough to do this. As soon as I received a few ounces of corn bread I would get away from that company as quickly as possible. I was only seventeen years old, but I did much better than many older and more experienced men. Never did I try to get a bigger share of bread than the other members of the several companies that I joined momentarily, only to sneak away from them at the first opportunity.

In one of the companies in which I registered myself I encountered an uncle, my mother's brother. This meeting was a hard one for both of us. When our company was directed to get ready for transfer to another camp, I told him that I was not going with the others. He begged me to go along, because he said I was too young to continue taking care of myself as I had done so far. It was certain that sooner or later I would be caught at my little trick, and my life would be forfeit. However, I felt that I had a better chance to survive by staying where I was, and I advised him to remain also. We talked in whispers so the guards could not overhear us. Neither of us could convince the other to accept his point of view, so we shook hands and parted. Nothing was heard of my uncle again. I am certain that he shared the fate of uncounted thousands of other Croatian war prisoners who were butchered there.

As usual, I got away from the "transferred" company before it passed through the gates of our place of detention. It became harder and harder for me to continue my game, however, for the number of prisoners declined noticeably. Off in the distance, a great deal of shooting made it quite clear what was happening to all of the registered companies. Soon there were so few captives confined here that everybody could get to the water fountain during the course of the day, if patient enough. No one who was "transferred" ever returned to the camp.

Early in June, an order was issued for all inmates to line up four abreast. There were approximately 6,000 of us remaining. Communist volunteers marched us out to an unknown destination. These men probably volunteered for the congenial duty of driving us along the highways and byways to indulge their natural passion for killing. Every night they killed some prisoners. During the daytime marches, anyone who collapsed because of hunger, thirst, or exhaustion was disposed of at once. Should one of us try to assist someone who had given out, both would be shot. If the guards were trying to frighten us by evidencing their ruthlessness, they did not succeed. It was evident that we could not avoid death, so we didn't worry about it. Many men sat right down when they became tired and told the guards to go ahead and kill them, which they did.

At night we usually camped in the market place of some village. Between dawn and sunset we habitually put in a good thirty miles of marching. Sometimes during these treks we were allowed a period of rest. Many men fell asleep when we halted in this manner, and often they never awoke from this slumber. Anyone who did not respond immediately when the guards told us to get going again was murdered on the spot. The guards always fired repeatedly into the bodies of such sleepers to make sure they were not merely feigning death. Our captors had plenty of ammunition and they used it freely. Wherever we stopped at night, the guards would make us crowd together in a very tight formation, so tight that no one could sit down even if he wanted to. Most of us didn't dare sit down, since the Communists kept machine guns trained on us, just waiting for somebody to do this. After a time they would tell us to lie down. Anyone who tried to rise for any reason following the execution of this order would be shot. Sometimes the guards missed the captive and hit those near him; we were crowded together as close as sheep in a pen. Every night we heard shots from close by. In the morning some of our fellow prisoners would be missing. Thus, we left our dead behind us as we continued our Calvary through Tito's Yugoslavia.

Whenever we passed through a Croatian village, the peasants would toss bread, smoked bacon, and other food to us. But if the toss was short, and anybody stepped out of the column to pick it up, he was killed then and there. When we came to a Serbian village, the inhabitants helped the guards maltreat us.

Our "Death March" took us through Varazdin, Koprivnica, Virovitica, and Podravska Slatina. In the latter place, we were permitted to rest in a ditch along the railroad track. Here we were visited by a Tito Youth Group, which was well armed and practiced on us in order to prepare for killing on a larger scale. These bloody juvenile delinquents fired their guns randomly at the prisoners. I can't begin to guess how many people they killed for no reason at all. Also, they practiced beating in our heads with rifle butts. Afterwards, survivors were given food, a rather surprising gesture on the part of our guards.

A freight train came along, and we were loaded into the cars. Those who had difficulty finding room were threatened with death by our proletarian escort. They kept cursing us, saying that they ought to kill all of us, only it was too much trouble burying those they'd already killed, without digging graves for us, too. We were loaded into the cars, one on top of another, as though we were logs. By the time the train arrived in Osijek, many men were dead. Since the heat was intense, whoever was buried under a pile of his comrades was likely to smother.

Those of us who survived were marched one July day to Zeleno Polje. Here we found many other prisoners. Thus a new column, 5,000 strong, was formed. New guards were assigned to this group, which was marched off in the direction of Pancevo in the old Banat. By the time we reached Vinkovci, the new guards had proved that, as killers, they were quite as efficient as the previous ones. I cannot estimate the number of their victims, because my mind had become an absolute blur. But I remember what I saw with my own eyes and what I heard. Every burst of gunfire meant that someone else had died; one volley followed another.

In Vinkovci, we were placed in an old brickyard which was fenced in with barbed wire. Here we were given haircuts and our clothes were steam-cleaned. Thus we were able to rid ourselves of lice which we had collected in abundance during the course of our march. Again a group of new guards relieved the most recent of our escorts. If anything, they were worse than either of the former crews. Yet, when we passed through the Serbian villages that lay between Vinkovci and Mitrovica, the villagers did more killing than the guards. These Serbian peasants would be waiting for us at the entrance to their villages. The Communist authorities always let them know we were coming a few days in before we got to these places. Also the "People's Government" would let the local residents know that they could do with us as they pleased. Therefore, they greeted us with hoes, pitchforks, axes, clubs, and every other kind of lethal weapon. In one of these Serbian villages, the Serbs murdered several hundred prisoners. This slaughter occurred at Laze, a town near Vinkovci. Here the Serbians looted us so effectively that most of us left virtually naked.

On our arrival in Sid, the Serbian residents tried to outdo the accomplishments of the inhabitants of Laze. Fortunately, it was already dark when we got to this place. Thus, the villagers could not gratify their lethal instincts too readily; sometimes, they even hit one another in the darkness. They soon desisted from their efforts to give us a permanent "home," or hell, in their settlement, and returned to their homes. We spent the rest of the night and the following day in a large, deep hole that had been dug for a brick factory nearby. It was excessively hot in there, since there was no breeze at all. Some Croatian women who lived in the vicinity brought us water, for which kindness the guards beat them, as well as us, with the butts of their guns.

Then, during the daylight hours, guards and Serb civilians vied with one another in shooting at us from the rim of the pit and maltreating us in every other way they could imagine.

By this time we who survived were only skeletons with a thin layer of skin over our bones. Death meant only a release from suffering to us. But I had relatives at Kukujevci, a village seven miles from Sid. By great good fortune my mother came to watch the passage of the "Death March." She brought a package of food with her. I hesitated to approach her, because usually such encounters ended with the prisoner being murdered before the very eyes of his loved ones. But the lure of the food was too great. I went right up to her. To my surprise, the guards did not stop me. When I greeted her, my mother asked me to be so kind as to try to find her son, Ivan Skoro, and to give him the package of food she had brought. She told me I could help myself to some of it too. Then I broke the news to her that I *was* her son. When I said this, she looked at me for a time, then fainted. This made me feel worse than anything that had happened to me so far. I was so shaken that I do not know how or when the column continued its journey from Sid. All I remember is that the heat was horrible and that we left many dead and wounded in the hole. Later, I learned that after recovering from her faint, my mother tried to find me among the corpses left in the hole. Then she followed the column to Kukujevci.

This village was one hundred per cent Croatian. Therefore, the guards forbade the inhabitants to stand in the street or even to watch from the windows as we passed. One prisoner was so thirsty that he jumped into the public well which was located alongside the road. Naturally, a guard shot him dead. From that moment on, this well remained unused by the local residents even though it had been in general use by the whole village up to this time.

When we arrived at the Serbian village of Kuzmin, we stopped in the market place to rest. A multitude of Serbs armed with big clubs beat us soundly. They also "identified" some of the prisoners and subsequently killed them. Other prisoners who protested against this savagery were shot by the guards.

From Kuzmin we went on to Mitrovica where we stayed for a full day. "Identifications" and ensuing executions took place there, too. A Serbian brigade relieved the guards who had brought us from Vinkovci. These new escorts outdid all of their predecessors in sheer bestiality. Whenever the guards had killed anyone up to this time, it was by shooting or by blows from rifle butts. At every opportunity, the Serbs now knifed us. I recall very well the appearance of one of these Serbians, although I do not know his name. He was tall, dark, and wore a mustache. Across his shoulders he carried a light machine gun, and he had a dagger in each hand. He kept sharpening these by rubbing one against the other. Although he kept yelling to us to stay four abreast, he himself pulled one man out of line and knocked him down. He knelt on the half-dead victim's chest and plunged one dagger into the man's side and the other into his neck. Slowly he pushed the blades towards one another until he was certain his prey was dead. He then got up and licked the blood off the daggers. His chest was bespattered with blood, and he seemed to have gone mad for he ran from one prisoner to another treating them in the same way. Finally, he became tired of killing in this manner. He put aside his daggers and started shooting captives with his machine gun. I am giving this description of what happened not from hearsay but from seeing it myself when and where it happened.

En route from Mitrovica to Ruma, we came upon a small pond. Its waters were calm and still, the July day was very hot, and our lips were parched with thirst. Without regard for the consequences, a number of prisoners broke out of line and ran towards the pond. The guards shot them down. But whatever the cost, the entire column suddenly disassembled as everyone raced to get to the water and satisfy his thirst. The Serbs kept firing at the thirst-crazed men until the pond was so filled with bodies that the water could no longer be seen.

Near Stara Pazova, there is a village which has a canal with running water in it. Near the canal the guards allowed us to rest. They then killed all prisoners who tried to get water. Thus, in these hot days of summer, our column of living dead men moved on from place to place barefoot, almost naked, starving, and dying of thirst. From Zemun, we went to Belgrade where we got new escorts.

This group wasn't as bad as the several guard details who had accompanied us up to this point. They used their gun butts to beat us to be sure, but their homicidal instincts were less developed than those of their predecessors. They took us across the Danube in ferry boats, which was not too difficult a task, since hardly a thousand of us were left out of the five thousand who had started out from Osijek.

When we arrived in Pancevo, the Communists gave us a little food of miserable quality. We slept in a large room which had a concrete floor that was scrubbed daily. Since we had neither sheets nor blankets, let alone mattresses, we had to lie on the bare floor itself. After five or six days there, we were transported by train to Bela Crkva near the Rumanian border. We were placed in a camp that was surrounded by barbed wire. There at least, we had straw to sleep on, but the food was as bad as before. In the morning we had to content ourselves with coffee that was black and bitter. At noon and in the evening we feasted on peas which had a worm in every grain. When we lined up before the cauldron to receive our portion, we could see floating worms covering the top of the soup. We used our spoons to remove the worms in the liquid, but still we found more in every bit of solid food. Also, we got a few ounces of very black bread, so black that we couldn't even guess what it was made of.

During our stay at Bela Crkva, we had to till the vineyards which the Communists had confiscated from the German families who lived here formerly. Many prisoners had received bad wounds in the course of our grueling marches, but they had to work anyway. The summer heat and the complete absence of medical care aggravated their sufferings. There was an ambulance for sick prisoners, but this did little good in the absence of medicine and physicians. Some of the wounds emitted an abominable stench as they festered. Many of these wounds were infected; they literally swarmed with worms. In view of such circumstances, it is not surprising that the sick and wounded died at the rate of around ten a day. We who survived had to dig graves for our late comrades and lay them in these last resting places. Some prisoners lost their eyesight or hearing, and not unnaturally, there were all kinds of mental breakdowns.

For the rest of the summer we labored in the vineyards, dug canals and irrigation ditches, and performed other tasks. When September came, we were taken back to Pancevo. Here prisoners born in 1926 or 1927, or later, were released because Belgrade had issued an amnesty for such people. I was among a group of 150 young men who were sent home. An equal number of older prisoners remained in the concentration camp at Pancevo. Thus out of 5,000 prisoners who left Osijek, scarcely 300 survived. I do not know what happened to the older men left behind at Pancevo.

While I was still in my homeland, I was able to listen to broadcasts in Croatian over the Paris radio. When the announcer read out the list of Croatian soldiers who were known to have been around Maribor in May, 1945, I recalled the hundreds and hundreds of dead men whom I had seen with my own eyes. Their relatives do not know, nor will they ever know, where they died or where their remains lie. I cannot remember the first or the last names of any of the people whom I saw slain during those tragic days. Since I expected death myself at any time, I had no interest in making new acquaintances.

After my release, I continued to live for thirteen years in my Communist-enslaved homeland. I kept hoping that in someway the regime imposed upon us against the will of every honest and patriotic Croatian would come to an end. Finally, I saw that this worst form of slavery known to history would continue indefinitely. Therefore, I decided to escape abroad and to return to Croatia only when the Communist regime fell. On October 26, 1958, my brother and I left the Domovina, perhaps forever. Now I am residing at Cremona, Villa Clari 8, Italy.

Signed: Ivan S. Skoro

Cremona, Italy
During the Christmas Season of 1958

Document XXII

Eyewitness Franjo Krakaj describes the Croatian troops' retreat, and their delusions in the attempt to surrender to the British. Many captives then enrolled in the "Thirteenth Battalion," that is, they were murdered. After this massacre, the "death marchers" began running away in all directions, but most of them were shot. Our witness and another prisoner ran through the woods until they entered a column of Croatian victims approaching Maribor. Krakaj was now in a real inferno that would defy even Dante's imagination; yet, he managed to escape from it. After wandering for several days, he and another escapee from the Maribor inferno found themselves in a new "Death March" near Celje. Krakaj eyewitnessed horrifying and unbelievably barbarous scenes which he describes with innate humor. This "Death March" took him to Samobor and Karlovac, on which stretch he joined a Work battalion. In this capacity he counted over 2,000 corpses of the murdered prisoners. From Karlovac, he went to the extermination camps in Sisak and Galdovo, where he worked on removing corpses from the rivers. Krakaj was then sent back to Karlovac, from Karlovac to Glina, and again to Karlovac. At Glina he and his companions experienced the brutalities of the Serbian population. Once more he was sent to Sisak; from there he went to Mostar. In Zenica he deserted from the Work Battalion, but was recaptured and assigned to the Thirteenth Krajina Brigade, commanded by a Croatian Partisan Antun Nozinic. This officer, as he himself boasted, murdered 9,000 Croatian war prisoners.

It was Saturday, May 5, 1945, when we received an order from General Headquarters to retreat from Generalski Stol and Vinski Vrh across the Dobra River to the outskirts of Karlovac. Here we fought a fierce battle with the Partisans. During the entire morning, their British Spitfire planes bombed and machine-gunned us. We remained entrenched along the Dobra until Sunday morning, May 6, and then gradually fell back on Karlovac. We evacuated this city on Sunday night and withdrew towards Jastrebarsko. After we had rested for a while, we continued our withdrawal on Monday, going through Prigorje to Samobor. Other Croatian units, which were retreating from the right bank of the Sava in the direction of Zidani Most, joined us at Samobor.

We reached Zidani Most without much difficulty; there I attached myself to a column in which my nephew was traveling. On May 10, we set out for Celje in Slovenia. There was now considerable confusion in the withdrawal, since many thousands of civilian refugees were getting in the way of our military formations. The soldiers did not have the heart to adopt ruthless measures towards this great mass of non-combatants and thus deprive them of all hope of escaping from the Communist killers who were following them. Anyway, it was apparent by this time that most of the more than half million people who had left the Fatherland would be able to get through to the British lines in Austria without undue embarrassment. At the time we thought that was all we had to do to save our lives.

While we were resting in Brezice, a captain, whose name I do not know, addressed us as follows: "Brothers, the war between Germany and England and her Allies is over. Now there is a new war underway. This will be a common war against Russia and Communism."

Somehow the idea that the British and Americans were going to use us to fight the Communists had gained wide credence among our leaders. I suppose this was a classic example of wishful thinking. Since the days of the Zrinis and Frankopans, the Croatians never have been political realists, but have lived in a world of political illusions. This belief that the Western Allies would have the sense to employ our Army, which was perfectly willing to continue the war against the Communists, if it could get modern, up-to-date weapons to do so, was one of the delusions which seemed to impress itself so readily upon the Croatian mentality.

Because of the military-civilian mix-up, I became separated from my nephew's column, which paused to assist some civilians. Since I was at the head of the formation, I took a route that I thought the main body was going to follow but did not. I spent the night in the woods a little distance outside of Celje. On the following day I passed through Pregarsko and reached Maribor. From this place, I went on to Dravograd.

Slovenian and Serbian Partisans attacked the group with which I now was traveling as we approached the bridge that spans the Drava River at Dravograd. We had to cross this structure under fire, throwing aside the Communist units which tried to bar our progress. On May 12-13, I fell in with another Croatian party which also had forced its way across the Drava in the face of enemy opposition. A Domobran captain from Lika gathered various detachments and individual parties under his command. We all followed him blindly down the main highway.

We ascended a hill, and the Lika captain stopped to survey the surroundings through his binoculars. Suddenly he exclaimed, "At last! There are the British." He pointed with his finger down into the valley below.

We felt greatly relieved, even happy, despite losing the war. Immediately, we went down the other side of the hill and indeed found ourselves surrounded by British troops. Our Domobran captain exchanged some words in German with one of the English officers. We were not asked to surrender our weapons, and that evening we camped along the road. Our captain remained with the British officers to whom he was trying to explain, in German, the pertinent facts relative to our situation and to that of our nation. Through gestures, the English soldiers told us to go ahead and eat, sleep, and not to worry about anything.

We still were laboring under the conviction that we would return to the Domovina as the advance guard of the Western Allies, who had too much sense to allow the Communists, of whatever nationality, to take over Central Europe and the Balkans. We knew that the British were helping the Greek Royalists against the Communists, and supposed they would do the same for us. What we did not realize was that we had no spokesman who was *persona grata* in London as King George was for the Greeks.

Waiting for our captain to rejoin us, we took a much needed rest. After an hour, he still had not returned and the British troops who had halted us disappeared. They took our captain with them, probably by force, since he certainly would have sent some kind of order to us if he had gone of his own free will to negotiate with higher British officers. Perhaps he did send a message, but the Englishmen did not deliver it.

Alarmed by his disappearance and that of the Britons, we packed up and prepared to move out. We assumed that we were in the British zone of occupation and therefore had nothing to fear from Yugoslav or other varieties of Communists. But we did not know the direction that we should take in order to reach the main British lines. Therefore, we stood around for some time debating whether or not to continue in the direction in which we were going, or turn back and retrace our steps.

While so occupied, a motorcycle with an attached sidecar pulled up in front of us. There was a Communist officer in this car who held up his hands in a peaceful gesture and said quickly to us, "Comrades, the war is over. You can go back to your homes. Nobody will bother you."

We were stunned by his appearance, for we realized at once that we were not in the British zone after all, but probably would find Partisan troops all around us. Since we were leaderless and ignorant of our exact whereabouts, and also because the Partisan's statement seemed to be delivered with complete sincerity, we decided to start back in the direction from which we had come in, that is, towards the homeland that we loved so dearly and from which we never had intended to depart for any length of time.

We had gone a little more than a mile when we encountered Partisan troops. They asked us to give up our weapons to them but assured us that we could proceed to our homes without fear of molestation. So, fools that we were, we tamely handed over our arms instead of using them.

The consequences of this surrender soon manifested themselves. Other Communists appeared to divest us of our clothing, knapsacks, watches, and other valuables. By way of exchange, they gave us their lice-ridden rags. Now we realized the trap into which we had fallen, but it was too late to remedy matters by fighting or seeking to escape. We were in the hands of our enemies. In this moment of despair, some lines from the *Last of the Barons* by Sir Henry Bulwer-Lytton came to my mind; I had read a translation of his historical novel and I now recollected that at the end Warwick turns to his men and says: "Commend your soul to God, for your bodies are the enemies."

The "Death Marches" began. As far as I could see, our guards were mainly Montenegrin or Dalmatian Partisans. One of them asked us, "Comrades, who wants to join the Yugoslav Army?" Still, we did not quite appreciate the gravity of our position. Thus, many Domobrans and others accepted this statement at its face value and declared their willingness to serve in Tito's forces. They were led away, to be incorporated into the Thirteenth Battalion, so we were told. At the time we did not know the sinister meaning of the name of this unit. But when we heard, soon after the departure of the "recruits," the continued firing of rifles, revolvers, machine guns, and all kinds of automatic weapons, we began to realize what assignment to the "Thirteenth Battalion" meant.

After the Partisan guards, who followed our column a hundred and fifty feet to the rear, began to kill everyone who lagged behind because of exhaustion, or who dropped out of line to look for water, I felt like volunteering for service in the Yugoslav Army too. A fellow sufferer dissuaded me from doing so, however, for he told me, "Don't go. They are killing whoever joins the 'Thirteenth Battalion'."

I don't know precisely where we were, or the day on which the incident occurred, but somewhere along the route I saw a Partisan staring at me very intently. Suddenly he began to shout:

"Comrade Commissar! Here is the Tabornik from my town!"[1]

I had never seen this man before in my life, or at least I do not remember it if I did. Nor do I have any idea where he came from. What's more, I never was a Tabornik at any time, nor did I even belong to the Ustasha Youth Organization. None of this prevented the Partisan from pulling me out of line and beating me. I heard the Commissar say, "To the Thirteenth Battalion with him!" My alleged fellow townsman kept

[1] A Tabornik was the leader of an Ustasha Tabor or camp.

right on whacking me with the butt of his gun. Finally, he pushed me in among a group of other prisoners who were all covered with blood and quite exhausted from the beatings to which they had been subjected.

Partisan guards herded us into a forest which stood on the top of a hill. I do not know the location of this place, but I remember that there were no houses in the vicinity. Among the rest of us in this group there was a very old man. I do not know who he was, but I never shall forget him as long as I live. Four Partisans armed with automatic weapons given to them by their British allies were following us at a distance of about sixty feet. The old man looked back at them and then said quickly to us, "They're going to kill us! I'll run towards the bastards; the rest of you can run away!"

The old fellow, who probably was a veteran of the war of 1914-18, actually did turn around and run straight at the guards as fast as his aging limbs could take him. One of the Partisans yelled at him to stop, but he kept right on coming and there was no doubt at all about his intention to wrest a gun from our captors. The Partisans began to fire, and undoubtedly they killed him. I did not see him fall, because the rest of us took advantage of his action to scatter in all directions.

Probably, there were no more than four or five of us who escaped unscathed. Bullets cut the air all around me, but I was not hit by them. Together with another prisoner, I ran through the woods for more than an hour. Then we collapsed from sheer exhaustion. Two hours passed before we could so much as speak to one another. Finally we got up and started to wander through the forest. We were hungry, thirsty, tired, unarmed, and afraid that we would be seen by a Partisan patrol, or by Communist sympathizers or "fellow travelers" who might turn us in to court favor with the victors. Whenever we became too tired, we would rest for a while, then go on again. All along the way we saw no houses at all, though we did pass one village which lay at the foot of a hill.

We spent the night in the woods and continued our journey the following morning. By noon of this day, we had passed five villages and a number of single houses scattered through the countryside, but we kept well away from all of them. Throughout the day, we tried to find the Drava River which flows by Maribor. This Slovenian territory was otherwise entirely unfamiliar to us, but we knew that if we followed the Drava we eventually would get back onto Croatian soil. At least a dozen times we came across small groups of people who had been murdered. Most of the bodies had been stripped, but the murderers had possessed the decency to leave the skirts on a few of the women whom they had killed. In one spot we found seven bodies, all with their hands wired behind them, arranged neatly side by side. In the forest, too, we came across many abandoned weapons. Most of the weapons were small arms, but we even encountered tanks that had been driven into the forest for a few feet.

We could have armed ourselves, but we decided against doing so. At this time we were still laboring under a major illusion: namely, that our group had just experienced bad luck in falling into the hands of sadists. Surely, if we could attach ourselves to a larger and more officially directed prisoner column, we could expect nothing worse than maltreatment! In the twentieth century no one killed prisoners of war any more. I still had not heard about the Katyn massacres perpetrated by the Russians early in the war, and I don't suppose my companion had either. So we thought that the best thing to do was give ourselves up peacefully, rather than die with arms in our hands, or let the Communists find us so equipped.

Finally, we did manage to join a prisoner column which was marching towards Maribor. The Partisan escort took us into the town and confined us in the courtyard of a building which was located on Koruska Street. It was a one-story structure which looked like an American ranch house; it had a number of apartments, and a large courtyard in which we were placed.[2]

On the morning we arrived, a commissar spoke to us. He told us that we would have to serve a term in the Yugoslav Army before we could return to our homes. Since I knew what such service meant, I did not respond to this offer of military employment. Everyone else kept quiet, too. Not one prisoner volunteered for the "Thirteenth Battalion." This made the commissar very angry. He said that all of us would have to join up and that on this same afternoon we would change uniforms. Our present "Fascist" attire had to be discarded.

The commissar spoke to us at 11:00 A.M. Around 2:30 P.M., we received orders to accompany our guards to the place where the new uniforms would be issued. I was in a group of fifteen or twenty persons who were escorted by two armed Partisans to a stable which was half an hour's walk from the "ranch" where we were quartered. There were six trucks standing in front of this stable which I saw leave, one by one, loaded with prisoners.

In due time they came back, empty.

My group was lined up outside the stable. We had to hand over whatever personal belongings had been left to us up to this point. Then we were taken inside the stable, one at a time. When my turn came to enter the building, I found a Montenegrin Partisan waiting for me. He wore a silver stripe and a star on his uniform. He asked my name and I gave it to him. Then he took me by the arm and told me not to be afraid. He led me into a separate room where seven other Partisans awaited me. I was told to turn around with my back to the Montenegrin and place my hands in the small of my back. When I did so the Montenegrin bound my wrists with wire.

---

[2] Probably the witness is describing here a replica of a Spanish-type "ranchhouse," such as are owned by many Croatians and Slovenes in California.—Editor's Note

I knew what was going to happen now, but I had delayed too long in putting up a fight. When he put his hand over my mouth and started to lead me to one side, I had the satisfaction of giving him a good bite. For that he hit me over the head with something, and the other Partisans seized me and threw me into the truck. In this vehicle there were prisoners who had preceded me into the stable; their hands were bound like mine. Some other captives were pitched in with us. Then, one by one, six guards armed with automatic weapons got in and we moved off.

After a ride of about twenty minutes, we were unloaded like sacks of wheat at Maribor Island, which is upstream from the town. As we approached this place, we heard the staccato firing of a machine gun, along with single rifle shots from time to time. So we had no doubt now concerning our fate.

I landed on my feet when I was tossed out of the truck. Thus, I was able to take a good look at a scene of horror that could have inspired a twentieth-century Dante. Right in front of me lay a group of thirty men who evidently had been shot immediately before our arrival. I saw that we were on the right side of the Drava River, in a sparse forest, rather than on the island itself. The woods extended upward to a mountain that towered over us. Could I return to this precise spot today I might have difficulty recognizing it, though I think I could correctly point out the exact location. At the time my attention was not concentrated upon the scenery. What absorbed my interest were several mass graves which had been dug about three hundred yards apart. Since they were almost filled with bodies, I could not determine how deep they were. I judge that each of them contained perhaps three hundred corpses. On top of these masses of cadavers, I could discern movement; some of the victims were still alive! Out of these grisly holes came screams, "Brother, kill me! Shoot once more!" I remember that cry being repeated several times. Also, there were unwounded men in the graves who were smothering as bodies were thrown on top of them. They were trying to make themselves heard too. Some intended victims were trying to get away into the woods and the Partisans were shooting at them.

Trucks drove up bringing other groups of prisoners. As the guards started to unload them, the volume of rifle and machine gun fire increased tremendously because these prisoners made a break for it as soon as they hit the ground. Although my hands were still bound behind my back, I also took off at a run. Bullets were whacking into the trees and cutting through the shrubbery all around me. I tripped over a fallen branch and fell down headlong. Probably this saved me, because the guards evidently thought that I was accounted for and turned their attention elsewhere. As I endeavored to regain my feet and slip off undetected among the trees, I noticed one of our men lying nearby on the ground. He was alive and unwounded but panting for breath. "Come, brother, show me the way to the Drava!" I called to him. We both got up and ran towards the river. When we reached it, we took shelter in the bushes along its bank because we spotted four Communists who were obviously searching for escapees.

We helped one another unfasten our bonds. Then we took off our trousers and shoes and swam downstream. I remember that we passed under three bridges, one of which was made of stone. Finally, we left the water in the vicinity of a factory. Here we found the bodies of some murdered prisoners, and were able to get new trousers from them.

For days we wandered through the woods without anything to eat. It was hot during the daytime, but turned much cooler at night so that we were unable to get much sleep, scantily clad as we were. Finally, we found ourselves on the outskirts of Celje. Since we did not know anyone to turn to, and believed that most Slovenes, except for Rupnik's White Guards, were Communist sympathizers, we seemed to have a choice of either dying of starvation and exposure or joining another prisoner column and hoping for the best. Surely this orgy of killing would not continue indefinitely! So we stuck our heads into the lion's mouth once again and slipped into the ranks of a column of captives which was moving from Maribor towards Celje. At first, the 8th Krajina Brigade escorted us, but soon a Dalmatian Brigade of Partisans took over from them. I noticed that there were quite a few Italians, former soldiers in Mussolini's Army, in this second formation. Whether it was the Krajina or the Dalmatian outfit that drove us on, we had to proceed at a run without getting anything to drink. Anyone who fell behind was killed at once.

On the way from Celje to Samobor, I was sent to rejoin the "Thirteenth Battalion" no less than three times. Divine Providence intervened again to save me on each of these occasions, one of which may be worth describing.

In the column to which I now belonged, I encountered an old man by the name of Zaresak. He was in his late fifties, a veteran of the war of 1914. During the struggle of 1941-45, he was conscripted by the Germans to chauffeur members of the Nazi Labor Chamber because he spoke and understood German. He was a native of Vares in Bosnia, and a good Croatian.

It also happened that among the Partisans who were escorting our column, there was a fellow by the name of Asim Poljanic, a Croatian who today is living in Zenica. He told one of the commissars who was with us that I had killed some people in this city. Old Zaresak saw what was happening and raised a great shout which caused all kinds of commotion among our guards, who thought the prisoners were starting to attack them. Under the cover of the resulting confusion, Zaresak pulled me into his section of the column. The group that I had been marching with was stopped while the guards ran around looking for me. With incredible rapidity, Zaresak outfitted me with a warm leather coat that the Partisans, in some incomprehensible manner, had missed confiscating. He also gave me a hat and glasses. Since I had on white,

German-kitchen trousers, I looked just like one of the other civilians who was traveling with us. This disguise fooled the Partisans completely, and they concluded that I had somehow made off into the woods during the outburst of excitement.

I was still in the woods all right, for the column to which I had attached myself was destined for service with the now grimly infamous "Thirteenth Battalion!" Two hours after Zaresak saved me, a female Communist from Dalmatia asked him, "Did you fight together with the occupiers?" He replied quite calmly, "Comrade, I was in the Work Chamber. The Germans forced me to drive for them because I remembered my German from Austro-Hungarian days and, of course, I couldn't refuse to chauffeur them unless I wanted to be shot."

The woman had a crazy look on her face as she listened to his words. After a while she said, "Since you were able to drive the Germans you must give me a ride, too." She made him take her on his back. I spoke to her, saying, "Comrade, come ride on my back and not on that of the old man."

"Your turn will come soon enough!" she told me.

I saw that she was a homicidal maniac, and since she was armed, and there were male Partisan guards around, there was nothing to do but shut my mouth and continue marching. Zaresak bore her on his back for more than a mile, but I could see that he was going to give out. When he finally had to stop for breath, she immediately killed him with her revolver. Then she perched herself on my back. I took a knapsack from another prisoner so that she could ride more comfortably. We progressed in this piggy-back fashion for about two miles, the woman's companions whipping me all the way as though I were a recalcitrant horse. As they did so they would shout "Hiya!" like cowboys in an American movie. Suddenly, the belts on the knapsack broke, and the woman tumbled from my back onto the ground, taking a bunch of my hair which she had gripped during the "ride" to steady herself.

I was sure that she would treat me as she had Zaresak as soon as she recovered. Therefore, I ran off like a madman. After hiding a while, I attached myself to another prisoner column without realizing that this one, also, belonged to the infamous Thirteenth Battalion. When I found this out, I escaped again. I then got into a Work Battalion. With this unit, I came to Samobor and went on to Karlovac, where we all were placed in the Luksic Camp. Since I had nothing better to do with my time on the march from Samobor to Karlovac, I counted the corpses that I saw along the route. I lost track of the number, but I remember that I had a final count of two thousand when my attention became diverted to other matters. At the camp in Luksic, carts would remove from fifty to sixty bodies every morning. Of course, people were "transferred" individually every night, too.

One good thing about Luksic was that we at least had water there. Too much of it in fact; four pounds of potatoes and a little corn were mixed into fifty quarts of water to serve eighty men at a time. Anyway, we did not stay here long. From Karlovac, we were sent to the Sisak camps by way of Kordun-Banija-Glina. When we arrived in Sisak, we were sent to the Teslic glass factory in Galdovo to pull corpses out of the Kupa River. Once the stream had been relieved of this old burden, it received replacements as more prisoners were murdered and thrown into the water. Such was life in the Work Battalions.

After this experience, those of us who survived were returned to Karlovac. When we passed through Pokuplje, I remember that the Croatian inhabitants of this place treated us very kindly. From Karlovac, we were transported to Glina and then back again. The Serbs living in Kordun beat us when we passed through, and I thought how right our old nobility had been when they protested to the Habsburg authorities in the sixteenth and seventeenth centuries against allowing Serbs to settle on Croatian soil. Near the old *granicari* (frontiersmen) town of Glina, Serbian women had poisoned the wells. Fortunately, we found this out in time, for most of us escaped this particular effort to make Croatian countryside safe for Serbians. Serbs of both sexes beat us continuously with hoes, hatchets, and revolvers whenever and wherever we encountered them in our own land, where their ancestors had once found shelter from the Turks. In Glina, we were brought into the courtyard of a school that had been demolished during the war. Here we had to run the gauntlet between lines of SKOJ[3] members. They beat us with belt buckles and wooden tennis rackets. This sport was repeated on several occasions. At Glina we had no rest, even at night, because the Serbian population of this place—the Croatian inhabitants seemed either to have left or been killed off—threw stones into our quarters at all hours. We received the same welcome whenever we passed through a Serbian village in the Kordun, the so-called cordon of frontier times.[4] On the other hand, the Croatian peasants everywhere showed great sympathy for us. Whenever they could, they brought us food and drink. Those of us who survived will be forever grateful to good Croatians who helped us survive these days of national tragedy, when we left dead colleagues behind us along a trail of "Death Marches."

---

[3] Federation of Communist Youth of Yugoslavia.

[4] The "cordon" in Habsburg times was a line of blockhouses *(cardaci)* and lookout posts along the Austro-Turkish frontier and the Granicari villages which stood in back of this line and which supplied guards for the "cordon" service. The "cordon" was not only a line of military defense against Turkish aggression. It also rendered all of Europe a service of inestimable value by stopping the recurrent plagues that used to sweep out of Asiatic Turkey to ravage the greater part of Europe. The sanitary precautions and means of disinfection employed by the "cordon" watch were centuries in advance of such media elsewhere in the world. It is significant that there were no more attacks of plague after the "cordon" was constituted towards the middle of 18th century. Both Croatian and Serbian Granicari were employed in the "cordon" service. —Editor's Note.

Eventually, we were sent back to Sisak to repair, as we were told, railroad tracks that extended from this old river port to Novska. Instead of repairing the existing tracks, we just tore them up and, as far as I know, they were never reconstructed. Then we went to Mostar via Novska-Slavonski Brod-Sarajevo.

When we got to Zenica, I "deserted" the battalion and found shelter for a time in my own home. But the Communists caught up with me at last, and in January, 1946, the officers of the 13th Krajina (Frontier) Brigade almost beat me to death.

The Commander of this Brigade was Antun Nozinic, who was a Croatian and a particularly despicable traitor to his country and his people. In 1943 he was serving in the Domobrans as a First Lieutenant. He participated in a battle that took place near Banja Luka between his battalion and the Partisans. In this fight, he went over to the latter and threw his own command into confusion. For this service, which saved them from the usual beating they received whenever they encountered our troops, the Partisans advanced him to the rank of Battalion Commander.

This "Hero of the Liberation" told me himself, "I have slain 9000 Ustashas and you are going to be 9001."

How I avoided this fate is a tale too long to tell here. Suffice it to say that, like the Abbe Sieyes during the French Reign of Terror of 1792-94, I lived. I only hope that no one replaced me as "9001" on Nozinic's inventory of victims.

Signed: Franjo Krakaj

Document XXIII

Over one-third of the following account deals with the retreat of the Croatian Armed Forces, their battles against the Reds, negotiations with both the British and Russians, and surrender to the British. The Partisans soon declared the captives as their prisoners-of-war, looting and maltreating them. The eyewitness and about 1500 other men eluded the Partisans and surrendered to the British at Klagenfurt. The British extradited them together with an estimated 4500 additional victims. These 6000 prisoners were divided into groups. Our witness was included in a column of about 3000 people that "marched" to Maribor. In this city he saw maltreatments of thousands of wounded soldiers; 1100 or 1200 of these wretches were thrown into the Drava. The witness gives a detailed description of the infamous anti-tank trenches which extended from Mt. Pohorje to the village of Ribnica and of his new "Death March" from Maribor to Ptuj and onwards. He ended the long trek by escaping in Osijek. The witness stresses that his column was 15,000 strong at Ptuj. About 9000 prisoners of this number were murdered in the Slovenian and Croatian countrysides. The account closes by emphasizing how many prisoners were murdered before the eyes of their parents, spouses, or children.

At the end of April, 1945, I was serving in a unit of the Croatian Armed Forces which received orders to retreat from Zlatar through Pregrada and Rogaska Slatina towards Celje in Slovenia.

We reached this Slovenian town on the 5th or 6th of May. Slovene Partisans held it, but they had to permit us to pass through or around the city without molestation in order to avoid annihilation at our hands.

On the next day, which was either the 6th or 7th of May, the German Army laid down its arms, while our Army continued to march northward to Austria where it intended to surrender to the British. The Partisans at Celje and elsewhere were now greatly emboldened. They began to bar the passage of and arrest Croatian non-combatants—male civilians, women, and children—who were following or mixed in among the last units of the Croatian Armed Forces. In Gustanj-Slovenjgradec, Tito's forces succeeded in annihilating the tail-end of our withdrawing columns in a narrow pass near Soteska. Along with three hundred soldiers who composed our rear guard, about 2500 male civilians, women, and children were slain in this twentieth century Thermopylae. "Marshal" Tito himself issued a bombastic proclamation concerning this great "victory" won by his Partisans.[1] The English, American, and other foreign presses dutifully echoed his boasts.

Meanwhile, the bulk of our Army was withdrawing through the mountains towards Slovenjgradec. Here they intended to reform so as to reach Dravograd in as compact a military formation as was permitted by the presence of so many civilians, and by the transportation chaos created by German abandonment of numerous vehicles along the main roads. It was said that all Croatians who wished to flee into Austria could obtain free passage at Dravograd.

But when the Armed Forces arrived at Dravograd, we found that the situation there differed from the one we had anticipated. First of all, a great many individual military units had arrived here in advance of the main Army. They got in our way because there were British troops in front of them who up to this time had refused to allow them to enter Austria. All of our men had their armament intact, but the English had the advantage of having hundreds of planes and tanks at their disposal, while we had no instruments of modern warfare available for our use. This technical lag was caused partly by the military parsimony displayed towards us by our German allies between 1941 and 1945, and partly by the refusal of the Balkan Wehrmacht, even in the moments of its own dissolution and surrender, to turn over to us, without a useless inter-allied fight, the armaments it still possessed. The result was that most of this equipment was either abandoned in such helter-skelter fashion as to impede the passage of the artillery and tanks we had, or else, it was turned over to the Partisans by our late allies.

---

[1] This great "victory" took place on May 15, 1945, the day on which the British and "Yugoslav" Communists had concluded the Bleiburg "deal". See Documents I, II, and III.

Ahead were the British. Behind us, Tito's "Liberation Army" was following very gingerly. Nonetheless, the Partisans were alert enough to pick up non-combatants or military stragglers. To our right were Russian Soviet units. Behind a small creek which lay to the left of us was the Bulgarian Army. We were in a trap all right, but we were still fully armed and our main force of 80,000 veteran soldiers could have put up a fight here and perhaps broken through into Austria under cover of night, when the British planes and tanks would have been less effective. But, for reasons best known to themselves, our generals forbade us to attack. As soldiers, we could only obey these commands.

Our local commanders informed us that the representatives of Dr. Pavelic's Government, and of our Military Headquarters, were negotiating with the British and the Russians. I do not know the names of the Englishmen whom our emissaries contacted, but I remember that General Sudar discussed the terms under which we were to surrender with Marshal Tolbuhin of the Russian Soviet Army. Tolbuhin demanded that we lay down our arms and accept confinement at Camp Tolbuch.

Before any agreement was reached, Tito's Partisans, always very daring fellows when they had plenty of allies to back them up, began to throw hand grenades into our tightly packed masses. Now, we had to counterattack. We beat the Partisans in a fierce fight and reached the small river behind which Bulgarians were massed. The Bulgarians got out of our way, and we continued in what we thought was the direction of the Austrian border. Only 15,000 of our total number participated in this final offensive of the Croatian Army. Its success indicates what an assault of our entire mass might have accomplished. I was in the van myself, and when I got through the enemy lines and reached the top of a hill, I looked back and saw the fighting continuing unabated behind and below me. I judge that we lost 2500-3000 in this engagement. Certainly the losses of the Partisans and their allies were considerably heavier, despite the disparity in armament.

It was nighttime, and we had to march without a compass. Of course, this Slovenian territory was unfamiliar to us; therefore, we made the tragic error of traveling in a circle. We ended up at the rear of the Bulgarian lines once again. Another battle ensued, in which we lost our heavy weapons along with another 1500 soldiers.

Again we battled our way through and continued our march to the Marenberg Valley. There were at least 90,000 Croatian soldiers and an undetermined number of civilians crammed into this valley. They were also trying to reach the Austrian border. There were many ambulances filled with wounded men, who had been brought from Zagreb or other places.

Here too, the Croatian troops found their way blocked by British troops with tank support. Since we now were in Austria, however, we were not concerned about this circumstance. Everyone said that both we and the Englishmen were awaiting the decision of the British Government concerning locations in which we were to be interned according to the laws of war. It was because of this that the segment of the Croatian Armed Forces with which I had been fighting joined the larger mass in the valley.

Shortly after dawn on the next day, we noticed that about a mile away from where we were camped, well behind the British tanks and artillery, non-British looking uniforms were to be seen. We still did not realize that the English were not going to honor the Geneva and other international conventions, so, when we received orders from our generals at about 3:00 P.M. to turn over our weapons to the Britons, we did so. As soon as we were disarmed, we were taken behind the English lines, six at a time. We had gone less than a mile when Partisans armed with automatic weapons appeared and declared that we were their prisoners. At once, they began to loot us of our clothes, pens, rings, watches, and money. They gave us the torn and lice-infested uniforms that they were wearing. We did everything we could to get word back to those troops which still had arms, to fight rather than surrender them; it was too late, however, to convey an effective warning.

The Partisans threw the wounded men out of the ambulance, and, without any regard for their condition, kicked, beat, and trampled these poor fellows, whose chances of recovery in many cases were precarious at best. On the stretchers that the invalids had used, the Communists piled their excess weapons.

All of the prisoners taken in my immediate vicinity were driven to Bleiburg. Thousands of our people were liquidated in the immediate vicinity of this place. Thus, the British certainly knew what was going on and must have approved it in advance. Or, at least they left a free hand to their savage "allies," just as they had to the American Indians favorable to them in the American Revolution and the War of 1812.

Some groups of our soldiers, who had tried to escape into the woods, but had been rounded up by British or Partisans, joined us at Bleiburg. Their faces were a picture of despair, and some of them looked as though they had lost their minds. They told us that the Partisans were shooting masses of people indiscriminately. Most of these shootings occurred between May 12 and 16.

Obviously, we had nothing to lose by trying to get away. Some fifteen hundred of us eluded our vigilant guards and made off towards Volkermarkt. Here we found the bodies of many people whom the Partisans had murdered. The Austrian inhabitants of this place told us how to get to Klagenfurt, the capital of Carinthia. We arrived there after traveling for two days through the woods. Here we were foolish enough to surrender once again to the British troops who were in this place. We still did not realize the infamous behavior English military authorities were capable of.

The Britons took away from us weapons we had procured during our journey from Bleiburg. They placed us in the Jager (Hunter or Pursuit)

Barracks, formerly occupied by Nazi troops between 1938 and 1945; here we remained for almost two weeks. The Englishmen then extradited us to their executioner allies.

There were about 6000 of us who were turned over to the Partisans. They beat us, looted us of whatever we possessed, and ordered us to start marching from Klagenfurt to Dravograd. During this long trek we received no food or water. Many of us were entirely naked, the Partisans having stripped some individuals even of their underclothing. Since Tito's people immediately collected every shoe they could find, all of us were also barefoot.

At Dravograd, we were split up into various groups. I was included in a column about 3000 strong which was sent to Maribor. In this Slovenian city, we were herded into a yard which stood in front of the cadet school that dated from Austrian times. Already, a number of wounded Croatian soldiers and some civilians were confined here. I believe that there must have been 3000 wounded men in the building itself, while at least 15,000 other Croatians were kept outside. The wounded received no medical care at all. It was a horrifying sight to pass through the school building, as groaning, suffering wretches lay about wherever the floors were still intact. You could smell putrefying human flesh, for gangrene had set in in many cases, and some soldiers had the courage to amputate their own arms or legs after these limbs had become completely black. Everyone was starving and dying of thirst. Finally, after we had stayed here for four days, a meager ration of soup and canned food was issued.

At the end of a week, the Partisans initiated a series of crimes more horrifying than I have ever seen either in war or peace time. They picked out Ustashas and distributed them in the first floor rooms according to the length of their membership in the Ustasha organization; the necessary data in this connection was obtained through interrogation. They then took the avowed Domobrans and civilians and confined them in the yard in front of the building. It was the evening of June 3, 1945.

The Partisans announced that the wounded were to be taken by train to Zagreb. Since we knew that the rail line between Maribor and the Croatian capital was destroyed in many places, we did not believe this assertion. Soon wagons belonging to the local peasants were brought up, and the wounded men were thrown into them in the most brutal manner imaginable. A number of us were assigned as hospital orderlies to accompany the wounded to the trains which supposedly were waiting for them. It was from two of these orderlies, Eugene Rajhl and Fabian Medar, that I obtained the story of what was done with helpless men whose only crime had been to incur wounds in the service of their country. Rajhl and Medar had served as orderlies in the Croatian Armed Forces. They noticed that the orderlies (some trained as they were, and others untrained), sent out with the first batches of wounded, did not return when the carts came back empty of prisoners. Nevertheless, they had no choice when their turn came but to get into the carts with the contingent of wounded for whom they were supposed to care. Here are Medar's words as I heard them many days later:

> We thought at first that perhaps they were going to take the wounded to Zagreb after all. Pretty soon, however, we found ourselves close to the Drava River. Here the wounded men were beaten over the head with iron rods and then thrown into the water. Some of the more serious cases were pitched in without the Partisans bothering first to kill them. Four of us (orderlies) were sent to a bend in the river which was about a hundred yards away from where the victims were disposed of, in order to consign again to the water those corpses which had become snagged on the river bank.

Rajhl and Medar did not see what happened to the other two orderlies who were assigned to this duty. When day broke, they found themselves alone. Probably, the executioners of the wounded soldiers had forgotten all about them. They were not familiar with Slovenia and did not know where to go or what to do. A day and night of hiding in the woods convinced them that the best possible choice they could make would be to return to the school and take their chances there, rather than starve to death in the forests. Therefore, they came back to join us survivors, to whom they told the story of the wounded veterans, murdered by Partisans.

I think that between 1100 and 1200 wounded men were removed from the school building and murdered in the manner described. When we examined the rooms in which they had lain, we found flies eating severed arms and legs.

Two days after this occurrence, the Partisans began to take the rest of us off in trucks, twenty or thirty at a time. No one knew where we were going. Some of us were detailed to collect long pieces of fallen telephone wire along the edge of the highway. These were cut into shorter lengths and placed in the cabs of the trucks.

The long slope leading up to Mt. Pohorje begins on the far side of Maribor. During the war, the Germans dug an anti-tank trench in the pass which leads to the village of Ribnica. This trench was two and a half miles in length. When I first saw it, I did not know how it was used. Only in 1947, when I was again imprisoned in Maribor for trying to escape from Tito's hell, did I discover the gruesome details of what had happened in this pass two years before. In 1947, I was serving a three-year sentence at forced labor to teach me to appreciate the "Socialist Paradise." I was sent to work at Pohorski Castle as an assistant to a bricklayer. One day, I went out with other prisoners to bring back logs from the Pohorje woods. In the course of this task, we approached the aforementioned pass and found that it was fenced with barbed wire to prevent access to it. Inside the fence, the ground was covered with traces of lime. Peasants in the village of Ribnica told us that after the war ended, the Thirteenth Proletarian Brigade had massacred thousands of Croatian soldiers in this place; victims were delivered into the hands of the Partisans by their British allies to whom the Croatians had surrendered in Austria. The bodies were thrown into the German anti-tank trenches and covered over with a thin layer of earth. Later, quicklime was dumped into this pit of horror.

Even today, all of the inhabitants of Ribnica know what was done in this place. Among other eyewitnesses, Frank Umetic, Janez Haluzan, and Stephan Golub are still living in this village.

At the Cadet School, we remained happily ignorant of many of the crimes enacted so close to us. About 7000 of us were formed into battalions and marched towards Ptuj. This was one of the "Death Columns" that were moving about the Croatian, Slovenian, and Serbian countrysides during the last half of 1945, and in 1946 and 1947. We provided a truly harrowing sight with our starved faces and naked bodies. Our column was a full seven miles long, and Tito's guards, armed with British-made or supplied machine guns, were stationed all along, in front and behind. Any attempt to escape or to get a drink of water from a well or brook meant a speedy, if not easy, death.

We passed the corpses of many people lying along the sides of the road. Since thousands of other prisoners were added to our column as we passed through Ptuj, Varazdin, Ludbreg, Koprivnica, Virovitica, Pdr. Slatina, Donji Miholjac, Osijek, and on to Vrsac in Serbia, there must have been more than 14,000 of us in all. But only 6000 survivors arrived at Osijek, where I succeeded in escaping.

The memory of what I saw between Maribor and Osijek will never leave me. I recall how the Partisans delighted in picking out victims whose homes were in villages or towns through which we passed. They would take them right to their houses, and shoot them there before their parents, spouses, or children. During the nights that we camped along the highway, the guards would fire their weapons among us indiscriminately. They said that they were doing this in order to "clean" their guns. Many prisoners dug up the ground with their finger nails in order to make holes in which they could lie and be relatively safe from this random shooting. But every morning when we were ordered to move on, there were dead men lying along the highway or in the fields nearby. Anyone who became too exhausted to continue was disposed of without mercy.

We were fed only twice during the long march from Maribor to Osijek. At Varazdin, we received two pounds of bread for every twenty men. When we reached Podr. Slatina we were given a little boiled corn.

Sometimes peasants would put jugs of water alongside the road, but the Partisan guards immediately rushed up to spill the contents along the dusty roadside. As they did so, they would curse us, call us bandits, and assure us that we were going to be allowed to die of thirst and hunger.

Signed: Zvonimir Skok

Kaiserlautern
March 6, 1953

P. S. This letter I have not written until today, because had I done so previously, while I was still living in Yugoslavia, I would have paid with my life for citing these few facts that I have given in the preceding account.

Document XXIV

The eyewitness A. Markotic first describes the Croatian troops' retreat from Zagreb and their bitter fight with the Partisans at Brezice. He relates also the difficulties that were caused by the German surrender at Zidani Most. In spite of the Partisans' insistence on surrender to them at Celje, the witness' column went farther and had another battle with the Reds at Hajren Kapela. Three days after this battle, the Croats surrendered to the British, who placed them together with about ten thousand Slovenian anti-Communist fighters. In a few days the prisoners were extradited to Tito's troops. They drove the victims in a train towards Jesenice. After a short ride, ten Croatian officers were murdered. The train stopped in Radovljica, and the captives now began their "Death March" through the Slovenian countryside. After reaching the Croatian soil, groups of fifteen to twenty victims were being taken out of the column and murdered. The tragic end of Colonels Petrovic and Hasic is also reported here. The witness was saved by a Croatian civilian who employed him and some other men on a mill job.

I arrived at Zagreb on May 8, 1945, as chauffeur for Colonel Djal, who was one of the commanders of the Ustasha rear guards. The Obrana had concentrated a formation of fast-moving tanks in the capital. At eight in the evening of this same day, we joined this column and moved out of Zagreb en route to Slovenia and Austria. Colonel Matkovic assumed command of the entire column.

Up to Brezice we encountered no resistance. Here, however, the Voyvodina Partisan Brigade, an almost entirely Serbian formation, attacked us. For three hours, a hot fight raged in the streets and environs of Brezice, killing and wounding many on both sides. Finally, the Communists had enough of this and sullenly drew off.

Our column was now able to proceed to Zidani Most without further incident. But beyond this point, our progress was blocked because the Germans in their retreat had abandoned vehicles and heavy weapons of all kinds, partially destroying many of them. To me, this final German act in the war always has seemed typical of the military stupidity and faithlessness of the Germans. If they had no further use for these weapons and vehicles themselves, the least they could have done was turn them over to us, their allies, intact. With German weapons and vehicles, we could have marched all the way to the Atlantic Ocean if we had to go that far to find someone besides the Communists who would accept our surrender. As it was, General Luburic had to order our pioneers to clear the road by finishing the job of destruction that the Germans had started.

When the pioneer detachments had cleared the road, Colonel Petrovic led the column on towards Celje in Slovenia. Communist forces held this town, and Colonel Petrovic demanded that they grant us free passage through Celje in order to prevent further unnecessary bloodshed, now that Germany had surrendered and the war was virtually over, even for Croatians, Serbians, and Slovenians. The Partisans countered his demand by insisting that we surrender to them. After the Partisans had disarmed us, they said that they would let us go on to Austria. Of course, Colonel Petrovic refused to accept this condition. Rather than fight our way through the streets of Celje as we had at Brezice, however, he sent our column around the town. Once beyond Celje we picked up the road to Klagenfurt in Austrian Carinthia.

We followed the Klagenfurt road until we came to Hajren Kapela. Here we encountered British soldiers who gave us food, the first we had received in many days. The Englishmen were kind enough to warn us that the Partisans were going to attack us, so that we would have to exercise great caution as we continued our march beyond this point.

At Hajren Kapela we effected a junction of our forces with those of Colonel Tomislav Mesic.[1] We were told that the British had supplied his troops with ammunition, because his forces had so little. At five o'clock in the afternoon of this day, the Partisans did attack our combined column. As usual, we drove them back, with only six men killed and two wounded in the action, while the ground was fairly littered with the corpses of those who wore the Red Star emblem. While we were fighting the Communists along the left side of the road leading to Klagenfurt, the British columns remained on the other side of the highway about a mile away from where the action was going on. They took no part in the combat at all.

Although the Partisans retreated in confusion, and the road ahead seemed to be clear as early as 8 P.M., we did not wish to expose ourselves to a night ambush. We remained on the battleground the entire night. Early on the following morning, the column moved on again towards Klagenfurt. There were about 20,000 soldiers and civilians in our group, but Colonel Mesic's troops lessened that number by detaching themselves from us and proceeding by a different route.

---

[1] Mesic today resides in Chicago, Illinois. He is one of the leading men in the United American Croatians organization.

At about two in the afternoon, we arrived at the banks of the Drava River. The bridge across it had been destroyed. Whether the bridge was demolished by the British or by the Partisans, we could not ascertain. Therefore, we had to proceed in the direction of Verlach, through the woods lining the bank of the Drava. Near a town called Kapela, we found a bridge spanning the Drava still standing. However, British troops held the end of the bridge that debouched onto Austrian territory, while the Partisans were guarding the Slovene part of the bridge. Of course, they did not want to allow us to cross into Austria. We could have thrown them into the Drava easily enough but, obviously, further armed action on our part was likely to complicate the conditions of surrender which we knew were facing us.

So we spent two days there negotiating with the Partisans. Finally, seeing that we were determined to cross, and knowing that they could not stop us from doing so, they retreated. Thus, at long last, we were able to do what we had set out from Zagreb to accomplish – surrender to the British.

The English troops allowed us to cross the bridge into Austria and continue our march to Klagenfurt. When we reached the town of Fipning, however, we found a British motorcyclist awaiting us. He directed us to a field where we found some Croatian troops and civilians along with about ten thousand Slovenian White Guards of the anti-Communist Slovenian forces commanded by General Rupnik.[2]

We waited for another two days on this field. On the third day, British soldiers conducted us to the town of Maria Elend. After a three-hour rest here, a number of empty boxcars arrived at the rail station. Colonel Petrovic told us that the British Command had ordered us to occupy these boxcars which, they said, were going to convey us to Italy.

We did not anticipate danger. On the contrary, we were very happy that the British had accepted our surrender. Naturally, we would never have surrendered to the Communists but, given the international situation, there didn't seem to be any point in fighting them any longer either. Thus, we were joyously singing old Croatian and Slovenian songs as we boarded the boxcars. We even set to work to decorate them, so jubilant were we at what we assumed to be the definitive end of the war.[3]

Once we were aboard the train, all of the officers were placed in third class coaches which were brought up from somewhere and joined to

[2] The extradition and subsequent wholesale massacre of these and thousands of other Slovenian anti-Communist troops are described in the volume, *Vetrinjska Tragedija* (Federation of the Slovenian anti-Communist Fighters. Cleveland, 1960). See also Supplement I, "La Tragedia del Pueblo Esloveno," in the book, *La Tragedia de Bleiburg* (Studia Croatica, Buenos Aires, 1963), pp. 175-185. Document XLIV of this volume also deals with the tragic fate of the Slovenian anti-Communist fighters.

[3] Compare this information with the first part of the account of Hasan Selimovic, Document XXVII.

the boxcars. Soon after the officers were separated from their men, British soldiers locked the doors of each of the boxcars.

This action aroused in us the first spark of suspicion concerning our fate. However, most of our people took the optimistic view that, after all, we were prisoners of the Englishmen and, certainly, they had to take precautions to see that none of us escaped their custody. We would have taken the same precautions had they been our prisoners, as indeed they would have been had we had the slightest intimation of what lay ahead of us when we still had weapons.

The trains remained motionless on the tracks for a long time. Then a locomotive with an attached boxcar came puffing into the station. Partisan soldiers came pouring out of the boxcar and most of them were deployed around the coach occupied by the officers.

The British troops who had been guarding us marched off. We were in the hands of the Communists! Only then did we comprehend how the Englishmen had deceived us!

Shortly after the arrival of the Partisan troops, the train finally got under way. We journeyed for scarcely half an hour, however, and had not even reached Jesenice, when we slowed down and stopped in a forest. The Partisans took ten officers out of our reach, tied their hands with wire, took all of their belongings, led them into the woods and shot them. Among the victims were Colonel Matkovic, Colonel Josip Mataja, Captain Tiho Kordic, First Lieutenant Bozicevic, First Lieutenant Kolaric, Second Lieutenant Stanko Segro, and Color-Bearer Luka Cop. I do not know the names of the three others who were shot.

Following this action, the train got under way again. We passed through Jesenice and arrived at Radovljica where our guards unloaded us. They lined us up into columns and marched us from the station through the town. The Slovenian population spat on us, mocked us, and struck us with clubs and other weapons. About a mile and a half from the town itself, there was a camp fenced with a triple row of barbed wire. There we were confined for the night.

On the following day, we were marched off again towards Zidani Most. Beyond this town we began to encounter the corpses of many Ustashas and Domobrans. They were prisoners who had preceded us in the return to our homeland after the British had turned them over to the Partisans. Once the Partisans were sure that there were no Englishmen anywhere in the vicinity, they robbed, tortured, and murdered these people. Just before we reached Celje, we came upon corpses of German, as well as Croatian soldiers. The Partisans had cut off the noses and gouged out the eyes of these victims.[4]

We crossed the Slovenian frontier into Croatian territory, where we were placed in various concentration camps. Here our already great sufferings were increased enormously. Except for a few crumbs of bean

[4] Many more details about such barbarities of Tito's troops can be read in the account of Josip Jelenic, *La Tragedia de Bleiburg* (Buenos Aires, 1963), pp. 294-297.

grain soaked with water, we received absolutely nothing to eat. Nor could we get any sleep, because throughout the night, our Communist guards roamed about us, awakening us and taking from us whatever we had of value. On the very first night that we were back in the Domovina, our captors began to take away groups of fifteen or twenty men. A few minutes after these unfortunates were led off, we always heard shots and cries which told us well enough what was happening.

One day, an immature fifteen-year-old Partisan youth took Colonel Petrovic's watch, ordered him to take off his trousers, and then with the assistance of other Red Guards, tied his hands with wire. Thus bound, the colonel was led away never to return. The same fate befell Colonel Avdo Hasic. During the five days that I spent in this hell, many other individuals and groups were treated in a similar manner.

On one occasion I happened to note a Domobran soldier hunting through a ditch in hopes that he might find a bit of food. He didn't encounter any, but he did come across a hand grenade. Instead of using it to kill some of our guards and trying to make a getaway, the poor fool put the grenade back where he had picked it up. Perhaps, he hoped to find a better moment to use it. But a guard saw what he was doing and, ignoring the man's excuse that he had come across the grenade only by accident, ordered him to be tied up and thrown into a nearby meadow. Here he remained for three days without food or water. Bound as he was, he naturally swelled up all over during this period of agony. Finally, the Partisans loaded him onto a cart and took him off to one of the various points of no return which awaited so many of our people.

There were a few Frenchmen among the Partisans, former German prisoners-of-war. Of course, they knew what was going on, and their attitude towards it was to be expected from descendants of people who had watched with equanimity massacres perpetrated by their Indian allies at Fort William Henry, Deerfield, and other places during the French and English wars in North America. Fortunately, however, they did ask the director of the concentration camp to detail several of our people to clean their quarters.

It was my good luck to be one of the prisoners chosen for this detail. Then, only a day after my assignment to this work squad, I experienced a further stroke of fortune. A private Croatian citizen who seemed to be on good terms with the Marxists, but who had some sympathy for us, too, found work for me and some of his other compatriots among the prisoners on a mill construction project.

We were employed for about a month on this job. Then, the Partisans brought us back to the concentration camp; few of my wartime comrades remained there. My wife and brother, too, had disappeared. I was told by a Slovenian Commissar that the Hercegovinian Partisan Brigade, composed of Hercegovinian Serbs under the command of a fellow by the name of Konjhodzitch of Mostar, had murdered about 1400 of the prisoners who had been confined with me before my departure for the mill job. This Slovene had fought in Rupnik's anti-Communist Army but, when he saw the war was lost, he managed to squirm into the ranks of the Partisans.

Divine Providence willed that those of us who had worked on the mill be allowed to return to this employment, our Croatian protector having again requested our services. But, after ten more days of labor, I found out that Communists were going to take us back to the concentration camp once more. I knew what that probably meant; thus, I decided to make a break for permanent safety, or at least find a quick end.

Again luck was with me, and I had relatively little difficulty in making my way to Italy. I have not been able to ascertain the fate of the other nine individuals employed on the mill construction project, but I know that they were sent back to the worthy imitation of Dachau and Buchenwald, where so many Croatian and Slovenian patriots met their tragic destinies.

Signed: A. Markotic

Fermo, Italy
May 8, 1946

Document XXV

This account of a Montenegrin nationalist first briefly corroborates the detailed stories of other eyewitnesses on the mass killings of war prisoners at Lasko, Slovenia. Then, the eyewitness depicts the massacre of several hundred Montenegrin nationalist troops at Zidani Most. The survivors were taken from here in a "Death March" which, amid usual brutalities and frequent murders, took them to Samobor, Croatia. The Croatian people, unlike those in Slovenia, showed great charity toward the "Death Marchers." On arriving in Samobor, our eyewitness was confined in the city's park which was converted into a concentration camp. There were thousands of war prisoners in this camp. Some victims were murdered by bullets; others were poisoned. The latter were taken by the Partisans to a "hospital" of no return. On one occasion, the witness saw a hundred and fifty of his co-nationals taken to be slaughtered. On another occasion, one hundred and forty Montenegrins, including our eyewitness, were led out to be slaughtered in the vicinity of Samobor. Colonel Vlado Dapchevitch, however, saved them temporarily. When the Montenegrins were liquidated, the Partisans took the Croatians out to be shot. On the twelfth day of his stay in Samobor, the witness escaped.

On May 15, I laid down my arms along with many other Montenegrin Nationalists or Royalists. There were about six thousand of us in the group in which I was included. We were driven through Dravograd to Maribor, where we stayed for two days in a concentration camp that was located on the outskirts of the city near the Drava River. Women and children, chiefly Croatians, were kept in one part of this camp.

The Partisans separated us into various categories, officers, intellectuals, the several branches of the military services, civilians, and so on. Thereafter, the mass killings began.

It was my luck to escape these. Together with a thousand other Montenegrins, I was taken from the camp and placed in a column which marched under conditions of great hardship towards Celje. Near Lasko, we were lodged in a large building which, with the courtyard that belonged to it, was converted into a concentration camp. This place was not well guarded, consequently many captives succeeded in escaping from it. We were subsequently transferred to a barracks that was close to a mine (I think this was at Hrastnik). There were three hundred students and "intellectuals" at this barracks; that is, there were that many individuals who acknowledged that they belonged to such a category. They were taken off by the Partisans "to work somewhere." Later on we learned that Tito's killers murdered them and threw their bodies into abandoned mine shafts.

From the barracks at the mine we were escorted to Zidani Most. Here we were placed in a large concentration camp that was approximately a half mile below the Zidani Most rail station. Germans and Croatians as well as Montenegrins were imprisoned in this place. We remained there for a day and a night during which time new escorts took charge of us.

These new guards belonged to the Fifth Montenegrin Brigade of Tito's Communist Partisan army. Also in this vicinity was the headquarters of the Partisan Third Division, which contained many Communist Montenegrins. Furthermore, the President of the Military Courts of the "Liberation" Army was also here. He was a Montenegrin by the name of Mirko Shukovitch, who came from around Kolashin. He came among us and interrogated every one of us individually. He asked us all about our family circumstances and past activities. Other Montenegrins visited us, too, for the purpose of identifying us.

Soon after this process of identification had begun, an officer started to call out names from a list which probably was prepared by Shukovitch. Everyone whose name was on this roll call was led to a forest across the street from the camp and shot there, almost within eyesight of us. The first group to be so disposed of included about fifty men. Among them were Zhariya Drashkovitch; an elementary school teacher from Lipovo by the name of Milovan Minitch; Peter Vlahovitch, a retired army captain from Kolashin; and Rade Radovitch, an elementary school teacher from Ravna Rijeka.

Other prisoners, who were eyewitnesses of the event, told me that prior to my arrival in this camp, the Montenegrin Communist General, Yankovitch, a native of the Zhablyak-Drobnyak district, found his three brothers, as well as a number of other relatives, among the Montenegrin Royalists. He had all of them shot at Zidani Most.

There were also Montenegrin commissars around here who posed a special danger because they were personally acquainted with many of us. Anyone whom they recognized was sent to be shot. Several hundred Montenegrins in all were executed in this camp, some before my arrival, others from the column which I had accompanied.

We survivors were thrust into a column that was moving towards Samobor. When we were only about six miles away from Zidani Most, the Fifth Kozara Partisan Brigade relieved our Montenegrin guards. This Kozara Brigade was composed chiefly of Serbs who lived in the vicinity of the Kozara Mountain. However some Montenegrin as well as both Muslim and Catholic Croatians were later included in this formation.

The most terrible sufferings to which I have ever been exposed now began. Our new Serbian Partisan guards were mounted on horseback and they carried long thick clubs with which they beat us unmercifully. They forced us to run practically all the time. Many captives could not keep us this pace and collapsed. Those who dropped dead of heart attacks brought on by this continued exertion were lucky. Those who momentarily ran out of wind were shot, beaten to death, or stabbed where they fell.

One day a Partisan noticed a small knife lying in the road. Of course no one was supposed to have a weapon of this sort on his person. He asked whose knife it was, and when he received no answer, warned us that if the "guilty" person did not confess, he would kill four of us. Still no one would acknowledge ownership of the knife, so he took the four men marching directly in front of me and mowed them down with his light machine gun.

So rapid was the pace that we had to keep up during our "march" that we threw away all belongings which the Partisans had left us. Every couple of yards along the route, we passed a dead man who had been unable to maintain the running gait that our guards forced us to adopt. We spent the first night of this ordeal on a large level space which formerly was used as an airport. On this night, a large number of prisoners were taken from among us and slaughtered in the near vicinity.

On the following day, we arrived at Samobor. We knew at once that we were now on Croatian soil because the inhabitants of this place, unlike those of the Slovene countryside through which we had passed, displayed great charity towards us. They tossed packages or bits of food to us and placed filled water containers for us all along the road near the town. However, our Partisan guards killed anyone who tried to drink from these vessels. I knew one of these victims, a fellow named Perovitch from Lipovo.

In Samobor, we were lodged in the city park, which had been converted into a concentration camp. This park was crowded with prisoners – we were told there were six thousand in all. Barbed wire fencing had been put up all around the expanse of grounds, but five meters inside this wire a thick white line was drawn. The guards shot on sight anyone who stepped over this line. Some of us risked doing this because we all were starving, and when the women of Samobor tossed food over the fence, captives scrambled for it without regard for the consequences. Such recklessness can be understood when it is borne in mind that some of us actually died of starvation.

Dysentery plagued us also. The Partisans brought us bottles of liquid oners who took a spoonful became ill. Then the Partisans took them off to the "hospital." No one ever came back from this place, if it really existed. A number of acquaintances of mine, among them Zhariya Min-which, they said, would protect us against this ailment. It did. All pris-itch, Slobodan Shtchepanovitch, Novelya Ilanchitch, and others were removed in this way.

We received our first provisional "hearing" in the park at Samobor. In this session we were asked to give our first and last names, place of birth, and the year in which we had been conscripted into the Montenegrin National Forces. The Partisans did not make any distinction between Montenegrin Royalists, Federalists, or Chetniks. They applied the insulting name "dyikani"[1] to all of us. After the interrogation, they led away a hundred and fifty men who acknowledged that they had served in the Montenegrin National Forces since 1941, that is, since the break-up of the first Yugoslavia. The Partisans shot these men in a kind of cleft in the hills that lies between the old part of Samobor and a destroyed building above the town.

On the seventh day of my sojourn in Samobor, I was taken out of the camp along with a hundred and forty men who admitted that they had fought against the Partisans since 1943. Guards were placed in charge of us to take us to the place where we were to "work." Hardly had we left the city, however, than another Partisan unit, about fifty strong, took over from our previous escort. These Partisans all carried light machine guns which they had obtained from the British, Russians, or Americans. They led us at first along the main highway, then made us turn off onto a country path. We must have been quite close to the place at which the Partisans intended to slaughter us when Lieutenant Colonel Vlado Dapchevitch, a brother of General Peko Dapchevitch, suddenly appeared in our midst. He ordered the column to turn back, saying that we were to undergo further questioning.

A violent quarrel ensued between Lt. Col. Dapchevitch and the commissar who had charge of the party that was supposed to shoot us. It reached the point where both men drew their guns and seemed almost ready to "shoot it out," like two characters from an American cowboy movie. The commissar insisted that he was in charge and that he himself had signed the order for our "liquidation"; therefore it was his duty

---

[1] Recalcitrant horses.

to execute this order. He was only a first lieutenant, however, so finally he gave way to his superior in rank and, much against his will, returned us to the camp.

In the days that followed, most Montenegrins were "liquidated" nonetheless. Then the Partisans began to take the Croatians out to be shot. As for myself, I succeeded in escaping on the twelfth day of my stay at Samobor. I do not believe that any of the Montenegrin comrades whom I left behind in this camp are still alive today. Never have I heard from or of any one of them. I fear that Lt. Col. Dapchevitch's gesture described above was in vain, except that it preserved my own life.

The facts cited above have been read to me and I find them faithfully recorded as I have related them.

Signed: B. D.

Rome, Italy
November 6, 1955

Document XXVI

Eyewitness Ante Dragosevic tells of the high morale of the Croatian Armed Forces and their delusions about the intended capitulation to the British. He also relates the astonishment and confusion attending the surrender to the Partisans. Dragosevic began his "Death March" at Bleiburg, and in four days arrived in Maribor. Here the Ustashas were separated from the Domobrans. Our witness was included among the latter. After spending one night in the warehouses along the railroad tracks and another in the girls' school building, the witness and his group were lined up in columns and "marched" to be slaughtered. A Serbian Partisan Major saved the victims and had them transported by train from Maribor to Zagreb.

We began our retreat from Zagreb on May 6, 1945, passing through Ilica to Zapresic, and then along the route Zidani Most-Celje-Slovenjgradec-Bleiburg. Although we did have to brush aside Communist resistance here and there, combat was rare. We captured one group of Partisans about seventy strong, and took them along with us to Bleiburg, where we released them. I remember that when we went through Celje, the Partisans were in possession of the town. Although they disarmed the German troops who were retreating along with us, they were afraid to oppose the passage of our contingent. Of course, Germany already had surrendered, whereas we had not, and the Communists were well aware of the combat readiness of the Croatian Armed Forces as compared to the remnants of the Wehrmacht.

The military morale of our troops was very high. As far as I could tell, it had remained virtually unaffected by the German collapse. Perhaps, this was because allegedly reliable information was circulating through our ranks to the effect that the political authorities of the Croatian State had made an agreement with the British for an honorable capitulation. The utterly idiotic idea prevailed that the Englishmen would allow us to rest up for a few days, and then supply us with new and better weapons than those we had. The rumors followed that the British were going to do this so we could help them and the Americans stop the Russians and Yugoslav Communists from overrunning Central Europe! I don't know who was responsible for the circulation of such fantastic absurdities as these, but I do know that both Ustashas and Domobrans devoutly believed that this would happen. They were convinced that the British and Americans comprehended the value of Croatia's freedom to their own countries. Thus, even though the Croatian troops were tired and hungry, their spirits were buoyed up by the knowledge that General Boban, a real tiger of a man, was in charge of the retreat, that Dr. Pavelic was conducting negotiations with the British, and that Archbishop Stepinac had stayed at home to protect Croatian interests in his capacity as a non-political personality.

Shortly after sunrise on May 15, we reached a small field about a mile and a half from the great meadow near Bleiburg. Following a short period of rest, we went on to the Bleiburg field, arriving between nine and ten o'clock in the morning. The great flat or rolling expanse of land on which we found ourselves, was packed full of troops and civilian refugees, many of whom were women and children. There was also a great number of vehicles and even some cattle. British planes hovered overhead, and we were foolish enough to greet their presence with enthusiasm, tossing our caps into the air and waving to them. A Croatian Air Force officer warned us, however, that the British were making a display of their military strength only to intimidate us into surrendering. The English planes flew very low over our heads several times.

About three o'clock that afternoon, we were advised that we were to lay down our arms, and display white flags. Afterwards we received orders to advance to the edge of the woods, where the process of surrender would be initiated. As we approached the woods I saw Yugoslav Communist troops standing in line along the border of the forest. Except for the Partisans we had taken prisoner, these were the first Communists I had seen for days. They seemed to be in a state of great confusion and trepidation. Evidently, they feared that we were going to break through their lines as we had during the retreat from Zagreb, whenever they had dared oppose our passage. They addressed us with great courtesy and even with submissiveness and humility. Without voicing any threats whatsoever, they asked us to surrender all of our weapons because the war was over and we were going to be allowed to return to our homes. They told us that we should not enter the woods, because these had been mined. We were fools enough to believe them, so we threw away our last chance to escape. Actually, we could have overpowered the entire Communist force, inadequately armed as we were.

Up to this moment, we had no idea that we were supposed to surrender to the Communists. In our naivete, we had assumed that the British would have the good sense to accept our surrender and thus secure valuable allies for themselves in the struggle that they must sooner or later engage in with the Russians. Now, however, we could see the Englishmen leaning against their tanks, smoking their pipes, and evidently taking great pleasure in seeing us faced with the choice of surrendering to their Communist allies of the moment, or engaging in a battle which could have only one eventual outcome, even if we managed to triumph at this time and place.

We were astonished to find that we were expected to capitulate to the Communists. Great confusion attended the surrender of our arms, which dragged on over a long period of time. The Communists addressed a number of questions to each man. About twenty yards away from where I was standing, a young Domobran lieutenant committed suicide in a fit of despair. This incident reveals the deplorable state of mind of all Croats present. Instead of killing Communists and putting up a fight for our lives, we were killing ourselves! The Domobran lieutenant was not the only one who took this way out of the predicament in which we suddenly found ourselves.

Dusk fell before the surrender of our weapons was completed. We were ordered to line up in columns of fours, and begin the march back to the Domovina. At first, the column moved very slowly, and we had a two or three-hour rest in a small town not far from Bleiburg. Around midnight, we received orders to move out again. We crossed the Drava River, passing through a small town where we saw British troops for the last time. Russian and Bulgarian columns were in evidence also, and the Russians had artillery in battle position along the left bank of the Drava.

Because of the slowness of our march, it took four days to cover the distance between Bleiburg and Maribor. I cannot say what units the Communist troops who were guarding us belonged to. They did not engage in conversation with us, but during the first part of our Calvary, at least they did not molest us in any way. Once they were sure that no English troops were nearby, and especially after they had passed the Russian columns moving in directions opposite to ours, they began to rob us of watches, rings, clothing, and other personal belongings.

Even today, fourteen years after these occurrences, I remember well the presence in the column of Major Josip Kuzela, Commander of the 8th Ustasha Brigade, Captain Kastelan, the heroic defender of Kostajnica in the 1945 fighting, Second Lieutenant Josip Dagen, the lawyer Bozo Mostovac, Karlo Starcevic, Second Lieutenant of the Zagreb Domobrans, Pavao Vidovic, and an Ustasha officer and his wife. There were also a number of other women in the column.

After the first four days, our guards began to maltreat us. I think it took them that long to get up nerve enough to do this, because on the first part of the march they seemed to be afraid that we were going to take their weapons away, and exchange roles with them. However, after four days and nights of marching with little rest, and almost no food or water at all, we had little fight remaining in us. Some of the men in our column were badly beaten. Those who fell out because of exhaustion were shot on the spot. After five days of almost steady marching, we received our first food, other than what we had been able to scrounge up along the route from sympathetic Slovenians. Our meal on this occasion consisted of a single piece of bread!

Following another all-night march, we arrived at Maribor on May 19, at eleven o'clock in the morning. As we crossed the bridge over the Drava, a young Ustasha officer jumped into the river. A hail of Partisan bullets followed him, but he may have made good his escape, judging by the villainous temper of the guards who pursued him when they returned to the column. We passed through Maribor, and stopped on a field half a mile outside the town. En route we asked an elderly Slovenian for water. He shouted at us, "There's no water for Fascists!" A young officer answered him, "Listen, friend, were we Fascists when Croatia gave shelter to thousands of Slovenian refugees when Hitler's troops occupied your country, and when we gave them food and jobs as well?" The Slovene did not reply immediately, but after a time he asked what part of Croatia we came from. "We are from all parts," the officer told him. Then the old fellow told a boy to get some water for us. While we were waiting in the field, a number of school children did bring us water.

On the field, the Ustashas were separated from the Domobrans and officers were separated from enlisted men. I was included with the Domobran officer group, which numbered more than two thousand men. Our captors led us from the field back over the bridge, to the Maribor freight station of the rail line. We reached this place at sundown and spent the night in the warehouses along the tracks. There were between sixty and eighty people in the room that I occupied.

The next afternoon, we were brought to a large building with a spacious courtyard. We heard that this was a girls' school dating from the days of the Austrian Empire. On one of the upper floors there was a large kettle in which beans had been boiled. Although they were already spoiled and mouldy, some of the younger officers ate several handfulls of this mess. They paid later on with stomach cramps and diarrhea for trying to satisfy their hunger.

We passed the night in the school building. The next morning, after we lined up in columns again, we were led away. At least our captors cheered us up by telling us that we were being sent to our homes in Croatia. We noticed, however, that we were being taken across the railroad tracks in an easterly or south-easterly direction. We had marched for about forty-five minutes when a Communist major stopped the column and asked where we were going. The Communist officer in charge of our group made a gesture with his arms as though he were raising a rifle to shoot someone. At once we "got the message"; we were being led off to our own execution!

Fortunately, however, the major was a former officer of the Serbian Royal Army. He asked the leader of our guards who had given the order to shoot us. When none of our guards answered him, he then demanded to know where the commissar who was supposed to be in command of the entire column was keeping himself. Just at this moment, the commissar rode up on horseback and asked why the column had halted.

A long and animated conversation between the major and the commissar ensued. Finally, the major came over to us and asked what army contingents we belonged to. We told him that we were all active or reserve officers of the regular Croatian Army, or Domobrans. Then he asked what regions of Croatia we hailed from. When he had ascertained that we came from various parts of the Domovina, and that we all would have to travel through Zagreb to get to our homes, he told us that he would arrange to have a train convey us near that city. He also informed us that whoever was charged with war crimes would have to stand trial, but that the rest of us would be allowed to go to our homes.

After this, the commissar ordered the column to return to the school building where we had spent the previous night. It was nightfall by the time we reached it. About four A.M., we were loaded into cattle cars and transported to Zagreb.

Signed: Ante Dragosevic

Rome, May 8-9, 1959

Document XXVII

The following account by Hasan Selimovic, opens with a description of the Croatian Exodus. The witness also describes his group's extradition from Klagenfurt by treachery. The horrors of murdering prisoners during the "Death March" from Jesenice to the extermination camp in Sent Vid near Ljubljana, as well as the Partisan atrocities in the camp itself, are vividly presented. The generosity of the people of Samobor is stressed in contrast to the brutalities of Tito's troops. The extermination camp in Precko and a mass grave of Croatian invalid and blind men are dramatically depicted. The account closes with the witness's transport to Serbia, his flight from the train, his later recapture in Banja Luka, and his especially moving presentation of a Catholic nun's tragedy.

Towards the end of World War II, I was commanding officer of the Pioneer Company of the First Ustasha Defense Brigade of the Croatian Army. We were stationed at Bosanska Dubica in Bosnia.

On either May 3 or 4, we received orders to withdraw from Dubica to Sunja. When we arrived at Sunja, we found that the collapse of Germany had convinced our own Government that it would be useless to try to defend the Domovina (homeland) against the hordes of Tito Broz, who had the Russians, Americans, and British behind him. Therefore, our entire Army had orders to evacuate the Fatherland.

My unit retreated from Sunja through Sisak, Ivanic-grad, Kerestinec, and further westward. At Sv. Nedjelja, we had a hot fight with the Partisans. Our hearts were full of bitterness at this time because we had just received the news of the fall of Zagreb to the Partisans. We threw Tito's forces back at Sv. Nedjelja, and went on to Zidani Most. Here we had to shoot our way through another host of Partisans. Major Matijevic, one of our most distinguished officers, fell in this operation.

We beat a path through to Celje in Slovenia, where we found that the Slovenian Partisans had captured a large German truck convoy; however, some of the Germans had refused to give up their weapons to the Slovenes. We confiscated these arms for our own use and by-passed Celje to get to Maribor. This city was also in the hands of the Slovene Partisans. Red stars, and Slovenian and Yugoslav flags could be seen all over the place. We tore them down, the Partisans fleeing before us without putting up much of a fight. From Maribor we marched along the highway that runs beside the Drava River to Dravograd, meeting no opposition along the way. The column to which my unit was attached was now under the command of Colonel Petrovic of the Domobrans or regulars, and Ustasha Colonel Avdaga Hasic from Klanj. Petrovic was a Hercegovinian Croat himself.

When we got to Dravograd, we found the entire valley surrounding it thronged with Domobrans, Ustashas, Germans, Serbian Royal Chetniks, and masses of civilians, mostly peasants and women and children. Our column did not allow itself to become involved with the heterogeneous groups which were overflowing the valley. We remained in the hills which overlooked the city from the right.

British troops barred the passage of all these fugitives across the Drava. We were told that our General Stancer was negotiating with the British Command. Soon, however, grenades were thrown from some quarter into the Croatian masses in the valley, causing a number of military and civilian casualties. As soon as our column saw what was happening, we charged without delay across the highway and seized the hills on the left side of the highway, routing the Partisans who had launched this treacherous and unprovoked attack.

Colonels Petrovic and Hasic decided that we had better go all the way to Klagenfurt to preclude any possibility of being surrounded by Yugoslav Communists, who obviously were gaining courage as they discovered that their allies had won the war. Since we had to cut our way through the thick Carinthian forests, and construct rafts to take us across the Drava stream, it took us four days to get to Klagenfurt. A number of Croatian officers and soldiers, who had escaped from a prisoner column that the Partisans were leading from Dravograd to Maribor, joined us when we left Dravograd. They told us how the Partisans had separated groups of 50 to 100 men from the other prisoners, led them into the woods, and machine-gunned them. Some of the intended victims escaped alive from these wanton butcheries, but the majority met death in the forests, as the Poles had met it at the hands of the Russian Communists at Katyn early in the war. The escaped prisoners said that the Partisans chose their victims quite arbitrarily. They warned us not to surrender to any of Tito's people under any circumstances. An Ustasha Color Bearer, Stipe Medic, a Sergeant Misetic, and a number of other non-commissioned officers and private soldiers were among the escapees whose names I recall. By this time, those Croatians who in one way or another had fallen into the hands of the Partisans realized what was in store for them. These Croatians were "cutting out" in large numbers from the various prisoner columns and concentration camps, which were not yet very efficiently guarded. Some of the captives escaped from the very brink of the mass graves in which the Communists intended to bury them. Many of them bore fresh wounds to prove their story. These people attached themselves to the numerous Croatian military units that still remained intact.

We were just about to enter Klagenfurt when a British patrol, mounted on motor scooters, met us. There seemed to be no reason to overpower this detachment, although we could have done so easily enough, despite the now inadequate state of our armament. We allowed them to conduct us to a war prisoner camp in the vicinity. This camp was situated in a large unfenced meadow. The Britons had no guards around the place. They merely enforced its separation from another camp which was located immediately across the road from the first one. There were about 3,000 men in this second camp, while ours was considerably larger. More than a hundred Croatian national flags fluttered over these camps, and Croatian military songs resounded everywhere, just as though we were commencing a war that we expected to win rather than finishing up one we had lost. No one anticipated what lay ahead of us.

We remained in this POW camp for approximately ten days. I do not recall the exact dates of our sojourn there; we had lost all track of time during our long retreat from the Domovina into Slovenia and Austria. One morning about ten o'clock, Colonel Petrovic lined us up into regular military formation so that we might listen to an address that a British Colonel was going to give us. Colonel Petrovic, an incurable optimist, told us that he believed we were to be transferred from Austria to Italy.

This opinion was confirmed by the British Colonel, who duly appeared and gave us a long harangue in his own language. Since Colonel Petrovic knew English well, he translated the Briton's speech for us. We were to be sent to Italy to join other Croatian troops who already had gone there. According to Colonel Petrovic's translation, the Englishman pointed out that food would be easier to procure in Italy than in Austria, which was no longer able to accommodate us. In Italy, we would receive new uniforms and undergo training for the new tasks that lay before us. The English Colonel who told us all this through Petrovic's translation was a tall, red-haired, pale, and emaciated-looking man of approximately fifty years of age. Naturally, we all were greatly pleased and enthused by the information that he gave us.

On the following day, a number of British trucks came to the camp to transport us to the local rail station. Since I was one of the first to get on the train, I do not know whether all the inmates of our camp were put aboard or not. Nor do I know if General Rupnik's Slovenian Domobrans, who were quartered in the establishment across the road from us, were removed by the British at the same time we were. We boarded the train with complete willingness, and no suspicion that anything was wrong although we were packed together like sardines. When the Englishmen told us not to let our feet dangle out of the windows and doors of the train, we at once obeyed their injunction.

We could not determine the direction in which the train started out. It stopped at two different stations along the run, which lasted about three hours. Finally, it halted again, and we were told to get out of the cars, which we did willingly enough, glad to stretch our legs in the open air.

To our consternation we found that the train was surrounded on every side by Partisans, armed with machine guns and other automatic weapons! Almost at once they began to rob us of our watches, fountain pens, clothing, and shoes. Though well armed, these Partisans were very poorly dressed. Most of them wore the *opanci* or pointed moccasins of the peasants, and spoke Serbian. There were some Macedonians and Albanians among them, too.

I do not know precisely where we were at this time. A high mountain loomed above us on one side, while on the other, a concrete bridge led across a deep ravine.

Pretty soon the Partisans separated about a hundred men from the rest of us who had been crammed into the leading cars of the train. Mainly officers who had refused to remove their insignia of rank were selected, but there were some noncoms and privates in the group, also. These people were taken to the rear of the train. Colonel Petrovic and his wife and daughter, and Colonel Hasic and his wife were included in this first group of victims. So were Lieutenant Colonel Oreskovic ("Gandi"), Commander of the motorized formations of the P.T.S. (Tjelesni Sbor or Dr. Pavelic's Bodyguard Brigades), Lieutenant Colonel Matkovic, Major Hadzija, Lieutenant Colonel Martin Kordic, and Color Bearer Stanko Petrina. These men were led first to the rear of the train and the others followed. While we could still see what was going on, the Partisans beat them, threw wire around their necks, and otherwise abused them. I am sure that once they were out of our sight, the Partisans murdered them. Since then no one has ever seen or heard of any of these unfortunate people.

All the rest of us were told that the train could go no further because the track ahead was damaged. We were lined up in columns of eight and marched on foot for about six hours. There were a number of old men, women, and children among us. Quite a few veiled Muslim women from Bosnia and Hercegovina marched side by side with their husbands, carrying their children in their arms. Also, there were pregnant women, some of them in their last months, in the column, which stretched out to the length of a full kilometer. Anyone who could not keep up, regardless of age or sex, was killed on the spot, either by machine gun, rifle fire, or clubbing over the head with gun butts. Old men, women, and infants were massacred in this way by the Partisan guards. I myself saw more than a hundred people butchered.

Indelibly impressed upon my mind is one horrible scene that took place as we were approaching the St. Vid camp. The commander of our guards, a Partisan captain, ordered the column to halt. We assumed that at long last we would be allowed to rest a little. Indeed, most of us were permitted to sit down in the road, or alongside it, for a few minutes. But the prisoners at the head of our grim procession were taken into an orchard ten or fifteen meters farther along the road. After they had been separated from the rest of us, we were told to get up and start moving again. As we did so, machine guns began to fire ahead of us. As we passed by the orchard, we saw heaps of corpses piled one on top of the other on the beautiful green grass, sprinkled with blood. I estimated that perhaps a hundred captives, including a number of women and children, were slaughtered at this place. Naturally, this massacre scene made a deep impression upon all of us. Women and children screamed and wept hysterically, while we soldiers threw tent covers over our heads to shut out this horrible sight.

Another incident that I recall distinctly is the slaying of the sister-in-law of Ustasha Lieutenant Marko Stojic. She was marching alongside of Stojic, one of those officers who could not bring himself to part with his decorations and rank insignia. But she induced him to give them to her, and tied them around her leg, in order that he would not be singled out as an officer by the Partisans. Unfortunately, they came loose and fell out onto the road somewhere along the route. It was her bad luck that some of the guards saw these objects drop into the dust. Always eager for loot, they picked them up. When they saw they were decorations, they took the woman out of the column and asked her to whom they belonged. This courageous Croatian woman returned no answer whatsoever to the Partisans, but only looked at them contemptuously. At once the guards began to beat her with their gun butts; then one of them smashed in her skull in full view of those of us who were passing by the spot where this murder occurred.

At sunset, we came to a clean, beautiful little town whose name I did not know at the time. The Slovene inhabitants of this place called us names and threw stones at us. On a hill overlooking the town, the Germans had erected military barracks earlier in the war. There were about fifteen buildings in all, including stables and warehouses. Later on, we found that this was the St. Vid prisoner camp. It was located close to the Slovenian capital, Ljubljana (known as Laibach in Austro-Hungarian days).

There was a double barbed wire fence around the camp, which was guarded by a large force of Partisans. Their commander was a Slovene major. We found many other Croatians in this place, who had either been picked up by the Partisans in the Klagenfurt valley, or been extradited from that area by the British. I also saw more than five hundred Serbs here. They were all young men who had served under the royalist leader, Dimitriyevitch.

On the night we reached the St. Vid camp, all women and children were separated from us and lodged in special barracks. Then an order was issued for everyone who knew a trade to report immediately to the camp authorities. About half a hundred bakers, mechanics, barbers, and so on complied with this command. Ten from my own barracks were among them, including a youth by the name of Klicic who came from the same village that I did, Gnjilavce, near Cazin. None of us ever found out what happened to these men. We assumed that they were killed, as were so many others in the St. Vid prisoner group. Later on I met Klicic's brother, while we were both confined in a district prison in Bihac. He told me that his family had not received a line from his brother since the war. They hoped, however, that he had escaped abroad. When I told him what I knew about young Klicic's experiences at St. Vid, he was filled with the gloomy certainty that his brother was dead.

On the morning after we arrived at St. Vid, the Partisans had us form a great circle. They told us that we were to separate into groups according to our places of birth. Once we were so segregated, we would be returned to our homes.

Instead of following this procedure, however, we were grouped according to military classifications: Ustashas, Domobrans, air force personnel, sailors and marines, gendarmes, police, and civilians. When we were sorted out in this manner, we were told to go back into the barracks. Two hundred and fifty Ustashas were led outside the gates of the camp, however. Among them were people I knew personally: Drago Krnjeta from Daruvar, Sergeant Milasinovic from the vicinity of Okucani, and Staff Sergeant Ante Abramovic from Orahovo. I am sure that this entire band of prisoners was murdered somewhere in the vicinity of St. Vid.

On the fourth day of our stay in the St. Vid enclosure, the Partisans took a large number of Croatian prisoners, myself included, to another establishment located near the Ljubljana railroad station. The Ljotic men were left at St. Vid, however.

The new camp had no barracks. It was just a field surrounded by barbed wire. There was a specially fenced in and guarded section where a few higher officers and their families were confined; among them were Lieutenant Colonel Ahmet Kapetanovic, and Minister of State Ivica Frkovic and his two daughters.

After a three-day sojourn in this place of detention, some three thousand of us were loaded into freight cars. A number of these cars, my own included, were open rather than closed vehicles. Guarded by Slovenian Partisans, they were all incredibly filthy and overcrowded. We were transported in these cattle cars and boxcars back to Croatia. Here we were unloaded, naked, barefoot, hungry, exhausted, and dying of thirst. From twilight until dawn, we were herded like human cattle along the road to Samobor. Many prisoners, including youths approximately eighteen years old, collapsed en route. The guards killed them as soon as they dropped out of the column.

It may be worthwhile to record here what a Partisan Second Lieutenant, a Muslim by the name of Omer Harbas from Turija near Bihac, told me long after the war. We met in the prison at Foca, while I was confined there as an anti-Communist, he as a petty postwar criminal. He described how he had served in the escort of a column of prisoners which was being taken from Zagreb to Daruvar.

> Determined to kill them along the road, we told those Croatian prisoners, whom we knew were anti-Communists, that we were recruiting them for service in our Partisan formations. We killed perhaps 5,000 and brought into Daruvar only a small number of survivors. These last were killed there. We had no feelings of remorse or pangs of conscience about doing this, for those prisoners were Fascists and sworn enemies of Communism. We had to exterminate them.

Such was the mentality of our Partisan captors, the darlings of the democratic press.

Just before my own column entered Samobor, a Partisan unit from Srijem (Sirmia) or eastern Croatia took charge of our party. I think this outfit belonged to the 25th Serbian Division. They mocked and insulted us, spat on us, pulled our hair, and beat us. We passed by a camp that extended along both sides of the road we were following, and came to another large prisoner establishment that was laid out on a big meadow. There was no fence around this camp, but it was strongly guarded by Partisan machine gun detachments. Several thousand starved, naked, and despairing men were crowded together here.

At this point, I perhaps should relate another anecdote that may shed a revealing light upon the conditions that prevailed in the prisoner camps at Samobor. During our retreat from Croatia, a short, weak youth by the name of Mato had joined us. He told us that he was a war orphan, a native of Slavonski Brod, but during the war he had worked in the shoe factory maintained by Pavelic's bodyguard Brigades in Zagreb. Probably he did work there because he knew the location of this establishment, at the corner of Draskovic and Jurisic Streets, as well as other details concerning it.

There happened to be a Partisan second lieutenant from his birthplace among the guards at Samobor. This fellow persuaded him to denounce various Ustashas who so far had succeeded in passing themselves off as Domobrans (regulars). He betrayed about thirty men in all, including Lieutenant Marko Stojic and Second Lieutenant Galic. General Sertic's chauffeur and I also had the honor of being identified in this process of delation. Previously, when we found ourselves in the hands of the Partisans getting off the train, I had managed to get hold of a navy jacket, taken the name of a friend who I knew had fallen in battle, and masqueraded successfully up to this point as a navy man from Sisak.

The thirty of us whom this little rat had betrayed were placed in the cellar of a two-story building, which had a yard with a cherry tree in it. It had one very small, barred window. For two days we were buried alive in this place. No one brought us food, water, or even any kind of receptacle in which we could relieve ourselves. We were able to talk to some other prisoners, who were lodged in an adjoining cellar which had a separate entrance. They told us that everyone who had been brought into the cellars ahead of us was going to be killed, and that the same fate was in store for us.

On the second day of our incarceration, at about 10:00 P.M., a tailor who lived in a house across the street appeared at the window of our cellar. In a low whisper he informed us that there wasn't much danger of our being killed now. "Marshal" Tito had delivered an address over the radio in which he called for the cessation of all "irresponsible" (i.e. non-official) killing. The tailor told us also that the citizens of Samobor were up in arms against the continued slaughter that had been going on in this vicinity. The valley nearby was so filled with rotting corpses, they were afraid that a pestilence, like those of the Middle Ages, before the Croatian Military Frontier was established, would occur. After he had given us this welcome news, the noble-hearted tailor brought us corn, slices of corn bread, and a bucket of water. For the first time in many days, we had something to eat and drink.

On the next day, the Partisans took down our names and personal data. Then they allowed us to go into the yard. Also, they gave us, for the first time since we had become prisoners, solid food—a little corn bread. Before this, when our various captors had given us anything to eat at all, it had been only the saltless, soggy, and insipid corn pap that Croatian peasants feed only to pigs.

At twilight of this same day, a so-called Partisan "delegate" appeared. He had with him a catalog of our names which he read off. He had us form up in military order, following which twelve heavily armed Serbian Partisans escorted us to the prison camp at Precko near Zagreb.

It is only a little way from Samobor to Zagreb. But on that short stretch, the guards murdered ten out of the thirty of us. They killed one man just before we got to Precko. I should say, however, that the population of Samobor and the vicinity, in marked contrast to the inhabitants of the Slovenian countryside, were very friendly. Whenever they could, they tossed food, cigarettes, and other necessities and luxuries to us. The Serb guards tried to stop them from doing this by driving them off. They arrested and imprisoned a number of women who refused to allow themselves to be intimidated by the threat of Partisan vengeance.

The Precko camp was situated in the barracks that had belonged formerly to the Honor Work Service. The buildings stood in a field that was encircled by barbed wire. One part of this camp was reserved for German prisoners. None of the prisoners were lodged in the barracks; instead all had to sleep out in the open.

On the day following our transfer to this place, a Captain Kajic took charge of us. He was the son of Stipe Kajic, former director of the prison in Bihac during the days of the Karageorgevitch Yugoslav state. Despite the fact that he had a criminal record, both in the old Yugoslavia and in the Independent Croatian State of 1941-45, Kajic had wound up as a Partisan captain. I must say that he did us the service of placing us with other Croatian prisoners, and that the Partisans under his command did not kill anyone here. Also, they gave us better rations of the corn pap for pigs than we had received elsewhere.

Nevertheless, I found the stay at Precko anything but pleasant; a Serb Royal Chetnik, a peasant from Nevesinje, gave me some horrible information while I was there. He told me that the camp authorities had sent him out to cut up some branches and twigs which were to be used to make brooms. While working among the former bunkers and trenches that lined the sand hills along the Sava River, he stumbled across some mass graves which were only sparsely covered over with earth. He dared to uncover them and found them filled with mutilated corpses, some without arms or legs. From the account that he gave of the condition of the bodies, it was evident that the Partisans had buried here the invalids whom they had removed from the Home for Invalids at Sv. Duh. The Serb showed me exactly where the bodies were buried, so that I might be able to find it at some future time without difficulty. Other inmates of the camp told me about similar atrocities that the Partisans had committed. They gave me the details of the slaying of fifty people who were blinded during the war, either because of wounds or through natural causes. Tito's executioners, after murdering these hapless victims, threw their corpses into the Sava. When some of the bodies were pulled from the river, the Partisans proclaimed that these blinded unfortunates were "victims of Ustasha bestiality."

There are a great many people who know about these crimes, in Precko itself as well as in other places. Among the willow trees, six hundred yards away from our camp, we could find at this time many crutches and canes which the victims had used to get around. Some remnants of these aids probably can still be found in this vicinity today.

They are pathetic, mute witnesses of one of the most atrocious crimes ever recorded in the annals of history.

On the third or fourth day that we spent at Precko, the camp commander called out the names of the thirty Ustasha men who had been brought here from Samobor. He called the names of the ten men whom the guards had murdered, along with those of the twenty of us who were still alive. We answered for them, saying that they had remained behind on the road we had traversed. Then he cursed our mothers and screamed hysterically, "Bandits! From the thirty—ten have fled!"

Soon afterwards, we twenty Ustashas were escorted to the railroad station along with 2,000 other Croatian prisoners. Here we were packed into freight cars in which we were conveyed to Karlovac. I found myself in the same car with a neighbor from Bihac, a tailor by the name of Safet Alijagic. Like me he is still alive today. I probably owe my life to him, since that little rat, Mato, had not known my name, although he did know that I was an Ustasha. Therefore, I still was using my alias, Catovic, and I asked Alijagic to refrain from telling my captors my real name and to address me always as Catovic. This he did, so the Partisans remained ignorant of my real identity.

When we got off the train at Karlovac, we were marched through the city to a camp that was located in the old P.T.S. barracks. This building stood just outside the city and overlooked the Karlovac-Duga Res highway. There were about 1,500 Croatians already here, all from General Rukavina's Lika Brigade.

On the day following our arrival, one hundred of us were detailed to pick up dry branches in the forest that lay behind the camp, between the Mreznica and Dobra rivers. Close by, there were hills covered with tall trees. During the war, the Italians had constructed bunkers here, which were still intact. Some of the detail noted that two of these bunkers were filled to the top with bushes, as were several trenches which had been dug in a zig-zag line between the bunkers. They started to collect these bushes and break off the branches, when they found to their horror that both bunkers and trenches were full of corpses still clad in Ustasha and Domobran uniforms. The hands of the murdered men were tied with wire. We risked making an examination of the bodies, and discovered that most of them had their heads beaten in, probably by gun butts. In four years of warfare, I never had come across such a horrifying spectacle as this.

Fortunately for us, our guards were not near by when we made this shocking discovery. They had gone off into some other part of the forest. We hastened to get as far from the scene of slaughter as we could, knowing that if the Partisans learned we had blundered onto the scene of the crime, they would deal out the same fate to us that the murdered men had met. Next, we picked up all the loose branches we could find and hurried back to the camp with them.

It is impossible to say how many bodies were piled into these bunkers and trenches. In the latter alone, I counted more than five hundred dead. Besides myself, Domobran Second Lieutenant Dragutin Fezic, Ustasha First Lieutenant Malin Malkoc, Ustasha civil administrator Husein Fajtovic, Ustasha Major Edhen Karikovic, an Assault Division Major and an Ustasha First Lieutenant of the P.T.S. saw what was in the bunkers and trenches. I cannot recall the names of the last two individuals, nor those of other members of my detail who looked into these improvised mass graves. Certainly, some of these other eyewitnesses are still alive today.

We remained in the Karlovac camp for ten days. During this time, we were forced to listen to lectures given us by political commissars. They told us that we were going to be enrolled in Tito's army. One night several hundred prisoners escaped. These escapees were mainly Ustashas from Lika. They took with them all the kitchen equipment and the entire supply of corn flour. Thus, we had nothing to eat the following morning. On this same day, the camp was broken up. We were told that we were going to be transferred to Zagreb.

Indeed, we were taken to the capital but we did not remain there long. Again we were loaded into cattle cars. When the train pulled out of Zagreb, our guards told us that we were en route to Serbia. We guessed that we were being sent to that land, because we could be murdered there more conveniently and with less fear of repercussions. Prisoners resorted to all kinds of devices to escape from the cars, and many of them succeeded. They fled wherever they could; I was fortunate enough to escape to Okucani. Here I found one of my wartime comrades, a veteran of General Metikos's Sixth Division, who arranged for my clandestine transport to Zaluzani near Banja Luka.

I remained in hiding for fifteen days in Banja Luka. Then an old neighbor of mine, Aziz Midic, who had become an agent of the OZNA (later called UDBA), Tito's secret police, denounced me. So, on July 25, 1945, I entered the so-called "Black House" of the Banja Luka prison.

On January 26, 1946, I was transferred to the prison at Bihac, known as the "Kula" (Tower). Then, on March 3, I was moved again, this time to the OZNA prison. Here something happened which I think should become a matter of public knowledge.

It was about 1:00 P.M. on March 13, 1946. I was confined in a cell with thirteen other men, most of them peasants from the surrounding district. Suddenly, without any kind of advance warning, our Partisan guards threw open the cell door and pushed a nun of the Congregation of the Precious Blood in among us. She wore full religious garb, and the red cord of the Order was tied around her waist. Terrified to find herself thrust among a group of men, she stood speechless, with her hands joined together in front of her, at the entrance to our dungeon. She was crying bitterly.

We were stunned to see a woman in here with us, a nun particularly. It was evident that she was going to share our imprisonment, with no facilities to insure any kind of privacy.

I approached the unfortunate Sister, introduced myself, and said to her, "Excuse me, Sister, but don't just stand there weeping. You are in prison, so the best thing to do is to sit down on the 'palace' (this was a kind of elevated platform where we slept on boards). Sister, do not cry, and do not have any fear. This is our destiny, and we must endure it."

She seemed to be somewhat encouraged by my words, but revealed that she was still frightened by keeping her hands joined together on her bosom. She told us that her original name was Mara Jelic, and that she was the daughter of Ivo Jelic of Zegar. Her religious designation was Sister Majella. She had been arrested the previous day on the charge that she sent sanitary and office equipment, including a typewriter, to Major Idriz Delic, a former teacher who had concealed himself in the forest of Pljesevica. Three other nuns and several men from the Zegar district were arrested with her. I remember that she said that one of these fellow sufferers was a shoemaker by the name of Andrija Konjevic.

Sister Majella had not been allowed to bring with her any change of clothing whatsoever. My mother had sent me a pillow case which I tore in half and gave to her along with one of my blankets. I also got some of the other men to help me put up a tent cover around her night waste container in order that this receptacle might be concealed as much as possible. Despite what we could do, the poor nun must have endured great torment, both of body and mind. For days she wept constantly and refused to take such food as we were able to get.

For a month and a half we all had to sleep together on the little platform. I slept on one side of Sister Majella, while the shoemaker from Zegar, Konjevic, who also was thrown into the cell with us, lay down on the other. Everyone in the cell block among these Croatian prisoners, regardless of whether they were Catholics or Muslims, treated her with the greatest respect, as though she were our own mother or sister.

Every one of the men who shared our quarters, and who still are alive today, can confirm the truth of the above story. Since we got to know one another quite well during our period of enforced association, I learned the names of all of them and I shall mention a few just in case any of the readers of this volume may meet one of these individuals somewhere. There was Rasim Cavcic, a peasant from the village of Cavcic and former headman of that village; the Communists later on sentenced him to a ten-year term of imprisonment for being an uncompromisingly patriotic Croatian. Ramo Amidzic, a peasant from Pokoj, was serving a sixteen-year sentence for the same reason; he survived this incarceration and today is back home in his native village. Mehmed Kulenovic, a businessman from Kulen-Vakuf, was jailed for eight years, but I believe he is living in Derventa at the present time. Konjevic, the shoemaker from Zegar, now is employed in the Shoemakers' Co-operative in Bihac. Another peasant, Maso Mijanovic, sentenced to twelve years for refusing to subscribe to the tenets of Marxism, eventually was able to return to his native Pokoj. There was also one man among us who never was tried for any dereliction whatsoever. Apparently, he was jailed only because he was a "capitalist." This was Hasan Ljubijankic, a businessman from Bosanski Novi, where he lives today.

The three other nuns arrested with Sister Majella were placed in other cells in the prison. All prisoners observed the most proper conduct towards them, and did everything they could to lessen the privations and indignities to which they were exposed. Most of the citizens of Bihac who found out what was done with these members of a highly respected religious Order were outraged and dared to condemn the Communist authorities openly. Consequently, a good many of them suffered severe punishment. Later on all four of the Sisters stood trial for their alleged "crime." They were sent to Stolac to serve the prison terms to which they were condemned. I did not see Sister Majella again until January, 1961. By that date both of us had been released, and I stopped to see her when I passed through the village of Zegar, where she was teaching. She thanked me most cordially on this occasion for the "brotherly and gallant conduct" that all of us had displayed towards her during those terrible days.

I am ready to confirm the testimony that I have given in these pages with an oath delivered before any legal forum. I have recorded in this testimony only the literal truth of my personal experiences during the last days of the Independent Croatian State, and the early years of the Communist regime imposed upon Croatia, Slavonia, Dalmatia, Istria, and Bosnia-Hercegovina by Tito Broz and his murdering bands.

Signed: Hasan Selimovic

Rome, April 25, 1961

Document XXVIII

Sead Zubcevic, as well as tens of thousands of other Croatian soldiers, surrendered to the Partisans at Dravograd. A portion of these captives were sent to Maribor, while about 35,000 of them were marched towards Celje and further to Zidani Most, Brezice, Samobor. As our witness and his long column were marching towards Zagreb, they were ordered to return to Samobor; from there they were driven to Velika Gorica; then, they were taken to Sisak. Here our eyewitness saw the abduction of masses of prisoners for the slaughter. From Sisak, Zubcevic was sent to Karlovac and then back to Sisak. During this stretch he saw the brutalities of the Serbian inhabitants of Vojnic and Vrgin Most. In Sisak, a new "Death March" was lined up and sent through Bosanska Dubica, Stara Gradiska, Okucani, Novska, Nova Gradiska to Osijek. Here the witness saw several thousand young Croatian recruits suffer from diseases, starvation and maltreatments. From Osijek, he was transported to Mitrovica; then, he and his co-sufferers were marched to Indjija for maltreatment by "Croatian" Serbs. The victims were then transported to Petrovaradin. After a twelve-day stay in this town, they were marched to Backi Jarak, Vrsac and Kovin, where they met survivors of the Maribor Massacres and various "Death Marches." While the witness was imprisoned at Kovin, Tito issued an amnesty. The account closes with a description of special sufferings of two priests, and emphasis on the Serbian civilians' brutalities and the Croatian population's hospitality towards the "Death Marchers."

I left Zagreb on May 7, at 10:30 P.M. As a Second Lieutenant of Infantry, I led my command on foot towards Krapina. Our objective was to get through to Austria. I believe that it was Saturday, May 12, when I arrived at Dravograd with my entire command intact.

It was here that the negotiations which led to the surrender of our Armed Forces had their starting point. As far as is known to me, our principal spokesman before the British Command was General Herencic. Somewhat later, Colonel Sudar also took part in negotiations with the British. The morale of our troops was very high at this time. Despite the surrender of our late German allies, we were prepared to continue the war indefinitely if we had to. Of course, few of us had given much thought to the odds against us, or to the fact that our lack of a war industry made prolonged resistance a virtual impossibility.

On May 13 or 14, Colonel Sudar told us that we had a choice of two alternatives. We could lay down our arms and surrender to the Yugoslav Communists. Or we officers could advise our men to take to the woods in small units and engage in battle whenever necessary until they established firm contact with the bulk of the English Army, which was pushing into southern Austria after receiving the surrender of the Germans.

By this time, most of our troops had already won through to Dravograd, beating and dispersing the Partisan formations which tried to stop them. Near this Slovenian city, everyone thought that the troops which had reached Austria ahead of us had already established liaison with the British, and that our Government, headed by Dr. Pavelic, had been interned in Klagenfurt. Therefore, we proceeded in the direction of the Carinthian capital. We were not aware that the troops which preceded us had indeed surrendered to the English, and then had been turned over to the Partisans by the Britons. The truth gradually became apparent to us on Tuesday and Wednesday, May 15 and 16, when we still were in the vicinity of Dravograd.

Both officers and men were overcome with gloom. I saw many of them weep, not from fright, but because they were ashamed of the plight in which our leadership had involved this last unbeaten force possessed by the losing side in the war. Some men refused to give up their arms; instead they went into the woods with them. What their ultimate fate was, I do not know. Had some higher officer possessed any initiative, and maintained his sang-froid, he could have formed a large army of men who still were willing to fight whomever they had to fight, no matter how hopeless the prospect of ultimate success might be. The worst thing about our situation, however, was that all of our commanding officers completely lost their heads when they found out that the British were not going to accept the Croatian Army as legitimate prisoners-of-war, but intended to deliver them into the hands of Tito's executioners.

In the prevailing state of confusion and absence of any kind of effective leadership, many of us did not know what to do. We began to lay down our arms, since it was evident that our commanders did not intend to organize mass resistance. We hoped for the best, since even if the British were turning our men over to the Communists, they surely would have exacted some kind of guarantee of humane treatment from the new regime in Belgrade. Such was the wishful thinking of which we were guilty at this time.

Soon we found out how foolish we had been not to keep our weapons, and use them if anyone tried to take them away from us. Communist escorts appeared, to start the disarmed masses marching along a route that was lined with Partisan formations. These "heroes of the Liberation" began to loot us of our possessions almost immediately. They took everything from our luggage to the shoes we had on our feet.

We were herded back to Dravograd like driven cattle. Once they had us in this Slovenian town, all officers, airmen, and anti-aircraft personnel were commanded to step forward; those who did so were driven off towards Maribor. Many officers and airmen or anti-aircraft gunners remained in Dravograd, however. Since the Partisans had stripped them of their uniforms and given them their own rags before arriving in the town, they were not easily identifiable, and were able to pass themselves off as common soldiers. I was one of those who was careful not to report himself as an officer. Later, I learned from survivors of the group taken to Maribor that the Partisans massacred everyone in the party, except the few who managed to escape under gunfire into the woods.

Those of us who had stayed at Dravograd were sent towards Celje. For a distance of about six miles we traveled without escorts, but then armed guards appeared to take charge of us. They looted us of whatever we had left upon our persons. We arrived in Celje after a day and a half of marching. The guards drove us through this city at a running pace, and killed anyone who could not keep up. I should mention that we were not allowed to have a drop of water all the way from Dravograd to Celje. Several times I saw murdered soldiers lying beside wells along our route. They still held water flasks in their hands. They were killed because they had tried to get a drink.

From Celje we went on to Zidani Most. We made this stretch without being allowed to rest for even a moment. All night long we tramped endlessly. We went right through Celje and came to Brezice, where we were finally permitted to pause briefly. About midnight, we were roused and driven towards Samobor. Some of our number were taken out of Brezice in another direction, however. I have never learned anything about their fate, but I believe they were slaughtered, like so many others.

When we left Dravograd, our column probably contained close to 35,000 prisoners. My estimate is based upon the observed length of the procession of captives, and upon the numbers marching abreast of one another. As we marched, however, our numbers diminished appreciably.

I shall always remember Samobor, because there we rested out on the meadows for a whole day and night, and recovered in some degree from the grueling exertions of the past few days. Here all civilians, men, women, and children alike, were separated from the military and taken to special concentration camps. A considerable number of younger soldiers were also segregated from the rest of us. Allegedly, they were going to be recruited into the Yugoslav Army. The rest of us were lined up according to the military districts to which we belonged, and then we were sent off in the general direction of Zagreb. But after a six mile march, we had to turn around and retrace our steps back to Samobor.

During all this time, we received nothing whatsoever to eat from our Partisan captors. Some prisoners had managed to conceal cans of food or squares of sugar upon their persons and they shared these treasures with as many of the rest of us as they could. Nevertheless, we all were in a desperate condition.

From Samobor, we were driven next to Velika Gorica, where we were confined in a sheep pen that was surrounded by barbed wire. We were packed like sardines into this small space, so crowded together that we had to try to stand erect simply because there was no room for anyone to sit or lie down. Such were the conditions under which we spent the night. At least our guards did begin to issue a few ounces of bread and some horrible soup to each prisoner. But most of us did not receive even this ration, for hardly had the distribution begun, than it was discontinued and we were ordered to get ready to make another journey.

Now they herded us towards Sisak. The heat was excessive and our thirst became unbearable. Many prisoners risked everything to get a drink of water, and paid with their lives for so doing, because the Partisans killed everyone who left the column.

In Sisak, I succeeded in getting away. Some women sheltered me there long enough for me to wash and rest a little while. Unfortunately, a Communist found out where I was, and turned me in. For some reason the local OZNA, which was composed principally of Croatian Communists, let me off with three days' imprisonment in their cells for this exploit. Then they sent me back to the concentration camp.

There were about 2500 Italian and German prisoners in this place, among them a German general. Many of the captives contracted typhoid fever. I saw an emergency "hospital" room where three dead men lay for a long time among the sick, because no one had bothered to take their corpses away. Despite the danger of infection and the blows that they received from the clubs of the guards, the Croatian citizens of Sisak persisted in bringing food to us. Every day, new prisoner columns arrived to further overcrowd our already jam-packed camp. The new arrivals were mainly young men, but their appearance was miserable.

At first, there was no cataloguing or grouping by military districts in this camp. One day, however, we received questionnaires that we had to fill out and return. At sunset on this same day, ten trucks pulled up before the camp gate. The camp commander called out the names of a number of prisoners who had returned their questionnaires. These men were ordered to get into the waiting trucks. Most of the prisoners on the roll call answered to their names, since they thought they were going to be transferred to another camp which might be an improvement on this hell-hole. Those who did not answer to their names, as well as those who had registered under an assumed name which had been called out, could not be rounded up, because it was almost impossible to identify individuals in this multitude. Fortunately, the camp administration had not grouped us into companies, battalions, and so on, so there was no way for them to check our identities.

I had anticipated that the prisoners whose names were called were going to be murdered, and when the questionnaires were issued, I did not register under my own name. When the roll call started, I whispered to two young men who were standing in front of me not to answer if their names were read out. The fellows who did report, and who were led off to the slaughterhouse in consequence, were members of Ustasha military units, or of the Domobran mountain brigades and the Eighth Hunter or Pursuit Regiment. This regiment defended Brcko with great heroism during the war, and also punished the Yugoslav Communist forces severely in the fighting around Tuzla. I learned from officers who were at large when the ten truckloads of youths were taken away that these soldiers were massacred quite close to Sisak.

After the departure of the young Ustashas and Domobrans, we were grouped according to our military districts. Then we were lined up in columns which were marched towards Srijem (Sirmia). Later on I learned that one of these columns went all the way to Macedonia. The Domobrans who had not been taken off with the Ustashas were combined with civilian prisoners, some of whom had just been rounded up in the regions around Sisak and Samobor. This special column was sent to Karlovac. I was fortunate enough to be included in this group, which was supposed to be integrated into the Second Yugoslav Army. Since ostensibly we were going to join them as soldiers of the "Liberation," our guards treated us somewhat more considerably than they had heretofore. We even got food along the route to Karlovac, not from our Partisan "comrades" of course, but from the Croatian population along the way, which cared for us with entire disregard for the consequences.

When we got to Karlovac, all men born between 1916 and 1928 were grouped together, along with the sick prisoners. I was among the latter.

We were taken to the concentration camp at Luksic, where again we were treated like slaves. Here we found many prisoners from the German Prinz Eugen Division, along with several hundred German officers whom the British had taken prisoner in Trieste. Officers were assembled in a separate group at Luksic. I was placed with them, together with many Germans, and eight officers of the Italian Army. We were sent to Sisak, from which I had come such a short time before.

This second journey to Sisak was the worst experience of my entire life. En route to this old Croatian town, the Partisans committed atrocities that I would not have believed had I not seen them with my own eyes. Both guards and the commissars who commanded them were "Croatian" Serbs, that is natives of this region, whose ancestors had been allowed to settle there by our ancestors. First they robbed the German officers of clothes and valuables which the British had not taken from them. Relatives of our escort showed up to help in this work of despoilation. This robbery kept them amused for a while, but that night they all set to beat us with heavy clubs. Several of the Germans were killed and many others were wounded, so that their officer colleagues had to carry them on tent covers the following day. Except for two fifteen-minute intervals, no carts were provided to transport the sick and wounded during the entire three days and nights that we spent in going to Sisak. To be sure, the Partisans allowed us to rest several times along the route. Apparently this unusual consideration was motivated by the desire to give the "Croatian" Serb inhabitants of Vojnic and Vrgin Most opportunities to maltreat us. To cite only one example, an Italian officer was walloped with heavy clubs and made to exclaim "Zivio Tito! Dobri Partizani!"[1] The rest of us were forced to sing derogatory songs made up by the Serbs, describing the national leaders and soldiers of the Croatian nation in an obscene and insulting manner.

Along the stretch of road that lies between Gora and Petrinja, the majority of the people were Croatian. They tried to bring us food, but the guards drove them off, saying, "You did not want to bring food to *us!*" During our three day stay in Sisak, however, we were fed twice daily, though in a fashion that would hardly have satisfied the demands of the pigs raised by the Croatian peasantry.

In Sisak, we encountered some Czechs who had served in the German Army during the war. There were also some Vichy French, and a number of General Vlasov's White Russian soldiers. Most Croatian officers in our group were conscripted into the Yugoslav Army and sent to Bosanska Dubica. Although we were supposed to be joining their army, I did not observe along the way any appreciable difference from our previous treatment. From Dubica we went on to Stara Gradiska, where we spent the night. On the following day, the Croatian population of the neighboring villages fed us in abundance. We went from Stara Gradiska

[1] "Long live Tito!" "The Partisans are good fellows!"

through Okucani to Novska, where we were lodged in a concentration camp for the night. During the night we received a good share of blows from our guards. We also felt the ground on which we were resting beginning to sink beneath our weight. The guards told us gleefully that we were sleeping over filled-in holes where many "Fascists" were buried.

From Novska, we were driven on foot to Nova Gradiska, where the Partisans themselves fed us—probably because they had become tired of fighting off the efforts made by the Croatian peasants along our line of march to supply us. Perhaps they thought that if they gave us something to eat we wouldn't look so starved, and therefore our fellow countrymen wouldn't feel so sorry for us. Also, we were taken by train from Nova Gradiska to Osijek. This was the first time that we had not been forced to march on foot.

In Osijek, there were several thousand Croatian prisoners who were living under conditions that defy description. Suffice it to say that they bore a much closer resemblance to partially animated skeletons than they did to flesh and blood human beings. Most of them were students who were recruited into the Croatian Armed Forces just before the end of the war, and had not even completed their boot camp training. Many Croatian women in Osijek risked their lives to toss bread and fruit over the fence to these starving wretches. It was soul-shattering to see how the young skeletons scrambled in the dust to pick up this food, and how avidly they devoured it. Only the women of Osijek dared to aid them in this way, because any of the male population which had not been killed or imprisoned did not dare show sympathy for their countrymen. For days on end, the women would stand outside the fence trying to toss food to my group, too. However, the guards drove them off with blows from their clubs and gun butts. We did get some insipid and saltless food, however. Life in the camp itself went on as usual—that is, the Communists maltreated us just as before. It would be repetitious to go into the details. I might mention, however, that at Osijek several nuns tried to give us food but they were prohibited from doing so by the guards, despite the fact that many of us were obviously exhausted and sick.

Along with other commissioned and non-commissioned officers of the former Croatian Armed Forces, I was transported from Osijek to Mitrovica by train. When we were sent to Indjija in order that we might be "identified" by Bosnian Serbs who recently had settled at this place. Of course, the Serbs did not recognize any of us and therefore could not identify us. This failure did not stop them from beating us as though they had indeed identified us as war criminals. On top of all of our other sufferings, dysentery (diarrhea) was rampant among us. Nevertheless, we were allowed to relieve ourselves only when we lay down at night.

From Indjija, we were sent by train to Petrovaradin. Here we found two thousand Croatian, and some German and Italian officers. Among the Croatian officers, were a number of men I knew. They had come to Petrovaradin in "Death Marches" other than the one in which I had participated, but according to what they told me, their experiences with regard to atrocities and mass killings of prisoners were the same as my own.

We remained in Petrovaradin for twelve days. During this interval, many Croatian women visited the prison camp, looking for their husbands or sons. It galled us bitterly to see how Tito's Communists cursed these ladies and slapped and beat them, while we were helpless to do anything but passively look on.

From Petrovaradin, we marched to Backi Jarak. There we were loaded into open railroad boxcars, and transported to Vrsac during a rainstorm. In Vrsac, the two thousand-odd Croatian officers were placed by themselves in an abandoned hangar. We were told that from now on we would receive as many meals as the regular Communists did. "Because of the scarcity of water," we were informed later on, it proved possible to give us only one feeding daily. This was sometimes lunch, sometimes supper. Other officers were brought in from various regions every day. There was a separate camp for non-commissioned officers at Vrsac, too. They told us that they were going to have to work for the Russians, and that they had Russian guards who beat them continually.

Eighty Domobran, and approximately a hundred Ustasha officers were separated from the rest of us and kept at Vrsac. The bulk of our group was taken to Kovin near Smederevo. There were many Ustasha officers with our column. They told me how they had saved their lives by hiding their real identities during the first days after the surrender. Some were able to pass themselves off as private soldiers; others were eyewitnesses of the mass killings of prisoners which took place around Maribor. They were survivors of slaughters there, and showed, to prove their stories, marks made in their flesh by the wire with which their wrists were tied when they were led to the places of execution. In one way or another, they had succeeded in cheating death. As Ernest Hemingway said of the Italians in World War I, it must be acknowledged that the Partisans in World War II were efficient killers as long as they were shooting at people who were not shooting at them. Nevertheless, the killings organized by Tito's people were carried out on such a mass scale, that with luck and ingenuity a resolute and daring fellow was often able to escape.

Among these Ustasha officer survivors, there were a number who had surrendered to the British in the vicinity of Villach in Austrian Carinthia. They said that the British told them they were going to be sent to Udine in Italy, and placed them in railroad cars with this understanding. At the third railroad station along the route, however, Partisans were waiting to take over the train. These Yugoslav Communists took the train column to St. Vid, where active Domobran and Ustasha officers were separated from the reserves. It was the reserve officers who were represented here at Vrsac in the greatest numbers. Most of the known active officers, that is, those who had served in front line units during the war, were taken away in trucks, usually at night, during the course of the "Death Marches."

We stayed in Kovin for twenty-five days, and I must say that here we received fairly decent food every day. A Yugoslav Communist delegation appeared in due time to question us about our past records. They told us that we would be drafted into the Yugoslav Army only as privates, or for special tasks which we were qualified to perform. Such tasks would be executed under military surveillance. They advised us also that it would be better for us if we demonstrated our interest in and devotion to Socialism. While the delegation was still interrogating us about what we had done in past years, a courier arrived. He bore an order to stop the questioning, for Belgrade had proclaimed an amnesty.

A process of releasing prisoners was initiated, but officers with the rank of major or above were held. Headquarters officers, judges, both those of the military and civil courts of the Croatian State, high officials, and some other prisoners of whom the Communists were particularly suspicious, remained in the camp too. I learned at a much later date that almost all of these men were sent to Belgrade.

Those of us who were released, were supposed to go back to our home territories and report ourselves to the local OZNA, or secret security political police. Of course, most of us did no such thing, for in our places of residence our anti-Communist sentiments and actions were known, and we were certain to be denounced as "war criminals" by local Communists or by individuals who wished to court favor with the latter. I understand that those who were foolish enough to return to their homes and report themselves to the OZNA were arrested. I heard also that a great many private soldiers of the wartime Croatian Army deserted the Yugoslav forces into which they were drafted after the proclamation of the amnesty.

In closing this testimony, I should like to call attention to a number of points which I believe are worthy of special notice. First, even at Kovin, long after the end of the fighting, some Croatian officers were liquidated. Just one day before we heard about the amnesty, forty officers were sent to Vrsac under strong Communist escort. Perhaps these men, too, were murdered at this late date. I wish to mention, too, that two priests, Jagodar and Eterovic,[1] were in the "Death Column" in which I myself marched. They were beaten more than the rest of us merely because of their calling.

On the "Death Marches," we experienced particularly savage treatment at the hands of Serbian elements living in the villages through which we passed. I remember that a Serbian peasant woman made off with the only shirt that I had, so I had to march stripped to the waist in all kinds of weather. Once our guards had supplied their own needs

[1] The brother of the author of Doc. LVIII.

with regard to footgear, they allowed the Serb peasants to take the shoes of any prisoners who still possessed such luxuries. The Serbs were careful to assure these individuals that they never would need shoes again, because everyone in our column was going to be killed. When we heard these Serbian peasants, we would ask the guards whether we were being taken to Bela Crkva, a notorious place of execution, or to the "Thirteenth Battalion."

On the other hand, I am glad to be able to state that whenever we passed through Croatian villages or towns, people would defy all the warnings and physical brutalities of the guards to bring food to us. Often they tried to feed as many as ten thousand prisoners at a time. Such generosity must have been a drain upon their own resources, in addition to exposing them to the danger of Communist reprisals. Even the children in these Croatian villages and cities vied with one another in bringing water to us, or doing us other favors.

Signed: Sead Zubcevic

Columbus, Ohio
September 20, 1964

Document XXIX

The following analyzes first the difficulties of the Croatian troops, chiefly caused by ten truckloads of wounded soldiers. The account then tells why this group surrendered to the Bulgarian troops at Dravograd. After the surrender, Tito's troops murdered about 2,000 captives, including seven truckloads of wounded soldiers. The Bulgarians, therefore, accompanied the prisoners twenty-three miles on their way towards Maribor. The rest of the way, the Partisans guarded the column. In Maribor, about ten thousand real or alleged Ustashas were led away for the slaughter. After a two-day stay in Maribor, about 20,000 captives continued their "Death March" and experienced usual Partisan atrocities. In the vicinity of Bjelovar, two hundred officers were murdered. In Bjelovar itself, large groups were separated from their co-sufferers and were presumably liquidated. From Bjelovar on, our eyewitness was included in a new "Death March". At Podravska Slatina, a group of victims were killed for reporting as good singers. The "marchers" arrived in Sisak practically naked, because the "Croatian" Serbs had looted them. The Serbs maltreated the prisoners through Fruska Gora, too. A little over 3000 out of 8500 prisoners arrived at Petrovaradin from Bjelovar. From this town, the witness went to Vrsac and then to Kovin. On August 8, 1945, he was set free. At the end of his account, our eyewitness stresses that all the atrocities he had seen or experienced were committed by Serbian Partisans.

During the war of 1941-45, I was a civilian citizen of the Croatian State. It was in this capacity that I left Zagreb on May 7, with the intention of escaping to Austria. I was in a column of approximately 20,000 mixed military and civilian refugees.

We got as far as Dravograd, but here we were cut off from the main body of the Croatian Army by the attacks of the Partisans. There were about ten truckloads of wounded men in our column, which the soldiers were unwilling to abandon to the mercies of the Partisans. Had they done so, the military part of our group could have probably cut its way through here, even though Bulgarian troops came up to support Tito's people.

Actually it was this development which proved to be our undoing. I cannot say that our higher officers displayed much presence of mind in the face of the disaster that had overtaken our nation, but at least they never would have surrendered to Tito's Yugoslav or Serbian and Slovene Partisans. But our officers thought they might be able to negotiate with the Bulgarians; they did not think the latter were real Communists. The Bulgarians in 1945 simply did what some Croatians wanted our nation as a whole to do in 1918,—that is, get on the winning side in order to escape the penalty for having fought on the losing side during the war years.

After they had talked with the Bulgarians, our officers told us that we had three choices. We could return to our homes and take our chances with the Partisans we would encounter while we were retracing our steps. Or we could hide out in the forests and either wage a guerrilla-type war against the Tito regime, or else try to escape abroad singly or in small groups, and lose ourselves in the free world. The final choice was to surrender to the Bulgarians who had promised to treat us in the manner prescribed for war prisoners under international law. In the latter case, the Bulgars would themselves escort us to Maribor and deliver us safely into the hands of the regularly constituted authorities of the new regime there. Thus, any Partisans who might want to work off old grudges against us would not have the chance to do so. Our officers appeared to think that from Maribor we would be sent by train back to our homes in Croatia. There, of course, we would have to undergo hearings which would be held to find out if any of us were guilty of war crimes, that is, of killing any Partisans or Communist sympathizers during the past four years.

Most of us decided to take our chances with the Bulgarians. This was a foolish resolve, because after we laid down our arms, the Slovenes and other Partisans fired continuously at us and killed two thousand soldiers and civilians, all of whom were unarmed, before the Bulgars could take over. Seven truckloads of the wounded men brought from the Zagreb hospitals were among these victims.

The surrender occurred on either May 11 or 12. Our Bulgarian captors lined us up in column formation and started us off on foot towards Maribor. Small detachments of Bulgarian troops were detailed to escort us, and one commissioned and one non-commissioned Bulgar officer was placed on each of the three remaining truckloads of wounded in order to protect these helpless invalids from further attacks by Tito's people, who were getting braver by the minute as they found that their allies had won the war for them.

Since we were still under the impression that we were going to be sent back to our homes from Maribor, and could easily escape en route if we saw that circumstances in the Domovina warranted this action, we passed up the opportunity to elude the vigilance of our Bulgarian guards. They had nothing against the Croats and probably would have let us get away if we had wanted to. But we were unarmed now, and most of us knew nothing about the Slovenian countryside, except that the villages through which we passed were filled with people who had climbed onto Tito's bandwagon. As is usually the case with new converts to a cause, they were vying with one another in demonstrating their Marxist convictions, so flight at this juncture seemed highly unsafe.

The Bulgarians accompanied us only about seventeen miles out of Dravograd. Then a large number of very well-armed Yugoslav Partisans took charge of us. From this moment on, the march accelerated. This meant that we had to move along at top speed with only five minutes' rest for every six miles we covered. All who could not maintain this killing pace were murdered by the Partisans.

When the bulk of the column reached Maribor, we were placed in a courtyard which belonged to a large military barracks; formerly the old Austro-Hungarian cadet school was located here. Soon after our entrance into this place, a considerable number of Partisan soldiers came among us to interrogate and identify individual prisoners. Ustashas were separated from Domobrans during this process. Since I had picked up a Domobran identification card, I passed myself off as an officer of this branch of the Croatian Armed Forces. I did this because I saw that everyone who was clad in an Ustasha uniform, or who was identified as an Ustasha by the Partisans, was being taken out of the camp and, presumably, killed. During the course of the first day and night that we spent in Maribor, ten thousand men were disposed of in this way. The Partisans themselves boasted about what they were doing. They said, "It is better to do it this way; there will be fewer of you now and you will proceed more easily."

The places of the victims were taken by new columns of prisoners which kept arriving at Maribor. I should mention that the guards incited a boy about thirteen years old to shoot approximately one hundred people with an automatic pistol right before our eyes in the courtyard. Evidently, this performance was designed to spread terror among us.

In between the killings, the Partisans looted us of everything we possessed. I saw the guards cut off the ring fingers of some men because their wedding bands or school class rings fitted too tightly to be removed by normal means.

On the afternoon of our second day in Maribor, twenty thousand of us were sent on foot towards Zagreb. We had received no food or water since our surrender, but fortunately a few people had cans or packages of food with them which they consumed before the guards could take them. Those who had no such supplies, and the weaker prisoners generally, could not keep up with the accelerated march and were shot when they stopped or collapsed along the route. Our Partisan escorts killed for sport as though they were a bunch of squirrel or rabbit hunters. Sometimes they would ask an individual if the march was tiring him. Should he answer in the affirmative, they would kill him on the spot. This, I presume, was their idea of relieving his sufferings. I should also mention that every morning when we left the field on which we had spent the night, a hundred dead men whom the Partisans had killed during the night would remain behind.

Before we came to Zagreb, the guards heard that sympathetic crowds were defying all warnings and lining the streets to do what they could for returning prisoners. To avoid such demonstrations, our column came to a halt and after a time was taken around the city. On the fourth day after we left Maribor, we arrived at Dugo Selo. Here we received a little warm food for the first time since the surrender almost two weeks before. All that we got was a kind of thick slop which was not sufficient to feed a third of us. Perhaps this was just as well because many of those who consumed this mess contracted dysentery as a result. When we were marched from Dugo Selo towards Bjelovar, this affliction weakened them further, causing them to give out more quickly than they otherwise might have done. Of course, they were butchered as soon as they fell behind the rest of us. So were two hundred officers who were taken into a forest as we were approaching Bjelovar.

On this stretch of the journey, however, our sufferings were somewhat relieved by the help given to us by heroic Croatian peasant women all along the way who supplied us with baskets of bread, cheese, and bacon, and jugs of warm milk. They persisted in doing this in face of Partisan threats to kill all of them.

At Bjelovar we were lodged in the courtyard of the Gendarmerie School. Here we were given real bread for the first time in two weeks. On the day following our arrival there, we ate warm food, no great quantity to be sure, but probably as much as our shrunken stomachs were able to digest. After the meal, the "hearings" commenced. All who had Domobran identification cards were separated from those who did not have them. The men who lacked cards were subjected to another interrogation and told that many of them would be shot as suspected Ustashas or other "war criminals." Those who were not liquidated were taken to Pozega. Some of them wrote to me later on that in this city they suffered greatly from starvation and disease.

Three hundred and fifty of us who possessed Domobran cards were formed into a Work Battalion, and assigned the duty of repairing damaged buildings in Bjelovar. On the day after our assignment to this task, a new column of prisoners arrived. There were about ten thousand men in this group, among them several hundred German officers and soldiers. Another day passed. Then, instead of going to work on the buildings of Bjelovar, we were lined up with the new column and marched through Virovitica, Podravska Slatina, and other places. At Podravska Slatina, a Montenegrin major addressed us, asking all who had good singing voices to step forward. Some poor fools, thinking that the Partisans were going to form a chorus, like those that are so popular among all the southern Slavs, hastened to comply with the Montenegrin's request. When they had identified themselves as the possessors of good singing voices, he cried out triumphantly, "Come on over here and sing for the last time!" He had his men lead these pathetic "songbirds" to one side, where they were immediately shot. The newcomers with whom we older prisoners were marching told us that before they got to Bjelovar their numbers were decimated by similar tricks played upon them by the Partisans.

From Podravska Slatina, we went across the Papuk Mountain and descended to the other side where we spent the night at an airport. There are a number of Serbian villages in this vicinity. Our Partisan guards made us lie down, while the Serb peasants took from us any blankets, shoes, shirts, or anything else our earlier captors had found no use for. Because of this new depredation, most of us were left practically naked. It was in this condition that we arrived at Sisak.

We remained in this north Croatian town for seven days. Every day we received a small piece of corn bread and a tablespoonful of corn flour. Since we had no containers in which we could cook this flour, we either toasted it or ate it raw. Our Partisan guards gave us no warm food, but the Croatian inhabitants of Sisak supplied us with everything that they could spare themselves. However, they were not able to do so for long, because the Partisans maltreated and even imprisoned many of them for the generosity displayed towards us.

From Sisak, we traveled across the Fruska Gora to Petrovaradin. On this stretch of our journey we were maltreated terribly by the Serbian peasants who lived in this part of the Croatian countryside. Our ancestors never should have allowed theirs to find shelter from the Turks in the days of Ottoman aggression. The least the Serbs did was to throw bricks and stones at us, and beat us with whatever weapons they could find.

After our arrival at Petrovaradin, many captives died of typhoid fever. I stayed for fourteen days in the fever-ridden concentration camp here. During this period, personal and official data concerning our pasts was compiled. One card filled with such data covering the past four years was sent to the OZNA at the birthplaces of the individual prisoners. Another such card went to the place or places in which he had been active during the war. An order was issued for all Ustasha officers and soldiers who had succeeded in concealing their identity so far to report themselves. Anyone who was later discovered to be an Ustasha would pay with his life for having concealed his membership in this most rabid of anti-Communist organizations. Despite what had happened to the Ustashas since the surrender, a hundred and sixty men now stepped forward to acknowledge their affiliation with this chief enemy of Communism. To our surprise they were not liquidated, and were left in the column with the rest of us. However, they had to do all the work around the camp.

We were supposed to get food every day in Petrovaradin, but there was always something wrong with the commissariat. One day there would be no food, the next there was food on hand but no water. We were lucky if we got one warm meal a day. The priests in Petrovaradin helped us out by sending us fruits and vegetables. The Partisan guards did not prevent them from doing this, but they watched carefully to see that no messages or letters were smuggled in with these foodstuffs.

At the end of two weeks, we prisoners were divided into two sections. One of these groups was composed of twelve hundred men, of whom two hundred were officers of the Croatian Army. I was included in the second group which contained nineteen hundred and sixty captives. The hundred and sixty were Ustashas, while the remainder were Domobrans, real, or alleged, like myself. Thus there were 3160 of us remaining out of the 8500 who had left Bjelovar together. Since escape was almost impossible after leaving this town, partly because of the physical exhaustion of the prisoners and partly because of the vigilance of the well armed Partisan guards, more than 5000 of our original column must have been killed or died of hunger, thirst, or other causes.

My group went from Petrovaradin to Vrsac, where the Ustashas were separated from the Domobrans. The latter were lodged in hangars that had belonged to the Croatian Air Force. I was told that there was another Domobran camp in Vrsac, besides one that accommodated noncommissioned officers exclusively. There were approximately one thousand men in each of these camps. Some of the Domobrans were put to work in the vicinity. They received better food than did the rest of the prisoners, but their ration was still only half of that given to the guards. Those of us who were not assigned to the work details fared just about as well as we had at Petrovaradin. At Vrsac, too, we suffered greatly from lack of water. In the morning everyone received a pint of water from the local wells, which he kept in a small pot.

Our stay in Vrsac lasted for approximately twenty days. Then all of the Domobrans were transferred to Kovin. Among us there were five Ustashas who had managed to keep their identities secret. The hundred and sixty known Ustashas remained behind in Vrsac. I have no information about their fate.

In Kovin we received very good food, but we had gone hungry for so long that a return to a normal menu caused many of us digestive troubles. We remained at Kovin until August 8, when we were freed on the basis of the amnesty granted by Tito. While we were at Kovin, reports on some of the prisoners were received from the various OZNA districts to which their data cards had been sent. Many of these men were allegedly taken back to Vrsac. I say "allegedly" because I know of one group that left for that place but never reached it.

The following categories of prisoners were not affected by the "Marshal's" act of grace but had to wait for his next spasm of leniency: battalion commandants and their assistants; the commanders of independent units such as the "Fleet Winged" divisions, the Black Legion, and so on; Croatian Armed Forces headquarters personnel; and the judges of the military courts. Such individuals had to prepare detailed reports concerning the operations of their units between April, 1941 and May, 1945, while they were awaiting Tito's decision about whether or not they ought to be killed. All reserve officers who had been mustered by the Croatian State could not be reemployed by the second Yugoslavia.

Those of us who were set free in August, 1945, were not allowed to dwell in the larger Croatian towns unless such places were located in the districts where we were born. I was allowed to go back to Zagreb which I reached without special trouble or inconvenience. At Kovin I had told the new authorities that my family was living in the capital. I remained there for only eight days because I was supposed to go to Tuzla which was in my district of birth. Conditions in Zagreb convinced me that there was no point at all in reporting at Tuzla. Many people were still being arrested in Zagreb, so I determined to escape to Trieste which I did on September 3, four months after the extinction of our national independence.

In closing this account I should like to stress one point. Apart from the bad treatment that we received at the hands of the population of the Slovenian countryside through which we passed, all of the brutalities described in the foregoing account of my personal experiences were committed exclusively by Serbian Partisans. As far as I know, all of our guards from the time the Bulgarians left us near Dravograd right up to the time that we spent at Kovin were members of this nationality.

Signed: V. V.

Fermo, Italy
September 9, 1945

Document XXX

Eyewitness K.L., after retreating first in a transport of 1,300 wounded soldiers and later in a column of about 15,000 troops, surrendered to the Partisans at the Yugoslav-Austrian border near Dravograd. He analyzes in detail the reasons that caused such a surrender. The prisoners were then driven towards

Maribor. After only making about 23 miles of their "Death March," an estimated 1800 prisoners were taken out of the column and shot. Six miles from Maribor, about 600 more victims were murdered. An additional 2,000 men were slaughtered near Celje. Just before the remaining captives reached the city of Pozega, 550 of them were liquidated in two Serbian villages. At Ruma, 700 were murdered. An estimated 5400 men arrived in Pancevo. Here, 600 prisoners died of various causes, including bullets. Less than 5,000 men survived the lethal orgies. From Pancevo they were sent to Kragujevac, where our witness labored for seven months and was finally set free.

At the beginning of May, 1945, I was taken to Zidani Most in a transport of wounded Croatian soldiers. The bridge across the river at this place was destroyed, so the hospital train was unable to proceed further. About thirteen hundred wounded men who were unable to walk remained aboard the train, since it was supposed that even the Yugoslav Partisans would treat them in accordance with international regulations governing the conduct of warfare. Since my wound was not serious enough to completely incapacitate me, I joined a column of Croatian troops which was retreating towards Dravograd. Later on, I learned that the Partisans killed all of the wounded men whom we left on the train.

The column to which I had attached myself was fifteen thousand strong. Without much difficulty, we reached Dravograd, where some officers went on into Austria to arrange the terms of our surrender to British troops who had entered that country.

In a short while they came back—to tell us that the Englishmen refused to accept our surrender! Instead the British Command insisted that we yield ourselves to the Yugoslav Partisans!

Our position was extremely precarious, because the British were in front of us with planes, tanks, and artillery, which we did not possess. Russian troops were to the right of us, the Partisans to the left. Also beaten Partisan units, whom we had dispersed on our march to Dravograd, had been joined by masses of new Yugoslav troops; these formations were following our rear. There was a division of opinion among our officers some of whom felt there was nothing to do now but fight to the end. The only question was whom to attack—the Russians, the British, or the Partisans—and in which direction? Heated arguments developed over this issue, since our High Command unfortunately seemed to have assumed that the English would accept our surrender as prisoners-of-war, and had made no plans whatsoever about what we should do if the Britons declined to do so. Other officers said that we might try to follow the British directive, and conduct negotiations with the Partisans. At least we might hear what they had to say. We could always refuse to lay down our weapons and put up a last-ditch fight, if we saw that the Partisans were as fanatical and lethally-minded as they had shown themselves to be during the war. But now since they, or, rather, their allies had won the war, and the fighting was over, at least as far as the necessity of continuing hostilities was concerned, even the Partisans could possibly be expected to become a little more human.

The arguments went on, expressing all kinds of wishful thinking. The crux of the situation was that we were the losers in the war, we had no hope of finding an asylum anywhere, and there was nothing left to die for. So, men clung to straws of hope in the attempt to secure their own personal salvation. Still, if we had possessed one officer of the calibre of the Turk, Mustapha Kemal Pasha, or the Fin, Baron Mannerheim, or even of one of the White Russian Commanders of 1918-21, we would have obeyed his orders to try to break through on one side or the other.

As it was, the counsels of those who wished to hear what the Partisans had to say prevailed. A Partisan officer addressed us in terms we could all understand, because he told us just what so many of us were hoping to hear. The Partisan said that the war was over and there was no necessity for further fighting. If we laid down our arms, we would be allowed to return to our homes and resume our peace time occupations.

The speech was fair enough. Since we were surrounded on all sides, and since both the British and Russians had artillery trained upon us and tanks ready to go into action against us, there really did not seem to be any point in fighting. Even if we overcame the odds against us, where could we go? And why risk everything and incur many additional casualties when, as the Partisan officer said, we could go back home and take up our lives where we had left them in 1941 when we marched off to war?

So, we surrendered our weapons, and were marched as war prisoners towards Maribor. After we had gone about twenty-three miles, we stopped on a big plain. Here, we stayed for a day and a night. While we remained at this place, an estimated eighteen hundred prisoners were separated from the rest of us, led into a nearby forest and shot. Following this episode we went on towards Maribor. We halted six miles outside the city, when darkness overtook us. Perhaps six hundred more of us were taken out of the column and killed.

Now, the hungry, thirsty, and exhausted survivors were forced to proceed at a running pace towards the town. We passed many bodies which were strewn along the sides of the road. Some people were killed by the Partisan guards right before our eyes. We went right through Maribor and on to Celje, where another two thousand men were separated from the column and slaughtered.

From Celje, we continued on to Bjelovar, from which point we were sent back to Zagreb. Afterwards, we were driven towards Slavonska Pozega. Before we reached this destination, we passed through two Serbian villages whose inhabitants used hatchets and hayforks on the prisoners. I would say that in the first village 350, and in the second, 200 men were massacred in this way. Those of us who got to Slavonska

Pozega went on, ever on, through Osijek, Vukovar, Backa Palanka, Novi Sad, and Ruma. At the last named place, the Partisans murdered 700 more of us near a brick factory. Other captives who tried to get a drink of water from a brook were butchered.

When our column arrived at Pancevo, it numbered only 5400 men, the survivors of our original 15,000. We remained in Pancevo for three months, working on various jobs. One night, 70 prisoners were shot. Others died of malnutrition, exhaustion, and diseases produced by the unsanitary and unhygienic conditions under which we had to live.

There were only 4800 of us left when we were transferred to Kragujevac, after the three-month sojourn in Pancevo. I worked for seven months in the mines and fields around Kragujevac, and then was allowed to go back to my place of birth in Croatia. I do not know what happened to those of my fellow prisoners who still remained alive at this time.

Signed: K. L.

Nuremberg, West Germany
October 30, 1954

Document XXXI

The Croatian soldier, U.D., and his group were captured by the Partisans at Dravograd. This group was divided into two sections: one of them was driven towards Maribor; and our witness' section went to Celje. From here the second section "marched" to Zidani Most. The witness wound up in the extermination camp in Krsko, where he saw masses of prisoners taken out to be slaughtered. The slaughter of about 8,600 victims was commanded by the Serbian Partisan Major Rade Brkitch. U.D. was saved from the massacre by a Croatian Partisan. Afterwards, the eyewitness "marched" to Vrapce; from Vrapce he was transported to Krizevci; then he "marched" again to Bjelovar. By either "marching" or riding in a train, he went through Virovitica, Daruvar and arrived in Pozega. In the last named city our witness saw prisoners dying from starvation, and about 500 being led out for the slaughter. The account closes with a description of the Yugoslav Army's units, to which U.D. was assigned after all the slaughterhouse orgies.

On February 28, 1942, I joined the Croatian Armed Forces and remained with them until the end of the war to make Croatia safe for Josip Broz Tito and his butchers.

When the retreat of our Army from the Domovina began during the first week of May, 1945, I got as far as Dravograd in Slovenia. Here, I was captured by the Partisan Fifty-Sixth Banat Brigade. This formation was composed chiefly of Serbian residents of the old Hungarian Banat of Temesvar. The commanding officer of the Brigade was one of our former lieutenant colonels. As late as 1944, he had commanded or taught at the Pioneers' School maintained by the Croatian Army at Srijemska Kamenica. Then, seeing which way the winds of victory were blowing, he had deserted to the Partisans.

Many Croatian prisoners, taken after the refusal of the British to accept the surrender of our Army, were brought to Dravograd. Here the Partisans divested them of their clothing and gave them whatever old rags they had themselves. One prisoner group was taken from Dravograd to Maribor. I was in another column which proceeded towards Celje. Enroute to this city, the Partisans killed individual prisoners who were unable to keep up with the rest of us. From Celje we went on to Zidani Most, where Slovenian militia men were waiting for us with clubs, which they used on us every time they had a chance to do so.

I wound up in the prison camp at Krsko. There were perhaps 10,000 Croatian war prisoners here, who were being shot in groups of five hundred at a time. There was a tunnel near the camp which had been there even before the war. The whole area was heavily mined. Sometimes the Partisans would detonate mines under the feet of the prisoners as they were driven into the forest.

The massacres which took place at Krsko were executed by the Second Battalion of the Seventh Krajina Brigade, a part of the Tenth Krajina Partisan Division. Commandant of this unit was Major Rade Brkitch, a Serb. One of the company commissars in the Second Battalion, First Lieutenant Milenko Dyunitch, personally murdered more than three hundred prisoners. This fellow was a native of Majkic Japra, near Banja Luka in Bosnia. From what I myself saw and heard while I was at this camp, I judge that about 8000 captives in all were slaughtered at Krsko.

I was led off to be shot in the forest, but a Croatian Partisan from Slavonia helped me to escape. Since I had no food and was not acquainted with anyone in this part of the country, I did not know what to do with my freedom. Finally, I succeeded in getting in among a group of Domobrans who were being escorted to Vrapce. We were placed in a detention camp there, and on the evening following our arrival, were jammed into railroad box cars and transported to Krizevci. The Croatian inhabitants of this town brought food out to the fair grounds as we were passing this memento of happier times, but the Partisans attempted to prevent us from getting it. However, our benefactors crowded against the guards and slipped the food to us.

After this welcome incident, we were marched towards Bjelovar. I became ill and could not continue with the foot column. Usually the Partisans shot anyone who dropped behind the main group, but another Croatian who had changed to the winning side in time, put me on a train which took me to Virovitica. Here, we all received a good clubbing from the Partisans, after which I went on by rail to Daruvar. From here, I had to march on foot to Pozega. The rest of my column arrived at Virovitica, thus it was in their company once again that I made the hike to Pozega.

Units of the Tenth Krajina Division escorted us all the way from Virovitica to the camp in which we were placed at Pozega. They did not perpetrate any mass slaughters along this stretch of our journey, but they did murder anyone who tried to get a drink of water along the way. Many prisoners died from starvation, and exhaustion.

There were 30,000 men in the Pozega camp, where we remained until July 17. I saw prisoners die from starvation every day. During the time that I spent in this place, about five hundred Croatians, most of them Dalmatians or Bosnians, were murdered after being "identified."

On July 17, I was assigned to the Reconnaissance Company, which was attached to the headquarters of the Seventh Krajina Brigade. My company commander was a fellow by the name of Radjan, while the company commissar was Rade Brkljac. Over one hundred former Croatian non-commissioned officers were detailed to this Brigade.

On March 13, 1946, I was transferred to the First Proletarian Division, a part of the Fourth Army. I was placed in the Third Battalion of the First Brigade and was posted to Materija in Istria. From this place, we moved on to Razdrto near Donja Vas. While I was stationed at Donja Vas, I succeeded in getting away to Italy. I was assigned to sentinel duty close to the frontier, and when I was relieved by another soldier, I simply walked across the line into Italian territory.

Signed: U. D.

Fermo, Italy
April 12, 1947

Document XXXII

The eyewitness L.Z., who in April, 1945, was drafted into Tito's Army, opens his account by depicting the Partisans' deceits and atrocities during the war. As a Partisan recruit, he learned of his comrades' brutalities from a very close range, especially at Maribor and at its well-known trenches. From Maribor, the witness followed a long column of "death marchers" on their way through Celje and Zidani Most to Zagreb. On this stretch he saw several hundred corpses of prisoners. At Ivanic-grad he did not see as many corpses, but even so, his description of the Partisans' brutalities gives a good insight into their super-Balkanese methods. Our eyewitness was one of the escorts of another "Death March", from Varazdin to Virje, during which trek he saw the atrocities of the Twelfth and Sixteenth Krajina Brigades. At the start of 1946, the eyewitness saw the unbelievably heinous cruelties of Tito's soldiers against women, children and old men in the Antunovac concentration camp near Osijek. In Vinkovci, he eyewitnessed the hanging of Mayor Toth and the Partisans dancing around the victim's scaffold.

In August, 1944, five apparent friends of mine invited me and three other young Croatians to attend the wedding of a companion, M. Turcinovic. This wedding was supposed to take place at the village in which Turcinovic's fiancee lived. Since we knew that Turcinovic was a Croatian, we didn't suspect foul play, even though the quintet that issued the invitation were mainly Serbs, that is, Serbs whose families had lived in Croatia for some time. When they tried to induce us to join the Partisans by making promises and threats, we should have been on our guard. But we were only out for a good time, therefore we just told them to shut up about the Partisans or they would get themselves into trouble with the authorities of the Croatian State. As loyal Croatians and anti-Communists, we naturally had no desire whatsoever to join Tito's raggle-taggle army. On the other hand, we did not suppose that these Croatian Serbs, even if they were potentially disloyal to the Croatian State, would dare to take hostile action against us at a Croatian wedding.

What we didn't know was that Turcinovic himself was a secret Communist, even though he posed as a good Croatian.

When we arrived at the girl's house, a group of Partisans came out of it. Our five Serbian "friends" helped them to overpower us. Furthermore, our friends proceeded to give us a good beating with wooden stakes. They used one of my three Croatian companions, for whom they seemed to have a special dislike, as a drum—that is, their idea of a joke was to play wedding music and pound him as they did so.

They wearied of this sport after a couple of hours and led us to the village of Crni Potok. Here, they continued to beat my poor friend terribly, along with one of my other companions. Finally, they shot them with revolvers which the regular Partisans carried. Among the murderers there was a Serbian Partisan woman from this locality, named Milka Kantar. The "friends" who had lured us into this trap were Yovo Peynovitch, Vaso Vuynovitch, and Stevo Zhigir, whose nickname was "Charuga." All three were Serbs, but I am sorry to say that Slavko Pokaz, and the fifth member of this precious quintet, whom I shall not name because he has some reputable relatives who were and probably still are good Croatian patriots, were Croatians themselves.

While the beatings and murders were taking place, my remaining friend and I were taken about fifty yards away. When we saw what was happening to our two friends, we took advantage of the unarmed condition of the men who were guarding us to run away into the woods. I succeeded in reaching my home, but the Partisans caught my friend and beat him soundly. They warned him that they would kill him if he tried to escape again. Therefore, he stayed with them and allowed them to place him in a school for non-commissioned Partisan officers, which Tito maintained at Papuk. Here, his Communist mentors endeavored to "re-educate" him. When he completed the course which qualified him to take a non-commissioned rank in the Partisan army, the Reds thought they had succeeded in making a Marxist out of him. They then sent him with an escort by the name of Zolarek to the village of Bukovlje, which is in the vicinity of my own home. They expected him to demonstrate his loyalty to the Partisan and Yugoslav cause by killing his own mother and his uncle, Dosen! Both of these relatives were declared to be notorious "Fascists" (i.e., Croatian patriots). The fact is that neither of them belonged to the Ustasha organization as the Partisans said they did. They were just loyal Croatians. Of course, my friend did not kill his mother or uncle, and he talked Zolarek into remaining with him at his home. Later, the Partisans killed Zolarek for this defection.

As for myself, I saw that there were too many Partisans in my part of the country for it to be safe for me. Thus, I went to Osijek and witnessed the fall of this city to the Partisans at the beginning of April, 1945. A little while afterwards, I was drafted into the Partisan army. I appeared before the military commission to begin my service along with an anti-Communist Croatian friend whom I shall designate as I. K. When we stood before the commission to be sworn in as soldiers, I. K. did not know the procedure observed by the Marxists and so raised his hand in the Croatian salute and thundered out "Spremni!" (Ready for the Fatherland). Because of this performance, the Yugoslav authorities certified him as "mentally unstable." They imprisoned him for six or seven months, but in 1946 the authorities allowed him to enter the officers' school in Osijek, from which he graduated as a second lieutenant of reserves.

I was assigned to the Supplemental Battalion and was sent to Maribor to join this unit with twenty companions. We arrived at this Slovenian city, sometime in May, 1945, after a difficult journey which we made partly by train and truck, but mainly on foot. We were ordered to halt under a clump of trees a mile away from the town, where we remained without doing anything for the entire day. We received food, but the armed "comrades," who in effect were our guards, took our shoes, valuables, and better pieces of clothing.

From the place where we had stopped, we could see a multitude of soldier prisoners whom the Partisans were guarding between the hill on which we stood and the Drava River. At first we did not know who the prisoners were, but later we were able to see that they were clad in all kinds of uniforms, Croatian, German, Serbian Chetnik, and others. They were confined in an improvised camp. At one end of the camp, a group of old civilians and some women and children were segregated from the military personnel. There were about a thousand of these non-combatants and perhaps four thousand soldiers and younger boys who were mixed in with the fighting men.

On the following day, we were told that we would have to bury some dead people who were lying at the foot of the hill on which we had spent the night. When we asked who the dead were, the Partisans growled, "Why do you ask about these bandits?" However, some of them told us that the dead men were the victims of a bombing attack. We descended the hill to do the job wished upon us and found several hundred corpses piled around a tree. Besides men who had been stripped of clothing down to their underwear, or whose outer clothing was badly torn, there were a number of women and children lying here. Most of the dead wore ordinary civilian clothing, but some were dressed in the remnants of peasant garb. It was evident that they were refugees who had sought to escape Tito's killers, but who had failed to do so, thanks to the incompetence of our national leaders. No wounds were to be seen on some of the bodies, but others bore the marks of knives or bullets. Many had their throats cut, while some had been decapitated. Certainly, they were *not* the victims of air bombings as some of the guards had tried to convince us! As a matter of fact, there were no signs of an air strike having been delivered at any time in this vicinity.

Together with fellow draftees, I had to throw the corpses into trenches that had been dug during the war for riflemen. These excavations extended in zig-zag manner along the bottom of the hill. Thirty or forty of us were employed in piling bodies, one on top of the other, into the trenches. Afterwards, we threw earth over them. I must have handled between twenty and thirty dead people on this day, some of them women and children. As we were performing our grim duty, another group was detailed to dig out a large hole that began where the trenches ended. To my horror I saw that this pit, too, was full of bodies. Since the dead in this hole were quite stiff or already putrefying, they probably had been killed days before. The entrails were cut out of some of the bodies.

We were still engaged in the task of burial at 5:00 P.M., when a hundred prisoners were brought to the newly excavated abattoir. We were told that they were going to help us inter the dead. But then these prisoners were lined up at the edge of the hole where the older corpses lay. Next they were looted of what belongings they had. Finally, the hundred prisoners were machine-gunned. I watched this slaughter from a distance of one hundred yards or less. Some of the prisoners threw themselves down flat and escaped the machine gun fire. They pretended to be dead, but the Partisans went from one apparent corpse to another and ran their bayonets through everyone whom they suspected of being alive. Screams rent the air, providing grim evidence that those who had dodged the machine gun fire had not eluded death for long. All of the new victims were thrown into the hole on top of the old corpses. Then the Partisans directed several more bursts of machine gun fire into the pile of bodies, just to make sure that they had not left anyone alive.

On the next day I witnessed the formation of a "Death Column." It was composed of Croatian soldiers, together with some Serbian Chetniks. There were no officers or Germans in this column. Both of the latter categories were left behind at Maribor. I do not know what happened to them ultimately. Some officers had concealed their identity by passing themselves off as private soldiers. Later, the Partisans made a search for them in the column to which I was assigned as a guard. There were some Germans in it, who pretended to be Croatians or Serbians. Before the "Death March" commenced, a number of Partisan officers and soldiers identified some of the captives as Ustasha or officers. Such individuals were murdered immediately without receiving even the semblance of a trial.

Finally, the column started off towards Celje. I marched at the rear of the long procession and had an excellent opportunity to count the people who were killed and left lying along either side of the road. These victims were people who had become too exhausted to keep up with the rest of the prisoners, or who had been obliged to stop to relieve themselves, or who had tried to get a drink of water. As we were approaching Celje, I saw a score of men who were mad with thirst throw themselves down beside a spring that was close to the road. With my own eyes, I saw the Partisan guards machine-gun all of them.

The column had to march night and day with halts of only a few minutes duration all the way to Zagreb. The prisoners were allowed to rest for ten minutes now and then, only to maintain some kind of cohesion in the column. Such stops were necessary whenever large intervals developed between the different sections of the procession. New escorts replaced the old ones every day, except for the Partisans who were mounted or walking. I lost count of the number of bodies that I passed during the course of the march from Celje through Zidani Most to Zagreb, but I know there were several hundred of them.

When we reached Zagreb, all the new recruits were taken away from the column and sent to Ivanic-grad. Here we were formally enrolled in the Yugoslav Armed Forces. We were given Partisan caps to wear to indicate our new status, otherwise, we were still clad in civilian clothes. While we were eating dinner at Ivanic-grad, we heard the sound of shooting from nearby. We got up and went to see what was going on. In the courtyard of a church, we came upon a score of Partisans who were blazing away at the doorway to a cellar. About ten corpses or so were piled up in front of the cellarway. As we watched this ghastly spectacle, an auto came up with two Partisan officers in it. They asked "What do the bandits want?" "They wanted air so we gave it to them," the guards replied.

Soon four trucks drove up. We had to load the dead and wounded onto them; then they were carried off to some undisclosed destination. One of the officers now shouted to whoever remained in the cellar, "Come out and get some fresh air!" Since the basement evidently was still overcrowded, the people in the rear must have pushed those close to the door out into the open. As soon as there were several men gathered in a group outside, the Partisans shot them. I saw this same scene enacted twice more. After the third group was disposed of, no one else came out of the cellar. Therefore, the Partisans opened fire through the doorway. No sounds could be heard from within the cellar; only the maniacal laughter of the Partisans disturbed the quiet of the churchyard. One Partisan went to the cellar doorway and yelled at the top of his lungs, "You see everything's all right now! You've got enough air! When you want more just let us know, and we'll do you a favor again!"

I do not know what became of the survivors in the cellar. We were transferred to Varazdin, where we were assigned to the Twelfth Brigade of the Twelfth Division of the Yugoslav Army. Our duty was to escort a column of prisoners to Virje. Here we were relieved by the Sixteenth Krajina Brigade, a predominantly Serbian command. My unit, too, had only a few Croatians in it. Most of the Twelfth was composed of Serbs, although there were also some Hungarians and Slovaks in it.

During the course of this escort duty, I again saw prisoners killed because they tried to drink water that peasants near Virje brought them. Some of the Partisan escorts also fired on the peasant women who threw bread, pastry, cherries, and other fruit to the captives. I remember, too, that I saw a Partisan sergeant knife a prisoner. A friend of the victim jumped onto the murderer, twisted the knife out of his hand, and killed him with it. Other Partisans gunned this courageous captive down on the spot and then shot thirty other members of the column by way of revenge. When the Sixteenth relieved us on a large field that was close to Virje, they took some more men out of the column and shot them.

After this "escort" duty, we got a two months' rest in the Voyvodina. In January, 1946, I was sent to Osijek. Near the artillery barracks here, I came upon some German prisoners who were locked up in a horse stable. They were getting practically nothing to eat; therefore many of them collapsed on the jobs to which they were detailed. They were horribly maltreated in other ways, too. At night they were not even allowed to leave the stable to relieve themselves. If they satisfied these needs, the Partisans made them eat their own excrement. Anyone who refused to so degrade himself was killed on the spot. Among these wretches I recognized a friend of mine, one Toni Vilger, who had worked in a bakery in my locality during the war. These Germans were taken off somewhere later in the year. We were told that they were sent back to Germany.

I also was an eyewitness of the transfer of the Tenjski Antunovac concentration camp near Osijek to Tenje. There were only women, children, and old men, chiefly Croatians, in the Antunovac camp. All of them who were unable to walk because of illness or exhaustion were left behind in the camp during the transfer, and slaughtered by soldiers of the regular Yugoslav Army. There may have been thirty or forty such victims. Their corpses were thrown into pigsties. I do not know if they were subsequently buried.

When all who could walk were lined up in column formation, I was one of the escorts assigned to it. Hardly had this sad procession moved out of the Antunovac camp, than an old man collapsed. He asked me to kill him so that his sufferings would be ended. I lifted him to his feet, but he could go only a few paces before he sank to the ground again. Unfortunately, the camp commandant, who was mounted on horseback, came riding up and saw that I was trying to help the poor old fellow. He yelled at me, "Why are you waiting? Kill him!"

Needless to say, I neither wanted to kill the old man nor did I have any intention of doing so whatever the personal consequences. When the commandant saw that I was not going to obey his order, he called to four soldiers who were standing near the entrance to the camp and told them to throw the poor octogenarian into a pigsty together with the other victims who had been "liquidated."

After this incident, I did not see anyone else killed in this particular group. However, these women, children, and old men were maltreated in the most brutal manner that could be imagined. For instance, they were compelled to go across the ice of frozen channels and streams. Sometimes the ice broke under their weight, and many of the miserable captives fell into icy water that came up to their waists. The winter of 1945-46 was a bitter one, and the shivering wretches literally froze in motion as they staggered along in their wet and ice covered clothes. The tempo of the march was fast, and the old men and women had to be dragged along by the younger women. Even so, they could hardly keep up during the nine mile hike to Tenje.

After this grueling experience, I was posted to Vinkovci. On the fair grounds, I saw the mayor of the city during the days of Croatian independence, Toth, hung before a mass of spectators. While many women in the crowd who knew or had been helped by him during the war wept at this sight, the Communists and their sympathizers danced around the scaffold.

This statement had been read to me, and I certify that everything contained in it is true. I am ready at any time to take a solemn oath to this effect and to testify to the accuracy of the events described before an international commission. Pending such an opportunity, I wish my name to be withheld from the general public, since I still have relatives and friends in Croatia who might be made to pay for my testimony.

Signed: L. Z.

August 22, 1962

Document XXXIII

A.R. first describes the surrender of the Croatian troops in the area between Celje and Maribor, then the "march" to Maribor and the separation of 500

Ustasha from 2000 Domobran officers in a Maribor park. He continues describing the classification of prisoners into active or reserve officers, and the liquidation of about 2,000 Domobran actives .The witness further depicts the concentration camp in Precko, the "Death March" from Zagreb to Bjelovar, murders of the captives on this stretch, and the concentration camp in Bjelovar. The account closes with another "Death March", from Bjelovar to Petrovaradin. From Petrovaradin the witness and a group of other survivors were taken to Vrsac, and finally to Kovin, where their "Death March" ended.

In 1945, I was serving as Color Bearer in the Twenty-Second Regiment of the First Assault Division of the Croatian Armed Forces. We left Zagreb on May 6, and retired in the direction of Austria. A week later, having covered the retreat of the main body of the Croatian forces, our rear guard unit was surrounded by superior Partisan forces, which cajoled us into surrendering to them instead of fighting it out to the end, as we should have done. They took our weapons, watches, and other valuables. I was quite amused at the time to note that a female Partisan was wearing several watches on each wrist and had a pair of revolvers tucked into her belt.

We officers were ordered to face the column about and turn it in another direction. We knew that we were somewhere between Celje and Maribor and soon learned that we were headed for the last named city. My part of the column was composed exclusively of Ustasha and Domobran officers. There were several members of my regiment among them.

En route to Maribor, we received no food and spent two nights under the open sky. When we were three miles outside the town, the Partisan guards made us proceed at a run, during which we discarded knapsacks, blankets, overcoats, and everything else that interfered with our running. Anyone who could not keep on running was shot without delay. Along the way we passed the bodies of other soldiers, who were probably from columns that had preceded us into the city.

About noon, we were brought to a park where two thousand Domobran officers were separated from some five hundred Ustashas. Among the latter were several of my schoolmates, such as First Lieutenant Peradinovic, a Slavonian Croat; Color Bearer Zlatko Volak, a radiotelegraphist from Banja Luka in Bosnia; his cousin, another Color Bearer (as was Ante Otkovic, who came from Celinac near Banja Luka), and a number of others whose names I do not recall now.

These Ustasha officers were murdered, probably shortly after our arrival in Maribor. None of the men whom I knew ever returned to their homes or were seen by anyone of whom I had knowledge after I left this camp. I survived to make inquiries, both oral and written, concerning my own friends, but to this day I have been unable to find out what happened to them.

On the first evening in Maribor, the Domobran group in which I was included was taken to a warehouse located alongside some railroad tracks. About three hundred officers preceded me into this place; many more came afterwards. I remember that I met an old friend here, but at this moment I cannot for the life of me recall his name, even though later on I served as a witness for his father in a court process in Banja Luka. I think sometimes that the experiences which I endured in 1945 have affected my retentive faculties permanently, for several times I have had lapses of memory in regard to names and identities. My battalion commandant, a Zagrebcanin, was in the warehouse too.

After two or three days and nights in the warehouse, we were transferred to a school building in the town. This was a two or three-story edifice with two entrances. Active officers were told to stand to one side and reserves to the other, while we were still outside the building. Anticipating that the active officers were going to be butchered in cold blood, I hastened to the right side among the reserves. Together with this bunch, I was taken through the right side entrance to the school. There were, perhaps, four hundred of us in this group.

The two officers whom I have mentioned above, and others whom I knew, stayed with the active officers, two thousand strong. I saw them being sent through the left hand entrance; that is the last I ever saw of any of them. When I inquired later on at Banja Luka about the friend whose name I can't recall, his father and sister told me that the news that I brought them concerning him was the only news they had heard of him since the end of the war. Nor did my battalion commandant ever return to his home in Zagreb. Several times, when I have had occasion to visit the capital city, I took pains to see his wife in order to ask if she had heard from him. But she knew only what I did, namely, that he had gotten to Maribor. Since the other active officers whom I knew were not heard from again either, I believe that the Partisans must have slaughtered them all on or about May 20, 1945.

As for the reserves to whom I had attached myself, we remained in the school building for a few days. Only on the third day there did we receive anything to eat—unsalted beans, which already were sour due to staleness and the spring heat. When we asked the cook who brought this mess to us why he had not fed us before, he replied that he had been unable to find us. We asked him also if he knew what had happened to the active officers, and he replied that he did not—as yet.

Although our previous captors had done a pretty thorough job of robbing us, the Maribor Partisans did their best to relieve us of anything the other "comrades" might have missed. There were fifty of us in the classroom where I slept; the other rooms in the place were just as crowded. At the end of the month (May), we were taken to the railroad station where we were loaded into boxcars. At least fifty men were placed in each car; then the doors were locked. A grueling overnight trip delivered us in ultra-exhausted condition to the Precko concentration camp in Zagreb.

After a several day sojourn in this hell-hole, many of us were lined up one evening for shipment elsewhere. Our guards started to bind the hands of the men at the head of the column, but for some reason stopped this procedure before they reached my position. We set out for Bjelovar about five thousand strong. Officers marched in front, NCO's in the middle, and Ustashas in the rear. I was about twenty rows from the front of the column. Our escorts were drawn from the Partisans' so-called Karlovac Brigade, which was composed of the worst villains I encountered anywhere in the "Death Marches" in which I participated.

We journeyed from Zagreb to Ivanic-grad via the state highway. When we got to Ivanic-grad, we turned to the right and executed a kind of long semi-circle through the forests. Every man of the Karlovac Brigade, especially commissars, tried his hand at killing us in cold blood, while we were going through these woods. Rifle and machine gun fire could be heard almost continuously. Two of the Partisans, Ljudevit Stefan and Boro Bjelkanovic, told me all about the slaughter in the forest. I saw how several officers were pulled out of the column before we reached Cazma, and murdered while I watched. Just before we entered Bjelovar, a Domobran colonel said something in a very bitter tone to the Brigade Commissar, who shot him down right in front of me, while we were crossing a railroad track.

The Croatian residents of Bjelovar welcomed us sympathetically. Therefore, the Partisans commanded us to keep our eyes fixed on the ground. An officer, who was a native of the town, saw his wife standing in the street and, forgetting himself, ran to embrace her. The Commissar pulled him roughly away from her and killed him instantly.

In Bjelovar we were taken to the barracks of the old Gendarmerie School, where we remained for a few days. One day, I saw a dead soldier lying in the courtyard through which we had to pass to get our noon rations. Now and then shooting could be heard during the night hours. Each shot that we heard probably meant that the life of another Croatian was being snuffed out.

From Bjelovar we were sent by train through Donji and Gornji Miholjac towards Osijek, but we entered the last named town on foot. Some prisoners were liquidated during this journey. I do not know of any killings that occurred in Osijek while we were there, although the Partisans could have committed some without our knowledge.

For two days we were quartered on a plain that lay alongside the railroad tracks, near a brick factory. From here we went by train to Srijemska Mitrovica, where we bivouacked on the ground floor of the S. Mitrovica prison. According to information that I received later on, some prisoners were liquidated on the night we spent here.

Our group was now composed exclusively of officers. On the day following our arrival at Srijemska Mitrovica, we went on to the castle at Petrovaradin. Here, for the first time, our names were recorded officially, and a check was made of our pasts. However, we did not have to answer roll call at this place. There were some 200 Ustasha commissioned and non-commissioned officers at Petrovaradin, and, in all probability, some Domobran officers were taken out of our group and placed with them. We know that they were beaten and tortured on the first night that we spent in Petrovaradin, because we could hear them screaming. Furthermore, the Partisans themselves boasted of what they had done to them. Later on, I was delighted to encounter a Color Bearer from Banja Luka who had survived the brutalities suffered by these officers on this night. He did not know what had happened to the rest of his comrades, but considered it probable that they were killed. I know that one good friend of mine, Ustasha First Lieutenant Ivan G., never returned to his home from Petrovaradin.

There were a few Germans, two generals among them, who were incarcerated in this old command post of the Petrovaradin Frontier Regiment, a largely Serbian formation in Habsburg times. We were kept here for nearly fifteen days, and then were marched to Vrsac, where we remained for a whole month. After this, I was taken with a group consisting almost exclusively of Domobran officers to Kovin. At this place, I underwent a short interrogation concerning my past, and then was amnestied. Most of the Color Bearers were so "pardoned" at this time. Higher officers were "tried" for the offense of having opposed Communism. Most of them were condemned to long terms of imprisonment or to forced labor.

From Kovin I went to my home. A year had not passed, however, when the Socialist authorities arrested me on the ground that I was an "enemy of the new Yugoslavia." For this "crime" I was sentenced to two years imprisonment. At my "trial," no charge other than serving in the Croatian Armed Forces during the war was brought against me. This fact in itself was considered proof that I was an incorrigible "enemy of the people."

It was only after I had lived for seven years under the reign of terror, organized by Tito Broz, that I succeeded in escaping across the Austrian frontier. Thus, I eventually was able to find the freedom which I enjoy today in Canada.

Signed: A. R.

Ontario, Canada
December 29, 1962

Document XXXIV

The following eyewitness account tells of a "Death March" which lasted two and one half years and took the survivors through scores of towns in "People's Republics" of Slovenia, Croatia, Bosnia-Hercegovina, Serbia and Montenegro. Croatian victims were murdered at most sites mentioned in this document.

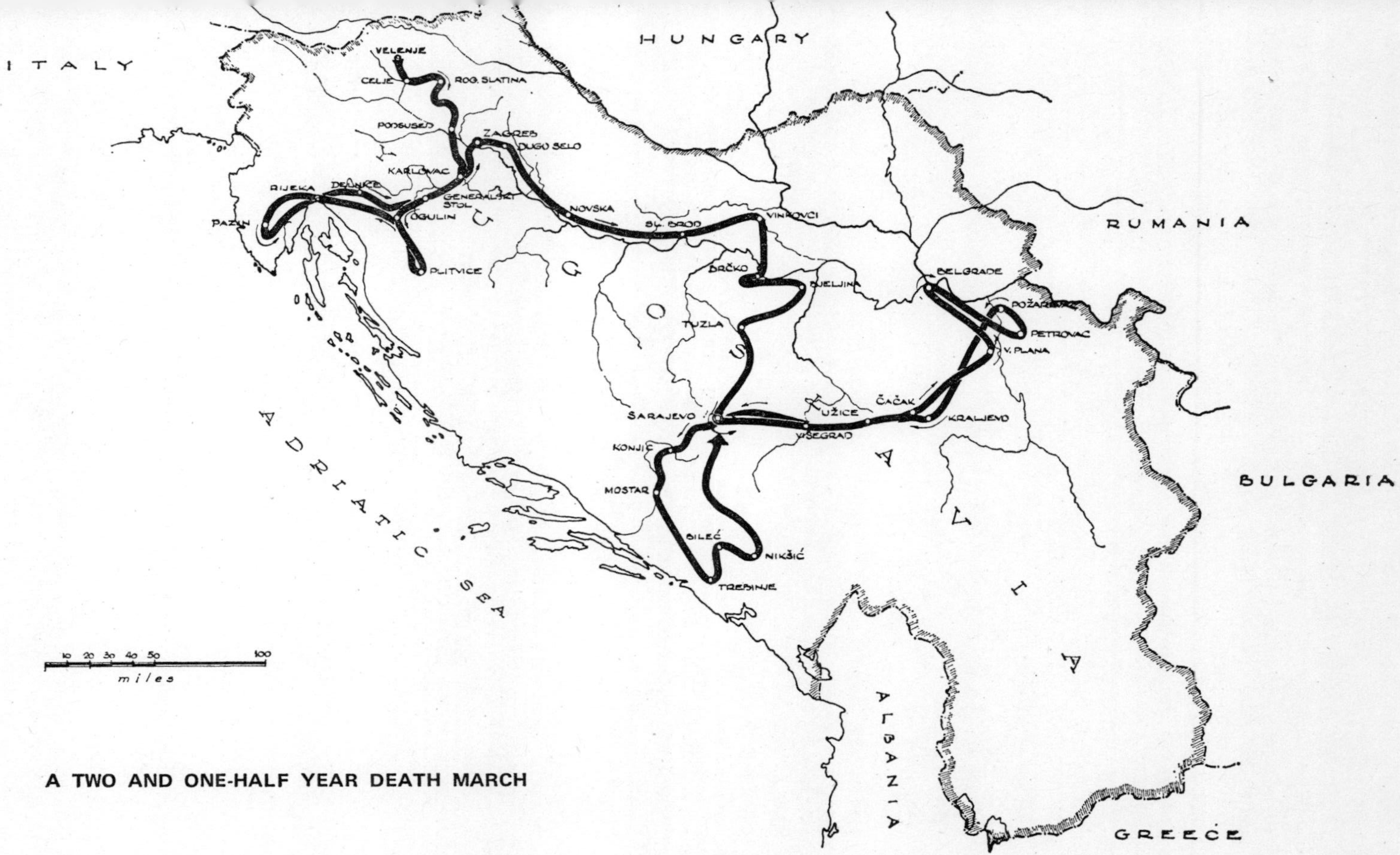

A TWO AND ONE-HALF YEAR DEATH MARCH

The retreat of my unit, the Second Battalion of the Fifth Croatian Pursuit or Hunter Regiment, began in the last days of April, 1945. At this time we were stationed at Vuka, between Osijek and Vukovar. We drew back to Djakovo, then to Selce, Kondric, Levanjska Varos, Rusevo, and Pleternica. As we were converging on Jaksic, we saw thirty-odd villagers whose throats had been slit by the Partisans. At the crossroads between Pozega, Kapela Batrina, and Slavonski Brod, we discovered another group of slaughtered civilians. I shall always remember these particular victims of the triumph of "democracy" in the last war.

We had orders to pull back through Novska and Okucani, in the directions of Zagreb. At the Ivanja River near the capital, we met the units of the First and Second Divisions which were commanded by General Boban. Together with his troops, we by-passed Zagreb, went toward Sestine and then on to Podsused, Krapina, Pusca Bistra, Klanjec, and Reichenburg.

We had planned to reach Celje in Slovenia and to regroup there, but huge masses of civilians, fleeing from the Communist dispensation that Russia and her democratic allies were wishing upon Croatia, hampered the movements of the military forces. Furthermore, my own unit was encircled by two Partisan Divisions, the sixth Banija and the Eighth Kordun. In these unfavorable circumstances, I became separated from my battalion and attached myself to one of General Luburic's groups.

The Reds already held the hills around Celje. Crossing the valley, our troops had to break through in order to reach the Austrian frontier and, as we thought at the time, safety. General Luburic issued clear, terse orders: "break through the Communist lines or die." We comprehended the situation perfectly and followed this brave general in an attack upon the positions commanded by the Partisans.

It was as hellish a fight as I have ever participated in. A full-scale battle raged for six hours without pause. While the Reds suffered more than twice the number of our casualties, we still lost an estimated 3,000 men here. Domobrans and Ustashas, surrounded by heaps of fallen Partisans, lay around everywhere.

Luburic's attack carried us through, and we left Celje behind and went on to Velenje. Here we encountered a column of Croatians who had reached Austrian soil, only to be turned over to the Partisans, after they had surrendered to the British. The captives were accompanied by Partisan guards, who took off into the woods as soon as they saw us coming. After this, the released prisoners told us that Tito's people already had begun to liquidate those Croatian soldiers who allowed the English to disarm them near Dravograd, Ravno, and elsewhere.

Receiving this depressing news left us in a quandary. We really did not know what to do. After some hesitation, we decided to go ahead, but we had gotten only as far as the end of the village of Velenje when we met another group of disarmed soldiers. They told us it was useless to go any further, because the British were extraditing to the Communists all troops and civilians who gave themselves up with the assumption that this war was like any other one in modern times; that is, that the worst that could happen to the losers was imprisonment by the victors. Of course, we all knew the Communist way of ending a civil war, or trying to do so. They had demonstrated these tactics very effectively in the Russian civil war of 1918-21, in Hungary in the time of Bela Kun, and in Spain during 1936-39. No Croatian in his right mind had any intention of yielding to Tito's people or the Russians. But we had committed the terrible fallacy of supposing that the British and Americans would honor the several international conventions which had prescribed the rules governing "civilized" warfare. In view of the millions of victims sacrificed to the Moloch of "democracy" during the French Revolutions, the Risorgimento, and the war of 1914-18, we should have known better.

Our military commanders, thoroughly disillusioned by the situation in which they found themselves, decided that individuals and small groups would have a better chance of survival than would large columns, which could be bombed from the air by British and American planes. We received orders to disband and to look out for ourselves as best we could. So, after all we had been through, and accustomed as we were to victory over our Communist opponents, our units now began to disperse. This in itself was indeed a sad ending to a long and bitter war.

Some soldiers went off into the woods individually or in small bands. Others decided to keep together for the time being and return to Croatia. Some Partisans appeared and assured us that we had nothing to fear. The war was over; and there would be no more killing. Thus, we let them escort us back to the Domovina. The Partisans were relatively few in number; most of them were mounted. Since they did not bother us all the way to Celje, we began to feel that perhaps we had done the right thing in returning to our country instead of trying to find asylum abroad, or losing ourselves in the forests, where we had little chance of surviving for long. Since we had nothing to eat, some men collapsed from exhaustion or hunger before we reached Celje. Others died of typhoid fever, which was probably contracted through drinking polluted water.

Before we got to Celje, however, the Forty-Fifth Serbian Division appeared on the scene to reinforce our original escort. The Serbs cursed us and struck us with their gun butts all the rest of the way into the town. When we entered this Slovenian community, they had us line up at attention on both sides of the main street. Then they robbed us of our clothes and valuables. All who resisted such treatment were beaten soundly or killed on the spot.

After this, a parade took place, featured by the appearance of many flags decorated with red stars and pictures of Stalin and Tito. The Partisan officers marched first in this triumphant procession, while privates followed behind them. The latter were attired in all kinds of uniforms.

The Communist sympathizers among the population of Celje tagged along at the end of the parade. There was a lot of singing, and I well remember one ballad that was recited again and again. It contained the lines: "Amerika i Engleska bit ce zemlja proleterska." (America and England will be lands of the proletariat.)

Indeed, all good Marxists had every reason to believe that Great Britain and the United States were exerting their best efforts to make the world safe for Communism at this time. No wonder that the Reds and fellow sympathizers everywhere have been so sadly disillusioned by American action in Korea, Vietnam, and Latin America! At that time, we felt it would serve the British and Americans right if their lands were to become the same sort of "Socialist Paradise" that they made out of Croatia by their policies and actions in 1945.

The good Communist citizens of Celje, feeling that they had plenty of armed protection, soon tired of marching. They devoted themselves to the more agreeable task of beating, cursing, and spitting on us. After all the fanfare ended, we were taken towards Grobelno, which is four miles distant from Celje. A German division which had surrendered to the Partisans was lodged in the villlage. Since their captors had given them food, they were faring better than we were. We Croatians had received nothing but an unending supply of various tortures since our surrender. Just as we were entering Grobelno, the column came to a halt. We could hear some Communists shouting out ahead of us, "Go back, bandits!"

Thus we were marched all the way back to Celje. En route, some men collapsed and were shot where they fell. I believe that it was May 17 or 18 when we were driven into the football and soccer stadium in this town. The soccer stadium still is located on the outskirts of the city. There were between fourteen and fifteen thousand Croatian soldiers crowded into this place. They were all barefoot, and had been stripped of their outer garments. We were brought into the stadium in pairs, with our arms lifted over our heads. Guards searched us to make sure that we had not succeeded in concealing anything of value from our previous captors. If they found anything that looked like a weapon on anyone, they killed him on the spot.

I know that more than a thousand of those who returned with me from Grobelno to Celje never reached the stadium. They were slaughtered along the way. A Communist officer, usually a Serb, but sometimes a Slovene, would yell out suddenly, "Kill that fellow whose head is sticking out above all the rest of the bandits!" Then another would cry, "Kill that little runt there!" Someone else would order that anyone wearing a beard, or someone who had been stripped of his shirt, should be done away with. Usually they did not shoot the individuals whom they singled out in this manner. To good Marxists, unnecessary expenditure of ammunition was "uneconomical" and smacked of capitalism.

Therefore, they knifed victims as a rule. Female Communists excelled in the slaughterhouse tactics employed on this march.

We remained in the Celje stadium for two days. Early on the third day of our detention there, a Communist officer mounted a platform and made a speech which went something like this:

> All of you who are gathered here are our enemies. We are the bosses now. We have received the permission of the Americans and British both, to do with you as we please. Therefore, we must find out, first of all, who is who. Have all commissioned officers gather together in one circle, non-commissioned officers in another. Let the Ustashas go to one side, the Domobrans to another. Those Domobrans who served during the years 1941-43 must form a separate group. Let the village militia assemble in one place, gendarmes in another, and civilians go off to one side. Whoever does not join his proper group will be shot immediately.

I do not know whether the officer who made this speech was a colonel or a general of the Partisan Army. Since I was unfamiliar with their rank insignia, he could have been either. We proceeded to execute his orders. There were a number of officers among us, but they or their captors had removed their insignia, so there was no way of telling them from privates. Some of them masqueraded successfully as the latter. Besides us Croatians, some of General Vlasov's Ukrainians, who had fought for the freedom of their country, were in the stadium, as were a contingent of Serbian Royal Chetniks, and a small group of Slovenian Domobrans, or White Guards.

When the respective groups were formed, Ustashas were taken out of the stadium and killed en masse. On the way to the scene of the slaughter, the Reds beat them with rifle butts, spat on them, broke their ribs, and so on. These known anti-Communist fighters were thrown into trucks and driven to the Savinja River. This stream was only about thirteen hundred feet away from the stadium. That night we heard screams and curses coming from that direction.

Following the butchery of the Ustasha men, the Partisans disposed of the hundred and fifty identified officers of the Regular Croatian Army. Every fifteen minutes a truck, which was a gift to the Communists from their Western Allies, pulled into the stadium to pick up a new batch of officer victims. Then it was the turn of non-commissioned officers, gendarmes, and the Domobrans who had served during 1941-43, to be slaughtered one after the other. Finally only old civilians, women, and children were left. These, too, were massacred, and new columns of war prisoners were brought into the now empty stadium to replace them.

Why did we allow ourselves to be led to the slaughter like sheep in a shambles? Well, the stadium was surrounded by a fence which was about eleven feet high. Outside this fence, barbed wire entanglements had been erected. Machine gun nests, approximately fourteen feet off the ground, were placed behind the barbed wire. Communist guards, armed with automatic weapons given to them by their British and American allies, were posted all around the stadium. Besides all this, many of us had received nothing whatsoever to eat and had gotten little, if any rest, for more than a week. No drinking water was available in the whole stadium. Some of us had typhoid. In short, most of us were dying of thirst, hunger, exhaustion or disease anyway. Thus, there were many who welcomed the prospect of a quick end to their suffering. This state of apathy towards everything which prevailed among us is indicated by the fact that a hole thirty feet long, fifteen feet wide, and nine feet deep had been dug by the Partisans at one end of the soccer field, and the corpses of those who died of starvation, thirst, fever, or exhaustion were thrown into this hole in front of our very eyes. Some of those who were tossed in on top of the others were still alive.

Apart from all this, we weren't absolutely sure that we were going to be murdered. Only twenty or thirty prisoners were removed at a time, and, for all we knew at first, they might be assigned to work details or, perhaps, transferred to a better place of imprisonment than this improvised concentration camp. During the six horrible days that I spent in the stadium, the number of prisoners was reduced every day, but new arrivals came from Bleiburg, Maribor, Ljubljana, and the Croatian Zagorje, a mountainous hinterland not far from Zagreb, to replace them. I think that the Communists slaughtered about twenty thousand Croatians and an undetermined number of other anti-Communist nationalities in this six-day period. Earlier in the war, trenches had been dug by the Germans along the Savinja River; it was there that the victims were butchered and hastily interred.

To this day, I really don't know why I wasn't massacred along with the rest. I think I was just overlooked, like a few other lucky ones. Undoubtedly, the fact that I continuously got away from any group whose turn for transportation was coming up, facilitated my survival. Perhaps, I was just fortunate. It was not yet my time to die.

Anyway, on the seventh day following the incarceration of my column in the stadium, I found myself in another column that was being directed from Celje towards Smarje. As we climbed the crest of a hill along this road, I took a quick look back at the part of the column that was strung out behind me. It stretched out more than two miles to the rear as we marched five or six abreast all this distance. Therefore, I estimate that there must have been about thirty-five thousand soldiers and civilians included in this one prisoner procession.

Along the way, many Slovenian peasants demonstrated their Marxist sentiments by beating us with big sticks, metal rods, and the like. Except for General Rupnik's White Guards and the many good Slovenian civilians who shared our fate as prisoners of the Reds, I, personally, shall never again have any feeling of sympathy for Slovenes who used to complain so much about "oppression" at the hands of the Austrians. There were just too many members of this nation who showed every quality of despicable and petty meanness. Some of the Slovene Partisans even tried to outdo the Serbs as killers of defenseless prisoners.

Of course, when it came to harassing and torturing captives, the Slovene civilians were only amateurs compared to Tito's military cadres. The Partisans had great sport in trampling upon those of us who collapsed and fell along the road. We tried to help one another keep up with the column, but we were all so weak that frequently someone who was carrying or supporting one of our weaker members would fall down along with whomever he was trying to help. When two or three people went down together in this manner, those behind the fallen members had to go around them without trying to pick them up. If there was any delay at all, the Reds would open fire with their machine guns and kill everyone who was in that part of the column. Of course, the people who were not hit by the machine gun bullets were confused and did not know whether to stay where they were or run ahead. All who stopped were shot down. Those who ran to catch up with the ranks ahead usually survived for a while longer. Many people who were only wounded were left lying in the road until other Partisans came along to finish them off, or throw them into ditches along the roadside, where they could die unassisted.

When we arrived at Smarje, I noted that our column was about a quarter of a mile shorter than when we set out. This meant that several thousand people were killed between Celje and Smarje.

From Smarje, we were taken along a country road which was lined with thick bushes and tall trees. Some Communists amused themselves by firing at us from the shelter of the foliage as we passed them. I found myself included in a group of six or seven thousand prisoners who were separated from the main "Death March" and sent towards Slovenska Bistrica. I do not know why we were so segregated.

We paused for the night in a camp that was located on a plain. Five of six hundred young Domobrans were killed during the few hours that we spent at this place. On the following morning, our guards received orders to take us back to Rogaska Slatina through Slovenska Bistrica. After an "accelerated march," we caught up with another Croatian prisoner column which was proceeding from Reichenburg towards Hrvatsko Zagorje.

We had passed through Reichenburg while we were retreating from Croatia towards Austria. At that time, we had found it empty. Now, however, it was packed with people. Most of them seemed to be Slovene Communists who welcomed us warmly with a whirlwind of blows from hoes, rakes, and other objects made of wood or metal.

Up to this time, the Forty-Fifth Serbian Division had continued to guard us. At Reichenburg they handed us over to the Eighth Kordun Division; the latter was one of the tougher Partisan units, composed of men who had been in the ranks of the Partisans since 1941. For four full years they had lived and fought in the mountains. During this time, they lost any semblance of humanity which they may once have possessed. As soon as they took charge of us, it seemed that all hell was unleashed upon us, or, as Sir Walter Scott wrote in his "Lady of the Lake":

> Within that dark and lonesome dell,
> Arose so wild and fierce a yell,
> It seemed that all the fiends that dwell,
> Had pealed the banner cry of Hell.

The Kordun men cursed us and beat us with such enthusiasm that some of them broke their rifles on our backs and shoulders.

It was to the accompaniment of scenes such as these that we finally set foot on Croatian soil again. As we passed through the Croatian countryside, things began to get a little better for us because the peasants and villagers, men and women alike, tossed corn bread and other food to us. To put an end to such hospitality, the Kordun men rained blows upon the heads of these people and even shot at them, while we starving prisoners scrambled around competing with one another, as we all tried to find the spot where a bit of bread had fallen in the dust.

When we arrived at Klanjec, another attempt to identify the prisoners was made. Here a considerable number of people were separated from the rest of us and taken off to be slaughtered. From Klanjec, the survivors went on across the Krapina River. At last, our long and painful march was halted temporarily at Podsused. Rumors spread that the Communists were either going to butcher the lot of us, or else throw us alive into the Sava River to drown.

There were Communist guards at the bridge near Podsused, standing at fifteen-foot intervals all along the bridge and the banks of the river near it. We were marched across in columns of fours. The Communists hit everyone they could reach with the butts of their rifles or other weapons. Some prisoners died of the blows they received; others were knocked unconscious. Whoever collapsed in such fashion was trampled upon by the guards.

After we had crossed the bridge, we found lines of Partisans waiting for us. These lines formed one behind the other, about sixty feet apart. Various captives were pulled out of our column, interrogated, and then, as a rule, murdered.

Early one June evening, we arrived at Samobor. Here, for the first time since we had fallen into the hands of the Partisans, we received warm food—spoiled corn flour cooked in gasoline barrels. Some of us ate this slop. Others, hungry though they were, could not stand the smell and ran past the barrels to get away from the mess. Soon afterwards, a number of prisoners who had partaken of this "specialty" died of some kind of poisoning.

We were confined in an old castle at Samobor. The seven thousand prisoners in this place ate anything which could take the edge off their hunger. Leaves, grass, and bark were on our menu. As usual, the Communists initiated an "identification" process. Various individuals were picked out and were led off, ostensibly to Okic, to be court martialed. They did not reach Okic, but were slain a mile and a half away from the castle.

I had savored the hospitality of this medieval relic for four days when, on the fifth morning of my sojourn there, the Reds lined us up in columns of fours and told us that we were to be sent to Jastrebarsko. We were marched to Zdencin, where boxcars were awaiting us at the railroad station. We formed groups of four and were "sorted out." Commissar Stanko Canak then demonstrated the heroism for which Partisans were celebrated in the Western press by beating prisoners over the head with his German-made revolver. When a captive fell under the weight of the blows, Commissar Canak jumped up and down upon the prostrate figure of his victim.

Eighty to a hundred prisoners were packed like cattle into each boxcar. In the stifling atmosphere of these conveyances, the heat of summer made our situation unbearable. While we were being loaded into the cars, the Communists would grab hold of heavily bearded men, or those whom they said were "indecently dressed," or anyone whose looks they especially disliked. Such individuals were beaten to death with clubs or rifle butts, or else had their throats cut.

Partisan "heroism" manifested itself also in the form of peppering the crowded boxcars with rifle shots. They made a great joke out of this, saying that they were shooting holes in the side of the cars in order to give us fresh air. Some prisoners died of bullet wounds, others from starvation, thirst, heat, or general exhaustion. A rumor went around that all Croatian war prisoners were going to be turned over to the Russians, against whom we had fought with at least as much determination as had the Germans. Our train was heading for a Russian zone of occupation. When they took charge of us, they would forward us to Siberia to perform forced labor in the mines and lumber camps. We also heard that we were going to be taken either to Petrinja or to Sisak, where we would be slaughtered.

When we were all aboard, the train started out. It went first to Draganic, then received orders to go back to Zdencin. From there it proceeded to Jastrebarsko and Ilovac. From the last named place, it departed for an unknown destination. Many prisoners believed that we were en route to Budapest. But, after traveling back and forth in this manner all night, we found ourselves in Karlovac when dawn broke.

The boxcars were opened, and we got out. Communist guards and Serbian inhabitants of Kordun and Banija were all lined up waiting for us. We had to pass between them, giving them a good opportunity to beat us with all sorts of objects. Some men were killed by their blows, others knocked unconscious, while all of us were badly banged up. In this state we arrived at the bridge which crosses the Kupa River. Since the old permanent bridge which used to span this stream was destroyed during the war, the structure that we had to cross was only of a temporary nature. Communist guards stood in two lines all along the bridge. Once again we had to "run the gauntlet" between them, going two at a time. Since there were no protective rails, the merciless beating caused many Croatian captives to fall into the Kupa and drown. Those of us who got across the Kupa found other Communists waiting. They beat us again and made us run, or at least tried to; most of us were so weary that we could hardly pull one leg after another.

When we passed through the streets of Karlovac, however, the inhabitants tossed bread and other food to us. The Communists fired at everyone who endeavored to catch or pick up these viands. Thus, many men died trying to get a bite to eat.

We were taken to the barracks that the Domobrans had occupied during the war. This building had suffered a good deal of damage from fire. Our guards pushed fifty of us into each room. Since the floors were half burned and in constant danger of collapsing, we were not kept in these barracks for any length of time. We were driven out onto the streets of Karlovac and across the bridges leading over the Mreznica and Kupa Rivers. Finally, the column halted at Turanj, where we were lodged in another military barracks in which there were already two thousand Croatian soldiers. They were animated skeletons. The living conditions in this camp were intolerable; there was not a tree in the barracks yard, so we were exposed to sun, wind, and rain according to the whims of nature. Once a day we received food of a sort. It, too, was cooked in gasoline barrels, and was an indigestible mess of spoiled beans, a kind of corn hodge-podge, and a few decagrams of corn bread.

In the Turanj camp, we were formed into platoons and battalions. I was assigned to the Sixth Reserve Battalion. Croatian civilians were not allowed to enter our encampment or prison. However, anyone who had a son, friend, or relative in the Eighth Kordun Division was allowed to visit us. Sometimes, they would give us a piece of bread in return for our last articles of clothing. Also, they would "identify" us, usually as Ustashas. These "identified" prisoners were herded down to the Kupa River, and slain on its banks. Typhoid fever caused many deaths, too. Women and children succumbed to this malady in great numbers, and, finally, all who were left alive were removed from Turanj. There remained in this place only young men between eighteen and thirty-five, who had the strength and stamina to endure the hardships and dangers to which we were subjected. While we were at Turanj, I estimated that approximately fifteen hundred Croatians were executed there, or at the neighboring camp at Dubovac.

From Turanj, those of us who survived were removed to a prison camp at Svarce. This place of detention was surrounded by barbed wire fences three to four meters high. Behind the wire, there were watch towers where guards armed with machine guns and other automatic weapons were posted. The Svarce camp was located on a plain which was entirely devoid of houses of any kind. We were watched here with special care, electric wires being intertwined with the barbed wire. Our days in this place were filled with the usual horrors.

After several days at Svarce, we were transferred to a stadium which stood in the middle of a plain. Here we were lined up in the units to which we had been assigned. We thought that we were all going to be killed, since the Communists had machine guns in position ready to fire. Instead, we were sorted out into new groups which were formed according to age and military districts. The latter were the same as those into which Royal Yugoslavia had been divided.

I belonged to the Osijek Military District. Therefore, I was transferred from the Sixteenth to the Fourth Reserve Battalion. In this unit, I met some old acquaintances. A Communist Colonel made a speech to us. He said that we were not prisoners any longer, but free men because there was now no danger to be feared from bandits and Fascists. Following this harangue, we received orders to march off by columns of fours.

It was just about twilight when we set off for Generalski Stol. We marched until midnight, when we halted to eat. Two hundred and fifty prisoners died hungry, however. They were taken from the column, led to the rocks overhanging the Mreznica stream, and murdered.

We survivors went through Generalski Stol, and on to Gornja and Donja Dubrava. Since the highway bridge that connected Donja Dubrava was destroyed, we had to use the railroad bridge to get across. Once on the other side, we did not pick up the highway again, but continued along a mere footpath or track. The guards told us that we were going this way because the highway was very dusty, and our lungs might suffer. We were convinced that there was some reason other than this for abandoning the main road.

The path that we were following led over a ravine that was about six hundred feet deep. We had to cross this place in pairs. Scrambling over sharp rocks, many prisoners did not make the crossing. Whoever collapsed and could go no further was knifed by the guards who brought up the rear.

We arrived at Ogulin, where the population gave us a friendly welcome, tossing parcels of food to us. Our Partisan guards beat or shot these benefactors, but the Communists could not stop the inhabitants from trying to assist us in every possible way. We were brought to a military barracks which was located in the center of the town. Here, three thousand prisoners were crowded into a small courtyard. The rest of us were taken to the Ogulin Gymnasium and put into an enclosed pen, surrounded by an exceptionally high barbed wire fence. Communist officers and soldiers "visited" us, as did civilians from the villages of Kordun and Banija. They came to us for the purpose of "recognizing" and "identifying" individuals who had committed "crimes." Naturally, anyone who was known to have killed a Partisan or Communist sympathizer was, *ipso facto,* a criminal, even though he had slain his man in battle.

One day we were given some kind of blue paper on which we were made to write down specific data concerning our past lives. Some prisoners carefully and completely filled out the questionnaire. These prisoners thought they would not be harmed since their only "crime" was that of defending their fatherland, Croatia. Many of us anticipated the worst, so we put down only those facts which could not possibly be held against us. When all the data sheets were finished and collected, they were sent to the county (opcina) authorities. Because of the abnormal conditions that prevailed in regard to transportation, it took a long time for the answers to come back. When the opcina replies did start to come in, prisoners had to go to divisional headquarters for questioning every day. After these hearings, the prisoners interrogated were "sent home." That is, they were either killed or transferred to another prison camp.

Ogulin stands on the Dobra River, which flows through a deep abyss, the Gjulin Ponor. This chasm extends along the left side of the highway leading to Ogulin, in Habsburg days the command post of the Ogulin Border Regiment of the famed Military Frontiers. On the right side of this thoroughfare can be seen the remains of the ancient city of the Frankopani (Frankopans), greatest of the Croatian noble houses, which contributed seven bans and many distinguished soldiers, clerics, administrators, and sponsors of Croatian cultural and educational life before the extinction of the clan in 1671.

Frankopangrad was in ruins, even in 1945. But the old walls, built of enormous stones, made ideal torture chambers, for screams of victims immured behind them could not be heard outside. When they had finished with the victims whom they "interrogated" in the gloomy chambers of this old noble stronghold, the Partisans threw what was left of them, living or dead, into the Gjulin Ponor.

The Reds did not dispose of all of us in this manner. They were nothing if not versatile in devising means of execution and finding a wide variety of places in which to employ them. They took those of us who had not been interrogated behind the thick walls of Frankopangrad and lined us up near St. Peter's Church, facing Ostarije. There were only a little over eight hundred of us left now, and we were drawn up in column formation four abreast. A Partisan officer delivered a speech in which he said that we were no longer prisoners, but were to be assigned to combat units of the Yugoslav Army. Then he added, "We ought to know which ones of you were in the Ustasha formations for even so much as an hour. Let such men, and also those who were only registered as future recruits for the Ustashas, leave the ranks."

Some men took this opportunity to identify themselves with the Ustashas, even though they never had any sort of connection with that organization. They had suffered too much to endure any more. All they wanted now was a quick end to their troubles and to lives that no longer seemed worthwhile. Some men who left our column on this occasion tried to get me to come along with them. One of my old friends, Ivo Safar, caught hold of my shirt sleeve and urged me to go with him and the hundred or so others who were reporting as Ustashas. But, I reasoned that while there's life there's hope, and knew that those whom the Partisans could not suspect of being Ustashas would live longer than the poor fellows who wanted to get it all over with. Therefore, I got Safar to remain with me in the column, instead of vice versa.

After the men who claimed to be Ustashas had fallen out of our column, they were lined up separately. An illiterate Partisan counted them off on his fingers, ten at a time. There were one hundred and eighty-three of them in all. The Partisan colonel then asked, "Is there anyone else? Let him report now if he wishes to go home to his wife and children, or to his parents, for it is a hard life to be a soldier in the Yugoslav Peoples' Army and to have to march twenty-five or thirty miles every day."

His words caused four more either credulous or despairing fellows to go over from our column to that of the Ustashas. The latter moved off four abreast towards Klek. We heard the following day that all of the presumed Ustashas were murdered when they arrived at this place. Later, we discovered that this rumor was true.

New prisoners were added to the column which once again reached a strength of fifteen hundred. We were divided into two groups. One of these remained in the Ogulin barracks, while the other was quartered in the Gymnasium. Some of us were assigned to guard detail, which watched the barracks, but had only empty rifles for such duty. And, whereas the regular Communist guards were changed every hour, we prisoners, who now were associated with them, had to stand out in the summer heat for four to five hours at a stretch.

New contingents of war prisoners, especially captives taken in Istria, kept arriving at Ogulin. We had to make room for them and were transferred to the small village of Ostarije. Among us, there was a priest who had concealed his identity until this time. Now he went to the parish priest at Ostarije and asked to be allowed to offer Mass to the prisoners. He received permission to do so, and some of us helped him to celebrate this low Mass. Some time later, the Communists found out about the ceremony. The prisoner priest, and some of those who had assisted him, were arrested and "transferred" (murdered).

Considerable numbers of Croatian soldiers, many of them descendants of the old *Granicari* (frontiersmen) of Habsburg times remained in the vicinity of Ogulin. They knew how to wage a guerrilla-type warfare in the woods, and they called themselves *Krizari* (Crusaders). These last defenders of historic Croatia gave the Communists much trouble.

For a guerrilla group to operate successfully against the power commanded by an organized state, it has to receive support either from the local population or from some outside source. During the war, Tito's Partisans received massive assistance of every kind from the Russians, British, and Americans. It was only this outside foreign aid which enabled them to hold out in the woods and mountains of Serbia, Montenegro, Bosnia, and Hercegovina until 1945. In Dalmatia, Istria, and Slovenia, of course, they were aided by the collapse of the Italians in 1943, and their surrender of huge quantities of arms, ammunition, and other war materials and supplies. Also large numbers of former soldiers of the Royal Italian Army joined them.

The Krizari received no help from the outside world. In fact, the Communists issued a stern warning to the population of Croatia to refrain from aiding the Krizari in any way. One day, the Krizari units entered the village of Skradnik and asked the inhabitants to give them food. Even had they not wanted to do so, the villagers had small choice in the matter. On the following day they dutifully reported what had happened to the Communist authorities in Ogulin. The Communists then initiated the practice of taking "hostages" from several villages in the vicinity. These "hostages," ten in number, were taken to the church at Ostarije and lined up in front of a long wall. There was one girl among these victims; the other nine were men. I think that the young woman's last name was Bozicevic. Ten regular holes were dug out in front of the wall. Four Communists were detailed to shoot each hostage.

We stood in nearby galleries to watch the scene enacted. Four of the victims knelt down to pray. The others stood erect and glared defiantly at the guards. A Partisan staff sergeant was among the four who were charged with shooting the girl, who was only about eighteen years old. Suddenly, he threw down his rifle and refused to go through with the execution. Then he was placed alongside the ten original victims and shot with them.

From this time on, any connection with the Krizari, whatever the circumstances, was made punishable by death.

After a time we prisoners, now, by the grace of Tito, Yugoslav soldiers, were sent from Ostarije to Josipdol, and from there to Licke Jesenice. We carried with us cauldrons, sacks of potatoes, beans, and other food. During the march, some men collapsed and had to be carried by others.

From Licke Jesenice, we went on to Saborsko. We had to follow a road that climbed steeply up into the hills; fifteen men who were unable to keep up with the rest were killed. When we got to Saborsko, we were detailed to the nearby village of Kiseljak. There were a number of lumber mills in this place, but during the war most of them burned down. We performed our military exercises among the rocks that dotted this vicinity. After these exercises, we had to work on the construction of barracks for the KNOJ (Communist National Defense of Yugoslavia). The KNOJ were the Yugo-Communist elite troops, a kind of gendarmerie like the Guardia Civil in Spain. They had the task of maintaining domestic security, that is, of murdering everyone who was opposed to the government in Belgrade.

The "Death Marches" of most of the Croatian prisoners ended in August, 1945. Ours was still a long way from its finish, however. At least prisoners no longer were murdered in such numbers as they were between May and August of this year. Two hundred and fifty of us were sent to the Plitvicka Lakes, and were quartered at Poljanak. We had to work day and night here on the construction of a barracks. A Captain of K.O.S. (Counter Intelligence Service), by the name of Marko Polovic, took a few of us away from Poljanak, ostensibly to transfer these few to another unit. None of these people were ever heard from again.

We remained at Poljanak until the end of January, 1946. Then we were led through Sertic Poljana and Saborsko to Licke Jesenice. From this last place, we ploughed through a snowstorm to get back to Ogulin. At this old Granicari town, we were loaded onto a forty-car train which took us to Rijeka. Our original column was enlarged by the addition of other batches of Croatian prisoners at Ogulin. A contingent of captives who had been held at Bihac joined us, too. There were roughly seventy prisoners in each car.

We were transferred to trucks at Rijeka, and driven to Pazin. One part of the prisoner convoy stayed there, while the rest of the trucks proceeded towards Trieste. I was in one of the vehicles headed for the latter destination. We stopped to dig trenches and to erect fortifications which, we were told, were necessary because the Yugoslav Army was going to attack the British in Trieste.

On the night of March 3, 1946, we were ordered to return to Pazin. On the way there, eighty-odd prisoners escaped. They went to Trieste to try their luck with the Englishmen again. After this, whenever the Communists had occasion to murder any of our number, they would say that they, too, had "escaped to the British."

From Pazin, three hundred of us were sent back to Rijeka. Then we were transferred to Kanfanar and again back to Rijeka. During these marches and countermarches, a hundred men were executed for daring to ask their Communist captors why they had not attacked Trieste. The rest of us were told that we, too, would be killed if our conduct was suggested that we might be Fascists, Nazis, or Capitalists.

These useless and continued marches were too much for many prisoners whose constitutions had already been undermined by privations to which they had been exposed during the past year. Many men, who had withstood incredible torments and hardships up to this time, collapsed on the streets of Rijeka. I was one of them. At long last, I, too, had reached the stage where I neither could nor would go on. As I lay down on the pavement, a Communist kicked me and ordered me to get up.

"I cannot get up," I told him. "Go ahead, kill me!"

Another Communist gave me a good boot, also. Then they walked off and left me lying there. A lady who lived nearby dared to bring me something to eat. Her husband and son, the latter a young man near my own age, had been murdered by the Partisans at the end of the war. Since it appeared that the Communists had all gone away, I accepted her invitation to sneak into her yard. With a bit of food in my stomach, and a little respite from marching, I experienced a miraculous recovery of strength. While I rested in her home, she told me how the Partisans had murdered the citizens of Rijeka in wholesale lots as soon as they entered the city at the end of the war. Since I didn't want to bring a similar fate upon her, I did not abuse her hospitality, but reported to the village of Skrljevo where the rest of my group had been taken.

I explained that I had inadvertently lost my unit, but had hastened to rejoin it as soon as I ascertained its whereabouts. This story earned me such a hard slap from a Communist officer that my nose began to bleed. Then two staff sergeants, Branko Vukobratovitch and Lyuban Mutich, gave me a good beating. Delegate Dragan Lapchevitch, who also was from the Eighth Kordun Division, helped them in this agreeable task. They only stopped beating me when some other prisoners, or impressed Yugo-Communist soldiers, if you prefer, who also had lagged behind the command, showed up late as I had.

From Skrljevo, we went by train through Delnice, Ogulin, Karlovac, Zagreb, Dugo Selo, Novska, Slavonski Brod, and Vinkovci to Brcko. Here we were placed in a military building for the purpose of cleaning out the refuse left by prisoners who had preceded us here. Also, the KNOJ had occupied this building for a while before being sent to the Majevica Mountain to fight off the attacks of the Krizari.

When we had finished this task in Brcko, we were lodged in private homes in the village of Gornji Zabar. During our stay at this place, at least two prisoners were "transferred" every week. That is, they were murdered by command of the notorious Captain of Counter Intelligence, Marko Polovic.

We were in Donji and Gornji Zabar, Upper and Lower Zabar, to serve as a defense wall against the Krizari, whom dyed-in-the-wool Communists feared greatly. Perhaps, we were not considered to be a reliable element for such an important task, for we were transported to Brezovo Polje, which is about fourteen kilometers distant from Brcko. This was towards the end of May or June, 1946; we remained at Brezovo Polje until the end of the summer. One day while we were there, an automobile stopped in front of the school building, where a group of one hundred and twenty prisoners was held. Marko Polovic was in the car; he ordered seventeen of the captives to be taken off to an undisclosed destination. That was the last seen of these people.

One of the seventeen was a member of the prominent Kelava family. Following his removal, I was called into the office of Commissar Milosh Kokir. Marko Polovic was with Kokir in this office. They accused me of being connected with Kelava. I denied this, and, for so doing, I got a brutal beating which left me covered with blood. Finally, I was knocked unconscious. According to what a girl told me later, four Communists then took me to a house in the neighborhood to recover.

When I had recuperated from this incident, I was sent back to my unit. Fortunately for me, Milosh Kokir was transferred. Commissar Fuad Rescic, a Muslim Croat from Bihac, replaced him. Like most Muslims, Rescic was quite a decent fellow, even though he had seen fit to join the Communists. He informed me that I was likely to be executed anytime. He helped me and another Croat from Karlovac, I.C., get a transfer to Bjelina. Here we scrubbed floors, cut wood, and did other hard work. Staff Sergeant Mehmed Coric, another Bosnian Croat, supervised our labors and treated us fairly.

From Bjelina, I.C. and I were escorted to Tuzla, where we were interrogated by the K.O.S. of the Eighth Kordun Division. We were asked about the conversations that we had had with recruits whom the Communists had brought to Bjelina. After this questioning, we were sent off to Sarajevo, where we were assigned to the Sixth Battalion of the Sixth Military District. We were placed in a camp which was fenced in with barbed wire. Here we shared a room with some other Croatians who had been taken prisoner in 1945.

We were kept in the Bosnian metropolis for two weeks. Then we were sent by train through Visegrad, Uzic, Cacak, Velika Plava, and Belgrade to Petrovac. This town stands on the Mlava River. When we got off the train here, the good Serbian inhabitants of the place turned out in force to beat us with big sticks, wooden poles, and other blunt objects. We survived this reception only to be herded to the depot of the forest railroad, where we had to perch on wooden beams that were being transported. Riding in this precarious fashion, with no safeguards whatsoever, some men lost an arm or leg by scraping it against some object along the way. Four of our number fell under cars because of this primitive mode of transport, and the very bumpy ride over tracks that were in a poor state of repair.

Finally, our grueling trip ended at the foot of the Homoljske Planine. From here, we headed along a poor and extremely narrow forest road towards Hladne Vode. At every turn, we came upon the bodies of people who had been killed quite recently. No one in my group was murdered by our guards, although everyone who dropped from exhaustion received a sound beating to inspire him to new and better efforts for President Tito.

On arriving at Hladne Vode, we were given wheelbarrows and other equipment with which we were to bring sand from the river. Each of us had to complete a "norm," which was two hundred wheelbarrow loads of sand. Everyone managed to meet this "norm" on the first day of work here, but, after that, some men began to collapse from sheer exhaustion. Of course, they were beaten thoroughly and brutally for being weaklings. A German prisoner-of-war group was engaged in this work, too. Our guards did not let us converse with them, but I don't think they were faring any better than we were. Branko Vukobratovitch, Dragan Lapchevitch, and Stevan and Nikola Podgrajac excelled in maltreating us.

At this point, I should mention that we had in our group of guards some Partisan officers who had contracted the so-called *Partizanska bolest* or "Partisan epilepsy." This was a kind of seizure or nervous breakdown which perhaps was brought on by participation in too much wanton killing. These people sometimes actually foamed at the mouth and howled like mad men. When they had their fits, they often gave a rambling but detailed account of the crimes they had committed. However, they often beat us while so doing. Then again, some of them would throw themselves into the river with the intention of drowning, and we had to jump in after them to pull them ashore.

I had to work on the sand detail for only two days. As might be deduced from the fact that I survived privations and exertions which proved too much for many others, I was a very strong young man up to the time of my capture by the Partisans. At this time in 1947, I was still fairly strong, despite all that I had gone through. Thus, I was put to work on a job that involved holing out a tunnel through a mountain cliff. Forty of us were assigned to this laborious task. Some of this crew lost their lives, and others their eyesight, before we finished this project. All of us who survived were beaten regularly by our Communist guards. I got an especially bad walloping because I had written to my father for the first time since I left Croatia in May, 1945. He wrote back scolding me for not finding anything better to do than to work in the People's Militia. I was forced to send him a second letter in which I suggested that he join the Peasant Cooperatives. This recommendation enraged him. He fired back a reply which asked why I had changed my views. Why was I now supporting the Communists? This correspondence resulted in my being summoned to the office of the commander of the work unit. Once again I was questioned about a lot of things, and then beaten because of my non-Marxist background.

At the end of August, 1947, we left Hladne Vode. We traveled by train through Petrovac, Pozarevac, Kraljevo, Cacak, Visegrad, and arrived finally at Sarajevo. Here we were placed in the Cengic-villa camp. Forty men were transferred into a "Disciplinary Battalion" in Butmir, which is near Sarajevo. Those individuals who had displayed evidences of "disobedience," especially if they had manifested such tendencies during "political" lectures, were sent away, probably to the mines on the Romanija Mountain.

Early in September, we departed by train from the Bosnian capital. We passed through Hadzic, across the Ivan Planina, through Mostar, Trebinje, and Bilec, arriving at Niksic. From there we were taken on foot northward to the foot of a mountain which stands close to the Zeta

River. For a little more than a month, we worked to construct a military airport at this place. While so doing, we received continual beatings, not only from our Communist guards but at the hands of Montenegrin civilians as well. Four of our number were led off and not heard from again. One of them was a medical doctor. Another hardy soul expressed a favorable view of the British and Americans during a "political" lecture, that is, a Marxist indoctrination session. He was taken to the office of the commander where he was beaten and tortured brutally. Then he was marched off in the direction of Niksic, where he was probably murdered.

These incidents inspired a panicky fear in us, since none could say what would happen next and to whom. At last, however, we were sent back to Sarajevo, where we underwent another interminable interrogation. We were photographed and fingerprinted. Some of us were assigned to the headquarters of the Sixth Military District. These men did not come back from this assignment. It is likely that they were liquidated.

On October 10, 1947, the few of us who had survived all the grueling experiences of the past two and a half years received military identification cards. These contained our personal data. The most important item was that we had served in the "People's Liberation Army" during the past twenty-nine months. My card was signed by Major Blamisa, Commander of the Sixth Construction Battalion.

At long last, the "Death Marches" were over. I was free to return to my birthplace to await new persecution by Tito's Yugo-Communists.

Signed: Ivan P.

Cleveland, Ohio

Document XXXV

The following account opens with a description of the Kanal extermination camp, where the eyewitness S.I. was imprisoned after the "liberation" of Zagreb. S.I. devotes over one-fourth of his testimony to an especially tragic case of a prisoner who was shot as he asked his mother to bring him strudel the next time she came to the camp. The witness then relates his "Death March," and the atrocities committed by the Thirteenth and Nineteenth Kordun Brigades in the Cazmanska Suma, Bjelovar, and elsewhere. From Bjelovar, the "Death Marchers" were conveyed by cart to Osijek; from there, they went on foot to Petrovaradin. Here, the witness was placed in a concentration camp, where he saw many prisoners die from typhoid fever or from the Partisan bullets. From Petrovaradin, a very long column of prisoners was taken to Vrsac. Two weeks later, they were taken to Kovin, where the eyewitness was set free.

When the Partisans entered Zagreb, I was arrested and imprisoned in the concentration camp at Kanal along with many other officers, soldiers, and civilians.

The treatment meted out to us in the Kanal Camp was indescribably inhuman. However ill we became, we had no medical care whatsoever, and we received almost nothing in the way of food. We also suffered greatly from lice and accumulated filth. The new Communist authorities especially exerted themselves to root out all so-called "Fascists" and their sympathizers. Every night they would take those they found away in trucks. Later, we were told what we had suspected all along; these victims were conveyed to places where they could be slaughtered and their bodies disposed of conveniently.

The Kanal Camp was guarded by Serbian and Macedonian units. Many horrible scenes were enacted at this camp, but there was one which even today stands out vividly in my mind. Many women, wives, mothers, daughters, sweethearts, or other relatives or friends of the prisoners gathered outside the barbed wire that surrounded the camp and peered through the barrier hoping to see their loved ones. Sometimes, when the guards were not looking, they tossed bundles of food or other necessities to us.

There was one woman who managed to give a package of food to her son; probably, she had bribed some of the guards to turn their backs while she did this. Her boy was a tall, husky fellow, an eighth grader in one of the local gymnasiums. His mother asked him what he wanted her to bring the next time she came to the camp.

"Strudel!" he answered.

A guard turned around and from a distance of about five feet shot the youth with his revolver. "Here's your strudel!" he shouted.

The young man fell to the ground, started up convulsively, as though he were going to attack his slayer, then fell back and lay motionless. His mother screamed, while everyone else stood there dumb-stricken, their faces ashen. All other prisoners left the vicinity of the fence and hurried back into the center of the camp.

Twelve days after this occurrence, I was sent to Bjelovar with other prisoners. Men from other places of imprisonment joined our column, until there were between eight and ten thousand captives included in it. Mounted Partisan escorts from the 13th and 19th Kordun Brigades accompanied us.

We marched on foot for thirteen miles, then traveled fifty more miles by rail. At about 5:00 P.M. the next day, we arrived at Bjelovar. There were no more than 6000 of us left to enter the prison camp, which was situated at the end of Zagreb Street. The elderly, the sick, and the exhausted lay along the route of our foot march. Often, we heard shots ring out behind or ahead of us as the guards finished off these people. We passed their bodies often enough, and sometimes saw the escort kill them in front of our very eyes. The worst slaughter occurred in the

Cazmanska Suma (Forest), where we had rested before picking up the train. When we entered Bjelovar, forty prisoners were shot in full view of the citizens of the town.

We remained in Bjelovar for six days. Then a new column was formed, loaded onto a train, and sent to Osijek. From Osijek we went on foot to Petrovaradin, where we were placed in a concentration camp in which I found some of my old colleagues. This camp lay outside an old fortress which dates from Habsburg and Granicari times. In it, we contracted typhoid fever. Since we received no medical attention whatsoever, an average of fifteen men died daily of this malady. The guards dragged off the sick and the dead together, pulling them by an arm or leg. Whenever someone suffering from a high fever asked for water, the Partisans would kill him immediately. Otherwise, however, the guards did not murder prisoners here as they did at so many other places.

From the prisoners held at Petrovaradin, a column of 10,000 men was formed. It proceeded on foot through Novi Sad and Titelj to Vrsac. Some of us were convinced that the column was being led northward to Russia. I was one of those who believed this. Therefore, I wrote a "last message" to my wife on a post card that I had concealed on my person. This card I hid under a stone near a bridge which spanned the Danube River. As I had hoped would be the case, some good Croat found it, and one way or another got it to my wife. She was greatly frightened to learn that I thought we were being taken to Russia.

Actually, my enforced journey had a happier ending. We were held at Vrsac for two weeks, then were sent to Kovin. There we remained for two and a half weeks, after which I was allowed to return to my home.

Many of my fellow prisoners were less fortunate.

Signed: S. I.

Rome, Italy
October 13, 1954

Chapter 8

Massacre Sites In Slovenia

Document XXXVI

M.M. opens his account by explaining why the Croatian troops and masses of civilians wanted to surrender to the Western Allies in Austria. The eyewitness then describes the Croatian surrender at Bleiburg and extradition of prisoners to Yugoslavia. He also depicts the Partisans' brutalities toward prisoners of war at Slovenjgradec and Alfentz.

On May 6, 1945, I was listening to a broadcast of the Zagreb Radio Station when it was announced that the retreat of the German armies in the Balkans caused the Croatian Government to order the evacuation of the capital. Friends called on me to discuss this unwelcome news. At this time everyone thought that the Army would have to retreat to Austria and that there the Western Allies would unite with us in order to check the spread of Communism. No one realized that Great Britain and the United States were so completely committed to their wartime Communist bedfellows that they would fail to take advantage of the opportunity to make use of the intact and unbeaten Croatian Army, which had fought successfully against many varieties of Marxists for four long years. The population of Croatia in general, and of Zagreb in particular, believed that the Government of Dr. Pavelic had concluded a "liberation" agreement with the British and American Governments, whereby they would aid us in establishing a democratic regime in the Croatian State.

Imbued with this conviction, a host of civilians joined the military caravan which was proceeding towards the Slovenian and Austrian borders. Naturally, this civilian influx hampered the operations of our military. Nevertheless, Tito's much publicized Partisan formations were not able to give us any great amount of trouble until after we entered Slovenia.

I myself saw nothing of the Partisans until we got to Celje. Here the Germans had turned over their armament and transport to the Slovene Partisans. The Croatian military, however, contemptuously refused the demand that they, too, lay down their arms at this point. Officers and men alike knew that Tito's people had not taken prisoners at any time earlier in the war, unless they wished to torture them to extract information from them. There was no reason to suppose that they would behave any differently now. Our military escort brushed aside the Partisans who tried to impede our further progress and we made our way to Slovenjgradec (Windischgratz).

We remained in this little city for a while and then went on to Dravograd. As we were approaching the bridge in Dravograd that leads across the Drava, a Croatian officer passed my particular group. In a loud voice he shouted out to us: "My friends, we have been deceived! Whoever wants freedom had better flee with us into the woods!"

I was so impressed by this warning that I turned back from Dravograd and sought to attach myself to some Croatian group which was not going to surrender tamely. After some searching, I was able to locate a body of troops led by a colonel whom I knew and trusted. Major K., a junior officer in this colonel's command, asked me to determine the extent of the Partisan concentration around Bleiburg. I was appointed as scout for this command and set out for Bleiburg to execute the assignment given me.

Since I had received almost nothing to eat and had very little sleep since leaving Zagreb days before, I became extremely tired and hungry. On my way towards Bleiburg, I came to a small hut in the forest. Its owner was a kind man who gave me some food, the first real meal that I had an opportunity to eat in many days. Then I decided I had better lie down for a while to recuperate from the exertions to which I had been exposed. I asked and received permission from the man who had befriended me to rest for a time in his dwelling. Actually, I fell into a deep slumber which lasted for almost two full days!

When I had awakened, the wife of the owner of the hut had just returned from Schwarzenbach, where she had gone to purchase flour. She told me that the Communists were loading all captured Croatian soldiers into trucks and sending them back to Croatia. Also, the British were disarming our soldiers but refusing to allow them to stay in Austria, or even to enter that country when they could prevent them from doing so.

I was not a professional soldier myself, and the alarming news conveyed to me by this woman caused me to deliberate for a long time about my own plight and that of my nation in general. It seemed to me as if the game were up; we had no place to go and no prospect of being able to wage a successful resistance for any length of time. I decided that I would go directly to the nearest Communist headquarters I could find and surrender there.

This was the greatest mistake of my entire life.

Near Schwarzenbach I ran into a young man attired in Partisan uniform. We struck up a conversation and I found that he came from a solidly Catholic family. He had joined the Partisans only because he was afraid of being shot by the Germans, whose stupid system of "reprisals" drove many non-Communists into Tito's ranks. As we were walking along, conversing amiably enough, another young man joined us. He was armed with a German machine gun. I accompanied this pair to Communist headquarters in Schwarzenbach. When we arrived there, the Partisans searched me and put me in a cell. Somewhat later they brought three other Croatians in to keep me company.

I think that we remained in the Schwarzenbach jail for about a week. On the last day we were there, we underwent a lengthy interrogation; after it was over, the same two Partisans whom I had met en route to this place came into our cell and beat us thoroughly. While they were doing so, I could hear other Partisans outside the cell suggesting that a woman by the name of Savka continue beating us after the two men were through. But she answered: "I can't beat them! I'm too tired!"

A few hours after this, we were taken into a courtyard where we joined a group of Croatian officers and soldiers. These prisoners also had been subjected to beatings and many of them were ready to collapse, partly because of the maltreatment they had received, partly because they had gone without eating, drinking, or sleeping for days on end. That fine female, Savka, had beaten them with a whip and club, while the Partisan guards kept guns trained on them. The guards only sought an excuse to shoot them at the first sign of resistance. Savka had so tired herself at this highly congenial task that she had no energy left to expend upon myself and my cellmates, when it was our turn to receive her attentions.

From the courtyard, we were taken to a larger building which was located in another part of the village. Another Communist military unit had charge of this place. We spent a few days here, then were taken by truck to another town whose name I do not remember. From this place we had to walk to Dravograd and from there to Slovenjgradec (Windischgratz).

Our captors lined us up in front of the Communist headquarters in Slovenjgradec. The commanding officer approached our group and said angrily to the soldiers who had conducted us there: "Why did you bring them here? You should have followed orders and liquidated them along the way! Don't bring any more of them here! As for this bunch, we'll keep them here tonight." I do not recall the name of this Communist Commissar, but I do remember hearing at the time that he was a former Serbian school teacher.

About seventy of us were confined in a large room, which I think had been previously used as a school room. Two Partisans guarded us carefully at all times. I suspected that we were going to be "liquidated" that night. Fortunately, however, the Partisans had a regular orgy in the courtyard and got so drunk that they were no danger to anyone. However, the men guarding us did not drink, and since they were armed with machine guns, we could not take advantage of the inebriates.

The next day, the Croatian officers and officials in our group were subjected to a special interrogation. One of them told me later how the Partisans beat him on this occasion. They knocked him down, trampled all over him, and broke several of his ribs. When they were through questioning him, they threw him to the bottom of the stairs head first. His hands were chained while all this was going on.

After we had been confined here for a few days, the guards told us that we were to be sent to work in the Voyvodina. Some of our group did go, but we learned later that the majority were "liquidated" after they got to this province. Several more days passed, during which we were split up into several smaller groups. Each group was placed in a separate room. There were now about twenty people with me. Every night screams uttered by men who were being tortured in neighboring cells could be heard. Towards midnight one evening, we heard the Partisans taking prisoners from the nearby rooms into the courtyard. The prisoners were left out in the open all night long. Somewhat later, one of the inmates in another room told me that he had seen the Partisans whip and beat the prisoners on the way to the courtyard.

One day we received orders to clean the yard and then to scrub down the interior of the building in which we were imprisoned. After this was done, we were taken to a work camp where we were put to forced labor. While we were so engaged, a Communist soldier approached our group, held up a pistol in front of us, and said proudly: "I killed 1200 Ustashas with this."

After a few days of hard labor, we were packed into freight cars and told that we were being sent to Maribor. Since there were only two guards with us, I thought that perhaps we were going to be sent to our homes. But when we got to Maribor, we were again confined in a carefully guarded prison. While we were incarcerated there, we had to work in the railroad yards during the daylight hours.

Our stay at Maribor was brief. Soon we were loaded onto trucks and taken to the Austro-Slovenian border. There were a number of Rumanians, Hungarians, and Germans as well as Croatians in our group. The Germans had built an underground factory at the town of Alfentz and we were put to work there.

The factory was guarded heavily. Even the village children were kept away from it so they could not slip food packages to us. One day a new prisoner from northern Croatia joined us. Since he spoke a different dialect[1] from the rest of the Croatian prisoners, the Communists evidently suspected that he was an "enemy of the people" and shot him.

I could continue this tale *ad infinitum.* It is the above-mentioned incidents, however, which have impressed themselves most indelibly upon my mind. I saw and experienced these horrible occurrences while I was a prisoner of the Partisans, during the most bloody days of the Communist rise to power in my native land. My experiences were far

---

1 Probably the man from northern Croatia was a "kaj" speaker. Most Croatians today use the "sto" dialect, but the "kaj" and "ca" are still spoken here and there (ed.'s Note).

less painful than those of thousands and thousands of my poor countrymen.

All the statements that I have made are, in God's name, true, and I am ready to swear that all I have told is, to the best of my recollection, in full accordance with the truth of events as they actually happened.

Signed: M. M.

Erie, Pa.
March 31, 1953

Document XXXVII

Partisan atrocities against the war prisoners at Ilirska Bistrica and Rijeka are described.

I was mobilized or conscripted into the Yugoslav Communist Army in October 1944. As a Partisan soldier, I moved with my unit through Hercegovina, Dalmatia, Lika, the Croatian Primorje (coastland) and northern Dalmatia.

After the end of the war, my detachment went to Ilirska Bistrica where we stayed ten days. During the time I spent there, I saw many captive Germans and a number of Croatian Domobrans. I saw no Ustashas; they were killed as soon as they were captured. About 20,000 half-starved German prisoners were taken to Rijeka. They presented a horrible sight with their skeleton-like faces and torn uniforms. Many of them had no shoes. Those who collapsed and could go no further were killed where they stopped. Many bodies were strewn on either side of the highway leading to the city. Their Partisan escort had no mercy for stragglers.

While I was stationed in Ilirska Bistrica, I got a pass to visit Rijeka, a famous old Croatian city which the Hungarians and Italians also claimed in the past. As I was walking back to Ilirska Bistrica, I saw a group of mass graves which were arranged to approximate a triangle. Some of these places of interment were between thirty and forty-five feet long.

Signed: B. B.

Rome, Italy
May 25, 1955

Document XXXVIII

This account reveals the slaughter at Kamnik of hundreds of Montenegrin and Croatian soldiers, among whom there were women and children.

At the end of the war we Montenegrins united with the Croatian Army and accompanied it during its withdrawal into Slovenia. Following the surrender of the Croatians to the British in Austria, we were disarmed by Yugoslav Communist forces at the Slovenian town of Celje. From there, we were taken to Kamnik with the understanding that we were to be sent from that point to our homes.

On May 13, some six hundred of us were crowded into a single building, where we were stripped of all our clothing except shirts and pants. Then our captors tied us together in fours. There were about thirty women and children with us who were treated the same way. That evening all of us, women and children included, were taken into a nearby forest.

Here, we were told to form a circle. When we had done so the Communists opened fire on us. I was hit three times in the forehead by the first wave of bullets, but evidently I have a very hard skull. However, I still bear a four-centimeter scar that shows where the bullets struck. Anyway, I collapsed on the ground and lost consciousness.

When I recovered my senses, I heard someone screaming. A Communist directed the beam of his flashlight into my face, but apparently thought I was dead, for he went off to check other "corpses." While I was lying on the spot where three of my brothers had fallen, I could hear, all around me, women and children screaming and wounded men begging to be killed. Also, I heard the Partisan executioners talking among themselves. They were quite upset because, when the fools lined us up in a circle and began firing they were spread out in a circle, too, outside of ours. Thus, in effect, they were shooting at one another as well as at us. Two Partisans were killed and two others severely wounded because of this bit of stupidity.

When morning dawned, I saw that two Montenegrins lying close to me had survived this holocaust also. They got up and hurried deeper into the woods. All of the Communists had gone so I, too, pulled myself together, broke the wire which tied me to my dead brothers, and fled into the forest myself. On May 22, I arrived safely in Austria.

Although all of the victims of the massacre in which I was involved were Montenegrins, I know that four hundred Croatian Domobrans were shot in the immediate vicinity on the same day, May 13.

Signed: M. M.

Linz, Austria
June 28, 1945

Document XXXIX

The following account of a Slovenian eyewitness first presents the pitiful condition of "Death Marchers" and then gives minute details about the massacres of Croatians and other prisoners-of-war at Bezigrad. The victims, among whom were many women, were shot, drowned, or killed in torture chambers. These Nazi-type slaughters of thousands of captives were in full swing in May and June 1945, but they were still in progress on a smaller scale as late as September of that year. Perpetrators of these slaughters were militiamen F. Sotosek, A. Sume, S. Krusc, and other Slovenian Communists. The account closes with a description of a massacre site at Prevalje near the Yugoslav-Austrian border, where about two thousand Croatian prisoners-of-war were murdered. At the very end of the account are details on the Partisans' files dealing with the Bezigrad massacres.

When Germany capitulated on May 6, 1945, various retreating armies were passing through Celje. There were Germans, Serbian Chetniks, Slovenian White Guards, and, most numerous of all, Croatians.

These several armies were proceeding from the direction of Zidani Most, Rogaska Slatina, and Maribor-St. Juraj respectively. They were heading towards Zalac-Slovenjgradec and Vojnik-Dobrna-Slovenjgradec. The Partisan fighters did not greatly bother the retreating columns much at first, except to snipe at them occasionally. As the refugees approached the Austrian frontier, however, many bitter battles were waged.

Some prisoners were taken by the Partisans in Slovenia. Later, the British repatriated into the hands of the Communists most of the Croatians and Slovenians who surrendered to them in Austria. I was living in Celje in Slovenia at this time and saw several prisoner columns pass through that town. They were in a pitiable condition, clothed in rags, starving, and exhausted. All along the roads they had traveled since falling into the hands of the Reds, lay the bodies of those who had been shot by the guards because they could not march fast enough or because they had dared to ask for water.

The Partisans at Celje were commanded by a fellow named Palcek, who came from Dramlje. He had his headquarters at Zgorno Sleme, close to his own home town. Other Partisan troops moved into this area later. I remember a brigade composed of Bosnian Serbs especially well. Their commander could not even write his own name; he just made a mark or drew a line when he was supposed to sign something. Nonetheless, he was appointed Commander of the Communist troops in Celje.

Most of the prisoners were taken to Camp Bezigrad near St. Anna, about three miles northeast of Celje. This camp was built by the Germans during the war. They had evacuated it at the beginning of May, leaving it fairly undamaged. The Partisans put barbed wire all around it so that flight was made virtually impossible. A road that led from Bezigrad to Blagojno went around the camp itself, which was located between Bezigrad and St. Anna, about a mile distant from either of these towns. In the camp were seven or eight barracks buildings, each about one hundred feet long. Near these barracks, there was a concrete water reservoir which rose a foot or two above the ground. There were two entrances to this reservoir.

Camp Bezigrad received its first prisoners on May 10, 1945, four or five days after the Germans capitulated. Very soon afterwards, perhaps on this day itself, the slaughters began.

The camp director was Franc Sotosek. He was between twenty-eight and thirty years old at this time, the son of a tailor from Blanc near Reichenburg. Later, he became director of the UDBA in Ljubljana and Celje. Also, he was a director of the Kmetijska Obdelovalna Zadruga Zasret, a worker's cooperative. I knew him personally. He was a tall, very strong fellow, with one bad eye. Sotosek's assistant was Anton Sume from Ljubecna. These two men were in charge of the mass butcheries that took place in or near Camp Bezigrad. They were assisted in the work of mass destruction by Militiaman N. Benesek from Dobje, or "Luka" as the Partisans liked to call it, and Stefan Krusc, also a native of Dobje.

Sotosek and Sume devised several methods of executing prisoners. Sometimes they had the militia guards crowd from one to two hundred men into the reservoir, which was built so low, they had to bend over double. Once they were locked inside, water was let in slowly until all were drowned. Then, other prisoners would go in to carry out the corpses and take them off to be buried together with people who were shot while the drownings were in progress.

Those prisoners who had the luck to be shot rather than drowned were stripped of their clothing at the camp. Then they were led off into a little valley which is fairly level and extends from the Bezigrad-Blagojno road below and around the camp running towards St. Anna. These prisoners were compelled to dig graves for themselves. After they had done so, the guards mowed them down with automatics and other types of weapons. The dead and the still living had a shallow layer of earth thrown over them. Since the Partisans were in a great hurry to get on with the killings, they did not trouble to bury the corpses very deeply.

There were other methods of killing captives put into effect by Sotosek and Sume, but I do not know their exact nature. I do know that in the camp there was a torture chamber, and that some people who were exposed to it died from the treatment they received.

The camp was very crowded; it may have contained as many as five thousand people at one time. As fast as one set of inmates was killed off, other candidates for death were shipped in. The majority of the individuals slaughtered here were Croatian soldiers, but there were some Slovenian Domobrans, a number of Chetniks who were captured near Zalac, and a few Germans. Many civilians, including a considerable number of women, were among the victims.

The residents of Celje knew all about the butcheries that went on, since they were performed in broad daylight as well as at night. Likewise, the people of Ljubecna, Blagojno, St. Anna, Zasret, and other nearby localities, were aware of what was taking place. Many of the inhabitants of these places saw the killings with their own eyes and some took snapshots of the scenes described. Tito's government sentenced anyone who was caught doing this to fifteen years imprisonment, but quite a few people were later found to have photos of the massacres in their homes.

All through May and June 1945, the mass executions continued. Slowly, they decreased in frequency and in the number of victims involved, but as late as September they were still in progress. In March 1946, the Yugoslav Armed Forces abandoned this worthy replica of the more notorious Nazi slaughter houses—Belsen, Buchenwald and Dachau.

Although access to Bezigrad was prohibited while the mass murders were going on, I had to discharge a number of errands for the camp authorities during this time. Thus I was in a good position to acquire knowledge of more details unknown to most of the residents of Celje.

After the camp was abandoned, I visited it in order to pick up discarded ammunition. I had ample opportunity to inspect Bezigrad itself and the areas where the butcheries had taken place and the mass graves were located. There are ten of the latter, each about seven hundred feet long and only six feet wide. They fill up one whole section of the valley mentioned above. The ground here is very unfirm underfoot, and anyone who walks on top of these mass graves is likely to fall down into them as the earth gives way beneath him. Often, when I had occasion to cross the valley, I could see heads, arms, and legs protruding from the long parallel trenches. Also, I frequently saw hungry dogs carrying off parts of the bodies.

The camp director, Sotosek, was quite an accomplished thief. He misappropriated the funds of the workers cooperative, of which he was a director, and sold things taken from the men he had murdered. Even the Tito government had enough of him, finally sentencing him to eighteen months imprisonment. One of the militiamen who took an active part in the murders, Stefan Krusc, is working at the present time in the Ulmann brick factory in Wolfsberg, Austria.

It will be seen from the foregoing narrative that I myself did not witness everything that went on in Camp Bezigrad. However, my uncle who was on duty at this place for four months, was also an eyewitness of the horrors that were perpetrated here. He gave me very frank accounts of what he saw. Since he is still alive today and a resident of Slovenia, I do not wish to have my name published at this time. The Tito regime always punishes the relatives of those who indict it in any way. Thus, it is able to employ an effective tactic of blackmail to insure the silence of many who are acquainted with the details of its crimes.

I have visited the site of the mass graves which are located precisely two and a quarter miles from Prevalje near the Austrian border. These graves are right at the Prevalje-Mezica road crossing, near the Austrian border, and close to the workers cooperative "Kraljevo," and a peasant house belonging to the Vodep family. There is also a partially destroyed church in this vicinity. About two thousand prisoners were killed here by a Bosnian Serb brigade. The peasants told me that the last man to be killed was the commander of the Croatian troops who were murdered. They did not recall his name.

There is one more circumstance that I should record. In the former Ravnikar building near the Policlinic, which the Celje UDBA used as their headquarters, a detailed record was kept of the executions carried out in Camp Bezigrad. It was in section Agit.-Prop., room four, on the shelf on the left wall, partition two. I actually had this record in my hands one time, but did not dare try to get it out of the building. It requires no imagination to comprehend what would have happened had I been caught with it.

This testimony has been read to me and I find that everything that I have said has been accurately and truthfully recorded.

Signed: K. L. V.

July 21, 1954

Document XL

Eyewitness S.P., and the Pioneers Company to which he belonged, surrendered to the Serbian Partisans at Celje. S.P. and a little over a hundred other young soldiers were separated from the main group and driven through Celje in the direction of Zagreb. After a five or six hour march, these young men were joined to a group of approximately one-thousand Croatian prisoners. This relatively short "Death March," during which twenty prisoners were murdered, was suddenly ordered back to Celje and taken to the soccer stadium. Here they found masses of other prisoners who were being "categorized" for slaughter. A witness' acquaintance helped him and a few other captives escape. Then they reported to the authorities as Partisans of the Eighth Kozara Brigade. As Tito's "soldier," S.P. not only saw how the "categories" of Croatian prisoners were led to slaughter, but, for four nights, was also a passive participant in the executions. The massacres which he saw carried out in the vicinity of Celje are therefore very dramatically described.

Young men born in 1928 were drafted into the Croatian Honor Work Service at the end of 1944. It was in this way that I found myself transported from Sarajevo to Zagreb. Here I found that some members of the Work Service were being sent to Germany to bolster the war economy of our flagging ally.

Since I had no desire to go to Germany, I decided to volunteer for service with the Ustashas. I was not quite sixteen years old at this time. The authorities assigned me to a Pioneer Company. I accompanied this unit on its retreat from Dubica to Zagreb in the first days of May, 1945.

We left Zagreb the night before the Communists entered this old capital of the Croatian Kingdom. The column of which our unit formed a part retired through Zidani Most towards Celje in Slovenia. We arrived at Celje after a four day march without having to do any fighting en route.

On the outskirts of Celje, however, we found that a force of Communists was holding a little bridge which led across the river. They had a tank with them which gave them the upper hand. Since it was after nightfall, we were unable to judge the strength of the forces opposing us.

The Communists told us succinctly: "The war is over. Surrender now, and go back to your homes. No one will be harmed in any way. Your wounded will receive hospital care." (We had with us an auto ambulance which was transporting four gravely wounded men).

We could tell that these Communists were Serbs by their Shumadian dialect. However, they seemed to speak fairly, so our commander, Branko, decided to negotiate with them rather than have us fight. We knew that the war was over indeed, and there did not seem to be any reason to prolong hostilities, if they could be avoided. But when Branko went to negotiate with them, they immediately pulled out pistols and shot him as he began to talk.

The loss of our leader caused us to surrender, because the Serbs told us that they had surrounded us to cut off our escape. Of course, all of us were very young people and fools enough to believe what they said, despite what they had done to Branko. We had separated from the rest of the column with which we had started out, so there were only a little more than a hundred of us, all under twenty. Many were only fourteen to sixteen years old.

That night the Serb Communists led us through the silent streets of the city of Celje. Towards morning they confined us in a large barracks which was located somewhere outside the far limits of the town. They told us they were going to escort us back to Zagreb. About eleven that night they did start us off in the general direction of the Croatian frontier. However, we noted that we were traveling along the side of the river opposite the one we had followed to reach Celje in our retreat. We marched for five or six hours along the left side of a railroad line. There were craters made by bombs or shells along the track. A number of Croatian soldiers who, like us, had been foolish enough to surrender to the Reds, rather than kill as many of them as possible even if they died themselves, were joined to our company of Pioneer recruits. There were now about a thousand of us altogether; we suffered greatly from hunger and thirst. I remember that many Slovene women brought us containers of water and drinking glasses, even though our Communist guards forbade them to do so.

During the march, the guards killed about twenty of us, just for sport, as hunters shoot squirrels or rabbits. All of these Communist guards were Serbs; they picked out the tallest men among us to murder. Some captives were killed, however, because they happened to be wearing good clothes which the Serbs wanted for themselves. When we observed what was going on, those of us who were well-dressed deliberately ripped or damaged our clothes to avoid attracting the lethal attentions of our guards.

Suddenly, we were ordered to halt. A courier riding a motorcycle brought some kind of order to the commander of our escort. He ordered us to turn around and start back towards Celje. We arrived there about midnight and were taken to an athletic stadium to spend the night. In the morning, a Serbian commissar made a speech to us from the grandstand of the stadium. He said that we were going to be separated into "categories," but that we had no reason to be afraid of this process by which Ustashas, Domobrans, Chetniks (Serbian royalists), and Germans would all be placed in separate groups. These several categories then would be subdivided according to years of enlistment in the several armed forces represented.

The "categorization" was duly carried out, and each group was placed in separate parts of the stadium. There were only five or six Chetniks, and about a hundred Germans among us. But there were so many Croatians and Slovenes, that the entire stadium was jam packed.[1]

We remained confined in this place for four days. During all this time, we had absolutely nothing to eat. No one dared to ask the Communists for food or any other comforts. There was a small pump on the stadium grounds, but to get a little drinking water it was necessary to wait in line for the better part of an entire day.

Every night the guards would take from eighty to a hundred captives, according to category, and lead them out of the stadium. We had an idea of what was happening to these people, so we all kept our eyes open, looking for an opportunity to get away. On the fifth night that I spent in the stadium, I had the luck to encounter an acquaintance from Sarajevo among the Communists who were guarding us. He permitted a few of us to scale the stadium fence and hide among the bushes outside. About an hour after we had made our "break," we heard several rifle shots in the distance. Then came a rapid burst of fire from automatic weapons. We knew that they were killing the detachment that had been taken out of the stadium that night; my countryman from Sarajevo who had allowed us to escape told us as much beforehand.

When daylight came, we decided that our best chance was to go boldly to the Communist barracks on the outskirts of the city and say that we were Partisan fighters who had become separated from our units. When we reported to the barracks, Communist officers asked us if we belonged to the 8th Kozara Brigade. We answered that this was indeed our unit and they took our word for it. They gave us enough to eat, but no clothing. I was wearing a German coat, the trousers of an Ustasha fighter, and a Domobran cap. I tore the frontal piece off the latter and sewed a red star in its place; fortunately, in the stadium I had found a red fez which provided sufficient material for the star.

---

[1] The "categorization" of prisoners in the Celje stadium and their subsequent wholesale liquidation is also well described in the first part of Document XXXIV.

Communist soldiers stationed in the barracks were almost all Serbians, although there were a few Montenegrins among them. On the first night we spent there, a platoon of some sixty or seventy guards filed out of the dormitories about twilight. They marched off to the stadium to escort the "category" of Croatian prisoners who were destined to be slaughtered that night. These Communist guards returned about two in the morning. They brought back with them good clothes, shoes, and valuables of all kinds which they had taken from their victims. I saw all this because I was on guard at the dormitories that particular night.

On the following evening at the same time, I was detailed to the guard group which was to carry out the nocturnal executions. We marched to the stadium and took out approximately one hundred men. The prisoners were lined up five abreast with a Red guard at the end of each file. Two guards armed with automatic weapons made up the rear of the column. We marched the prisoners around the city for four or five hours to tire them out. Finally, the column halted in front of a large one-story building. The captives were taken by twos into this structure. Inside they were beaten and stripped of all their clothing down to their underwear. Few Serbians bother to wear underwear, and I presume this is why most of the prisoners were allowed to keep their shorts and undershirts. When they had been stripped, their hands were bound behind their backs with wire. Then they were tied together in pairs, arm to arm.

There were about fifty or sixty Serb Communists inside the building. Among them were twelve or fifteen officers and commissars; there was also one woman Communist. She was from Dubica in Bosnia, and she advertised her presence by shouting at the prisoners on every possible occasion. She went around arm in arm with another Communist from Dubica; his first name was Sakib, but I did not learn his surname.

After the prisoners had been tied securely, they were taken out a rear door and marched into a sparse grove of trees, two or three hundred feet away from the building. Here they were killed. For four nights in a row I had to be a passive participant in these massacres. On the first two nights of such duty, we found two holes already dug to accommodate the corpses. These holes were approximately twenty feet long, six feet wide, and four and a half to six feet deep. The third and fourth nights, we had to dig the holes ourselves; there were five in all, because they were considerably smaller than the holes prepared for the first two nights I witnessed the executions.

The slaughters were carried out in the following manner. First, victims were forced into the holes in which they either knelt or stood up according to their degree of strength and reservoir of courage. The executioners shot them, either through the head or in the mouth. Some victims were stabbed to death, too. One eighteen-year-old Serbian juvenile delinquent attained great popularity among the guards, because of the pleasure he took in killing prisoners with his dagger. This sadistic pervert would utter cries of pure joy while he was picking out captives to kill.

Some of the prisoners did not die immediately. Screams came from the holes after every volley as those who were wounded begged to be killed. I especially remember how one wounded man kept howling from beneath a group of dead bodies. A Serbian went among the corpses stabbing with his bayonet in the darkness, until he finally found and killed the yelling man.

I witnessed all of this from very close range. Sometimes I was no more than thirty to forty-five feet away from the death holes. One night I had to go to the very brink of a pit in search of a shovel. I could see the prisoners kneeling or standing in the hole and the executioners at work among them. On the fourth night of my duty, one man managed to loosen the wires which bound him and escaped into the darkness. We received strict orders to keep quiet about this occurrence.

Neither I nor most of the other Communist guards did any of the killing. There were only about twenty Reds in all, chiefly officers, who acted as executioners. The rest of us had the job of throwing three or four inches of earth over mass graves after each night of slaughter. During my four nights of duty, I saw four large and ten smaller holes in all. A short distance away from the place where these murders occurred, was another large section of freshly covered earth; there were other graves in the vicinity. Of course, I did not dare to ask about the nature of these places.

In my guard platoon I recall especially a pair of twins, about twenty years of age. Their name was Stipetitch, I think. They came from Imotski, and had an uncle who owned a night club in Sarajevo before the war.

After my four-day tour of duty with the execution and burial squads, I was transferred to Zagreb. I was housed in barracks near the zoological garden, and was later assigned to a tank unit.

Signed: S. P.

October 2, 1955

Document XLI

Eyewitness I. M. and his group surrendered to the British at Tamsweg, Austria, on May 12, 1945. Nine days later, however, they were extradited to Yugoslav troops. Past Jesenice, the officers and drivers were separated from the rest of the prisoners and conveyed to Koruska Bela. Here the drivers were separated and driven first to Ljubljana, then to Sezana near Trieste. On June 20, the witness and other prisoner-drivers were assigned to drive trucks. On July 5, he and four other colleagues were taken to be shot at Donji Logatec near the Slovenian capital. The four driver-prisoners whose names are given

below were shot. Our witness, however, escaped and later was granted asylum in Italy.

During the war of 1941-1945 I served as a police driver in Zagreb. On May 7, 1945, I left Zagreb with other members of the police department in accordance with orders received from the Government of the Croatian State.

Our column reached Slovenia and then Austria in safety. On May 12, we surrendered to British forces at Tamsweg, Austria. Five days later, the English confiscated our weapons and on May 21, the commandant of the camp in which we were confined notified us that we were to leave all our wagons, cars, trucks, and other vehicles in Tamsweg. This British officer assured us that on this same afternoon his countrymen were going to transport us to another Croatian camp in northern Italy.

Indeed, the British did take us by truck to Rosenbach, which we reached at eleven o'clock that night. Here, the English delivered us into the hands of Yugoslav Communist forces who had trains waiting for us.

About a third of our number were civilians; the rest were military or police personnel. The trains started towards Ljubljana, but at the third station that we reached after passing Jesenice, the Reds ordered everyone except officers and drivers to get off the trains. After they had done so, the officers and drivers were placed in a special train and conveyed to Koruska Bela. Here, the officers had all their valuables taken away from them; then they were separated from the drivers.

We drivers were loaded into trucks and driven to Ljubljana. After a night in this town, we were sent on to Sezana near Trieste. All drivers and a few other men were locked up in a shop for a while.

Later, I was assigned to an automobile unit which was located in Donji Logatec near Ljubljana. On June 20, I was put to work driving a truck at this place, where there were a number of other prisoner-drivers. We were so employed until July 5. On that day a Communist first sergeant came to our quarters and told us that five of our number were being assigned to a Partisan division that was stationed in Donji Logatec.

Before our departure, we had to report to the commandant of the automobile unit. He gave us our letter of transfer to the new command in the presence of five Communist soldiers who were armed with machine guns. I noticed that the letter he handed us did not bear a seal. This fact aroused my suspicions, which were augmented when they took our working clothes away from us.

The five of us were escorted out of the village by the five armed Communists. I saw that we were going in a direction that was altogether different from the one in which the division to which we were to report was located. I asked one of the guards where they were taking us and he replied that we were en route to the Lika Division. Since I knew that there was no such division in Tito's army, I had a fairly good idea what was in store for us. Since our guards were armed and we were not, there did not seem to be much that we could do about the matter, however.

When we came to the last house in the village, the guards said they were going to take off two of the drivers to bring them to the new trucks that they were going to drive. In a few minutes the guards returned, but there was no sign of my companions. They took off the other two drivers and I remained alone with two of the guards. After I had asked them several times what actually was going on, they told me that we were all going to be shot. Having said this, they conducted me into the house mentioned. Here I found the militia commandant of the Ljubljana OZNA. He interrogated me, asking what I had done during the past four years. I told him that I had been a driver for the Zagreb police force. He remarked that then I had spent too much time transporting bandits and that I would not do so anymore. After this, the guards took my watch and my money. They wanted to appropriate my ring, too, but they couldn't get it off my finger. Then they bound my hands behind my back with wire and led me out of the room. As I came out into the air, I heard the pounding of machine guns. I accused my escorts of murdering my driver colleagues. They replied that they were going to murder me, also.

We walked along a little ways and the Reds dropped a few feet behind me. They were talking among themselves and I knew that they were debating about the most convenient place to kill me. Therefore, deciding that I had nothing to lose by making a break for it, I ducked in between a clump of trees and ran for all I was worth through the woods. Since the guards wasted a lot of time firing their machine guns at me before they started in pursuit, I had a good lead. None of their bullets hit me, and I succeeded in outrunning them. Although my hands were badly swollen, I managed to loosen my bonds after about three hours.

I arrived in Trieste on July 9. From there I was transferred to the refugee camp in the Italian, formerly Austrian, city of Udine on July 12. I was sent from there by airplane to Rome, which I reached on July 21.

The other four drivers who were with me when we were taken from Donji Logatec to be killed were: First Sergeant Petar Mikulic, born in 1913 near Mostar; Policeman Marijan Dzijan, born at Brcko in 1914; Policeman Mate Balen, born at Slavonski Kobas in 1919; and Driver Nikola Kurtov, born at Zagreb in 1917. They were all murdered at Donji Logatec as indicated above on July 5. I am sure they received no more of a court trial than I did.

During the time that I spent in Donji Logatec, a number of other drivers disappeared in the same manner. Ostensibly, they were "transferred to other units." Since I never saw or heard anything about them again, I assume that they, too, were killed.

This statement has been read to me and I declare that it corresponds to the true experiences that I had and to which I am willing to swear. A proof of the accuracy of my story can be found in the fact that the scars caused by the wire with which I was tied are still clearly visible on my hands and wrists.

Signed: I. M.

Rome
August 21, 1945

Document XLII

This account of a Slovenian eyewitness contains valuable details on two very large groups of Croatian prisoners, one numbering about two thousand and another about seven thousand, who were dumped down mine shafts at Lasko and Hrastnik. The witness also tells of a mass grave at Kosice, near Celje. His testimony closes with a general statement on the pitiful conditions of other groups of Croatian prisoners of war.

After World War II ended in May 1945, I saw with my own eyes what the Yugoslav Communists did to their opponents. They committed such horrible crimes that words cannot be found to describe these outrages in the detail that they deserve.

Men, women, and children, most of them Croatians, who fled to Austria to surrender to the British rather than the Russians, were turned over to Tito's Yugoslav Communists by the Englishmen. The Reds returned the captives to Yugoslavia where they inflicted inhuman tortures upon most of them. There are three mass graves of such victims that I know about myself. These are at Lasko, Hrastnik, and Kosice.

The prisoners were brought to Lasko in trucks every night during an entire week. When they were unloaded from the trucks, their guards threw them down a mine shaft which was more than three hundred feet deep. At least three thousand living men, women, and children were hurled down this shaft. The guards would toss hand grenades on top of every batch of twenty or thirty such victims. When the shaft was practically choked with corpses, it was closed up.

At Hrastnik, this procedure was repeated, but on a larger scale. Seven thousand people were thrown into the mine shafts there. At Kosice, near Celje in Slovenia, a group of approximately one hundred war prisoners was murdered. The Communists threw only a light blanket of sand over their bodies, so that starving dogs were able to dig up the corpses. It is impossible to say what happened to smaller groups who were delivered into the hands of the Yugoslavs by the British. It suffices to say that there were innumerable instances of torture and slaughter which have never been recorded.

I am willing to swear to the truth of everything that I have stated above. Furthermore, I am prepared to assume both moral and material responsibility for my testimony in this regard.

Signed: J. F.

Le Fraschette di Alatri
September 11, 1952

Document XLIII

This brief testimony corroborates what the previous document has stated concerning the massacre of Croatian victims at Hrastnik.

At the end of May 1945, long columns of Croatian war prisoners were moving through Slovenia in the direction of Zagreb. About one mile north of Hrastnik, there is an abandoned coal mine. I estimate that seven thousand of these prisoners were massacred here. Their bodies were thrown into the mine openings. The mine was then dynamited to cover up the traces of the crime.

One of the chief executioners in the butchery effected here was Lojze Ovnik. He is working at the present time for the glass factory in Hrastnik.

Signed: S. F.

Nurnberg, West Germany
October 28, 1954

Editor's Note: The author of this brief account of the massacre that took place at Hrastnik is himself a Slovenian resident of this town.

Document XLIV

The first of this extremely valuable testimony tells how sixty to seventy men of the Eleventh Dalmatian Brigade were selected to form an "Extermination Company." The eyewitness belonged to the Eleventh Brigade; therefore, he and his companions escorted the exterminators first to Podutik where truckloads of Slovenian and Croatian prisoners-of-war were brought, shot, and dumped into a deep pit. Then the witness' company was transferred to Kocevje. Here, for eight days, the witness watched trains bringing Croatian, Slovenian and some Serbian prisoners-of-war in unbelievably pitiful condition. Among them there were women and teen-age boys. All these masses of prisoners were taken to be slaughtered at Kocevski Rog. The exterminators boasted of having killed thirty to forty thousand captives. For this "feat" they were rewarded with a vacation on scenic Bled.

After completing four years of secondary school studies at Vela Luka, I lived at home with my parents until September 10, 1943. On that day I was forcibly drafted by the Yugoslav Communists, who had appeared in Vela Luka after the surrender of Italy to the Western Powers earlier this month and after Italian troops serving in Dalmatia had either surrendered or gone over to the Partisans.

I was assigned to the Twenty-Sixth Dalmatian Division, but since I was under age, I was detailed to work in the British hospital on the island of Vis.[1] After the fall of Gospic to the Communists in March, 1945,

---

[1] Better known, perhaps, in the western world as Lissa. It was off this island that in 1866 the Austrian fleet under Admiral Tegetthof completely defeated a larger Italian squadron. The Austrian vessels were manned chiefly by Dalmatian Croats.

I was transferred to the Eleventh Dalmatian Brigade, which was based in Gospic. I participated in battles that this unit fought in the vicinity of Trieste. Following the capture of Trieste, we advanced through the valley of the Soca (Isonzo) River all the way to the village of Kranjska Gora. We arrived here on either May 15 or May 16, and I remained with my unit at this place until the German and White Russian troops under the command of General Vlasov had surrendered in the nearby mountains, which extended into Austrian Carinthia.

We crossed the frontier line into Carinthia, and I was stationed in the vicinity of Klagenfurt for six days. Here I witnessed the surrender of the Croatian troops to the English who extradited them into the hands of the Yugoslav Communists.

After the disarmed Croatian soldiers had been turned over to Tito's people, the Western Allies did not allow us to stay in Carinthia. We were sent back to Yugoslavia via the Jesenice tunnel. After a one-day stop at the border, we went on to Kranj by foot. This was about May 24 or 25. We remained for another day at Primskov near Kranj. Here, orders were received by the Brigade Command that the most trustworthy Communists, whether officers or privates, should be selected from all four battalions of the Brigade. These reliable elements had to carry out a "confidential task."

A special company was formed from the men picked out. Second Lieutenant Jokovic, who came from my own village, let me know right away that these men had been selected to kill Croatian, Slovenian, and German war prisoners. The Third Company of the Third Battalion, to which I belonged, was assigned to escort and protect the newly formed company of executioners, which numbered between sixty and seventy men. Its commander was Captain Nikola Marsic, who was a native of the Makarska coastal district. Formerly, he had been vice commander of the Second Battalion. The company Commissar was Ivan Bokez, nicknamed "The Montenegrin." In supreme command of this detail was Major Sima Dubajic of the War Operations Section of the Headquarters of the Fourth Army.

It must have been May 26 when the "extermination company," escorted by my own Third Company of the Third Battalion, set off for Ljubljana. We arrived at the Slovenian capital at about five P.M. The trucks carrying us stopped in front of a concentration camp. This place of detention contained many wooden barracks, which housed great masses of war prisoners, as well as many civilians, including women and children. Entire families were incarcerated here. I learned that this was the St. Vid concentration camp and that the gymnasium of the Ljubljana Church Diocese was located here.

The camp was entirely surrounded by barbed wire. All of us, with the exception of the "extermination company," were forbidden to approach the prisoners or to communicate with them in any way. However, the exterminators were allowed to enter the enclosure in order to loot the prisoners of their watches, fountain pens, rings, gold, jewelry, and other valuables.

We spent the night of our arrival in barracks. At 6:00 A.M. the following morning, four truckloads of prisoners and a truck loaded with the "exterminators" left the camp. The nickname of "Crna Marica" (Black Maria) was given to the prisoner trucks; all of us knew that the passengers had been taken off to be killed. At 10:00 that morning, our Third Company was loaded into two trucks to gather up and load the clothes of the slain prisoners. We went about one mile in the direction of Ljubljana, then turned to the right and proceeded about two miles further along a rather wide country road, until we came to a peasant house that stood in an orchard. Behind this house there was a forest with a big field adjacent to it. Some three hundred feet from the house, a deep hole had been dug.[2]

Our trucks stopped at the house, where I saw a prisoner group about fifty strong. They had been stripped of their clothes, their arms were bound with wire, and they were tied together in pairs. It was evident that they had been beaten by their guards. They all looked quite depressed; indeed, they had good reason to feel that way. Some who had collapsed from exhaustion were placed between stronger pairs in order that the latter could carry them to the death pit that had been prepared. All of the victims were ordered to chant in unison "Sjeno-slama-kuca-jama" (Hay-straw-house-hole). As they reached the pit, the "exterminators" shot them down, and they fell into the great yawning cavern that had been excavated for them.

We remained here throughout the day. A new group of trucks would arrive every hour. In all, about forty truck-loads of victims were brought to this place before sundown. These death wagons were escorted by Slovenian courier troops, who were commanded by a blond-haired Slovene captain. He looked like an Austrian or a German and had received a citation as a Partisan fighter as early as 1941.

That evening the "exterminators" boasted that they had killed between eight and ten hundred men. They accomplished this massacre with British-made light machine guns to which silencers had been attached in order to muffle the sound of the firing. Usually, the victims were shot in the back of the head, but some of them jumped alive into the hole, even though it was a good fifty yards deep. At frequent intervals, the "exterminators" tossed hand grenades that the British had given them on top of the masses of bodies in the pit. Most of the people murdered here were anti-Communist Slovenes, but there were some Croatian soldiers among them.

About 11:00 A.M., I approached the hole and looked down into it. Before I could note any details other than a mass of bodies covered with blood, Bokez and Captain Marsic ran up to me and began to beat me furiously with the butts and barrels of their service revolvers. I fell to the

[2] Compare these details with the information in Document XLV.

ground, bleeding quite profusely. After this incident, our escorting company was moved some distance away from the death hole and none of us were allowed to go anywhere near it or to watch the massacres that continued to be perpetrated throughout the day.

When evening came, we were put to work packing up the greenish uniforms that the massacred men had worn, along with their other belongings. About eight P.M., we returned to St. Vid and the concentration camp. This same evening Major Dubajic ordered that future killings be carried out farther away from the city. He was afraid that the civilian population would find out what was going on, because the scene of the executions effected during this day was hardly four miles distant from the town. I overheard other Communists discussing the advisability of dynamiting the hole and the corpses in it to obliterate all traces of the massacre. Actually, a peasant had brought quick-lime to the place during the massacres; the lime was poured over the bodies to keep flies from being attracted by the blood and to eliminate the stench that would emanate from the decaying corpses.

On the day following the mass slaughters, we were sent by train to Kocevje. This town had been fairly well shot up during the war so the best place that could be found to house us was a partially destroyed military building, half a mile outside the community. Previously, German troops had been stationed here. The "exterminating" company had preceded us to Kocevje, but we did not see them there. I heard that they were encamped in a forest two hours distant. During the war, the Slovenian Communists had posts in the center of this great woods, named Kocevski Rog.

My company was assigned the duty of standing by while Slovene Communist escort troops took new batches of prisoners into the military building where we were being accommodated. Once they had them inside, the Slovene Reds would strip the prisoners of their clothes and all valuables; they collected from them some twelve pounds of gold in all. The Commissar of the Third Company, Ljubo Barbaric, a Croat from the island of Hvar, was made responsible for the custody of all valuables. We were told that clothes taken from the prisoners were to be exchanged for military uniforms.

Our job was to guard the prisoners until trucks arrived to take them away from this place, and then to load them onto these trucks. During the eight days that we remained at Kocevje, ten or more trains came in on the rail line every twenty-four hours. Each of these trains was composed of between ten and twenty boxcars, all well nailed up and sealed, and loaded with prisoners. The captives came from Ljubljana and other places. Most were men, but there were some women among them. These unfortunate females were subjected to mass rape as soon as they were brought to the building which we were guarding. There were also many fifteen or sixteen year old boys among the prisoners. I know that the blond-haired Slovene captain saved one of these boys from being shot, probably because he was acquainted with him or his family.

There were more Croats than Slovenes among the prisoners with whom I came into contact. Also there were some Serbian Chetniks brought here. I do not know to what units they belonged. We heard that during our eight-day stay, thirty to forty thousand prisoners were slaughtered in two nearby mountain ravines. The commander of our company was another Croatian, Ivo Frankovic, from Hodilje on Peljesac Peninsula. I do not know how he felt about the murders that he knew were being carried out at the expense of his countrymen.

On the eighth day of our stay at Kocevje, a dance was arranged to honor and amuse the "execution company." Women were brought for them, and the men swaggered around boasting that they had "liquidated" thirty to forty thousand people during the past eight days. I judge from the number of prisoners I saw taken out of the building we were guarding that there must have been more than thirty thousand victims. Since we shipped more than twenty railroad car loads of clothes from this place, it would appear that this estimate is not too far off the mark. I saw only about ten or fifteen women among the captives, but there were certainly more who were murdered here. Naturally, I did not see every arrival, since I was not on duty all the time. I know that the women were not stripped of their clothes in the vicinity of the building where we were stationed, but were conducted fully garbed to the place of execution. They were dishonored again in the ravines close to their final destinations.

There was another Croat Communist by the name of Bozo Kacic from Hvar who bragged about what he had done to the women prisoners. Those that I saw all looked miserable and wept almost constantly. They were the widows of Croatian officers who were massacred at Kocevje. I saw no children, these evidently having been separated from them. Most of these officers' widows were dressed in civilian attire, but some wore military slacks and boots; I assume that they had found such garb more practical than conventional feminine wear during the retreat from Croatia. We of the escort company were not allowed to approach the women at all; evidently, the "exterminators" were keeping them for themselves.

There were about two hundred boys between fourteen and sixteen years old who wore the uniforms of the Ustasha youth. All of these boys were killed, except for the one spared by the Slovene captain. They all kept saying that they were innocent of any wrong doing. Many of them cried like the women.

The condition of the railroad boxcars in which the prisoners were brought to Kocevje was horrible. Since their guards did not allow them to leave the cars, even to relieve themselves, the filth in them was indescribable. During the days that they were locked in these abominable pest wagons, the captives received neither food nor water. I do not know if they were fed after they reached the concentration camp or not. Some men lost consciousness or went mad while they were locked in the cars. Others collapsed from heat and exhaustion after they were pulled out of the railroad wagons. Such victims would be beaten by their escorts, who then would load them onto stronger fellow prisoners. All the prisoners were well aware that they were being led to death. Some of them looked as though they would make a fight for their lives, but most were so tired out and weakened by lack of food and drink that they did not seem to care greatly what happened to them, but only hoped it would happen quickly. Many men warned the "exterminators" that a day of reckoning for the atrocities committed would arrive. Other said that they had committed no crimes and had saved even Communists from execution at the hands of the Ustashas during the war. They asked that their lives be spared, but they might as well have saved their breath. No one was spared except the boy previously mentioned. There was no questioning of the prisoners, nor did any of them receive any kind of trial, nor was there any selection made among them. Everyone who was brought to Kocevje was doomed to die. Domobrans, Ustashas, Serbian Chetniks, General Rupnik's soldiers[3] and a variety of other anti-Communists were all killed together. Some German soldiers, most of them officers, were brought to Kocevje too. Two or three Ustasha colonels were among the victims, but I do not recall their names.

I heard that quite a few of the captives made attempts to escape just before they were to be shot. Some of these men timed their tries so well that they actually got away into the woods and mountains. Others were shot down by the guards as they fled. I am glad to be able to say that I risked my own life to allow some prisoners to escape from the building in which we guarded them until the "executioners" could take them off to the human stockyards where they were disposed of.

This company of slaughterers was active at Kocevje for only eight days. The day on which the final massacre took place was a Saturday; five or six high-ranking Communist officers visited the military building where the prisoners were housed before execution on this day. Among them was a Serb from Kordun, Colonel Dule Korac, whom I knew. Two or three well-dressed civilians accompanied the officers. The whole party was welcomed by Major Dubajic and Commissar Bokez. These high-ranking Red officers had come to check on how we had packed up the uniforms and valuables of the victims. They devoted great attention to the gold that had been collected from the murdered people. Commissar Bokez handed everything over to them without keeping so much as a fountain pen for himself, and they offered him no rewards.

---

3 General Rupnik organized a force of "White Guards" or Slovene anti-Communists who collaborated with the Germans during the war. The Slovenes did not like the Nazis, but thought that they might secure the freedom of Slovenia if they cooperated loyally with the Wehrmacht.

However, I was able to ascertain on good authority that, after this episode, Bokez never had any difficulties with the Communist authorities to whom he had turned over the confiscated valuables.

The inspecting commission spent hardly half an hour in our building. From here they went to the forest to see the mass graves in the ravines. I was told that they had come to Kocevje to see how the killings had been carried out and to make sure that all visible signs of the massacres, that is the ravines into which the bodies had been thrown, were covered up. Before they left Kocevje, we heard several loud explosions in the forest. We assumed that bombs or dynamite had been used to topple masses of rocks onto the thousands of corpses choking the ravines. The commission did not return to Kocevje after its inspection of the places of slaughter.

On Sunday morning at seven o'clock, the "exterminator company" left by train for a vacation at Lake Bled. I didn't know this at the time, but learned it only much later when these killers rejoined their old companies, which had been sent to Macedonia in the meantime. They told us that as a reward for the massacres they had committed at Kocevje they had received twelve days vacation on the island of Bled, where they were lodged in a former luxury hotel. They received good food, went swimming, had sail boats at their disposal, and saw plays performed for their special benefit every evening by a group of amateur actors provided by the Headquarters of their Division (the Twenty-Sixth Dalmatian Division). In addition, all of the "exterminators" received two or three decorations from the Tito Government, along with gold watches, cameras, and other presents of value.

Among these much decorated "exterminators" was a twenty-two year old courier from Brigade Headquarters, Ante Cepic, unfortunately another Croatian like myself. He was a youth leader also and came from Makarska, like Captain Marsic. From this time on, the "exterminators" remained the most trustworthy of all Yugoslav Communists. I heard, however, that some of them became epileptic later on—perhaps the so-called "partizanska bolest" (Partisan sickness), from which they suffered, was a form of nervous breakdown.

The Third Company remained at Kocevje until the evening of the same Sunday on which the "exterminators" departed from the scene of their crimes. We boarded a train which took us to Kranj, where we stayed for ten days. Then we were sent on to Tetovo in Macedonia, which we reached on July 7. Scenically, the region around Tetovo could not compare with the Kocevje district, but if I had to go back today to either place, I would choose Tetovo a thousand times before I would ever return to Kocevje. At least the former has no particularly unpleasant associations connected with it.

I do not know whether the Communists carried out any massacres at Kocevje before or after the eight days of slaughter that I have referred to above. But I do know what happened during those terrible eight days of murder, rape, and pillage. I am willing to testify with my own signature to the exactness and truth of what I have said above. Also, I am ready to testify to these facts before any authorized international commission, and to risk my life, if by so doing I can bring to justice at least some of the "exterminators" and the people who charged them with their inhuman duties.

Signed: I. G. I.

August 14, 1953

Document XLV

In the following account of Tito's former soldier, Ignac Jansa, there is a detailed description of the exhumation of a mass grave at Podutik near Ljubljana. In May, 1945, large groups of war prisoners were dumped in a Podutik abyss. On June 20, 1945, their exhumation was ordered by Chief of the Slovenian UDBA, General Macek, because the Ljubljana's water supply was contaminated by the victims' putrefying corpses. Captain Lenart was in charge of this unpleasant duty, carried out by some eighty German prisoners-of-war. Our witness was Lenart's chauffeur; he is therefore able to give us minute details not only of the exhumation operation, but also of the Podutik massacre itself.

Because of the German occupation of Slovenia and the crimes carried out by the Wehrmacht in that land, I enlisted in the Partisan forces on May 12, 1944. I was assigned to the 3rd Miners' Company in the Gorenjsko formations. My unit was stationed at Mezakla near Bled. On April 8, 1945, I was wounded in an attack we made upon the German Gendarmerie station at Gorjak. Even today, I am suffering from the effects of the wounds that I received on that occasion. After five weeks of hospitalization, however, I was well enough to be appointed assistant to the Partisan commander at Jesenice. I remained at this place until June 1, 1945, when I was transferred to Trzic. Here I was supposed to be detailed to UDBA service in Carinthia. But I had no liking for such duty and on June 15 I succeeded in obtaining an assignment as chauffeur for the UDBA headquarters in Ljubljana.

Here I became the personal chauffeur for Captain Lenart. Prior to the war, he was a carpenter by trade. Now he was in charge of the exhumation of the masses of war prisoners whom the Partisans had murdered the previous month after the so-called "liberation" of Ljubljana. At that time, the corpses had been thrown into a ravine. The result was that Ljubljana's water supply became contaminated as water flowed down to the town from the vicinity of this vast charnel house. When chemical analysis of the polluted water revealed that decomposing bodies were causing the trouble, General Macek, chief of the Slovenian UDBA, ordered the corpses to be cleared out of the ravine and buried more suitably in regular pits dug for that purpose.

It was Macek who assigned Lenart to this disagreeable duty. Since I had never liked Macek from the first day that I joined the Partisans, I kept away from him as much as possible and never did learn why Lenart, who had held a high position in Gorica, was picked for this new duty.

Twice a day I had to drive Lenart from the "Slavija" Bank, where the UDBA had its headquarters, to a peasant's house near Podutik. The abyss in which the corpses had been thrown was only about three hundred meters away from the peasant's home. This place of mass murder was actually barely two miles distance from Ljubljana and only half an air mile from the Ljubljana-Vrhnika road! No wonder the city water supply was contaminated!

The ravine which contained the bodies had a wood scaffold erected over it. On this scaffold there were long ropes and some steel tongs about a yard long. The tongs were fastened to the ropes and lowered into the ravine. German war prisoners were let down by other ropes into the pit, so that they could put the corpses inside the tongs which were then closed to hold the decaying flesh fast. I saw with my own eyes how the tongs could pull up several bodies at the same time. This remarkable accomplishment was facilitated by the fact that the Partisans had tied victims together with wire by threes and fours before killing them. Also, I saw how the tongs brought up separated arms and legs and other parts of the putrefying corpses. It was a horrible sight and the stench that came from the ravine was suffocating.

One view of this process of exhumation was enough for me. As a matter of fact, I had to sneak up on the place and keep myself out of sight to see anything at all, since "spectators" were not allowed to watch what was going on. However I knew Sergeant Anton Burja who was the son of an innkeeper from Zasip near Bled. He told me many of the gruesome details connected with the work of clearing the ravine and reburying the remains of the dead. Burja knew what he was talking about, because he belonged to the group of Communist guards who kept watch over the German prisoners who had to do the "dirty work" in the ravine.

There were about eighty of these Germans who were employed in the work of exhumation. They labored in two shifts daily. I calculated that if they worked for fifteen days they could recover between one and two thousand corpses. Knowing the methods of the UDBA as I do, I am quite sure that after the German prisoners had taken the bodies out of the ravine, cleaned it, and had buried the bodies in a new hole they were forced to dig, they were shot themselves and thrown into the same hole. The number of guards watching the Germans was approximately equal to that of the POW's themselves. These guards were all very young and had absolutely no conception of ethics, morality, compassion, or any other human qualities. Indoctrinated in Marxism and deliberately "blooded" by the Communists, who had trained them to kill unarmed prisoners during the recent massacres, they knew only to do what they were told and to enjoy doing it. Hence, they were much more trustworthy than older men, who, even if they were Marxists, were also more capable of thinking for themselves and weighing the results and the justice of their actions. Burja told me that Lenart had ordered the guards to keep a sharp watch on the Germans to see that they did not escape. Indeed, some of them were shot every time an escape attempt was made. I know that one of the guards did kill a German over a very trivial matter. This guard was from Zirovnica and only about fourteen years old, a typical little "trigger happy" Marxist rat.

For ten days I had to pick up Lenart at his apartment in Ljubljana at 7:00 A.M. every morning. Then I drove him to the scene of the slaughter, where we stayed until 8.00 or 9:00 A.M. After he had inspected the work of digging up and reburying the bodies, we would return to town. Again in the afternoon, I drove him out to the peasant house near Podutik and here we remained from about 2:00 to 4:00 P.M.

After ten days of this duty, another UDBA officer and his chauffeur took over for us in the exhumation proceedings. I continued to be employed as chauffeur at UDBA Headquarters until August 20, 1945, when I was demobilized.

This oral statement of mine has been read to me and I found it to be factually correct in all of the details cited.

Signed: Ignac Jansa

Rome
October 31, 1953

Document XLVI

Although M. L., a former Partisan and author of this testimony, was not able to see as many details of the infamous massacres at Kocevski Rog as are given in Document XLIV, nonetheless his account is very important because it corroborates what Doc. XLIV has stated.

A couple of days after Italy had capitulated to the United States and Great Britain in September 1943, I was inducted by force majeure into the ranks of Tito's Communist Partisans. This incident occurred at Blato. Together with fourteen other fellow townsmen, I was assigned to the First Proletarian Brigade, which had its headquarters at Prisik near Duvno. Since one of the new inductees protested against being mobilized, the Partisans shot him in the Blato cemetery. His name was Nikola Cetinic Krnjan, the sacristan of the church at Blato. His murderer was Ivan Jurjevic, nicknamed "Crnogorac," or "The Montenegrin," but he was actually a Croat from Lubarda on the island of Korcula.

From Duvno we were sent into the mountains above Biokovo. Since we hadn't volunteered for service, but had been inducted forcibly, the Proletarians did not trust us. I was assigned to the Third Company of the Third Battalion. Mirko Gabric from Metkovic was our company commander at this time. After he was killed in a fight with the Croatian troops at Ostra Glava near Knin, Captain Nikola Raos from Makarska took over the company. Before the war, he had been a shoemaker. The political commissar of the Battalion was Ljubo Barbaric from the island of Hvar. Grga Markitch, a very cruel man, was Brigade Commissar. He came from Desne on the Neretva River. Later, he died of a brain tumor.

My company went via Knin to Brlog in Lika. Since I was a good soccer player, I was permitted to play in three matches that our team played with the Tank Brigade Eleven. Somewhat later, I was sent to Senj and then, in February 1945, to the island of Krk (Veglia), once the property of the great Croatian noble house of the Frankopans. As the war neared its end, I was ordered back to the mainland.

After Trieste fell, we proceeded to Klagenfurt in Carinthia, where we remained for two days. From here we moved to Jesenice and Kranj in Slovenia, and by the end of May we were at Ljubljana.

It is very probable that at Kranj the most trustworthy Communists were selected for the secret task of executing war prisoners. We were not supposed to know anything about this matter, but we heard that a new company was being formed for a "confidential" mission; and gradually the whole truth leaked out.

In Ljubljana I was lodged with two fellow soldiers near the bath house "Ilirija." We were charged with standing watch over three hundred and twenty automobile tires that were stored in a warehouse. After four days of this duty, I was sent with the rest of the Third Company to Kocevje, where we billetted in private homes. This was at the end of May, 1945.

I was assigned to the home of a postal clerk who knew Dalmatia well, because he always went there during his summer vacations. My company's first duty was to escort newly arrived prisoners from the railroad station to a barracks and then to a building situated outside the town. Here they had to undress; then their arms were tied with wire. They were loaded into trucks and driven to a ravine in the forest where all of them were murdered. I do not know how far away the ravine was from the city, but it must have been quite far, since we did not hear any sound of firing. Later, I heard from the lips of the murderers themselves that some of the prisoners were shot at the edge of the ravine and others were thrown in while still alive, while some jumped down of their own will. The command of our company was taken over at Kocevje by Ivo Frankovic, a Croat who had deserted from the Domobrans to join the Communists at the end of the war—just in time to get on the winning side. He told me that one day a prisoner seized a gun from one of the executioners and killed him and two other Communists, then got away into the woods. The rest of the Red Guards directed a veritable hurricane of fire after him, but he made good his escape.

I do not know exactly how many train loads of prisoners arrived during the seven or eight days that we remained at Kocevje. Usually, these prisoner trains pulled in to the station either late in the evening or just before dawn. The Communist authorities did not want the civilian population of the town to know what was going on. From ten to twenty boxcars were included in each train and the prisoners arrived completely exhausted and almost starved to death. They knew what was in store for them but they were too tired and dispirited to care. As far as I could tell, there were more Slovenes than Croatians among the prisoners. These Slovenes were the White Guards of General Rupnik. I saw some women and adolescent boys among the captives. One such youth, a boy of fifteen or so, was pulled out from among the prisoners by a Slovenian officer. The Slovene asked the boy what his name was and where he came from. The young fellow replied that his name was Dolic, he was a Croat from Zagreb, and was a member of the juniors of the "Corcordia" soccer team.[1] Through the good offices of the Slovene commander, he was sent to a Slovenian unit that was escorting the trains to Kocevje; I think the Slovene himself may have been the officer in charge of this unit.

I had to escort the prisoners from the train to the barracks and to their final place of detention. Since I did this just one day, I can only guess the number of prisoners who were brought to Kocevje to be slaughtered. From other people who were there, I gathered that as many as twenty thousand may have been butchered. A special company of hardened Marxists was formed for the purpose of carrying out the mass executions. A certain Albert Stambuk was the Assistant Commissar of this unit. On the day I was detailed to escort prisoners from the station, he told me that among the newly arrived captives he had seen the pastor of my own native parish. Assistant Commissar Stambuk said that he had told the priest what was in store for him and added: "My heart will be content when I kill him!" Indeed, on the following day he told me that he had murdered the old cleric and was very content that he had done so. On another occasion, I saw Stambuk carrying a bag filled with gold watches, gold and silver coins, necklaces, bracelets, foreign currency and many other valuables. It was rumored that he had sent six gold watches to his home, which was in Pucisce.

I had a great deal of contact with Stambuk because he was billeted in the home of a postal clerk where I, also, was putting up. One evening he was lying on the sofa in this house and seemed to be feeling very sorry for himself. I asked him what his trouble was, and he replied,

---

[1] I think that it is this same Dolic who today is playing for the "Lokomotiva" soccer team in Zagreb.

"Poor me! I'm tired out from having to do so much killing. I've had to work all day long walking prisoners along, undressing them, killing them and shoving them into the ravine."

"That's not my trade," I answered him. "I can't do that sort of thing. And who put you up to doing it?"

"As a Party member I was given this task, and I must perform it," he replied. "No one who is a Communist can refuse to kill if he is ordered to do so!"

This Stambuk in 1947 was Commissar of the Auto Company stationed in Kranj. As far as I know, he is still alive and doubtless enjoying the fruits of his crimes. He was fairly typical of the individuals who made up the "Extermination Company," a special unit formed, I think, at Kranj, to murder the prisoners. I do not know the names of all of the "Exterminators," but I am acquainted with a few of them. Second Lieutenant Daniel Jokovic from Vela Luka and Djuro Maric of Varazdin were two of their number. Maric was a former Domobran, who, like Ivo Frankovic, had defected to the Communists at the end of the war. I ran into him in Zagreb in 1947. He invited me to look him up if I ever came to Varazdin and told me that his home was located in the center of this old city.

As to Major Sima Dubajic, I do not know whether he took part in the Kocevje massacres or not. An alcoholic Serb of medium height with black hair and mustache, he behaved very roughly toward his own soldiers. On one occasion he slapped me.

The "exterminators" were rewarded for perpetrating the horrible butcheries at Kocevje by being given several days of vacation on the scenic island of Bled in the Slovenian Alps. Afterwards, they were sent back to their old commands, which in the meantime had been transferred to Tetovo in Macedonia.

The above statement was read to me after being typed. I confirm with my word of honor that everything said herein presents a truthful record of my recollections of the events of 1945 in which I was an unwilling participant.

Signed: M. L.

September 5, 1953

Document XLVII

The following dramatic account entitled "The Facts About Tito," appeared in the September 1965 issue of *The St. Clair and Superior News,* (Cleveland, Ohio), pages 1 and 6. It deals with extradition and subsequent wholesale murder of thousands of Slovenian anti-Communist fighters at Kocevje, one of the most infamous massacre sites not only of Slovenians but also of an even larger number of Croatians and several thousands Serbians.

With all the favorable reports appearing regularly in the American press regarding the Yugoslav dictator Tito, the "liberator" of Yugoslavia, it is only fitting that our public learns the true story about this Communist leader and about the crimes he committed against Slovenian, Serbian and Croatian nations during the last World War. Over half a million people fell victim to his bands, and their blood stirs me to tell this story to the still free world.

During the last war, I was a member of the Slovenian Home Guard, an army of some 18,000 officers, non-commissioned officers and soldiers, organized for the sole purpose of defending the Slovenian countryside against marauding Communist bands, since the occupying powers could not or would not provide such protection.

Under the leadership of General Leon Rupnik, whom we affectionately called our father, we almost completely cleaned out the Slovenian territory. But in 1945, international communist brigades came to Tito's rescue and we had to leave our country. Together with us and under our protection, thousands of civilians also fled the country in hope of finding freedom and peace in foreign lands.

When we arrived in Austrian territory, we were accepted by the British Eighth Army and directed to the Vetrinje (Viktring) field, where our army and some 15,000 civilians camped in the open. The British demanded that we surrender our arms, which we did, under the sole condition that none of us would be returned to Yugoslavia. The British, however, did not respect our wishes and some 12,000 of our soldiers were returned to Yugoslavia and there slaughtered by Tito's Communists.

This shameful act was performed by treachery. The British told us that we were being sent to Italy, where other detachments of our army had arrived. Instead, we were transferred from the lorries to the freight wagon on the railroad station Podrozca, the last stop before the Yugoslav border. The wagons were then locked. Following our encagement, a howling band of Communist Partisans, yelling for our blood, came out of the building.

The train started, but soon stopped again, in the middle of the tunnel between Austria and Yugoslavia. We heard the yelling, cursing and laughing of the Communists, who were dragging some of our unfortunate friends out of the wagons and beating them up in the tunnel. Before Jesenice, the first Slovenian town, the train made a few more stops. Each time we were beaten, robbed of our valuables, and spat upon by the Partisans and their sympathizers.

Sometime after midnight, we arrived in Kranj and were transferred to a nearby military camp. During a short walk, we were greeted at this late hour by a band of frenzied civilians who threw rocks at us, while the Communist commanders made us run and walk just as it pleased their fancy.

When we arrived in the camp, one of the commissars pulled out of our ranks a seventeen year-old boy, France Koman, beat him mercilessly, and shot him in the head. Then this beast, who could kill a man just as easily as a fly, told us that if there was anybody else who would like to get shot in the head, "he would gladly oblige him." We dug a grave and put the martyred body of our friend into it.

For three more days, the beatings and plundering continued, but no one was interrogated, tried, or sentenced. On the last day of May, the commissars gave us sheets of paper with orders to write our personal data and history. We were also told to state when and why we joined the Home Guard. One of the Commissars, without reading a single paper, declared, "You have already been sentenced, and you shall learn your sentence when it will be executed." We spent the night in prayer and terror.

On June 1, 1945, some 1,500 of us were taken on the first transport and brought to Ljubljana. Since one of the railroad bridges was destroyed, we had to transfer to another track. During this journey through Ljubljana, a mob of Communist sympathizers again attacked us physically. By the end of the day, we were again loaded in freight wagons, and while waiting for the train to move, heard the bells of the Ljubljana churches ring the "Ave Maria"—Angelus. Although we knew these were the last bells we were to hear, their sound nevertheless filled us with confidence and quiet. We arrived at Kocevje at dawn of the second day of June, 1945. The high school building was already packed to the attic with other unfortunates, and, in groups of 150 to 200 men, we were taken to the place of massacre. They tied our hands with telephone wire and stacked us, like firewood, on trucks. A priest, also one of us, gave us general absolution, and we started to sing folk songs and religious hymns. Soon the trucks moved in the direction of Rog, a forbidding primeval forest area south of Kocevje.

After a long ride, during which four Communists, who rode on top of us in the back of the truck, showed their sympathy for us with rifle butts and boot kicks, we suddenly heard the noise of machine guns, burp guns, and hand grenades. The end was near, and we started to sing our last hymn:

> Blessed art Thou, Oh Mary,
> Thus said the angel;
> When the last bell tolls,
> You will come for us . . .

They threw us off the trucks and took all our better clothing and shoes; then they tied us together in pairs and made us march towards a cave, some 15 or 20 yards wide. Along the path leading to the grave, the Communists were standing, playing with knives and heavy sticks to "show us the way."

I offered a short prayer to our Mother of Mount Carmel, whose medal I still wore around my neck, then started to walk with my companion towards the edge of the grave. There, two Communists with burp guns were dispatching the already half dead warriors. They shot at me, also, but, somehow the hand of God interceded, and I fell alive and unhurt on the mass of dead or dying bodies. Five days and four nights I spent among my dying friends. Many of them were still alive, moaning and praying. Whenever somebody cried out loud, the Communists would start throwing hand grenades in his direction, thus mutilating the dead even further. Throughout all this time, I did not hear any cursing or begging for mercy, nor did anybody call for God's vengeance upon the Communists. More than once, however, I heard the words, "Father, forgive them, for they know not what they do."

On the fifth day, the grave was mined and blown up to cover and hide it forever. During the explosion, a giant tree fell into the grave, allowing just enough room for me to crawl out and save myself. Thus, through the Grace of God, I was saved from the grave on June 6, 1945.

Twenty years have passed since the "hammer and sickle" replaced the Cross of Christ over Slovenia. They have killed the Home Guard, but they will never defeat us.

I, therefore, publicly demand an answer from dictator Tito to these questions:

Why did you slaughter us in such a criminal and shameful manner?

Why didn't you go before a court of justice, prove our guilt, and demand such a horrible death?

Why don't you admit this crime and relieve the relatives of the slaughtered, many of whom still cling to a mad hope for the return of their loved ones?

Why don't you, before the world, declare the guilt of the Home Guard and justify the sentence pronounced and executed upon them?

It is an uncontrovertible truth that 12,000 men of the Slovenian Home Guard had to meet their death because they were honest, peace-loving and conscientious patriots, defending their national and religious heritage and because they were uncompromising in their fight against Communism.

And it is further indisputable truth that ALL THESE THOUSANDS OF MASSACRED MET THEIR DEATH AT THE HAND OF COMMUNIST BUTCHERS WITHOUT ANY DUE PROCESS OF LAW WHATSOEVER!

I have written this account because there is no hope that either Tito or any of his henchmen will ever admit its authenticity. It is, nevertheless, a truthful account of what happened to me and my fellow countrymen in June of 1945. Writing these lines, I only wanted to pay homage to the memory of the slain and to enable anybody and everybody to judge for himself what kind of life and freedom we can expect under a Communist regime.

Signed: Milan Zajec

Document XLVIII

The massacres at Krsko and Kostanjevica, Slovenia, and killings in a "Death March" through Croatia were committed by the Third Battalion of the Seventh Krajina Brigade.

I was born on January 2, 1922, at Bileca. On September 28, 1942, I joined the Croatian Army in Sarajevo. I served in Bosnia until the Army evacuated this section of Croatia and retired northward. In the retreat I was captured by the 10th Krajina Division of Tito's Communist Army. Since I was a Bosnian, my captors seemed to have thought I was a Croatian Serb. Therefore, they assigned me to the 3rd Battalion of the 7th Krajina Brigade. I accompanied this unit all the way to Slovenia. Therefore, I was a witness of the many atrocities that the Third Battalion committed against the members of the Croatian Armed Forces. At Krsko and Kostanjevica, this command massacred more than two thousand prisoners. Many of the victims were under eighteen.

The massacres at Kostanjevica were carried out by detachments commanded by Captain Petar Duitch of Bosanska Krajina, and the commander of the 3rd Battalion, Mitar Bakovic, from Duvno. Lieutenant Milisav Gjukitch of Bosanska Krajina carried out most of these executions.

The Third Battalion also had to escort Croatian war prisoners from Zagreb to Osijek. The Battalion committed a series of murders along the way. These wanton killings were executed by members of the Communist Party and SKOJ (Federation of Yugoslav Communist Youth).

Signed: A. K.

Rome, April 12, 1947

Document XLIX

This testimony of Marko C., who is still kept in a concentration camp, was smuggled out of Yugoslavia. It deals with a massacre of over nine hundred Croatian prisoners at Brezice, Slovenia, where the eyewitness himself was shot and presumed dead. Since he was not lethally wounded, he managed to escape from the pile of corpses. After wandering through the woods, he reported as a Partisan and was taken to a Zagreb station of the Yugoslav Secret Police, the OZNA (later UDBA). From here he escaped at once. Later he found a temporary shelter in a Zagreb hospital. Then he lost himself among the inhabitants of Zagreb and thus found safety from death, but not from imprisonment.

I, Marko C., am a Croatian from the vicinity of Bihac, in Bosnia. During the war I served in a Domobran Regiment of the Croatian Armed Forces. Together with my comrades, I went into Austria after the collapse of our German allies. We understood that the British would intern us as prisoners of war if we gave up our arms to them.

Instead, the Englishmen delivered us into the hands of the Yugoslav Communists. Under the escort of these elements, a column of approximately nine hundred Croatian soldiers was conducted from Maribor in Slovenia back towards the Croatian frontier.

When we arrived at the Brezice airport, the whole lot of us crowded into a hangar. As soon as night fell, our guards told us to don Communist uniforms because we were going to be taken into the Yugoslav Armed Forces. As a preliminary measure, we had to take off all our Croatian uniforms and were left wearing only underpants and shirts. When we had done this, a hundred prisoners at a time were sent into the "dressing room," where we were to be outfitted with our new Yugoslav uniforms.

While the rest of us were waiting for the first hundred to get dressed, we heard rifle and machine gun shots. The firing went on for a little while, then everything became very still. We could not tell exactly where these shots were coming from. After a time, Partisan guards came to take another hundred prisoners to the "dressing room." We realized what had happened and understood that we had reached the end of the line.

The younger prisoners, many of them were only boys who had been picked up in the last recruitment, began to cry, while the older men bowed their heads in prayer and prepared quietly to meet their Maker. One by one the hundred lots were led off, until finally only the last hundred was left in the hangar.

And now our turn came. We were tied together in threes and led in groups to trenches which had been dug to protect the airport during the war. When my trio reached the trench line, corpses were piled almost to the top. The Communists fired into our backs and we fell on top of the still warm and bleeding bodies of our comrades.

No bullet found its mark in my flesh. However, the two men to whom I was tied were both hit and fell into the trench dragging me down with them. I lay quietly on top of the dead men, hoping against hope that some way or another I would be able to extricate myself from this charnelhouse. After a time, however, the Partisans poured another volley of shots into the trench just to make sure that no one was still alive. This time, two bullets lodged in my back, but fortunately they did not hit vital places. Some time afterwards, ten more prisoners were brought to the trench and shot. They fell on top of me and my dead comrades. I remained there protected by their own bodies.

When the executioners left, there didn't seem to be anyone around to throw dirt on top of us; for all I know they intended to bring more victims here to be executed before they covered up the trench and its grisly contents. I didn't wait to find out what was going to happen, but managed to untie myself and climb out of the trench. I found that I did not appear to be wounded seriously, although I was covered with blood, some of it my own and some that of my dead comrades. Of course,

I could not bandage the back wounds that I had sustained. I wandered about looking for a house or for someone who might be kind enough to administer first aid and, hopefully, give me clothes to put on; I wore nothing but undershirt and shorts and the night was getting very chilly.

After I had gone into the woods a mile or so, I saw a campfire somewhere in the trees ahead of me. I crept up close to it and saw that several German soldiers were warming themselves around it. When I made myself known to them, they bandaged my wounds, fed me, and gave me a German uniform to wear. I remained with them until dawn, by which time the bleeding from my wounds had stopped.

I now took my leave of the Germans and made my way towards Zagreb, hiding in the woods whenever I saw or heard Partisans along the way. For a while I was able to avoid using the roads and to stay under the cover provided by the forests. After a time, however, my wounds began to pain me and I decided to take my chances on the highway, in the hope that a vehicle would come along that might transport me to our capital city.

Since the loss of blood seemed to have weakened me considerably and there was also a chance that my wounds might be infected, I realized that I had no time to lose in securing medical attention of some kind. Therefore, I quite boldly stepped out in front of a truck that was full of Communist soldiers and threw up my hand to halt it. I introduced myself to them as a member of a Communist unit that I was fairly certain was some distance away from this vicinity. Even though I was clad in a German uniform, they believed me, for at this time Tito's people, including the Slovenian Communists, were wearing all kinds and combinations of uniforms. Convinced that I was one of their own, the "comrades" let me get into their truck. In order to stave off any questions about my unit, I made a great show of suffering, groaning, grunting, and grimacing with pain. Apparently, my "act" was not too convincing, for as soon as we passed the Zagreb customs house, one of the older Communists stopped the truck. He ordered me to get out and follow him.

He conducted me to a house which, I found out afterwards, was a branch depot of the OZNA. He told me to sit down on a bench in the corridor while he went into a room, to report to the OZNA officer in charge, I presume. As soon as the door closed behind him, I rose from the bench and nonchalantly walked out of the nearest street door. Once on the sidewalk, I proceeded to lose myself among the passing pedestrians.

I knew that the German uniform was bound to make me an object of suspicion sooner or later, even though many Partisans were wearing Nazi garb. I made my way to the house of a family with which I was acquainted. They gave me a civilian suit for which I thanked them wholeheartedly. Not wishing to endanger their own safety any more than I already had, I then left their residence and reported to a hospital.

Luck was still on my side because there was a Croatian nurse on duty at the reception desk here. I told her frankly that I was a Croatian soldier and explained to her how my wounds had been incurred. She registered me as a Partisan fighter and assigned me a bed. Although I was safe for the moment, I soon found out that I could not remain in this hospital for any length of time. This same nurse had provided a similar "escape hatch" for eleven other Croatian military refugees. The Communist authorities were beginning to get suspicious because a number of "Partisans" without identification of any kind had appeared out of nowhere, asking for medical treatment of one sort or another.

All of the patients began to be summoned into the hospital office to check up on their identities. OZNA men questioned everyone who claimed to be a Partisan concerning the unit in which he had served during the war, as well as his reasons for being in the hospital. Whenever someone was unable to prove he was what he claimed to be, he was at once labeled an Ustasha and taken off to be killed.

On the fourth day of my sojourn in this hospital, the good Croatian nurse advised all of the individuals whom she had sheltered to leave immediately because very shortly we were going to be questioned, and would undoubtedly be arrested afterwards. She got civilian clothes for us from the hospital storeroom and provided us with white hospital coats to put over these garments. Thanks to her kindness, all of us were able to walk out of the institution unmolested and make our way to safety.

Signed: Marko C.

January 28, 1962

Document L

The massacres at Sevnica, Slovenia, the "Death March" from Sevnica to Pozega, and the "crowning" with caps made out of barbed wire at Osijek are revealed.

I was born in 1927 in the village of X in the Travnik district. Unfortunately, I cannot supply precise data and names in the following record because of the danger—more accurately, the certainty—of reprisals being taken against my relatives in the homeland.

In October, 1943, I was called up for military service in the Travnik district. I passed the physical examination and was assigned to the German Prinz Eugen Division. I neither requested this assignment, nor was I pleased by it. Since I was wounded at Oroslavlje towards the end of the war, I was allowed to return home for recovery. Afterwards, I couldn't manage to get out of this unit until it started to retreat in May, 1945. Then I attached myself to a Croatian battalion from Kupres.

Somewhere around May 10, I cannot remember the exact date now, we were in front of Dravograd, which was in plain view from the hill on which we were bivouacking. Thus, we were able to see that the surrender of Germany and the certainty of our own eventual defeat was causing our commanders to give up and surrender to the Partisans. Therefore, with ten or so of my comrades, I changed into civilian clothes. A Slovene peasant gave me his old, worn-out suit for my brand new suit. I got rid of my weapons, a German M. P. and an Italian "berett," disassembling them and scattering the parts about everywhere.

We wandered through the woods until we were stopped by some Slovene Partisans. We surrendered to them, since they had their guns trained on us. They conducted us from one place to another for four or five days, until we found ourselves in the Sevnica camp.

This camp was located in the school which stood on the right side of the Sevnica-Zidani Most road. The school building was a two-story edifice, at least I remember it as such, with a great courtyard fenced in by barbed wire. Partisan guards, armed with machine guns, were on duty at all time. There was another camp in the former German Army barracks in Sevnica. The courtyard of the school camp was thronged with prisoners, Croatian for the most part, but was also occupied by a sprinkling of Germans. While most of the Croatians were soldiers, there were quite a few civilians and a good number of women and children.

Together with many other compatriots who were confined in the above-described school, I saw how a large number of heavily armed Partisans led six or seven Ustashas out of the nearby forest. The Ustashas still had their weapons and would not surrender them. Among them was an officer, a man of middle stature with a big mustache. The Partisans were arguing with the Croats, trying to get them to give up their arms. They surrounded the Ustashas on all sides.

The Croatian group stood with their M. P.s in their hands, turning one way and the other, and keeping a wary eye on the Partisans. Suddenly, they opened fire and killed a great number of the Reds, so that there was a whole pile of Communist corpses. The fighting continued until Tito's people had killed the last Ustasha. We in the camp had to bury them.

We became faint from hunger, because we received nothing to eat here for the first three or four days. However, the wife of one of my friends, F. M., along with other women and children, was allowed to go into the town and beg for food. Thus, she was able to bring us a little bread or onions to eat. When we were herded to the public food warehouse one day to clean it, we found it completely ruined. But we also found some little paper sacks containing a whitish substance which we thought was flour. We took this "flour" back to the camp to boil it, but discovered that it was gypsum. We were so disappointed and generally miserable that we wept.

One afternoon after a few days of starvation, the Partisans began to distribute some unsalted soup to us; it was made from horse and mule meat.

The guards at the Sevnica camp were mainly Serbs. I could tell this from the dialect they spoke. There was one Croat among them, however, a Partisan lieutenant or sub-lieutenant by the name of Jozan Vidak. He came from the village of Puticevo near Travnik. Today he is employed in the match factory at Dolac. His brother, Andrija, was sentenced to twelve years imprisonment for having served with the Ustashas in the war. I must say that Vidak did not kill anyone, as far as I know, but, on the other hand, he did nothing to help us in our misfortune nor did he take any notice of us.

When we arrived at the camp, no one troubled to ask us our names, and no one wrote down any details concerning our "guilt." After we had been in the place for a day or two, four Partisans took a young man dressed in the uniform of the Ustasha "Black Legion" into an empty classroom on the first floor of the school. None of us saw him again until a day or two later, when he appeared dressed as a Partisan among the other Partisans. Then I recalled that he had spoken a Serbian dialect used by few Croatians. This youth proceeded to point out individuals who allegedly had served with him in the same "Black Legion" unit. The technique of choosing the candidates for execution was very simple. Every good physical specimen among the young men, especially if he was unfortunate enough to have long hair, was declared to be an Ustasha. Those so designated were killed on the evening of the following day. Together with my near neighbor, T., I was among those elected for execution.

As soon as the young Partisan pointed out someone, two other Partisans would grab this victim and drag him into a vestibule of the school where his hands were bound with wire. Then he was taken to a special room which was guarded by two Partisans armed with hand machine guns. T. and myself were taken to this room and tied up for the entire night. There were about 120 of us picked out for execution which apparently was set for the following day.

When morning broke, two or three Partisans, probably officers, placed themselves before the door of the room in which we were confined. They wrote down the name, branch of service, place and date of birth, and the unit in which each individual had served, taking us one by one to compile this information. This procedure was by no means a judicial one, for no one raised the question of crimes committed, nor was any kind of evidence of guilt submitted or asked for. T. and I and two or three others were listed as "minors," since we gave our year of birth as 1929. We were released from our bonds and placed with some other people who had not been condemned to death.

That same evening about ten o'clock, the men destined for death were led down to the lower floor with their hands still tied. As they were going down the steps, their captors struck them with gun butts so that some men cried out in pain. Everyone in the building heard these cries. The doomed captives were led off into the night. It was not half an hour later that we heard machine gun fire, and knew that our compatriots had been murdered.

At about six o'clock the next morning, the Partisans picked out twenty or twenty-five strong young men, myself among them, gave us shovels and hoes, and took us to the bank of the Sava. I was frightened when I trod the sandy ground some fifty meters away from the river and saw lying near the overgrown young willows there the bodies of the entire group of 120 men who had been slaughtered the night before. They had been machine gunned. In addition, one had received his *coup de grace* by a pistol shot in the head. Flies were buzzing around them, and it was evident that some of them, probably in their death throes, had kicked or torn up the grass or ground around them. The scene of this massacre was perhaps one or two kilometers distant from the town of Sevnica.

Our Partisan escorts ordered us to dig a hole in the immediate vicinity of the place of execution. We dug a "grave" among the willows, about three or four meters wide and long enough for the purpose. Then we had to throw the corpses, their hands still bound with wire, into the pit. We covered it up with hardly half a meter of sandy earth. Even today, I would be able to recognize this tragic burial mound if it had not been effaced in some way later on.

I was acquainted with one of the victims, Ante Fisic, the son of Pero and Janja X. He was born in 1924, not far from Travnik. His two brothers probably met a similar fate, because they did not return to their homes after the war. They simply "disappeared."

Twice more I was sent to bury murdered victims of the Communist authorities. The same number of captives, 120, were interred on each of these occasions. All three mass graves were dug near the bank of the Sava within an area of approximately 500 meters. With me on the second burial detail was J., who still lives in Yugoslavia today, and holds state employment there. I know his exact capacity and address. Also T., the fellow prisoner whom I mentioned earlier, lived to make his peace with the Tito regime which murdered so many of his comrades. He is also living in the Domovina at the present time. There are other people, too, women especially, still alive in the fatherland today whom I know well, and who survived the horrors of the Sevnica Camp and can testify to what went on there. I can reveal their names only when it is possible to give guarantees for their lives and freedom and protect them against the vengeance that the Communists reserve for all who tell what they know.

After the above-mentioned massacres in Sevnica, we the survivors, were thrown into open railroad cars in which we traveled to the Zeleno Polje at Osijek. We received neither water nor food on this journey. I think that I remained in this place about fifteen days. Among the various tortures that I suffered here, I shall mention only that the Partisans presented my group with a "cap" which was made out of barbed wire. They forced the captives to put this "cap" on one another and to press it with rods. Even a very weak blow would pierce the victim's head as the "cap" pressed down on it. I had my head injured in this way until, with blood streaming down my face, I fell to the ground.[1]

From Osijek our train took us to the concentration camp at Slavonska Pozega. On the way, Serbian peasants attacked us with stones in one or two villages at which we stopped or through which we were passing very slowly.

In Pozega I was discharged from the camp after a few more days of suffering. I owe my release to the fact that I had given my birth date as 1929. Therefore, I was included in the freeing of this age group. Actually, I was two years older than most of the others in the bunch. When I reached home, my weight was only 48 kilograms (106 pounds), and I was so weak and ill from malnutrition and privation that I had to crawl on my hands and knees a distance of several kilometers. Today I weigh 87 or 88 kilograms (close to 200 pounds), which is just a bit too much for one of my height.

While I was in Pozega, I took care of a school friend, N. Dilber. Because lice had gotten into his ears and had bitten right through them and he was burning up with fever resulting from typhus, Dilber appeared to be dying. Yet, he is alive today. When I met him later in Travnik he said, "I am eating with your teeth."

Signed: H. M.

February 24, 1962

[1] The tortures of this kind, in addition to the crucifying of several Croatian officers, are even more fully described by Joseph Hecimovic in his book, *In Tito's Death Marches and Extermination Camps,* p. 66.

Chapter 9

The Maribor Massacres

Document LI

This account by the Croatian Franciscan, Vendelin Dr. Vasilj, relates how the hospital train of the Obrana defense troops retreating from Zagreb was stopped at Hoce near Maribor. Most combatants, in order not to jeopardize the position of the sick, wounded, and non-combatants, took off to the nearby woods. The rest of the contingent was captured by the Slovenian Partisans in Maribor. The lot of the captives was not too bad before the arrival of the Serbian Reds of the Fourth Voyvodina Brigade in Maribor. At their arrival, however, the wounded and sick were mercilessly treated. The witness, under an assumed name, decided to serve the spiritual needs of the Maribor Catholics in St. Peter Parish. While he was performing his services, he saw the Partisans' atrocities against Croatian prisoners-of-war and learned many details of the massacres at the anti-tank trenches. Dr. Vasilj closes his testimony with a passage on the persecution of Slovenian Catholics. Then he states why he escaped from Yugoslavia.

I was the chaplain of the Ustasha Obrana defense formations. On May 7, 1945, I left Zagreb on the hospital train belonging to this unit. The commander of the train was a military doctor, Colonel Dr. Sime Cvitanovic. Aboard the train, which pulled out of the Zagreb rail station at 10:00 A.M. on this day, were about five hundred wounded or sick soldiers. An escort of two hundred well armed soldiers, commanded by several outstanding officers, accompanied the convalescents. In addition, there were approximately seven hundred women, children, and other civilian non-combatants. These people boarded the train at the last moment before it left the station. There were forty or fifty priests among these people.

The train was well supplied with food and hospital necessities. We rolled slowly northwards, heading for the Austrian frontier. It took us two and a half days to cover the distance between Zagreb and Maribor in Slovenia. The Slovenian train conductors apparently obeyed instructions they received from the Partisans to delay us as long as possible at each station we came to. The purpose of the delay was to prevent our making early contact with the British who, together with Russian troops, were moving from Graz towards Maribor.

Before we reached Maribor, strong Communist forces stopped the train at Hoce. They demanded the complete disarmament of all military and civilian personnel aboard the train. If we accepted this stipulation, they would allow the train to proceed. Major Jakov Barbaric, the commander of our escort, had a difficult decision to make. All the soldiers wanted to engage the Communists, throw them aside, and take the train on through. Barbaric realized, however, that overwhelming Partisan, Russian, or Bulgarian forces might be encountered before the train reached the Austrian border. The position of the sick, wounded, and non-combatants would be compromised by a military escort which had just gained a victory over the Partisans. On the other hand, he assumed that even the latter would not take out their war-time spite on non-military personnel. Therefore, he decided to take his soldiers into the woods and lead them towards Austria on foot.

Even if we had possessed a sufficient quantity of arms, there were few of us left aboard who could have put up any kind of resistance. Therefore, those of us who carried various weapons gave them up to the Partisans without argument. When they were sure that we were all disarmed, the Communists, true to their word in this instance, permitted the train to go ahead to Maribor.

When we pulled into the Maribor station, we found that Bulgarian troops had taken possession of it. All passengers were obliged to disembark and were taken to a concentration camp which the Germans had established here during their occupancy of the town. Once we were imprisoned in this place, Tito's people took over and began to rob us of all valuables. They stripped men, women, and children alike of their clothing, and left the wounded naked and without bed coverings.

On the first day of our incarceration, men and women were strictly segregated. None of us received any food for three full days. Fortunately, some people who had managed to conceal a few edibles in one way or another shared what they had among the rest of us. The wounded and sick men were not fed either. Nor did they receive water to drink, or any kind of medical care, because all physicians and nurses assigned to the train in Zagreb were led away the first evening.

Apart from this neglect of our primary necessities, the Communists did not behave in a particularly cruel manner towards us at first. On the fourth day of our confinement, however, the Fourth Partisan Brigade, which was composed chiefly of Serbs from the Voyvodina, took over the control of the camp. The commander of the Army to which this unit belonged was General Kosta Nadj. His men searched industriously to find anything of value we might have left and threatened us with all kinds of dire punishments.

During the retreat from Zagreb, a barber named Kokic, who came from Zavidovic, had gotten aboard the train, which had need of a barber to service the patients. Whether he was a Partisan Communist spy or not I do not know, but our Serbian guards used him to designate all officer personnel who were among the convalescents. These officers, when pointed out by Kokic, were separated from the rest of us.

The arrival of the Fourth Brigade nullified the efforts made by a young Slovenian priest, Father Z.D., to secure humane treatment and professional medical care for the wounded and sick. With the help of the Bishop of Maribor, Josip Tomasic, he negotiated in our behalf with the Slovene Communists. Also, he asked that all priests whom we had with us be set at liberty. The command of the Fourth Brigade put an abrupt end to the talks he was having with the local Communist authorities.

I saw that our delivery into the hands of these Serbs had greatly endangered our situation. When I found out that I was not going to be allowed to minister to the wants of the sick and wounded, I decided to escape. Thanks to the help given me by a very energetic and determined Sister-nurse, I was able to make my preparations for doing so. There were five Sisters on the hospital train when it left Zagreb, but when we arrived in Maribor they were freed by a Slovenian Communist officer. Instead of seeing to their own safety, they maintained contact with those of us who still were prisoners. They busied themselves with smuggling food, advice, and instructions to us.

I want to stress that the conduct of Slovenians towards us was relatively correct, and unquestionably, this tolerant attitude, which characterized even professed Communist elements among the Slovenes, considerably facilitated the work of the Sisters. I saw that everyone except die-hard Marxists expected the British to occupy Slovenia at any moment. They were not at all sympathetic towards the Tito regime and disapproved of the way in which we prisoners were being treated. The actions of the Fourth Brigade, in particular, aroused their profound disgust.

On the Sunday after we arrived at the camp, all male prisoners were paraded through the streets of Maribor, presumably for the purpose of demonstrating the might of Marxism. There were about fifty priests who were put at the head of the column. After being paraded through the city all through the afternoon and evening, we were returned to our place of detention around midnight.

I had a presentiment that our destinies were going to take a turn for the worse after this incident. On the next day I got away with the help of Sister ---- and found shelter at the Franciscan monastery in Maribor. Here I registered under an assumed name. Because of the lack of Slovenian priests, many of whom fled to Austria, I took over parish duties at St. Peter's Church. I went there every day and remained all night long at this post on Saturdays and Sundays, when many of the faithful took advantage of the darkness to discharge their religious obligations with less fear of Communist molestation.

After my escape, the remainder of the priests were sent back to Croatia, together with the sick and wounded. Ostensibly, they were to be returned to Zagreb. Later, I learned that some of the more seriously wounded were thrown from the train into the river when the bridge over the Sava was reached. At least one priest, Dr. Ivo Guberina,[1] was executed in Zagreb.

While I was officiating at St. Peter's, I had a good opportunity to see what was going on in Maribor. From May 13th through the night of the 18th, columns of prisoners passed constantly through this city. They marched barefoot and were obviously exhausted from lack of food and water. Of course, they had been robbed of everything they possessed except a few rags of clothing. A great many of these prisoners were taken to the Cadet School in Maribor. Here they were confined in the open schoolyard without food, adequate clothing, drink, or any roof but the sky over their heads. Many of them died in the Cadet School of thirst, starvation, or exposure.

From May 15 on, the prisoners at this school were divided into Ustashas, officers, and Domobrans. Then they were slaughtered in groups. Most of the massacres took place at night in Tezno on the outskirts of Maribor. The killings took place principally at the anti-tank trenches dug by the Germans when they held the city. Machine guns, knives, and various other lethal weapons were employed in these mass executions. Most of the killing was done by the Serbs of the Fourth Brigade, but Slovenian Communists had a hand in it too.

Of course, the inhabitants of Maribor knew what was taking place on their own doorsteps. They were horrified by the massacres, but too cowed to protest against them. I risked investigation by writing letters to the military Commander of the City and to the Headquarters of the Fourth Brigade, protesting against the executions that were in progress. Of course, I signed these letters with my assumed name. The letters went unheeded by the authorities.

While I was discharging my duties at St. Peter's, I often had occasion to witness the corpses of Croatian and German soldiers floating in the Drava. I was told that the corpses accumulated and formed a regular log jam at a point about six kilometers east of Maribor. They finally had to be removed from the water.

At Tezno, however, the massacred soldiers were thrown into the anti-tank trenches and covered over with a few shovels of earth. Since hungry dogs and other animals got at the bodies and since the corpses later decayed, quick lime had to be poured over them, and then more earth thrown on top of them. According to the Communists themselves, between thirty and thirty-five thousand Croatians were slaughtered in the area around Maribor during the second half of May. These figures corresponded with the estimates made by trustworthy residents of Maribor, who were in a position to find out some of the facts about the matter.

I obtained a first hand account of the massacres from one of the survivors, Lieutenant S. Together with an officer colleague, he was

[1] Dr. Ivo Guberina, a noted Croatian author and professor, is one of eleven other priest-martyrs of the Catholic Diocese of Sibenik who were killed by the Partisans.

wounded by the Partisans' first shots into his prisoner group, which had been marched to the place of execution. Both men dropped to the ground and feigned death. Under cover of darkness, they were able to crawl into the woods and find shelter in a nearby village. Since they did not want to compromise their benefactors, they decided to pose boldly as wounded Partisan fighters. They reported as such to the hospital in Maribor, where they received treatment for twenty days. Then anti-Communist personnel on the hospital staff helped them to be repatriated to Croatia.

This account of the mass slaughters perpetrated at Maribor can be corroborated by many residents of this city. After the end of hostilities, the Communists arrested and imprisoned large numbers of Slovenian Catholics. Entire families were thrown en masse into various prison camps because they had opposed or refused to collaborate with the Partisans during the war. In the parish at which I served, I had to witness several generations of the same family being led off to imprisonment and probably death. At least 13,000 Slovenes were incarcerated at the Sterntal camp, where they were systematically starved and finally clubbed to death.

I had the dubious satisfaction of learning from the newspapers, as well as from a clerk at OZNA headquarters, that the Communist authorities were diligently seeking to locate me, because I had written three anti-Marxist books in previous years. Since all of the functions of the Catholic Church were subjected to special surveillance, it was only a question of time before someone recognized me and betrayed me to the OZNA. I anticipated this action by escaping to Trieste on September 3, 1945.

Signed: Fr. Vendelin Dr. Vasilj[2]

Chicago, Illinois

Document LII

Railroadman B. J. first tells of the difficulties encountered by a Croatian hospital train passing through Slovenia. Then he corroborates the information given in the previous Document on the "Death Marches" in general and on the Maribor Massacres in particular. After a nine-day stay in Marbor, B.J. was lined up in a "Death March" that went in the direction of Zagreb. At Vrapce, however, he escaped and entered the Croatian capital without Partisan guards. The regin of terror in its many forms caused him to leave Zagreb and go to Sibenik. His account closes with a passage on two prisoner-of-war camps along the road that took him to Sibenik.

---

[2] Dr. Vasilj is a member of the Croatian Franciscan Province in Hercegovina, which, because of its loyalty to God and Croatia, was hardest hit by the Partisans of Josip Broz Tito. Over sixty Franciscans of this Province, twenty-eight at Siroki Brijeg alone, were murdered by Tito's troops.

I was drafted into the Croatian Armed Forces during February, 1942, and was assigned to the Second Railroad Battalion which was commanded by Ante Vokic.

On Sunday, May 6, 1945, I ascertained that preparations were being made to evacuate Zagreb. In accordance with a directive issued by General Moskov I went to the railroad station where I boarded a hospital train. Wounded men belonging to the P.T.S. (Pavelic Body Guard Brigades), members of the Ustasha Youth, and the Auxiliary Services of the P.T.S. were already aboard. At midnight the train pulled out of Zagreb and by morning had reached Brezice. The train commandant was a medical major whose name I cannot recall.

Since there were many trains on the tracks that led from Zagreb through Brezice to Zidani Most, we made slow progress on Monday. I am sure that some of the Slovenian conductors were Partisan sympathizers and deliberately held up the journey at various points. Of course, it was difficult to be sure of this, because we had to slow down to let other trains pass by us and often had to back up onto other tracks to let Zagreb-bound trains through. There was danger of being bombed by British or Russian planes too. Thus, it was almost evening when we arrived at Zidani Most.

Our train remained at the Zidani Most station for only half an hour and then went on towards Celje which we reached on Tuesday morning, May 8. The many automobiles around the station at Celje accomodated some of our refugees. After a short stop in this Slovenian town, the train continued towards Maribor. At the fourth rail station out of Celje, the train was halted for an entire day. When we asked the reason for the delay, we were told that the locomotives had to go on to Pragersko to take on water or they would not be able to pull the cars any longer. As dusk fell on May 10, the hospital train of General Luburic's Obrana formations pulled up near our own train. The Obrana train was under the command of Colonel Dr. Sime Cvitanovic. In this transport was the chief of the main railroad station in Zagreb, Zembic; Major Mirko Blazevic; Lieutenant Colonel Bilobrk; Director of the Wagon-lits Society; Captains Prpic and Ferencic, and a considerable number of Ustasha officers. There were also priests, the Obrana's hospital personnel, and the families of various officers and officials.

By some jockeying back and forth, the Obrana train got on the tracks ahead of us. Their train was armored and I decided to get aboard it. Just before it became completely dark, the Obrana train started moving towards the Austrian frontier. Much later I learned that the P.T.S. hospital train had to return to Celje where the Partisans commandeered it and brought it back to Zagreb. Some of the officers aboard fled from the train at Celje, but others were returned to the Croatian capital by the Partisans.

The Obrana train drew into Pragersko, where we spent the night of May 10. We heard that the German troops had evacuated the place some time before and that the Slovenian Partisans were in control of it. They did not bother us during the night, and when morning came we were able to repair the damaged tracks which had caused the delay. On we went towards Maribor. We ran into a group of armed Slovenian Partisans at the first station beyond Pragersko, who refused to allow the train to proceed further. They demanded that we surrender our weapons and promised that if we complied with this request, they would let the train continue on to the Austrian city of Klagenfurt. Dr. Cvitanovic talked with them for some time and finally a compromise agreement was reached. Officers were allowed to retain their weapons, while the rest of us were to surrender ours.

At noon on May 11, our train started off again. But we only reached one station down the line before we had to stop again and wait until 4:30 P.M. Partisan troops appeared at this station to guard the train. When we saw them take up positions around us, many officers and soldiers, and even some of the wounded men who were able to walk, left the train and disappeared into the woods along the track. Among those who got away were Lieutenant Colonel Bilobrk, Major Blazevic, and a large group of soldiers who had kept their weapons.

It was late in the afternoon when the Obrana train started moving again. This time it went all the way down the line, until it came to the first station out of Maribor. Here other Partisan formations stopped it and checked to see who was still aboard. They asked the remaining officers to give up their side arms. Some of them complied, others did not. There were no lights where we stopped, and something had gone wrong with the train lighting. The hospital nurses took advantage of this circumstance to help the officers change into civilian clothes. Later on this same night the train went on to Maribor, but now it was so strongly guarded that it was no longer possible to escape from it.

When we arrived in Maribor, the Partisans told Colonel Dr. Cvitanovic to leave the train. They took him and his teen-age son into a room in the railroad station. I do not know what happened to them afterwards.

Apart from the wounded who were left on the train, there were some 1500 of us who were removed from the cars at Maribor. We were led out four at a time and were not permitted to take any luggage with us. Soon we were confined in a small hall in the customs warehouse building, which stands near the Maribor rail station.

During the first six days we were lodged here, the Partisans supplied us with food and warm water—all mixed together. That is, the warm water had a little flour—the so-called *tarana,* or pap, floating in it. We were permitted to go to the rest room once daily. Even though a barbed wire fence surrounded the warehouse, we were guarded whenever we made this daily trip to the lavatory or water fountain. Women and children were crowded with us during the initial forty-eight hours of our sojourn in the little hall assigned to us. They were treated no better than the soldiers were. On the third day of our incarceration, they were placed in a separate room. On the ninth day of our imprisonment, we began to receive a daily breadless ration. Usually what we got was the "tarana."

From the third day on, officers, non-coms, and privates were taken from among us after Partisans from various regions had "identified" them. Also, we were robbed of everything that we possessed. When Serbian units arrived in Maribor, we began to have a particularly difficult time. They removed groups every day and night and probably killed them. Nine days after our departure from the train there were only 300 civilians, real or pretended, remaining of the 1500 aboard when we pulled into Maribor.

A Major Chule, who came from Hercegovina, distinguished himself by continually leading off groups of three to five men. I am fairly certain that he had all of these individuals tortured and murdered.

However, there were some prisoners taken away who eventually rejoined us. They told us that the Partisans had maltreated, tortured, and finally killed many of those who had been on the train with us. Ustasha Color Bearer Fabian Rastegorac told us how the Partisans had taken him to a cellar, where they tied him up and subjected him to the most brutal tortures. His wrists bore the marks of the wire with which his captors had bound him. In some way or other, he managed to get away and sneaked back into our quarters to tell us about his experiences. We managed to keep him concealed among us for some time.

Those of us who were not taken away to be interrogated as he had been, had to supply data concerning ourselves too. Whenever the Partisans suspected that a prisoner was an Ustasha, they used every trick they could think of to make him admit that he was a member of that organization and that he had knifed or otherwise killed many people. They made no real effort to find out whether or not he really was a murderer; they just wanted to make him admit that he was one. The Serbian Partisans excelled in subjecting us to various brutalities and tortures, while the Croats and Slovenes, even if they were Marxists, behaved much more decently towards us.

While we were in Maribor, I heard that the five or six hundred wounded men who had remained aboard the Obrana train after we left it had been sent to a hospital in Zagreb. Later on I was told that they were probably murdered outside the capital. I know that while the train was still standing at the Maribor station, an older nurse, whose name I cannot recall, was murdered. Several of the younger nurses were taken away by the Partisans; I do not know what happened to them. Of course, the Partisans took all of the medical and sanitary supplies from the train, thus leaving our wounded without these vital necessities. They also stole all of the food that was on the train, so nothing was left to feed the wounded.

On the ninth day of our imprisonment, war prisoners began to come in from Dravograd. Since there was no room or food for this influx of captives, the women and children already here, together with seventy of us who were railroad, customs, or treasury employees of the Croatian State, were sent on to Zagreb on foot. Jelic, a pharmacist, was in charge of us. We made this march without receiving food or clothing from our captors.

There were some Croatian soldiers who escaped from the prisoner columns which were brought to Maribor from Dravograd. They told us that after the surrender at Bleiburg and Dravograd, the Partisans treated everyone quite decently as long as there were British troops nearby. As soon as the Englishmen were out of sight, however, the Partisan guards made the captives run almost constantly and killed those who could not keep up. They threw the bodies of the people they killed into the Drava River. According to what we heard from the prisoners who were brought into the barracks, approximately thirty-five Domobrans, Ustashas, or civilians were killed between Dravograd and Maribor. The prisoners whom we saw were barefoot and almost naked.

Those of us who were sent to Zagreb passed through Bistrica and Hum on the Sutla River in order to cross the Croatian frontier. At Pregrada, Partisan militia men and members of the OZNA checked our identifications and made a minute search to find anything of value we had succeeded in concealing from our previous captors. They swore that they would ferret out every Ustasha among us and that none would succeed in escaping the "vengeance of the people."

On May 21, those of us who remained alive came to Podsused. Here we were split up into several smaller groups. Some other prisoners joined us and we were led into a park, where we were lined up in columns of fours. Off we started for Vrapce, where we had to undergo another interrogation concerning our identities. I knew that my status as a member of the Railroad Battalions was enough to secure my execution if I were identified, so I sneaked out of the park into a courtyard where there were a number of young Ustashas and Domobrans whom the Partisans had already selected to serve with their own troops. Each one of these young boys was given a Partisan cap with a red star on it. In this group, I found Sergeant Rukavina of the P.T.S. Security Service. We escaped together and made our way to Zagreb, arriving there on May 22.

In the capital I found that all the schools and every large building of any kind was crowded with war prisoners, civilians, women, and children. As yet there was no organized Communist or Socialist government in the city. But the Partisan troops and the OZNA were arresting and imprisoning people right and left, and robbing them of everything they had. Tito's people searched every house on the pretense that they were looking for caches of arms and hidden Ustashas; they were actually looking for loot of every description. The population was panicky and unable to resist these searches and arrests. No one's life was safe. Many Zagrebcani told me how the Partisans and the OZNA would block off sections of the city at night and then round up the inhabitants of this area and take them off to concentration camps. The trams were kept running all night to facilitate the procedure. My wife told me that one could easily count the number of homes and families which did not lose one or more of their members then. It was a real reign of terror. After all the reading I had done about the French Revolution, I only now came to understand for the first time what life in Paris between 1792 and 1794 must have been like.

Since the Partisans had blockaded the capital and no one was allowed to go into the countryside to get food, starvation conditions prevailed. Even the peasants were not allowed to bring anything in to Zagreb.

Because of the general conditions of insecurity that prevailed in the city and the danger that I might be arrested myself any night, I exerted myself to forge a false travel permit. With this fake document I rode to Sibenik in a truck with a Zagreb businessman and his wife. On the way, we passed two prisoner of war camps. There were approximately one thousand Domobrans in each of these places of detention which were located on a large plain. Barbed wire fences surrounded them. I saw local Serbians, especially children—real little monsters from an early age on—throwing stones at the Domobrans behind the wire. Many of the Domobrans were clad only in underpants and torn undershirts. We also saw groups of Domobrans and some German war prisoners repairing the road along which we traveled. Such work groups were guarded by strong Partisan detachments.

This report of my experiences was given from October 18 through October 22, an interruption having occurred on October 21, 1945.

Signed: B. J.

Fermo, Italy
October 22, 1945

Document LIII

When the Croatian contingent to which the witness T. Z. Z. was attached had surrendered to the British, Tito's people came out of hiding and lined up the prisoners in a column. The prisoners were driven towards Maribor amidst maltreatments and killings. About six miles from Maribor, a prisoner killed a Partisan officer, for which a long segment of the column was liquidated. Our witness and a group of other captives buried the dead in three pits along the road. In Maribor, the prisoners were divided by military districts. T. Z. Z. was grouped with the Zagreb district from which 520 men were selected for various types of work. A hundred of them, for instance, tended horses; one-hundred and fifty stored the uniforms of the executed victims; sixty other workers buried the murdered prisoners for fifteen days. The witness gives many details about how his group of twenty men one night tied truckloads of victims before their execution at the notorious anti-tank trenches. After this horrifying night, the witness succeeded in getting the job of tending the horses. During his two-month stay at Maribor, he learned more facts about the Maribor Massacres. In 1953 he visited these sites which he describes at the end of his account.

I was drafted into the Croatian Honor Work Service shortly after the beginning of the year 1945. Sent to Germany for training, I heard over the German radio network the news of the unconditional surrender of Germany early in May. Two days after this announcement came on the air, the entire personnel of the Honor Work Service camp was en route back to Croatia. We hoped that we would arrive there in time to participate in the anticipated defense of our homeland, Croatia, against the Communist hordes let loose on Europe by Nazi stupidity and Anglo-American benevolence towards everything Marxist.

On May 8, we reached the Slovenian city of Celje. It was bedecked with red flags hoisted by the Slovenian Communists. Nevertheless, the Croatian Armed Forces were not molested as they retreated through this place. From these retiring formations, we learned of the decision taken by the Pavelic Government to evacuate the Armed Forces from Croatian soil in order to spare the population the horrors of civil war. The troops invited us to join them in their withdrawal into Austria. They told us that they soon expected to return to the Domovina and to free it from the Communist regime that was being established there by Tito Broz.

We decided to accept their invitation, and joined the long columns of military and civilian fugitives who started from Celje towards Ljubljana. When we were about six miles from the Slovenian capital, we heard that the Russians had entered this city. The military men decided that they would turn northwest towards Dravograd instead of fighting their way through, in order to give the civilian refugees who were accompanying the military columns a better chance to reach Austria without suffering casualties. En route to Dravograd, we had to fight a number of battles with Communist units who often had the roads blocked or mined. Our technicians uncovered the mines and encircled dangerous places along the route with stones to keep people away from them. All of this took time. On the third day after we left Celje, we stopped near a Slovenian village which was built on the slopes of a hill. The villagers placed containers of water along the road for our use. When we started to sample this water, we noticed that it smelled badly. Some of us became convinced that the peasants had poisoned the water. Soon an order was issued forbidding anyone to drink from these containers.

We reached Dravograd after five days march only to find that our leaders now had decided to surrender to the British. After we had surrendered, Tito's people, who had hidden behind the skirts of the British until they were sure we weren't going to put up a fight, lined up a column of us prisoners, and drove us from Dravograd towards Maribor.

Along the road, the Slovenian peasants cursed us and sometimes attacked and beat us. Their greatest benevolence was to give us a piece of hard bread in exchange for cigarettes, shoes, and other articles of wear or use that our Communist guards had not already pilfered from us. I shall never forget the inhuman behavior of these peasants in our moments of greatest adversity.

Our escorts were drawn chiefly from the Twelfth Division of the Third Yugoslav Army. The men in this unit were mainly Serbs from the old Hungarian Voyvodina; quite a few of them were Hungarian speaking. The Divisional Commander was a short, stocky man with a heavy black mustache and a savage face. I remember him well, and I recall that he came from the vicinity of Majur near Srijemski Karlovci.

At this point I should like to stress the fact that the ethnic Magyars or Hungarians from the Banat, most of whom had been conscripted by force into the Communist Army, behaved very decently towards us. They protected us from the Serbs as much as they could, and gave us a fair deal in bartering bread for cigarettes. The Serbs from Sirmia (Srijem) were the worst of all our captors. Yet, there was one good fellow even among them, a Sergeant Stojanko, who did not take a hand in the constant murder of prisoners that went on during the journey to Maribor. Any Communist Partisan guard in the escort could kill prisoners at his pleasure. Since this indiscriminate butchery was too sporadic to get rid of us quickly enough, the Divisional Commander, or the commissars who accompanied the column, designated individuals and groups who were to be separated from the rest of us and killed along the wayside. The worst of all the Reds was Zora, a woman from Sirmia. She held some kind of low-commissioned rank in the Partisan Army and flaunted it by riding a horse. I recall that as we were marching eight or more abreast, she had an exhausted soldier taken out of my file. After the guards had thrown him into a ditch alongside the road, she shot him. A couple of hours after this occurred, she had another man pulled out of my file. The rest of us were carrying this poor fellow to keep him from collapsing. She shot him, too. She continued to display her sadistic mania by killing several other soldiers along the route. Later, I ran into her in the hospitals of Novi Sad and Petrovaradin, where she was supposed to be a nurse. I wonder if any of her patients recovered! If they weren't Communist party members, I am sure they didn't. For her efficiency as an escort of the prisoner columns, she had received the rank of captain when I saw her in the hospitals. Later, in April 1948, I saw her again while I was serving my term in the KNOJ (Communist People's Defense of Yugoslavia).

This slut was only one of many, both male and female, who, thanks to our own stupidity and that of our leaders, now had the opportunity to wreak upon us all the stored-up hatred which they had accumulated through the Marxist indoctrination to which they had been exposed. Any prisoners who became sick, weak, exhausted, or unable to walk for any reason were killed in full view of the rest of us in the column. It is impossible to say how many people were butchered along the route. There were times when I did not see a dead body for as much as two or three hundred yards. Then again, I saw several corpses lying together, or at fifteen to twenty-yard intervals.

We got nothing to eat or drink all the way to Maribor. Our thirst became so unbearable that, despite the threats of our guards, we would rush to get some water whenever we came to a well or a stream. Our "disobedience" was answered by volleys of shots, which often left piles of corpses around the watering places. Sometimes the guards would allow prisoners to go for water when we came to a village along the route. Then, while these men were drinking, the Reds would amuse themselves by shooting them.

Somehow, one of the prisoners had managed to conceal a revolver on his person. A day before we reached Maribor he killed a particularly cruel Partisan officer with this gun. The Divisional Commander, a commissar, and that slut Zora hurried up to find out who had killed their "comrade." The prisoner who had done the killing had hidden the revolver again and didn't confess his guilt. Nor did any of us want to betray him. Thus, the Commander lined up a special group about a hundred and fifty yards in length. This segment was separated from the rest of the column by twenty-yard intervals to front and rear.

I was standing just four to five rows behind the isolated group, so I had a clear view of the performance that was now enacted. Two Partisans brought up a heavy machine gun with which they opened fire at close range upon the prisoners who had been in the vicinity of the killing. There were several hundred victims of this reprisal. Later, my own group, which consisted of members of the Honor Work Service, had to bury the people shot here. We interred them in three pits, which were dug about fifteen yards off the road some six miles out of Maribor. Over the mass graves, we placed bunches of green grass in an attempt to make the abattoirs blend with the surrounding greenery.

We spent the night on a meadow close to a crossroads a few miles out of Maribor. There were about twenty thousand prisoners collected here. The following morning we were lined up in groups according to the military districts to which we had belonged in the days of the Croatian State. Together with almost all of the other members of the Work Service, I had the good fortune to be grouped separately in the Zagreb district. Since we were only a para-military formation, we were kept apart from the soldiers as such.

After we had been lined up to the satisfaction of our captors, they led us across a concrete bridge which spanned the Drava. We had to go right through the city of Maribor to reach this bridge. When we had crossed it, we had to cut across some railroad tracks which led into Dravograd. A mile and a half away from the Maribor-Trieste highway, our column was conducted into a large barbed wire enclosure. This place was located on a kind of plain where there were neither houses nor trees visible as far as the eye could see. I think this was the Maribor rifle range.

We had to wait a few hours here. Then the stocky Divisional Commander with the big black mustache came to select five hundred and twenty Honor Work Service men for his "Work Battalion."

This battalion was transferred to the barracks that the German troops had so recently occupied. It was located on the road that led into Maribor and was approximately half a mile distant from that city. The barracks consisted of two three-story buildings, one of which had the form of an irregular quadrangle, while the other was a square edifice. Behind the barracks there were two stables, each of which could hold fifty-six horses. A stone building, which had probably been a chapel in Austro-Hungarian days, was now being used as a blacksmith shop and as an ammunition warehouse.

We slept in the stables and on the first floor of the quadrangle building. Various duties were assigned to us. Approximately one hundred men were charged with the care of the horses. Twenty others had the task of transporting sacks and cans of food from the silos near the railroad freight station. A hundred and fifty unfortunates had the disagreeable job of storing and packing the uniforms and belongings that were taken from the people who were executed. Still others had to store the arms and ammunition. Of course, the worst function of all was discharged by the burial details. For fifteen consecutive days, sixty members of our battalion had to tie together the victims of the daily or nightly massacres, pile them into mass graves, and throw a layer of earth over them.

We "workers" had no choice but to allow ourselves to be incorporated into Tito's Armed Forces. The food that we received was insufficient in quantity, though not bad in quality. We were treated fairly well also, especially by the Hungarian Communists who were assigned to guard us. Some prisoners were badly used, however. On one occasion, two members of the "Work Battalion" hid one can of food a piece on their persons. When they had the bad luck to be detected, the Divisional Commander assembled the entire battalion and the Communist military units guarding it. He pronounced the sentence of death upon our two comrades for their "theft," ordered them to kneel, and then had the female Partisan, Zora, shoot them. This bitch had trouble with the mechanism of her machine gun and came out with a series of sacrilegious blasphemies before she could get it working.

One night, while we were asleep in the barracks, a Communist guard roused us. Twenty of us were picked out at random and loaded onto a truck. Together with six or eight guards, we drove to the vicinity of the concrete bridge that led over the Drava. I remember that we passed under a railroad bridge and then traveled some distance further on an unpaved road. I think that the entire journey must have taken more than an hour. Finally, we came to a large meadow which was fenced in by barbed wire. Behind this area there lay a forest of tall fir trees. There were three brick barracks with vault-like roofs, made out of boards and covered over with roofing paper, inside the enclosure. Probably, these buildings were hangars belonging to the Maribor airport.

Our guards conducted us into one of the barracks, where they conferred with four Communist officers who were posted there. Half an hour later, a truck bearing forty-five to fifty men pulled up in front of the hangar. There was a large group of Red guards accompanying the prisoners, who were soldiers of the Croatian Army. Their arms had been bound with wire, which cut deeply into their flesh. They were shabbily and scantily dressed. Some of them were tight-lipped and silent; others warned their captors that sooner or later all "Titoists" would get their just reward. Since they spoke the "kaj" dialect, it was evident that these victims came from around Krizevci or Zagreb.

We of the former Honor Work Service were ordered to untie the hands and arms of these men. Then they had to take off all their clothes except their underwear. Since some refused to obey this order, we had to undress them by force. Following this process, we received orders to tie them up again, this time with their hands behind their backs. We had no choice but to do this, though we made sure that the wire did not tear into their flesh as before.

The bound men were driven over to a corner of the hangar. Here they waited while two other truckloads of prisoners arrived and were disposed of as the first had been. Finally, we had to load all of the tied up captives onto the trucks. A board, called a "walk plank," was fastened to each truck.

On the following day, we were informed by the burial details that these victims of Marxist theory and practice had been taken to the anti-tank trenches and executed there with every refinement of cruelty. The trenches were only about half a mile away from the hangars.

The scene described above was repeated seven or eight times on this particular night. There were long waits between the time that the three trucks took off with the stripped and bound prisoners and returned with new batches of candidates for the slaughterhouse. Although we were certain in our own minds what the fate of these men was going to be, it was only when we heard, towards dawn, the noise of continued firing of automatic weapons that we abandoned all hope for them. It was a particularly terrible ordeal for me, because my brother, a second lieutenant of the Tjelesni Sbor (Bodyguard Brigade of the Poglavnik), was among the prisoners.

We went back to the barracks on foot, arriving there a little before 6:00 A.M. On the way, we passed a group of sixty men of the "Work Battalion." This was the burial detail which had a two-fold task; first to pack the victims' clothes, then to bury the corpses. They told me later that men were shot while they were still in the trucks. Some of the bodies were toppled into the trenches from the "walk planks," while others were thrown over the sides of the vehicles into ditches. A layer of less than two feet of earth was piled over these abattoirs, which were about nine feet deep by six feet wide.

I tried especially hard to avoid a repitition of this experience. Although I never in my life had tended horses, I succeeded in obtaining a job in the stables. Because of my inexperience I received many beatings from a Communist non-commissioned officer who was in charge of this detail.

I found a number of opportunities to talk with the members of the burial squads. They were mainly young peasants between the ages of seventeen and nineteen. They had to spend the entire night or day at the hangars burying victims, and when they received anything to eat, they had to consume it surrounded by corpses. They had about fifteen days of this duty, although the killing lasted for only ten days. The rest of the time they were kept busy levelling off the terrain and packing up the clothes of the massacred men.

I remained in Maribor for about two months. On several occasions I was told that the terrible stench that emanated from the decaying bodies made it absolutely impossible to use the roads around Tezno or through the nearby forests. We also heard that the population of Maribor was profoundly shocked by these killings. The bulk of the Slovenes are a highly civilized people, of course, and many of them sympathized with us openly. They gave water to the prisoners who were led through the city on the death marches organized by the Tito Government, and they bartered bread for cigarettes, despite Communist injunctions against doing so.

Following a two months stay at Maribor I was sent to Petrovaradin and from there to Novi Sad. At the latter place, I was included in an amnesty which was proclaimed by the regime in Belgrade. It was a little over a month and a half after the Maribor butcheries. I returned to my home in Zagreb only to be imprisoned in this city.

I visited Maribor again in 1953, after the end of my prison term. Despite the risk involved, I made it my business to visit the places where the horrible massacres had taken place. When I went to see the former hangars, I found the "TAM" automobile factory occupying the site where they had stood. The mass graves and the forests near them were fenced off by barbed wire, but an automobile road cut through the forests from the factory.

The above testimony was read to me, and I find it in accordance with my verbal report.

Signed: T. Z. Z.

February, 1956

Document LIV

The undersigned, Slavko Skara, opens his account by relating the Croatian troops' retreat, their battles, and General Servatzi's order for surrender to the British. According to Skara, about eighty percent of Croatian troops did surrender and the other twenty percent took off into the woods. After the surrender, the usual "Death March" brutalities were started by the Partisans. Amidst all these brutalities, the witness arrived in Maribor and was placed in the Tezno concentration camp. A Croatian Partisan was the commander of the camp, but he did not harm the prisoners. On the contrary, he showed his rage against the slaughters in Maribor. He even took the witness to the infamous anti-tank trenches and told him that about sixty-five thousand victims lay there. After a two-month stay at Maribor, Skara and about two thousand other prisoners were lined up in another "Death March" in which an estimated fourteen hundred were murdered. For Skara, this bloody trek ended in Pozega; his persecution, however, continued. Our witness closes his account by giving us a list of the Croatian patriots from his native village who in various brutal ways were murdered by the Partisans.

I was included in one of the columns that was moving through Slovenia towards Austria during that fateful second week of May, 1945. Sometimes we had to fight pitched battles in order to throw aside Partisan formations that tried to hold up our march. Most of the time, however, we were not molested. The Reds had no stomach to engage the "Crnci" and "Luburicevci" of Generals Boban and Luburic who were covering our flanks. When we got close to Dravograd in Slovenia, however, we had to stop for two days because our leaders were negotiating with the Western Allies. On the third day here, Communist artillery, which had been brought into position during our halt, opened fire upon us. Kocha Popovitch, a Serb, was the Partisan commander. In ten minutes time we suffered heavy casualties, both military and civilian. There was nothing for us to do but continue our retreat towards Dravograd; the disintegration of the Balkan Wehrmacht had resulted in the blocking up of all the main roads as abandoned German vehicles prevented our artillery from keeping up with the infantry columns.

Before we reached Dravograd, a number of British airplanes flew low over us, although they had the grace to refrain from dropping bombs. Also, the British had more than a hundred tanks drawn up to oppose our further progress. The tanks we had been able to get from the Germans during the war had been sent to stop the Russian and Bulgarian advance into Sirmia, so if we had tried to fight we would have been at a great disadvantage. Furthermore, there didn't seem to be any reason to do this, since we knew that the war was lost. A British General assured our leaders that if we laid down our arms no harm would come to us.

Our commander at this point was General Servatzi. He accepted the words of the Briton at face value and issued the order to surrender to the British, whose devotion to fair play was a popularly cherished fiction in Croatia, Slavonia, and Dalmatia up to this time. Nevertheless, Servatzi may have had his doubts about the Briton's good faith. In his communique to the troops directing them to surrender, this Croatian General added: "Some troops do not want to lay down their arms. Let them go wherever they wish!"

Most of us had no anticipation of what was going to happen. The war was over, we were the last force on the losing side still in the field, and our never too numerous planes, artillery, and tanks were not available to us at all. Even if they had been, it seemed that there was nothing left to fight for now that we had left our own country. This was the twentieth century, not the days of Alexander the Great or the Romans who formed their prisoners in precisely defined lines to have their throats cut. Presumably, all we had to worry about was a period of confinement in prison camps, and the problem of making a living after we were released from these. Therefore, about eighty per cent of the troops accepted Servatzi's surrender order, while the rest followed his hint to keep their arms and go into the nearby forests.

A few minutes after we had begun to stack our arms, Red commissars appeared. They started lining us up in columns and putting us on the road to Maribor. Eight women Partisans armed with long poles stood along the road on which the column was marching. They sang scurrilous songs, mocking the Ustashas, and struck the prisoners with the poles.

As we got farther down the road, I began to see corpses every ten paces or so along the line of march. There were sometimes ten or more disfigured bodies lying together. Often, the hands of these victims were tied with wire. The Drava River was filled with floating bodies of this kind. Mutilated corpses also lined the banks of this stream.

Those of us who survived the death march between Dravograd and Maribor were exhausted from thirst, hunger, and continuous marching without pause. At Maribor we found more suffering in store for us. We were sent into the various concentration camps located there. I went to the Tezno camp which was located about two miles outside of Maribor. There were perhaps two thousand Croatian war prisoners here. Providence willed it that the commander of this place should be a Croat. Though professedly a Communist, he was basically a good man, and saw to it that no one did us any harm. After a few days in this camp, I was assigned to work as a cook. I was interviewed by the commandant himself in a warehouse located on the camp grounds. When I was brought before him, the commander of the prison guards was with him, but this individual was sent out of the room while I talked with the Croat commander.

He offered me a chair and asked if I would like something to eat and drink. Needless to say, I replied that I would—I had not had a morsel of food and hardly a swallow of water for several days past! After I had refreshed myself, the commandant told me not to be afraid of what was going to happen to me but to tell him the truth about myself.

At this point I was firmly convinced that my days were numbered anyhow; I had nothing left to hope for or to lose. Therefore, I informed him quite frankly that I was a member of the Ustasha and so were all three of my brothers. He asked why I had described myself as a Domobran (regular) when I arrived at the camp. I replied that I had done so because, from what I had seen along the route from Dravograd to Maribor, I was certain that any Ustasha who had been fool enough to surrender would be killed without mercy, if his identity were discovered.

From this moment on, the camp commander became my very good friend. He promised that as long as we remained under his supervision none of us would be harmed.

Below the camp there was a large thick forest. Every day and night we could hear the firing of machine guns from these woods. Now and then, screams could be heard rising above the sound of the shots. Naturally, I wanted to know what was happening out there. I asked the commander about the screaming. He did not say a word in reply, but after a few days he had me accompany him in an old car on a drive in the direction of this forest. When we came to the edge of the woods, he told the driver to wait there with the car. The two of us got out and made our way through the trees into the heart of this dark and forbidding place.

We had gone about six hundred feet into the forest when we came upon a horrifying scene. An anti-tank trench had been dug in a meadow that lay behind the thick dense fringe of woods. This trench was fully two and a half miles long and was filled almost to the top with disfigured and bloated corpses. They were so badly decomposed by the heat that one could not have recognized his own brother among them. Of course, the stench emitted by the putrefying bodies was unbearable. However, I was so shaken by this grim sight that I was hardly conscious of the smell of death as distinct from its appearance. My three brothers had arrived in Maribor with me and I realized that undoubtedly they lay somewhere in this mass grave.

I looked at the camp commander who obviously was also strongly moved by this charnel house. He said to me in a sombre voice, "Someone will pay dearly for this innocent flower of youth that lies here!"

Despite the danger of my own position, I could not refrain from asking him, "Commander, is the entire Croatian Army buried here?"

Without looking directly at me, he replied in a low voice, "Not all of it, but as far as I can remember, sixty-five thousand of them are here!"

His answer left me petrified and I could not bring myself to ask him any more questions.

We remained in the Tezno camp for two months. Then, the entire two thousand of us were sent on another "Death March," to serve as a lesson to the potentially rebellious inhabitants of the socialist paradise created by Tito and his henchmen with American, British, and Russian assistance. The new sufferings to which we were exposed included beatings, insults, wanton killings, and the continual danger of being trampled under the hooves of our guards' horses. Because of the treatment to which we were exposed, only six hundred of us survived to reach the Zeleno Polje near Osijek. After a few days there, we were driven like cattle from Osijek to Slavonska Pozega. Many other columns had preceded us to these places and we heard stories concerning the slaughter of hundreds of prisoners every night.

We spent fifteen days at Slavonska Pozega. Then our Communist guards assembled two hundred and eight of us who had held commissioned or non-commissioned rank in the Croatian Army. They told us that the Peoples' Committees located in our places of residence had certified that we were good men and ought to be released. They wanted us to return to our homes.

We thought that this announcement was designed to lull us into a false sense of security, so that we would allow ourselves to be placed in trucks and conveyed into the woods on the pretense that we were being taken to our homes. Then, we feared that we would be killed en masse.

But to our overwhelming amazement, we were actually turned loose and apparently free to make our way back to our native localities as best we could!

I don't think that many or any of us did what the Communists expected us to. We knew what we could expect from the common criminals who constituted the membership of the "People's Committees" and "People's Courts" of our places of residence. Therefore, we went to any place in Yugoslavia rather than our native habitats. I, for one, stayed clear of my Dalmatian birthplace, concealing myself in Bilogora until September 12, 1945.

On this day, Tito's secret police discovered and arrested me. They threw me into one prison after another, until finally I was brought to Split to be tried as a "war criminal" and "enemy of the People." Since I had done nothing during the war that any soldier on active service might not have done, it was hard to prove anything against me except that I had been an Ustasha. This fact in itself was enough to expose me to torture of various kinds at the hands of my interlocutors, but they got nothing out of me that way. Surprisingly enough, some witnesses dared to testify to my innocence of wrongdoings of which all Ustasha were supposed to be guilty. Nonetheless, I was sentenced to three years forced labor. Presumably, this was the punishment I deserved for having fought on the losing side in the war.

It was 1952 when I finally returned to my native village in Dalmatia. When I asked there about the present whereabouts of my old school friends and military comrades, I found that they either were known to be dead or else had "disappeared." I shall not attempt to enumerate all of these individuals by name, but perhaps the data that I can supply in regard to the following eighteen people, all of whom I knew well, will be revealing and have certain value for posterity.

Frane and Jure Banovic were killed because they made many donations and contributions to the Croatian Armed Forces during the war years. No one knows what was done with their bodies. Marko Bobanovic, son of the late Gajo, was killed because his son was a soldier in the Croatian Army. While he was on furlough from the Army, Mile Skara was caught and shot by the Partisans during the war. Marko Zilic was arrested while he was having supper one evening after the war. He was led off and shot. An elderly veteran of the Austro-Hungarian Army of World War I, Joso Krstenac, was killed by the Partisans during the war in the same way. Grga Bacic was murdered in front of his house for no known reason. Mile Peraic was overpowered by several Communists on his way home from work one evening and murdered by them. His thirteen-year-old son tried to defend him, but the killers bound him with wire and threw him down a ravine. Ljubo Zagorac was picked up by a Communist detail on his way home from his fields. His ears, nose, and genitals were cut off and his captors then tried to make him eat these severed parts of his anatomy. Even Niko Peraic's dog had to share the fate of her master and mistress. The Communists killed Niko first, and next threw his body into a large hole. Then they slew his wife and dumped her corpse on top of his. Finally, these upholders of the "People's Justice" butchered the Peraic dog and sent her to accompany her masters in death as she had in life. Stones were heaped upon the common grave of the three victims. Juko Kulas, both of his sons, and Ruza Peraic were crucified by the Partisans who also evidenced their proletarian instincts by gouging out the heart of Joso Matosic.

I could go on and relate the fate of many other people whom I once knew. But I think that this cross section of victims of the American and British-backed Tito regime may suffice to show what the triumph of the Communists in the last war meant. I selected the names of the above-mentioned individuals from many others because they all were good, honest, human beings whose only crime was that they happened to be patriotic Croatians.

I have not written this report for the purpose of opening old wounds. But peaceful, truth-loving people everywhere must know what the victory of Communism implies. What happened to the Croatians at the hands of the predominantly Serbian Yugoslav Communists can happen to any people who fall under Communist domination anywhere in the world.

Signed: Slavko Skara

Alsdorf, West Germany
August 30, 1961

Document LV

The first fourth of this account by Croatian cadet G., deals with the Croatian troops' evacuation of Zagreb, their battles with the Partisans at Dravograd, their talks with the British at Bleiburg, and their surrender to the Sixteenth Voyvodina Division. The Partisans of this unit were in charge of the prisoners' column, to which eighty-two cadet officers, including our witness, were attached. They were marched through Dravograd to Maribor. When they arrived there, the witness and a large group of other young prisoners were assigned to the unpleasant jobs in warehouses. G., for instance, disinfected bloodstained uniforms that had been stripped off prisoners. During this work, he learned about the horrifying massacres at the anti-tank trenches. At the end of July, our eyewitness was transported from Maribor through Slovenia and Croatia. In mid-August 1945, G. was set free at Osijek.

I, the undersigned, am a surviving witness of the occurrences of May 17, 1945. In the following report I have recorded events as they impressed themselves upon my memory. I have limited myself in this account to episodes involving the Croatian Armed Forces, in general, and the detachment to which I belonged, in particular.

The military evacuation of Zagreb was effected at the end of the first week in May. My detachment left the capital on the 8th, after the Germans had blown up the arsenal which was housed in the Prince Eugen Barracks in Cernomerac. We had orders to retire towards Zapresic where we would receive further directions. We knew that the Croatian Army Command intended that the forces under its control should make contact with the British. We surmised that we would return with the latter to Zagreb.

I was one of four hundred student officers of the Armed Forces. Although we were accompanied by some civilians, we retreated in a compact body. The civilians were mainly the wives of Army officers and the parents of some of the cadets.

Just as we were crossing the Croatian-Slovenian border, the order reached us to proceed towards Klagenfurt in Austria. Still maintaining our military formation, we passed through Celje where we ran into Partisan detachments. These Communist formations did not attempt to interfere with our march towards Dravograd.

We experienced our first difficulties as we approached Dravograd. Bulgarian troops, who were accompanying the Soviet armies which had attacked the Croatian state from the north and east, barred the Drava crossing. Since the bridge was still intact at this point, we determined to fight our way across the stream. My close friend, Senior Lieutenant S. N., opened fire upon the Bulgars with his four howitzers. I do not believe that the Bulgarians cherished any animosity towards the Croatians or had any wish to fight them. In any case, they beat a quick retreat. We did not cross the river anyway because we learned that large masses of Russian troops were approaching, and that we were bound to run into them on the far bank.

Following a wait of four or five hours, we began moving along our bank of the Drava in the direction of Klagenfurt. Because we did not wish to march in formation along the highway and thus expose ourselves to sniping on the part of the Slovenian Partisans who were gathering in the hills nearby, we broke up into small parties and made our way through the woods over difficult terrain. Thus, we avoided being shot at by the Communists who stayed well out of our way, evidently having no stomach for an engagement on equal terms among the trees and thick shrubbery.

We had our first exchange of fire with the enemy only as we neared the Austrian frontier. I am not familiar with the details of this encounter. From this time on, the group to which I was attached remained out of contact with the other cadet parties and their civilian accompaniment.

Our march was held up for several hours for unexplained reasons on May 14. We still had not run into Communist opposition of real consequence. On the following day, May 15, we came to a huge field which lay outside the town of Bleiburg. Here we were ordered to form up by unit. I do not know how many people were gathered together on this vast meadow. I heard later that close to 200,000 refugees of all categories had assembled here, but I cannot affirm that this figure is correct. Our ranking military officer was General Herencic, while Professor Daniel Crljen was the civilian representative of the Pavelic regime. We were told that these two were carrying on negotiations with the British Command and that we had halted our withdrawal into Austria for this reason. The purpose of regrouping into our proper units was to facilitate a surrender to the British Army that we had anticipated for some days past.

Most Croatians possessed a truly touching faith in the British sense of military honor and fair play, supposedly inculcated on the playing fields of Eton, Harrow, Sandhurst, and other English academic establishments. Hence, we had no apprehensions about our fate. We knew only our gladness that the war was over, even though we had lost it, for the long marches of the past week, accompanied by lack of food and water or a place to rest at night, had worn us out.

At 4:00 P.M. we were still engaged in reforming our units. Suddenly, we were told to furl our Croatian flags and to run up white emblems of surrender in their stead. Likewise, we had to stack our weapons for delivery to the British. The war was over, and though we had lost, we had nothing to fear.

Up to this point in my life, I had always been an optimist. Therefore, I assumed now that everything had been arranged by our Command and that we had nothing but a period of temporary detention to worry about. It was only when I noticed that it was not Englishmen, but men of the Sixteenth Voyvodina Partisan Division, who were collecting our piled up arms that I began to feel uneasy.

Once we were disarmed, the Communists had us form up in columns of eight. We started out towards Dravograd. I was included in a group of eighty officer cadets, all from the original unit which had left Zagreb on the 8th. We marched under the leadership of First Lieutenant Nicholas Obad. The Communists were amazed at the precision and order of our march. In retrospect, our attitude at this time seems tragically futile. Yet, at that moment in history, our only thought was to demonstrate to Tito's assorted collections of Marxists that we had formed part of a well organized Army compared to which they were only rabble. Unfortunately, that rabble was supplied, armed, equipped, and backed politically by the three major world powers: Russia, Great Britain, and the United States.

From Bleiburg and Dravograd we continued along the Drava bank to Maribor. During the first phase of our march, I did not see our Communist captors commit any atrocities, although they did not allow us to eat or drink. I cannot say precisely when they began to single out certain prisoners whom they stripped of their clothes and valuables and then shot alongside the road, or in the adjoining woods. I do remember that on May 17, I was barefoot and clad in nothing but my underwear.

The "comrades" approached us from time to time and committed all kinds of brutalities. As torturers, the female "comrades" distinguished themselves; their bestiality was unbounded.

En route to Maribor, Lieutenant Commissar Yovan Yovanovitch, a native of Stara Pazova, appeared among us. Until Easter, 1943, he had been a fellow student of mine at the Officer Training School in Zagreb. He was the only member of the Orthodox Church who attended this school, as far as I know. As a former fellow student who knew us well, Yovanovitch was relatively decent in his conduct toward us. He told us that we were being taken to prison camps where we would be investigated individually. Any persons who were proved to be war criminals would be punished. Those who were not charged with war crimes would be sent to their homes. This piece of information cheered us up greatly, because we knew that we were not guilty of anything save being identified with the losing side in the war. After Yovanovitch left us, however, the "comrades" continued to strip us and beat us. We endured this treatment without fighting back because we thought that once we had reached the camps and were under the eyes of some kind of authority, this would cease.

Then the Reds began to shoot whomever they happened to feel like shooting. In the beginning, they took individuals out of the formation and killed them in the nearby woods. Later, they fired directly into the prisoner column. This shooting was entirely indiscriminate. They seemed to be worried lest they had overlooked something of value that we might have, so, from time to time they stopped different sections of the column in order to make minute investigations of our persons. Due to these search procedures, the column split into several segments. Those left in the rear were ordered to run to catch up to the forward parts of the column. Anyone who lagged behind was shot without warning.

Our greatest suffering came from thirst. There were wells close to the highway, but Communist machine gun detachments were stationed before each of them. Also, the Drava closely approached our line of march at many places. To fall out of the column in order to obtain water meant certain death. Some of the more decent of our guards told us that the commissar who had charge of the column had issued specific orders that we were not to be allowed to stop to drink anywhere. He was a Serbian from Belgrade.

We arrived in Maribor about noon of the 19th. Here we were separated into four groups, officers, Ustashas, gendarmes, and Domobrans. I was among the latter. We were treated rather more leniently than were the other groups, because we were younger.

After this classification, which was conducted by a commissar, we found ourselves grouped into units of approximately one hundred each. The Communists allowed us to designate one of our number to command us. We chose Simon Suic, an Ustasha lieutenant, who hailed from Dalmatia. He had graduated from the officer school in Zagreb ahead of me. We sat or lay on the ground waiting to see what was going to happen now. Again the "comrades" searched us to make sure they hadn't missed looting us of something worthwhile.

On the evening of this day, Communist headquarters in Maribor issued a call for laborers. Eighty-two of us were assigned to this detail which proceeded under heavy guard to the barracks which stood near the Franciscan church in Maribor. Here we were received by our new commander, "Comrade" Carl.

We were put to work at various unpleasant and tiring jobs. After working all day, we were allowed to return to the barracks at night and sleep there. During the first few days of our employment, there was wild shooting all around the city. The guards told us that these shots were being fired in victory celebrations. Later, we found out the truth—anti-Communist Croatians and Slovenes were being liquidated.

I did not see the ill-famed anti-tank ditches where the massacres took place. However, I had no trouble discovering what was going on. My place of employment was the Communist clothing warehouse located in the former "Hitler Square" in Maribor. While the Germans were in control of this town, the headquarters of the Gestapo were located here. For eight days I was occupied with the cleaning and disinfection of uniforms taken from members of the Croatian Armed Forces. It was with deep horror and vain sentiments of rage and regret that I had to throw the bloodsoaked uniforms of Ustashas, Croatian gendarmes, Domobrans, and German Gestapo alike into the steam ovens and, after they were cleaned, load them into wagons.

One of the wagon drivers was a Slovenian civilian from Maribor. I accompanied him on each of the four trips that he made daily to a large clothing warehouse that was located just outside of Maribor. Here, the cleaned uniforms were pressed and distributed to various Communist units. Naturally, I found out a good many things from the Slovene during these trips. Civilians in the neighborhood also told me that on the nights of May 20-24 inclusive the slaughter of all Ustasha prisoners had been effected in the above mentioned anti-tank trenches dug originally by the Germans near Maribor.

I learned from my several informants that General Kosta Nadj, Commander of the Third Yugoslav Army, was in charge of the destinies of those of us included in the work detail. As traitors (to Karageorgevitch Yugoslavia which the Communists themselves hated), we Croatians could all expect punishment. Those of us who bore a lesser degree of responsibility for this "treachery" had to be "reeducated." Major "traitors" would be executed or assigned to forced labor groups.

The director of the clothing warehouse was a Slovene by the name of Steharnik. A junior officer of the former Yugoslav Army of 1919-41, he was married to a woman from Belgrade. I remember that he had a female assistant named Lyubica. She was the usual type of bitch one finds among the "comrades." There was also a guard, Novakovic, who had charge of me personally during the trips I made with the uniforms. He was not a Communist himself. Involved in black market operations in Austria during the war, he had been arrested by the German authorities in Vienna where he was imprisoned. When the Russians captured Vienna, they found him in prison and assumed, therefore, that he was at least a Socialist, if not an outright Communist. They freed him, and he returned to Maribor as a "patriot." He behaved quite decently towards me, and I am thankful that I had the good luck to be assigned to his custody.

I worked at the warehouse until the end of July. At this time, about three thousand Croatians were concentrated at Camp Tezno near Maribor. This was the last Croatian group left in Slovenia. We were placed under the command of a commissar by the name of Matthew who had us loaded onto freight trains. For three days and four nights we stayed aboard these trains which pulled slowly through Zidani Most, Zagreb, Brod, and Vinkovci, among other places. Finally, we were unloaded at Osijek where a camp had been established at the Kolar brick factory. The head of this newly founded place of detention was a Communist militia lieutenant, Ilias. We were treated somewhat better at this camp than at the last one, but we had to be careful concerning what we said or did since spies were planted in our midst.

From Osijek we were transferred to Pozega. Here, we had to undergo another investigation. Twenty-five of us were separated from the rest and sent to the prison maintained by the Communist militia in Osijek. A further investigation dragged out here over a two week period. Then we were freed. I arrived at my home on August 19, 1945. Thus, my participation in the death marches that followed the end of hostilities in

May came to a more fortunate close than that of many of my old comrades from the officers' school who were no more guilty of war crimes than I was.

Signed: G.

Document LVI

Stjepan Maric tells how the Seventh Croatian Division and a great number of other Croatian troops surrendered to the Partisans near Dravograd. Then, mounted Partisan guards accompanied them towards Maribor amidst usual "Death March" brutalities. About three miles from Maribor the exhausted marchers were forced to run. After this, Maric and several hundred other prisoners were taken to the Maribor airport to work on filling some three hundred holes that had been made during the war by bombs. A considerable number of our eyewitness' co-workers were taken off by the Partisans to join tens of thousands of other Croats being murdered in the area; some others escaped into the woods..After a three month labor at Maribor, Maric and close to two hundred other captives were transported to Osijek like cattle for the slaughter. Here, the witness was at long last released and sent home.

During the war of 1941-45, I served in the 7th Croatian Division which was commanded by General Pericic. When the collapse of Germany became imminent, we started to retreat northwards from Capljina. Our route went through Mostar, capital of Hercegovina. At the Grubisno Polje in Hercegovina, we were heavily engaged with the Partisan troops and I was wounded. However, I was able to stay with the Division which went on to Sarajevo and then to Zagreb.

In compliance with orders issued by the Government, we evacuated Zagreb on May 8, 1945, and retired towards Celje and Dravograd in Slovenia. On the way, we had a few skirmishes with the Reds, who were not able to interrupt our progress. We halted our retreat before we reached Dravograd because our civil and military authorities were trying to negotiate with the British and Americans for surrender to their troops. We wasted several days here until the British, using low flying planes and a formidable array of tanks and artillery, finally induced us to surrender on the premise that we would be prisoners-of-war.

A great number of Croatian soldiers laid down their arms on a big field near Dravograd. After they had done so in the belief that they were surrendering to the British, Yugoslav Communists appeared to organize the prisoners into columns. I was included in one of these groups which started to march to the Slovenian town of Maribor.

As soon as our Communist guards were sure that the British were out of sight and hearing, they began to rob us of our watches, rings, money, and fountain pens, together with everything else of value, including our shoes and clothes. Although the road that we traveled was known to be mined, we had to stay on it. There were three stretches along this route where people stepped on mines and were blown up.

We spent the first night of the march to Maribor in a village. On the next morning we set off again, accompanied by mounted Partisan guards. They killed anyone who could not keep up with the column. Anyone who tried to quench his thirst at a brook, stream, or well along the route was also killed on the spot. Besides their guns, our captors had long whips ending in pieces of lead. They used these on every possible occasion, so that many of us soon were bleeding profusely from gashes they inflicted.

A Croatian soldier from Hercegovina became so infuriated by the blows he received that he attacked one of the Partisan guards and pulled him from his horse. When he had him on the ground, he snatched a big knife that the Communist had stuck into one of his boots and killed the man on the spot. Then the Croat ran towards the bank of the Drava, dove into it, and swam across to the other side. The Partisans fired furiously after him, but he made good his escape.

When we were about three miles distant from Maribor, our guards ordered us to start running. In order to keep up, we had to throw away the rest of our belongings. In this manner, we were brought to a big prison camp where we were divided into two groups. The Ustashas were lined up on the right side, while the Domobrans were assembled on the left. I took my place with the Domobrans.

After the separation was complete, several hundred of us were marched off in the direction of the Maribor airport. Along the way, I saw the Partisans taking small groups of prisoners towards the Drava River along whose banks they were shot. There were many corpses floating in this stream.

When we arrived at the airport, we were put to work filling up holes in the runway. For the first time in four days of captivity, we received some food—two pounds of bread for every ten men. Also, we were given some spoiled cheese. A Partisan officer informed us that we were considered captives rather than enemies. He told us, too, that after we had filled in the holes at the aerodrome, we would be returned to our homes.

There were approximately three hundred holes made by bombs dropped by Allied airmen during the war. They were usually about six feet deep and ten feet in diameter. It took us a good three months to fill them up. There were only about a hundred and fifty of us left at the end of this time, since many men escaped while others were taken off in a black automobile nicknamed "Black Maritza." None of these individuals ever returned to our ranks.

Often, while we were working at the airport, we heard continuous shooting from the middle of the afternoon until around ten in the evening. We were informed through various sources that Croatian military personnel were being murdered en masse. One of our fellow workers at the airport, Stjepan Bakula, was able to go into the town at night to exchange cigarettes for bread. There he heard about the mass killings and passed the information he received on to us. Through him, we learned that tens of thousands of officers and soldiers had been slaughtered by the Partisans. A similar account was supplied to us by Ivan Galic, who was a native of the village of Galic-Vinjani near Posusje. Galic was later stricken by an attack of typhoid fever and, during periods of delirium, he used to babble and rave about the killings. He recovered from the fever, but was then taken off in the "Black Maritza" and never again heard from.

After about three months, we were transferred to one of the Maribor prison camps. Here, we received almost no food at all. The Communist guards assigned to this place were an exceptionally brutal lot. Fortunately, I did not remain there very long. I was one of a group of seventy-three Croatians and a hundred and three Italians who were packed into locked boxcars and shipped to Osijek like cattle to the slaughter. During the journey to this place, we received only crumbs of bread and a truly microscopic quantity of water. Since there were no sanitary facilities provided, we had to relieve ourselves right in the congested boxcar. When we arrived at Osijek, we were so stiff and exhausted that we couldn't scramble out of the cars fast enough to suit our captors, who consequently gave us a good beating.

At least the worst of our troubles were now over. We remained in Osijek for only ten days, then were sent to Pozega, where we remained imprisoned for another month. Finally, I was released at Pozega and was able to return to my home.

Signed: Stjepan Maric

Rome
February 13, 1953

Document LVII

Dimitrije Pejovic, a Montenegrin prisoner-of-war, in the first third of his report describes the retreat and battles of the Croatian Armed Forces and the Montenegrin Brigade against the Partisans. On the night of May 14-15, the Croatian warriors were ordered to cease fire. In the second third of his account, Pejovic corroborates what so many other eyewitnesses had stated concerning "Death March" atrocities from the Austrian-Yugoslav border to Maribor. The last and the most important part of this testimony deals with the witness' escape from an imminent slaughter and with his description of the anti-tank trenches and other abattoirs at Maribor.

On May 5, 1945, my unit of the Croatian Armed Forces marched out of Zagreb en route to Ljubljana. When we arrived at Zidani Most, we received orders to take the Celje road. We were informed that the Partisans had already captured the Slovenian capital.

Celje was in the hands of the Communists, too, but General Luburic's Croatian forces and the Montenegrin Brigade, which was commanded by Lieutenant Janjitch, forced them to give up the town after a brief encounter. We continued our retreat in the direction of Maribor.

When we came to the Maribor-Dravograd crossroads, we met several thousand anti-Communist Russian Cossacks. We joined them in their procession from Maribor, and our combined forces moved on towards Dravograd.

Two miles out of this town, we ran into strong Communist formations. Although we could have forced our way through easily enough, as we had at Celje, our leaders knew that the war was lost and that the Germans had already quit. Therefore, they considered it best to try to make an agreement with the Reds, so that we could continue our march into Austria without further bloodshed.

Two days were spent in negotiating with the Partisans opposing us. Of course, these people were only stalling for time until they could receive reinforcements. On the third day that we remained here, they told us that at 3:00 P.M. they would open their lines and let us go through without resistance.

Many of us had no faith in any promises that the Partisans might make. Therefore, we were prepared when they attacked us in force half an hour before the time scheduled for our penetration of their lines. A fierce battle raged throughout the afternoon and into the night. Finally, General Luburic's troops broke through the Red front and sent Tito's people flying helter skelter into the woods. We did not suffer too heavily in this fight, but I remember passing many dead and wounded Partisans.

The Austro-Slovene frontier lay close to Dravograd. We had another skirmish with the Partisans before we reached the boundary line, and once again brushed their forces aside. On the night of May 14, word reached us that our leaders had established contact with the British to whom we were going to surrender. Further fighting was prohibited by our Command.

Midway through the following morning, we suddenly found ourselves in the hands, not of the British, but of Yugoslav Communists. They informed our leaders that the British, American, and Russian forces had made an agreement whereby all anti-Communist military units and civilian refugees would be taken to Maribor, where the Tito Government would examine their cases individually.

Since our commanders appeared to feel that the Partisans were acting in good faith, we left our ammunition and arms at the border that same night. Then, as prisoners of war, we were herded back towards Maribor by Montenegrin Communist guards.

When we arrived at Dravograd, all women and young people up to the age of seventeen were separated from the male prisoners. The women were sent by train to Maribor, but the children rejoined us a little later on.

That evening we marched about four miles outside of Dravograd, before we stopped for the night. On the following morning we continued our "march" towards Maribor. Along the route, we saw piles of corpses, mostly those of Croatian soldiers. Many of these victims still wore their uniforms, but their shoes had been removed. There were air shelters, built by the Germans, along the way, too. Since we could see arms and legs hanging out of the windows, and heads, too, here and there, these shelters seemed to be filled with bodies. It is impossible to estimate the number of corpses we had to pass. The Communists saw to it that we did not approach the dead too closely.

At Maribor we were joined by another group of Croatian soldiers. Our entire column was now ordered to proceed on the run, instead of walking as before. In this fashion we were crowded into some military barracks where we were overjoyed to find our wives. They had come to Maribor by train.

Our elation was short-lived, however. The Reds again separated all the women and youth up to seventeen from the rest of us. They were taken out of the city and then sent to their homes. When the escorts got back to the barracks, they looted us of all our valuables. Likewise, they beat us for no reason at all. The female Partisans surpassed the men in savagery and bestiality.

Somewhat later, we were lined up according to our military districts and told that we were going to be transported to our places of origin. I remember that the first to leave were soldiers who came from the village of Berane. The rest of us followed, individually. Two lines of Partisans awaited us outside. They conducted us to another part of the city where we were taken into a courthouse. Here we saw big piles of Montenegrin uniforms, some of them almost five feet high.

Inside this building, we were ordered to remove all of our clothes except our underwear. This done, the Partisans began to beat us again. Grouping us together by threes, they then tied our hands with electric wire. They kept on beating us as they loaded us into trucks. There were twenty-four prisoners and three armed Partisans in the truck in which I found myself.

After the truck began to move, I managed to release my hands and wrists from the wire with which they had been bound. Having done so, I helped five other men escape their bonds. I asked a Partisan guard where we were going; he replied bluntly that we were going to be shot. Since we obviously had nothing to lose, I joined four other prisoners in jumping the guards and the driver. We threw them out of the truck, although one of them managed to hang on to his machine gun and fired a burst after us. We got away unharmed.

We were about four miles out of Maribor when this incident took place. It seemed best to abandon the truck and make our way on foot, which we did, after freeing the rest of the prisoners. As we moved through the woods, we saw German soldiers shoveling earth onto freshly dug graves a short distance from the road. Also, we saw holes from which there protruded the heads, legs, and arms of various victims. We had to go right through the area where the massacres were taking place and had a good opportunity to witness the extent of the bloodbath. It is my estimate that there were 50,000 Croatians dumped into the anti-tank trenches the Germans had scooped out during the war. Half a mile away from this mass abattoir, at least 7,000 Montenegrin royalists lay dead. On one occasion, I witnessed from nearby the slaughter of a number of women and children. What had these innocents done to merit execution? I felt like an animal in a slaughterhouse.

For a good ten days we made our way through the forests and mountains. Finally, we crossed the Austrian border at the Gorenska Preca and reached the British zone of occupation. Although it was against our better judgment to do so, we were so hungry and exhausted that we gave ourselves up to the British again. We were taken before the commanding officer in this sector. A major and two captains were with him. I spoke enough English to be able to tell them everything, just as I had seen it happen. All of the Britons were horrified to hear what their Partisan allies had done.

I swear on my honor that the facts I have related above are true. I am ready to go with an international commission to those places where I know the massacres occurred. I shall be glad to testify to what I saw and, if the necessary excavations are undertaken, there will be no difficulty in proving the truth of my statement. I certify that all the details cited above were read to me and were recorded truthfully.

Signed: Dimitrije Pejovic

Villach, Austria
June 20, 1945

Chapter 10

The "Liberation" of Zagreb

Document LVIII

The Rev. H. Eterovic opens his account by depicting the exceptionally high morale of the Croatian troops at the time of the evacuation of Zagreb. The Partisans, on the other hand, entered the Croatian capital with fright and anxiety; they soon concentrated their attention on lootings and plunderings. In mid-May, 1945, columns of prisoners-of-war began arriving in Zagreb and for a week and half filled Zagreb streets at all hours of the day and night. Then the Communist Government directed all Domobran (regular) officers to report for service in the Army of "new" Yugoslavia. These officers, most of them reserves, were not heard from afterwards. Two months after the "liberation," the entire population was classified into supporters of Communism, "gray masses" and anti-Communists. The account closes emphasizing the fact that for over two years after the war, the activities of the Tito regime were directed chiefly towards the liquidation of all real, potential, or imaginary enemies.

I am a Dominican Father, a survivor of that community which suffered so greatly during the bombardment of the Dominican monastery adjoining the park at Maksimir in Zagreb by Allied airmen on February 22, 1944.

Throughout the last days of the Independent State of Croatia, and during the first years of the post-1945 Communist regime, I continued to reside in Zagreb. However, at Christmas and at Easter the Church authorities sent me to various places in the provinces to serve the spiritual needs of churches, which remained without pastors after the spring of 1945.

The following are the recollections of this eventful period as they have remained in my memory.

While the wartime Croatian State administration was operating, a considerable number of the inhabitants of Zagreb stood opposed to it, either openly or secretly. The dissatisfaction with the regime of Dr. Ante Pavelic increased more and more as the war approached its end. Some Zagrebcani imagined that the establishment of a Marxist government in Croatia would effect a relief of existing abuses and a better observance of law. They thought that the prospective new order would bring to the capital, in particular, a way of life that would correspond more closely to that of pre-1918 Zagreb than did that of the Ustasha dispensation of 1941-1945. They expected that the Croatian Peasant Party would set the tone of the changes that could be anticipated.

These dissident elements had not counted on the fact that the scum of the central Balkans would arrive in Zagreb after the withdrawal of the Croatian Armed Forces. This region has all too often distinguished itself by the production of the worst sort of riff-raff. Immediately as they entered the capital city, this miscellany of desperados, cutthroats, sadists, and political fanatics began a reign of terror such as had not been seen in Zagreb since the Mongol invasion of the thirteenth century.

Prior to the appearance of these "modern Huns," the attitudes of the Zagrebcani towards the expected Partisan takeover had differed considerably. Some people took a very optimistic view of the situation and thought that Tito's people would behave quite decently once the war was over. Others had a more realistic outlook, but still hoped that some slight improvements over wartime conditions would follow the return of peace. In my own opinion, the majority of the citizens of Zagreb who stayed in the city to welcome the new authorities were Partisan sympathizers, although it should be recognized that not everyone who took a favorable view of the Partisans had identical ideas about them. For some time, Tito and his more intelligent disciples contrived rather successfully to play the "all things to all men" role. Thus, a good many Croatians who had no use for Marxism in any form, nonetheless allowed themselves to be persuaded that, with the advent of Communism or Socialism, an era of lesser evil would be inaugurated. Then, there were the wives, children, and other relatives of members of the Croatian Armed Forces, both dead and living, who thought that it would be wiser for them to remain at home than to join the military exodus, which, as a matter of fact, was greatly hampered by the influx of civilian refugees.

Yet, in the final analysis, the attitude of the population of Zagreb was determined chiefly by the announcements put out over the Zagreb radio station. Right up to the last minute, Ustasha guards stood around this center of information, which continued to ask one and all to behave with composure and discretion even after the Croatian Army had evacuated the city. Thus, pro and anti-Communists alike labored under the impression that it would be better to remain quietly in their homes, than to join the retreat or expose themselves to the various risks attendant upon appearance in the streets during the first hours of the entrance of the Communists into Zagreb and the transition from Ustasha to Marxist regime.

The prevalence of this general attitude explains why the streets of the capital were completely deserted when the entry of the Partisans into the city was effected. Even out and out Marxists were afraid to show their heads, because they had observed that the Croatian troops, who only two or three days earlier had passed through or around Zagreb on their retreat from the south, bore no resemblance to a defeated army, or to one in flight. Unlike the Germans, who were fast becoming a disorderly and disorganized mob, the Croatians had kept their formations intact and, despite the military parsimony of their Teutonic allies, they were fairly well equipped and armed, and entirely disciplined and obedient to the orders of their commanders. Not for nothing had the Croatians been the last troops to withdraw from a lost field during the long centuries of Habsburg rule. The habits of iron discipline ingrained by service in the old Imperial-Royal Army had passed over into Croatian military tradition as a permanent legacy. Thus, in May, 1945, the withdrawing formations looked more like troops who were anxious for and preparing to initiate new combats, than units which found themselves on the losing side in a war. Not a trace of fear or even anxiety could be detected among the Croatian soldiery. On the contrary, a spirit of Homeric heroism and that readiness for combat which appears in epic poetry of ancient Greece and other nations was evident. Even the strongest Communist sympathizers were intimidated, because they were prey to the uneasy suspicion that these retreating troops might about-face at any moment and make a quick end to the Marxist establishment in the Balkans, before the Russians, Americans, and British could arrive on the scene in time to save their Red proteges.

Especially terrifying to all Marxist sympathizers was the appearance of the "Crnci" and "Maksovci" ("Luburicevci") groups during the retreat. These units formed the rearguards of the retiring army and, as a general rule, they were the last armed men to pass through the city. They were organized into detachments of twenty or thirty men, almost all of whom carried light machine guns. One glance at them was enough to persuade any onlooker that they were enraged over the course that events were taking and were in a thoroughly savage humor. En route through the city they would open fire on anyone whom they detected peering at them out of a doorway or window. However, it must be remembered that the "Maksovci" and the other groups did not fire directly upon those whom they caught watching their withdrawal. They peppered the areas immediately below or around the windows and doorways with bullets, but I do not believe that a single person was killed or wounded by their discharges. Nevertheless, the lesson taught served as an effective deterrent to idle military curiosity; not even the stoutest Marxist dared to indulge his desire to harass the retreating troops.

When the Partisans began to enter the city, there was heavy firing heard from the direction of Dubrava. A little later, a battle developed around the radio station where some die-hard Ustasha elements offered strong resistance to the takeover. I had the opportunity to listen to the radio broadcasts, which continued while the fighting was in progress, and I heard the Communists, after they had won control of the Station, cursing the "Ustasha mothers" of the defenders and personnel of the network. Some Croatian spokesmen answered the Marxists back very sharply. There remains in my mind a jumbled impression of confused quarreling and a mutual exchange of insults going on over the air waves. Most of this action occurred around ten or eleven o'clock P.M. on May 8, 1945.

Soon after the fighting ended around the radio station, the Communists began to send out their own broadcasts. These were intended primarily for those of Tito's troops who had already entered Zagreb, or who were about to do so. The Partisans were asked to refrain from plundering the population of the city and to restrain their conduct in general. Individuals who did not comply with these instructions would be hanged or shot.

On the following day, May 9, about 10:00 A.M., individual columns of Partisans began to filter through the streets of the city. I remember that one such column came from the direction of Dubrava towards Vlaska Street. Another column surrounded and seized the railroad station. These Partisan formations looked scared to death. Even though the streets were empty and no resistance was being offered anywhere, Tito's people were noticeably "jumpy" and seemed to expect an ambush at any moment. Many of them would not cross a street, except at full speed and all bent over, as though they anticipated a hail of bullets around their ears.

The first Red units to enter the city were not composed of Croatian Communists. They were mainly Montenegrins, or people from other areas to the south of the Croatian territories. Their appearance produced an impression incomparably worse than that made by any unit in the Croatian Armed Forces. Many of these Partisans were barefoot, and almost all were dirty, unshaven, and clad only in rags. Their faces reflected a mixture of savagery and fright. Their actions at the main railroad station were really quite ludicrous. This station was entirely empty, but the Partisans crept cautiously from one boxcar or pile of wood to another and were ready to bolt whenever they heard the least suspicious sound. Indeed, their entry into Zagreb bore no resemblance to that of a victorious army or the "heroic seizure" that Tito's publicists began to talk about later.

Such behavior naturally influenced the attitudes of the citizens of Zagreb, including those who were Communist-orientated. Even the most fanatic Marxists stayed off the streets and made no attempt to greet the entering "comrades" or to exhibit any rejoicing at the takeover. One had the impression that they still half expected the Croatian Army to return suddenly and send this raggle-taggle though well-armed (by Russia, Great Britain, and the United States of America) collection of guerrillas flying back to those parts of the Balkans, from which they had so recently emerged.

Three or four days after the appearance in the metropolis of these mixed Balkan units, Croatian Communist formations from Dalmatia and Slavonia began to enter the city. These men presented a far better appearance both in dress and conduct. For the first time since the beginning of the war in 1941, I saw mounted Communists wearing boots. Horse and boots were a sign of rank among Croatian Partisans. Still later, motor vehicles and tanks poured into Zagreb. The citizens were horrified when the latter tore up the secondary streets which could not support the weight of these metal monsters.

Despite the warnings issued in regard to plundering, the Partisans almost immediately began to take the shoes of all the male inhabitants of the city they could find. In those first days of the "liberation," it seemed that the Partisans were unable to look anyone straight in the face. They had eyes only for footgear, and they made any passer-by who was wearing good shoes take them off instantly. Especially in the southern part of the city, many apartments were plundered. It seems that the poorer elements of the population, those living in the several suburbs, especially at Trnje, suffered most heavily from this indiscriminate looting. I heard that the Communist authorities severely punished some of the looters. At least they saw to it that news was spread around that plunderers were being shot or hanged.

While all this was going on, the optimistic mood, prevalent among such a large part of the city's population since the end of hostilities had become imminent, changed gradually into disappointment, despair, and, finally, panic.

Five or six days after the entry of the first Partisans into Zagreb, columns of captured German and Croatian soldiers began to arrive from the northwest. Lined up in columns of fours, they passed through the city at all hours of the day and night. These processions of captives filled the main streets for a period of about ten days. My impression was that the number of these soldiers was immense. Yet, I do not recall that I saw many Ustashas among them. It is the Domobrans whom I remember most distinctly. There was no mixing of Croatian with German captives. Each nationality proceeded in separate columns and along different streets. Not many Communist guards were in evidence. Those who were present hardly could be detected among the multitude of prisoners.

The Germans were very visibly more war-weary and depressed than the Croatians. The latter were unshaven and very tired from lack of sleep, as well as food and water. They marched heavily, dragging their feet, and they had no smiles or greetings for the spectators who lined the sidewalks to see them pass. Still, they retained their military appearance; obviously they were soldier-prisoners. The fact that they were in Zagreb and in their own country provided them with a ray of life and hope. On the other hand, there was no trace of humanity in the countenances or general appearance of the Germans. They looked like animated corpses moving mechanically wherever they were driven by a remote, directing Intelligence. My impression was that the numbers of German and Croatian captives passing through the capital were approximately equal. I heard, too, that German soldiers who were not needed for labor on public works (such as the concentration camp and execution places) were slaughtered en masse at various places in the interior of the country. The abysses found on the Adriatic islands served as convenient places of disposal, also, for surplus prisoners-of-war.

Few people appeared on the streets to witness the passage of these masses of war prisoners through the city. The population preferred to look at the columns from behind closed windows. Nowhere did I see anyone offering food or water to the prisoners, who obviously were literally dying of thirst, hunger, and fatigue.

The "Great Fear" had permeated Zagreb in May 1945, just as the original sensation of this name had spread through the French countryside in the summer of 1789. But there was a more solid foundation for the 1945 emanation of the "Great Fear" than there was for its 1789 counterpart.

Some executions were carried out during the first days of the occupation. I was told that these killings took place only in the park at Maksimir. Apart from the passage of the prisoner columns, whatever happened was effected out of the sight and hearing of the city population, as far as I can remember.

About a month after the end of the war, the Communist Government directed all Domobran officers to report to the local authorities. It was announced that they were needed for service in the new Yugoslav Army. Many of these men were reserve officers who had never been in active service in the Croatian Armed forces. Some were old men who had fought in the Austro-Hungarian Army in 1914-18, but who were not called up in 1941-45. They were registered in the last reserve of the Croatian State, only for use in case of dire emergencies. These emergencies never occurred since Croatian political authorities decided to evacuate the country rather than defend it to the last gasp. Included among the Domobran "officer" group that had remained in Zagreb were a number of veterans who had seen service in the first part of the war, but who subsequently had been invalided out or otherwise retired from military life.

Because of the presence of all these categories of former or potential warriors in the population of the capital, a great number of men reported to the barracks located between Maksimir and Dubrava. I remember that they formed a column at least a mile long.

None of these men ever returned to their homes, nor did I nor anyone else among the civilian population of Zagreb learn anything concerning their fate. Not unnaturally, the entire populace was horrified by this incident. From the moment that these unfortunate victims of military and political bureaucracy vanished into thin air, fear and foreboding reigned supreme in what once had been "gay Zagreb."

After a few months, everyone had to get a new identification card. Everyone, without exception, received such an identification card complete with a photo and index of physical characteristics. Three kinds of cards were issued, though the number, placed in the seal of the card, was so small and inconspicuous that many people either did not notice it or, if they did, attached no importance to it. Yet, these numbers were of vital significance for the fate of the postwar population of Croatia.

The number "1" placed on an identification card meant that the individual to whom it belonged was an active member of the Yugoslav Communist Party, or at least was in good standing with the new authorities, because of wartime services in their behalf; "2" was inscribed on the cards of politically insignificant people, members of the so-called "gray multitude" or "gray masses." But a "3" on a card meant that the person who owned it had been identified in some way with opposition to Marxism and that he had to be watched closely.

Of course, I received one of these identification cards. As a Dominican, my number naturally was "3".

I lived under the Yugoslav Communist regime for more than two years. During this time, I can recall no work of reconstruction being carried out. To the best of my recollection there was no rebuilding going on, although the Tito regime received enormous shipments of goods of all kind from the UNRA. Tito's adherents took everything that was edible, wearable, or usable in any personal way among the UNRA packages and distributed it among the Party members and Partisan veterans and their families. The rest of the population received nothing whatsoever from the UNRA shipments, which could have been donated outright to the cause of Marxism in Yugoslavia, for all the good they did non-Marxists.

Between the end of the war in 1945 and the latter part of 1947, the activities of the Tito Government were directed chiefly towards one end —the liquidation of all real, potential, or imaginary enemies. Night arrests, abductions, and executions were the order of the day. It was the Reign of Terror of 1793-94 all over again, only it lasted much longer and the Yugoslav Communists or Socialists were far more sanguinary than were even the most fanatical of their Jacobin prototypes.

In short, it was a time of "purges" carried out on a mass scale. I can supply the details relative to several such purges but, in view of the multiplicity of evidence offered by eyewitnesses and survivors in these pages, it does not seem necessary to do so here.

This summary of my recollections of the years 1945-1947 has been read to me. It represents a faithful rendition of my personal experiences and impressions. Therefore, I am ready to confirm this deposition under oath, and I also stand ready to testify to the accuracy of the facts that I have related before any person or institution of authority.

Signed: Rev. Hyacinth Eterovic

Lynch, Nebraska
January 1, 1961

Document LIX

The first half of this testimony by a woman eyewitness deals with the "liberation" of Zagreb in May 1945. In the second half, the eyewitness, because of the Reign of Terror in the Croatian capital, finds herself in the Croatian provincial towns where she both saw and heard of "Death March" atrocities. Our eyewitness' story corroborates not only the previous document, but also many other accounts included in this volume.

I was first a citizen of the Austro-Hungarian Monarchy, then, after 1918, a subject of the Serbian dominated Serb-Croat-Slovene State which, in 1929, changed its name to "Yugoslavia." During the years 1941-45, I continued to live in what became the independent Kingdom of Croatia. After the Communist takeover in 1945, I remained in the new Yugoslavia until 1950.

I was an eyewitness of the Communist entry into Zagreb. They filtered into the town from several directions, by way of Sljeme, Sava, Kustosija, and through the park of Maksimir. They came into the city cautiously and quietly and yelled threats at anyone who looked at them out of a window. The streets of Zagreb were entirely empty. Passers-by were rarer than stray dogs. What impressed me most about the Partisans was their cursing, which included the most foul profanity, particularly directed at all Croatian mothers, whom they evidently held responsible for breeding this anti-Marxist species. The women Communists were worse than the men, both in language and actions.

Even though Dr. Pavelic and his Government had ordered the city to be evacuated without resistance, there was some fighting in Zagreb. I recall that there was a great deal of shooting, a pitched battle, in fact, around the radio station and that it was very dangerous to appear on the streets. If you passed a Partisan without greeting him, you would be arrested immediately and probably never seen again. On the other hand, if you called out a blithe "Hello, comrade!" or "Greetings, comrade," then you would be allowed to go your way without question.

Several days after the entrance of the Communists into the capital, those Croatian troops who had surrendered to the British Army in Austria or Slovenia and who had been handed over to the Partisans by the British, began to arrive in considerable numbers. For a month this influx of extradited military and civilian personnel continued to throng into the city.

The appearance of these captives was miserable beyond description. They were driven through the streets, so that everyone could see them. Then they were crowded into concentration camps, which were located at various points in the city and its suburbs. Their Partisan guards kept beating them with gun butts, pushing them, and yelling obscene threats and insults at them. Sometimes, the spectators were driven back by the guards so that they could not get a close view of what was going on, but on other occasions, the population was invited to see for themselves what the fate of enemies of the regime was likely to be. Evidently, the

Communist authorities were trying to employ the "strategy of terror" in order to intimidate the Zagrebcani, most of whom were known to be anything but Marxist-orientated.

I noted that a large number of the Croatian soldiers, as well as the German captives who were being brought in, were almost completely nude. Some actually had been stripped to the skin by their captors and could not hide their nakedness at all; others had nothing but a rag tied around their loins, while a great many were clad only in their underwear. I remember particularly a high-ranking German officer who had lived in Lovacki Rog during the war years. He was a good man and used to give us fodder for our pigs and other animals. Also, he saw to it that we were paid good wages when we had to do work for the Germans. I think that, perhaps, this man was an Austrian originally, rather than a German from Germany. Now, he, too, wore nothing but a dirty towel tied around his waist. I recall that his legs were badly bruised and bleeding, since the Partisans had struck him repeatedly with their gun butts and even used their bayonets on him.

From time to time we dared to toss food of one kind or another to the unfortunate men. If the Partisan guards saw us doing this, they would beat both the prisoners and the onlookers. Those bitches, the women Partisans and Communist hangers-on, would shoot everyone indiscriminately right on the spot. Some of the male Partisans, especially if they were Croatians themselves, would allow relatives of the prisoners to give them a piece of bread now and then. One always had to wait for hours to get a chance of this kind, however.

I remember particularly how both Croatian and German soldiers were driven barefoot through Draskovic Street, which was littered with broken glass from the windows of the stores and homes lining it. All of these incidents were only a prelude to the real Reign of Terror which set in after the Communists were sure that the Croatian Army had disintegrated, thanks to the cowardice or imbecility of its commanders and the Government that they served. I believe that for a few days the Reds really did not think they would remain in possession of Zagreb for any length of time and were more concerned with looting it while they had the chance than they were with liquidating their wartime enemies who, they thought, still might gain the upper hand.

Once they were sure that they were in the Croatian capital for a lengthy stay, the OZNA (secret police) and other Communist agencies began to arrest people in their homes. As a rule, these arrests were effected under cover of darkness, so that few spectators could see what was happening. Then the Red authorities began to evict people from their apartments. Some men fought rather than submit tamely to eviction, but, eventually, they were killed and thrown out of the windows along with their children and wives or parents. This sort of thing went on for several months. It was an era of continual tension and constant suffering. No one felt any sense of security. The Communist terror was aimed particularly against Croatian intellectuals and former officers and soldiers of the Armed Forces, but everyone who was suspected of anti-Marxist inclinations was a target for reprisals, too. The Communist-Socialists kept proclaiming at every opportunity that they were going to liquidate everyone who "breathed the Ustasha and Fascist spirit."

The atmosphere of Zagreb became too much for me to stand. Thus, I contrived to get away to the Podravina where I drifted from one place to another during the fall and winter of 1945-46. I found that conditions in the provinces were, if anything, worse than those in the capital itself. The military prisoners disappeared from Zagreb after a while. A great many of these former soldiers were transported from the concentration camps to Maksimir, or to places outside the city, where they were butchered like sheep in a slaughterhouse. Large piles of corpses were thrown into a great pit, which was dug behind the Mirogoj cemetery in the direction of Remete. Rains filled the hole with water after the bodies were pitched into it. Rather than remain in this place of horror, a good many of the people in the vicinity sold their homes for whatever they could get. Residents of Zagreb who knew or thought that relatives or friends had been killed and buried in this hole used to come to it and light candles as they prayed for the souls of the victims. When the Communists found out about this, they hid nearby and fired without warning on such visitors.

This same thing went on in the great cemetery at Mirogoj proper. Here were buried the Croatian veterans of the Austro-Hungarian Army of World War I, as well as the casualties of World War II. The Communists pulled out the crosses decorating the graves of these fallen heroes, made great piles of kindling out of them, and set them alight. Then the Reds used tanks and tractors to plough up the military part of the cemetery. I know that they followed this same procedure wherever they knew that the dead from either war were buried.

Not all of the prisoners were killed near Zagreb, however. "Death Marches" were organized by the Tito Government. That is, the prisoners were driven like cattle through the Croatian countryside en route to some great abattoir and even to other parts of the new "Peoples' Republics." The Government intention was to impress everyone with the consequences of opposition to the Socialist dictatorship. My cousin, Franjo S., was one of those who participated in these death marches. However, he was luckier than most because he was set free when his guards discovered that, although he had been mobilized into the Croatian Army during the war, he had deserted and hidden himself in the countryside. He told me that before he was released, his column passed through a number of Serbian villages. When the prisoners asked the women of these places for water, they usually got it—mixed with quick lime. Those who drank this brew would soon have cramps and collapse along the roadside. The guards killed everyone who fell out of the column in this way.

At one place that my cousin's column visited, the prisoners begged a Serbian woman, who was working around a bread oven, to give them some water. She filled her shovel with glowing embers and threw them on the captives.

I saw myself how these columns of death traversed the Podravina. The corpses of people who couldn't keep up were left in ditches along the line of march. Nearby residents would come out after dark and bury them as decently as possible somewhere in the woods. I remember three murdered Slavonian prisoners being buried right on little Orlovac Street in Ksaver. I witnessed many atrocities, but my mind refuses to recall all of the details when I try to remember them at one time. What does return to mind again and again is how the Partisan guards would whisper to the men they were guarding that the latter ought to make a break for it. The guards would look the other way and let all who dared to flee get away safely. Of course, whoever believed what his guards told him would be mowed down before he got very far. Nevertheless, some prisoners really did escape into the woods, and often they killed guards who tried to follow them through the forests, ambushing them and beating in their heads with tree branches, or overpowering them with their bare hands.

Out in the countryside and in the small villages and towns, I often saw bodies piled up in peasant carts. The wheels of these vehicles were greasy with blood because, as a rule, the dead men were badly mutilated and had bled from many wounds. Some of the victims were still alive when I saw them.

I know, also, that the Partisans often threw bound prisoners into bath houses or other places that could be flooded with water. When such treatment was resorted to during the winter months of 1945-46, the legs of the doomed men would freeze quickly. Then the guards poured hot water over the frozen limbs. If a Croatian asked for a cigarette he got one—lighted end first! Let him express displeasure with this procedure and the whole cigarette would be shoved down his throat.

I suppose that to a civilized public, such as we thought existed in the Western World before 1914, many of the facts that I have recorded above will seem incredible. Yet, I swear that they occurred, even though anyone who did not live through them may find it difficult to believe that the allies of the supposedly humanitarian Western democracies could have behaved as they did. I want to take this opportunity to say myself that there were good men among the Communists; in fact, there were and are all kinds of believers in Marxism. The Bosnians were the best of all of Tito's people, especially the relatively few Muslim Communist soldiers that he had under his command.

I am ready to affirm with an oath taken on the Gospel that the facts I have described above took place just in the way that I have told them.

Signed: B. M.

Omaha, Nebraska
February 16, 1961

Document LX

The following Document comprises two very detailed accounts concerning the three hundred wounded Croatian soldiers who were brutally removed from hospital beds at Rebro, Zagreb, and murdered in the Maksimir park.

During the war of 1941-45, the Rebro Hospital in Zagreb contained large numbers of military patients. Wounded Germans as well as Croatians were cared for here.

When the order to evacuate Zagreb was given early in May 1945, all patients who could be moved without serious danger were sent on ahead of the withdrawing army, traveling either by motor truck or by train. Those whose condition was serious enough to preclude evacuation remained in the hospital to await the entry of the Partisans into the capital.

Among other colleagues of mine who were employed in the Rebro Hospital at this time were Doctors Boris Krznar and Vlado Polic. It was from them that I later learned the fate of the badly wounded men who had to be left behind to the mercy of the Partisans.

When the Communists entered Zagreb, they brought with them a number of severely wounded Partisans who urgently needed hospitalization. Therefore, on the night of May 9-10, they ordered the hospital personnel to place all of the Croatian and German patients on the sidewalk in front of the entrance to the main building. They were to be transferred to another hospital in order to make room for the incoming Communist wounded; this is what the Partisans said.

At about 2:00 A.M., all hospital personnel were told to leave and go to their homes; medical personnel from the units of the "National Liberation Army" were to take over the care of the patients, many of whom were in casts or otherwise completely bedridden. Instead of obeying the orders of the Communists, Doctors Krznar and Polic, together with other hospital personnel, concealed themselves in the building and, by surreptitiously peering out of the darkened windows, were able to see what was going on in the street below them.

There were about three hundred wounded men lying on the sidewalk. Soon after two o'clock, a number of motor lorries pulled up. About ten minutes passed; then the Partisan guards began to load the hospital patients onto the trucks. The night air was rent by frightful screams and moans as the wounded were dumped one on top of the other into trucks like chopped blocks of wood. The Partisans showed them no consideration whatsoever; they even went out of their way to deliberately hurt the helpless men, some of whom had undergone serious operations during the past twenty-four hours. When all were aboard, the trucks drove away, and agonized groaning and shrieks of pain of the wounded men drowned out the noise of the motors. This process of removing three hundred serious hospital cases from their beds into the street and onto the trucks took no more than an hour.

Doctors Krznar and Polic made it their business to find out where their recent patients had been taken. They learned that they had been handed over to the special task force of the Thirteenth Battalion, now commonly referred to as the "Death Chamber." The wounded men from the Rebro Hospital were driven out to Maksimir Park, where they were killed that same night. Their bodies were flung into a hastily dug mass grave and covered over with quick lime.

To this day, in the Rebro Hospital there still remain complete files on all patients who were treated there during the war years and who were discharged in regular manner from this institution, after their wounds had healed. Thus, since the files relating to these men showed no official discharge by the hospital authorities, it was a simple matter for Doctors Krznar and Polic to ascertain the exact number of severely wounded patients who were removed from the hospital and butchered on this night.

During the war, the Rebro institution was a military hospital assigned to the use of the Croatian Army. Its director was a Dr. Papo, who is presently a Professor at the Army Medical Academy in Belgrade. Doctors Krznar and Polic survived the occupation and eventually were able to escape abroad.

A footnote of interest to this affair is that while this mass removal and execution was in progress, Dr. Mile Budak, Dr. Pavelic's physician, was concealed in the cellar of the Rebro Hospital.

Signed: P. G.

Rome, Italy
March 22, 1962

Supplement

To the above cited testimony I, L. Ambrenac, son of the late Josip Ambrenac, wish to add that one of my classmates from the non-commissioned officers' school was among the hospital patients who were slaughtered on this night. His name was Marko Kozjak, nicknamed "Cvorak," and he came from the village of Morovic near Sid Kozjak. He was wounded during the severe battles that took place around Veliki

Grdjevac and his left leg had to be amputated below the knee in an operation that was performed hastily on the battlefield itself. Then, he was rushed to Rebro, where he underwent three subsequent operations. There the Communists found him and killed him along with his fellow patients.

I learned of Marko's fate from my close neighbor, Stjepan Matosevic, who was an eyewitness of what happened to the Rebro patients. Matosevic was an officer in the Croatian Army, but he refused to obey the order to surrender to the British that was issued by the Croatian political and military authorities. Instead, he succeeded in passing himself off as a hospital orderly attached to the "National Liberation Army." In this capacity, he remained for eight months at Rebro, had easy access to the files of the patients, and was able to see with his own eyes what went on.

The man who told me all this, Stjepan Matosevic, joined the anti-Communist Krizari (Crusaders), who continued to fight the Tito regime after the end of the war. He was captured by the Communists in the spring of 1946, and sentenced to death by an army court at Novi Sad. He was shot at Rit along with two other Crusaders, and a feminine member of their band, the brave Marica Subotic, a native of the village of Nijemci.

Signed: L. Ambrenac

Rome, Italy
March 22, 1961

Document LXI

The undersigned Croatian, S. M., hid in Zagreb during the Croatian exodus and saw the city's "liberation" by the Partisans. In the first week after the take-over, plundering was the chief occupation of the Tito troops. After this, arrests of thousands of people took place and the concentration camps were filled to overflowing. Croatian associations were banned, many priests were imprisoned, and Catholic Sisters were expelled from the hospitals. "Death Marches," passing through the streets of Zagreb, increased the gloom of the once gay Zagreb. Since the eyewitness was a chauffeur, he was saved from the tragic end of a multitude of Zagreb inhabitants and was put to work for the truck division. One night, S. M. transported Croatian victims to be slaughtered in the vicinity of Vojnic. Among these victims was his own brother, Richard, whom he spotted during the repair of a flat tire. He had his brother help him in the repair during which he agreed with him on a signal for escape from the slaughter. Just before arriving at the slaughter site, one prisoner did escape from the eyewitnesses' truck. After these horrifying experiences, S. M. reported sick and managed to be declared mentally ill. When he was sent to the mental hospital in Vrapce, he escaped to Italy and, on the day of his escape, wrote this valuable testimony.

From the early part of November 1944, I served in the Croatian Armed Forces as a commander of the Transportation Division in Zagreb. When the evacuation of the city was ordered during the first week of May, 1945, I was up to my ears in work assigning and routing vehicles and seeing to it that they were properly serviced. I was so busy right up to the last second that I did not think about escaping from the city myself until every last military and civilian vehicle had left.

Suddenly, I realized that I was left stranded without any way of getting out of the town except by making good use of my legs. Since the obviously jumpy and nervous Partisans were already filtering into the streets, an escape on foot did not seem practical. Since the Communists were filled with hatred for all Croatians, they would no doubt fire at anything that moved.

Therefore, I hid for three weeks in the home of a friend who was not identified with the Pavelic regime. Since my presence under his roof involved a constant threat to his own security, however, I decided I would have to take my chances with the victors in the war. I succeeded in leaving the home of my friend unseen by anyone, and reported to the Communist authorities. I told them that I was a chauffeur. Since they had need for such people, they accepted me without much questioning and assigned me to the First Company, Second Battalion, of the Second Army. As a chauffeur attached to this command, I had every opportunity to see what went on in Zagreb and its environs. What I had observed from the windows of my friend's house during the first three weeks of the occupation had aroused in me the determination to commit to memory an exact recollection of the succession of events that attended the "liberation." Since I was an eyewitness of the details that attended the Communist takeover right from the beginning, and since I lived through this period myself, my testimony may possess some value for posterity. The following are my honest recollections of the happenings of these terrible days.

First of all, although the Croatian military and political authorities ordered the capital to be evacuated to save it from destruction at the hands of the British, American, and Russian air forces, there was some fighting in the city. Some Croatian patriots were either unwilling to go into exile or foresaw what was going to happen after the Pavelic regime executed its intention of surrendering the Armed Forces to the British. Therefore, they chose to kill as many Partisans as they could, and die armed.

Despite the prohibition against looting issued by the Communist authorities, houses and stores were plundered from the very first day. After several days of occupation, this looting was organized by the authorities themselves on a systematic basis. The homes of those people whose relatives had served in the Croatian Armed Forces were the first to suffer pillage and vandalism.

The new government closed up all stores, explaining this action on the ground that an inventory was necessary. Actually, the Partisans and ranking members of the Communist Party closed off the stores for their own use. They entered them at their pleasure, day or night, and took whatever caught their eyes. To be sure, the Communist brass issued "receipts" for these arbitrary confiscations of property. Such "receipts" gave the purchaser's name, the price of the articles taken, and the name of the store. Store owners were assured that Partisan headquarters would honor these chits and pay the amounts shown on them. Of course, whenever a merchant dared to present such a "receipt" for payment, the local authorities told him that the buyer's name was unknown to them and that there probably was no such person. If he did exist, it was up to the store owners to find him; the regime certainly was not going to assume the responsibility of doing so. Actually, many of the names recorded as those of "purchasers" were well known to the administration, and could have been located easily enough had they not been *personae gratae* in Marxist circles.

After the first few days of the occupation, officially supervised details took all goods that were left in the stores and loaded them into trucks. They explained that all available commodities had to be deposited in government warehouses. From these places they would be reissued in fair proportion to the various merchants. To further exemplify the egalitarian tenets of Marxism, all banks were looted systematically, and the machinery was removed from state factories and machine shops, as well as from private establishments. Wine and liquors were removed from inns and restaurants and placed at the disposal of the Red officers' messes. No one was compensated for the losses he sustained through this wholesale appropriation.

Despite the systematic official pilfering, the population of Zagreb was lulled into feeling a certain sense of security, because few arrests were made during the first six or eight days of the "liberation." That is, there were relatively few individual or personal arrests. Of course, mass arrests began on the very first day that the Communists entered the capital.

These mass arrests took place in the following manner: the new Marxist authorities issued an official announcement to the effect that all owners of factories, shops, or stores were expected to place their privately owned bourgeois establishments at the disposal of the regime. Such owners had to be present at their places of business to attend to the necessary details of operation. Militiamen then appeared at these places of business to arrest all the owners who appeared, and the entire personnel of the enterprise as well. The arrestees were placed in concentration camps where they were interrogated. Those who expressed sympathy for Marxist principles and practice were released fairly quickly. Thus, the belief gained ground that to survive all one had to do was proclaim himself an ardent Marxist. Thus, his past associations would not be inspected too minutely. In some businesses, however, notably publishing concerns, the entire staffs, including laborers, were suspect and, even if released from the prison camps, were not allowed to return to their former employments.

During the third week of the occupation, all privately owned vehicles were confiscated. It was announced, too, that no one would be allowed to possess more than two suits. Whatever clothes one had over this limit were to be turned over to the state. At this time, too, the Communist soldiers began to stop pedestrians on the streets in order to rob them of their watches, rings, and other valuables. Women even had to take off their earrings and other jewelry, if they had any, and hand it over to the proletarian military. Likewise, everyone who was wearing good shoes had to donate them to the Red soldiers.

Meanwhile the OZNA (Secret Police) had begun to operate. Committees of real or professed Communist sympathizers were formed in each street. These committees denounced whomever they didn't like to the OZNA which carried out night arrests of the suspects. Many thousands of people were arrested thanks to this process of delation; only a few returned to their homes. No one except the Communist authorities and the execution squads knows what happened to the others.

The concentration camps were filled to overflowing with refugees and deportees from Slovenia. Conditions in these camps were appalling. The prisoners had to spend the nights in the open air, even when it rained. They received (if they were lucky) a quarter of the bread allowance issued to the Partisan soldiers. Their only other food was a little watery soup. Since this concoction was very salty and since they were given water only every third day, they suffered severely from thirst. Later, the prisoners were allowed to accept food brought to them by friends or relatives, but such visits could occur only twice weekly. The citizens of Zagreb were not permitted to come near the concentration camps. If for some reason they had to pass by them, they had to ignore the prisoners completely because guards shot without warning every chance passer-by who evidenced curiosity concerning camp conditions. In the Kanal concentration camp there was a cellar in Barracks No. 6 where interrogations of prisoners were conducted. It was said that no one ever returned from these hearings.

Everyone in Zagreb who was not a Communist suffered from the prevailing food shortage. For instance, my mother received two and a half kilograms of flour and a half liter of oil once every two months. These allotments had to suffice for five people. Vegetables and fruit could be bought in the markets, but neither lard nor meat was available. At first, there were some potatoes on the market, but soon the peasants refused to bring them into town to show their opposition to forced collectivism. On one occasion, at Tresnjevka, I saw a Communist woman soldier shoot a peasant woman who was selling green vegetables a little above the price fixed by the government.

All Croatian associations were banned and the members of the singing association "Zvonimir" were arrested. In fact, most of the members of Croatian social organizations wound up in the concentration camps. Some sports clubs and athletic societies, such as the Croatian Academic Sports Clubs, were disbanded; others were reorganized under new names. A radio singer named Andrija Konc was sentenced to six months of forced labor. I myself saw him sweeping the streets of Zrinjevac. A number of priests were arrested and imprisoned. Among them were several whom I knew, including Reverend Matej Vodanovic, a Franciscan; he was the pastor of the parish that is attached to the Monastery of Our Lady of Lourdes.*

All of the nurses and orderlies at the Catholic Hospital of Rebro were thrown into the Kanal concentration camp. The religious sisters who served here were released with the insulting remark, "You can go out into the world now and become prostitutes." On the day following the arrests, some of the nurses were released, but the interns were not seen again. Likewise, the nurses were expelled from the Salata medical school and hospital. Communist party members took their places, whether they knew anything about nursing or not.

The lot of any distinguished individuals who had chosen to remain in Zagreb was a hard one. Such outstanding personalities as the industrialist, Arko, and the famous Dr. Sercer, committed suicide. Professor Mladin Anzel of the University was set to work by the Communists, removing mines placed by the Germans in the high school on Domagoj Street. All judges of the military courts were taken to the concentration camp at Savska. Here, their hands were bound and then they were sent to Maksimir to be shot. It was well known that practically all railroad officials were anti-Communists, as were the majority of the post office personnel. Therefore, almost all of these people were transported to the concentration camps. From here, many were taken out to be shot. This was especially the horrible fate of women postal employees. Their particular purge was organized by a former Post Office official, Nada Galajer. She now is the wife of Colonel Holjevac, Military Commander of Zagreb.

The personnel of the Forestry Service had a hard time of it, too, because the new Director of the Ministry of Forestry was an old Communist Party member who had escaped into the woods when the Pavelic regime took over in 1941. He now revenged himself upon all captured Forestry men.

The case of Petar Begovic, an engineer and a Captain in the Transportation Division of the Croatian Armed Forces during the war, was exceptional. He was arrested during the Communist takeover of Zagreb but at the end of nine days of internment he was released and restored

*Reverend Vodanovic, member of the Franciscan Province of Holy Redeemer in Dalmatia, was shot in February, 1947. Thus, he joined thirty other martyrs of his religious community who had been murdered by the Tito troops.—Editor's note.

to his old rank. He is the only Croatian military officer I know about whose rank was recognized by the Communist authorities. An old classmate of his at the military academy saved him. This classmate had become a major in Tito's forces during the war, although he was actually a strong anti-Communist. After the fighting ended, he wished to escape abroad but could not bring himself to abandon his parents, especially since his mother had contracted a serious illness during the war.

For some time after the end of the fighting, groups of Croatian soldiers who had surrendered to the British and had been turned over to the Yugoslav Communists, continued to be brought into Zagreb. I recall seeing one such group being led down Zvonimir Street en route to the airfield, where they were to do forced labor. Although they were very tired, hungry, and thirsty, they retained their military dignity and smartness, and sang Croatian marching songs as they passed through the street. Probably, they were all murdered later in an unknown location.

A machinist from Bjelovar, Ivan Stajninger, told me that, while riding in a locomotive along the rail line outside of Bjelovar, he had seen a number of Communist soldiers, and had heard shooting from the woods there. Above the shots, he heard the screaming and crying of women. He concluded that they were being executed by the Communists. Also, he saw his own son, Marian, in a prisoner column. A few days after he gave me this information, Stajninger escaped into the forest with an anti-Communist Croatian group.

Although the Reds accepted my services as a chauffeur, they did not permit me to do any driving at first. Since I had time on my hands, I spent it repairing an old truck. While I was engaged in this work, the Communists discovered that I had been an officer in the Croatian Army. Probably, they wished to liquidate me immediately, but they needed chauffeurs badly, so after about two weeks I was put to work in the truck division. The company and battalion authorities promised that if I became a Communist, my rank would be recognized in six months time.

My initial job was to transport arms from Cernomerac to Maksimir, and to the Savska Street headquarters of the former Bokinj Company. While I was engaged in this work, I saw two or three thousand boys and girls of the Ustasha Youth Group of Zagreb in Maksimir. They had been returned from Slovenia and Austria by courtesy of the British. Among them was the daughter of an Ustasha Colonel. She managed to give me a letter she had contrived to write to her father. I intended to free her, but found no opportunity to do so since I had Communist guards watching me all the time. These young people were living their last days under horrible circumstances. They were hungry, thirsty, lice-ridden, and had no place to rest or sleep except on the bare ground of the park.

My superiors seemed to trust me and soon put me in charge of the transportation column. On the morning of July 11, the battalion commander ordered me to take six trucks and drivers and to carry a hundred and fifty extra gallons of gasoline, since we were to make a longer trip than usual. At 12:30 P.M., I received the command to start the column moving towards the concentration camp at Precko. Here, I was to report to a Brigade Commander who would give me further instructions.

We arrived at the Precko camp without incident. When I reported to the Commandant, I was told that I was to transport military personnel from the camp to Karlovac. There were some twenty-five thousand regulars of the Croatian Army and Air Force in Precko at that time. A number of Ustashas, who disguised themselves as regulars after the surrender, were included among them. All of these former members of the Croatian Armed services were now wearing Yugoslav Communist army caps, complete with the red star. They had been told that they were going to be distributed among the various individual brigades of the Yugoslav Army to finish out their periods of military service in this manner. My brother, Richard, who was an Air Force Sergeant during the war, was at the camp at this time. I did not know this then, but found out about it later.

The prisoners were assembled and told that they were being transferred to Karlovac. Immediately afterwards, one hundred and thirty men were crowded into my six trucks, along with thirty Communist soldiers and six commissars. These Communists came from the vicinity of Zagreb for the most part.

Since the tires on our trucks were very poor, we had a number of flats. I asked one of the commissars to assign someone to help me fix one of these flats. Just at that moment, I spotted my brother in one of the trucks. Without telling the commissar who he was, I pointed him out and said that I knew he was a good mechanic. The commissar allowed him to assist me with the repairs.

After we had gotten the column going again, Richard sat in the cab with me and related the happenings of the last few weeks concerning the Croatian Army, which had evacuated Zagreb in perfect order during the first week of May. He said that the prisoners at Precko had received nothing to eat for the past two days. He was worried about what the future had in store.

We arrived at Karlovac at eight that evening, but had to wait until a major of the militia appeared at 10 A.M. He told us, "Comrades, this brigade is filled up. You will have to go on to Vojnic where you will wait for the Eighth Division. You will become part of the Thirteenth Battalion of this Division. The Thirteenth is composed exclusively of Croatians. You will have it good, and you will get good food."

Later, the designation "Thirteenth Battalion" became a phrase of ill omen, because everyone who was sent to this formation was murdered.

We moved out of Karlovac, taking the road towards the Petrova

Gora in the direction of Vojnic. When we were about fifteen kilometers outside of Karlovac, it began to rain. The major said that we would have to stop until daylight broke because of the poor state of the roads and the condition of our truck lights. He went on to Vojnic, while a number of the rest of us took shelter in a barn that belonged to a Croatian Serb farmer of this vicinity.

On the following morning, July 12, a commissar gathered all the drivers together and told us where we could get some breakfast. However, he warned us not to say anything about eating to the prisoners, since there was not enough food for all of them. We remained until noon at our overnight stopping place, then moved on a short distance and stopped again.

Nothing happened until about 4:30 that afternoon when a truck loaded with thirty Serbian Partisans armed with machine guns joined us. Later, I discovered that they belonged to Tito's secret police. They took counsel together about two hundred meters away from us. I became suspicious and asked a commissar what these men from Vojnic were doing here. The commissar answered that there were Ustasha remnants in the neighborhood and that the Serbs had been sent here for security reasons.

His explanation did not satisfy me and I had a gloomy foreboding that the prisoners were going to be slaughtered. Still, why had they been given Communist caps and officially assigned to definite military units? I returned to my truck, where I found my brother in a dark frame of mind. I confessed to him that I, too, had my suspicions about the meaning of the arrival of the Serbs at this lonely place. Richard said that he didn't like to die without fighting, as though he were a coward, after he had survived four years of pitched battles and guerrilla warfare. A commissar noticed us talking together and asked what "this fellow" was doing near me. Was he my assistant? I answered that he was not. The commissar ordered Richard to get out of the truck and join the rest of the prisoners. As he was getting out of the truck, I whispered to him that I would give him a signal if I found out that the prisoners were really going to be shot. He muttered that he would try to escape even if he were shot on the spot. After he had gone, I found that he had left his jacket, pen, and a pack of cigarettes on the seat.

The prisoners were ordered to line up in rows. While they were doing so, I asked the commissars point-blank if a mass execution was going to take place here. Although they did not give me a direct answer, I could tell from their manner what was going to happen. Therefore, I gave the prearranged signal to Richard.

The Communist soldiers commenced to push the Croatians into a nearby barn, where they were kept until six that evening. Wire was cut into half yard lengths and was used to tie men two by two. As soon as they were tied, they were forced into the trucks where they had to kneel down as the remainder of the wire was used to bind their feet.

Since the Communists performed the job of tying up the prisoners very brutally, wrists were cut badly. Anyone who resisted was beaten with gun butts.

Darkness soon fell over this grim scene. I was commanded to turn on the lights of my truck, which was facing the door of the barn. The prisoners were taken out of the trucks by pairs and shoved back into the barn again. Then it was noticed that one man had escaped. The Partisans cursed horribly and went out looking for him, but the night had swallowed him up. I hoped that this escapee was my brother, whom I could not see anywhere among the other prisoners. I had my own worries, too, for a commissar asked me where I had been during the past four years and, not believing my answer, said that I ought to be shot, too.

At 11:00 P.M., my truck was loaded again. The column started out, four of the other trucks preceding mine. We went about three miles and then all except the first truck stopped in the woods. After a time the first truck came back—empty, save for the guards. The second truck then took off. Eventually, it, too, returned without its load of prisoners and so on until it was the turn for my own truck. I was ordered to drive on for a few miles. Finally, I was commanded to stop in a thickly wooded area. The legs of the prisoners were untied and they were taken about five hundred yards into the woods. I heard shots and cries, curses, and yells of rage. Most of the Croats were beaten over the head with the gun butts of their guards. By twelve midnight the liquidation was completed, and the executioners started back to Vojnic.

We drivers stayed the remainder of the night in the same barn that we had used twenty-four hours before. The next day we returned to Zagreb. On the way back, the Communist guards divided among themselves the money and valuables they had found on the prisoners. They tore up and threw away a number of prayerbooks that the Croatians had carried.

This was the last time I had to make an expedition of this kind. Later, the drivers in my unit told me that, after this first experience, Croatians were not employed to transport prisoners destined for execution.

Back in the capital I reported sick. Actually, I was in a virtual state of shock. A doctor sent me to the hospital maintained by the Sisters of Mercy. They could find nothing visibly wrong with me here, but I confided to one of the nuns that I wanted to be certified as having experienced a nervous breakdown. The doctor in charge, a Croatian himself, was obliging enough to make the desired diagnosis of my case and to report it to my superiors.

I was sent to the mental hospital at Vrapce but, instead of going there, I succeeded in making my way to my home. Here, I hid in the house of a friend for a while, then took refuge for two weeks in a Catholic rectory. Then I heard that drivers were needed for the coastal city of Split. I reported to the hiring place under an assumed name. My intention was to get away to Italy, but I found no opportunity to execute such a maneuver. However, I did discover that it was possible to secure a travel permit through making use of the services of the International Red Cross. As soon as I knew this, I went to Red Cross headquarters and told the director there that I was a native of Split and wished to secure permission to travel to that place. I received the necessary permission; then, by careful manipulation I changed the place of destination on the permit from Split to Trieste. From Trieste I escaped to Italy on September 12, 1945.

This report was read to me and I confirm that it has been written the way I gave it.

Signed: S. M.

Fermo, Italy
September 12, 1945

Document LXII

The undersigned, Maca Koracevic, describes the loss of her husband and general slaughterhouse procedures in postwar months in Zagreb. She gives us also her observations on the city's "liberation," on jails, and on concentration camps, especially the Kanal camp. Her husband was confined in this camp until July 13, 1945, when he and many other victims, without having stood a trial of any kind, were taken to be slaughtered. The account closes with a brief description of the commander of the Kanal camp.

It was during the first part of July, 1945, that I learned the British had extradited my husband into the hands of the Yugoslav Communists. I remember the time and place of this incident as though it had occurred only yesterday. It was early in the morning, right after the night curfew had been lifted. The streets were empty of civilians because the Communists had the habit of picking up people at random for questioning. Despite the danger attendant upon such action, I soon went out into the street to look for my husband's place of detention.

While I was walking down Marticeva Street, I saw two young boys between fourteen and sixteen being led along by two Communist guards, who were armed with machine guns. The hands of these two youths were bleeding profusely, because they were tied tightly with rough wire which was cutting deeply into their flesh. Despite the danger of my own position and my worry concerning the fate of my husband, this depressing spectacle moved me greatly. I could not stop my tears, although the authorities of the "People's Republic" had issued strict orders forbidding anyone to cry during this joyful period of "liberation." We were supposed to radiate happiness and thankfulness at the "deliverance." I do not know the fate of these two boys, but I can sorrowfully guess.

The jails in Zagreb were filled to capacity at this time. Ten thousand more Croatian prisoners crowded the concentration camps at Precko, Mirogoj, and Kanal. I located my husband at the Kanal camp. We, the wives and relatives of the inmates of this place, stood out under the hot July sun from early in the morning until the night curfew fell. While we waited, strung out in long lines one behind the other, we saw prisoner groups being taken off to other prison camps where they could be murdered less conspicuously during the night. Every night, too, we saw trucks loaded with fifty or sixty prisoners leaving the Kanal camp. As these prisoner vehicles passed under the bright street lights, we could see that thousands of the prisoners had their hands tied behind their backs with wire. Of course, no one in Zagreb who was not a Communist was supposed to know what was going on, but we took turns in hiding ourselves behind buildings that were located close to the camp, and along the route we knew the trucks would have to take to get away from the city and other inhabited areas.

On July 13, it was my husband's turn to join the long list of victims of the naive Croatian belief in the British spirit of fair play, and the well advertised civilizing processes of the democratic way of life. Included in my husband's death group was Vlasta, the nineteen year old fiancee of Vinko Marovic. I believe that my spouse and Vlasta, as well as their fellow prisoners, bravely met the "death in the forests" that awaited them at the hands of their British, American, and Russian-subsidized executioners. Without having stood trial of any kind, all were shot the night of the 13th.

Although we were not able to follow the death trucks to the place of execution, Vlasta's mother and I exerted ourselves to find out where the killings had taken place and what had been done with the bodies. Our endeavors finally resulted in a confrontation with the commander of the Kanal camp, a former police officer of the pre-1941 Yugoslav state. I shall never forget this man and how his hatred for everything Croatian flashed so expressively from his deep-set eyes as long as I live.

Signed: Maca Koracevic

Santa Rosa, California
October 15, 1961

Document LXIII

This account deals with the wanton killing of seventy Croatian young girls and also with a slaughter of an uncounted number of wounded soldiers.

On Sunday, May 20, 1945, two weeks after the entry of the Partisans into Zagreb, I was a mechanic in charge of a garage located at 18 Solovljev Street in Zagreb. I was standing in the doorway of the garage, close to a Partisan guard who wore a British uniform.

A feminine acquaintance happened to pass by and was imprudent enough to greet me with an "Hello, Kreso!" She then realized what she had done and practically ran to the corner of Draskovic Street, glancing back fearfully at the guard as she did so.

When he heard the greeting, the guard started nervously and gave me a piercing look. Then he began to walk back and forth along the sidewalk, staring at me constantly as he did so. Naturally, I broke out into a real sweat, my mind filled with the most gloomy presentiments. Suddenly, the guard stopped squarely in front of me and began to speak in a very agitated voice. Obviously, he was laboring under the strain of some great inner emotion:

"I haven't been able to sleep for several nights," he told me, and then stared gloomily at the sidewalk for several seconds. Finally, he continued in a low monotone:

"Take the night before last, for instance. We drove seventy girls from the Institute (Internat) in Preradovic Street by truck out into the country. All of these girls were between sixteen and twenty years old. We shot all of them on the first curve past Velika Gorica, on the road to Kravarsko. The screams of these young girls, 'What is our guilt? What are we accused of? Why do you want to kill us?,' are still echoing in my ears, and I cannot forget how they clung to one another, trembling and weeping."

The Partisan's face was a study in gloomy retrospection. After a time, he went on in a subdued voice:

"In this same vicinity we shot the wounded soldiers whom we took out of the Zagreb hospitals. They didn't ask for mercy. The more lightly wounded ones even dug the holes into which their bodies were to be thrown. Some of them tried to hit us with the shovels when they got a chance. Since our officers didn't think it was necessary to waste bullets on them, some of the more severely wounded cases were thrown into the ditches and buried alive."

The only question I asked the guard was where he originally came from, since I could tell by his accent that he was not a native of Zagreb. He replied promptly, "I am a Croatian from Djakovo (in Slavonia)."

Soon after this incident, the Croat from Djakovo was replaced by another guard. I did not see my informant again, although I continued to work as a mechanic in the garage until July 20, 1945.

This anecdote, therefore, has no ending as a piece of fiction would, nor is it intended to point out any kind of moral. I am merely repeating the conversation as it occurred, because I think the facts that were revealed to me in this chance meeting should not sink into historical oblivion. The victims mentioned are nameless, but the manner of their deaths should not be forgotten, either by any loyal Croatian who had the fortune to survive the grim events of 1945, or by those who have to bear the responsibility for these wanton killings which lacked even the justification of political necessity.

Signed: Kresimir Babic

Geelong (Victoria), (Australia).
February 13, 1963

Document LXIV

The massacre of 5,000 disarmed Croatian soldiers at Sestine, near Zagreb, is revealed.

When the Independent State of Croatia existed, 1941-1945, I was a soldier in the Domobran divisions of the Croatian Army. After the fall of Zagreb in May, 1945, about five thousand of us, either drawn from the rearguards of various units or stragglers from the several branches of the Armed Forces, surrendered to the Partisans at Sestine near the capital.

Hardly had we laid down our arms, when General Dyoko Yovanitch, Commandant of the Sixth Proletarian Division "Nikola Tesla," issued the following order verbatim, "All the bandits who served in the Croatian Armed Forces must be shot."

As far as the prisoners taken at Sestine were concerned, Yovanitch's order was carried out to the letter. With my own eyes I had to watch as Communist guards led the prisoners off to dig their own graves. For days on end, I had to listen to the chain volleys which put an end to the lives of these unfortunates.

The only prisoners at Sestine who were not executed in this manner were several hundred skilled workers whom the Reds needed to keep their transport and communications units functioning. As an auto mechanic and chauffeur, I had the good fortune to be included among those whose lives were spared.

I was assigned to the First Brigade of the "Tesla" Division and remained with this unit for six months, working either as a mechanic in the workshop at Sestine, or as a chauffeur.

The Commander of the First Brigade was Major Milosh Cankovic, from Ploce, in the Lika area of western Croatia. Commissar of the Brigade was Andrija Muhek, from Marija Bistrica, in the Zagorje region of Croatia. Later, Muhek was transferred to another unit and Major Bosko Kerkez of Kordun replaced him as Commissar in our command.

Altogether, I served in the First Brigade for a year and a half. During this time I, of course, enjoyed no rights or privileges like leaves of absence, town passes, etc. Eventually I was released from the Brigade and received permission to obtain civilian employment. Communist security police and intelligence men always kept a close watch on everything I did. Nevertheless, I found an opportunity to elude their vigilance and escaped across the Austrian frontier. Now I am happy to be able to live in relative freedom, far away from the Communist dictator and his executioners.

Signed: S. Sostaric

Stuttgart, West Germany
April 4, 1956

Document LXV

This brief Document relates the massacre of an estimated 5,000 Croatian civilians and disarmed soldiers between Gornji Iskavac and Kravarsko.

During the month of May, 1945, a great number of motor trucks passed through the forest which lies between Gornji Iskavac and Kravarsko near Zagreb. Soon after the arrival of a truck in this forest, volleys of shots were heard by the inhabitants of the two villages which are located in this area. Some of the more intrepid villagers tried to enter the forest to find out what was happening. They were stopped by Partisan guards who told them that the Zagreb section of the OZNA (Yugslav Secret Police) had taken over the forest. No one was allowed access.

In this lonely woods, five thousand or more citizens of Zagreb and former Croatian soldiers were murdered. It is likely that my brother, too, was killed here sometime in May, after his arrest in Zagreb by the OZNA.

Signed: B. I.

Nuremberg, West Germany
November 2, 1954

Document LXVI

The undersigned, R.M., did not surrender at the time of the Bleiburg catastrophe, but rather hid in the village of Jablanovac near Bistra. On May 23, 1945, the "people's" authorities discovered him and confined him for two days in the concentration camp at Jankomir. From there, our eyewitness was transferred to the infamous Precko camp, where he heard of mass liquidations, witnessed many atrocities and saw the groups of prisoners led to be slaughtered. R.M. states the purpose of these mass slaughters of Croatian war prisoners. The Precko camp was first guarded by the Serbian Partisans. Their Croatian comrades, who were not as brutal, soon relieved them. As a member of the Youth Brigade of the Third Assault Partisan Division, R. M. discovered that there were almost no men in the villages around Sisak and Kostajnica. On

March 12, 1946, the witness was assigned to the First Battalion of the First Brigade of the First Proletarian Division. He closes his account by listing the names of the leading officers of these units, pointing out the anti-American propaganda of their commissars, and stating the causes that induced him to leave Yugoslavia.

I entered the Croatian Army on December 15, 1941, and served in the garrison at Bjelovar, until the evacuation of the Domovina in May, 1945. I was in a column which got as far as the village of Zapresic. There we received word that our Government and Military Command had been unable to arrange our surrender to the British, who insisted on turning us over to the Partisans. After some debate our column split up, some of the men deciding to go on to Austria, where they still hoped to find asylum, while others determined that they would take their chances on remaining in the homeland.

I was not foolish enough as to trust my life to either the British or their Partisan proteges. But I could think of nothing better to do than hide in the house of a patriotic Croatian peasant in the village of Jablonovac near Bistra. On May 23, 1945, the "People's Militia" of the village, as fine a group of scoundrels as I ever laid eyes upon, discovered my whereabouts and took me to the concentration camp at Jankomir. This place of detention was only temporary, so, after a two-day stay, I was transferred to the infamous Precko camp. Here I remained until June 26.

During my sojourn in these two Communist prison camps, many residents of Zagreb or its suburbs visited them. They were looking for friends or relatives, so they brought packages of food with them as a rule. If they could not find those for whom they had prepared these gifts, they would distribute the food among the other prisoners, all of whom were quite literally starving because the Partisan authorities refused to supply them with anything to eat. Although I did not witness the incident myself, I heard that the Partisans shot a young man just as his mother was giving him a package of food she had brought.

We were exposed to very brutal treatment besides the hunger which prevailed among us. The Ustashas especially had a hard time of it. First they robbed us at Jankomir, then repeated the process, if we had anything left, at Precko. At the latter camp, they separated the Ustashas from the Domobrans. However, they grouped those Domobrans who had served in the Croatian forces since 1941-42 with the Ustasha unit. These veterans had given the Partisans many thorough thrashings in the battles fought during the war. Actually, if the Germans hadn't been so stupid and interfered with our operations at every juncture because they were afraid we would become too independent of them, we could have completely wiped out Tito's forces long before the end of the war. I myself think it was the deeply ingrained fear of the battle-tired Croatian units that motivated the Partisans to perpetrate the hideous massacres of 1945 and succeeding years. They were afraid we would succeed in overthrowing the Communist dictatorship established by Tito if they allowed us to live. Even if our men agreed to accept his rule temporarily, they would turn against him and the Communist Party eventually. The Partisans knew better than to think they could face up to the Domobran and Ustasha regulars in a war in which the odds were even approximately equal. Therefore they were determined to "liquidate" all the old Croatian veterans, while they still had the backing of their British, American, and Russian allies.

Therefore, everyone who had participated in the defeats inflicted upon the Partisans during the war was singled out and marked for execution. Such prisoners were separated from the rest of us; I do not know what happened to them. However, captives who had surrendered to the British in Austria, and who were turned over to the Partisans by the Englishmen, told me about horrifying massacres which took place at Dravograd, Maribor, and Celje in Slovenia, through which they themselves had passed on their way back to the Domovina. They had not witnessed these butcheries, but they had seen masses of prisoners taken off in trucks and then heard the sound of continuous shooting in the distance.

I learned also that in the woods near the Precko camp itself, the Partisans had murdered seven hundred and fifty Domobrans who had served in the Croatian Army since 1941. Furthermore, I could see for myself how small groups of the Precko inmates were led off with their hands bound almost every day. They never came back to join us, so we assumed that they were "liquidated." Officers of the Croatian Army who were not removed in this manner were put to work performing all the menial labor in the camp. I remember that men like Colonel Greguric of the First Mountain Brigade of the Seventh Mountain Division, Lieutenant Vidakovic from the same unit, Captain Pataki, and Major Krtovica were among the targets of Partisan spleen. There were perhaps seventy officers in all who were not liquidated immediately. Later they were taken to Mitrovica; I do not know what happened to them there.

The food given to the prisoners at Precko was of extraordinarily poor quality and insufficient quantity. We saw no bread for ten days at a time. Our rations included a little black coffee and flour boiled in water. Wounded Croatian soldiers were brought from hospitals in the vicinity and placed in a special part of the prison camp, separated from the rest by a wire fence. Those who could find a place in the barracks in this part of the enclosure slept there, while the others remained outside on the ground. Of course, no one had any blankets. Typhus sufferers were sent to a special barracks, too, but neither doctors nor medicine were supplied for them or for the wounded men. Therefore, many died from typhus, exposure, malnutrition, or other remediable causes.

While men were dying every day from one or the other of these afflictions, those of us who survived were assembled periodically so that we could hear lectures which extolled the virtues of Soviet Russia. Of course, the lecturers venomously attacked the former Croatian and the first Yugoslav regimes.

At first, camp was guarded by Serbian Partisan units, but these were soon relieved by the Zumberak Brigade. The officers and soldiers from Zumberak were not as brutal as the Serbs, since they were themselves Croatians from the northwestern part of our country. In fact, many of them had served in the Croatian Army until the later stages of the war, when they had seized the opportunity to get on the winning side.

On June 26, I, too, was drafted into this Brigade. But about July 1, it was dissolved and its members were assigned to the Youth Brigade of the Third Assault Division. Initially I was attached to an automatic weapons company, but later on I was transferred to a mine laying command. The divisional commander was a Croatian, Major Franjo Rofler, who had himself served in the Croatian Regular Army until late in the war. Dushan Zhivada was divisional commissar, Major Sretan Zharkovitch functioned as lieutenant commander of brigade, and Major Lyuban Vukitch assisted him. All three of the last named were Serbs. The commandant of the mine laying or throwing company was Valentin Pogadic, who had no rank in Tito's army. He was a former Ustasha who had joined the Partisans in order to save his life when they captured him. Another turncoat was the company commissar, Ivan Barkanj, once a pilot in the Croatian Air Force. He appeared to be a dedicated Communist now, but nonetheless he did not persecute us any more than he had to. Also he dared to say more than once that the Croatian Army was not so bad.

As a member of the Youth Brigade, I had to participate in the surveillance of the Croatian villages around Sisak and Kostajnica. My own unit did not kill anyone in discharging this duty, nor did it loot or pilfer. The villagers told me, however, that Serbian Partisan units which had passed through this territory before us had mercilessly looted every village they had come to. There were almost no men left in these hamlets—one saw only women and children. The women cursed the commissars and the system they represented. Once when I was being entertained in a house in Kozji Brod, a young girl entered and greeted everyone present in the old Croatian rather than the prescribed Marxist manner. Fearing that this might be a trap, I addressed her as "comrade" and remarked that the salutation she had used was no longer proper. The young woman answered fearlessly: "Excuse me! I am not your comrade. Your comrades are the Partisan girls who sleep with you under the trees. I am a Croatian girl and for me my manner of salutation is proper. Those who do not wish to listen to it can turn away."

She went on to say that her brother and her fiance were both Ustashas. They were killed, as were all the other men in the village. Only the girls remained; life for them in the "Socialist Paradise" was not worthwhile. Finally she said directly to me, "What is in my heart is on my tongue. I am not afraid to die."

While I was serving with the Youth Brigade, we were sent to the village of Majdan near Bosanski Novi to work in the woods. We were not allowed to keep our weapons on us while we were so employed. Only the officers remained armed. They told us that there were wolves in this vicinity. Indeed there were, but they were human anti-Communist wolves—the dreaded Croatian Krizari, or Crusaders.

At Majdan we were assigned quarters in the home of a Serbian who belonged to the Communist Party. He refused to put us up, telling our commandant that as a good Communist himself he did not have to stand for this imposition. The Commandant told him to shut up and we moved in as ordered.

At this time, the Government in Belgrade was moving a part of the population of old Serbia to the Voyvodina, which is in the northeastern part of the present Yugoslav state. Some Serbs emigrated willingly. One of them went to the Voyvodina to look over the situation there and found that the newcomers to this area were being put into the Communist "kolkoz," or collective farms. Therefore he changed his mind about going northwards. Other Serbians sold their property, except for two thousand pounds of personal belongings, which they were allowed to take with them.

On March 12, 1946, the Youth Brigade of the Third Assault Division underwent a reorganization. I was reassigned to the mine throwing company attached to the First Battalion of the First Brigade of the First Proletarian Division. Gayo Voyvoditch was divisional commander, Lieutenant-Colonel Komen Zhugitch functioned as divisional commissar, Major Voya Abramovitch was brigade commander, brigade commissar was Major Bozhidar Shevo, Second Lieutenant Bozho Orlanditch acted as battalion commander, and Captain Dragisha Milutinovitch was battalion commissar. My company commander, Lieutenant Boshko Bolyevitch, acted as commissar of this unit too. All of these officers were either Serbs or Montenegrins.

I served with this unit until May 9, 1946, when I managed to escape from it. We were stationed between the villages of Herpelj and Kozina at the time. Our several units of occupation wore different insignia and were known by different names. The outfit to which I belonged was called "Tiger B." At the regular indoctrination meetings, the commissars explained why we were not permitted to converse with civilians. They said that the Americans were imperialists and oppressors of the people, as the Austro-Hungarians had been in former times. The Americans only pretended to be allies of the proletariat and of the Yugoslav state. Therefore the war was not over yet.

Although I did not dare write home in order to inform my relatives and friends of my whereabouts, I received news that the Partisans had wiped my village, among others, off the face of the earth. This information, and my general antipathy for the Communist cause, induced me to desert my new unit and to leave Yugoslavia. I risked this desertion and escape because I am opposed to Communism unalterably and for the duration of my life. Also, I do not wish to live in any kind of a Yugoslavia.

Signed: R. M.

Fermo, Italy
April 1, 1947

MASSACRE SITES OF THE CROATIAN VICTIMS

Chapter 11

Massacre Sites in Croatia

Document LXVII

The undersigned "Croatian" Serb, Dusan Vukovic, joined the Partisans' Svilaya-Mosor formation in September, 1943. Towards the end of 1944, he was transferred to the Eight Brigade of the Twentieth assault Division. Vukovic tells of the battles at Knin, Gospic, and Rijeka. After the battles, masses of prisoners were murdered. At Knin, approximately one thousand Serbian Chetniks, seven hundred Croats and over 1,500 Germans were murdered. At Gospic, four hundred Croatian prisoners were killed as a revenge for having fought with determination. At Ilirska Bistrica, north of Rijeka, thousands of German and Croatian prisoners-of-war were shot. Our eyewitness, who had participated in these massacres, describes them with minute details. According to his testimony, at Sent Petar in the Kras, too, about a thousand prisoners, mainly Germans and some Croatians, were liquidated. In June, 1945, Vukovic was transferred to the Protective Battalion of the Second Partisan Army and stationed in Zagreb where, at the city's Command Headquarters, he eyewitnessed the liquidation of five hundred prisoners. He watched other massacres of both military and civilian groups. The eyewitness heard about the massacre of the wounded soldiers from trustworthy sources and was disgusted by this more than by any other massacre. At the end of the account, Vukovic explains why he fled to Italy and decided to give this testimony.

I joined the "Svilaya-Mosor" Partisan formation in the village of Maovice at the foot of the Kozjak Mountain in September, 1943. At the time I was not yet eleven years old. My older brother was already serving with the Partisans and it was this fact, together with the unbridled character of the life I was living, that explains my enrollment in the ranks of Tito's Army. I want to stress that I was not forced to take this step because of the conduct of either the Croatian Army or of the Italian forces in the vicinity. Neither of these armed forces bothered my village at all.

The commander of the "Svilaya-Mosor" group was Captain Bogdo Njegus who came from Drnis in Dalmatia. Today he is director of the Croatian Geological Institute, which is located at 3b/V on Djoric Street in Zagreb. Our political commissar was Mile Njegic, a native of Miocic.

Late in 1944, I was transferred to the Eighth Brigade of the Twentieth Assault Division, which was attached to the Eighth Corps of the "People's Liberation Army." General Petar Drapsin commanded this Partisan formation. Our units were supplied by the British Armed Forces.

Marshal Alexander, the English commanding general, asked us to advance towards Rijeka by way of Knin and Gospic in the interior part of Dalmatia. By so doing, we could help to form a ring around the enemy forces which were withdrawing northwards.

When we took Knin, we captured a number of Germans and Croatian Ustashas and Domobrans, as well as a large group of Serbian Chetniks, who were under the command of Voyvoda Momchilo Dyujitch. Major Marinkovic, who was chief of the Knin military district, had these captives massacred in groups of fifty to a hundred at a time. The execution details worked in shifts. Despite my youth, I was assigned to the duty of shooting the prisoners, too, but when I took the heavy German-made machine gun, the so-called "Sarac," I found it was too heavy for me to handle. Therefore I did not participate directly in the executions, though I did witness what went on.

I judge that my unit murdered 700-1000 Chetniks, perhaps 700 Croatians, and more than 1500 German soldiers, along with about ten Italians who had stayed with the Germans after the Italian collapse in 1943. The Chetniks belonged to the "Dinara" Division. Since I am very well acquainted with the vicinity of Knin, I can still locate the exact spot where the massacre took place.

About a mile and a half from the town, there is a place called Borici. The German prisoners were forced to dig large pits here. Then the captives were tied together by telephone wire in groups of tens. As each batch of bound men was led to the edge of one of the holes, a guard would shoot the first man in the file. As he fell, he would pull the other nine into the excavation with him. Then the executioners would discharge bursts of machine gun fire into the bodies of the still living victims. They also threw hand grenades into the holes. Some very dramatic scenes were enacted as the tied men were brought to the brink of their common grave. I remember that the different nationalities met death in ways that evidenced their national characteristics. Some of the Germans and Italians begged for their lives, insisting that they had never harmed anyone. Most of the Croatians maintained a glum silence though some of them cursed us and tried to kick their guards. The Serbs screamed defiance and outdid the Croatians in their swearing. However, they went to meet their end without mercy.

From Knin, we advanced towards Gospic where the Croatian Armed Forces offered savage resistance. We engaged in running battles with them all the way from Knin to Gospic. Whenever we managed to capture an Ustasha, we were allowed to do with him as we pleased. I saw how our men tied the Ustashas to pine trees and then very slowly drove their Italian daggers into the hearts of the victims. The purpose of this vivisection, I was told, was to provide an object lesson in the functioning of the heart, like biology or physiology students are exposed to in a university laboratory. The Domobrans were treated less cruelly, especially when the Partisan officer in command of a unit that captured them was a Croatian himself. If he was a Serb, the Domobrans fared badly, too. Although the Croatian Partisans did spare some of their Catholic co-nationals, they vied with their Serbian comrades in maltreating any Muslims whom they captured. Finally an order was issued that if the commander of a unit were Croatian, the political commissar attached to it had to be Serbian, and vice versa.

Sometimes I saw individual prisoners being led to one side, away from the main group of prisoners. When they were a short distance away, the Partisans would shoot them in the back and say that they had done this because the victims had tried to escape. Some of the older Partisan fighters did not report willingly for assignment to the execution details. Nevertheless, they obeyed the express orders issued by their commanding officers or commissars for such duty. Our superior officers justified the executions by asserting that the men whom we killed had murdered innocent people and that there was no possibility of correcting their "fascist," "monarchist," and antisocial behavior and instincts.

At Gospic, the Ustashas fought with a determination that even they had never before evinced. The battle here was simply tremendous, the hottest in which I have engaged at any time. Even before the fighting started here, we knew what we would encounter because the Ustashas of Gospic were well known warriors. They would let us get within thirty feet of the places in which they had entrenched themselves, and then would blow our whole unit apart with continued firing. Very few of them fell into our hands alive, because they fought as long as they had a breath of life in them, or else killed themselves with their last bullet. Only twenty-five or thirty men, completely out of ammunition, and all more dead than alive, were captured out of the whole force that defended the town. We "liquidated" all of these exhausted fighters on the spot.

Since we had sustained very heavy losses in the battle, we revenged ourselves upon the population of Gospic. We followed instructions given us by the OZNA to dispose of these people in different ways. Sometimes we gouged out the hearts of the victims and hid the bodies in the debris of buildings destroyed in the fighting. Apparently the OZNA wanted to create the impression that they had perished when the walls and floors collapsed. Other corpses were concealed in caves in the mountain a mile away from Gospic. I saw one Ustasha who was skinned alive and then hung on a tree branch with his own skin. I believe that about four hundred of the citizens of Gospic were murdered, most of them in a very sadistic manner. Also, I should like to mention that I saw officers attached to a Russian delegation that came to check on the Partisan operations photographing the bodies in the caves. Probably they used these photographs later to fool their Western Allies into thinking that the Ustashas or other Croatians had committed the murders.

After we had recovered from the fighting at Gospic, we went on towards Senj and Novi Vinodol. Then we joined other Partisan formations which were closing in on Rijeka. The Croatians gave us a bitter battle in the Katarinc section of Rijeka. From this city we advanced to Slovenia. When we entered Ilirska Bistrica, we captured a large number of German as well as Croatian soldiers. A relatively small number of Germans were separated from the rest and grouped together according to the trade they had professed in civil life. For instance, the unit to which I was attached took charge of the chauffeurs and mechanics. The rest of the captives were shot in the immediate vicinity of the town. I noticed that the Croats wore German uniforms, but had the Croatian coat of arms on their sleeves. Probably only two per cent of these prisoners of war were spared and sent to Zagreb.[1]

Most of the victims were shot, but before receiving this final *coup de grace* they underwent horrible tortures. With my own eyes I saw the Partisans cut off noses and ears and gouge out eyes. They cut symbols of various kinds into the flesh of the captives, too, especially when they thought they had Gestapo personnel in their hands. A brief explanation for the necessity of massacring the war prisoners was provided for the benefit of the Partisan recruits enrolled in 1945.

Of course the prisoners received no trial of any sort. The manner of their deaths was left to the personal initiative of the local commanders who themselves had express orders from the headquarters of the Eighth Corps to liquidate all prisoners. I cannot estimate the number of victims, because they were disposed of over a considerable period of time and by various execution details. Frequently, we heard heavy and prolonged bursts of gunfire, so I think that a very large number of captives must have been liquidated. I know that a thousand German prisoners were killed at Sent Petar in the Kras district. Some Croatians were murdered here, too. As far as I can remember, we had orders not to kill the civilians who were retreating with the Croatian Armed Forces. Sometimes we even gave food to these people. On the other hand when they were closely and inextricably mixed up with military personnel, they were killed too.

Here are the names of the Partisan units which carried out the principal massacres, and also the names of the officers and commissars who commanded them:

First Battalion (my own unit) of the Eighth Brigade, Twentieth Assault Division of the Eighth Corps of the Fourth "People's Liberation Army"; Commander of the Twentieth Division, Colonel Bogdan Pecetic; Commander of the Eighth Corps, General Petar Drapsin, and its Commissar, Vladko Cetkovic; Commander of the Eighth Brigade, Lieutenant-Colonel Ivo Purisic from Muc, and its Commissar, Dragutin Crnogorac of Kninsko Polje. My own battalion commandant was Mile Knezevic who came from Maovice. The Commander of the Second Battalion of our Brigade was Dane Bogunovic, a native of Vrelo in the defile of the

[1] Compare this information with Document XXXVII.

Zrmanja River; Commissar Rancic from the village of Vojnic in the Sinj district was associated with him in the direction of this unit.

Twenty-Sixth Division of the Eighth Corps, Divisional Commander Marko Bace. Commander of the Eighth Brigade of this Division was Major Sima Dubajic from Bukovica.

Eighth Kordun Division, Commander Joze Skocilo, Commissar Djuro Kladarin (today director of the newspaper *Zagrebacki Vjesnik*).

Sixth Lika Proletarian Division, Commander Dyoko Yovanitch from Kořenica (at present chief of the Zagreb Military District), Commissar Rade Zigic.

Eleventh Corps, Commander Vjeceslav Holjevac.

Fourth Montenengrin Proletarian Brigade, Commander Lazo Lopatchitch.

Some units of the Nineteenth Division and of the Seventh Banija Division had a hand in the massacres too.

In June 1945, I was transferred to the Protective Battalion of the Second Army and was stationed in Zagreb. The commanding officer of the Second was General Ivan Gosnjak, its Commissar was Zigic, and the headquarters chief was General Ivan Sibl. At the city Commando Headquarters, I saw a group of five hundred prisoners liquidated. They were killed in small groups and had to await their deaths under the most horrible conditions imaginable, because of the cramped quarters in which they were confined. The massacres were carried out on the bank of the Sava River, or in the woods of the park at Maksimir. The prisoners were conveyed to the latter place by trucks called "Maricas." Vjeceslav Holjevac took a leading role in the direction of the liquidations.

One execution drama stands out particularly in my mind. The OZNA chief who arranged the slaughters carried out around Ilirska Bistrica was Mile Beljan, a Serb from the village of Miocic near Drnis. In the Zagreb killings, however, the officers of the Military OZNA were Novica Radovic (presently serving in the Court Guard at Sisak), Rade Lyubichitch, and Stevo Nisevic. One day they showed me a group of young Ustashas, none of whom was more than sixteen years old. "Look, Dusan," they told me, "there are young Ustashas, too." Then they had the boys led to the bank of the Sava, where a priest heard their confessions and gave them absolution. Once this was over, the Partisans bayoneted them and threw their bodies into the Sava. The same fate befell the priest.

Another group murder I remember vividly was that of a large group of wounded Croatian soldiers who had served as volunteers on the Eastern Front. They were hospitalized in Zagreb when the Partisans entered the town. First they were taken to the prison on Petrinja Street; then they were conveyed somewhere else to be shot. I did not witness this slaughter myself, but I heard about it from trustworthy sources and, young as I was, this particular episode disgusted me more than any of the other experiences described above.[2]

---

[2] See Document LX.

While I was in Zagreb, I had ample opportunity to watch the massacre of both military and civilian groups. I should mention that the executioners habitually took any valuables which were on the persons of the people they killed. They used the butts of their guns to knock the gold dentures out of the teeth of the victims. German officers, in particular, were treated this way.

I joined the Partisans in good faith, although without any real cognizance of what I was doing or what the war was all about. The things that I saw while I was serving with the Twentieth Division (Eighth Brigade) and the Protective Battalion of the Second Army did a good deal to shake my boyish trust in the cause with which I had identified myself. Still, there seemed to be no place for me except in the army. So I continued to serve for some years in various capacities. Finally, I became chief of the Escort Department of the State Secretariat for the Interior Affairs of The Federal People's Republic of Yugoslavia.

By this time I was no longer a boy, but rather a full grown young man, able to do his own thinking and to distinguish right from wrong. Because of the independence of mind I was developing, I had some disagreements with my colleagues and superior officers. Therefore, I found it expedient to leave my post and flee to Italy.

I have reported the facts cited above of my own free will according to the dictates of my conscience. I have not tried to conceal anything that happened, not even those actions in which I participated myself, because I want to be of some use in the fight against the reign of terror which made me its dupe while I was still a child. I decided to give this report after much mature deliberation. Today the memories of my youth seem repugnant to me and I realize that many things which I experienced then, and of which I thought little at the time, were very reprehensible.

I confirm with my own signature the literal truth of the statements that I have made above. These statements have been recorded faithfully and have been read to me. I declare myself ready to testify to these same facts before any authorized commission or tribunal.

Signed: Dusan Vukovic

Document LXVIII

The undersigned Muslim Croat, E. F. D., along with several Croatian soldiers, two Germans, and six Italians, surrendered to the Partisans of the Eighth Brigade, Twenty-Third Serbian Division, at Derventa. The two Germans were shot on the spot. Other prisoners were taken through various villages and towns in Bosnia. At the village of Zuljevica, the eyewitness saw a new group of thirty Croatian prisoners-of-war; all thirty were murdered. Our eyewitness and his companions were about to be slaughtered at Sveta Nedjelja, when he escaped. Although he later pretended to be a Partisan, he was arrested and placed in an OZNA (secret police) prison in Samobor. Here he found about two hundred Croatian captives. E. F. D. managed to escape from this captivity to Mostar. Before leaving, however, he visited Samobor, learned of a concentration camp and mass liquidation of prisoners, went to Zagreb, revisited his acquaintances in Samobor and then went to Mostar. Here he was arrested and imprisoned among many other Hercegovinian Croats. The witness closes his account by describing his meeting first with a Serb, former member of the above mentioned Brigade, then with Croats, relatives of his co-sufferers in Samobor.

I was mobilized into the Croatian Domobrans in September, 1942. My first assignment was to the Motorized Battalion in Zagreb. Then I went to Sarajevo in the Auxiliary Company of the Third Army. Afterwards I served in the garrison battalion at Sinj, from which point I was returned finally to the Auxiliary Company. When Sarajevo was evacuated in April, 1945, I retreated with this formation to Zenica and from there to Doboj and Derventa.

As my command was entering the last town, we found that the Partisans were already in possession of the place. I had to surrender to them along with several other Domobrans, two members of the German Balkan Wehrmacht, and six Italians. The latter were German prisoners up to the time of the German collapse.

Our captors were the Seventh Partisan Brigade of the Twenty-Third Serbian Division. They took down the data which we supplied concerning our past service and also questioned us in regard to the trades that we had professed before the war. They wanted volunteers who were qualified mechanics or specialists in other lines. To save our lives we had to "volunteer" for duty with them. I should mention that they did not interrogate the two Germans at all; they simply led them out to a nearby field and shot them amid the cornstalks. The order to shoot these prisoners was issued by the commander of the Escort Unit of the Eighth Brigade of the Twenty-Third Serbian Division. He was a tall, husky fellow, who wore a heavy mustache. I believe that his name was Zeco, but perhaps that was just his nickname. He usually went around in the company of his father who dressed in civilian clothes. A Partisan non-commissioned officer—I think he was a sergeant—volunteered for the murder detail; it was he who did the actual shooting. Almost all of the men in this division were Rumanians, or at least spoke Rumanian; they came from the eastern part of Serbia, or the old Banat of Temesvar of Hungarian days. There were some genuine Serbs among them, however, mainly from the vicinity of Kragujevac.

After the two Germans were shot, the Partisans intended to liquidate the six Italians. However, I asked the sergeant who had killed the Germans to spare the Italians because, as German prisoners themselves, they certainly had not served against Tito's forces, at least not since the Italian surrender in 1943. The Serbians knew that a close working cooperation had existed between them and some of the Italian units even before this time, and besides, many of Mussolini's soldiers joined the Partisans in 1943 or afterwards. So they decided to send the Italians to Derventa to repair a bridge there.

All of this occurred at Novo Selo where our captors had brought us. The streets of this place, as well as of other Croatian villages, were completely deserted. Almost the entire Croatian population of this countryside seemed either to have gone into hiding or to have retreated with the Armed Forces.

The Eighth Serbian Brigade took us prisoners to Prnjavor where we rested for a short while. Then we went on to Banja Luka, where we were placed on a train at the Kraljev Drum railroad station. The train carried us to Prijedor; from there we were marched to a Muslim village where the population welcomed us with kindness and gave us supper. The people in this place displayed a very cool attitude towards the Partisans.

We spent the night in this Muslim community and went on the next day to Blagaj and Zuljevica. Here we heard that there was heavy fighting around Bosanski Novi where the Ustashas and a Cherkez (Circassian) unit under German command were battling the Partisans. The latter had suffered many casualties. I myself saw several large piles of Partisan corpses. Later, these bodies were buried in the nearby hills. So severe were the losses suffered by Tito's people here, that real pandemonium reigned in the ranks of the Communists whose commissars had to use their pistols to check the flight of the Partisan troops and force them to return to the battle line.

Since Zuljevica was a Serbian village, the population welcomed the Partisans and showed them great respect. I was the only prisoner left with this group now; my fellow captives either escaped or were transferred to another unit. A guard stayed near me at all times.

About sunset one day, a group of approximately thirty Domobrans arrived in the village. They wore new German uniforms and told me that they belonged to the Fourth Mountain Brigade. While detailed to defend a bunker, they were cut off from their unit which retreated unexpectedly from Bosanska Kostajnica. They held out until they ran low on ammunition and then decided to surrender to the Partisans. I asked if there was anyone from Hercegovina among them. One young Muslim said that he was from Jablanica. He showed me a photo of his wife standing with a child in her arms in front of their house. I do not recall anything about the other members of this command. They did not anticipate the fate that was in store for them and lightheartedly lit a fire to keep warm, because the nights were cold that spring of 1945.

Commander Zeco had accepted the surrender of the thirty Domobrans, but only so they could be killed without danger to their captors. He ordered that their hands be tied with wire. Then the Domobrans realized what was going to happen. They told the Serbs that they were innocent of any crimes and had served only as simple soldiers in the defense of their country. Also, they called attention to the fact that they all had wives and children at home. Their pleas were ignored as six or seven Partisans armed with Russian-made light machine guns took them off in the darkness towards the railroad tracks. They shot them down about a hundred and fifty feet away from the local river. In the village, we could hear the sound of the shots and see the flashes of gunfire. After the bursts of machine gun fire, a few individual shots sounded out from time to time. Either someone had escaped, or else they were killing those victims who were only wounded.

Some time later the executioners returned. They carried with them the blood-stained trousers, coats, and belts of the murdered Domobrans. The killers were all between twenty and twenty-one years of age, except for two who were perhaps about eighteen. I soon found out that these two youths never missed a chance to participate in a shooting party. One of them wore a single decoration, while the other, a blond, sported a pair of these testimonies of Partisan valor. This fellow was an altogether different type from the other Rumanian-speaking Partisans.

I marched with the Escort Company of the Eighth Brigade from Bosanski Novi to Dvor where we spent the night. On the next day we advanced to Gvozdanjsko and Glina. At this old border town, the Serbian inhabitants joyfully acclaimed the Partisan liberators. They even organized a celebration in their honor. This event took place in the city square on May 1.

From Glina we marched to Pisarovina by way of Vojnic. We remained in Pisarovina the entire day and learned that the Fourth Battalion of the Eighth Brigade was battling against Ustasha troops in the immediate vicinity. The Escort Company received orders to dig trenches deep enough for a man to stand in them. These trenches were dug at the end of the village, which is close to the road that leads to Zagreb. Since we had to work quickly and I was not accustomed to this kind of labor, I soon became exhausted. Fortunately, a Serb by the name of Danitchitch helped me; he was much huskier than I was, even though we were the same age. Danitchitch was not a Marxist, but had been mobilized forcibly into the ranks of the Partisans. He was a fine fellow who never took part in the killing of prisoners in all the time that I knew him.

On the following day, we advanced via Rakov Potok to Sveta Nedjelja. On the way we passed a number of Partisan units, among them the mobile hospital of the Twenty-Fifth Serbian Division. It was transporting a large number of wounded Partisans in peasant carts. Most of the Partisan units that we met came from Serbia proper, but some of them were Bosnian Serbs.

One Partisan formation was being guided by a peasant of the vicinity. He became tired, or else did not want to accompany Tito's troops any further, so he told them that he was unable to go on. He suggested that they find another guide. For this they killed him.

At twilight we arrived at Sveta Nedjelja, where we remained for two days. We slept in a new building which was uninhabited when we entered the village. On the first morning in this place, a young man dressed in civilian clothes was brought to the room I was occupying. He told me that he was a Domobran, that his home was not far from Sveta Nedjelja, and that this was where the Partisans had caught him. He was firmly convinced that the apparent victors in the war were going to allow him to return to his home without imprisoning him for any length of time.

After we had breakfasted on the morning of the second day in Sveta Nedjelja, Commander Zeco informed us that we were going to be transferred to another unit. Only when our captors started to tie our hands with wire did we realize the meaning of the word "transfer." I dropped to the ground and used my fists and feet to keep myself from being tied up. The sergeant who had given the order to bind us cursed me and struck me twice with a heavy military shoe. Finally, he gave up trying to secure me, and allowed all of us to proceed untied. While this fracas was going on, the above-mentioned Danitchitch stood by without either helping me or assisting the other Partisans.

We left the village with the two eighteen-year-old Partisan juvenile delinquents following about nine feet behind us. They were armed with light Russian machine guns. Once outside the village, they ordered us to bear to our left towards a forest. I whispered to the young Domobran from Sveta Nedjelja that we had better make a break for it, because we were being led to a place of execution. He refused to follow my advice because he still placed literal reliance upon the statement of Zeco that we were being transferred.

As soon as we entered the forest, I swung around abruptly and threw my Domobran coat over the head of the escort, who was a pale, weak-looking fellow. Then I hit him on top of the head with all my might and ran as fast as I could downhill in among the trees. Shots rang out behind me, but I was not hit. I dashed through the woods and came to an open plain over which I saw that I would have to pass to reach another clump of trees. Bullets were still flying all around me, but I succeeded in crossing the open space and dived in among some thick thorn bushes in the second forest. I had found an excellent hiding place, since it apparently did not occur to the Partisans that anyone would try to penetrate such a prickly growth of shrubbery. I could hear the two escorts yelling out to one another as they looked for me, but they did not call in any of their Partisan fellows to join in the pursuit. Probably they reported to their commander that they had completed the liquidation.

I stayed among the thorns and brambles that whole day without a bite to eat or anything to drink except my own urine. Later I discovered that I was quite close to a spring. When evening came, I calculated that the escorting company would be well away from this district. So I extricated myself from my improvised shelter and wandered through the woods until I happened upon a peasant who was working in a vineyard. I conversed with him for half an hour, telling him that I was a Partisan soldier released only recently from a hospital, and that I was trying to rejoin my unit which had gone to Slovenia. He took me to his home on the other side of the Samobor-Zagreb road and gave me milk and cornbread for supper.

While I was eating, a Partisan artillery patrol stopped at the house. I told them the same story I had related to the peasant, but of course I could not show them a hospital release. Therefore, they took me to their commander who forwarded me to the OZNA in Samobor. The OZNA men imprisoned me with some two hundred other soldiers and civilians. I remained in their prison for two days and nights. Both the commander of this place and his men were from Zumberak. He told me that some of the civilian prisoners were going to be sent home and that they would be supplied with passes to insure their safe conduct.

Anything looked better to me than an OZNA prison, so I mingled with the civilians as inconspicuously as possible. Since I had lost my Domobran coat in the manner described, I didn't look much different than they did. I even gave my own name when we "civilians" were lined up to receive our passes, and I secured one that gave me permission to go to Mostar. On this pass there was a seal which bore the Partisan five-beam star. The pass also contained a recommendation that the bearer should not be interfered with in any way, but should be assisted to return to his home. I cut a five-beam star out of red cloth that I managed to get hold of and affixed this insignia to my Domobran cap. Thus attired, I was able to leave the prison twice a day without being challenged by the guards. I went into the city where I learned that on the outskirts of the community there was a concentration camp which contained German as well as Croatian soldiers. Thanks to my improvised star, no one stopped or questioned me when I entered this camp. There were more than two hundred prisoners there at the time. Among them I recognized my close compatriot, Safet Cuskovic, from Mostar. His brother-in-law was with him. They took me for a Partisan at first.

Nevertheless they asked me to bring them some food, for they had received nothing to eat for more than two days. Without revealing my identity, I obtained some potatoes and salt for them from houses in the neighborhood. I returned to the camp with this food, which I gave to Cuskovic and his brother-in-law, as well as to some of the German prisoners. One of the Germans had an extra pair of very good trousers with him which he gave to me along with a pair of shoes. Since my clothes were in tatters, this was a fortunate acquisition.

I told Cuskovic that I was going to Zagreb in the near future. He asked me to contact his wife and sister who lived on Preradovic Street in the capital. I assured him that I would do so.

The discipline maintained in this camp varied in strictness. Now and then selected groups were taken outside the barricade to be "transferred." The sound of shooting could be heard in the forest adjoining the town after such "transfers," so it was assumed that these prisoners were shot.

The war was over and there was no fighting going on that would account for this gunfire. During one of my visits to the Samobor camp, I met a professor who was a native of a village in the Zagorje. He told me that every time shots were heard in the forest, groups of prisoners were being liquidated. I cannot assert positively that what he said was the truth. However, on one occasion I saw the Partisans give a merciless beating to a young man of the Honor Work Service who had gone under a bridge outside the camp to relieve himself. They charged him with intending to escape, and beat him over the head with their fists and gun butts until he collapsed. His friends had to carry him back into the camp.

Finally, I was allowed to leave for Zagreb equipped with my officially authorized and issued pass. In the capital city, I visited Cuskovic's wife and sister as I had promised to do. I told them that their husbands were in prison in Samobor. They were quite upset by this news and asked me to wait until the following day so they would have time to prepare good food for their spouses. They worked all that night putting up various delicacies, meat dishes, coffee, etc. I returned to Samobor the next morning, but found that all the prisoners had been "transferred," supposedly to a place near Karlovac. I was convinced that all the captives had been murdered, but did not have the courage to say this to Cuskovic's wife and sister. Therefore, when I went back to Zagreb I did not see or send word to these women but rather took a bus to Slunj and Sibenik. I spent a night in Sibenik where the OZNA imprisoned every traveler on the bus except me. My pass certainly worked wonders for me!

From Sibenik I took another bus to Split, Livno, and Bugojno where I boarded a train which brought me through Travnik and Sarajevo to Mostar. Here in my own town, I was arrested by a Communist street patrol two days after my arrival.

I did not dare to show these new captors the pass I had obtained in Samobor. The data that appeared on this document, especially my place of birth, was fictitious. Therefore, the patrol incarcerated me first of all at Militia headquarters and then handed me over to the OZNA on Santic Street. There I was interrogated chiefly by OZNA Color-Bearer Gavro Papo, a native of Mostar. He is still a very high official of the UDBA (successor to the OZNA) and is stationed in Sarajevo.

After two nights in the OZNA prison, I was transferred to the Celovina, the old city jail in Mostar. From there I was sent to the "Northern Camp," which was the main point for the assembly and questioning of soldiers and civilians in this part of the country. During the fifteen days that I remained in this place, I witnessed daily "selections" of people who were taken off to unknown destinations. Prisoners in the camp, as well as people living outside it, told me that many liquidations were being effected in this area. Officials of the Croatian Government and men whose daughters were married to high-ranking Ustashas were taken from the room in which I was confined. One of them was Pero Musa, whose daughter had married an Ustasha official by the name of Barbaric.

Musa, however, got off with twenty years' imprisonment for the offense of allowing his offspring to marry this man. Also imprisoned in my cell was Jozo Merdzo, who had held official position in the Pavelic regime. He also drew a twenty year term while his brother, Ivan, received a shorter sentence.

The commander of the camp was a Mostar Serb, Tasko Zurovac. Today he is living in Zagreb. Most of the other camp officers were Serbs from Gacko and Bilec.

I had the good fortune to work off my punishment by labor service in the Yugoslav Army. In April, 1948, I was serving as a mechanic and was transferred (in the legitimate sense of the term this time) to an auto platoon at Zajecar. One afternoon, I was unloading military supplies at the railroad station there. A group of peasants dressed in national costumes was waiting for the passenger train at this station. Among them I recognized Danitchitch, the former Partisan soldier who had assisted me in the digging of the trenches at Pisarovina three years before. I went up to him and asked him if he recognized me. He said that he had seen me before, but couldn't remember where. I introduced myself to him and recalled to his memory the days of our joint service in the Escort Company. He seemed greatly bewildered and told me that he had assumed I was killed at Sveta Nedjelja by the two young executioners. I related the story of my escape to him. He invited me to visit him at his home which was in the village of Kobimica. All I had to do was to ask for "Trubac" (Tuba Man); everyone in the place knew him by this nickname. He assured me that he would supply me with details concerning the Partisans who reported that they had killed me. The pale one whom I had knocked senseless hailed from Donji Milanovac and was still alive.

Danitchitch knew all of the other Partisans who had served in the Escort Company of the Eighth Brigade of the Twenty-Third Serbian Division, whose special duty it was to liquidate prisoners. While we were talking, the train arrived and we said goodbye to one another. I did not see Danitchitch again after this meeting for, after all, he was a Serb, although apparently a good enough fellow. Still he might decide to ingratiate himself with the authorities by denouncing me, if I took him at his word and visited him in his native village.

When I was finally discharged from Tito's Army I visited Mrs. Cuskovic in Zagreb. I asked her about the fate of her husband, but she told me that the message that I had brought to her was the last she had received from him. Both Safet Cuskovic and his brother-in-law—the husband of Safet's sister—must have been murdered by the Partisans on the same night that I left Samobor to go to Zagreb.

To provide a guarantee for the truth of the above cited testimony, I swear to its veracity on my honor and confirm this oath with my signature.

Signed: E. F. D.

Rome, Italy
April 18, 1961

Document LXIX

The undersigned, C. S. F., was captured on May 8, 1945, in Opatija. Following his capture, he was confined five days in the Pension Victoria in Lovran, two days in the Villa Kuben in Opatija, and three days in Martinscica. From Martinscica, he was transferred to the jail on the Via Roma in Rijeka where he stayed for thirty-five days in the company of some two hundred other Croatian prisoners. About a hundred of these prisoners were first tortured terribly and then led away to be slaughtered. The other hundred prisoners were sent to Opatija and finally to the camp in Martinscica. In the "Lazaret" section of this camp, there were 600 to 700 Croatian prisoners-of-war. In the "Vodovod" section, there were a thousand prisoners, mainly Germans and some Croatian Legionnaires. Gradually, they were being killed in order to make room for new arrivals. The "Vodovod" prisoners were liquidated in the mountain ravine known as "Urinj". The "Lazaret" inmates were murdered on the military rifle range at Poljana. The eyewitness was taken again to the jail in Rijeka, but this time was set free.

During the war of 1941-45, I served at first as a sergeant of Domobrans in the Croatian Army. Then I was promoted to lieutenant and attached to the command of Colonel Res, who was a liaison officer assigned to the Second Italian Army which had its headquarters in Susak near Rijeka (Fiume). Colonel Res was afterwards given the rank of Military Commissioner in which capacity he continued to represent the Croatian State at Italian Headquarters, until the withdrawal of Italy from the war in 1943. Later, he was the Croatian representative at the German Command for Trieste and the Kvarner (Quarnero) region at the head of the Adriatic Sea.

On April 27, 1945, the Germans blew up the bridge that spans the Rijecina River and retreated northwards. At this time I was still stationed in Susak. The Partisans did not enter this city until the evening of the 28th. I rejoined my family in Opatija (Abbazia) and witnessed the arrival of the Partisans in this town. On May 8, I was arrested together with my brother-in-law, Alfonso Parin. We were taken to the Hotel Palme, which the local OZNA used to contain its prisoners until they could be interrogated. I was not questioned here, but on this same night was driven to the Pension Victoria in Lovran where I remained for five days. Afterwards more than a hundred of us were taken to the Villa Kuben in Opatija under cover of night. Following a two-day confinement here, we were transferred to a prisoner camp at Martinscica. After three days there we were ordered to walk to the Gendarmerie station on the Boulevard in Susak. When I arrived there, I was taken almost immediately to the Central OZNA headquarters for Istria and the Croatian Littoral. They kept me in their jail on the Via Roma in Rijeka.

There were approximately two hundred of us in the jail where I remained for thirty-five days. Half of the prisoners were designated for execution. Before they were killed, they were subjected to horrible tortures. Screams and oaths resounded from the rooms in which they were "interrogated." Among the victims was an Italian school inspector, a

German by the name of Kaiser who had represented various German commercial enterprises and who owned a villa in Opatija, and the owner of the restaurant "Mali Raj," which was located on Punta Collova between Opatija and Icici.

The remaining hundred of us were eventually transferred back to Opatija. En route we stopped to rest at Punta Collova. Darkness had fallen when the Communists brought us to a spot where the Germans had shot thirteen of the comrades earlier in the war. Our captors ordered us to lie down with our faces to the ground. When we had done so, they trampled all over us and beat us with their gun butts for a quarter of an hour, screaming, "Inhale the blood of our comrades whom you bandits shot on this spot and then threw into the ravine!" All of us thought that the Reds were going to kill us here, but they did not go that far. Instead they conveyed us to the Villa Kuben in Opatija. From here we were taken to the Martinscica camp.

This place of detention was located in the lowlands which face the sea. It was divided into two sections. On the right hand side of the road leading out from Susak was a fenced-in area which was known as the Lazaret. Civilians, Domobrans, and some members of the Susak Ustasha Brigade were sequestered here. There were between six and seven hundred prisoners in all. On the left hand side of the highway, Germans and Croatian Legionnaires of the Blue Division, which had fought in Russia, were confined in an open area called the "Vodovod" (water line). They numbered perhaps a thousand in all. These captives received much worse treatment than we did. They suffered greatly from hunger and thirst. Frequently I saw how the Germans, who had been stripped of all their clothes, would run pell-mell to a stream that flowed nearby the camp whenever their guards gave them permission to do so.

My relatives were sometimes able to come to the camp to visit me. Several times when I was waiting at the gate for them to appear, I saw new batches of German prisoners arrive to replace the earlier groups which were sent to Kostrena. I would estimate that in three days' time as many as two or three thousand Germans passed through Martinscica. When I left this place on the third day of my stay there, a good six hundred Teutons were still incarcerated in the "Vodovod." Since I am a former soccer player and accustomed to estimating attendances at games, I believe that the figures I have given above are fairly accurate.

Great masses of Germans were killed during the three nights that I spent at Martinscica. On every one of these evenings, we could hear the chain shooting of automatic weapons from the direction of the mountain ravine known as the "Urinj." It is located on the right side of the Susak-Kostrena highway at the foot of the coastal rampart which rises up near St. Barbara at Kostrena. This ravine is connected with the sea and is only half a mile from the prisoner camp. The inhabitants of Kostrena, as well as the people who lived in neighboring villages like Zurkovo, St. Lucia, and so on, told us that the Partisans brought the prisoners to the ravine in trucks, or else marched them there in foot columns. They were killed during the night hours and thrown into the "Urinj." It was chiefly Germans who were murdered here. The killers belonged to the KNOJ (Communist National Youth of Yugoslavia). Later on, truckloads of quicklime were poured into the ravine, because of the abominable stench that emanated from the decaying corpses which filled it. Nevertheless, it was feared that the bodies, if left unburied, might cause a plague, so after two or three months, cemetery laborers were brought from Susak to load the remains onto trucks in order that they might be taken elsewhere to be buried. They had to construct a road from the highway to the ravine to gain access to this great open grave. Despite the grisly nature of their task, some of the "graveyard detail" were so hardened that they searched among the putrefying remains for money, rings, and other valuables.

Later on I was returned to the jail on the Via Roma in Rijeka. Here I found other prisoners from the Martinscica camp, including Davor Parisic who today is living in Trieste. A professor whom I shall designate only as "I," a Dr. "K," and other people who are still residing in Yugoslavia, were in this jail, too. Some of the inmates were at Martinscica before I came there. They told me that during their stay at this place many civilians and Croatian war prisoners were taken in small groups from the "Lazaret" section of the camp to be killed at Poljana. Then, when the German prisoners started to arrive, the scene of the mass slaughters was shifted to the "Urinj" ravine. After the Germans were disposed of in the manner related above, the butchery of Croatian civilian and military personnel was resumed at the Poljana location, where the military rifle range was used as an abattoir. Two tailors, I.R. and A.E., who today are residing in Susak and Rijeka respectively, informed me about these matters. K.I., who presently is living in Crikvenica, confirmed what they told me.

A friend helped me to get out of the little jail on the Via Roma. While I was free, I went to see the bodies of two slain soldiers whom the women of Veprinac had found in the valley below the village church. The corpses were covered over with leaves and tree branches. Local Communist authorities declared that the two dead men were victims of the Germans. But tatoos on their arms, the German trousers that they wore, the German socks that were still on their feet, and the general appearance of their remains assured me they were German war prisoners whom the Partisans murdered in this lonely spot.

I am ready to testify personally to the truth of the facts that I have cited above before any international commission charged with the investigation of war crimes. However, I must stipulate expressly that necessary discretion must be observed by such a body in order to prevent reprisals against my relatives who are still residing in the old Domovina.

Signed: C.S.F.

October 1, 1955

Document LXX

This account opens with a detailed description of the extermination camp at Mirkovci, in the northern corner of Croatia, where eight thousand Croatian victims were subjected to indescribable horrors. The director of this camp was a Croatian Communist, Djuro Skreblin. The majority of the officers and soldiers detailed to watch the camp were Serbs. From May 9 through June 1, 1945, all eight thousand prisoners were liquidated in the vicinity of Mirkovci. After this massacre, the authorities captured former enemy soldiers for "service" in the infamous Thirteenth Battalion. The eyewitness was one of the "recruits" but, because of a letter from the "People's Committee," he was set free. Other recruits, about twenty thousand of them, were liquidated at Lepa Bukva, in the Gorski Kotar. Towards the end of his testimony, our eyewitness describes how, during the massacres in Slovenia, he was once saved by Slovenian Partisans and another time by a Croatian Partisan woman. The testimony closes with a description of the Opleniski Vrh abyss into which about fifteen hundred Croatian prisoners-of-war were thrown alive.

During the retreat from the Domovina of the Croatian Armed Forces in 1945, a number of our rear guard or stragglers were captured by the Yugoslav Partisans. Ustashas and Domobrans, who until the last moment had remained in their homes close to the Slovenian frontier, were among those taken. All of these captives were crowded together into the prisoner-of-war camp at Mirkovci, which is between Krapina and Zabok in the Hrvatsko Zagorje (Croatian hinterland). There were approximately eight thousand prisoners here in all. The camp was surrounded by an electrified barbed wire fence. Armed guards were posted all along the wire at five yard intervals. There were barracks in this place, but the windows and doors were broken so that the shelter they offered was inadequate in cold or rainy weather. Since there were no beds left in them, the inmates had to sleep on the floors.

At first the soldiers imprisoned here were not allowed to have any contact with the civilian population. Nonetheless, the people living in the vicinity came in masses to see if they had friends or relatives among the imprisoned. They used to crowd around the guards asking them questions. A hundred or so prisoners took advantage of this practice to escape. Most of them were caught and killed in a very horrifying manner.

The Croatian civilians in the vicinity brought countless packages of food to the camp. They were deceived by the Partisan guards, who promised to give these packages to the people for whom they were intended, but used them themselves. Meanwhile the starving prisoners had to eat grass or bark from the trees. Soon all of the food was gone; the eyesight of some of the prisoners was affected, apparently because of malnutrition. I saw this phenomenon myself because one of the guards, who was an acquaintance of mine, was not able to endure the horror of the treatment that the captives received. Therefore, he allowed me to smuggle in packages of food to as many men as I could. Those who had gone blind could still smell the food, even if they could not see it. It was a tragic sight to see these blind skeletons groping feebly for a bite to eat and to know that there was no hope for any of them.

Conditions in the camp soon became so bad that the Partisans spread the rumor that a number of prisoners had contracted typhoid fever. They protested that it would be better to destroy these prisoners like sick animals rather than to allow the disease to spread. So they threw most of the original eight thousand captives into trenches that had been dug nearby.

Because my home was only a fifteen minute walk from the Mirkovci camp, I was well informed about the details of the slaughter and the identities of those responsible for it. It was Djuro Skreblin, a Croat from Brezova, who, as camp director, issued the order for the liquidation of all "bandits." Skreblin, who has a finger missing from one hand, surpassed in brutality even the Serbian Partisans who carried out the executions.

I tried to establish contact with the Croatians who were included among the Partisans guarding the camp. I knew that they would be willing to contrive at the escape of as many of the captives as possible. However, my efforts in this direction were unsuccessful because the majority of the officers and soldiers detailed to watch the camp were Serbs who suspected the loyalty of their Croatian comrades to Yugoslavia. So I had to give up my attempts lest I compromise some of the Croatian Partisans. Also, I was in grave danger myself because I had served in the Honor Company of the Twelfth Ustasha Infantry Regiment in the "Dr. Pavelic" barracks.

The martyrdom of the prisoners at Mirkovici lasted from May 9 through June 1, 1945. I do not believe that any of the eight thousand prisoners confined there survived. Many local residents sturdily protested to the Yugoslav authorities that they could testify unconditionally to the fact that men whom they knew among the captives were innocent of any war crimes. Such heroic gestures were completely useless and even dangerous because the invariable reply was that the "People's Republic" would destroy not only the prisoners, but also everyone who spoke up in their behalf. So after a while no one dared approach the camp any more. As lies concerning the contagious diseases prevalent in this place of horror circulated, people were afraid to even bring food packages to the vicinity.

One day the authorities issued an order for all those who had served the enemy during the war and were still at large to report themselves. I waited for a few days to see what was going to happen to the men who obeyed this instruction. According to what I heard, some of them were allowed to return to their homes, while others were assigned to serve in the Thirteenth Battalion. At the time I assumed that this unit was a work battalion so I reported in to Krapina. My two brothers accompanied me there; they were sent back home. As I had expected, I was posted to the Thirteenth Battalion.

One of my brothers suspected the true character of this formation. He urged the referent, a Croatian whom I shall designate here only as "M," to tell him frankly where I was being sent. The referent gave him a long-winded explanation and then suddenly asked my brother if he were willing to sacrifice his life for mine. Finally, he told my brother that if he could secure a guarantee of my character and innocence of war crimes from our local People's Committee he might be able to save my life.

It was in this way that my life was spared and I have survived to this day to tell what I know about those most inhuman of monsters, the Partisans commanded by Josip Broz Tito.

Let me tell you about the fate of the men assigned to the "Thirteenth Battalion." Fortunately, I did not get my information first hand or I would not be relating this story today. A friend of mine, whom I shall call D. R., told me all about this "unit." D. R. is himself a Croatian who joined the Partisans at the end of the war in order to save his own skin. He was detailed to escort the prisoners sent from Krapina to the "Thirteenth Battalion" to the so-called "Lepa Bukva" near Maceljska Gora. Every day the Partisans brought people from the several regions of the Hrvatsko Zagorje to this place. These captives were tied together by twos, wire being used for this purpose. They lined up in two big circles around the "Lepa Bukva" which is a ravine in the mountains. The guards would shoot one of the bound prisoners, or bludgeon him to death, and he would fall into the abyss and pull his living partner in with him. Quicklime eventually was thrown over the bodies. D. R. was not able to endure this slaughter for long, so he deserted from Tito's army. Afterwards he told me what he had seen.

It was the concensus among the inhabitants of the vicinity that twenty thousand prisoners were butchered in the manner described above. I know of six Croatian soldiers from my own hamlet who were murdered at the "Lepa Bukva."

Perhaps it will be asked how I, a known Ustasha, succeeded in escaping the fate that overtook so many of my comrades. Well, the circumstances of my own capture placed me in a relatively favorable position right from the outset. There were four of us who were caught by the Slovenian Partisans at the Maribor railroad station, while we were waiting for a train to take us to Celje. I identified myself to the Slovenes as a Domobran rather than as an Ustasha, and since they didn't know much about either one of these branches of our Army, they were taken in easily enough. As the Slovenes were leading us off, a column of Serbian Partisans came up to the railroad station. They demanded that the Slovenes turn us over to them to be killed, but the Slovenian Partisans flatly refused to comply with this request.

On the following day a Slovenian Partisan detachment conducted my three companions and myself outside of the city. Four German prisoners were added to our number, and a Serbian Color Bearer joined our escort.

He shot all four of the Germans while they were still fully clothed. Then the Partisans ordered us Croatians to undress and we knew that our turn was coming. As the Serb leveled his machine gun to dispose of us, a girl who wore the insignia of a Partisan Captain came running up. She asked us who we were and where we came from. We replied that we were Domobrans from the Krapina district. Thereupon she grabbed the Serbian's machine gun and shouted angrily at him, "You're not killing men from my own region!"

And so we had her to thank for saving our lives.

In closing this account, I shall skip over the various vicissitudes that I experienced after this near escape from death. Although there were plenty of people who knew that I was an Ustasha, they did not betray me to the Yugoslav authorities or the Partisans that they commanded. Even so I would have wound up in the Thirteenth Battalion had it not been for my brother's intercession in my behalf as described above.

Some time after the war and the orgy of political murder instituted by Tito and his henchmen, a friend, "M. J.," took me to the Opleniski Vrh (peak) in the mountainous region of the Gorski Kotar. He showed me a deep hole, three feet wide by three feet long, and the Devil alone knows how deep, high up in the mountains there. He told me he was present when the Partisans, after the end of the war, threw fifteen hundred living Ustasha prisoners down this hole, which was the opening to a great abyss that the murderers partially covered up after they had committed their crime. They threw bombs on top of the victims whom they pitched into this pit of horror.

What I have related above is not all that I know about the atrocities perpetrated by the followers of Tito Broz after the war of 1941-45. I could write a whole book on this subject. And perhaps some day I shall, if the one in which this record is contained does not serve the purpose of indicting for all time to come the Master Criminal of the twentieth century, Josip Broz Tito, and his murderous crew of sadistic and fanatical killers.

Signed: B. P.

Allgau, West Germany
December 16, 1962

Document LXXI

Described here is the massacre of twenty-seven Croatian war prisoners, at Klanjec.

I was only ten years old in May, 1945, when the Partisans of the Twenty-Sixth Montenegrin Brigade murdered twenty-seven Croatian war prisoners in my birthplace, Klanjec. Five of these prisoners were killed on the highway down which a prisoner column was driven. There was an uncle of mine among these victims.

The twenty-seven Croatians murdered by the Montenegrins came from different Croatian provinces, some of them from the Hrvatsko Zagorje, or hinterland. Several were natives of Klanjec.

I heard that many other war prisoners were liquidated in the neighboring village of Vampas near Truheljske Toplice. Since I was not there, I do not know the facts concerning this reported massacre. But I do know very well that the twenty-seven referred to above were disposed of in Klanjec; I confirm this fact with my oath and signature.

Signed: Zvonimir Gajsak

Rosebery, N. S. W., Australia
September 21, 1963

Document LXXII

The massacre of Croatian prisoners-of-war at Sosice in Zumberak is described by S. P.

I survived the retreat and surrender of the Croatian Army in 1945 to find myself in a "Death Column," which Tito's Partisans drove before them like a herd of cattle destined for the slaughterhouse. By a bit of luck, I managed to escape from this column and to reach my home.

Not long after my return, I was drafted into the Yugoslav National Liberation Army. When I had completed this unwelcome obligation, I visited acquaintances who lived in Zumberak. They gave me the following eyewitness accounts of the cruelties perpertrated by the Partisans upon the Croatians who were captured in 1945.

It was about May 20, 1945, when the Partisans began bringing trucks filled with Croatian Nationalists of all categories to this region. The captives had their hands tied to sticks which were set below their knees. They were brought along the road that leads from Zagreb through Kerestinec, Jaska, Karlovac, and Samobor. Women working in the fields heard their husbands, sons, or brothers call to them as the trucks passed by. Some of the prisoners were able to shout a last goodbye to their wives or children as they passed through their native villages.

The truck loads of victims were all brought to Sosice. Ten minutes from the center of this village there is a deep abyss (no one ever has ascertained its exact depth), which has an opening only about two feet in diameter. This chasm is located between Sosice and the neighboring village of Gornje Selo on a plateau which is filled with rocks and bushes.[1]

---

[1] Sixteen years ago, Thomas Reskovac of Cleveland, Ohio, visited the Sosice massacre site and took moving pictures of it. He showed the movies to a large audience in the Croatian Liberty Home on 15711 Waterloo Road. He even lectured on the massacre. Not long ago John Prcela, who had seen those pictures and heard Reskovac's comments on the massacre, asked him for the photos for publication in this volume. Reskovac, in order not to endanger the lives of his relatives in Zumberak, refused to give them. His story of the massacre, however, was by far more detailed than either this or the next Document.

When the trucks reached this abyss the victims were unloaded. First, the Partisans beat and tortured them. My informants, who witnessed from a distance what was going on, said that the Partisans used sledge hammers, axes, knives, gun butts, and revolvers upon the prisoners. After Tito's "Heroes of the Liberation" became tired of torturing their prey, they threw them alive down into the abyss. This procedure was repeated daily for an entire month. Local Communists from Zumberak participated in these butcheries. A certain Trubinac Sr., of Sosice, especially distinguished himself in the fine art of killing bound and exhausted, starving, thirst-crazed men. Later, the local butchers became agents of the OZNA (later UDBA) or of the K.O.S. (Counter Intelligence Service).

To this day access to the abyss between Sosice and Gornje Selo is strictly forbidden to all by the Communist authorities of this region.

Signed: S. P.

Rome, July 9, 1952

Document LXXIII

The first part of this document corroborates the previous testimony. The second part, dealing with the massacres at Cemernica, is complemented by Document LXXVIII.

I am one of those Croatians who survived four years of battles against the Communist enemies of our country. In the retreat into which we were forced by the collapse of Germany in 1945, I got as far as Dravograd. When someone issued an order to us to surrender here, I refused to comply because I foresaw that the British would hand us over to the Partisans. So I made my way back through Slovenia to the Domovina, where I hid out in the woods and mountains.

While doing so, I busied myself gathering eyewitness testimonies of the happenings that are described in the work of Dr. Oton Knezovic, *Pokolj Hrvatske Vojske 1945* (The Massacre of the Croatian Army in 1945), which was published in Chicago a year ago. I wrote down these testimonies myself or collected them from the depositors themselves and concealed them in a safe place. If we live to see Croatia freed from the Communist terror which oppresses her, these eyewitness accounts of the barbarities and mass butcheries of 1945 and succeeding years will be made public. I concerned myself especially with gathering information about those Croatians who were murdered by the UDBA long after the end of the war to make Croatia safe for Tito and his butchers.

Since I have noted that Dr. Knezovic says nothing in his book about the killings that took place at the Sosice abyss in the Zumberak region, I am going to relate the following account here.

In 1948 I had a meeting with some former Croatian soldiers, who were still hiding out in the Zumberak area. They took me to a place where there is a deep hole in the ground into which several thousand Croatian war prisoners were thrown, still half alive, during the late spring of 1945. We dug down into this hole until we came to some beams which had been placed to bar further excavation. There was something less than two feet of earth piled on top of these beams. The Communists who took part in the massacre of our soldiers here are still alive and residing in Zumberak.

I shall also tell of a place in Cemernica, between Karlovac and Vrgin Most, where there was a concentration camp after the war. Several thousand Croatian soldiers were slaughtered in this camp by the Partisans after the end of formal hostilities. These soldiers were handed over to Tito's people by the English after they had reached Austrian territory. They were returned through Slovenia to Glina and Karlovac and brought from those places to the Cemernica camp. Eight groups of soldiers of the various branches of the Croatian Armed Forces were murdered here. One band of some 200 military men succeeded in getting away from this camp. They scattered far and wide, all of them finding refuge somewhere, chiefly in Bosnia, Hercegovina or the mountainous Lika region in western Croatia. In this group of escapees were two Muslim Croats from Stolac. They were with me in the mountains in 1948 and told me about their experiences at Cemernica.

Signed: Ilija Barbaric

Sao Paulo, Brazil
July 8, 1961

Document LXXIV

The following testimony deals with the shootings of Croatian prisoners-of-war in the vicinity of Rakov Potok and Kerestinec. In the latter part of May, throughout June, and well into July, 1945, these massacres assumed massive proportions and were carried out daily. They continued, although on a smaller scale, in the second half of 1945, too.

For nearly two months following the fall of Zagreb to the Communists, columns of Croatian prisoners coming from Slovenia could be seen passing along the road leading from Sv. Nedjelja through Stupnik close to the capital.

These prisoners presented a sad spectacle indeed. They were hungry, thirsty, and clad only in rags and tatters; their captors had taken everything they owned that was at all usable. These captors, or guards, were usually Serbian Communists, who kept peasants living along the route from supplying the captives with food, water, or other necessities and comforts.

When anyone became exhausted and was unable to keep up with his column, the guards would tell him to drop out along the roadside and wait until a truck came along to pick him up. Such exhausted individuals would be collected in groups along the side of the road. After night fell, they were taken into nearby woods where they were shot or bayoneted.

We heard this shooting going on in the forests and thickets around us every night. Usually the butcheries took place between 11:30 P.M. and 2:00 A.M. They occurred in the vicinity of Rakov Potok and especially in the Stupnicka Suma (forest) and the Makaronka Bushes between Paucnjak and Rakov Potok.

After the killings, the corpses were thrown into the so-called "Dekungi" trenches. These excavations stretched from the Kalinovac crossing for a distance of one full kilometer along the roadside. They ended near the home of the Kavur family on the outskirts of Stupnik on the Zagreb-Karlovac highway. The trenches—more properly speaking, ditches—were approximately three feet wide by four to five feet deep. Some of them stretched out to a length of twenty to fifty feet and were dug in a zigzag manner. These trenches or ditches were not connected with one another. Stretches of unexcavated land separated them. All of the holes were dug on the right side of the Zagreb-Karlovac road, save those near Kerestinec, which were on the left side of this highway.

During the latter part of May, throughout June, and well into July, 1945, passers-by noted that every day one or more of the trenches was being filled in and covered up. Within a two-month period, the entire group of diggings was no longer noticeable.

Although they heard the firing going on in the woods adjoining the highway almost every night, no one in the vicinity paid much attention to the holes along the roadside, until dogs began to dig into them. The war had brought privation to the canine as well as to the human population and the more enterprising members of the former species soon began to pull corpses or parts of bodies out of the hastily covered mass graves. Shocked peasants tried to place heavier coverings of earth and stones atop the funeral blankets to cover up these common graves more thoroughly. Yet, during August and September it became impossible to go anywhere near these trenches or holes, and wide detours had to be used because of the awful stench of decaying flesh which poisoned the air. Finally, the "People's Authorities" sent trucks from Zagreb loaded with carbolic acid which was poured over the improvised mass graves.

Although the covering of the "trenches" ceased when the prisoner columns came to an end, the shooting out in the forests continued. None of us living in this area ventured to find out what was going on in the Makaronka Thickets, but, until December 1945, there was a great deal of shooting every night in that vicinity. Because of the prevailing food shortage, people went into the woods during the daytime to look for mushrooms or to secure wood for fuel or building purposes. Almost always, they came upon new, freshly covered holes or ditches dug deep in the forests.

By this time, of course, everyone knew what was going on. The men shot during the gradually cooling nights of the late summer and the autumn of 1945 were not residents of the villages dotting our countryside. They were brought by truck from various extermination camps, chiefly from those located near Zagreb.

I do not know whether carbolic acid was poured over these graves later on, or whether the bodies were reburied.

Signed: S.V.

Rome

May 1, 1952

Document LXXV

The undersigned, Kruno Vucicevic, who at present lives in California, refused to surrender to the Partisans in May, 1945, and went with sixty-two of his troops into Croatian forests. Early in June, Vucicevic and his soldiers found several hundred Croatian "Death Marchers" who had been murdered at Gracanica. On June 22, he reported to the OZNA (secret police) in Kutina where he became one of their 180 prisoners. The following day all of these prisoners were searched, one murdered, and the rest taken towards the village of Sveti Kriz. Here, the Serbian Partisans wanted to murder the whole group, but a Croatian Communist from Lika saved them. At Klostar-Ivanic a detachment of the Thirty-First Serbian Division took charge of them and brought them to Sesvete near Zagreb. Our eyewitness stayed nineteen days in the Sesvete camp, during which period he saw hundreds of prisoners taken to be slaughtered each night. On the seventh night he himself was ordered to join such a group; he hid in a toilet, instead. Afterwards, he slept in the open in order to save his life. On the nineteenth day of Vucicevic's stay in the Sesvete extermination camp, the Partisans, in order to prove to a delegation of the International Red Cross that this was a "transitional" camp, took our witness and some three hundred other prisoners to Zagreb, first to the Kanal and then to the Precko concentration camp. Vucicevic and twenty-five other men escaped from Precko into the Croatian forests. While wandering in the forests, our eyewitness visited the Sesvete massacre site; it is with a detailed description of that infamous place that he concludes this valuable testimony.

We retreated through Zagreb on Monday, May 7, 1945. The Partisans were already in the city and we had a brisk skirmish with them on Vlaska Street. During the course of this day, we withdrew without further fighting to Cernomerec and Samobor. Then we went on to Slovenia, passing through Zidani Most and Celje.

When we arrived in Celje, we heard that the Western Allies were handing all Croatians who surrendered to them over to Tito's people. Therefore, we decided that we would not surrender even though the war was hopelessly lost and there was nothing left to fight for. In my capacity as First Lieutenant, I brought my sixty-two men back to Croatia with their arms and equipment intact. We ran into the Partisans at the village of Klanjec near Stubicka Toplica, killed some of them, and lost two of our own men. This experience caused me to keep my command under cover during the daylight hours. Hereafter, we moved only at night.

Sticking to the woods, we marched from the vicinity of Klostar to Ivanic. We stopped at the village of Osokova near Kutina and then proceeded towards Gracanica. Early in June, some twenty or twenty-five days after our return from Celje, we approached Gracanica about 6:30 one morning. As we neared the place, we came upon the bodies of from 300 to 500 men. Most of them lay face down in the fields near the village. When we examined the bodies, we found that they had been mowed down by machine gun fire. There were corpses all along the way from Gracanica and Osokova to Sisak.

The peasants of Gracanica told us that a column of Croatian soldier prisoners had attempted a mass escape, and that their Partisan escorts had gunned down many of them. However, a soldier who succeeded in escaping from the column and joining my group, told us a somewhat different story. According to him, the Partisans began to shoot the prisoners during a rest period that had been allowed to them. This soldier's name was Zvonko Banic. After questioning him, I came to the conclusion that not one but two columns of war prisoners had passed through here and that this fact accounted for the discrepancy in the stories told by the peasants and by Banic. Banic stated that his column had rested near the railroad tracks, but the bodies we found in the fields were not in this vicinity at all.

I kept my men in the woods around Kutina, Repusnica, and Krc for eight more days. During this time I managed to see my fiancee who lived with her mother in Kutina. They told me that Tito had proclaimed a general amnesty. Anyone with a questionable record during the war would be tried in the regular law courts.

When I acquainted my men with this news, they decided that we should disband and everyone should go to his own home. Once there, the best thing to do would be to report to the local Communist authorities and hope for the best. In the absence of outside support, further armed resistance appeared futile. We shook hands, took our leave of one another there in the woods, and then went our own way. It was a sad ending to a hard war and a valiant effort to establish an independent Croatian State.

On June 22, I reported to the OZNA at Kutina. This security police organization had an office here; the Thirteenth Serbian Division was quartered in the village of Ciglanica nearby. From what was said to me, especially by my fiancee and her mother, the OZNA at Ciglanica liquidated everyone who was brought before them. Nobody survived their "interrogations."

I underwent my interrogation at Kutina. Afterwards, I was locked up in a building which was formerly a tavern and store. There were about one hundred and twenty prisoners here; on the night of my arrival sixty more joined us. Around 9:00 P.M., Partisans armed with clubs came into our confine and began to beat us. The prison commandant interrupted this process and forbade the Partisans to beat us any more since "Communists don't act as Fascists do." This man was an old-line Communist from Repusnica. He was of Czech origin, but had taught school in Croatia before the war.

On the morning of June 23, the whole one hundred and eighty of us were lined up, three abreast. The Partisans began to search us and to confiscate any valuables that we had. One Croatian officer had a watch which probably was a keepsake. The Partisan who was conducting the search of our persons ordered the officer to take off his watch and hand it over. When the Croatian refused, the Partisan took him out of line and killed him with a rifle shot. His body was allowed to lie where it fell. I had a watch, too, an Omega, which my brother had given me as a birthday gift the year before. Warned by the fate of my fellow officer, I let the Partisans take my watch without putting up an argument. However, I managed to save my fountain pen by tossing it to my fiancee who had come to watch what was going on.

We were taken under escort towards Kriz-Novoselec. The commander of our guards was a Croatian from Gornja Jelenska in Lika. He was a veteran Communist, but not a bad fellow at all. He allowed us to rest from time to time and to get water during our long march. That night we reached the village of Kriz where the Thirty-First Serbian Division was stationed. When we entered the village, a Serbian lieutenant came up to our commandant and told him that the Serbs would take over the duty of watching us during the night so the escort could get some sleep. Behind his back, we made gestures to the Croat Communist that if he consented to this offer the Serbs would kill us during the night. Evidently our commandant knew this himself, because he told the Serb that there were many honest people in our column who did not deserve death. He went on to say that honest people were shot only by Fascists. The Serb went off cursing all Croatians, Fascist, Communist, or anything else.

On the following morning, we moved towards Klostar-Ivanic under the same escort we had had the previous day. But after we had followed the main road for a while, detachments from the Thirty-First Division took charge of us. They told us that we would not have to walk any longer; we would ride instead. Indeed, they loaded us into a few railroad cars which were attached to a locomotive. Then our train quite literally raced across a repaired railroad bridge nearby, backed up and came over it again, then shot like a thunderbolt across the structure once again. This procedure was repeated four times. Twice we went across at full speed, while the other two times we proceeded quite slowly. Obviously, our train was being used to test the strength of the repaired structure and we were being utilized as human guinea pigs in this interesting experiment. Fortunately, the bridge didn't give way as the Serbs evidently hoped it would. Perhaps, it was from sheer disappointment that they beat us over the head with their pistols and rifles. Also, once the bridge proved to be safe enough, we didn't ride any more. We walked as we had before the "experiment."

Our guards took us to Sesvete where we were placed in a concentration camp. This place was known as the Badel Factory and was about nine miles east of Zagreb. The Badel plant was an alcohol factory which belonged to Marijan Badel, the father of one of Tito's "Heroes of the Liberation." Two or three unfinished two-story buildings and some wooden barracks surrounded by a seven-foot high wall were included in this establishment. There was also a long building which was fenced in by barbed wire. It stood on the left side of the Dugo Selo-Zagreb road. On the other side of this road, the OZNA and the camp administration had their headquarters. Barbed wire, five meters in height, surrounded the wall of the factory, and small holes had been bored into this wall. The barrels of machine guns appeared through these apertures. Thus, escape from this place was practically impossible.

Our guards led us into the camp and left us there. The place was already filled to capacity. According to what I heard from other prisoners, there were 6000-7000 people crowded together here. My own estimate agrees with theirs. During the nineteen days I remained in this hell-hole, five more transports of prisoners arrived. Over five hundred captives were included in each of these new batches of prisoners. No one was transported away from the camp throughout this entire period; that is, there was no organized transport of prisoners. Nor, so far as I know, did anyone succeed in escaping from this place. Yet, despite the new arrivals, the camp slowly emptied. Before I left there, the population had fallen to half its original number. This fact was evident from the increasing number of vacancies in the barracks.

Camp life was very hard. No one could go outside the barbed wire. During the daytime we were permitted to move freely about the camp, but we were confined to our quarters at night. I received no food for three days, but later I was given small amounts at irregular intervals. There wasn't enough food to feed everyone every day. Thus, some people always got left out and went hungry. The "food" that we got consisted of warm, dirty water in which there floated a bit of barley, potatoes, beans, or dough. Only during the last few days that I spent here did we get bread. This bread was made of corn flour and was only half-baked. We could tell how many people disappeared every night once the bread rations started to arrive, because there was supposed to be a ration for the exact number of prisoners counted the day before. On some days as many as one hundred loaves would be left over. Since each loaf was used to feed six prisoners, you didn't have to be a mathematician to figure out that six hundred souls had disappeared during the night.

Our guards belonged to the Thirtieth and Thirty-First Serbian Divisions, the same ones which later guarded me at the Precko and Kanal Camps, and in Zagreb. They spoke the Serbian "Ekavski" dialect exclusively. Not one could be heard using a Croatian dialect. The camp commander was, I think, the divisional commander also. He was a man of about fifty years of age, with brown hair, Mongoloid features and pronounced cheek bones.

I have said above that there was no "organized" transport of prisoners from the Badel Camp. With the influx of new arrivals, it remains to be explained how the "vacancies" that we noted came about.

On the first night that we spent at the factory, four trucks entered the camp at about 10:30 P.M. Two of them were Czech Skoda vehicles, while the other two were of German make. Thirty armed guards followed them on foot. Without notice, these guards put between forty and sixty prisoners in each truck, selecting them entirely at random. An escort of American-made jeeps filled with Partisans armed with automatic weapons appeared to accompany the convoy. Any captives who refused to get into the trucks were beaten over the head with gun butts. Once in these conveyances, the captives' wrists were bound with wire. Some of the prisoners put up a fight or voiced loud protests. I noticed that there was blood on the bumpers of one of the Skoda trucks. As soon as the Communists saw that we were looking at this bloody bumper, they chased us off and took the vehicle out of the camp to wash it.

Soon after the trucks took the prisoners away, we heard the firing of automatic weapons from the direction of a forest that lay behind the parish church. It seemed to be about 500 yards away from the barracks. Later, I visited the mass grave of the victims who were disposed of on this night and found that the killing had occurred almost two miles away from us. The shooting went on for several minutes. However, for a long time afterwards, single shots could be heard from time to time. The trucks returned later on that night and took away more prisoners. Again we were horrified to hear shooting in the distance.

We survivors calculated that 300-500 men were slain every night. Perhaps the number of victims was greater on one evening, when six rather than four vehicles were employed to cart away candidates for the slaughterhouse.

On the seventh night of my sojourn at Badel Factory, forty to fifty armed guards entered the small ground floor stock room where five hundred of us were trying to find space to lie down. It was about 11:00 P.M. The guards took the men on the left side of the room first, but soon they turned their attention to the other side where I was reclining facing the wall. Someone kicked me and cried out, "Get up, comrade!"

A flashlight was directed at me, so I pretended to be awakening from a deep sleep, blinked my eyes, and asked drowsily, "Why? Where?"

"Transfer to the Thirteenth Battalion," came the gruff reply.

I knew what that meant! I got up and went towards the door through which they were taking the prisoners to the trucks. I had nothing to lose so I walked right by the guards stationed there. One of them stopped me and asked, "Where do you think you're going?"

"To the toilet."

He asked me what room I was quartered in and if I was from the group that was being loaded into the trucks. I told him that I came from another room, from which I knew a selection of victims had been made previously. He let me go, supposedly to my "room." Instead of going there, or to the toilet, I went up to the second floor of the building. Since it was dark, he probably couldn't see where I went.

On the second floor, I lay down on top of a human pile, since the entire floor space was already taken up with occupants. At first, the inmates of this place resented my arrival, but after a while, they contrived to make a little room for me so I could squeeze into position on the floor. Of course, I was unable to go to sleep.

An hour later, the trucks came back to the factory. It was just my luck that the next prisoner group which was catalogued to be shot was drawn from Room No. 2 on the second floor—the one in which I now was lying! This time, however, I wasn't picked to go. From the window in our room I could see the trucks below and their jeep escort. I watched them pull out and drive towards the church. Before they reached it, they made a right turn into the nearby forest.

After the experiences of this night I did not sleep in any of the buildings. Instead, I got some boards, put them over bags of cement in a kind of outhouse, and concealed myself there at night.

During the entire nineteen days that I remained at the Badel Factory, no interrogation or trial of prisoners took place. We were all to be liquidated, it seems, although our guards never said as much to us. Of course, we had to give our names to the OZNA commandant, and there were periodic roll calls to find out who had been killed and who was still alive. Whoever did not answer when his name was called was crossed off the list and presumed to be dead. Some officers and men took different names every day. I used that of a war colleague, Janko Valentic, who I knew had been killed during the fighting on the Papuk Mountain. Later, I answered the roll call under the name of Anton Medved.

Of course, everything done in this camp was not this haphazard. I remember that after the second day of my arrival, all commissioned and non-commissioned officers were ordered to report themselves. No one did so because everyone knew that certain death awaited such people. Whenever anyone was found to be an officer, he was taken to OZNA headquarters, and that was the last seen of him.

Also, I recall that on my fourth day here everyone who belonged to the Eighth Hunter or Pursuit Brigade, the First and Fourth Mountain Brigades, the Thirteenth Ustasha Brigade, and the Seventh Mountain Division of General Pericic was ordered to report. Obviously, this roll call was designed to catch any members of these elite Croatian units which had repeatedly inflicted heavy losses upon the Thirtieth and Thirty-First Serbian Divisions. This was a great opportunity for the Serbs to take revenge on their now disarmed adversaries—if they could find them. None of the older veterans of these Croatian commands reported themselves. However, some naive youths who had been recruited into the First Mountain Division in 1945 did disclose that they had served briefly with that unit. Since they had not participated in any of the fighting (their duties being executed behind battle lines while they were undergoing training), they thought that their captors could not charge them with any crimes. Despite their youth, the Communists taunted them with being murderers, and separated them from the other prisoners. On the afternoon of my fourth day, these two hundred and fifty thin and maltreated boys were taken off to the abattoir to be slaughtered. Their death was the saddest episode of my entire experience in the camp. The guards made no secret of the fact that the boys were murdered. They referred to these poor fledglings, whose wings were cut before they learned to fly, as "Fascist bandits."

After the massacre of these youths, we discussed among ourselves the question of genocide. Did Tito and the Communist regime in Belgrade plan to extirpate the entire Croatian nation to perpetuate the Yugoslav fraud, dreamed up by the propaganda agencies of the Western Allies during the war of 1914-18? It looked as though this was just what Belgrade had in mind. In time, Marxism might make Yugoslavs out of Serbians, Montenegrins, and Slovenes, but it would be a hard job to amalgamate Croatians into this amorphous nationality.

On another occasion while we were at the Badel camp, the Partisans called for all Ustashas, gendarmes, airmen, legionnaires who had fought against the Russians on the Eastern Front, and Navy men to report themselves. At least a thousand men obeyed. They did so out of utter despair, calculating that they might as well get their suffering over with. Among these were men who had never belonged to one of the organizations mentioned. They simply decided that they were going to be killed anyway, so the more quickly the better. Life at Badel Factory wasn't worth living.

Then something entirely unexpected happened. An hour after they had been separated from the rest of us, they were returned to our midst and nothing happened to them for identifying themselves. I do not know the reason for the leniency displayed towards them.

Among those I know were executed while I was at Camp Badel, I should like to mention the names of the following Croatian patriots:

Tomo Klepic from Dubrava near Cetingrad; Dane Cindric of the PTS (Pavelic Bodyguard Brigades), a youth of nineteen or twenty years; the thirty-year-old Tomo Medved, a Domobran; Ustasha Color Bearer Lenes, who was a Muslim from Kljuc; Domobran Sergeants Alic from Sanski Most and Ivan Solicki of the Third Battalion of the First Mountain Brigade. I have forgotten the names of two non-commissioned officers of the Third Company, Second Battalion, Fourth Mountain Brigade, but I know they both came from Slavonski Brod.

On the nineteenth day of my incarceration at the Badel Factory, I answered roll call under the name of Anton Medved, because I had heard a rumor that a Red Cross delegation was due to visit the camp and that three hundred prisoners were to be sent to Zagreb to provide this international committee with proof that our camp was "transitional." Indeed, it was, but the only transition that had taken place in it so far was from life of a sort to a miserable death. The camp commandant with the Mongoloid features gave the three hundred departees a little address before leaving: "We have screened the camp and identified those who were criminals," he said. "Your names are unimportant. You are no longer prisoners but national soldiers."

Of course, this was whitewash designed to be translated for the benefit of the foreign Red Cross visitors. As soon as the latter left Sesvete, the executions were resumed.

When I left the Badel Factory there were still a number of my good friends there. Among them were Ivan Sakavski from Banja Luka, who was a Domobran Sergeant; an Ustasha Major whose nickname was "Lugar" (Forest Man), and who had commanded our forces at Garesnica during the war; and a Muslim Ustasha Colonel, who in 1943 was the Commander of Bihac. Of course, the two Ustasha men had assumed false names. I do not know their ultimate fate.

We were escorted from Sesvete to Zagreb by the Partisans of the Thirtieth Serbian Division. Although we arrived in the capital on the same evening, they delivered us to the Kanal Camp the following morning. I remained at Kanal for only two days; then I was transferred to Precko. After a six-day sojourn here, I was sent to a camp at Bjelovar. I stayed there for twenty days during which time I was able to find out that my weight, which during the war was normally around 205 pounds, was down to 120.

Despite what the Serb commandant had said when we left Badel Factory, our situation had not changed for the better. Executions were going on at Kanal, Precko, and Bjelovar, too. Therefore, I joined a group of twenty-five other men and escaped from this place. We took shelter in the forests. Our plan was to flee to Italy.

As we wandered through the woods, we approached quite closely to Sesvete. Despite the danger involved in so doing, I wished to visit the mass grave of my fellow prisoners, especially since I was thought by the Communists to be lying in it myself. I orientated myself by using the church as a landmark, and then went in the direction I had seen the trucks turn when I had watched them from the second floor window of the factory building. I remembered, too, the direction from which the shooting had seemed to be coming. After some searching through the woods, I found the great mass graves, just after crossing the Sesvete-Zagreb highway where it runs over the hills. The graves were in a valley filled with oak trees, a lot of bushes, and marsh vegetation of various kinds. In the center of this valley was a large grass and weed covered plain. Although there were no houses in this vicinity, some little girls were pasturing their cows less than a mile away from where I was standing with my companions, two other Croatian soldiers, Mile Matanic and Ivica Bozicevic.

We approached the girls in order to find out the exact location of this valley. They told us it was about a mile and a half from Sesvete.

The graves themselves were fifty feet away from the edge of the surrounding forest. The largest one was approximately a thousand feet long by ten feet wide. It ran parallel to the line of trees that marked the beginning of the woods. Already grass was growing at one end of this great mass grave. In some places the earth had sunk a foot or so. On the side of the abattoir away from the woods, the natural beauty of the valley remained unspoiled. At one end of the great pit the grave made a rectangular turn which was about forty feet in length. Half of this part of the hole was filled with earth; the other half was empty. Therefore, I could see that the depth of this part of the burial trench was approximately eight feet. Near this section of the hole there was a large amount of quicklime.

Further investigation disclosed that there was a typical country road running right up to this mass grave. Trucks could use this path without too much difficulty. There was no reason to ask anyone about the nature of this great digging; an indescribably abominable stench emanating from thousands of putrefying corpses told me well enough that I was standing close to all that remained of so many of my colleagues from the Sesvete camp. And here was the grave where, I, too, would have been lying at that very moment except for a bit of luck.

Since the grass close to the great grave was neither trampled nor cut, it was evident that no one visited this place of tragedy. Yet, I am convinced that the inhabitants of Sesvete know what is here and will respond with accuracy to an interrogation concerning the crimes committed, if they are guaranteed immunity from punishment for so doing.

As for myself, I shall be ready at any time to testify under oath to the truth and validity of this report before any Free World Forum.

Signed: Kruno Vucicevic

Aversa, Italy
May 17, 1961

Document LXXVI

Thirty mass graves of Croatian prisoners-of-war at Vojnic are discovered.

In December, 1945, I left my native village, Jezerane, with a few companions in order to seek work. Our little group included Dane Lelic, who was also a native of Jezerane, and several people from the hamlet of Sveta Nedjelja, which is in the district of Drizpolje Brinje. Among the men from this place were Vlado Sebalj, his brother, Toma, and their father, Jure. John Sebalj, nicknamed "Longo," and Joseph Sebalj were also with us.

We went on foot to Josipdol where we picked up the train to Vojnic. Here we found work—cleaning the tunnel through which the railroad tracks ran on the route between Vojnic and Petrova Gora.

One day while I was strolling close to the tunnel, I saw a pool of water in which human intestines were floating. Actually, this pool had been formed by heavy rains which had washed away the thin layer of earth, only ten to fifteen inches thick, which had been thrown on top of a huge mass of bodies. I investigated more closely and found that there was a great common grave, about one hundred and fifty feet in diameter, quite close to the tunnel. In the vicinity there were approximately thirty more such holes, all between thirty-five and fifty feet in diameter.

Not far away from the spot which had first attracted my attention, I encountered a woman who was tending a flock of sheep. Her name was Eva. I introduced myself to her as a Serb; she then related the story of the holes and their contents in these words:

"Immediately after the war, the Partisan soldiers brought Croatian civilians and soldiers from Karlovac to the Vojnic area. They hit them over the head with big sticks, then they shot them and threw them into these holes that you have seen around here. When one group of captives had been disposed of in this way, they would go on to deal in the same way with the next bunch and so on, until all of the holes were full of bodies."

There was a fellow by the name of Milosh Vukobratovitch working with us on the tunnel job. He came from Vojnic and during the war he had been a Partisan officer. I asked him what kind of people had been killed here and thrown into these pits. He replied:

"Croatian criminals who belonged to the Domobrans and to the Ustasha Army."

Despite the danger to my own person that such an answer involved, I could not help retorting angrily, "They were not criminals but only innocent victims of your precious Tito!"

All of the men from Jezerane and Sveta Nedjelja whose names I have supplied above saw the holes and what was in them. I confirm the report which I have given of this matter with an oath and my signature.

Signed: Tom Krakar

Document LXXVII

The massacre of wounded Croatian soldiers and of two Catholic nuns who had taken care of them, are discovered in the vicinity of Sisak.

Several days after the Partisan seizure of the city of Sisak in northeastern Croatia, passers-by discovered a great number of horribly disfigured corpses near the Staklana glass factory on the right bank of the Sava River.

The throats of many of the victims were slit, their eyes were gouged out and their teeth knocked loose from their mouths, probably to facilitate the removal of gold dentures. Severed arms and other disparate pieces of human anatomy were strewn all around. Knives were still thrust into the wounds of some of these bodies.

The inhabitants of Sisak said that the dead men were wounded Croatian soldiers who were left behind in the hospitals of Sisak and vicinity, when the Croatian Army evacuated this sector in May, 1945. All casualties able to travel were removed in ambulances or hospital trains, but there were many whose condition did not permit their being moved, especially since the Croatian military authorities expected even the Communist Partisans to respect the laws of war with regard to the treatment of wounded prisoners.

Among the corpses were those of two nuns who had cared for the wounded in the Sisak hospital during the war.

The commander of the Partisan division which massacred these helpless and seriously wounded or ill men was a Slovene by the name of Podkrajsek. He had only Serbs under his command. The bodies were laid to rest in a common grave near the bank of the Sava.

Signed: P.J.

Nuremberg, West Germany
Nov. 3, 1954

Document LXXVIII

The massacres of four thousand Croatian captives in the village of Cemernica near Topusko are divulged.

I, the undersigned, formerly Tito's soldier, declare the following which I myself saw or heard from my war companions:

In the village of Cemernica, some four miles from my birthplace, Topusko, the National Liberation Army had established a concentration camp. They sent to that camp usually those Domobrans and Ustashas who were under twenty years of age. No one emerged alive, and we Partisan called it "the liquidation camp." It was located in an isolated spot, some distance out of the village, about a mile and a half away from a nearby forest. The Partisan guards used to take the prisoners into the woods and murder them. Also, they took some of their captives to points beyond the Toplicka Kosa, where they buried the bodies in trenches or threw them into natural holes in the ground.

A Partisan lieutenant, Ilija Rakaric, during a visit home, said to me: "Look, Ivan, what we Croatians have to undergo. In Cemernica, the Partisan authorities are having our young Croatian people killed without giving them any kind of judicial trial. And these victims are still really children rather than grown-ups. Is this what we Croatian Partisans have been fighting for?"

Other witnesses told me that there were usually several hundred and sometimes thousands of prisoners at the Cemernica concentration camp. All of the captives were murdered in the most atrocious ways. Serbian Communists led by Milutin Vuyosevitch, Stole Janjanin, and other Serbs from around Topusko committed these crimes. The Cemernica camp, which obtained Croatian soldiers from many other camps, came under the authority of the Banija military district. According to information which I received from people who knew, that is Partisan guards at this camp itself, four thousand people were slaughtered here alone. My brother, Luka, who was later at Lepoglava with a Serbian Partisan who participated in these mass murders of young Croatian soldiers, confirmed the reports that I received from other sources. He told me that the High Command of Tito's National Liberation Army ordered the butcheries.

Signed: Ivan Dragicevic

Document LXXIX

During the evacuation of Zagreb in May, 1945, the eyewitness P. J. did not retreat with the Croatian Armed Forces. He was captured by the Partisans and, with approximately one hundred other prisoners, was sent towards Belgrade. On this trek they saw corpses of over five thousand Croatian victims whom the Partisans had murdered in the forest between Galdovo and Brezovica.

During the war of 1941-45, I served in the Croatian Navy which possessed both coastal (Dalmatian) and inland detachments. The latter were charged with duties which largely involved river service.

At the end of the war, most of our naval units were withdrawn from the coastal areas into the interior, and accompanied the rest of the Armed Forces in their withdrawal northwards to Slovenia and Austria. At the end of the first week in May, 1945, when the Croatian Government issued orders for the evacuation of Zagreb, I decided to remain in the capital since I did not want to face an uncertain future as an exile living abroad.

Soon after the Partisans entered the city, I was arrested and sent towards Belgrade in a small column that contained a hundred other prisoners. We passed through Sisak and Galdovo and were approaching the Brezovica Forest, when we became conscious of an abominable stench that polluted the air. As we continued our march through this forest, we came upon piles of human bodies, all completely stripped of clothing. I would estimate that there were between five and ten thousand corpses in this forest. Those that I saw at close range had been shot; bullet holes were plainly visible on many of the bodies.

One of our Partisan guards told us: "For three hours we were killing them with heavy and light machine guns."

The corpses lay piled one on top of the other for a distance of about a mile. As far as I could see these victims were all males. I assume that they were Croatian soldiers who surrendered or thought they were surrendering to the British at the end of the war, but who found themselves in the hands of Tito's Partisans after they had laid down their arms.

I am not certain of the exact date when the prisoner column to which I belonged went through this forest, but it was around May 20, 1945.

Signed: P.J.

Nuremberg, West Germany
November 2, 1954

Document LXXX

Here are described the liquidations of 1,718 young recruits in Virovitica, and the massacres in Dubrovnik and Mostar.

D.D.W., the wife of a merchant, had been living in the Croatian town of Virovitica for ten years past. She related to me the following sequence of events that occurred in this city after its final conquest by the Reds in 1945.

Tito's Partisans entered Virovitica along with Russian troops. On some occasions earlier in the war, they had been at the gates of the city, but, heretofore, they had always been thrown back. As in other parts of the Croatian territories which the Partisans could not take until the Government in Zagreb ordered the beginning of the great retreat, all young men capable of bearing arms were now mobilized. Part of the Croat youth went to the Domobrans, part to the Ustashas. Among them were boys eighteen years old and even younger. They were quartered in the military barracks at the end of Matija Gubec Street, a road that extends towards the nearby Hungarian frontier.

These young boys, who were called up for military service at the end of the war, were forgotten by the very authorities who mobilized them.

Left without orders or leadership of any kind and having received no weapons or training, they were easy victims of the Partisans, who murdered them and threw their bodies into a mass grave in the vicinity. Later, it was ascertained that this abattoir contained 1,718 corpses.

These ill-fated youngsters were not the only victims of the triumph of "democracy" in Virovitica. Those citizens who had discharged their duty by defending the town against the attacks of the Reds were also butchered when captured. The names of many of these people were given to me, but I have forgotten them in the years that have passed since the end of the war. However, the director of the Croatian Food Administration was known personally to me. This man was arrested on May 1, 1945, and hung publicly in the square of the city for the entertainment of the proletariat. Furthermore, his wife declared that she visited her native village, fifty kilometers distant from Virovitica, to look in the fireplace at the home of her brother, a sawmill proprietor and a member of the German minority in Croatia, for gold and banknotes hidden there since the beginning of the war. On her journey there she found that Serbian peasants had seized the houses and land all around the village. During the war, these peasants had fought as Partisans and had lived in the forests; they now helped themselves to the property of the dispossessed Croatian peasantry. Thus, in the territory around Pitomaca and Virovitica, a stronger Serbian enclave than ever before arose on Croatian soil.

Among the young Ustasha and Domobran recruits slaughtered in the barracks on Matija Gubec Street in Virovitica was an N. Kovacic, the son of Niko and Kata Kovacic, a couple who owned some small properties in Dubrovnik-Lapad on the coast. This young man had volunteered for service with the Ustashas in 1942, when he was only nineteen years old. On my last visit to Virovitica in 1950, I tried to find someone who knew something about his fate, since his parents were known to me and had asked me to do this. Unfortunately, all I could discover was that he was in the barracks when the massacre took place and was never seen again afterwards.

From Niko and Kata Kovacic and other friends in Dubrovnik, I learned the following details concerning the Partisan occupation of that town: The Partisans entered Dubrovnik without a struggle on October 19, 1944, and immediately began to arrest and imprison patriotic elements. A few days later, sentences of death were pronounced against these unfortunates. These sentences were posted on the walls of the city. The most distinguished people of Dubrovnik, among them a former mayor, the current assistant mayor or burgomaster, two other city officials, the priest on the island of Lapad, noted Franciscan and Dominican lecturers, a news dealer, the director of one of the local gymnasiums, a former mayor of a Serbian town, a pharmacist whose son had joined the Chetniks and later had fled abroad, and many other eminent local personalities were among those condemned. All of them were murdered under the most brutal circumstances.[1] Later, it was discovered that the greatly beloved priest, Don Djuro Krecak, asked the remaining victims to sing a church hymn before his own death. He began this solemn requiem himself, and others joined in the chorus.[2] The Partisan executioners then came among the singers, and, as they killed them, listened with pleasure to the death rattle of those who did not die instantly. Some of the victims were still living when they were thrown into an open grave.

About sixty-five people were executed on this particular occasion. Later, many others were dispatched without either reason or trial. It was said in the town that 170 people were murdered during the first days of Communist rule. Many Croatian nationalists were taken to the island of Korcula to be judged while others were imprisoned in Split. All met a violent death.

In the summer of 1945, Dubrovnik became a charnel house. Macedonian recruits for Tito's army were paraded through the town in a long procession. They came on foot through Niksic to Dubrovnik and from there were taken by ship to Split and Rijeka. They were assigned quarters in barracks which the Italians had built on Lapad while awaiting this transport. One morning an epidemic broke out in one of these barracks, where the recruits had already noted a poisonous stench in the air. Whole truckloads of dead or half-dead recruits were brought to the hospitals in Dubrovnik. Over 170 men lost their lives in this outbreak, which can perhaps best be described as plague. I myself conversed with one of the Macedonians who survived this episode. He told me that the Reds had purposely exposed the recruits to disease arising from the presence of many half-buried corpses in the vicinity of the barracks. The Macedonians had not enlisted willingly in Tito's forces, and this served as warning to their countrymen not to try to evade forced conscription. In this connection, it should be mentioned that Macedonians attacked the Germans when Nazi forces retreated from Greece. Also, they harassed the Partisans who rushed down from Montenegro to cut off German detachments.

It is worth knowing that after the Partisans took Dubrovnik in October, 1944, they were thrown into a panic by a report that a German troop command stationed in the vicinity of Herceg-Novi was going to retreat through Dubrovnik. The Germans decided to go through Mostar, however.

Mostar was "liberated" in February; that is, the Domobrans and Germans evacuated it. The Partisans held great celebrations in honor of this liberation in which 2500 Domobrans and Germans allegedly were

---

[1] See a detailed account of the Dubrovnik massacres in the book, *La Tragedia de Bleiburg*, pp. 197-199, by Fr. Lino Pedisic, O.F.M.

[2] The Croatian martyrs at many other places, including Sinj, the hometown of one of the editors of this volume, died in similar fashion during the days of "liberation." —Editor's note.

killed.[3] It was also declared that 1200 had fallen in the defense of Dubrovnik and that 6000 were reported dead when Sarajevo was taken in April, 1945. The accuracy of these figures can be gauged by the fact that only twenty-six defenders were killed when Dubrovnik fell, because the Partisans waited for Croatian forces to evacuate the town before they moved into it, so fearful were they of engaging in open combat with the national army. Undoubtedly, the Partisans claimed victories in imaginary combats, and publicized the heavy "losses" sustained by the enemy to cover up the subsequent executions of non-combatants, buried in graves designated as those of "military casualties."

D. D. W.'s commentary ends with declarations made by people who proved to me the falsity of Partisan reports about heavy losses sustained by the Croatians and Germans in the battles for Dubrovnik, Sarajevo, Mostar, etc. Finally, the commentary relates how the Chetniks, in 1945 and 1946, were still plundering UNRA shipments and other convoys.

The above recital has been signed in full consciousness and understanding of the fact that I may later be asked to corroborate this statement.

Signed: Gerhart Terborg

Rome
March 9, 1954

Document LXXXI

This testimony provides significant details concerning one of the Pozega concentration camps, a modern inferno where the guards of the Tenth Division of the First Partisan Army made the prisoners suffer from thirst and uncleanliness, starved them to death, and murdered them by bullets and also by purposely spreading deadly diseases.

In the second half of May, 1945, I was included in a column of Croatian war prisoners who were marched from Bleiburg through Celje to Slavonska Pozega. When we arrived at the last named place, we were placed in a concentration camp which was situated near the Orljava River, not far away from the present location of the modern prison.

There were approximately eleven thousand inmates in all, chiefly Croatian Ustashas and Domobrans, although there were other Croatian elements, as well as some anti-Communist Serbians and Slovenians. Not

---

[3] The killings of the war prisoners at Mostar are by no means alleged ones. See Paul Prcela's (the brother of the editor of this volume) eyewitness account in *La Tragedia de Bleiburg,* p. 206. There are many other detailed eyewitness reports on these and other pre-Bleiburg massacres in the files of the Committee for Investigation of the Bleiburg Tragedy, but we have not included such reports in our book, since we have sought to emphasize the postwar massacres in Tito's new Yugoslavia. We have included, however, the above and a few other reports on pre-Bleiburg massacres, because they are necessary for a historical understanding of later happenings.

one of these prisoners was completely clad. They had purposely torn everything but their underwear to prevent their guards from confiscating it.

On the second day of my stay in this camp, I saw several Croatian doctors with whom I had some association when I was engaged in hospital work. There were around ten of them at the camp, but today I can recall the names of only three, Doctors Dufek, Hilak and Sokac.

The living conditions in the Pozega camp were totally unbearable. Well-armed Partisan guards surrounded the place, but they did not dare to approach the barbed wire enclosure because dysentery and typhoid fever were rampant among the closely packed prisoners and they were afraid of becoming infected themselves. Since there were no medicines available, people died every day. They were buried right in the camp itself and the presence of these inadequately interred corpses probably helped to spread disease among us, as our captors perhaps intended that it should.[1]

We prisoners had to report our actual numbers each day. In order that we might receive extra loaves of bread for our one meager meal, we always turned in a count that was considerably above the real number of live prisoners on any given day. That is, we drew loaves for men who had died that day or the night before. This was possible because we had to bury the dead ourselves and our guards did not keep a close check on the interments for fear of catching something.

The only food we received besides the half-baked bread consisted of a watery bean broth. These rations were not distributed according to roll call, but were brought up in army carts and placed close to the barbed wire. The guards would toss the bread over the wire, while a few prisoners were allowed to go outside in order to carry the soup cauldron into the camp. Only those captives who had containers of some kind, or who could borrow one from someone else, got the broth. Since I had no such container of my own and found it difficult to secure the loan of one, I never did manage to get a drop of this miserable soup during my entire stay in the camp.

---

[1] The authorities of the camp spread deadly diseases among the victims not only by leaving corpses unburied for days, but also by administering deadly shots to the living inmates. These methods of wholesale liquidation of prisoners in the Pozega extermination camps are described by Ivan Madjarek in his article, "Eksterminacija Hrvatskih Zarobljenika Bakterioloskim Sredstvima"—(Extermination of the Croatian Prisoners by Bacteriological Means), *Hrvatska Drzava* (Berlin-Munich, July-August 1966), nn. 139-140, page 3. According to Madjarek's article, the poisonous shots were administered by express orders of the Yugoslav Army's General Headquarters. The orders were further given by Colonel (now Lt. General) Vojo Todorovic, commander of the Tenth Krayina Division which was in charge of the Pozega extermination camps. Drs. Aljasa and Griner "vaccinated" the prisoners each time they visited the camps. The technical part of such a "sanitary" extermination of prisoners was in the hands of General Gojko Dr. Nikolis, Chief of the Yugoslav Army's Sanitary Department. Madjarek states that an estimated 60,000 Croatian prisoners were exterminated at Pozega by "medical" injections and bullet shots.—Editor's note.

Every evening, guards under the command of a Captain-Commissar would come to the enclosure and pick out from seven to ten prisoners at a time. Anyone who identified himself as a Croatian was eligible for inclusion in these groups. "You are a murderer and criminal!" they would tell him, and lead him outside the gates with his fellow national malefactors. Usually these selections took place between five and six o'clock in the evening and half an hour after the prisoner groups were taken off, we would hear screams coming from some point not far away. While I was confined here, not one prisoner who was removed from the enclosure in the manner described ever came back to it. The doctors whom I have named above are still alive today; and they know what went on here as well as I do.

As I have indicated above, the prisoners who died of typhoid, dysentery infection, or other causes were not buried immediately. Often they were left lying in our midst for a full two days. Only when the fly-infested corpses began to decay in the heat of the sun and to emit a nauseating odor, did we receive orders to bury them. We had only little pointed poles with which to dig the mass graves of these victims of the latest effort to make the world safe for democracy. With such instruments, it was difficult to dig the holes deep enough. There were at least thirty such shallow pits covered over with mounds of earth before I left the camp.

Although the Orljava stream was hardly sixty feet away from us, there was a complete absence of hygienic precautions in this modern Inferno. Our guards would not allow us to fetch water from the river, either for washing or drinking purposes. Two hours after we had our solitary meal of the day, they would bring drinking water to us. Meanwhile, since we were exposed to the rays of the blazing hot sun, some prisoners lost their minds. Often they would utter cries of despair, and beg someone to kill them. There was always some stronger personality who was able to ease the tension felt by such sufferers.

The camp was located on the right bank of the Orljava between this stream and the railroad tracks which run towards Pleternica. We were able to see the factory chimneys of the city of Pozega, an old Croatian town. Our enclosure occupied a large treeless meadow which was fenced in with barbed wire outside of which there were numerous armed guards. These guards belonged to the 10th Partisan Division, which was attached to the Command of the First Army which had its headquarters in Zagreb.

As related above, the Partisans picked out Croatian prisoners every evening and took them away from the camp. The screams which we heard told us that these people were subjected to torture of various kinds before they were killed. Bursts of gunfire signalled the final extinction of their lives. I was able to ascertain that the spot where they were massacred was in the immediate vicinity of the camp itself, in a small forest which stands on the right bank of the Orljava.

There were other prisoner concentrations around Pozega, but we had no contact with our fellow sufferers in these places. I remained at

Pozega for only ten days and then was sent under armed escort towards Kovin under cover of night. No food was issued to us during this journey. Otherwise nothing happened to me that has not been told by other survivors of those grim days of 1945. Similarly, there is nothing particularly noteworthy about the story of my survival to the present time. Therefore I am going to end my relation at this point with the promise that I am ready at any time to confirm under oath the truth of this report which I typed myself.

Signed: P.G.

Document LXXXII

This account of a former Croatian Krizar (Crusader) opens with a description of how twenty-five Ustashas surrendered to the Twentieth Serbian Brigade at Slavonski Dubocac. It also tells of the massacre of these prisoners-of-war by the same unit. The eyewitness then gives horrifying details on "Death Marchers" who were brought to this Bosnian village and were beheaded with hatchets or shot with bullets. These small-scale slaughters went on at Dubocac for over five weeks. The account closes with a list of the witness' co-villagers who were murdered by the Partisans both during and after World War II.

Sometime between April 20 and May 1, 1945, twenty-five Ustashas who were under the command of Color Bearer Luka Raso surrendered to the Twentieth Serbian Brigade at Slavonski Dubocac.

Prior to their surrender, the Ustashas were holding out against the Communist troops in the forests. Since the Serbian Partisans were unable to round up these Ustasha stragglers from the main body of the Croatian Army in any other way, they went to the relatives of these men, who were local residents. The Serbs told their families that if the Ustashas surrendered they would not be harmed in any way. When their civilian relatives communicated this information to the Ustasha fighters, the latter decided that since there was no chance of winning the war further resistance was useless. So they surrendered, most of them bringing their arms with them. A few, however, concealed their weapons in the woods before they gave themselves up to Tito's people.

Escorts detailed from the Twentieth Serbian Brigade took them from Slavonski to Bosanski Dubocac. Immediately after their arrival at the latter place, the Serbs took them half a mile out of town upstream along the Sava River. I saw them myself as they passed through Bosanski Dubocac.

At twilight on this same day, their guards machine gunned them. On the following morning, at about 10:00 A.M., I saw the bodies lying seminude, all in one big pile. Three of the victims were Bosnians, while the rest came from Slavonski Dubocac or thereabouts. Relatives identified the bodies and transported them back to Slavonia for burial.

A little later, at the end of May or the beginning of June, I saw columns of Croatian war prisoners being brought back from Bleiburg, Maribor, Celje, and other points. Many of these captives were escorted first to Derventa. I believe that the chief of the OZNA at Derventa at this time was Omer Porobic. He had the prisoners bound with wire and tied to peasant carts; they had to move rapidly to keep up as the vehicles jounced along over rough paths from Derventa to a field half a mile away from my home town, Bosanski Dubocac. Because the war captives had received nothing to eat or drink since their surrender days before, and had obtained very little rest, they were worn out. Many could not keep up with the swiftly rolling carts and collapsed only to be dragged along on the ground behind these crude wagons.

Five and a half miles from Derventa and half a mile from Bosanski Dubocac, a field known to local residents as "Rakinac" stretches downstream along the Sava River. It was to this place that the captives were led, one or two hundred at a time. They were brought here after night fall. Together with other villagers, I saw the columns of victims pass through Bijelo Brdo.

Croatian soldiers and officers who had refused to surrender to the English, the Russians, the Partisans, or anyone else were in this vicinity too. I was a "receiver" (jatak) for them. One night in the early part of June—I cannot recall the precise date—I followed a prisoner column from Bijelo Brdo to "Rakinac." With me were the Krizari or "Crusaders" (anti-Communist fighters or remnants of the Croatian Army) Nikola Pejic and Ilija Pranic. Both of these men were natives of Bijelo Brdo. We arrived at the "Rakinac" field about 2:00 A.M., and concealed ourselves in a forest of willow trees that bordered it. The night was clear and visibility was good. The two "Crusaders" crept close to the spot where the column had halted.

A horrifying sight met our eyes. The Partisans were beheading the victims with hatchets or shooting them. I remember how the captives were singing as they passed through the village of Bijelo Brdo. They were not singing on the field at "Rakinac," but I did not hear them beg for mercy either. They seemed to shout as one man: "Long live Dr. Pavelic! Long live Croatia!"

I saw approximately one hundred men slain on this night in the manner described above. Uniformed Partisans did most of the killing, but some of the murderers wore civilian clothes. The chief executioners were Tair Sinanovic from the village of Bosanski Dubocac and Luka Tomitch from the hamlet of Pajlovac in the Derventa district.

Two or three days later I returned to the scene of the crime. Evidently the killers had thrown the bodies into the Sava whose current carried them downstream. Many corpses had drifted in among the bushes that grow down to the water's edge on the banks of the river. Some of the dead men that I saw were naked, while others still wore their Croatian uniforms. Also a number of severed heads were lying around on the field since the butchers apparently had not thought it worth the effort to toss them into the river. A few complete cadavers were left on the field for two or three days, too, until the killers found the leisure to throw them into the water after their comrades.

These small-scale mass slaughters went on at Dubocac for five or six weeks. My fellow villagers said that from five hundred to a thousand captives passed through our locality during the early part of the period mentioned. Later smaller groups were brought to the banks of the Sava to be "liquidated," and after the "liberation" effected by the Partisans of Tito Broz, the following inhabitants of Bijelo Brdo met their end too:

Ilija Pejic—knifed at Pjelovac by Drazha Mihailovic's Serbian Chetniks.

Nikola Pejic, "Crusader"—died fighting against the OZNA in 1947 at a battle waged in the village of Korace.

Ivica Pejic, Ustasha Color Bearer—disappeared but place of death unknown.

Jure Pejic—place and manner of death also unknown.

Mato Pejic—killed by the OZNA in Derventa in 1945.

Marko Pejic was tortured by the OZNA before he died. He was given the "water treatment," that is, the OZNA operatives forced him to drink and drink until the water ran from his nostrils and he gagged with nausea. Then they crushed the bones of his arms and legs and drove needles and nails beneath his finger nails. When all of this could not make him disclose the location of the "Crusaders," they beat him savagely with anything that they happened to lay their hands upon. I was an eyewitness of this grisly proceeding because I had to bring water to the victim so he would regain consciousness and thus endure more torture. He told the OZNA men nothing; they finally took him out into the forest where his body was found two days later. The villagers buried him.

Marko Pejic, police commandant in Derventa in the days of the Pavelic regime, was hanged on June 24, 1945. While he was dangling from the scaffold, the rope broke under his weight. Luka Tomitch pulled him up again and completed the job.

Jozo Pejic and Jakob Pejic disappeared also. Ilija Pranic I was killed in 1947 in the battle against the OZNA (UDBA) at Korace. Ilija Pranic II was led off by the OZNA and not seen again. The same fate befell Pavao Pranic. Ivo Tigorcic was delivered into the hands of the OZNA in Derventa. Jozo Jerkovic fell as a "Crusader" at Bijelo Brdo. Marko Jukcic, Roko Pranic, Stipe Pranic, Marko Pranic, Ilija Cabraja, Stipe Cabraja, Jozo Blazevic, Franjo Blazevic, Ante Gavra, Jozo Sedlic, Ante Stjepanovic, and Ivan Zeba were all led away to be killed by the OZNA. The latter also arrested Pero Zeba; he has not been heard from since. Ilija Vuleta and Mato Goga were hanged with Marko Pejic at Derventa. Marko Vuleta and ten other members of this clan "disappeared." Vid Peric was killed by the OZNA and Ivo Pejic was strangled by other Communists on the bank of the Sava. Pavo Matkovic fell at Bijelo Brdo in 1945. Jozo Paradjik, Stipan Matkovic, Pavo Cundra, Marko Cundra, the brothers Franjo, Mato Dadic and others whose names I do not now remember were led off by the OZNA or the Partisans and presumably killed.

Besides the victims enumerated above, twenty other men disappeared from my village in 1945 and afterwards. In December 1946 a mass arrest of men, women, and children was effected. All of the arrested people were taken to prisons and concentration camps. They were suspected of being receivers of the "Crusaders," and had to spend four months in prison in consequence.

This was my village after the "liberation." Before the war this place had approximately two hundred and fifty houses. Between 1941 and 1948, two hundred of the inhabitants were killed. Half of these were murdered by the OZNA; others were killed by the Partisans after they had surrendered as prisoners of war in 1945.

I hereby affix my signature to this document as a guarantee of the truth of the facts that I have related.

Signed: J.I.

Udine, Italy
December 27, 1955

Document LXXXIII

The tragic fate of sixty-three young Croatians between Okucani and Lipik is recorded by a Montevidean.

In the second half of June, 1945, a group of captured Croatian Domobrans was employed in gathering hay at Kukujevci. The main encampment of these prisoners was at Ergeli in Lipik, near Pakrac, in Slavonia.

On June 27, when the mowing was almost finished, part of the captives were subjected to an examination or hearing which was conducted by Stevo Bosanac, a native of Rajici near Okucani, Pane Zestic from present day Novo Selo (formerly Spanovica) close to Pakrac, and a third Serbian Communist whose name I cannot recall.

Early in the morning on Saturday, June 29, this group was made ready for departure from their camp. At about eight o'clock that morning, they set out towards Nova Gradiska in the company of ten well armed Partisans. In Nova Gradiska they were forced into a cellar, where they remained confined through July 1. On July 2, thirty heavily armed Partisans conducted the entire group towards Okucani. They arrived there about 11:00 A.M. and were herded into an orchard near the forest railway line which runs uphill to Psunj.

At 5:00 P.M. on this same afternoon, the young Croatians were loaded into open railroad cars while their escorts, all thirty of whom carried automatic weapons, placed themselves at the front and rear of the train. The train started out along the tracks that lead from Okucani to Lipik. Soon the train turned away from the Okucani-Lipik highway and began to enter the wooded region. One of the prisoners unexpectedly jumped from the train and fled towards the western side of the forest. The Partisan guards were taken by surprise and before they could grasp what was happening, the young Croat, running for his life with a speed that approached the pace of light itself, had penetrated so far into the woods that the shots they fired after him went wild, except for one which nicked his heel. He disappeared quickly and completely from their sight.

The train slowly neared the twelve kilometer line while the guards kept their machine guns trained upon the hungry, thirsty, and tired, but still proud Croatians. Finally, the train came to a stop. The guards leaped to the ground ahead of the prisoners and with leveled guns ordered the latter to descend slowly from the train, in pairs, a good distance from one another. The Croats were bound with wire and, after they had all disembarked, the train continued on further into the forest.

With their wrists bound together, the young Croatians were driven by their guards a kilometer or so to a barracks which had been used as a headquarters by Partisans operating in this forest during the war. They came to the right side of a little brook, where there was an underground bunker covered with thick planks and supported by heavy posts. The entrance to this place was cleverly masked with earth and bushes.

Here the young Croatians, most of whom were between 18 and 28 years of age, and a few only 16 or 17, found their last resting place. Their only crime was that they were born Croatians, and that they had loved and defended their fatherland with arms in hand. They met their gruesome end at about 7:00 P.M., July 2, 1945. The young man who escaped from the train fled along a little stream that runs below Bijela Stijena, until he was seen by a group of Serbian Partisans. They overpowered him after a short struggle and subjected him to questioning during the course of which they killed him. They buried him in a plum orchard near the scene of the crime. This young fellow was sergeant of the Fourth Company of the I Mountain Group of the Croatian Army during the war.

Recording witness of this testimony: Vjekoslav Cecelja

Montevideo, Uruguay
August 15, 1963

Ed. Note: The identity of the person who has supplied the details of this butchery cannot be revealed because of the danger of reprisals being taken by the Tito regime against his family. The informant knows precisely where the sergeant of the I Mountain Group and his sixty-two companions are buried; he dared to visit the hidden bunker secretly and found that the bodies had not been moved. This testimony is of great importance, since it is probable that few people know of this particular crime and it is unlikely that agents of the authorities in Belgrade can find the graves and obliterate the evidence at this late date.

Document LXXXIV

The undersigned, B. M., in May, 1945, surrendered to the British at Ancona, Italy. Later, he and 254 other Croatians, who were confined in a camp at Gruno Appula, decided to take their chances in Yugoslavia. In mid-August they and an additional five hundred Croatian prisoners-of-war sailed across the Adriatic to Dubrovnik. Here they were divided into five groups. Our witness was included in a group of 113 men who were sent to Mostar. In this town, all Hercegovinian and Bosnian Croats were taken out. Other men went to Doboj where they were placed in an OZNA (secret police) prison that was overcrowded with Croatian victims, including women and children. From Doboj, B. M. was sent to Brod and then to Mitrovica, where his group was reduced to just fourteen men. The fourteen were now confined in a concentration camp that had over four thousand prisoners. B. M.'s and his companions' jobs here was to dig graves and bury corpses, for twenty to thirty people died daily in this camp. From Mitrovica, our eyewitness and a group of 1,200 were sent to Klenak where the guards broke his collar bone. As a result, he lay in bed for six days. One night the guards took him through the woods. Convinced that he was going to be killed, B. M. refused to follow the guards, who left him alone. He walked from this spot and made it to Indjija, where his collar bone injury was treated in a hospital. During this confinement, an international commission visited the hospital and learned of B. M.'s difficulties. A British member of the commission promised him a release from the hospital within ten days. As soon as the commission had left, the witness was punished for his confession, but he was also freed as he had been promised. Once he became "free," he was not able to find any job. Therefore, he fled from Yugoslavia and found refuge in Trieste.

Together with other Croatian naval personnel who had come from Trieste, I surrendered to the British at Ancona in May, 1945. All of us were sent at first to a POW camp near Taranto. Later, we were transferred to another such camp, which was located at Gruno Appula in the vicinity of Bari.

In August, a Yugoslav Partisan captain visited our place of detainment at Gruno Appula. He was accompanied by Captain Miskulin, a former officer of our own Croatian Air Force, who evidently had gone over to Tito in time to avoid punishment for having fought on the losing side in the war.

As delegates of the Yugoslav Government, these men called upon us to return to Yugoslavia. They assured us that no reprisals would be taken against any of us who were not "war criminals or butchers." Two hundred and fifty-five of us decided to take our chances back in the old country, rather than to waste any more of our lives in the prison camp at Gruno Appula.

A few days later, our group of returnees was joined by some five hundred Croatian boys, all of whom were between sixteen and eighteen years of age. They were from the Medjumurje region[1] and had escaped from there to Austria, where the British had made prisoners of them.

In mid-August, our combined group, totalling more than seven hundred people, was loaded onto a French ship at Bari. We sailed across the Adriatic to Dubrovnik where accommodations were found for us in an empty hotel building. After we had remained in this edifice for five or six days, our Communist guards divided us into five groups. I was in the first group which contained one hundred and thirteen men.

Our detachment was sent to Mostar in Hercegovina. Here, all of the Hercegovinian Croats were separated from us and taken off by the OZNA (Yugoslav Partisan Secret Police). I do not know what happened to them. The rest of us were transported to Sarajevo where we, too, were handed over to the OZNA in that town. They took charge of the Bosnians in our group and sent those of us who came from other parts of Croatia on to Doboj.

At Sarajevo, sixty Partisans armed with Russian-made automatic weapons had reinforced the detachment which was guarding us. They locked us in freight cars which took us from Sarajevo to Doboj. Since leaving Mostar, we had received nothing to eat but bread and water. Thus, we were feeling very weak and miserable. When we reached Doboj our guards took us to the OZNA prison which was already badly overcrowded. Many women and children were included among the prisoners. About eighty of us were packed into a cell which could not have contained fifteen people in any kind of comfort.

Fortunately, we remained only fourteen hours in this twentieth century Black Hole of Calcutta. Then we were sent on to Brod in Slavonia. During this journey, our Partisan guards robbed us of all valuables. En route to Brod we heard heavy gunfire coming from the hills through which we were passing from time to time. When we asked our guards about this surprising volume of fire, they replied that there were bands of Ustashas, as well as Green Cadre men,[2] who were still holding out in the hill country.

At Brod our group was split up into several sections. Each of these was sent to a different destination. The section to which I was assigned

---

1 The Hungarians and Croatians have disputed the ownership of this territory since the seventeenth century. During the war of 1941-45, the Hungarians occupied it.

2 The "Green Cadres" was a name applied to deserters from the Austro-Hungarian Army in 1918 who banded together and lived in the woods, preying on the countryside, and sometimes attacking Imperial-Royal installations. The name was revived during World War II to apply to non-Communist and anti-Ustasha elements who fought for their own hand as the "Green Cadres" had done in 1918.

moved to Hrvatska Mitrovica, where again we were divided. My group was reduced in number here from twenty-eight to fourteen.

I was interrogated for the first time by a Serbian OZNA lieutenant at Mitrovica. During the interrogation, the OZNA men slapped our faces and maltreated us. Six days after our arrival in this town, we were transferred to a camp situated near the penitentiary which stands on the Vasariste. There were approximately four thousand Croatians, a few hundred Germans, and perhaps eighty Italians confined here.

Although I had brought eight suits of clothes with me back to the homeland, I now had only a pair of shorts, a mazri shirt, and a pair of torn shoes to wear. The rest of my gear remained in the hands of various OZNA men or Partisan guards. In our new camp, the prison commandant called us "Englishmen" and set us to work digging graves and burying all the bodies we could find in the vicinity. Many of these had remained unburied since the end of the war and were in a frightful state of decomposition. Furthermore, a horrible epidemic of fever broke out in the camp where conditions soon became unbearable. We received little food, and what we got was disgusting. Our breakfast consisted of "soup," which was really nothing but colored water, while for dinner we got unground wheat cooked in water. Some thirty pounds of this wheat was dumped into two hundred and fifty gallons of dirty water. Thus, each of us received only a few grains per meal. We also received four ounces of bread daily; it was made from corn flour. Because of the conditions to which we were exposed, and the fact that we had no heat to protect us from the cold weather that was setting in, twenty to thirty people died every day.

Our day began at four A.M. At five, we began our work which, after a time, was changed from grave digging to repairing roads or building siloes. After about a month of this, we heard that we were going to be visited by a commission of the International Red Cross which has its headquarters in Switzerland. All of us who had returned voluntarily from Italy agreed that when this commission appeared, we would complain to it about the treatment we had received. But before the commission arrived, some twelve hundred of us were loaded onto a special train and sent off to Klenak to fell trees.

At Klenak, the OZNA began to question us individually. They asked me why I had not fought in the ranks of the Partisans during the war. I said that I was a Croatian and had been drafted into the Armed Forces of the Croatian State. Besides, throughout the entire course of the war, I had never once seen a Partisan. I'd read what the newspapers had to say about them, but that was the extent of my information concerning these heroes of the foreign press.[3]

---

[3] This testimony is important because it underlines the fact that the Anglo-American Press during the war greatly magnified the extent and importance of the Partisans and their "Army of Liberation," organized by Tito with Russian, English, and American assistance. Anyone who believed what he read in English about the exploits of

They didn't like my answers, so I was slapped in the face and beaten. After this manhandling, the sub-lieutenant of the OZNA who had conducted the questioning said to the guards in the room, "Take him to his place." They led me down a flight of stairs. Suddenly, I felt a terrible blow on my right shoulder. I think that one of my guards had meant to bash in my head with his gun butt. However, in the semi-darkness of the staircase, he missed my head and struck me on the shoulder, instead. I fell down the rest of the stairs and fainted. When I recovered consciousness, I found myself in a cellar. My shoulder pained me horribly, and I was not able to move my right arm. I realized that my collar bone was fractured.

Some time later I was taken to a hut which, like other structures of this kind in the camp, had no walls, but only a roof supported by posts around which barbed wire had been wrapped. Because of the lack of walls, we suffered greatly from wind and rain. I lay in this place for six days without receiving any medical aid. Finally, a major attached to the Third Yugoslav Army Corps of Novi Sad happened to pass by the hut in which I was confined. Since I knew that he came from a part of Serbia that had belonged to Hungary up until 1918, I thought he might be more civilized than the troglodytes from Serbia proper. Thus, I called him, and he came over to our enclosure. He asked me what was wrong with me. Of course, I did not dare tell him that a guard had broken my collar bone with the butt of his rifle for, had I done so, my present guards would have taken quick action to remove the evidence in the case. Therefore, I told him that while felling trees in the forest, one of these trees had fallen on me. The major remarked that I was obviously a liar, but that, nevertheless, he would have me sent to a hospital the following day.

He was as good as his word, but when my guards led me off through the woods the next day, saying that they were taking me to the rail station, I suspected that they were going to kill me. I knew that there was a much shorter road that led to the station. Since I thought I was going to die anyway, I balked and refused flatly to go any farther with them. After some argument among themselves, they went off and left me alone in the woods, telling me to get to the hospital without any help from them.

I succeeded in making my way to Indjija, where a number of houses had been converted into hospitals for war invalids. There was a Croatian medical captain here who directed three German POW doctors to attend to my case.

They reset my collar bone and, while I was convalescing under their care, I heard that the Red Cross Commission finally had arrived. Great

---

the Partisans would have imagined that they controlled all of Croatia outside of Zagreb itself. In fact, many Anglo-American papers and periodicals did make just such an assertion! The fact is that the Partisans were known to the greater part of the population of the State of Croatia only by hearsay until the end of the war.

preparations were made throughout the hospital for the reception of this Commission. On the day that it visited us, we received much better rations than usual. The Commission itself was composed of a British major, a Swiss who wore civilian clothes, and a Partisan colonel. They stopped at my bedside, as they did at others, and the Partisan Colonel, mistaking me for a German, addressed me in that language. I did not answer him until he repeated the question, then I replied in English with which I have some acquaintance. I told him that I was a Croatian, not a German.

He shouted back at me demanding to know why I was ashamed to speak my own language if I were a Croatian. I said frankly that after all that had happened to me I was ashamed to admit that I was a member of any Southern Slav nationality, and that any language sounded better to me than my own. Then I told him my story, speaking now in Croatian.

The other members of the Commission seemed to be interested in my case, because I had spoken English at first. They asked that my story be translated to them. I told the Partisan colonel that although I did not speak English fluently I could understand that tongue fairly well, and that I would know whether he translated my statements correctly or not. As far as I was able to tell, he did give the Englishman and the Swiss an honest account of what I said. As soon as he was acquainted with my experiences, the British major protested sharply against the treatment to which I had been exposed. The Partisan colonel made various excuses, saying, among other things, that it was impossible that things had happened to me the way they had, that foreigners were not acquainted with the circumstances in regard to the Croatians, who were a nation of villains, and so on. Nevertheless, the British major assured me that I would be released within ten days time, since my shoulder now was healing up nicely.

Two days after this visit my cousin was arrested because he gave me some cigarettes through the barred window that was provided for interviews with people from outside the hospital. Also, they confined me in the cellar to punish me for this incident, and I remained here for the remainder of my stay in the hospital. Since up to this time I'd been allowed to smoke, I understood that my cousin and I were being punished for the statements I had made to the Commission. But when the ten-day interval referred to by the British officer was up, I was given my release papers and discharged from the hospital. Before I left the vicinity, the camp commandant at Klenak warned me what would happen if I ever returned to his "little Dachau."

I went back to my home in Petrovaradin where I reported to Militia Headquarters in order to secure an identity card. The Militia authorities sent me to the OZNA, whose chief refused to give me a card. He told me, "We'll see. If some old woman comes to accuse you, you'll know what to expect."

Fortunately, I hadn't made any such enemies during the war, so after a while, I got my card. Since my collar bone now had healed up altogether, I appeared before the local People's Liberation Committee in order to obtain a job classification, which they refused to issue me. Thus, although I am an experienced auto mechanic, I had to work as a laborer in the vineyards. They advanced no reason whatsoever for refusing to put me in my proper job category.

When the harvest season in the vineyards ended, I went back to the People's Liberation Committee to try to get an appropriate classification once more. They asked what I had done and where I had been during the war. I replied that I had served in the Croatian Navy and that after the end of hostilities I had surrendered to the British. When they heard this they told me, "Let Churchill give you a classification then. If he didn't assign you one, we can't."

Without a work classification permit, it was impossible for me to find anything to do around Petrovaradin. Therefore I became a vagrant, wandering to Osijek, Zemun, Belgrade, Zagreb, Ljubljana, Jesenice, and Rateche-Plavnica. Since all of these places were industrial centers, I hoped that I might be able to find some kind of job in one of them. But without an official classification, I couldn't get one. At the Labor Office in Zagreb, a clerk did offer to assign me to "pioneer" work on the Brcko-Banovici railroad line. I told her that in such a job I would receive no wages but only some kind of lodging and food of a sort. Since I needed new clothes and had to support my mother and sister besides, this sort of employment would be inadequate for my needs. The clerk shrugged her shoulders and said, "Then we cannot do anything for you, comrade, seeing that you are from such a big family."

When I came to Rateche-Plavnica and met with the same result in my efforts to find work, I made up my mind to get away from this Communist hell and escape across the frontiers. However, I was arrested here and put through an oral and written cross-examination. I naturally denied that I had any intention of going abroad and, since they couldn't get me to change my story in this regard, I was passed on from one OZNA office to another until I finally wound up in the central OZNA establishment in Ljubljana. Here, I had to undergo more cross-examinations, after which I was turned loose, but with the injunction that I leave Slovenian territory without delay.

I made my way to Zagreb, where I was able to borrow a thousand dinars. With money in my pocket, I made up my mind to risk everything on another escape try rather than slowly starve to death in Tito's "Socialist paradise." I bought a ticket to Susak, from which point I went on to Rijeka. From here I was able to sneak across the frontier line and get to Trieste.

Signed: B. M.

Rome, January 4, 1947

Document LXXXV

In the beginning of May, 1945, the undersigned, J. N., and thirty-nine other Domobrans were captured by the First Proletarian Division. The forty prisoners were taken to Sisak and placed among 140 additional captives. Seven days later, sixty-four men of this total were sent to Kutina. Here, our witness' fellow villager secured for him release and got him to join the Kutina Partisan militia. As a militiaman, J. N. guarded one of the columns of prisoners that was to be sent to Serbia. He learned from the prisoners of the liquidation of two hundred "Death Marchers" at Ivanic-grad. "Death-Marches" that were rolling through Kutina for three weeks were guarded by the Partisans of the Montenegrin Division. Later, J. N. was transferred to Ivanic-grad, Garesnica, and finally to Base No. 2 of the Yugoslav Army in Bjelovar. Here, thousands of Croatian women were bringing food to the Croatian war prisoners who were either in the former Gendarmerie School or were marching through the area. The Partisans of the Third Montegrin Division guarded the Gendarmerie School extermination camp and at night liquidated prisoners. They even killed several women who had brought the food and had also spoken in defense of the prisoners. J. N. closes this testimony by stating that after the end of hostilities, the Partisans murdered twenty-six people in his native village of Kruzac. In March, 1946, the witness escaped from Yugoslavia.

I joined the Croatian Domobrans on September 28, 1941, and served in garrison units at Brcko, Brod, Doboj, and Okucani. During this period of service, I heard of the way in which Tito's Partisans killed Croatian soldiers who surrendered to them at Tesanj and Okucani.

At the beginning of May, 1945, my unit retreated through Garesnica to Cazma, where forty of us were captured by the First Proletarian Division. This outfit turned us over to some Sisak Partisan units which escorted us to the prison camp in Sisak. There were 140 prisoners, most of them Croatian military men, incarcerated here. After a seven-day stay at this place, 64 of us were sent to Kutina.

Because the Kutina district was my place of birth, a fellow villager who had joined the Partisans secured my release and got me into the Kutina militia. There were detachments of this militia force stationed in Ivanic-grad and Garesnica. Zvonko Bezjak was militia commandant, while the commissar was a Serb from Garesnica.

At this time, columns of Croatian war prisoners and civilians who had surrendered to the Partisans in Slovenia were being escorted through the Kutina region. Our commissar ordered us to take charge of one of these columns which was being sent to Serbia. Also he commanded us to strip the captives of their clothing and valuables, and especially to deprive them of their shoes. Likewise, we had orders to keep the civilian populace from approaching them or supplying them with food.

Over sixty Croatians, both men and women, were shut up in the jail at Kutina. The Partisans maltreated these people and called them "Fascists," "murderers," and the like. Actually they all were honest peasants of the region, whose only crime was that they were loyal to the idea of Croatian nationality and independence.

The soldiers and civilians captured in Slovenia were subjected to the most brutal treatment while they were passing through Kutina. At this time, the notorious Third Brigade of the Montenegrin Partisan Division was in our district. These Montenegrins robbed the local peasants and villagers of food, clothing, horses, and everything else they could carry away with them, because the war prisoners had nothing left for them to take. The Croatian soldiers and civilians taken in Slovenia were in miserable condition, starved and nearly naked. I saw hundreds of them dressed only in underpants; they all were barefoot.

For three weeks, the prisoner columns continued to roll through Kutina. I remained in the area during this period because the Montenegrins were assigned to escort the prisoners to Serbia and we militia men thus were relieved of the duty wished upon us by our commissar. As a militiaman, I had ample opportunity to see and even converse with the captives. Many of them begged me to give them a piece of bread, which I did whenever I could without another guard seeing me. The prisoners had made the entire journey from Slovenia to Kutina on bare feet, which had become torn to ribbons, a mass of blood and sores. Mounted Partisans had accompanied them all the way. They told me that during a halt at Ivanic-grad, a commissar had two hundred of them taken out of the column and killed on the spot. The reason for this butchery was that the exhausted and starving captives had not maintained the column of threes in which he had aligned them.

The militia unit in which I was serving was composed of men drawn from the surrounding villages and towns; we acted as police. Later, I was assigned to the detachment at Ivanic-grad and then was posted to Garesnica. The commandant here was a Serb who robbed the local residents of their food and other belongings. Thus he provoked bitter hatred that was directed not only against himself, but also towards us and the entire complex of authority in Tito's Yugoslavia.

From Garesnica, I was transferred to Bjelovar where Base No. 2 of the Yugoslav Army was located. The commandant of this base was Captain Stevo Vuckovic, while the base commissar was Zdenko Cerha. Among the units stationed at this center were the following:

Waggoners' Company; Commander, Djuro Posavac. This unit was equipped with horses, harnesses, etc.

Work Company; Commander, First Lieutenant Vaso Pocuc, Commissar Stevo Stanionkovic. This outfit numbered eighty-six men, most of them Croatian prisoners.

Cattle Depot Company. This was a detachment which was charged with the care of the stables, the cattle belonging to the Base, etc.

I was assigned to the Work Company. Since we were practically all former Croatian soldiers, we were given the most arduous jobs such as the loading or unloading of heavy weapons. We were fed very poorly.

While I was so employed, many peasants brought food to the base warehouse. I had occasion to talk with them and found that they were anti-Communist without exception. They told me that more than 5000 Croatians were imprisoned in the former Gendarmerie School. The officers were taken from this concentration camp and marched all the way to Serbia. This information awakened my interest in this place of confinement. When I went to look it over, I saw great numbers of people bring food to the prisoners. On one occasion an incident took place here which caused something of a sensation, even in the Socialist hell that Tito had made out of Yugoslavia.

Thousands of women came to the barbed wire fence which surrounded the camp in order to toss packages of food over it to the captives. The guardsmen pushed the women back, cursed them, and drove them off. But the women refused to leave the vicinity of the camp and kept shouting at the top of their lungs, "Let the Domobrans out! Why do you torture them? They are guilty of nothing at all!" The guards became so enraged by these words that they opened fire on the women and killed several of them.

The Third Montenegrin Division had its headquarters in Bjelovar, a Croatian city. Soldiers from this division were assigned to guard the prisoner camp in the Gendarmerie School. Many people said that the Montenegrins took prisoners away into the surrounding hills under cover of night and killed them there.

A friend of mine visited Bjelovar and told me all about the situation in my native village, Struzac. I learned that the Partisans had killed twenty-six people there after the end of hostilities. Also they had made off with my only possession—two cows. Since my brother fell fighting against them in 1944, there was nothing left to tie me to the place of my birth. I welcomed my transfer to Slovenia, which took place in March, 1946, because I knew that it would be easier to escape to the non-Communist world from that region than from any other that was subjected to the authority of Tito and his killers.

Signed: J. N.

Fermo, Italy
April 13, 1947

Document LXXXVI

The undersigned, J. O. M., describes the massacres of the population at the villages of Drenovci, Tovarnik, and Soljani. The witness emphasizes the fact that the Partisans, with the help of local Croatian Serbs, murdered at least fifty to sixty Croats in every single village of the province Srijem.

When my native village of Drenovci was captured by Tito's troops in April, 1945, I was absent from home. Later I heard the details of the seizure from fellow villagers, particularly my cousins, and some of my close friends. This is what they told me:

On the first night that the Partisans took over the control of Drenovci, they carried out a massacre of the inhabitants. This butchery was organized on the basis of a "black list" which was prepared in advance by local Communist sympathizers. I know the individual who took the chief part in arranging the proscriptions that were effected in Drenovci.

Fifty people were arrested and tied together in pairs with wire. Then they were led out of the village in the direction of Sumanovac. On the way they were shot and buried in a common grave. Although this massacre was perpetrated secretly at night, murder will out. Through some Communist indiscretion the local peasants found out where the grave was located. Relatives of the victims went there by night to unearth the corpses and transfer them to the Drenovci cemetery. Vendelin Sajbl, the village barber, was tied to the arm of his son, Ilija,[1] who was a theology student at the seminary in Djakovo. The boy's belly was ripped open and his entrails had been cut out. Since the remaining members of the Sajbl family had all left the village, other peasants reburied father and son in a large cabinet that they procured for this purpose.

Ivica Sajbl, Vendelin's oldest son, was not at home when the Titoists captured the village. But after he had remained in hiding in Osijek for some time, he was imprudent enough to come back to Drenovci, where he hid in the attic of his home. Of course, someone betrayed his whereabouts to the Communists who searched the house, found him, and placed him under arrest. Although several months had passed since the slaughter of his father and brother, Ivica's name still was on the black list prepared before the end of the war. Therefore, he was taken from the village, supposedly to be placed on a train at the nearest rail station so that he could stand trial at a larger town. En route to the station a guard shot him, allegedly for trying to escape. Later the guard himself acknowledged that he had received orders to liquidate Ivica. "If I had not killed him, my superiors would have killed me," the guard said.

Massacres similar to the one that I have described above were perpetrated in every other Croatian village in the province of Srijem (Sirmia). Fifty to sixty persons, chiefly peasants, were liquidated in each of these communities. Occasionally as many as a hundred or more were butchered. Tovarnik was one place where a slaughter on this scale was carried out. The Partisans had prepared a black list for every one of these Croatian settlements. There have been many Serbs in this easternmost part of the Croatian national territory since Turkish times. Evidently the Serbian Communists were determined to make it an almost completely Serbian province by wiping out all the potential leaders among the Croatian population. Of course, many non-Communist Serbs saw eye to eye with them on this matter and this black list procedure

---

[1] Ilija Sajbl is one of nine members—eight of them priests—of the Djakovo diocese who were murdered by Tito's troops.

probably explains why so many Croatian Serbs from this territory joined the Partisans in the later stages of the war. Tito's people exercised much ingenuity in concealing the facts concerning many of these killings and burial places.

In the village of Soljani, the Partisans slaughtered a great number of people, but I do not know the names of any of these victims. According to what eyewitnesses told me, they were abducted from their homes in the dead of night and taken out onto a field where they were shot. Soon afterwards, the local Communist authorities had the field plowed and wheat planted over the burial place. No one had any idea that a mass of victims of the theory and practice of Marxism lay beneath the gently waving stems of wheat.

Yet this butchery, too, did not remain a secret for long, and all the elaborate precautions taken by the Communists to keep the facts from becoming known were entirely in vain. On the night that the victims were taken from their homes, a dog belonging to one of them trailed after his master. A day or two later the animal returned home in a very excited state. It seized its late master's wife by her skirt and tried to pull her outside the house. She realized that the dog wanted to lead her to her husband, so she followed. This intelligent pet led her unerringly to the plain where the prisoners had been murdered. When he began to dig up the earth, his mistress guessed what had happened. She went back to the village, got a shovel, and asked several men whom she knew she could rely on to aid her.

A little digging uncovered the bodies which were laid one beside the other. Of course the faithful dog's mistress found her spouse among them.

Signed: J. O. M.

Rome, Italy
June 27, 1962

Document LXXXVII

The first and main part of this testimony by J. B. K. deals with the massacre of four hundred inhabitants of Srijemski Karlovci by the Partisans. The witness gives minute details of the massacre site, of the atrocities committed, and of the victims murdered there. A list of victims with whom J. B. K. was acquainted is also given. The second part of the testimony describes the pitiable condition of "Death Marchers" who went through Karlovci towards Novi Sad. A moving episode occurred when a woman, at the exclamation "Mother!" ran toward her son and, for this, was struck so hard by a Partisan that she fell senseless. The account ends by emphasizing that the Serbian peasants never missed an opportunity to beat and torture their disarmed Croatian enemies.

During the first part of the war of 1941-45, I worked on a peasant farm in Germany. In the late fall of 1943, I returned to my home, Srijemski Karlovci, and lived there with my parents until the Partisans of Josip Broz Tito took the town in October, 1944, at the time of the grape harvest.

I have vivid memories of this event. The Croatian defenders of this predominantly Serbian locality waged a bitter battle in the vineyards around the town for a while, but late in the afternoon on which the fighting started, the Partisans broke into the city itself. They were attired in uniforms of various kinds and some of them wore civilian clothes. A great part of the local Serbian population welcomed them joyfully and many volunteers entered their ranks to replace the casualties they had suffered.

While it was still daylight, they began to seek out the Croatian and Serbian anti-Communist inhabitants in their homes. Whenever they were able to lay their hands on such people, the Partisans bound them and took them off to be killed, as we all knew they would be. Many of the arrested men were conducted along the street on which I lived. I remember how blood was dripping from open wounds made by the wire with which Tito's executioners had bound our neighbor, Djuro Krizan. That same night, two brothers, Ilija and N. Brigarski from Karlovci, whom I saw escorting him as he passed by our house, hung him on a chestnut tree near Kraljevo Brdo along the road that leads from Karlovci to Belgrade. They stripped the skin off his back and other parts of his body. Then they beat him to death while he hung from the tree.

The details of this murder were related to me by a sixteen-year-old youth, N. Beta, whose arm was paralyzed. He watched the commission of this crime from a nearby vantage point.

Most of the massacres that followed the Partisan occupation of the town took place on the hill called Doka, which is about one half mile out of Karlovci in the direction of Bukovac. Local and non-resident Partisans carried out the killings after night fell. Although I knew the names of several of the murderers at the time, eleven years have passed since then and I cannot recall them at the moment. Perhaps the names of these killers will come back to me later.

On the first day that followed the Partisans' capture of Karlovci and the subsequent massacres, the wives of some of the victims came to the scene of the slaughter that had taken place on the Doka hill. One of my cousins was among these women. When they located the mass grave, they saw that something was moving beneath the shallow covering of earth, and realized that some of the victims were not dead. But Partisan guards came up and drove them away from the grave, striking them repeatedly with the picks and shovels with which (as we learned later on) the murdered people had been forced to dig their own graves. Everyone present at this scene recalled that there was a great deal of blood around the grave, which made it easy to locate. Later the Partisans poured quicklime over it.

Among the Croatians of Karlovci who were murdered by the Partisans after the capture of the town, I was acquainted personally with the following: Stevo Seder, a peasant, perhaps forty-five years old; Marko Lukasic, also a peasant; Ivan Kamra and his two sons, one fifteen, the other seventeen years old; Rajcingar, another peasant who, however, lived on Donja Svapska Street in the city itself; Jasa Krenajs, a retired peasant about sixty years of age; a miller by the name of Bencinger who was around fifty years old, and his wife who was approximately the same age; Vinko Tot, another old peasant; and Andrija Polozanac, a district clerk, whose fingers were chopped off by the Partisans while they had him in their custody. Tito's people revived an ancient form of punishment in disposing of Djuro Balanov, a wealthy peasant of the village of Maradik. They tied each of his arms and legs to a horse and then whipped the animals so that they pulled in opposite directions until they had torn poor Balanov apart. One of the members of the locally prominent Harasti family was also killed.

There were about four hundred executions in all. All fathers of families, and all boys sixteen or seventeen years old, who lived on Gornja and Donja Svapska Streets, were liquidated. Only widows, younger children, and a few very old men were left alive on these streets. Of course the older boys and some of the other male members of these families were serving with the Croatian Armed Forces and thus escaped this particular massacre. The victims were chiefly Croatians, but some anti-Communist Karlovci Serbs were included among them. The executioners were mainly Serbs; they were aided by Gypsies with criminal records, who discharged their debt to society in this facile manner. A couple of women and some adolescent boys were among the victims of the "triumph of democracy" in Karlovci.

I was only twenty-one years old when the events that I have described occurred. Apparently none of the local Communists knew about my stay in Germany or I, too, probably would have been liquidated. As it was, I was able to continue to live quietly in Karlovci until the end of the war.

A month after the fighting had ended, long columns of Croatian war prisoners were led through the city enroute to Novi Sad, the "Serbian Athens" of Hungarian days, when Hungarian Serbs were somewhat more civilized than their descendants in 1945. The Croat captives presented a horrible spectacle. They were starving, clad in rags, covered with lice, and many of them were sick as well. Their Partisan guards killed everyone who collapsed or dropped behind the rest. On one occasion I saw a barefoot young man whose feet were bleeding badly, and who had not a stitch of clothing on him except underpants, glimpse his mother standing alongside the street through which the column was passing.

"Mother!" he exclaimed.

The poor woman ran toward her son, but a Partisan hit her so hard with the butt of his rifle that she fell senseless in the street.

I think I should mention, too, that the Serbian peasants who lived in the vicinity of Karlovci conducted themselves like wild beasts, never missing an opportunity to beat or otherwise torture their disarmed Croatian enemies.

Signed: J. B. K.

November 9, 1955

Document LXXXVIII

The massacre of several thousand Croatian war prisoners in the Golubova Suma near Bosanski Brod is tragically revealed.

After the end of the war of 1941-45, the new Yugoslav authorities established a concentration camp at Bosanski Brod, designed to serve as a transitional place of detention for Croatian war prisoners. Until the winter of 1945-46, such captives continued to be brought to this Bosnian camp. The place contained five barracks and was located close to the stocking factory on Kardelj Street. It was also near the buildings which stand along the thoroughfare that was subsequently renamed in honor of the wartime Communist propagandist and apologist, Milovan Djilas. Fifteen hundred feet away from the barracks was the Golubova Suma (Pigeon Forest).

The prisoners brought to this camp were starved, clubbed, and exposed to all kinds of hardships. Since there was no room in the barracks to accommodate all of them, a great many men had to stay out in the open, even during driving rain storms. Several thousand captives were murdered in the Golubova Suma. Near this woods, bombs dropped by planes during the war had left many craters. The Partisans would kill the prisoners, then pile between forty to eighty corpses at a time into these holes and cover them over with a sparse layer of earth. Since there were not enough bombholes to take care of all the bodies, some of the Croatian war prisoners had to dig their own graves near the brick factory which stands near the Sava River, about a mile from Slavonski Brod.

Partisan officers from pre-1918 Serbia directed the butcheries that were carried out at these places. Their commandant, however, a fellow by the name of Momcilo, was a native of Bosanski Brod. As this orgy of slaughter neared its peak, Momcilo was allegedly transferred to Serbia. Nothing was heard of him after his departure from Bosanski and Slavonski Brod.

All of the residents of this small Bosnian town know about the gruesome mass slaughters which were carried out by the Serbian Partisans here. I do not consider it necessary to sign my name to this report, because reprisals would be taken against my relatives and old associates, some of whom have been unable to get out of the Tito-made hell that once was Croatia and Bosnia. However, since the Committee for the Investigation of the Bleiburg Tragedy has my signed testimony, if it is absolutely necessary to establish my identity to guarantee the authenticity of this relation, it can be done without difficulty.

Signed: S.S.

Document LXXXIX

The undersigned Muslim Croat, Abid Dizdarevic, opens his testimony by explaining why two concentration camps were necessary in Bosanski Novi, and why both of them became extermination camps for the Croatian prisoners-of-war and for arrestees in general. Groups of prisoners were led to be slaughtered every night during the thirty day period that Dizdarevic's father was an inmate in one of the camps. The massacres were perpetrated in the vicinity of each camp near Ciganluk (today's Kovacka) Street and at Srednja Ada. In 1952, Yugoslav Reds, during excavation, tried to attribute the Ciganluk victims to the Ustashas. In 1956, they charged the Ustashas, too, for the skeletons found at Srednja Ada. At the end of his testimony, Dizdarevic demonstrates that the mass slaughters of the Bosanki Novi victims who had been neither tried, or identified were perpetrated in 1945 and 1946 by Yugoslav Reds.

At the close of the war of 1941-45, die-hard Croatian elements held out to the end at Bosanski Novi against the attacks delivered upon this town by the National Liberation Army of Marshal Tito, who had largely Serbian troops (including some former Chetnik opponents) under his command.

Soon after the siege was over, the OZNA (forerunner of the UDBA secret political security police of today) opened a concentration camp in the city. This camp was situated on the left side of the street that runs from the railroad station into the main part of the town. It was only about two hundred meters from the station, on the right bank of the Sana River. Formerly gardens and fields had stood here. The camp was surrounded by barbed wire and was well guarded by Partisan troops. The camp command was located in a one-story house which had usually lodged the veterinary ambulance (ambulanta) of the town.

Bosanski Novi is one of the most important rail centers in Bosnia. Through it passed men who were returning by train to their homes in various parts of Bosnia. Thus, the OZNA camp originally was designed to be a transitional detention point from which prisoners, after interrogation, could be sent on to their various places of residence. Many war prisoners were brought here, along with civilians who had tried to escape from Yugoslavia by retreating with the Croatian Armed Forces. The camp filled up so rapidly that there was not enough room in it to accommodate all of the captives brought to Bosanski Novi, despite the way in which these unfortunates were jammed together, literally one on top of the other. Therefore, the OZNA chief, Semso Kapetanovic, brother of Hajro Kapetanovic, who today is Minister of Finance for the People's Republic of Bosnia-Hercegovina, opened a subsidiary camp near the rectory of the Orthodox parish in the city.

Both camps were overcrowded. At times, there were more than three thousand prisoners in them. These inmates were exclusively Muslim or Catholic Croats. They were young men for the most part, but there were a few older people. Usually the OZNA released the latter rather quickly and sent them home. However, new groups of war prisoners and civilian arrestees kept arriving every day, so the congestion increased. Perhaps it was lack of space more than any other factor which induced the OZNA to initiate the mass slaughter of prisoners.

Every night, well armed OZNA operatives would enter the camps and shine their flashlights into the faces of the prisoners as the latter lay sleeping on the ground. They would kick awake whomever they liked and take them outside the enclosures. Prisoners who tried to protect themselves against the night chill by throwing overcoats over their heads were presumed to be "criminals" trying to hide their identities, and were the first to be led off. The stronger and younger men were special targets of OZNA vindictiveness. Thirty to sixty men were taken in this manner every night. None of them were interrogated, or received any sort of trial; usually the OZNA did not even bother to find out their names.

Half an hour after the victims were taken off, the shooting began from a point not too distant from the camps. The Gypsies who lived on Ciganluk Street (which today is called Kovacka Street) saw how captives were executed each night, and how the corpses were thrown into holes made by bombs during the war. Now the textile industry halls stand where the massacres took place. Not all of the executions took place there, however; some prisoners were slaughtered at Srednja Ada and along the banks of the Una River near the confluence of that stream with the Sana.

The number of victims taken from the two camps must have exceeded a thousand in all. Since the bomb holes were large and especially deep, they could accommodate that number of bodies quite easily. And the killings continued for quite a number of nights.

I was not an eyewitness of the proceedings that I have described above, but I heard about them from my father who spent an entire month in the first OZNA camp. He told me, too, that the prisoners were poorly fed and badly treated, even when they were not taken out to be killed. Other people in the village in which I lived confirmed his story. Some of these individuals had undergone periods of imprisonment in one or other of the camps, or had seen captives being led off to execution. There were people who had spied on the massacres as they were being committed, and who had excavated and reburied some of the bodies later on.

The textile factory which I have mentioned above was erected (with the money of American taxpayers) in 1952. At the beginning of the summer of that year, the foundations were dug for the columns which today support the textile industry halls. During the excavation, bones of hundreds of men piled together in a common mass grave, were uncovered. The "People's" authorities at once issued an announcement that the remains were those of people killed by the Ustashas in 1941. Since the officially controlled Yugoslav press did not comment on the discovery of these bones at all, this statement is an obvious lie. Had the victims of the Ustashas been interred here, the newspapers would have made a *cause celebre* out of this affair and the government writers would have produced whole books to describe this "Fascist" crime. I might mention, to prove my point, that none of the bones of these alleged victims of the Ustashas were transferred to cemeteries maintained for the dead of the National Liberation Army, as was done with the remains of other presumed "Fascist" victims. For example, in 1958 five children were killed by the explosion of an old grenade which they dug up. These innocents were declared "victims of Fascism" too, and were interred in the Partisan cemetery near Vidorija. The population of Bosanski Novi knew very well whose bones the money of the American taxpayers had unearthed.

Also, when the canal was dug through Srednja Ada in 1956, numerous skeletons of recent interment were found. Of course, the authorities declared that these remains also belonged to "victims of Fascism." Again, none of the bones uncovered were reinterred in the cemeteries of the Partisan casualties of 1941-45. The inference is plain.

The recording of this report was carried out in accordance with my recollections of what was told to me by my father and fellow villagers who themselves lived through the episodes that I have described above.

Signed: Abid Dizdarevic

Rome

December 7, 1960

Document XC

This account by Nezir Medic first relates the precarious conditions of the Croatian Armed Forces at the end of World War II, which caused a part of his detachment to withdraw from Croatia, and another to surrender to the Partisans. Since Tito's people were imprisoning or murdering masses of Croatians, the witness' father fled into the forests, and the witness himself stayed home. Later, he was arrested and "tried" along with about two thousand other arrestees. All of them were divided into three groups. Groups No. 1 and 2 were sent to a prison camp in Teslic, and eventually released. Group 3, to which our witness was assigned and from which he escaped, was taken to Derventa, where its members were tortured and killed. Among the victims was Medic's uncle, Hasan Mujic, and an acquaintance, Mustafa Polic.

During April, 1945, there was continuous fighting around Zavidovic between the Domobrans and Ustashas on the one hand and the Partisans on the other. At the time, I was only seventeen years old. However, I fought in the Domobrans alongside my father.

The Balkan Wehrmacht of the Germans was collapsing at this time, as was the Reich itself. Therefore, it was only a question of how long we could hold out, unaided as we were, against the Serbian, Slovenian, Bulgarian, and Russian Communists, and their British and American allies.

It was only at the end of the first week in May that the Croatian State began to disintegrate, but when it gave orders for the still intact Armed Forces to evacuate Croatia, the end of the Army was near, too. One part of the Croatian forces fighting around Zavidovic withdrew in the direction of North Seher. The rest of us decided to surrender to the Partisans, since there was no hope of winning the war and we did not want to go into exile.

After the Army had withdrawn from the country or laid down its arms, the Partisans seemed to be intent upon wiping the Croatian people, as well as the Croatian State, off the face of the map. They went into the villages and threw into prison or killed nearly every Croatian. My father became ill at the end of the war, which was one important reason why he and I surrendered. A Partisan soldier told him that the lives of all those who were sent to the concentration camps were in jeopardy. As a Domobran, my father knew he was bound to be imprisoned. Thus, he fled into the forests, despite his weakened condition.

I did not accompany him, because we thought that even though I had served in the Domobrans, too, my youth would prevent me from being punished too severely. But I was arrested along with practically every other Muslim or Catholic. At least we got a trial in a regular "People's Court," which is more than many Croatians did. Our names were read off and every third man was put to one side. There were approximately two thousand of us who were subjected to this process. We were separated into two groups after the "trial." One group, the No. 1's and 2's, was sent by truck to Camp Teslic. The second bunch, which was made up of No. 3's, traveled in railroad boxcars to Derventa.

I was among the No. 3's. But I ran away from this column, remained in hiding for two days at the homes of relatives, and then concealed myself in my own home. Three months later, the people who had gone to Camp Teslic came back home. Those sent to Derventa were never seen again. According to the peasants who lived in the vicinity of this town and around Prnjavor, the Communists first tortured the No. 3's in the cellars of the local residents, then killed them. Among the victims was my uncle, Hasan Mujic, an invalid because of wounds suffered on the Russian front, and a man by the name of Mustafa Polic from Potklec, whom I also knew.

Signed: Nezir Medic

Document XCI

The first half of this testimony, delivered by Safet Bayin on the Podgraci massacre, is written in the third person. The testimony opens with a brief description of "Death Marches" and introduces us to the tragic fate of an estimated 3,500 Croatian war prisoners. On the stretch from Pozega to Podgraci, these prisoners were subjected to unbelievably savage atrocities at the hands of Serbian Partisans and civilians. Bayin learned the minute details of the tortures and subsequent massacre of the Podgraci victims from a few escapees. He had a special interest in learning about the Podgraci massacre, because his brother Hasan was slaughtered there. The second half of the testimony is presented in the first person on the basis of what Bayin saw while he was employed at Podgraci—a large field of bones of the unburied victims. Here the eyewitness tells us how he managed to learn about the massacre itself. A Serbian from the village, who was Bayin's machinist-helper, gave him a great deal of first-hand information. Later, Bayin was tried for having listened to the story. Authorities, however, talked his informant into retracting what he had told. This revealing document ends with an explanation of the primary reasons that drove Bayin to flee from Yugoslavia.

After the end of the war in 1945, the Serbian Partisan troop units commanded by Generals Kocha Popovitch and Peko Dapchevitch murdered many of the disarmed Croatian officers, soldiers, and civilians who were turned over to them by the English. They killed most of these victims in Slovenia, where the British had few if any observers. Those whom they did not kill were marched from Bleiburg to Dravograd, Celje, and Maribor and, finally, to Slavonska Pozega. Here they were placed inside a barbed wire enclosure which did duty as a concentration camp. This place was lacking in shelter against inclement weather and was nothing but a mudhole, not fit for pigs to wallow in.

Among the captives who survived the Slovenian massacres were my brother, Hasan, and another close friend of ours who came from our home district of Jajce in Bosnia. They were included in a column of 3500 Croatian Domobrans, all between twenty-one and twenty-five years of age. It took them ten days to cover the distance between Bleiburg and Dravograd and Slavonska Pozega. They arrived at the latter place in desperate condition, since the Serbs hardly fed them at all throughout this long and arduous journey. There were 20,000 other Croatian prisoners in the Slavonska Pozega camp when my brother and his fellow sufferers arrived there. During the ten days that they remained in this place, hundreds of captives were slaughtered every night. Perhaps 500 prisoners died also of illness, exhaustion, or hunger in this period of time.

On May 23, a number of Partisan officers, among whom were Jovo Byelitch, Mile Tendyeritch, Cedo Kopar, and a so-called Muslim by the name of Kovacevic, came to the camp. This Kovacevic hailed from the village of Bosanska Dubrava, which is located between Bosanska Gradiska and Banja Luka. These Partisan officers asked all Croatian prisoners from Bosnia and Hercegovina to step forward. When they did so, Byelitch delivered a brief address to them, saying, "Comrades, we are all aware that you are sons of our liberated Bosnia-Hercegovina. From 1942 to 1945 you fought against the National Liberation Army because of ignorance and the influence of errors of judgment. We do not consider you criminals, and I am authorized by our Supreme Commander, Josip Broz Tito, to save you from death by sending you to fell trees for two months. The freedom of all of you is guaranteed. Your closest relatives will be allowed to visit you and to bring you packages of food and clothing."

The Bosnian and Hercegovinian prisoners were glad to hear what Byelitch said, even though some of them were skeptical. Three hundred Partisans of the First and Second Kozara Brigades took the Bosnian and Hercegovinian Croats to the railroad station, where they loaded them onto boxcars. After three days of beatings, thirst, and hunger, the train conveying them arrived in Okucani. From there they proceeded on foot to Bosanska Gradiska. Three captives who were natives of the last named place asked their escorts to give them permission to get something to eat from their homes, so that they would have the strength to make the twenty mile trek from Bosanska Gradiska to Gornji Podgraci. The Partisans told them that they would be fed when they got to the latter town, so they could not leave the ranks at Bosanska Gradiska.

However the three prisoners had an idea of the kind of dinner they would get at Gornji Podgraci, so about 11:00 A.M. they tried to escape into some prune orchards and gardens that lay along the line of march. The guards picked them off before they had gone forty yards. Then the Partisans warned the other captives that they would be shot, too, if they tried to get away or violated in other ways the rules of discipline demanded by the National Liberation Army.

As soon as the prisoner column arrived in Gornji Podgraci, they were taken in front of the Serbian Orthodox Church and divested of their clothing right down to their underwear. A few of the bolder or more indifferent prisoners asked Mile Tendyeritch the reason for this procedure. By way of reply, he drew his dagger and killed these "disobedient" men on the spot. Then he told the remaining captives they would be treated in the same way in the abandoned Sipadov saw mill (Sipadova Pilana) nearby. The rest of the nearly naked prospective victims were too worn out from many days of thirst and hunger and the long exhausting marches to voice any protest.

Their well armed guards were now reinforced by other Partisan troops. They drove the prisoners into the saw mill. While this was going on, Commander Byelitch, who came from the neighboring village of Jablanica, cursed, screamed, blasphemed, and yelled as though he had suddenly gone mad. He shouted at the prisoners that this was not 1941 when all of them had enlisted in the Croatian Army and became Ustashas. Literally foaming at the mouth, he declared that they had fought under Pavelic's command against the "people" right up to the last minute of the war until they, together with their German and Italian allies, found themselves defeated. He added in a somewhat more controlled tone: "You are now in the hands of the peoples' justice and exposed to the vengeance of the Kozara region, which will be enacted against you. The surviving fighters from Kozara and the local Serbian population will try you."

As he uttered these words, Byelitch and Tendyeritch pulled out their daggers and began to stab the prisoners closest to them. Some of the captives were taken out singly to a nearby brook where they were killed. By midnight, 400 victims had been disposed of in one way or another. After this hour, mobs of Serbians armed with axes, hay-forks, sickles, knives, and clubs charged in among the remaining victims and killed 200 more of them. Whoever survived was marched along the narrow railroad tracks that led deeper into the Kozara Mountain. A thousand of them were shot a mile down the tracks in a ravine that runs for approximately 600 feet along the right side of the rail line. About 1900 other prisoners were taken down a track which splits off to the left from the main line. They were lined up in groups of two hundred apiece in another ravine a mile and a half down the line. It was at this point that my acquaintance, whom I have mentioned above, made good his escape, along with another Croatian who came from the nearby village of Ivanjska.

I should have mentioned earlier that before Byelitch and Tendyeritch let the prisoners know what was going to happen to them, they took the precaution of having their wrists bound with wire, even though most of the victims were too exhausted to put up a fight for their lives. My friend, however, and his fellow captives got rid of their bonds and ran into the woods. Their Serbian guards kept yelling "Halt! Halt!" and fired salvos of shots after them, but the fugitives were not hit. By the evening of the following day, they reached the Muslim village of Kozarac, which is located at the foot of the far side of the Kozara Mountain near the railroad tracks which connect Zagreb with Banialuka. Thus they escaped death.

Eight other prisoners took advantage of the confusion produced by the flight of the first two to get away also. Unfortunately these men were not familiar with the Kozara Mountain which is thirty miles long by fifteen miles wide. They wandered through the valleys and along the paths of this territory, until they came upon some shepherds whom they asked to give them a bit of bread. But the shepherds betrayed their presence to the Serb peasants of the Kozara region, who set upon them with axes and killed them.

The Podgraci massacre and accompanying atrocities lasted from May 26 to May 29. Yovo Byelitch and Mile Tendyeritch were proclaimed national heroes for their organization of this slaughter. As such, they still enjoy unlimited privileges, along with the survivors of the Sarajevo assassinations of 1914. It is well to understand that Tito's Yugoslavia cherishes several distinct murder cults.

The two Croatian Domobrans who escaped the Podgraci slaughter in the manner described above are alive today. It is from them that I learned about the horrors which were enacted on the Kozara Mountain at the end of May, 1945. Then, in 1957, in my capacity of skilled machinist, I was employed by the industrial lumber concern "Vrbas" to work on the construction of a twenty-six mile long road between Gornji Podgraci and Ivanjska. I was stationed right in Gornji Podgraci, where my job was concerned with the operation of Diesel motors. One of the residents of this village acted as my helper and I soon gained his confidence. He told me stories about himself and the Kozara region, in which he stressed the heroism of the Serbs who constitute the entire population of Gornji Podgraci. It was he who gave me the details of the killing of the eight Croatian refugees from the general massacre mentioned above. I paid careful attention to what he told me, and encouraged him to supply me with more details about the slaughter enacted here twelve years previously. Everything he related to me corresponded closely to what I had learned from the escaped Domobrans.

Since I promised to teach him all about the operation of Diesels, I succeeded in getting him to take me to the spots where the massacres had occurred. He showed the place from which the two Domobrans had made their get away, and pointed out where the other eight men had escaped. Also, he took me to the ravine on the right side of the railroad tracks, where the remains of the victims of the butchery still reposed. The Serb Partisans and the villagers who perpetrated the massacre did not take the trouble to bury their victims, and my machinist-helper told me that in June, 1945, both the dogs and wolves of the neighborhood gorged themselves on Ustasha meat. Throughout the summer, no one could approach this area, which is called the "Ustasha Avram" (synagogue), because of the horrible stench of putrefying flesh that emanated from it. The trees are so sparse in this ravine that it resembles a desert, since it is white throughout its length of 450-600 feet from human skulls and rain-washed bones.

I walked around this scene of slaughter for half an hour, thinking about the death of my brother, Hasan, and the other Croatians who had died here. Never can I forget either of the two ravines on the Kozara which were still white with the skulls and bones of murdered prisoners of war, all of them natives of Bosnia and Hercegovina. This, I reflected, is the Serbian way of making good their ridiculous claim to the Serbian identity of these two old Croatian provinces—a claim which despite its lack of foundation has received wide credence in the English and French-speaking worlds.

After I had returned from the mountain to Gornji Podgraci, I could not refrain from commenting upon the massacre. I told my helper that the men killed on that occasion were not Ustashas but Domobrans, and that no one but Serbs would have stripped them of their clothing in front of a church and then slaughtered them without any kind of investigation or trial. He stared at me and shrugged his shoulders, as if what I said were of no importance.

On the following evening I was watching an American movie. The commander of the local militia had me taken from the theatre to the militia station where he interrogated me. He finished his investigation by telling me that I would be sent in chains to the UDBA director in Stara Gradiska. I got word of what had happened to the construction director who was my employer. This fellow talked my machinist helper into retracting the statements which he had made to the militia commander concerning my observations on the massacre. My precious assistant lied cheerfully, in the way that only a Serb can, saying that he had been drunk and didn't really remember what I had said to him while he was in his cups. He'd awakened with some kind of confused impression that I had criticized the "justice enacted by the people." But on thinking it over, he had come to realize that he had dreamed the whole thing.

So the Communist court of Stara Gradiska found me innocent and set me free. It is lucky for me that the influence exerted by my employer was enough to dissuade the court from making a further investigation. If they had discovered that I belonged to a well known Croatian Ustasha family in Bosnia, I would have been sentenced to at least a five year term of imprisonment. A court martial held at Bugojno on April 15, 1945, had condemned my father to be hung, and a year later I had been accused myself of helping the Krizari. As it happened, this charge was false because I had never even heard of the Krizari until this time. Even so the OZNA men had worked me over; their commander, a Serbian by the name of Milan Mancitch from the village of Drinic near Bosanski Petrovac, displayed special diligence in beating me. It was only because I was a minor, and because of the intervention of some of my neighbors who had ingratiated themselves with the Communist authorities, that I escaped death on that occasion. So, if they had gone into my past, it can be seen that I would not have fared well at the hands of the court in Stara Gradiska eleven years later.

My experiences in the Kozara area, combined with what I had learned from other sources, filled me with disgust for Tito's Yugoslavia. In October, 1959, I crossed the Slovenian border into Austria as had our Armed Forces and civilian refugees fourteen years before, when I was still a boy. I was luckier than they had been in finding refuge on the soil of the old Habsburg lands. But I decided that I had had enough of the Old World, and on June 9, 1960, I arrived in Canada. Here I am free to describe the ghastly and perfidious massacre of the 3500 Croatian Domobrans whose deaths were a result of the Bleiburg betrayal and catastrophe.

Signed: Safet Bayin

Uranium City, Sask., Canada
December 30, 1961

Document XCII

The following testimony by Safet Jaskic concerning the massacre of approximately four thousand Croatian war prisoners at Podgraci, Bosnia, is written in the third person except where Jaskic quotes the eyewitnesses of this most horrifying slaughter. Two of Jaskic's informants, inmates in a concentration camp in Bosnia, were escapees from the massacre. The third informant, who is presented towards the end of this account, was a Serbian peasant who had dared condemn his Serbian co-nationals for their exceedingly savage liquidation of Croatian victims. He was imprisoned for his honesty. Even though the account is not written in the first person as all other Documents are, this account nonetheless is one of the most important testimonies of this volume not only because of the facts recorded in it but also because of Jaskic's very dramatic presentation.

In order to avoid possible misunderstandings, I wish to state at the outset of this relation that I am ready to repeat this report verbally or in writing before any competent international commission which may be charged with the investigation of war crimes. But to avoid jeopardizing the safety of individuals who are still living in Tito's Yugoslavia, I am not going to mention specific names here or indicate certain precise dates and circumstances connected with my postwar imprisonments in Banja Luka, Zenica, or other places. I shall be glad indeed to supply all of this specific data when and if an international commission undertakes an investigation of what Tito and his Partisans did after the close of hostilities in 1945.

While imprisoned at one of the places mentioned above, I had repeated conversations with D.I.G., a fellow captive. During 1941-45, this Bosnian Croat served as a private soldier in the Domobran units of the Regular Croatian Army. Along with another Croatian from Bosnia, A.D.S., this prisoner, who at the time I knew him faced a long term of incarceration, was an eyewitness of a mass killing which I believe was not equalled by any other of the long chain of massacres perpetrated by the Yugoslav Communists after the end of World War II. So far as I know, D.I.G. and A.D.S. are the only survivors of this slaughter. During our many conversations, they related the whole story to me in detail. They felt a pressing need to perpetuate the memory of their dead comrades by testifying spontaneously to the terrifying circumstances which they had lived through themselves.

D.I.G. was included in a column of perhaps 15,000 Croatian war prisoners who were marched from Dravograd to Slavonska Pozega. Along the way, the column thinned out as the Partisan guards murdered many of the captives without giving them any kind of trial or hearing. By the time the column reached Slavonska Pozega, it was down to half of its original number.

At Pozega the prisoners were placed in a concentration camp, where they were given absolutely nothing to eat or drink by their Partisan captors. It was only the assistance they received from the Croatian population of the surrounding territory that enabled some of them to survive for a time.

Both of the above mentioned witnesses concurred in stating that on June 21, the Partisans stretched a rope from the gate all the way through the middle of the camp. Whoever stood on the right side of this rope was led outside the camp and lined up in front of the barbed wire fence that surrounded it. D.I.G. and A.D.S. both were in this right hand group. A Communist officer, who seemed to be in a very agitated frame of mind, spoke to the prisoners who had been taken out of the camp. He told them that the People's authorities had decided that even though they were wartime enemies, they would be accepted into the Armed Forces of the Yugoslav State and henceforth would be regarded as free citizens of the Yugoslav Republic. Some prisoners had their doubts about the sincerity of this speech. Others, especially the younger men, took an optimistic view and thought that their lives were safe.

On this same morning, the prisoners taken from the camp were formed into a column and led off under strong escort towards Stara Gradiska. The journey to this place lasted two days. D.I.G. and A.D.S. estimated that there were 4,000 Domobrans in the column. Since they had no opportunity to count the "Death Marchers" with precision, this figure represents only a guess on their part. On every stretch of this journey, the Croatian population brought the prisoners bread and other food. Strangely enough the Communist guards did not interfere with these charitable actions, as they had during the marches through Slovenia and on the return to Croatian territory from that land. This leniency heartened the captives, more and more of whom came to feel that their long journey would have a happy ending.

The column crossed the Sava River near Bosanska Gradiska; then it was permitted to rest for a long time. As the guards loaded cases of ammunition onto the backs of some of the prisoners, the march was resumed. All captives had to take turns in rotation at carrying the ammunition cases.

Once again the column enjoyed a long rest. Sometime after June 23, it arrived at the village of Podgraci which lies at the foot of Mount Kozara. The captives were led past a large lumberyard into a valley which was surrounded by dense woods and shrubbery on all sides. Several hundred Partisan guards were distributed along the flanks and rear of the column; waiting in the valley itself were many hundreds of Serbian peasants. The number of these Serbs increased every moment, as new arrivals kept coming up. Women, youths, and old men from nearby villages were included among these peasant masses. Obviously the People's authorities had invited them to assemble at this place. They carried hatchets, pitch forks, picks, metal rods, clubs, and other lethal weapons.

Suddenly a Partisan officer gave a signal to the peasants. The numerous women and youths among them began to howl,"Butchers! Ustashas! Knife them all! Revenge! Revenge!" These yells and screams of rage were interspersed with obscene gestures and torrents of curses, as well as by the brandishing of weapons carried by the peasants. Some of the Serbs kept repeating, "So you want to join our Armed Forces!" While all this was happening, the prisoners were naturally looking for a way to escape from the situation in which they found themselves. But the hundreds of Partisan soldiers who surrounded the column carried light machine guns, and attempted escapes could result only in disaster.

The commissar in command of the guard detail ordered the peasants to tie the captives together by pairs. Telephone and other types of wire were used for this purpose. As the prisoners were tied together in this fashion, they were led deeper into the surrounding woods in groups of ten. Each group was escorted by a Partisan guard armed with a machine gun and by several Serb peasants who carried blunt or pointed weapons. Soon screams and curses could be heard coming from every part of the nearby forest. Women, youths, and old men vied with one another in knifing the victims or smashing in their skulls. Most of the bound men were too exhausted by the privations to which they had been exposed since the first part of May to resist, as they certainly would have done under other circumstances. The two survivors of this massacre, D.I.G. and A.D.S., told me it was impossible to escape. Even if a prisoner did manage to wrest a machine gun away from the guards, he was too worn out to seek safety in the woods, and could only die trying to kill as many Serbs as possible. The Partisan soldiers did not participate in the killings unless they were directly attacked by desperate captives, but they prevented the escape of any individuals with stamina enough to try. The brutality displayed by the Serbian women and children who took part in this butchery defies description, and adds one more of the many black marks chalked up against the record of the Serbian nation in the twentieth century. Both surviving witnesses agree on all of the essential details concerning this savage massacre of half starved, exhausted, and bound men. It must be stressed that most of the victims were not Ustashas. They were chiefly Domobrans of the last recruitment carried through by the Croatian State in 1945. They were very young men who had hardly been afforded an opportunity to participate in the final battles of the war. There were, however, some Croatian gendarmes among these prisoners.

My two surviving eyewitnesses were among the last of the captives to be taken into the woods. Therefore, they had ample opportunity to observe the bestial rage of the Serbian populace and to listen to the terrible screams and yells of agony that came from the surrounding forest, as the victims were beaten to death or literally cut to pieces. But although they knew what was in store for them, my informants did not know what to do about it. It so happened that the Serb peasants tied D.I.G.'s left wrist to the right wrist of A.D.S. Fortunately the people who bound them together in this manner did a sloppy job and the wire was loose around their wrists. As they were being led into the woods, they succeeded in ridding their wrists of the wire, but they kept their wrists together as though they still were tied.

"As our escorts engaged in an excited debate," eyewitness D.I.G. said to me, "we took advantage of their preoccupation of the moment to jump out of line and to get as far away as we could from the spot where we were to be slaughtered. By the time our escorts became aware that we had broken away and the Partisans began to shoot at us, we were a good distance away from them. Bullets were buzzing all around us but the dense foliage of the forest and our desire to live saved us."

Obviously, it was sheer luck that they were not hit by the first shots fired by the guard. Once they had disappeared among the trees and bushes, however, they did not have to worry about pursuit. If their guard and the peasants with him left the other eight intended victims in this particular group, these wretches, too, might get away. Of course the woods nearby were full of Partisan guards and Serbian peasants who had led other groups away to the several abattoirs; these were warned by shots and shouting that some prisoners were making a break. There was a flurry of aimless shooting and yelling in all parts of the forest. "After about ten or fifteen minutes we could not hear any footsteps behind us or any yelling from close at hand, but only shooting in the distance," witness D.I.G. continued to tell me.

Although they had felt very tired before the mass slaughter started, the two ex-prisoners now found the strength to continue their flight to freedom well into the evening hours. Throughout the night, they remained in the forest, where perfect quiet reigned all around them. (This was a Serbian forest and the Serbs have a reputation for killing everything that lives, even the birds, in the woods around their homes. A Serbian forest can always be identified by the stillness and absence of life that reigns within it.) While they rested, their thoughts turned to their butchered comrades and they resolved that if they lived long enough to do so they would transmit to posterity the story of this mass slaughter. They believe that they were the only captives who managed to escape out of the whole column. They do not know where their massacred colleagues were buried or who buried them.

On the day following their escape, they proceeded slowly in the general direction of Banja Luka. About midnight they came to a village. All of the villagers were sound asleep. Since both men were wearing the remnants of Domobran uniforms, they knew that if this was a Serbian village, as was probable in this part of Bosnia, they still were in deadly danger. Somehow they had to get hold of civilian clothes.

At one end of the village stood a house, whose construction and more orderly arrangement and upkeep suggested that it might be the dwelling of a Croatian, rather than a Serbian family. The escaped prisoners decided to take a chance and knocked on the door of this house. After a time a woman told them from behind the closed door that her husband and other men from the village had been summoned by the People's Committee of this place to pursue "two Ustashas" who, as the woman said, had escaped from some prison and were hiding in this forest. Because of their presence in the vicinity, her husband had told her not to open the door to anyone after he left. Fortunately, she had no inkling that the two escapees were right here on her own doorstep! Since the woman's accent and dialect proclaimed her to be Serbian, the former prisoners (who were neither Ustashas or refugees from an ordinary prison) bade her a hasty goodbye and hurried away from this region. They realized that the Yugoslav authorities everywhere, when they learned of the escape, would make every effort to silence such dangerous witnesses of their postwar crimes. From the viewpoint of Belgrade and the local Communist authorities, they would have to be apprehended at any cost. Of course the Yugoslav authorities misrepresented the facts in the affair, even to those Serbian elements which had not participated in the slaughter. They identified the two escapees as "Ustashas" and "fugitives from prison."

Since the former prisoners knew the fate that awaited them if they were caught, they overcame their growing fatigue and put as much territory as possible behind them. When day broke, they had already passed around to the right side of the city of Banja Luka. As they continued their flight through the forests and mountains, they blundered upon a party of one hundred armed soldiers. By great luck these were Ustashas who belonged to the command of General Boban and who had refused to surrender when they found that the English were going to turn them over to the Partisans. They had made their way back into Bosnia, and were now slowly feeling their way westwards in the hope of escaping to the free world. It was a joyous meeting for D.I.G. and A.D.S., who kissed and hugged the Ustasha men to whom they related their gruesome experiences. Boban's soldiers gave them food and drink and suggested that they join the Ustasha party and go abroad with it. The two fugitives decided, however, that odds were against the Ustashas making good their try for freedom. They agreed that it would be wiser to go to their homes and wait for Tito's bloody reign of terror to come to its inevitable end.

They lived to regret this decision; although they did succeed in reaching their homes, they were soon arrested and sentenced to long terms of imprisonment. Fortunately, their new captors did not know they were eyewitnesses of the slaughter at Podgraci.

It was during this subsequent imprisonment that I became well acquainted with the two men. We exchanged the details of our several tragic experiences with one another. Even at this time we gave much thought to the question of conveying to the general public facts concerning the horrible crime committed at Podgraci. In case they did not survive themselves, they took pains to acquaint me in intimate detail with everything that they themselves had experienced. I cannot reveal at this time the exact date, place, or other circumstances of my association with D.I.G. and A.D.S. Although they are living today in circumstances quite different than those which prevailed when I knew them, they are still ready and willing to give testimony in regard to the Podgraci killings. Naturally authorities in Belgrade will go to any lengths to silence such dangerous witnesses, if their identity should become known prematurely.

At this time, I feel I should give the details of a conversation which I had in prison in 1948 with a Serbian peasant confined along with me. He came from a village in the Kozara-Prosara region. More than sixty years old, he was serving a sentence of several years when I met him. Although he was a Serbian, I had known him and enjoyed good relations with him for more than twenty years prior to our encounter in the same prison in which D.I.G. and A.D.S. were confined. He was one of the finest members of his nation I have ever known, a member of the Orthodox Church, and a good one, honest as the day is long, and broadminded with respect to national questions. Since I knew that he had not served as a soldier since the war of 1914, and did not belong to the Chetniks of Mihailovic either, I wondered why the Communist authorities had imprisoned him. Therefore I asked him the reason for his sentence. This is what he told me:

"When the war ended I went back to my native village of ----. Although I was not a Communist, the Comrades soon gave me a post on the People's Committee of the village. As a committeeman, I had to send orders to various men and women to report to the People's Committee to carry out certain duties. One day late in June, 1945, we received an order from above that 'all inhabitants living at the foot of the Kozara Mountain and around Prosara' must assemble at an appointed time at the lumberyard in Podgraci in order to kill the Ustashas. The population of this district had to bring hay-forks, picks, knives, and other weapons with which they could carry out this killing of the Ustashas who were about to be brought to this place. All of them were to be slain, without exceptions and without the expenditure of ammunition. Many people obeyed the summons to go to Podgraci; others, more honest folk, did not want to go there and stayed in their homes.

"When I myself saw what was being done to disarmed and exhausted men at Podgraci on that horrible day, I protested, telling the people: 'Do not do that! That's a crime. A terrible revenge will be taken upon us, the Serbs. A more horrifying evil will befall us than this if we get our just deserts for what we are doing here!'"

"I meant no harm to anyone by these words. Instead I said them because I wished everyone well, as I have throughout my entire life, during which I have tried to look straight into the eyes of every honest man and to avoid evil. This honesty, however, did not help me one bit after I said these things. For my frank words the Communists 'tried' me and sentenced me to serve this term of imprisonment. It is for this reason that I now am in here with you!"

I have given this report conscientiously and according to my recollection of the exact stories told me by D.I.G., A.D.S., and the old Serbian peasant whom I shall designate only as J.D.G., even though he is probably dead now. I shall always be ready to testify under oath to the truth of the record that I have given above and to repeat the details before any authorized international forum. Two, and perhaps all three, of the witness quoted are still alive today and can be contacted personally by anyone who wishes to make a serious investigation of the Podgraci massacre.

Signed: Safet Jaskic

Osnabruck, Germany
January 28, 1963

Appendix A

My Last Message

Editors' Note: Slavko Kvaternik, as a young man, was a member of the Croatian Party of Right. This nationalistic and patriotic group was founded by Dr. Ante Starcevic after the conclusion of the Nagodba or Compromise between Hungary and Croatia-Slavonia in 1868. Its program was one of uncompromising opposition to the Nagodba, and to both Austria and Hungary, although Starcevic and most of his followers were willing to accept the sovereignty of the Habsburg dynasty on the condition that the ancient Triune Kingdom of Croatia, Slavonia, and Dalmatia had an equal status with Austria and Hungary in the Habsburg complex. After Dr. Starcevic's death, his party split into two factions. Those elements which grouped themselves around Dr. Joseph Frank, a Croatian Jew, continued the Starcevic policy of hostility towards Hungary but saw that Croatia-Slavonia could not under any circumstances separate from Austria. They hoped that by following a pro-Austrian policy they would be able to secure the reunion of Dalmatia, which belonged to the Austrian half of the Monarchy, with Croatia-Slavonia, which was part of the Hungarian Kingdom though, insofar as domestic affairs were concerned, an autonomous unit within it. It was to this Frankist faction that Slavko Kvaternik belonged when he married the daughter of Dr. Frank.

During the war of 1914-1918, Kvaternik served as an officer in the Austro-Hungarian Army in which he was known as a "Draufganger," or one of the most daring and toughest of commanders. In the postwar period he became associated with the Ustasha group of Croatian nationalists who replaced the Frankists as the main standard bearers of the idea of Croatian independence. When the Germans attacked the Serb-Croat-Slovene state in 1941 Kvaternik helped to disorganize the Yugoslav Army and to set up the revived Kingdom of Croatia. Although this revived Croatian state had to function as a German satellite for the remainder of the war, Slavko Kvaternik was one of the few individuals of any nationality who dared to speak out frankly and openly to Adolf Hitler himself, as Hitler has acknowledged in his rambling "Conversations." Promoted to Marshal, Slavko Kvaternik for a time was the highest military authority in the Croatian state. Owing to policy disagreements with the Pavelic government, he not only remained in the background in the second half of the 1941-45 period, but was even exiled to Slovakia. After the German collapse in the spring of 1945, he was taken prisoner by the United States forces, imprisoned in Salzburg, extradited as late as September 9, 1946, to Communist Yugoslavia, tried as a war criminal—the usual accusation levied by the "People's Courts" against every enemy of orthodox Marxism—found guilty, and eventually executed in 1947.

While Marshal Kvaternik was awaiting execution, his relatives received scant reports on his condition. Out of these reports this "Last Message" to the Croatian nation and people was composed. It was first published in the *Hrvat-*

ski Kalendar of 1950.[1] This is an almanac of the Croatian Franciscans in Chicago, Illinois. The following translation of the Croatian original is the only version of Kvaternik's last words that has appeared in English. It should be of particular interest to professional military men, such as Slavko Kvaternik was, for it demonstrates graphically what any soldier who opposes Communism can expect his fate to be in the event of the eventual defeat of the army in which he is serving.

I am so oppressed by sufferings of various kinds that I don't believe that I'll be able to endure this confinement much longer. It appears that I shall not be brought before the court again. Since they cannot find valid evidence to convict me of the crimes with which I have been charged, it is likely that they will simply dispose of me here in the prison. I have been given medicines which, I am told, will cure me of my physical ills; it seems to me that I am being poisoned rather than helped by these remedies.

I asked to be allowed to talk with Archbishop Stepinac. They would have allowed me this privilege had I been willing to agree to make undignified declarations and to meet other conditions that they demanded of me. Of course I refused with indignation and contempt to oblige them in this matter.

Then, when I requested a confessor, they brought to me a very suspicious fellow indeed. I addressed to him some questions of general character concerning the principal teachings of the Catholic Church. Since he was unable to give me any kind of intelligent answer I refused to make my confession to him. Evidently he was an agent of the OZNA who was posing as a priest in the hope that he might be able to extract some kind of a compromising confession out of me.

They tried this trick on me again, bringing to me a person who wore the robes of a Franciscan. When I asked him to show me his Cross, he replied that he never carried one. He did not possess a stola either. Nevertheless I asked him to give me a prayerbook in order that I might prepare myself to make my confession to him. He told me that it was not necessary to consult a prayerbook before making the confession, so I sent him packing too.

Afterwards I saw that I had done well for I had made my last confession to our beloved priest and national hero, Vilim Cecelja,[2] and this is my last comfort as I prepare to make my exit from this hell. I pray

[1] Two Croatian writers have informed the editors of this volume that Marshal Kvaternik's "Last Message" was not written by him but was put together by Dr. Ante Niksic, a prominent Croatian exile (now deceased) in Buenos Aires, on the basis of various details from various letters. Even so, the message sheds much light on Kvaternik's and his nation's tragedy. We have therefore decided to include it in this Appendix.

[2] Reverend Vilim Cecelja, director of the "Caritas Croata" in Austria, was imprisoned over a year together with Marshal Kvaternik in Salzburg. They were separated on September 9, 1946, when the latter was extradited by the United States occupation forces to Yugoslav Communists.

to God daily in behalf of our martyred people and for our poor, suffering Croatian land and my last prayer will be for them.

Three days ago towards midnight a dark complexioned man, rather tall and with a savage look about him, came into my cell. While an escort stood awaiting him in front of the cell door, he began to load his service pistol with bullets in a most ostentatious manner. He told me that he had come to shoot me and asked if I wished to make any last wishes before he did so. I said to him that I had none and that I was thankful that by the infinite mercy of God my sufferings finally had reached their end. When he heard me speak thus the fellow left my cell uttering a variety of oaths and blasphemies that no one but a Marxist could think of.

Despite what I said to him I did have one last request that I should have liked to have had granted. It was that Generals Percevic, Navratil, and I be allowed to wear Croatian military uniforms, even though they lacked our insignia of rank. This request was not granted for my captors said that they had no such uniforms. My appeal was made in accordance with internationally accepted conventions governing the rules of war, but it was to no avail. So we are not to be allowed to die as Croatians.

I am suffering a great deal from malaria and from spells of dizziness. My captors have been so kind as to give me various pills and shots—after receiving which I invariably feel much worse than I did before. One result that they seem to produce is vomiting.

I believe that an important cause of my poor physical state is that I am not allowed to sleep. Every time that I doze off they shake me awake. I have the feeling that I am being poisoned too. They have refused me the services of two physicians in whose integrity I have confidence.

A friend smuggled a message into my cell. It was to the effect that I should ask for nothing. To request anything, whatever its nature, would be the surest way to get myself liquidated. As it is I have to sign records all the time. Some of these are supposed to relate to the "check-ups" that the doctors have given me; I don't even know what the contents of some of the other "records" were. Unfortunately, I have neither the desire nor the energy to raise questions about anything any more. I am altogether apathetic. I have friends outside who are willing to risk anything to get me out of here. They prepared a plan of escape for me. It was well designed and I think it would have worked. But I refused to try it for if I did escape, it might cost the lives of several young Croatians.

In days to come Croatia will need new workers and new fighters. But I am a worn out old man who already has given all that he had to give for his people and nation. My day is done, and whatever good I have done, or whatever harm I may inadvertently have done, belongs now to the judgment of history. There is no point in causing any of my friends or young Croatian patriots in general to sacrifice their lives to save mine, which is much less valuable. Tito's people, like most cowards, are always trying to find excuses for perpetrating new massacres. I shall seek my happiness, not in escape from this jail but in life to come when I may meet again those Croatian officers and generals who were knifed or otherwise murdered in Belgrade, along with so many other Croatian martyrs. Let our blood be the last that suffering and oppressed Croatia has to shed before attaining the freedom and happiness that we have sought for her!

I feel that what strength I have is giving out and I apprehend that my end is near. Therefore I am sending to you my dearly beloved, my last greetings. All of my activities were designed to secure the freedom of my country. Still today I am conscious of what I did when I took upon myself the responsibility of proclaiming the national independence of Croatia.[3] I did not take this action arbitrarily on my own account or in my own interests, nor on the advice or with the help of any foreigners whatsoever. Whoever asserts that I acted either in my own behalf or in that of foreigners does not comprehend the irresistible aspirations of the Croatian people to be free and master in their own homeland. Above everything else the Croatians want the national independence of their country.

The uprising staged by Croatian troops in Karlovac in the fall of 1939 was a portent of things to come. It was a clear sign that the tide of national feeling could not be dammed up by the artificial restrictions imposed by the Serbian dictatorship, nor could the course of this national tide be turned into the waters that the Serbians desired. From this day on it was evident that the fate of the totalitarian and aggrandized "Great Serbia," known to the Western World as "Yugoslavia," would be sealed by the bullets and rifles of Croatian soldiers who were only waiting for the right moment to strike at the hydra-headed monster of 1918.

Between April 6 and April 10, 1941, the most accurate and inspiring of national plebiscites in the history of the Croatian people was carried out.[4] No one can hold this plebiscite against us for twenty-three years of slavery gave us the right and the obligation to free our people whenever the opportunity offered; to act in any other way would be to mark us out as a nation that does not deserve freedom. Those who are our friends will not hold our actions of 1941 against us for they know how much we had to suffer and how much we love our own country. We

---

[3] On April 10, 1941.

[4] Marshal Kvaternik is referring to the joy and enthusiasm with which an overwhelming majority of the Croatian people welcomed his proclamation of the Croatian national independence. Archbishop of Zagreb, later Cardinal Stepinac, on numerous occasions expressed similar views in reference to the establishment of the Croatian State in 1941. At his Communist-held trial in 1946, he re-echoed the same sentiments of Croatian national aspirations: "The Croatian nation unanimously declared itself for the Croatian State and I would have been remiss had I not recognized and acknowledged this desire of the Croatian people enslaved by the former Yugoslavia."

were sorry that our goal of national independence had to be realized during a war that was not provoked by us, that we did not want, and in which we had no wish to be involved. Those who took our freedom from us and who tortured, hanged, and murdered so many Croatian patriots between 1918 and 1941 bear the responsibility for what happened in 1941. This was the harvest they reaped for their persecution of us in and out of court, during church processions and funerals, and even at the election polls. I am positive that the more talented statesmen in the western democracies foresaw—they must have foreseen—what was going to happen. After the assassination of Stjepan Radic,[5] an Englishman himself admitted as much to me. Furthermore it ought to be remembered that when we struck in 1941, the United States of America was not involved in the war. We counted upon receiving moral aid and sympathy from this great and free nation, the greatest of world powers, which has given bread to so many Croatians.

We had no reason to enter the last war which was a clash between the major powers of the world. All insinuations that we participated in the struggle in the hope of securing territorial gains, or in order to impose Croatian rule upon non-Croatian peoples, are base calumnies. I want to take this opportunity to admit one thing, which, in fact, I perceived clearly in the fall of 1939, and this is that Germany sinned greatly in attacking Poland. By so doing, apart from the wrong done to the Polish people and state, the defense of the West against Soviet Russian aggression was fatally weakened. In this first act of the war the key to the eventual German failure is to be found.[6]

Another fatal mistake made by the Axis was its treatment of Croatia and Slovenia. Particularly the demand made by Italy, or rather by the Italian Fascists, for our Croatian Dalmatia was utterly insensate. I never reckoned upon the Italians being so stupid as to grab the most purely Croatian and most culturally advanced of all Croatian provinces. In their seizure of Dalmatia I saw the greatest and most dangerous evil that could possibly have befallen us. This act demonstrated the basic inability of the Axis to settle world affairs wisely and honestly. I did what I could to impede the Italian takeover of Dalmatia and to prevent the other evils that befell us through our association with the Axis. I helped whomever I could help; I protected whomever I could protect. Everyone who has taken the trouble to inform himself as to my activities knows this well; above all, the good Lord, who is my best witness, knows it best.

---

[5] Radic, leader of the Peasant Party, the majority faction in Croatian political life after 1918, was murdered along with other Croatian deputies during a session of the Serb-Croat-Slovene Skupshtina or Parliament in 1928.

[6] In order to keep the record straight and to avoid misunderstandings as to the fraternal sentiments felt by almost all Croats for the Poles, the editors feel obliged to point out that neither the English, the French, nor the Americans could or did do anything for Poland in 1939. Obviously, therefore, the Croatians could hardly have been expected to give material help to that nation.

I think that some of my collaborators and friends are still alive today. They know how, despite the pressure applied by the Axis Powers to make things take place in our country not according to democratic principles but in conformity with the practices that prevailed in the Axis Powers themselves, we never stopped working to effect our final liberation from their tutelage. I thought that Croatia, like Denmark and other small nations, would be able to find a haven of peace amid the whirlpool of war. It is too bad that Germany did not know how to conserve her great forces for the inevitable conflict with Soviet imperialism. It pains me when I see who today are considered to be war criminals. For the guilt of the last war is almost as much Russia's as Germany's. After all, Germany's first ally in the war was Russia and it was Russia who partitioned Poland with her.

I freely admit that I agreed to permit Croatian volunteer troops to fight against the Soviets in 1941 and in succeeding years in order that they might do their bit to free mankind from a great Asiatic lie, and from the greatest terror and slavery that ever has prevailed at any time anywhere.

I am a soldier and I do not like to discuss politics anymore. However in this connection I have to add one last word and it is this: In essence the Croatian people are addicted to democratic principles. The greatest sons and most illustrious intellects of Croatia were permeated by democratic principles. Ante Starcevic, Stjepan Radic, and many younger men, who today are continuing to work for the salvation of Croatia, are numbered among them. Every Croatian knows that democracy is the primary condition for the peace, happiness, and freedom of our country and people. Stjepan Radic knew how to express in a couple of words that which is engraved deeply upon the Croatian national soul. How proud we Croatian officers and political representatives were before and during World War I, when in Sabor[7] he opened every speech he made with the words: "Highly Respected National Parliament!" May the Lord rest his soul; perhaps in a few days time I'll be in his company again!

All that I did was done in the belief that I was acting for the good of my fellow Croatians and of our common fatherland. I am firmly convinced that when the Croatian people finally obtain the freedom for which they have fought and suffered, they will establish on our national territory a firm fortress of peace and progress. May God grant that this day of freedom will come soon! May the Croatian people as a nation emerge unscathed from this greatest catastrophe of all the centuries. May they never allow their enemies to rule over them! May they be wary

[7] The pre-1918 Croatian diet or legislature and one of the oldest parliamentary bodies in Europe. The noted medievalist, Dr. Dominic Mandic, has adduced evidence to indicate that the Croatian Sabor may date as far back as the eighth century, if not before. See his *Hrvatski Sabor na Duvanjskom Polju g. 753* (Buenos Aires, 1960) (The Croatian Sabor held on the field of Duvno in the year 753 A.D.).

of whatever the Serbs have to say to them, for the Serbs deceived us in the basest way right up to the final minute of the war. And still today, as exponents of Bolshevism, they are continuing to spread a network of poisonous intrigue in order to annihilate our Croatian land and national consciousness.

My last greeting to all of my beloved ones, to my children first of all, and then to my friends and collaborators, my brother officers, and to all Croatian soldiers right down to that youngest Croat soldier who to the last drop of his blood will stand as a guard of the Eternal Croatia!

God and the Croatians!

Slavko Kvaternik
Field Marshal of the
Croatian Armed Forces

Written in prison during Holy Week, 1947.

Appendix B

Resolution*

On The 15th Anniversary of the Croatian Genocide, The Bleiburg-Maribor Massacres

WHEREAS on this May 30 day, a befitting annual observance has been set by the American people to commemorate and honor the war dead of this great country, we as American Croatians join in this memorial observance and express our deepest gratitude for the sacrifices of all those Americans, since the founding of this Nation, who gave their lives for the preservation of future generations, and for the democratic ideals embodied in the Constitution and the American way of life; and

WHEREAS the freedom seeking Croatian nation, from which we are descended, has also a special meaning to us, the assembly thus finds it especially fitting to honor the Croatian war dead, particularly the over 150,000 Croatian soldiers, representing a whole generation of Croatian youth, who in May 1945, after the end of World War II hostilities, fell victims to "Serbo-Partisan" Communist treachery and virtual genocide for the recreation of the synthetic State of Yugoslavia; and

WHEREAS the perpetrators of genocide utilize mass murder with the intended result of the liquidation of a nation, and in this case, the then Independent State of Croatia, the assembly therefore wishes to emphasize to America and the free world the reason given for this horrendous crime by reiterating the words of Tito's henchman, Milovan Djilas, in charge of the genocidal operation against the Croatian nation, who said: "Croatian soldiers must die in order that (then defunct) Yugoslavia may live"; and

WHEREAS genocide is an international crime of the worst nature, violating all the inalienable divine, civil, and human rights of men and nations to existence, the assembly herewith demands that the Croatian genocide remembered as the Bleiburg-Maribor Massacres be investigated by the American Government with all possible swiftness, and further

*See *Congressional Record*—House, June 2, 1960, p. 10922.

demands that the administration and Congress vigorously use every means available to bring Tito and his Communist conspirators to justice, and to help restore an independent Croatia from its hellish prison of Yugoslavia. Elemental justice demands this, since it was the imprudent World War II Anglo-American recognition and support of Tito and the "Serbo-Partisan" Communists which helped precipitate these massacres and the forceful subjugation of the Croatian nation into a second and more tyrannical Yugoslavia.

UNITED AMERICAN CROATIANS OF CLEVELAND

John Prcela, President
Nikola Frigan, Vice President
Ivan Coric, Secretary

Cleveland, Ohio—Hotel Statler-Hilton
May 30, 1960

Index

Note: The names of Partisan units, and the names of individual Partisans are italicized so as to make these names stand out in contrast to other names. Many surnames have been spelled phonetically in the text. In those instances, the correct native spelling also appears in parentheses adjacent to the phonetic spelling throughout the Index.

[redacted] 49271

Preela, & Guldenshn